Lecture Notes in Computer Science

Vol. 1: GI-Gesellschaft für Informatik e.V. 3. Jahrestagung, Hamburg, 8.–10. Oktober 1973. Herausgegeben im Auftrag der Gesellschaft für Informatik von W. Brauer. XI, 508 Seiten. 1973.

Vol. 2: GI-Gesellschaft für Informatik e.V. 1. Fachtagung über Automatentheorie und Formale Sprachen, Bonn, 9.–12. Juli 1973. Herausgegeben im Auftrag der Gesellschaft für Informatik von K.-H. Böhling und K. Indermark. VII, 322 Seiten. 1973.

Vol. 3: 5th Conference on Optimization Techniques, Part I. (Series: I.F.I.P. TC7 Optimization Conferences.) Edited by R. Conti and A. Ruberti. XIII, 565 pages. 1973.

Vol. 4: 5th Conference on Optimization Techniques, Part II. (Series: I.F.I.P. TC7 Optimization Conferences.) Edited by R. Conti and A. Ruberti. XIII, 389 pages. 1973.

Vol. 5: International Symposium on Theoretical Programming. Edited by A. Ershov and V. A. Nepomniaschy. VI, 407 pages. 1974.

Vol. 6: B. T. Smith, J. M. Boyle, J. J. Dongarra, B. S. Garbow, Y. Ikebe, V. C. Klema, and C. B. Moler, Matrix Eigensystem Routines – EISPACK Guide. XI, 551 pages. 2nd Edition 1974. 1976.

Vol. 7: 3. Fachtagung über Programmiersprachen, Kiel, 5.–7. März 1974. Herausgegeben von B. Schlender und W. Frielinghaus. VI, 225 Seiten. 1974.

Vol. 8: GI-NTG Fachtagung über Struktur und Betrieb von Rechensystemen, Braunschweig, 20.–22. März 1974. Herausgegeben im Auftrag der GI und der NTG von H.-O. Leilich. VI, 340 Seiten. 1974.

Vol. 9: GI-BIFOA Internationale Fachtagung: Informationszentren in Wirtschaft und Verwaltung. Köln, 17./18. Sept. 1973. Herausgegeben im Auftrag der GI und dem BIFOA von P. Schmitz. VI, 259 Seiten. 1974.

Vol. 10: Computing Methods in Applied Sciences and Engineering, Part 1. International Symposium, Versailles, December 17–21, 1973. Edited by R. Glowinski and J. L. Lions. X, 497 pages. 1974.

Vol. 11: Computing Methods in Applied Sciences and Engineering, Part 2. International Symposium, Versailles, December 17–21, 1973. Edited by R. Glowinski and J. L. Lions. X, 434 pages. 1974.

Vol. 12: GFK-GI-GMR Fachtagung Prozessrechner 1974. Karlsruhe, 10.–11. Juni 1974. Herausgegeben von G. Krüger und R. Friehmelt. XI, 620 Seiten. 1974.

Vol. 13: Rechnerstrukturen und Betriebsprogrammierung, Erlangen, 1970. (GI-Gesellschaft für Informatik e.V.) Herausgegeben von W. Händler und P. P. Spies. VII, 333 Seiten. 1974.

Vol. 14: Automata, Languages and Programming – 2nd Colloquium, University of Saarbrücken, July 29–August 2, 1974. Edited by J. Loeckx. VIII, 611 pages. 1974.

Vol. 15: L Systems. Edited by A. Salomaa and G. Rozenberg. VI, 338 pages. 1974.

Vol. 16: Operating Systems, International Symposium, Rocquencourt 1974. Edited by E. Gelenbe and C. Kaiser. VIII, 310 pages. 1974.

Vol. 17: Rechner-Gestützter Unterricht RGU '74, Fachtagung, Hamburg, 12.–14. August 1974, ACU-Arbeitskreis Computer-Unterstützter Unterricht. Herausgegeben im Auftrag der GI von K. Brunnstein, K. Haefner und W. Händler. X, 417 Seiten. 1974.

Vol. 18: K. Jensen and N. E. Wirth, PASCAL – User Manual and Report. VII, 170 pages. Corrected Reprint of the 2nd Edition 1976.

Vol. 19: Programming Symposium. Proceedings 1974. V, 425 pages. 1974.

Vol. 20: J. Engelfriet, Simple Program Schemes and Formal Languages. VII, 254 pages. 1974.

Vol. 21: Compiler Construction, An Advanced Course. Edited by F. L. Bauer and J. Eickel. XIV. 621 pages. 1974.

Vol. 22: Formal Aspects of Cognitive Processes. Proceedings 1972. Edited by T. Storer and D. Winter. V, 214 pages. 1975.

Vol. 23: Programming Methodology. 4th Informatik Symposium IBM Germany Wildbad, September 25–27, 1974. Edited by C. E. Hackl. VI, 501 pages. 1975.

Vol. 24: Parallel Processing. Proceedings 1974. Edited by T. Fer VI, 433 pages. 1975.

Vol. 25: Category Theory Applied to Computation and Control. Proceedings 1974. Edited by E. G. Manes. X, 245 pages. 1975.

Vol. 26: GI-4. Jahrestagung, Berlin, 9.–12. Oktober 1974. Herausgegeben im Auftrag der GI von D. Siefkes. IX, 748 Seiten. 1975.

Vol. 27: Optimization Techniques. IFIP Technical Conference Novosibirsk, July 1–7, 1974. (Series: I.F.I.P. TC7 Optimization Conferences.) Edited by G. I. Marchuk. VIII, 507 pages. 1975.

Vol. 28: Mathematical Foundations of Computer Science. 3rd Symposium at Jadwisin near Warsaw, June 17–22, 1974. Edited by A. Blikle. VII, 484 pages. 1975.

Vol. 29: Interval Mathematics. Procedings 1975. Edited by K. Nick VI, 331 pages. 1975.

Vol. 30: Software Engineering. An Advanced Course. Edited by F. L. Bauer. (Formerly published 1973 as Lecture Notes in Economics and Mathematical Systems, Vol. 81) XII, 545 pages. 1975.

Vol. 31: S. H. Fuller, Analysis of Drum and Disk Storage Units. IX, 283 pages. 1975.

Vol. 32: Mathematical Foundations of Computer Science 1975. Proceedings 1975. Edited by J. Bečvář. X, 476 pages. 1975.

Vol. 33: Automata Theory and Formal Languages, Kaiserslautern May 20–23, 1975. Edited by H. Brakhage on behalf of GI. V 292 Seiten. 1975.

Vol. 34: GI – 5. Jahrestagung, Dortmund 8.–10. Oktober 1975 Herausgegeben im Auftrag der GI von J. Mühlbacher. X, 755 Seiten 1975.

Vol. 35: W. Everling, Exercises in Computer Systems Analysis (Formerly published 1972 as Lecture Notes in Economics and Mathematical Systems, Vol. 65) VIII, 184 pages. 1975.

Vol. 36: S. A. Greibach, Theory of Program Structures: Schemes Semantics, Verification. XV, 364 pages. 1975.

Vol. 37: C. Böhm, λ-Calculus and Computer Science Theory. Proceedings 1975. XII, 370 pages. 1975.

Vol. 38: P. Branquart, J.-P. Cardinael, J. Lewi, J.-P. Delescaill M. Vanbegin. An Optimized Translation Process and Its Applicatio to ALGOL 68. IX, 334 pages. 1976.

Vol. 39: Data Base Systems. Proceedings 1975. Edited by H. Hasselmeier and W. Spruth. VI, 386 pages. 1976.

Vol. 40: Optimization Techniques. Modeling and Optimization in the Service of Man. Part 1. Proceedings 1975. Edited by J. Cea. XI 854 pages. 1976.

Vol. 41: Optimization Techniques. Modeling and Optimization in Service of Man. Part 2. Proceedings 1975. Edited by J. Cea 852 pages. 1976.

Vol. 42: James E. Donahue, Complementary Definition gramming Language Semantics. VII, 172 pages. 1976.

Vol. 43: E. Specker und V. Strassen, Komplexität von Ents problemen. Ein Seminar. V, 217 Seiten. 1976.

Vol. 44: ECI Conference 1976. Proceedings 1976. Edited by Samelson. VIII, 322 pages. 1976.

Vol. 45: Mathematical Foundations of Computer Science 197 Proceedings 1976. Edited by A. Mazurkiewicz. XI, 601 pages. 197

Lecture Notes in Computer Science

Edited by G. Goos and J. Hartmanis

45

Mathematical Foundations of Computer Science 1976

Proceedings, 5th Symposium, Gdańsk, September 6–10, 1976

Edited by A. Mazurkiewicz

Springer-Verlag
Berlin · Heidelberg · New York 1976

Editor
Antoni Mazurkiewicz
Computation Centre
Polish Academy of Sciences
P.O.Box 22,
00-901 Warszawa/Poland

AMS Subject Classifications (1970): 02C99, 02E10, 02E15, 02H10, 18B20, 68A05, 68A10, 68A20, 68A25, 68A30, 68A45, 94A25, 94A30

ISBN 3-540-07854-1 Springer-Verlag Berlin · Heidelberg · New York
ISBN 0-387-07854-1 Springer-Verlag New York · Heidelberg · Berlin

Printed in Germany
Printing and binding: Beltz Offsetdruck, Hemsbach/Bergstr.

FOREWORD

This volume contains papers which were contributed for presentation at the Symposium on Mathematical Foundations of Computer Science — MFCS'76, held in Gdańsk, Poland, September 6-10, 1976. This symposium is the 5th in the series of annual MFCS symposia organized in turn in Poland /every even year/ and Czechoslovakia /every odd year/. The aim of these symposia is to promote and to develop the mathematical approach to the basic computational phenomena.

The articles in these Proceedings consist of a number of invited papers and short communications concerning mathematical results motivated by practical problems and related to:

- Programs and computations,
- Programming languages,
- Data bases and information retrieval systems,
- Analysis and complexity of algorithms,
- Formal languages and automata.

The scientific interest in the above topics is increasing rapidly; an example of this interest can be seen in the number of papers submitted for the Symposium. The Program Committee has been forced to reject more than half of them /sometimes valuable ones/. The main guideline for selecting papers was their orginality and relevance to the subject of the Symposium.

The Symposium is being organized by the Computation Centre of the Polish Academy of Sciences in cooperation with the University of Gdańsk.

The organizers of the Symposium are grateful to all authors for their valuable contributions and to all people who helped in the organization of the Symposium. The main part of the organizational work has been done by the following members of the committee: E.Czuchajew , P.Dembiński /Vice-Chairman/, C.Góral, W.Kwasowiec, J.Leszczyłowski , W.Lipski,Jr. , A.Mazurkiewicz /Symposium Chairman/, A.W.Mostowski , B.Rykaczewska, J.Winkowski /Program Chairman/. The organizers are specially indebted to J.Winkowski, who has taken the greatest part in the preparation of this volume.

The help of Springer-Verlag, which has produced these Proceedings is highly appreciated.

Antoni Mazurkiewicz

Warsaw, May 1976

CONTENTS

Invited Lecturers

Communications

EXERCISES IN DENOTATIONAL SEMANTICS

K.R. Apt

J.W. de Bakker

Mathematisch Centrum, Amsterdam

1. INTRODUCTION

The present paper is a progress report about our work on semantics and proof theory of programming languages. We study a number of fundamental programming concepts occurring e.g. in the language PASCAL, viz. assignment, sequential composition, conditionals, locality, and (recursive) procedures with parameters called-by-value and called-by-variable. Our goal is the development of a formalism which satisfies two requirements

- Semantic adequacy: the definitions capture exactly the meaning attributed to these concepts in the PASCAL report.
- Mathematical adequacy: The definitions are as precise and mathematically rigorous as possible.

Of course, full semantic adequacy cannot be achieved within the scope of our paper. Thus, we were forced to omit certain aspects of the concepts concerned. What we hope to have avoided, however, is any *essential* alteration of a concept for the sake of making it more amenable to formal treatment.

Our approach follows the method of denotational semantics introduced by Scott and Strachey (e.g. in [12]). Moreover, we investigate the connections between denotational semantics and Hoare's proof theory ([6]), in sofar as pertaining to the concepts mentioned above.

As main contributions of our paper we see

- The proposal of a new definition of substitution for a *subscripted* variable. This allows an extension of Hoare's axiom for assignment to the case of assignment to a subscripted variable. (This idea is described in greater detail in [2].)
- The proposal of a semantic definition and corresponding proof rule for recursive procedures with an adequate treatment of call-by-value and call-by-variable. (We believe these to be new. The proof rule is based on Scott's (or computational) induction, which is well-understood for parameterless procedures, but hardly so for procedures with parameters. In our opinion, neither the papers of Manna et al. (e.g. in [10,11]) nor those of e.g. De Bakker ([1]), Hoare ([7]), Hoare and Wirth ([8]), Igarashi, London and Luckham ([9]) give the full story on this subject.)

It will turn out that our treatment of procedures is quite complex. However, we doubt whether an approach which is *essentially* simpler is possible. Of course, we do not claim that our formalism is the last word, but the programming notions involved *are* intricate, and we feel that essential simplification could be obtained only by changing the language.

The paper has the following outline:

Section 2 gives the syntax of the various language constructs. Also, a careful definition of *substitution* is given which is needed for the treatment of assignment, locality and parameter passing.

Section 3 is devoted to the definition of the denotational semantics of the five types of statements. We introduce the semantic function M which gives meaning to a statement S, in a given *environment* ε (a mapping from variables to addresses) and *store* σ (a mapping from addresses to values), yielding a new store σ' : $M(S)(\varepsilon,\sigma) = \sigma'$. For assignment, sequential composition and conditionals the definitions are fairly straightforward. It is also reasonably clear what to do about locality, but the treatment of procedures may be rather hard to follow. Some of the causes are:

- When applying the usual least fixed point approach, one has to be careful with the types (in the set-theoretical sense) of the functions involved.
- The notion of call-by-variable (the FORTRAN call-by-reference) requires a somewhat mixed action to be taken: When the actual parameter (which has to be a variable) is subscripted, the subscript is evaluated first, and then a process of substitution of the modified actual for the formal is invoked.
- The possibility of clash of variables has to be faced. (Cf. the ALGOL 60 report, sections 4.7.3.2 (Example: b int x; proc P(x); int x;b...e;...P(x+1)...e) and 4.7.3.3 (Example: b int x; proc P;b...x...e;...b int x;...P...e...e).) These problems are not exactly the same as encountered in mathematical logic; in particular, they cannot simply be solved by appropriate use of the notions of free and bound occurrence and of substitution, as customary in logic.

Section 4 introduces the proof-theoretical framework. It contains the "Exercises in denotational semantics": For each type of statement, a corresponding axiom or proof rule is given, and it is required to show its soundness. Also, a modest attempt at dealing with substitution is included. In fact, for two rules (sequential composition and conditionals) the proof is easy, for the assignment axiom we refer to [2], whereas the remaining three cases should, at the moment of writing this, be seen as conjectures since we do not yet have fully worked out proofs available. However, we are confident that the rules, perhaps after some minor modifications, will turn out to be sound.

It may be appropriate to add an indication of the restrictions we have imposed upon our investigation. There are a few minor points (such as: only one procedure declaration, i.e., not a simultaneous system; only one parameter of each of the two types, etc.). Next, things we omitted but which we do not consider essentially difficult (such as type information in declarations) and, finally, a major omission: We have no function designators in expressions, nor do we allow procedure identifiers as parameters.

There is a vast amount of literature dealing with the same issues. Many of the papers take an *operational* approach, defining semantics in terms of abstract machines.

This we wholly circumvent in the present paper, though it is in fact needed for the justification of the least fixed point approach to recursion (to be given along the lines of De Bakker [1]). Many others take their starting point in some powerful mathematical system (universal algebra, category theory), but tend to fall short of a treatment of the subtler points of the programming notions at hand. A proof-theoretic approach can be found e.g. in Hoare and Wirth [8] or Igarashi, London and Luckham [9], but we must confess not to be able to follow their treatment of procedures and parameter passing. There are also a few papers dealing with the relationship between semantics and proof theory, such as Donahue [4], Cook [3] and Gorelick [5]. Again, the approach of these papers differs from the present one. E.g., the first one omits treatment of recursion, and the other two treat locality in a way which differs from ours (cf. the block rule in our section 4). On the other hand, we recommend the papers by Cook and Gorelick for a discussion of substitution, a topic to which we pay little attention below.

2. SYNTAX

We present a language which is essentially a subset of PASCAL, though there are some notational variants introduced in order to facilitate the presentation. We start with the following classes of symbols:

SV = {x,y,z,u,...}: the class of *simple variables*,
AV = {a,b,...} : the class of *array variables*,
B = {n,m,...} : the class of *integer constants*,
P = {P,Q,...} : the class of *procedure symbols*.

For technical reasons which will become clear below (def. 2.1, def. 3.3), we assume some well-ordering of these four sets.

Using a self-explanatory variant of BNF, we now define the classes V (*variables*), IE (*integer expressions*), BE (*boolean expressions*), and S (*statements*):

V (with elements v,w,...) $\quad$ v::= $x \mid a[t]$
IE (with elements r,s,t,...) $\quad$ t::= $v \mid n \mid t_1+t_2 \mid t_1*t_2 \mid \underline{\text{if}}\ p\ \underline{\text{then}}\ t_1\ \underline{\text{else}}\ t_2\ \underline{\text{fi}}$
BE (with elements p,q,...) $\quad$ p::= $\underline{\text{true}} \mid \underline{\text{false}} \mid t_1=t_2 \mid t_1>t_2 \mid p_1 \supset p_2 \mid p_1 \wedge p_2 \mid \neg p$
S (with elements $S,S_0,\ldots$) $\quad$ S::= $v:=t \mid S_1;S_2 \mid \underline{\text{if}}\ p\ \underline{\text{then}}\ S_1\ \underline{\text{else}}\ S_2\ \underline{\text{fi}} \mid$
$\underline{\text{begin}}\ \underline{\text{new}}\ x;\ S\ \underline{\text{end}} \mid P(t,v)$.

Remarks

1. We shall use the notation $t_1 \equiv t_2$ ($p_1 \equiv p_2$, $S_1 \equiv S_2$) to indicate that t_1 and t_2 (p_1 and p_2, S_1 and S_2) are identical sequences of symbols.
2. Whenever convenient, we shall use parentheses to enhance readability or to avoid ambiguity. Syntactic specification of this is omitted.
3. (Variables) Note that we have *simple* variables (x,y,z,u) and *subscripted* variables (a[t],b[s],...), and that an arbitrary variable v may be both simple or subscripted.

4. (Expressions) The syntax of *IE* and *BE* has been kept simple on purpose. A minor extension would be to introduce additional operations. On the other hand, the inclusion of functions designators within *IE* or *BE* presumably would constitute a major extension, requiring substantial additional analysis below.
5. (Statements) In *S* we have: assignment, sequential composition, conditionals, blocks, and procedure calls. The last two cases require further comment:
6. (Blocks) We restrict ourselves to declarations of simple variables without type information. This is motivated by our wish to treat declarations only in sofar as needed for the analysis of parameter passing.
7. (Procedures) *Throughout the paper, we restrict ourselves to the case that we have only one procedure declaration*, given in the form

(2.1) $\quad P \Leftarrow \mathit{val}\ x \cdot \mathit{var}\ y \cdot S_0$

with the following conventions

(α) $P \in P$, $x,y \in SV$, $S_0 \in S$, with $x \not\equiv y$.

(β) S_0 is the *procedure body*, x the formal value parameter, y the formal variable parameter.

(γ) In a *call* P(t,v), t is the actual (∈ *IE*) corresponding to the formal x, and v (∈ *V*) corresponds to y.

(δ) The declaration (2.1) is assumed to be "globally" available; a call P(t,v) always refers to (2.1) as corresponding declaration.

(In PASCAL, one would write for (2.1):
<u>procedure</u> P(x:integer,<u>var</u> y:integer);S_0).
Extension to a treatment of *systems* of declarations is reasonably straightforward (see e.g. [1]), and omitted here mainly for reasons of space; extension to any number of (value and variable) parameters is trivial.

Substitution plays an important role below, both in semantics and proof theory (assignment, locality, parameter mechanisms). In particular, we define
- S[v/x]: substitute the (arbitrary) variable v for the simple variable x in S;
- s[t/v] and p[t/v]: substitute the integer expression t for the variable v in s or p.

The first kind of substitution is defined in the standard way using the notions of free and bound occurrence of a simple variable in a statement (An occurrence of x in S is bound whenever it is within a substatement of S of the form <u>begin</u> <u>new</u> x;S_1 <u>end</u>. All other occurrences of x in S are free.) The second kind of substitution, which includes the case of substitution for a *subscripted* variable, was introduced in De Bakker [2]. We refer to that paper for a detailed account of this, in particular of its application in proving correctness of assignment statements.

DEFINITION 2.1. (Substitution in a statement)

a. $(w{:=}t)[v/x] \equiv (w[v/x]{:=}t[v/x])$

b. $(S_1;S_2)[v/x] \equiv (S_1[v/x];S_2[v/x])$

c. (<u>if</u> p <u>then</u> S_1 <u>else</u> S_2 <u>fi</u>)[v/x] ≡ <u>if</u> p[v/x] <u>then</u> S_1[v/x] <u>else</u> S_2[v/x] <u>fi</u>

d. (<u>begin</u> <u>new</u> z;S <u>end</u>)[v/x] ≡ <u>begin</u> <u>new</u> z;S <u>end</u>, if x ≡ z
≡ <u>begin</u> <u>new</u> z;S[v/x] <u>end</u>, if x ≢ z and z does not occur free in v
≡ <u>begin</u> <u>new</u> z';S[z'/z][v/x] <u>end</u>, if x ≢ z and z occurs free in v, where z' is the first variable ≢ x not occurring free in v or S

e. P(t,w)[v/x] ≡ P(t[v/x],w[v/x]).

DEFINITION 2.2. (Substitution in an expression)

a. The definitions of s[t/v] and p[t/v] are straightforwardly reduced by formula induction to that of w[t/v], for some w ∈ *V*.

b. We distinguish two cases: v ≡ x, and v ≡ a[s].
 (α) x[t/x] ≡ t, y[t/x] ≡ y (x≢y), a[s][t/x] ≡ a[s[t/x]]
 (β) x[t/a[s]]≡ x, b[s'][t/a[s]] ≡ b[s'[t/a[s]]] (a≢b),
  a[s'][t/a[s]] ≡ <u>if</u> s'[t/a[s]] = s <u>then</u> t <u>else</u> a[s'[t/a[s]]] <u>fi</u>.

Examples

1. (<u>begin</u> <u>new</u> y; x:=a[y]; P(x+y+z, a[x]) <u>end</u>)[y/x] ≡
 <u>begin</u> <u>new</u> y'; y:=a[y']; P(y+y'+z, a[y]) <u>end</u>.

2. x[1/a[a[1]]] ≡ x, b[2][1/a[a[1]]] ≡ b[2],
 a[a[2]][1/a[a[2]]] ≡ <u>if</u>(<u>if</u> 2 = a[2] <u>then</u> 1 <u>else</u> a[2] <u>fi</u>) = a[2] <u>then</u> 1 <u>else</u> a[<u>if</u> 2 = a[2] <u>then</u> 1 <u>else</u> a[2] <u>fi</u>] <u>fi</u>.
 Observe that the last expression is semantically (section 3) (though not syntactically) equal to <u>if</u> a[2] = 2 <u>then</u> a[1] <u>else</u> 1 <u>fi</u>.

3. DENOTATIONAL SEMANTICS

For any two sets *K*, *L*, let (K → *L*) ((*K* $\xrightarrow[\text{part}]{}$ *L*)) denote the set of all functions (all *partial* functions) from *K* to *L*.

We define the meaning *M* of the various types of statements in our language yielding, for S ∈ *S*, as a result a partial function *M*(S) operating on an environment-store pair yielding a new store: *M*(S)(ε,σ) = σ'.

As starting point we take the set *A* = {α,β,...} of *addresses* and the set *I* = {ν,μ,...} of *integers*. Again, we assume these to be well-ordered. Let Σ = {σ,σ',...} be the set of *stores*, i.e. Σ = (*A* → *I*), and let *Env* = {ε,ε',...} be the set of *environments*, i.e., of certain *partial*, 1 - 1 functions from *SV* ∪ (*AV*×*I*) to A. More specifically, we require that each ε is defined on a *finite* subset of *SV*, and on *all* elements *AV* × *I*. Thus, for each x ∈ *SV*, ε(x) ∈ *A* may be defined, and for each a ∈ *AV* and ν ∈ *I*, ε(a,ν) *is* defined. (For a subscripted variable a[s], if s has the current value ν, ε(a,ν) yields the address corresponding to a[s]. The assumption that ε(a,ν) is always defined stems from the fact that we study (explicit) declarations of *simple* variables only. Array variables may be considered as (implicitly) declared globally.) Next, we introduce

- For each $t \in IE$ its *right-hand* value $R(t)(\varepsilon,\sigma) \in I$,
- For each $v \in V$ its *left-hand* value $L(v)(\varepsilon,\sigma) \in A$,
- For each $p \in BE$ its *value* $T(p)(\varepsilon,\sigma) \in \{T,F\}$.

DEFINITION 3.1.

a. $R(v)(\varepsilon,\sigma) = \sigma(L(v)(\varepsilon,\sigma))$, $R(n)(\varepsilon,\sigma) = \nu$ (where ν is the integer denoted by the integer constant n), $R(t_1+t_2)(\varepsilon,\sigma) = plus\ (R(t_1)(\varepsilon,\sigma),R(t_2)(\varepsilon,\sigma)),\ldots,R(\underline{\text{if}}\ p\ \underline{\text{then}}\ t_1\ \underline{\text{else}}\ t_2\ \underline{\text{fi}})(\varepsilon,\sigma)$

$$= \begin{cases} R(t_1)(\varepsilon,\sigma), & \text{if } T(p)(\varepsilon,\sigma) = T \\ R(t_2)(\varepsilon,\sigma), & \text{if } T(p)(\varepsilon,\sigma) = F \end{cases}$$

b. $L(x)(\varepsilon,\sigma) = \varepsilon(x)$, $L(a[s])(\varepsilon,\sigma) = \varepsilon(a,R(s)(\varepsilon,\sigma))$

c. $T(\underline{\text{true}})(\varepsilon,\sigma) = T,\ldots,T(t_1=t_2)(\varepsilon,\sigma) = equal\ (R(t_1)(\varepsilon,\sigma),R(t_2)(\varepsilon,\sigma)),\ldots,$ $T(p_1 \supset p_2)(\varepsilon,\sigma) = (T(p_1)(\varepsilon,\sigma) \Rightarrow T(p_2)(\varepsilon,\sigma))$, where "$\Rightarrow$" denotes implication between the truth-values in $\{T,F\},\ldots$.

For the definition of assignment we need the notion of *variant* of a store σ: We write $\sigma\{\nu/\alpha\}$ for the store which satisfies: $\sigma\{\nu/\alpha\}(\alpha) = \nu$, and, for $\alpha' \neq \alpha$, $\sigma\{\nu/\alpha\}(\alpha') = \sigma(\alpha')$.

Using the notations and definitions introduced sofar, it is not difficult to define the meaning of the first three types of statements. We shall use the convention that $M(S)(\varepsilon,\sigma)$ is undefined whenever ε is undefined on some variable which occurs free in S or S_0. A similar convention applies to L, R and T.

DEFINITION 3.2. (Assignment, sequential composition, conditionals)

a. $M(v{:=}t)(\varepsilon,\sigma) = \sigma\{R(t)(\varepsilon,\sigma)/L(v)(\varepsilon,\sigma)\}$

b. $M(S_1;S_2)(\varepsilon,\sigma) = M(S_2)(\varepsilon,M(S_1)(\varepsilon,\sigma))$

c. $M(\underline{\text{if}}\ p\ \underline{\text{then}}\ S_1\ \underline{\text{else}}\ S_2\ \underline{\text{fi}}) = \begin{cases} M(S_1)(\varepsilon,\sigma), & \text{if } T(p)(\varepsilon,\sigma) = T \\ M(S_2)(\varepsilon,\sigma), & \text{if } T(p)(\varepsilon,\sigma) = F. \end{cases}$

For blocks and procedure calls, some further preparations are required. First of all, we require that, for each ε, $A \setminus \text{range}(\varepsilon)$ is infinite. Moreover, for each ε, each $y \in SV$ not in the domain of ε, and each $\alpha \in A$ not in the range of ε, we use the notation $\varepsilon \cup \langle y,\alpha\rangle$ for the extension of ε defined also on y (and yielding there α). This allows us to give

DEFINITION 3.3. (Blocks)

$M(\underline{\text{begin}}\ \text{new}\ x;S\ \underline{\text{end}})(\varepsilon,\sigma) = M(S[y/x])(\varepsilon\cup\langle y,\alpha\rangle,\sigma)$, where y is the first variable in SV not in the domain of ε, and α is the first address in A not in the range of ε.

The last - and most difficult - case is that of procedure calls. Complications are

- The standard least fixed point treatment of recursion can be given only in terms of a somewhat hybrid entity: a function which expects linguistic objects (elements of IE and V) as arguments, and yields an element of $(Env \times \Sigma \xrightarrow[\text{part}]{} \Sigma)$ as value.

- The possibility that the actual parameter t has (free) occurrences of the formal x.
- The concept of call-by-variable which, contrary to call-by-name, does not allow straightforward substitution but requires prior evaluation of the subscript in case the actual is a subscripted variable.

Let us consider the declaration $P \Leftarrow \mathit{val}\ x \cdot \mathit{var}\ y \cdot S_0$, with $S_0 \in \mathcal{S}$. In general, S_0 will contain "inner" recursive calls of P, i.e.,

$$S_0 \equiv \ldots P(t_1,v_1) \ldots \sim \ldots P(t_i,v_i) \ldots \sim \ldots P(t_n,v_n) \ldots$$

Let us use, for any $S \in \mathcal{S}$, the notation $S[P\to X]$ for the result of replacing all occurrences of P in S by X, where X is an element of the set $\mathcal{X} = \{X,Y,\ldots\}$ of *procedure variables*. This result is no longer an element of $\mathcal{S}$, but it is easy to extend the definition of $\mathcal{S}$ yielding $\mathcal{S}_{ext}$ containing both $\mathcal{S}$ and all elements of the form $S[P\to X]$.

We shall define the meaning of the procedure P to be an element of a certain subset of the set $\mathcal{H} \overset{df.}{=} ((\mathit{IE}\times\mathcal{V}) \to (\mathit{Env}\times\Sigma \xrightarrow[part]{} \Sigma))$. In fact, we consider the subset $\mathcal{H}_{vi}$ consisting of those elements η of $\mathcal{H}$ which are *variable invariant*, i.e., which satisfy $\eta(t[y/x],v[y/x])(\varepsilon\cup\langle y,\alpha\rangle,\sigma) = \eta(t[y'/x],v[y'/x])(\varepsilon\cup\langle y',\alpha\rangle,\sigma)$, for all y,y' which do not occur free in t, v or S_0. Furthermore, we order $\mathcal{H}_{vi}$ by putting $\eta \sqsubseteq \eta'$ iff $\forall t,v[\eta(t,v) \subseteq \eta'(t,v)]$. Let $\theta,\theta',\ldots$ be elements of the set $(\mathcal{X}\to\mathcal{H}_{vi})$. Thus, it is meaningful to write $\theta(X)(t,v)(\varepsilon,\sigma) = \sigma'$. For each $\theta \in (\mathcal{X}\to\mathcal{H}_{vi})$ and each $S_{ext} \in \mathcal{S}_{ext}$, we define a mapping $\mathcal{M}(\theta)(S_{ext})$ in the following way:

- For S_{ext} of one of the first four types, $\mathcal{M}(\theta)(S_{ext})$ is the obvious analogue of $\mathcal{M}(S)$. E.g., $\mathcal{M}(\theta)(v{:=}t) = \mathcal{M}(v{:=}t),\ldots,\mathcal{M}(\theta)(\underline{b}\ \underline{new}\ x;S\ \underline{e})(\varepsilon,\sigma) = \mathcal{M}(\theta)(S[y/x])(\varepsilon\cup\langle y,\alpha\rangle,\sigma)$, where $y = \ldots$ and $\alpha = \ldots$.
- $\mathcal{M}(\theta)(X(t,v)) = \theta(X)(t,v)$.

Actually, we shall mostly use θ's of the special form $\theta = \langle X,\eta\rangle$, where we have $\langle X,\eta\rangle(X) = \eta$, $\langle X,\eta\rangle(Y)$ is undefined for $X \not\equiv Y$.

Let, for Φ a monotone element of $(\mathcal{H}_{vi} \to \mathcal{H}_{vi})$, $\mu\Phi$ be the least fixed point of Φ, i.e., the least element of $\mathcal{H}_{vi}$ satisfying $\Phi(\mu\Phi) = \mu\Phi$. Let us, finally, write $\underline{b}\ \underline{new}\ x,y;S\ \underline{e}$ as short hand for $\underline{b}\ \underline{new}\ x;\underline{b}\ \underline{new}\ y;S\ \underline{e}\ \underline{e}$, provided that $x \not\equiv y$.

At last, we have enough background to give

DEFINITION 3.4. (Procedure calls) Assume the declaration (2.1). Then $\mathcal{M}(P(t,v)) = (\mu\Phi)(t,v)$, where Φ is the following (monotone) function:

$$\Phi = \lambda\eta\cdot\lambda t,v \cdot \mathcal{M}(\langle X,\eta\rangle)$$
$$(\underline{begin}\ \underline{new}\ u_1,u_2;u_1{:=}t;u_2{:=}s;$$
$$S_0[P\to X][u_1/x][v_1/y]\ \underline{end})$$

where u_1,u_2 are the first two variables not occurring free in t, v or S_0,
where if $v \equiv z$ for some $z \in \mathit{SV}$, then $s \overset{df.}{\equiv} u_2$ and $v_1 \overset{df.}{\equiv} z$,
where if $v \equiv a[r]$ for some $a \in \mathit{AV}$ and $r \in \mathit{IE}$, then $s \overset{df.}{\equiv} r$ and $v_1 \overset{df.}{\equiv} a[u_2]$.

Example. Consider the declaration

$P \Leftarrow$ *val* x • *var* y • if $x \geq 2$ then P(7,y) else if x = 1 then
i:=i+1;P(x-1,a[y]) else y:=0 fi fi .

Then M(P(x+5),a[i])) = ($\mu\Phi$)(x+5,a[i]), where we have, e.g.,

$\Phi(\eta)(7,y) = M(<X,\eta>)(\underline{b}\ \underline{new}\ u_1,u_2;u_1:=7;u_2:=u_2;\ \underline{if}\ u_1 \geq 2\ \underline{then}\ P(7,y)\ \underline{else}\ \underline{if}\ u_1 = 1\ \underline{then}$
$i:=i+1;X(u_1-1,a[y]\ \underline{else}\ y:=0\ \underline{fi}\ \underline{fi}\ \underline{e})$

and

$\Phi(\eta)(x+5,a[i]) = M(<X,\eta>)(\underline{b}\ \underline{new}\ u_1,u_2;u_1:=x+5;u_2:=i;\ \underline{if}\ u_1 \geq 2\ \underline{then}\ P(7,a[u_2]\ \underline{else}\ \underline{if}\ u_1 = 1$
$\underline{then}$
$i:=i+1;X(u_1-1,a[a[u_2]])\ \underline{else}\ a[u_2]:=0\ \underline{fi}\ \underline{fi}\ \underline{e})$.

4. APPLICATIONS TO PROOF THEORY

We introduce the kernel of a system of axioms and proof rules to show the correctness of programs in our PASCAL-like language, and offer as exercises the proofs of the soundness of these axioms and rules.

The formal system is taken from Hoare's axiomatic treatment ([6,7]) of the inductive assertion method. (Subsequent elaboration of his system may be found e.g. in [8] and [9].)

What we view as our extension of the theory as previously developed, is the following:

- An extension of Hoare's axiom of assignment to the case of assignment to a subscripted variable
- A rule for recursive procedures which extends Scott's induction principle to procedures with call-by-value and call-by-variable parameters.

Let p,q $\in$ *BE*, S $\in S_{ext}$. A *correctness formula* is a construct of the form {p}S{q}. Arbitrary correctness formulae are denoted by $\gamma,\gamma_1,\gamma',\ldots$, and finite sets $\Gamma = \{\gamma_1,\ldots \gamma_n\}$ of such formulae are called *axioms*. Outermost parenthesis in $\{\gamma_1,\ldots,\gamma_n\}$ are sometimes omitted.

The proof rules of our system are of the following two forms:

(4.1) $$\frac{\Gamma_1}{\Gamma_2}$$

(4.2) $$\frac{\Gamma_1 \to \Gamma_2}{\Gamma_3}$$

DEFINITION 4.1.

a. $M(\theta)(\Gamma)$ holds iff $M(\theta)(\gamma)$ holds for each $\gamma \in \Gamma$.

$M(\theta)(\{p\}S\{q\})$ holds iff for all ε defined on all free variables of p,q,S and S_0, and for all σ, we have $T(p)(\varepsilon,\sigma) \Rightarrow T(q)(\varepsilon,M(\theta)(S)(\varepsilon,\sigma))$.

b. Γ is valid iff $M(\theta)(\Gamma)$ holds for all θ.

c. $\frac{\Gamma_1}{\Gamma_2}$ is sound iff, for all θ, $M(\theta)(\Gamma_1)$ implies $M(\theta)(\Gamma_2)$.

d. $\frac{\Gamma_1 \to \Gamma_2}{\Gamma_3}$ is sound iff soundness of $\frac{\Gamma_1}{\Gamma_2}$ implies validity of Γ_3.

We now present the axioms and proof rules for the five types of statements and, moreover, a proof rule dealing with substitution. (It is possible to refine the last rule (see [3,5]); however, in the form as given it is sufficiently powerful to allow meaningful application of the procedure rule.)

Assignment $\{p[t/v]\}\ v{:=}t\ \{p\}$.

This axiom, though syntactically identical to Hoare's assignment axiom, is in fact an extension of it since it also covers assignment to subscripted variables. Example: {<u>if</u> a[2] = 2 <u>then</u> a[1] = 1 <u>else</u> <u>true</u> <u>fi</u>} a[a[2]]:=1 {a[a[2]]=1}. For details see [2].

Composition $$\frac{\{p\}S_1\{q\},\{q\}S_2\{r\}}{\{p\}S_1;S_2\{r\}}$$

Conditionals $$\frac{\{p\wedge q\}S_1\{r\},\{p\wedge\neg q\}S_2\{r\}}{\{p\}\ \underline{\text{if}}\ q\ \underline{\text{then}}\ S_1\ \underline{\text{else}}\ S_2\ \underline{\text{fi}}\ \{r\}}$$

These two rules are easily seen to be sound.

Blocks $$\frac{\{p\}\ S[y/x]\ \{q\}}{\{p\}\ \underline{\text{begin}}\ \underline{\text{new}}\ x;S\ \underline{\text{end}}\ \{q\}}$$

where y *is some variable which does not occur free in* p, q, S *or* S_0.

This rule was first given in Hoare [7]. It is not so easy to grasp all its consequences. Let us point out, e.g., that the fact that it leaves declaration (2.1) unaffected ensures that in a program such as <P ⇐ *var* x · *val* y · ... z ..., <u>b</u> ... <u>b</u> <u>new</u> z; ... P(t,v) ... <u>e</u> ... <u>e</u>>, a clash between the global z of the procedure body, and the local z valid at the moment of call, is avoided. (As we see it, this problem is incorrectly dealt with in [3,5].)

Procedure calls. Assume (2.1), and let S_0 have the form as described before definition 3.4. Assume we want to prove {p} P(t,v) {q}. Let $p_0 \overset{\text{df.}}{\equiv} p$, $q_0 \overset{\text{df.}}{\equiv} q$, $t_0 \overset{\text{df.}}{\equiv} t$, $v_0 \overset{\text{df.}}{\equiv} v$.

$$\{p_1\}\ X(t_1,v_1)\ \{q_1\},\dots,\{p_n\}\ X(t_n,v_n)\ \{q_n\}$$

$$\rightarrow$$

$$\{p_0\}\ \underline{\text{begin}}\ \underline{\text{new}}\ u_1^0,u_2^0,u_1^0:=t_0;u_2^0:=s_0;$$
$$S_0[P \rightarrow X][u_1^0/x][v_1^0/y]\ \underline{\text{end}}\ \{q_0\},$$

$$\dots$$

$$\{p_n\}\ \underline{\text{begin}}\ \underline{\text{new}}\ u_1^n,u_2^n;u_1^n:=t_n;u_2^n:=s_n;$$
$$S_0[P \rightarrow X][u_1^n/x][v_1^n/y]\ \underline{\text{end}}\ \{q_n\}$$

$$\{p_0\}\ P(t_0,v_0)\ \{q_0\}$$

where, for each $i = 0,1,\dots,n$, *the* u_1^i, u_2^i *do not occur free in* S_0, t_i, v_i, p_i *or* q_i, *and where the* s_i *and* v_1^i, $i = 0,\dots,n$, *are derived from the* v_i *in the same manner as in def. 3.4.*

Observe that the p_i, q_i, $i = 1,\dots,n$, are assertions about the *inner* calls, whereas the p_0, q_0 are assertions about the *outer* call. Therefore, the p_0, q_0 do not play a part in the induction hypothesis. One should also observe that the rule remains valid when the formulae $\{p_i\}\ P(t_i,v_i)\ \{q_i\}$, $i = 1,\dots,n$, are added to its conclusion (i.e. to $\{p_0\}\ P(t_0,v_0)\ \{q_0\}$).

Substitution

$$\frac{P \Leftarrow \mathit{var}\ x \cdot \mathit{val}\ y \cdot S_0,\ \{p\}S\{q\}}{P \Leftarrow (\mathit{var}\ x \cdot \mathit{val}\ y \cdot S_0)[v/u],\{p[v/u]\}S[v/u]\{q[v/u]\}}$$

where v *satisfies the following requirement: None of the simple variables occurring in* v *occurs free in* S, S_0, p *or* q.

We hope that the notation in this rule - which extends the definitions given so-far - is self-explanatory: Above the line, calls of P refer to declaration (2.1), but below they refer to the declaration $P \Leftarrow (\mathit{var}\ x \cdot \mathit{val}\ y \cdot S_0)[v/u]$, where a natural extension of def. 2.1 is assumed.

We are confident that the proofs of the soundness of the block rule, the procedure call rule and the substitution rule, will offer no difficulties.

REFERENCES

1. De Bakker, J.W., *Least fixed points revisited*, in λ-Calculus and Computer Science Theory, Lecture Notes in Computer Science 37 (C. Böhm, ed.), p.27-61, Springer (1975).

2. De Bakker, J.W., *Correctness proofs for assignment statements*, Report IW 55/76, Mathematisch Centrum (1976).

3. Cook, S.A., *Axiomatic and interpretive semantics for an ALGOL fragment*, Technical Report no. 79, University of Toronto (1975).

4. Donahue, J.E., *The mathematical semantics of axiomatically defined programming language constructs*, in Proc. Symp. Proving and Improving Programs, p.353-370, IRIA (1975).

5. Gorelick, G.A., *A complete axiomatic system for proving assertions about recursive and non-recursive programs*, Technical Report no. 75, University of Toronto (1975).

6. Hoare, C.A.R., *An axiomatic basis for programming language constructs*, C.ACM 12, p.576-580 (1969).

7. Hoare, C.A.R., *Procedures and parameters, an axiomatic approach*, in Symp. on Semantics of Algorithmic Languages, Lecture Notes in Mathematics 188 (E. Engeler, ed.), p.102-116, Springer (1971).

8. Hoare, C.A.R. & N. Wirth, *An axiomatic definition of the programming language PASCAL*, Acta Inf. 2, p.335-355 (1973).

9. Igarashi, S., R.L. London & D.C. Luckham, *Automatic program verification I: A logical basis and its implementation*, Acta Inf. 4, p.145-182 (1975).

10. Manna, Z., S. Ness & J. Vuillemin, *Inductive methods for proving properties of programs*, C.ACM 16, p.491-502 (1973).

11. Manna, Z. & J. Vuillemin, *Fixpoint approach to the theory of computation*, C.ACM 15, p.528-536 (1972).

12. Scott, D. & C. Strachey, *Towards a mathematical semantics for computer languages*, in Proc. of the Symp. on Computers and Automata (J. Fox, ed.), p.19-46, Polytechnic Inst. of Brooklyn (1971).

W-AUTOMATA AND THEIR LANGUAGES

Wilfried Brauer
Institut für Informatik
Universität Hamburg
D-2000 Hamburg 13

0. Introduction

The classical finite-state acceptors, the Rabin/Scott automata (in short RSA), and their languages (the RSL's) have many nice properties, e.g.

- nondeterministic and deterministic RSA are equivalent; there are simple methods to construct new RSA from given ones; almost all problems concerning RSA are decidable; RSA can directly be interpreted as (right-linear) Chomsky grammars;
- there are elegant algebraic characterizations of RSL's in terms of congruences, syntactic monoids, the rational operations etc.;
- the class of RSL's has interesting closure properties.

Many attempts have been made to construct automata or grammars which are more powerful than RSA but have basically the same constituents (finite-state machine or finitely many right-linear productions) - the power being gained by a more complex method of acceptance or generation of languages, e.g. by [1)]

- using several RSA more or less in parallel (e.g. multi-tape, multi-head, or the multiple finite automata of CH),
- using right-linear productions in parallel (e.g. equal matrix, right-linear simple matrix, or the n-parallel right-linear grammars of RW),
- using index grammars with right-linear productions or applying the idea of index grammars to the above mentioned parallel grammars (LA),
- using RSA with additional peripheral devices each of which being solely described by a language over the set of its actions (KS).

The algebraic tools have been applied to other classes of languages, e.g.

- to linear context-free languages (BH),
- to context-free languages (in short CFL's); in particular the syntactic congruences of CFL's have been studied in depth, but only recently a suitable generalization of the notion of congruence relation by which CFL's can be characterized in a way similar to RSL's has been found (OP).

New multiplications on the set of all words over a finite alphabet have been introduced s.t.[2)] the rational operations and the congruences of finite index define new languages

1) Only some recent or supposedly less well known papers are cited; for more information see BR and SA.

2) "s.t." abbreviates "such that".

having many of the properties of the RSL's (e.g. the k-linear grammars of Amar/Putzolu, the σ-regular languages of SC, the quasi-regular sets of WE) and automata over such monoids have been defined (e.g. SM, WA).
Following Eilenberg and Schützenberger recognizable and rational subsets of arbitrary monoids have been investigated - rational subsets of free commutative monoids have (under the name of semilinear sets) become an important tool in formal language theory. The literature on these subjects is abundant, dispersed and heterogenous.

In the following I'll outline how W-automata (the nondeterministic finite automata over monoids introduced in WA) can serve as a basis for a general theory encompassing many of the things mentioned above and giving rise to new results and problems (for more details see BR).
In section 1 some of the classes of monoids which play a rôle in the application of the theory to formal languages are presented. In section 2 W-automata are defined and it is briefly reported how notions and results from RSA theory can be transferred to W-automata. Section 3 contains some hints on the application of the theory to formal languages. In section 4 remarks on open problems and directions of further research are made.

1. Some classes of effective monoids

A monoid is a pair $(M,\circ)$ - M a set, $\circ$ an associative binary operation (normally called multiplication) on M s.t. M contains an identity e for $\circ$; if $\circ$ is understood, we denote the monoid by M.
Let W(X) be the set of all words over the (finite) alphabet X. A monoid M is called effective, if there is an injective mapping i of M into some W(X) and an algorithm that computes $i(m \circ m')$ for each pair i(m), i(m') of representations of elements from M. (i is called an effective representation of M.)
W(X) with the concatenation of words as multiplication and the empty word Λ as identity is called the free monoid generated by X, denoted by F(X).
For each monoid M and each subset X of M there is a unique homomorphism $h_{X,M}$ from F(X) to M. The set $X^* = h_{X,M}(F(X))$ is the submonoid (of M) generated by X; the set $X^+ = h_{X,M}(F(X) - \Lambda))$ is the subsemigroup generated by X. If $X^* = M$, then X generates M.
There are several methods for constructing effective monoids:
(1) WS-multiplications on W(X). (This is a generalization of methods introduced in SC and WE): A W-mapping is a computable mapping f: W(X) $\longrightarrow$ W(X) s.t.
(i) f(w) is a piecewise subword of w; let $\overline{f}(w)$ be the rest of w obtained by erasing the letters of f(w) in w, then $f(\overline{f}(w)) = \Lambda$.
(ii) For each pair u,v from W(X) s.t. $f(v) = \Lambda$, there is exactly one w in W(X) s.t. f(w) = u and $\overline{f}(w) = v$.
(iii) For all w,w' in W(X) we have:
If $w \neq w'$ and f(w) = f(w') then $\overline{f}(w) \neq \overline{f}(w')$.

Example: Let $k,m,n \in \mathbb{N}$ [3]. For $w \in W(X)$, $|w|$ [4] $< k+m+n = s$ put $f_1(w) = w$ and for $v \in W(X)$, $|v| < s$, $x_i \in X$ put $\overline{f}_1(vx_1 \dots x_{jk}x_{jk+1} \dots x_{jk+jm} \dots x_{js}) = x_{jk}x_{jk+jm}x_{js}$, where $js+|v| = |w|$. Then $f_1(vx_1 \dots x_{js}) = vx_1 \dots x_{jk-1}x_{jk+1} \dots x_{jk+jm-1}x_{jk+jm+1} \dots x_{js-1}$, and f_1 is a W-mapping.

A W-mapping f defines a multiplication $\circ_f$ on W(X) s.t. $W_f(X) = (W(X), \circ_f)$ becomes a monoid (called a WS-monoid on X):

$$u \circ_f v = \begin{cases} u & \text{if } f(v) = v \\ \text{that } w \text{ which fulfils } f(w) = u \text{ and } \overline{f}(w) = v & \text{if } f(v) = \Lambda \\ (u \circ_f f(v)) \circ_f \overline{f}(v) & \text{if } \Lambda \neq f(v) \neq v . \end{cases}$$

Example: $f(w) \circ_f \overline{f}(w) = w$ holds for all $w \in W(X)$. If $|\overline{f}(w)| = 1$ for all $w \in W(X) - \Lambda$, then $W_f(X)$ is a free monoid.

It is obvious that WS-monoids are effective.

(2) Quotients of F(X) by simple relations. Let R be a finite set of pairs of words over X. Two words u,v in F(X) are R-adjacent iff [5] there is a pair (r,r') or a pair (r',r) in R s.t. $u = u_1ru_2$ and $v = v_1r'v_2$. The relation of R-equivalence is the reflexive and transitive closure of the relation of R-adjacency. The set F(X)/R of R-equivalence classes with elementwise multiplication of classes forms a monoid (the quotient of F(X) by R).

If $R \subseteq \{(xy,yx) \mid x,y \in X\} = C$ then F(X)/R is a literal monoid (see CF), if R = C then F(X)/R is the free commutative monoid generated by X. To show that a literal monoid is effective, define a total ordering < on X and call a word $x_1x_2 \dots x_n$ ($x_i \in X$) well arranged, if $(x_ix_{i+1}, x_{i+1}x_i) \in R$ implies $x_i < x_{i+1}$ for $i = 1, \dots, n-1$. Each R-equivalence class contains exactly one well arranged word - this relation defines an effective representation of F(X)/R.

If $X = \{x_i \mid i = \pm 1, \dots, \pm n\}$ and $R = \{(x_ix_{-i}, \Lambda) \mid i = 1, \dots, n\}$ or $R = \{(x_ix_{-i}, \Lambda), (x_{-i}x_i, \Lambda) \mid i = 1, \dots, n\}$ then F(X)/R is the involutive monoid generated by X or the free group generated by $\{x_1, \dots, x_n\}$ respectively (for n = 2 the involutive monoid is the bicyclic monoid). For both versions of R a word is called R-reduced if it is not R-adjacent to a shorter word - the mapping of an R-equivalence class to the one R-reduced word it contains is an effective representation of F(X)/R. The R-equivalence class containing Λ is the Dyck set or the symmetric Dyck set on X respectively.

In the theory of asynchronous automata the relation $Q = \{(xx,x) \mid x \in X\}$ is of interest.

(3) Cartesian products of effective monoids. The Cartesian product $M \times M'$ of two monoids

---

3) $\mathbb{N}$ is the set of natural numbers, $\mathbb{N}_0 = \mathbb{N} \cup \{0\}$

4) $|w|$ is the length of w

5) "iff" abbreviates "if and only if".

with componentwise multiplication is called the direct product of the monoids.
The Cartesian product $W(X)^2$ of two exemplars of W(X) augmented by a new element 0 can be furnished with the following multiplication (see NP):

$$(u,v)\circ 0 = 0\circ(u,v) = 0\circ 0 = 0$$

$$(u,v)\circ(u',v') = \begin{cases} (u,wv') & \text{if } v = wu' \\ (w'u,v') & \text{if } u' = w'v \\ 0 & \text{otherwise} \end{cases}$$

This defines the polycyclic monoid P(X) which is the syntactic monoid of the Dyck set on $X \cup \overline{X}$ where $\overline{X} = \{\overline{x} \mid x \in X\}$.

A property of great importance (introduced by McKnight/Storey) is equidivisibility:
A monoid M is equidivisible iff
$a\circ b = c\circ d$ (for $a,b,c,d \in M$) implies the existence of $s \in M$ s.t. $a\circ s = c$ and $s\circ d = b$ or $a = c\circ s$ and $s\circ b = d$.
It is known that free monoids, groups and the bicyclic monoid are equidivisible but not the literal monoids or the direct product of monoids. It is easy to show that WS-monoids and involutive monoids as well as F(X)/Q are equidivisible but not the polycyclic monoids.

2. W-automata and some of their properties

Def.1: A W-automaton (in short WA) over the monoid $(M,\circ)$ is a quintuple $A = (Z,X,t,S,F)$ where
Z is a finite set (of states), $S \subseteq Z$ and $F \subseteq Z$ are the sets of initial and final states respectively,
X is a finite subset of M, the input set,
$t = (Z\times X, Z, \tau)$ is a correspondence (multivalued mapping) from $Z\times X$ into Z (the transition correspondence) with $\tau \subseteq Z\times X\times Z$ as its graph - the elements of τ are the transitions of A.
A is locally deterministic iff t is a partial (single-valued) mapping.
A is weakly complete iff $pr_{1,2}(\tau) = Z\times X$ [6].
A is initial iff $|S| = 1$.
The global transition correspondence $t^* = (Z\times M, Z, \tau^*)$ is defined in two steps:
(i) Consider X as an alphabet generating F(X) and put
$\tau_F^0 = \{(z,\Lambda,z) \mid z\in Z\}$, $\tau_F^1 = \tau$, and for $n \in \mathbb{N}$
$\tau_F^{n+1} = \{(z,wv,z') \mid$ there is a $z'' \in Z$ s.t. $(z,w,z'') \in \tau^n$, $(z'',v,z') \in \tau\}$.
Then $\tau_F^* = \bigcup\{\tau_F^i \mid i\in \mathbb{N}_0\}$ and $t_F^* = (Z\times F(X), Z, \tau_F^*)$.
(ii) $t^*(z,m) = \bigcup\{t_F^*(z,x_1x_2 \ldots x_n) \mid x_1\circ x_2\circ\ldots\circ x_n = m,\ x_i \in X,\ n\in \mathbb{N}_0\}$.
A is complete iff A is weakly complete and X generates M.
A is deterministic (or a DWA) iff t^* is a mapping.

---

6) pr_i and $pr_{j,k}$ are the projections from a Cartesian product to its i-th factor or to the Cartesian product of its j-th and k-th factors respectively.

A is a CDWA iff it is a complete initial DWA.

A is multiplicative iff $t^*(t^*(z,m),m') = t^*(z,m \circ m')$ for all $z \in Z$, $m,m' \in X^*$.

Examples: 1) A two-tape automaton in the sense of Elgot/Mezei (in short a 2-EMA) is a WA over $F(X) \times F(X) = F(X)^2$.

2) A nondeterministic generalized sequential machine or a sequential transducer with accepting states (an a-transducer) can be viewed as an initial WA over $F(X) \times F(Y)$.

Prop.1: (i) A locally deterministic WA need not be deterministic.

(ii) WA are not necessarily multiplicative. A weakly complete DWA is multiplicative. If M is freely generated by X then A is multiplicative.

(iii) If A is a multiplicative WA then the correspondences $t^*_m = (Z,Z,\tau^*_m)$, $\tau^*_m = pr_{1,3}(\tau^* \cap Z \times \{m\} \times Z)$ for $m \in X^*$, form a finite monoid, the transition monoid T(A) of A, which can effectively be constructed if M is effective.

(iv) If in M it is undecidable whether the intersection of two finitely generated subsemigroups is empty, then it is undecidable whether a WA over M is deterministic.

(v) If M is effective and if multiplicativity of weakly complete WA is decidable, then it is decidable whether a weakly complete WA is deterministic.

The proof is a straight forward application of ideas known from the theory of RSA and of linear CFL's, the condition in (iv) holds for direct products of free monoids (as a consequence of the unsolvability of Post's correspondence problem).

Examples: 1) 2-EMA are not multiplicative; it is not decidable whether a 2-EMA is deterministic.

2) A WA over a WS-monoid $W_f(X)$ s.t. $|\overline{f}(w)| = 1$ is multiplicative.

Def.2: The language accepted by the WA of Def.1 is $L(A) = \{m \in M | t^*(S,m) \cap F \neq \emptyset\}$.

Two WA over submonoids of M are equivalent iff they accept the same language.

A subset L of M is acceptable, D-acceptable or CD-acceptable iff there is a WA, a DWA or a CDWA A respectively s.t. $L = L(A)$.

Acc(M), DAcc(M) and CDAcc(M) denote the sets of acceptable, D-acceptable and CD-acceptable subsets of M.

A subset R of a monoid M is recognizable if there is a homomorphism h of M into a finite monoid s.t. $L = h^{-1}(h(R))$. The set of all recognizable subsets of M is denoted by Rec(M).

The set Rat(M) of all rational subsets of the monoid M is the least class C of subsets of M satisfying:

(i) The empty set and each single element set is in C.

(ii) If U,V are in C, then $U \cup V$, $U \circ V$ and U^* are in C.

Examples: Let $X = \{a,b\}$.

1) The WA $A_0 = (\{z\},\{(a,b)\},t_0,\{z\},\{z\})$ over $F(X)^2$ where $\tau_0 = \{(z,(a,b),z)\}$ accepts $L(A_0) = \{(a^n,b^n) | n \in \mathbb{N}_0\}$

2) The WA $A_1 = (\{z\},\{aba\},t_1,\{z\},\{z\})$ over $W_{f_1}(X)$, where f_1 is the W-mapping defined

in the example to 1,(1), with the restriction k = m = n = 1, and where $\tau_1 = \{(z,aba,z)\}$, accepts $L(A_1) = \{a^n b^n a^n | n \in \mathbb{N}_0\}$.

Prop.2: (i) Rat(M) = Acc(M). If M is finitely generated then Rec(M) = CDAcc(M) $\neq \emptyset$.
(ii) CDAcc(M) $\subsetneq$ DAcc(M) $\subsetneq$ Acc(M).
(iii) CDAcc(M) is not closed under product or under submonoid generation. DAcc(M) is not closed under product.
(iv) CDAcc(M) is a Boolean algebra of sets.
Acc(M) is not closed under intersection or complement.
If M is finitely generated, L $\in$ Acc(M), and L' $\in$ CDAcc(M) then L $\cap$ L' $\in$ Acc(M).
(v) For each multiplicative WA over an effective monoid (by means of the transition monoid or of the power-set construction) an equivalent CDWA can be constructed.

Remarks on the proof: For (i), (iv) and (v) the same simple constructions of automata as in the case of RSA are used - if M is not finitely generated then there is no CDWA over M.
The first parts of (ii) and (iii) are easy. The second parts are obtained by proving that for X = {a,b,c} and Y = {a,b} $P = \{(uc,vuw) | u,v,w \in Y^+\} \notin DAcc(F(X)^2)$ but $P \in Acc(F(X)^2)$.

Lemma: If M is an equidivisible or a literal monoid and A and A' are CDWA over M, then there is a multiplicative WA over M accepting L(A)∘L(A').

The proof is very simple - as in the case of RSA A and A' are connected by e-transitions from all final states of A to the initial state of A' (with some amendments in the literal case).

Together with prop.2 this gives a very simple proof for two theorems by McKnight/Storey (proved by semigroup theory) and Fliess (proved by Hankel matrices and power series - see FL):

Prop.3: (i) If M is a finitely generated equidivisible monoid s.t. the single element subsets of M are recognizable, then Rec(M) = Rat(M).
(ii) The product of recognizable subsets of a literal monoid is recognizable.

By applying prop.3 (i) to WS-monoids we obtain several results by Amar/Putzolu, Schnorr (SC) and Wechsung (WE) as corollaries.

Furthermore, from prop.3 (i) one easily deduces that the first of the two axiom systems for rational expressions given in SL is correct when applied to a monoid fulfilling the condition in prop.3 (i), while the second is not (for more details see VO).

Prop.4: Let X be a finite subset of a monoid (M,∘) and, for $m \in X^*$, define
$p(m) = \min\{k \in \mathbb{N}_0 | x_1 \circ x_2 \circ \ldots \circ x_k = m, \; x_i \in X\}$.
Then for each $L \in Rat(X^*,\circ)$ there is $n \in \mathbb{N}_0$ s.t. for each $m \in L$, fulfilling $p(m) \geq n$ the following holds:
There are $u,v,w \in X^*$ s.t. $m = u \circ v \circ w$, $v \neq e$, $p(u \circ w) \leq n$ and $u \circ v^k \circ w \in L$ for all $k \in \mathbb{N}_0$.

The proof is almost the same as for RSA - if M is effective and L is given by a WA then n,u,v,w can effectively be constructed.

By applying this to direct products $F(X)^n$ or WS-monoids one easily obtains hierarchy results on language families as developed in RW and SC (cf. 3).

<u>Prop.5</u>: Let A and A' denote arbitrary WA over an effective monoid M.
(i) It is decidable whether L(A) is empty (or infinite).
(ii) If the condition of prop.1 (iv) holds, then it is undecidable whether $L(A) \cap L(A')$ is empty (or infinite).
(iii) If A and A' are multiplicative then it is decidable whether they are equivalent.
(iv) It is decidable whether a WA over M is deterministic, iff it is decidable whether the intersection of two rational subsets of M is empty.
(v) Multiplicativity of WA over M is decidable if equivalence of WA over M is decidable, and this is decidable if $R \subseteq R'$ is decidable for rational subsets R and R' of M.

The proofs are quite easy - they use constructions known from the theory of RSA or of linear CFL's.

As a corollary to prop.3 (i), prop.2 (iv) and prop.5 (i), (iv), (v) we obtain:
For WA over monoids satisfying the condition of prop.3(i) it is decidable whether they are deterministic and whether they are multiplicative.

3. Some applications to formal language theory

3.1 It is well known that <u>linear CFL's</u> can be represented by 2-EMA (i.e. by WA over $F(X)^2$), namely a subset L of F(X) is a linear CFL iff there is a WA A over $F(X)^2$ s.t. $L = \{u\tilde{v} \mid (u,v) \in L(A)\}$, where $\tilde{v}$ is the mirror image of v;
A is said to represent L.
Since the structure of ambiguous CFL's and the origin of ambiguity of CFL's is almost unknown, it is interesting to investigate the class of linear CFL's represented by DWA; some of the results obtained so far (HW) are:

- Each unambiguous linear CFL can be represented by an initial DWA; this implies that the deterministic 2-EMA introduced in DI in order to study linear CFL's are a proper subclass of the class of initial DWA.
- Each n-bounded CFL has a degree of ambiguity $\leq \binom{n}{2}$, and if it is linear it is representable by an initial DWA.
- Using the notion of iterating pairs, a particular notation for linear CFL's represented by WA over $F(X)^2$ having only trivial cycles in their graph (accepting only rational sets of star height 1) has been developed, which allows for the formulation of criteria guaranteeing that a language is unambiguous or that a union of languages has a given finite degree of ambiguity. Finite unions of unambiguous languages described in this formalism are representable by initial DWA.

3.2 <u>Language families having properties like RSL's</u> (in particular closure under the Boolean and the rational operations, decidability, existence of a complete and correct axiom system for finite expressions denoting them, algebraic characterization by congruences of finite index) can easily be defined using WA over WS-monoids, since the single element subsets of WS-monoids are CD-acceptable.

For example let $d = (s_1, \dots, s_n, d_1, \dots, d_n) \in \mathbb{N}^n \times \{-1,+1\}^n$ be given. Then a W-mapping f_d can be defined as follows: Put $s = s_1 + \dots + s_n$. Decompose each $w \in W(X)$ into $w = w_0 w_1 w_1' w_2 w_2' \dots w_n w_n'$ s.t. $|w_0| < s$

$$|w_i| = \begin{cases} ks_i, & \text{if } d_i = +1 \\ s_i & \text{otherwise} \end{cases} \qquad |w_i'| = \begin{cases} s_i, & \text{if } d_i = +1 \\ ks_i & \text{otherwise} \end{cases}$$

where k is defined by $(k+1)s + |w_0| = |w|$. Then define

$$f_d(w) = w_0 v_1 v_2 \dots v_n, \quad \text{where } v_i = \begin{cases} w_i, & \text{if } d_i = +1 \\ w_i' & \text{otherwise} \end{cases}.$$

The WS-multiplication $\circ_{f_d}$ is very similar to the associative partial operation $\circ$ of SC, and the acceptable subsets of $W_{f_d}(X)$ are exactly the $\circ$-regular sets of SC. The WA over $W_{f_d}(X)$ can be regarded as <u>deterministic (n+1)-head automata</u>: heads 1 to n always move simultaneously, where d_i denotes the direction into which head i moves, and s_i is the number of symbols head i reads in one step; head 0 only reads the first part of length $< s$ of the tape in one step and does not move.

Another class of W-mappings (the associated WS-monoids of which are free monoids) is defined as follows (WE):

Let $t: \mathbb{N}_0 \to \mathbb{N}_0$, s.t. $1 \le t(n) \le n$ for $n \in \mathbb{N}$, be computable. Then $f_t(x_1 \dots x_n) = x_1 \dots x_{t(n)-1} x_{t(n)+1} \dots x_n$ defines a W-mapping f_t s.t. $|\overline{f}_t(w)| = 1$ for $w \neq \Lambda$.

3.3 Languages generated by <u>n-parallel right linear grammars</u> (RW), by <u>right-linear</u> or <u>one-sided-linear simple matrix grammars of degree n</u> can be described in terms of WA over $(W(X)^n, \circ_d)$, where $\circ_d$ is a multiplication defined as follows: For $d \in \{-1,+1\}^n$ let $(u_1, u_2, \dots, u_n) \circ_d (v_1, v_2, \dots, v_n) = (w_1, w_2, \dots, w_n)$ where

$$w_i = \begin{cases} v_i u_i, & \text{if } d_i = +1 \\ u_i v_i & \text{otherwise} \end{cases}.$$

Many of the known results on these families are simple corollaries of the propositions given in 2. The WA over $(W(X)^n, \circ_d)$ can be interpreted as nondeterministic n-EMA - a word has to be decomposed nondeterministically into n pieces, and some of the pieces may have to be reversed before they are written onto the input tapes of the n-EMA.

3.4 <u>Pushdown automata</u> (in short PDA) can be viewed as WA over $F(X) \times P(Y)$ or $F(X) \times I(Y')$, where $I(Y')$ is the involutive monoid generated by Y'. The first assertion follows from algebraic considerations combined with the second one. The second assertion is verified as follows: Let X be the input and Y be the pushdown alphabet of a given PDA - we can assume that the PDA only writes or reads single letters on the pushdown store. Then to each $y \in Y$ we can associate two symbols <u>pushy</u> and <u>popy</u>. Let $Y' = \{\text{pushy}, \text{popy} \mid y \in Y\}$. Then the relation $P = \{(\text{pushy popy}, \Lambda) \mid y \in Y\}$ on $F(Y')$ describes the essential feature of the PDA - the PDA can obviously be interpreted as a WA over $F(X) \times I(Y')$, where $I(Y') =$

$= F(Y')/P$. A language L is accepted by the PDA by empty store iff $L =$ $= pr_1(L(A) \cap F(X) \times \{e\})$. Several results on CFL's are immediate consequences of the properties of WA given in 2.; e.g. since each pushdown alphabet Y can be encoded in terms of a fixed alphabet of two letters, each Y' can be encoded in terms of a fixed four-letter alphabet V; thus each W(A) over $F(X) \times I(Y')$ can be viewed as a WA over $F(X) \times F(V)$, and $L \subseteq F(X)$ is a CFL iff $L = pr_1(L(A) \cap F(X) \times D)$ where A is such a WA, and D is the Dyck set on V. Since there is a canonical injection of $F(X) \times F(V)$ into $F(X \cup V)$ there exist fixed homomorphisms h_1 and h_2 from $F(X \cup V)$ to $F(X)$ and $F(V)$ respectively s.t. we obtain: $L \subseteq F(X)$ is a CFL iff there is a rational subset $R \subseteq F(X \cup V)$ s.t. $L = h_1(R \cap h_2^{-1}(D))$. In the same way we see that $L \cap R$ is a CFL if L is a CFL and R is rational, or that the set of words left on the pushdown store by a rational set is rational.

3.5 Since Turing machines are equivalent to PDA with two pushdown stores the _type-0 languages_ can be characterized by WA over $F(X) \times I(V)^2$, where V and I(V) are as in 3.4. Several results on type-0 languages can easily be derived from this fact: e.g. in the same way as in 3.4 we can deduce that there are two CFL's L_1, L_2 in $F(X')$ and a homomorphism h from $F(X')$ to $F(X)$ s.t. for each CFL $L \subseteq F(X)$ there is a rational set $R \subseteq F(X')$ s.t. $L = h(L_1 \cap L_2 \cap R)$. Most of the results in SV can be obtained in a similar way.

4. Concluding remarks

The theory presented may help to solve some more known problems, it gives rise to quite a number of new questions and it offers several ways for further research:
The general theory of WA over arbitrary effective monoids should be pursued, e.g. by attacking the following questions:

- Which conditions on monoids M other than equidivisibility ensure Rat(M) = Rec(M) or imply that Rat(M) is a Boolean algebra ?
- Are there other properties of RSA which hold for WA ?
- What is the effect of restricting the structure of a WA by imposing a structure on the set of states (e.g. disjoint union of several sets as with Rabin/Scott's two-tape automata, or Cartesian product of several sets) ?
- What is the effect of changing the mode of acceptance, e.g. by requiring $t^*(s,m) \subseteq F$ as in WO ?

The theory of WA may possibly be generalized to cover partial monoids (i.e. sets endowed with an associative partial binary operation) or even to use more general algebraic structures (this is closely related to the problem whether some of the methods and results from OP can be transferred to nonfree algebras).

Another problem is, how the methods and results from LA can be generalized to WA and their languages.

The theory of WS-monoids is only in its infancy; in particular W-mappings have to be studied along the lines of WE and with respect to complexity problems.

The properties of WA over particular monoids like $(W(X)^n, \circ_d)$, $F(X) * I(Y')^2$, $F(X)^n * I(Y')$ (which represent n-tape PDA) and the WS-monoids should be investigated in detail, especially in order to apply the results to formal language theory as indicated in 3.1 - 3.5.

As WA over $F(X)^2$ are closely related to linear CFL's and to generalized sequential machines, their properties are of great interest; some of the open questions in this field are:

- Are there linear CFL's of unbounded ambiguity representable by DWA ?
- Are all linear CFL's of bounded ambiguity representable by DWA (This is closely related to the question of Eilenberg whether each CFL of bounded ambiguity is a finite union of unambiguous CFL's) ?
- Is the equivalence of DWA decidable ?

References

BH F.Bartholomes, G.Hotz, Homomorphismen und Reduktionen linearer Sprachen, Lecture Notes in Operations Res. and Math. Systems 32, Springer-Verlag, Berlin 1970

BR W.Brauer, Automatentheorie, Teubner Verlag, Stuttgart, in preparation

CF P.Cartier, D.Foata, Problèmes combinatoires de commutation et réarrangements, Lect. Notes in Math. 85, Springer-Verlag, Berlin 1969

CH K.Čulik, I.Havel, On multiple finite automata, in W.Händler, E.Peschl, H.Unger, 3.Colloquium über Automatentheorie, 19.-22-10.1965, Birkhäuser, Basel, 1967

DI Y.A.Dikovskii, A Note on Deterministic Linear Languages, Systems Theory Research, A Translation of Problemy Kibernetiki 23, Novosibirsk 1972, pp. 295-300

FL M.Fliess, Matrices de Hankel, J.Math. pures et appl. 53, 1974, pp. 197-222

HW C.Hoffmann-Walter, Deterministische Zwei-Band-Automaten und Eindeutigkeit linearer Sprachen, Diploma Thesis, Inst.f.Inf. Univ. Hamburg, Dec. 1975

KS R.Kurki-Suonio, Describing Automata in Terms of Languages Associated with Their Peripheral Devices, Computer Sc.Dept., Stanford Univ., Techn. Rpt. STAN-CS-75-493, May 1975

LA M.Lahnstein, Keller-Stack-Automaten und indizierte parallele Sprachen, Diploma Thesis, Inst.f.Inf. Univ. Hamburg, to be published as Techn. Rpt. IFI-HH-B, 1976

OP M.Opp, Charakterisierungen erkennbarer Termmengen in absolut freien universellen Algebren, Doctoral Dissertation, Inst.f.Inf. Univ. Hamburg, Techn. Rpt. IFI-HH-B-20/76, Feb. 1976

RW R.D.Rosebrugh, D.Wood, Restricted parallelism and right linear grammars, Utilitas Math. 7, 1975, pp. 151-186

SA A.Salomaa, Formal Languages, Academic Press, New York, 1973

SC C.-P.Schnorr, Freie assoziative Systeme, EIK 8, 1967, pp. 319-340

SL A.Salomaa, Theory of Automata, Pergamon Press, Oxford, 1969

SM J.M.Smith, Monoid Acceptors and Their Relation to Formal Languages, Ph.D. Dissertation, Univ. of Pennsylvania, 1972

SV W.J.Savitch, How to make arbitrary grammars look like context-free grammars, SIAM J. Comput. 2, 1973, pp. 174-182

VO H.Vogel, Zur Theorie der rationalen und deterministischen Mengen, Diploma Thesis, Mitt. Ges. Math. Datenverarb. 18, Bonn. 1972

WA S.J.Walljasper, Non-deterministic automata and effective languages, Doctoral Thesis, Univ. of Iowa, AD-69 2421, 1969

WE G.Wechsung, Isomorphe Darstellungen der Kleeneschen Algebra der regulären Mengen, Mitt. Math. Ges. DDR, 1973, Nr.2/3, pp. 161-171

WO D.Wotschke, A characterization of Boolean closures of families of languages, in: Böhling, Indermark (eds.), 1. Fachtagung über Automatentheorie und formale Sprachen, Lect. Notes Comput. Sc. 2, Springer-Verlag, Berlin, 1973, pp.191-200

On Semantic Issues in the Relational Model of Data

J-M.Cadiou

IBM Research Laboratory
San Jose, California 95193

Abstract

This paper discusses the semantics of Codd's relational model of data, considered as being time-independent properties of the relations describing the data. The paper emphasizes those properties which are expressible in terms of the relations present in the data base, as opposed to the properties which relate the data base to the outside world. Among the semantic properties being discussed are the functional dependencies, the weak dependencies, the integrity constraints and the cross-referencing of the data base entities.

1.Introduction

The relational model of data was introduced by Codd in a fundamental paper[6], then expanded and further studied by him in a series of subsequent papers ([7] through [13]). We will not discuss here the advantages of this representation over other approaches to data base architecture : they are thoroughly discussed in the above references and in [15], and are outside the scope of this paper.

In the relational model, the data is viewed as being arranged into a collection of time-varying relations of fixed format, whose 'meaning' remains constant. This 'meaning' is what is usually considered to be the 'semantics' of the data. Rephrasing this sentence slightly, we can (informally) define the semantics of the relations in a relational data base to consist of the time independent properties of these relations.

Let us illustrate the concepts introduced above by taking a simple example from a department store data base. The information that an employee belongs to a department of the store might be kept in a relation:

ASSIGNED(EMPNO,DEPTNO)

More precisely, the fact that employee number x belongs to department number y would be represented by the occurrence of a pair (x,y) in that relation. The set of pairs present in the relation will vary with time, as employees change departments, leave the company, new employees are hired, etc... , but the 'meaning' of the presence of a pair (x,y) in this relation will remain the same as time varies (namely : employee x belongs to department y). This meaning is part of the semantics of that relation.

Given a relational data base, one can divide its semantic properties into two classes :

a) those which are expressible in terms of the relations of the data base,
b) those which require concepts 'outside' of the data base relations.

An example of a) would be the assertion that an employee belongs to only one department. An example of b) would be the fact that employees are humans.

This paper will concentrate on properties of the first class.

Semantic properties of the second class have been studied in [22],[23],[24]. They appear to be useful for supporting natural language front-ends to a relational data base management system, such as the RENDEZVOUS system proposed in [12] and currently under development at the IBM San Jose Research Laboratory .

We believe that the difference between properties of class a) and b) is mainly a question of scope and not of nature, and we conjecture that the relational model can also serve as a basis for representing the 'outside' knowledge as well. This, however, will not be pursued further in this paper.

We will first present a formalism for representing time-varying relations in terms of schemas and instances (Part 2). Then, we review the principal known results on functional dependencies (Part 3) and weak dependencies (Part 4), and the associated decomposition theorems. The dependencies are viewed as constraints which restrict the possible instantiations of the schema. In Part 5, we will discuss integrity constraints, which are a very general class of semantic properties expressible in terms of the relations in the data base. Part 6 will discuss the concept of entity in the relational model. In particular, it is shown how entities can be uniquely cross-referenced in the data base once appropriate domains have been specified as entity-domains, and a certain equivalence relation provided between attributes on these domains.

2.The Relational Model: Formalism

2.1 The relational model of data as initially developed by Codd[6] can be viewed as consisting of a schema together with rules of interpretation.

The data base schema consists of a finite collection of relation schemas and a set of domains. Each relation schema consists of a relation name R,together with a finite set of attribute names X={A1,A2,...An},(all distinct within that relational schema),and a 1-1 mapping D of this set of attribute names into the set of domains.The informal interpretation of that mapping will be that,if an attribute name A of a relation schema maps into a domain D(A),then values for that attribute must belong to that domain.Two attribute names within the same relation schema may map into the same domain. There is no particular significance (other than mnemonic) to the fact that attribute names belonging to different schemas are the same. We will tend to use letters R,S,T for relation names,A,B,C,... for attribute names,X,Y,Z for sets of attribute names,when discussing properties of the relational model.Examples will be given with intuitive mnemonics to illustrate the discussion.

The rules of interpretation are restrictions on the relations which are admissible instances of the schema. These restrictions are of a semantic nature. Parts 3 and 4 are essentially devoted to a discussion of the different ways of representing these constraints (dependencies, integrity constraints, etc...) .

2.2 If n is a positive integer, an n-ary mathematical relation over the sets D1,D2,...Dn is a subset of the cartesian product D1 X D2 X... X Dn , (n is called the degree of the relation). An element of such a relation is called an n-tuple,often tuple for short.Such a tuple is of the form $u=\langle u1,u2,\ldots,un\rangle$,with $ui \in Di$. We will usually denote mathematical relations by small letters r,s,t tuples by small letters u,v,w and omit 'mathematical' when no confusion is possible.

An <u>instance</u> of a relation schema R(A1,A2,...An) is a finite relation over D(A1) X D(A2) X ... X D(An) , where D is the domain mapping of the schema. A time-independent property of a schema is a property which holds for all instances of the schema.

If a relation r is an instance of a relation schema R(A,B,...), and u is one of its tuples,then the i-th element of u is often designated by the corresponding attribute name between brackets:u[A] instead of u1,etc... Thus, the order in which the attribute names of R have been placed is unimportant. If $u \in r$, and Y is a subset of the attribute names of R, say Y=[C1,...,Cm], then the expression u[Y] denotes the set {u[C1],...,u[Cm]}.

The <u>projection</u> of the relation r on the set of attributes Y,denoted r[Y],is the set {u[Y]} for $u \in r$.

2.3 It is convenient to represent a relation r which is an instance of a schema R(A1,...,An) by a table whose column names are A1,...,An and whose rows are the tuples of r,where,for every tuple u r,the value of u[Ai] appears in column Ai.

Every instance of R can be represented by such a table,but it is important to note that the converse is not true. For a table to represent a relation,the following must hold:

1- No two rows of the table are identical.(A relation,being a set, does not have duplicate elements).

2- Every column Ai of the table must only contain elements of the appropriate domain D(Ai).

Several tables may represent the same relation,since order of the rows in the table is unimportant. Permuting the columns is immaterial too, provided the column names are permuted in the same way.

Consider as an example the relation schema PART(NAME,COLOR,QUANTITY) with the corresponding domains suggested by the attribute name mnemonics. Then the following table can represent an instance of that schema:

r :

NAME	COLOR	QUANTITY
Pen	Blue	30
Pencil	Red	25
Pen	Red	25
Pencil	Green	20

The projections s=r[COLOR,QUANTITY] and t=r[NAME,QUANTITY] can be represented by the tables:

s :

COLOR	QUANTITY
Blue	30
Red	25
Green	20

t :

NAME	QUANTITY
Pen	30
Pencil	25
Pen	25
Pencil	30

2.4 Joins. Let S(X) and T(Y) be two relation schemas in the same data base, with attribute names A in X and B in Y, such that D(A)=D(B). A and B are said to be joinable. Let s and t be respective instances of S and T. The natural join, join for short, of s to t on A=B, denoted s[A=B]t, is a relation defined as follows:

1-It is an instance of the schema J(X' ∪ M ∪ Y'),where X' is the complement of A in X, Y' is the complement of B in Y and M is an attribute name not in X' or Y'. X' and Y' are supposed disjoint, otherwise a renaming has to be performed.

2-It satisfies the following condition: whenever there is a tuple u in s and a tuple v in t such that u[A]=v[B], then there is a tuple w in the join such that:

w[X']=u[X'], w[M]=u[A]=v[B], w[Y']=v[Y'] .

For example, if we consider again the previous relations s and t, the join s[QUANTITY=QUANTITY]t is the relation represented by the table:

NAME	COLOR	QUANTITY
Pen	Blue	30
Pen	Green	30
Pencil	Blue	30
Pencil	Green	30
Pencil	Red	25
Pen	Red	25

The new attribute name for the joined column has been chosen identical to the common attribute name of the joined columns in s and t. The tuple w=<Pencil,Blue,30> of this relation is obtained from the tuples u=<Blue,30> of s and v=<Pencil,30> of t.

The above example shows that, in general, it is not true that a relation is recovered by taking the join of two of its projections on their common attributes.

2.5 It should be observed that the above formalism does not capture the idea of an unnormalized relation of the kind defined in Codd's original paper[6]. Informally speaking, unnormalized relations can have attributes whose values can be relations. While it is certainly possible in the above formalism to have a domain D(A) having relations as elements, it is not possible to impose a structure on those relations. The definition of 2.1 could easily be extended however to cope with this problem by allowing the set X of attribute names of a relation schema R to include relation names. In [6], Codd shows how, under very general conditions, unnormalized relations can be transformed into normalized relations of the kind discussed in 2.1 through 2.4 . Using his terminology, all the relation schemas discussed in this paper are in First Normal Form (1NF).

3. Functional (Strong) Dependencies

.3.1 The functional dependencies in a relation are an important part of its semantics, and easy to formalize in mathematical terms. This is probably why a considerable amount of work has been devoted to them. The advantage of such a formalization is that reasoning can be performed on these dependencies in a purely formal way, without any need for remembering the underlying semantics which led to their original establishment.

It is important to realize that the functional dependencies are not derivable from the data, although examination of the data may suggest potential dependencies. The functional dependencies are time-independent properties, which are asserted because of knowledge about the world modelled by the data base. Not only do they hold for the past, but they must also hold in the future.

The proper formalization of the dependencies is therefore at the schema level, to reflect the fact that they hold for all relations which are acceptable instances of the schema.

The theory of functional dependencies is now reasonably well understood. In [16], Delobel and Casey proved a theorem relating the system of functional dependencies to the propositional calculus. In [2], Armstrong gave an axiomatization of the functional dependencies. Recently, Fagin [18] has established the completeness of Armstrong's axioms and given an elegant proof of the Delobel-Casey theorems. He has also given a very direct relationship between the system of functional dependencies and the propositional calculus.

Following Fagin, we use the term strong dependency for the relation between attribute names which formalizes the concept of functional dependencies.

Given a relation schema R, a strong dependency is a statement of the form:

A1A2...An --> B1B2...Bm ,

where A1,A2,...An,B1,B2,...Bm are attribute names of R. We say that a relation r which is an instance of the schema R is compatible with the dependency statement, if it is such that, whenever two tuples u and v of r agree on A1,A2,...An, (i.e. u[Ai]=v[Ai] for each i), then they also agree on B1,B2,...Bm, (i.e. u[Bj]=v[Bj] for each j).

If X,Y are sets of attribute names A1,A2,...An and B1,B2,...Bm respectively, we often use the notations X-->A, A-->Y, X-->Y in place of (respectively) A1A2...An --> A , A --> B1B2...Bm , A1A2...An --> B1B2...Bm .

Strong dependencies are 'context-independent' in the following sense : if R(X) is a relation schema, P(Y) its projection on a subset Y of X, and U,V two sets of attribute names in Y, then U-->V in R iff U-->V in its projection P .

We will use this property in the decomposition process of Section 3.5 .

3.2 Armstrong's Axioms. Completeness.

Armstrong's system of axioms for the theory of strong dependency statements is equivalent to the following, in our notations :

(S1) A1A2...An --> Ai , for each i in [1,n]

(S2) A1A2...An --> B1B2...Bm
iff A1A2...An --> Bj , for each j in [1,m]

(S3) A1A2...An --> B1B2...Bm and
B1B2...Bm --> C1C2...Cp imply
A1A2...An --> C1C2...Cp .

This set of axioms is complete (Fagin[18]),in the sense that given a relation schema R and a set of dependency statements DEP, then every dependency statement which holds for every instantiation of R compatible with DEP is derivable from DEP by using this set of axioms.

In fact Fagin shows that there is a complete analogy between this formal system and the implicational statements of the propositional calculus. The '-->' relation (strong dependency) behaves exactly as the '==>' relation (Propositional implication) in the propositional logic.

Precisely stated, Fagin's theorem says that a dependency d is a consequence of a set of dependencies DEP if and only if the formula d is a logical consequence of the set of formulae DEP, where the correspondence between d,DEP and d,DEP is the following:

Column Names A,B,C ..... Propositional Variables A,B,C

Strong Dependency --> ..... Propositional Implication ==>

A1...An --> B1...Bm ..... $A1 \wedge \ldots \wedge An \Rightarrow B1 \wedge \ldots \wedge Bm$

3.3 Keys. The dependency statements of a relation determine the keys of that schema.

A key of a relation schema R is a collection K of attributes of R such that, for every attribute A of R :

(1) K --> A holds
(2) No proper subset of K has that property .

Condition (1) says that a key uniquely determines its tuple.

A schema can have several keys. In that case they are called candidate keys. One of them is selected as the primary key. There is no mathematical reason for selecting one candidate key rather than another for becoming the primary key, but there may be practical or semantic ones. In particular, it is required that no field of a primary key take a 'null' (undefined) value, in order to guarantee distinctness of tuples in a relation (see Codd [11]).

3.4 Operations on a Data Base. To motivate the following Sections, it is interesting to briefly describe the types of operations which are performed on a data base. (We are excluding here operations which modify the data base schema).

There are basically two types of operations : read and write.

The read operations (queries) do not modify the data, and are of less concern to us here. The write operations are usually separated into updates, insertions and deletions. They can be thought of as transformations on relations which preserve compatibility with the dependencies of the schema.

Tuple insertion and deletion have the obvious meanings. Updating a tuple consists in changing some or all of the values of the elements of the tuple. An update is logically equivalent to an (uninterrupted) deletion- insertion pair, if side effects are ignored.

Let us briefly examine some of the problems which can arise when such operations are performed on a data base schema with strong dependency statements.

As an example, we take the relation schema:

OFFER(SUPPLIER,PART,CITY,QUANTITY)

with the dependencies:

SUPPLIER --> CITY
SUPPLIER,PART --> QUANTITY

where the intended meaning of tuple ⟨s,p,c,q⟩ in an instance of this schema is that supplier s, which is located in city c, is offering part p, of which he has q available. (This interpretation is merely to illustrate the problems in a more concrete setting, as the dependencies are the only aspect of the semantics which will be used here). The only candidate key is SUPPLIER,PART and therefore it is also the primary key.

Let us consider the following instance of this schema:

r:	SUPPLIER	PART	CITY	QUANTITY
(1)	S1	Wheel	San Francisco	15
(2)	S2	Battery	Warsaw	25
(3)	S3	Tire	Paris	20
(4)	S1	Gearbox	San Francisco	30

Here are some of the problems which can arise in this schema :
If supplier S3 ceases to supply tires, we must delete tuple (3). However, we then lose the information that S3 is located in Paris. (Deletion problem).
Similarly, if we acquire the information that supplier S4 is located in London prior to knowing what parts he offers, then we cannot store the information in this schema, because null values are not allowed in primary keys (Insertion problem).
Also, if supplier S1 moves to San Jose, we must update tuples ((1) and (4)). In general we have to update all tuples of r in which S1 participates. This is a time-varying number. (Update problem).
If supplier S2 starts supplying Battery Chargers, we must look up the data base in order to find out in which city he is located before we can insert the tuple. If a complete tuple is provided, we still have to look up the data base to make sure that the 'CITY' field of the tuple is Warsaw. (Insertion problem).
In this example, all the problems come from the same source, namely that CITY depends on SUPPLIER alone. The idea which comes to mind is to keep this information separate. Taking the projections s=r[SUPPLIER,CITY] and t=r[SUPPLIER,PART,QUANTITY], we get:

s: SUPPLIER	CITY
S1	San Francisco
S2	Warsaw
S3	Paris

t: SUPPLIER	PART	QUANTITY
S1	Wheel	15
S2	Battery	25
S3	Tire	20
S1	Gearbox	30

It is easy to see that all the above deletion, insertion and update problems have now disappeared. Furthermore, the original relation r can be recovered by joining s and t on column SUPPLIER, so there has been no loss in decomposing r into s and t. Sections 3.5 and 3.6 present the main results known about decomposition of relations.
The reader may wonder what happens in relation t if we acquire the information that S3 also offers Tubes, but without knowing in which quantity. One way to proceed is to further decompose t along SUPPLIER,PART and SUPPLIER,QUANTITY. This is not necessary, however, and the problem can be solved by introducing a 'null' value in the QUANTITY field of the tuple of t, which is possible, since QUANTITY is not part of a primary key of the relation schema.
Problems associated with file operations have motivated a good deal of the data base relational theory. The reader is referred to the original papers of Codd([7],[9],[11]), and to Date[15], and Heath[21] for a more complete coverage.

<u>3.5 Decomposition</u>. <u>Boyce-Codd Normal Form</u>. As was shown in the previous example, decomposition of a relation into 'simpler' relations can eliminate certain undesirable properties. This has motivated the investigation of various decomposition techniques, leading to several so-called 'normal forms': Second Normal Form or 2NF, Third Normal Form or 3NF (Codd[7],[9]), Boyce-Codd Normal Form or BCNF (Codd[13]), which can be obtained by using strong dependencies only, and Fourth Normal Form (Fagin[19]), which requires another kind of dependency and will be studied in Section 3.6.
In this section, we will study the decompositions which make use of strong dependencies only. In any of these decompositions, each step consists in replacing a relation schema by two of its projections, in such a way that no information is lost. More precisely, any relation which is an instance of the original schema can always be recovered from the decomposed relations by appropriate joins.

The basic decomposition step is justified by the following theorem, which appears to have been noted for the first time by Heath[21] :

Theorem : Let R(X) be a relation schema, U,V,W be a partition of X, and assume that the strong dependency statement U-->V holds for R(X). Then any relation r which is compatible with R(X) is the natural join on U of its two projections r[U,V] and r[U,W].

The proof is immediate. We only supply it to exercise some of the definitions. It suffices to show that the join is contained in the original relation r, since the converse is always true.

Let x = uvw be a tuple in the join. By definition of the join, we must have:

uv ∈ r[U,V] and uw ∈ r[U,W]

By definition of the projections we must have two tuples of the form uvw' and uv'w in r. But, since r is compatible with R(X), r verifies the dependency U-->V, which implies that v = v'. Hence uvw ∈ r . □

We will express the previous property by saying that, if U-->V holds for R(X), U and V disjoint, then R is non-loss decomposable into R[U,V] and R[U,W], where W is the complement of U and V in X.

Since projections inherit strong dependencies, as was noted in Section 3.1, the same process can be repeated on the projections R[U,V] and R[U,W]. After any number of such steps, one obtains a collection of relations, which represents a non-loss decomposition of the original relation.

Notice that, in such a collection, there is always one of the relations which contains a key of the original relation.

The decomposition process is not unique: for example, R(ABC) with A-->B and C-->B can be decomposed into either R[AB],R[AC] or R[AC],R[BC] .

The decomposition process is finite, but the questions of how and how much to decompose are far from trivial.

In the example of the schema of Section 3.4, it was clearly desirable to decompose OFFER(SUPPLIER,PART,CITY,QUANTITY), with the dependencies SUPPLIER-->CITY and SUPPLIER,PART-->QUANTITY, into the two projections S(SUPPLIER,CITY) and T(SUPPLIER,PART,QUANTITY). What was happening there was that the attribute CITY depended on part of the key SUPPLIER,PART. A relation schema where this does not happen is said to be in Second Normal Form (2NF).

To define 2NF precisely, we need the notions of prime attribute and of full dependency :

A prime attribute of a relation schema is an attribute which belongs to at least one candidate key of the schema.

If Y and Z are collections of attributes of a relation schema R(X), we say that Z fully depends on Y if Y-->Z holds in the schema, and Y'-->Z holds for no proper subset Y' of Y.

Definition of 2NF: A relation schema is in 2NF if every non prime attribute of R is fully dependent on each candidate key of R.

This definition is due to Codd[7]. (Note that all the relation schemas in this paper are already in First Normal Form, in Codd's terminology: see Section 2.5).

It is always possible to transform a relation schema into a collection of 2NF relation schemas by a series of non-loss decompositions. However, 2NF relation schemas can present problems which are in many ways similar to those encountered in Section 3.4 . As an example, let us consider the schema R(SUPPLIER,CITY,POPULATION), with the dependencies SUPPLIER-->CITY and CITY-->POPULATION , where the intended meaning of a tuple ⟨s,c,p⟩ is that supplier s is located in city c which has population p. The only candidate key of that schema is SUPPLIER, and therefore it is in 2NF. Yet, the same problems which we discussed in Section 3.4 also occur here: if we delete the last supplier in a given city, we also lose the city's population, etc...

The source of the problem here is that POPULATION does not depend directly on the key SUPPLIER. In [7], Codd formalized this notion using the concept of transitive dependency, and defined Third Normal Form (3NF) to characterize schemas where these dependencies do not occur. The reader is referred to Codd's original paper [7] for a precise definition of 3NF.

As it turns out, it is possible to eliminate further anomalies by adopting a slightly different characterization of Normal Form, generally referred to as Boyce-Codd Normal Form (BCNF). Codd's definition of BCNF is the following ([13]) :
A relation schema is in Boyce-Codd Normal Form (BCNF) if whenever a collection of attributes V depends on a disjoint collection of attributes U, then so does every other collection of attributes W. (In other words, for all U,V,W with U and V disjoint : U-->V implies U-->W).

BCNF is slightly different from 3NF, particularly in the treatment of prime attributes. (What Heath calls 'Third Normal Form' in [21] is actually BCNF, not 3NF). There are schemas which are in 3NF but not in BCNF, for example:

R(ABC) with AB-->C and C-->B .

However,any schema in BCNF is also in 2NF and 3NF. It turns out that it is not possible to go beyond BCNF by using strong dependencies alone.

There are many ways, in general, in which a relation schema can be decomposed into a collection of BCNF schemas.
Following Codd, we say that a decomposition is in optimal BCNF if it consists of relation schemas in BCNF and no such decomposition exists with fewer relation schemas.
This prevents, for example, breaking the schema R(ABC), with A-->B and A-->C, into R1(AB) and R2(AC). R is already in BCNF and, if the above dependencies are all we know about it, presents none of the problems previously discussed. (We allow nulls in fields other than in primary keys).
Optimal BCNF is not unique, as shown by our earlier example R(ABC) with A-->B and C-->B .
It does not either solve all the problems associated with file operations discussed above, as we shall see in the remainder of this Section and in the following.

When decomposing a relation schema, some of the functional dependencies may be 'broken', as Codd noted in [7]. He gives the example R(ABC), with AB-->C and C-->B: decomposing R into R1(AC) and R2(BC) 'breaks' the dependency AB-->C. More precisely, the two projections R1,R2 and their internal dependencies do not capture the entire original schema.
Such dependencies seem to occur in the real world, as in the following example, due to Date [15] : T(STUDENT,COURSE,TEACHER), with the dependencies STUDENT,COURSE-->TEACHER and TEACHER-->COURSE. The meaning of a tuple ⟨s,c,t⟩ in this relation is that student s takes course c from teacher t. The dependencies reflect the fact that, in the particular environment modelled, a student does not take the same course from several teachers, and that a teacher only teaches one course.
A problem with T as it stands is that there is no way to keep the information that a teacher is assigned to a course before there are students registered in it. This is a classical problem with a schema not in BCNF.
If we then decompose T into its two projections T1(TEACHER,COURSE) and T2(STUDENT,TEACHER), which is a non-loss decomposition, another problem appears : updating T2 cannot be done without performing checks involving T1. For example, if we suppose the state of T1 and T2 to be :

t1: TEACHER	COURSE	t2: STUDENT	TEACHER
Finicky	EE185	Sloppy	Finicky
Soporific	EE185	Hazy	Soporific

then inserting the tuple ⟨Sloppy,Soporific⟩ in T2 is illegal, because Soporific teaches EE185 and Sloppy already takes EE185 from somebody, namely Finicky. Thus, the (external) dependency STUDENT,COURSE-->TEACHER would be violated by this insertion.
Of course, given T1,T2 and the interrelational dependency STUDENT,COURSE-->TEACHER, the necessary information is there for the system to check for this kind of problem. This is a performance (or complexity) issue, not a logical impossibility. The point is that decomposition has complicated the situation in

this case.

A possible solution, at least for this case, might be to stay with the original relation T, without decomposing it, and to supplement it with a relation T'1(TEACHER,COURSE). T'1 would only be used to hold the information that a teacher teaches a course when no information is available on students taking the course. Thus, a teacher would never be in T and T'1 at the same time. This kind of constraint is expressible by integrity constraints of the type discussed in Part 4.

Yet another possibility might be, again in this particular case, to model the reality by a different schema, involving the notion of 'offering' rather than 'course'. The difference is that the dependencies now become :

TEACHER-->OFFERING and OFFERING-->TEACHER . There are two possible decompositions, none of which presents a problem.

It is open to question whether it is always possible (and practical) to replace a schema which has 'dependency breaking' problems by one which does not.

3.6 Weak Dependencies. There are certain semantic properties which, while having a 'dependency' flavor, fail to be captured by the strong dependency concept. Let us consider the following example:

R: EMP	CHILD	SAL	YEAR
John	Paul	15K	1974
John	Mary	15K	1974
John	Paul	16K	1975
John	Mary	16K	1975

The meaning of tuple $\langle e,c,s,y \rangle$ in this relation is that employee e has a child named c and has earned amount s in year y. The only non-trivial minimal strong dependency in this schema is EMP,YEAR-->SAL, leading to the decomposition R1(EMP,YEAR,CHILD) and R2(EMP,YEAR,SAL), which are both in BCNF. Yet, R1 presents obvious operational problems: the meaning of the YEAR field in a tuple of R1 is rather obscure. Adding the fact that John has a third child will result in two new tuples to be inserted in R1, if non-loss decomposition is to be preserved.

Clearly, YEAR should not be present in R1, and BCNF decomposition should not be done in this case.

Actually, R is non-loss decomposable into R'1 and R2:

R'1: EMP	CHILD
John	Paul
John	Mary

R2: EMP	YEAR	SAL
John	1974	15K
John	1975	16K

R is recoverable by joining R'1 and R2 on EMP, but this decomposition is not obtainable by using strong dependencies, as we do not have EMP-->CHILD in R. Schmid and Swenson[24] noticed and recommended this kind of decomposition, on semantic grounds('repeating characteristic object types').

It is possible to generalize the notion of dependency in such a way that it provides a necessary and sufficient condition for non-loss decomposition. This generalized dependency has recently been introduced by Fagin, in [19], where he calls it weak dependency. We will first introduce it informally, then give a precise definition. Let U,V,W be a partition of the set of attributes of a relational schema R. Let us call V(u,w) the set $\{ v \mid uvw \text{ is a tuple of } R \}$. In general this set depends on v and w. We say that V weakly depends on U , denoted U-*->V , when the set V(u,w) depends on u alone. What this means is that, for every w,w', V(u,w)=V(u,w') . (Incidentally, notice that this set could depend on u alone, and also depend on w alone without being reduced to a singleton, because of the discreteness of the domains). Weak dependency is, in this sense, a 'set' dependency. In the above example, the set of children of an employee depends on the employee alone. This is the intuitive basis for Schmid and Swenson's 'repeating characteristic object types'(repeating groups)[24].

The following definition of weak dependency is easily seen to be equivalent to

the previous one:
Definition: Let U,V,W be a partition of the set of attributes of R. Then U-*->V iff whenever there are two tuples of R agreeing on U, say:

$$uvw \text{ and } u\underline{vw} ,$$

then R also contains the two tuples:

$$u\underline{v}w \text{ and } uv\underline{w} .$$

The reader may convince himself that, in the previous example, EMP-*->CHILD and EMP-*->SAL,YEAR .
Strong dependency is a special case of weak dependency (i.e. U-->V and U and V disjoint imply U-*->V) . Notice that V and W are symmetric in the above definition: U-*->V iff U-*->W . For this and other reasons, the symmetric notation U-*->V|W is often more convenient to use.
The notion of weak dependency leads to the following decomposition theorem :
Theorem (Fagin[19]): Let U,V,W be a partition of the set of attribute names of a relation schema R. Then, R is the join on U of its projections R1[U,V] and R2[U,W] iff U-*->V|W .
Using this Theorem, it is in general possible to decompose a relation into a collection of relations in Fourth Normal Form, where Fourth Normal Form is defined as follows (Fagin [19]) :
Definition: A relation schema R is in Fourth Normal Form (4NF), if, whenever there is a non-trivial weak dependency U-*->V in R, then, for every attribute A of R, the strong dependency U-->A also holds. (A trivial weak dependency U-*->V|W is one in which either V or W is empty).

A relation in 4NF is always in BCNF, but the converse is not true , as the previous example shows. It is always possible to decompose a schema into a collection of schemas in 4NF (non-loss decomposition), by repeating the above basic step.
Weak dependencies are substantially more complex than strong dependencies in their behavior. First, they are context-dependent, in the sense that non-trivial 'new' weak dependencies may appear in projections, which is never the case for strong dependencies. For example, in a relation R(ABCD), we may have A-*->BC and not A-*->B, but A-*->B may hold in the projection of R on attributes ABC.
Thus, to be able to repeat the decomposition process as far as possible, it is in general necessary to have the weak dependencies in the projections in addition to those of the original relation.
Also, the axiom system for weak dependencies is more complicated than its counterpart for strong dependencies. The following set of axioms for weak dependencies is due to Fagin and Howard, and they have proved its completeness in [20].

(W1) U -*-> $\emptyset$

(W2) U -*-> V implies U -*-> W ,
where W is the complement of U and V

(W3) $\left.\begin{array}{l} U \text{ -*-> } V \\ W \text{ -*-> } X \\ V \cap W = \emptyset \end{array}\right\}$ imply U -*-> $V \cap X$

Axiom S2 of strong dependencies only holds in one direction for weak dependencies : U-*->V and U-*->W imply U-*->VW , but the converse is not true.
Similarly, transitivity does not always hold for weak dependencies. However, the following 'partial transitivity' does hold : if U-*->V and V-*->W, and if U and V are disjoint, then U-*->W holds. (Notice that if U and V were not disjoint, U-*->W would not be defined).
Finally, the interaction between strong and weak dependencies seem to be quite complex. For instance, adding weak dependencies to a set of strong dependencies may cause some new strong dependencies to appear, as shown by the following example : U-->W and V-*->U imply V-->W.
A complete set of axioms for weak and strong dependencies together has recently been discovered by Fagin.

4. Integrity Assertions

Weak and strong dependencies are special cases of a much more general kind of statements which can be used to express semantic properties of a data base : the integrity assertions.

Sometimes called integrity constraints ([17]), such statements can be any time-independent assertion about the data base which is 'computable' from the relations and the values in them. It can involve either values from one state (state assertion), or values from several states (transition assertion).

An example of a state assertion might be : 'The number of employees in any given department must never exceed 100'. An example of a transition assertion might be that the salary of an employee is never decreasing. Typically, transition assertions involve two states of the variables , 'old' and 'new'. Notice that, conceptually, a transition assertion on a data base can be regarded as a state assertion on an augmented data base where a (virtual) attribute has been added to every relation in order to keep track of the states through which the data base goes. (Of course, we do not suggest that this should actually be done!)

To make the definition of integrity assertions precise, one has to say what it means for an assertion over a collection of relation schemas to be 'computable'.

The notion involved here is a special case of that of a 'computable' data base query. In turn the latter is equivalent to the notion of definability of a relation schema in terms of the data base schema : a query is an extraction from the data base of tuples of values $\langle x1,...,xn\rangle$ satisfying an assertion $P(x1,...,xn)$, which must be 'computable' from the data base. Those tuples form a relation definable in term of the data base relations.

In [8], Codd proposes a relational calculus, based on the predicate calculus, and which, in effect, defines a class of 'computable assertions' about a data base schema. He also defines a relational algebra, based on some primitive relational operations (cartesian product, union, intersection, difference, projection,join, division). This defines a class of relation schemas obtainable from those of a data base by repeated application of the operations of the algebra. He further shows that these two notions of definability are equivalent and proposes them as a basis for characterizing the expressive power of a data base query sublanguage (relational completeness).

A number of relational data base query languages have been proposed (ALPHA [10], SEQUEL [4], QUERY BY EXAMPLE [25], DEDUCE [5]), all of them relationally complete.

It should be noted, however, that the concept of 'computability' involved here is more restrictive than the usual notion of computability. No recursive definition of relations is provided : the transitive closure of a relation, for example, is not definable in the relational algebra of [8]. (QUERY BY EXAMPLE, however, has recently been extended to handle transitive closure [26]).

Integrity assertions have important operational consequences:

- an operation which would violate an assertion should be prevented, such as trying to decrease the salary of an employee,
- appropriate deletions/insertions/updates should be triggered: if there is an assertion stating that any supplier present in the OFFER relation must be present in the SUPPLIER relation, then deleting a supplier from the SUPPLIER relation should cause all of his occurrences in the OFFER relation to be deleted. This integrity assertion can be expressed by stating that the projection on S# of the OFFER relation must be included in the projection on S# of the SUPPLIER relation.

The reader is referred to Eswaran,Chamberlin[17] for an extensive discussion of integrity assertions.

5. Interrelational Semantics : Domains, Entities

5.1 The domains of the relational attributes carry important interrelational information. The domain of each attribute is specified as part of the data base schema definition (see Section 2.1). The terminology used in the present paper is in agreement with Codd's later papers[7],[9] and differs slightly from that of his original paper [6], where he used the term 'underlying domain' for what we have been calling here 'domain', and 'domain'(possibly qualified by 'role') for what we have been calling 'attribute names'.

One of the purposes of introducing these domains is to indicate comparability of attributes, within the same relation schema or across schemas. This is reflected in the definition of the join operation (See 2.4), as well as that of other relational operators, (union,intersection,difference,division : See [8]). Recall that the join of two relations R and S on two attributes, or sets of attributes, A and B, is the relation containing a tuple w for every pair of tuples u of R and v of S which match on A and B : w is obtained by taking the 'union' of u and v, where the duplicate elements of u on A and v on B have been collapsed. A and B must be on the same domain for that matching to make sense.

Consequently, two attributes which are intended to be compared for equality should be assigned the same domain, and, conversely, assigning different domains to two attributes will prohibit joins on them. The assignment of domains to attributes is one more way, for the data base designer, of conveying semantic information.

Domains have types of values associated with them : numeric, character. Numeric domains often have unit types (weight, length, time, etc...) Different attributes on the same domain can have different units(lbs,kgs,tons,etc...), and conversion formulae should be provided for comparisons.

Of course, equality is not the only permissible comparison : each domain could have its set of comparators. In fact, one may want to introduce comparability information involving several domains : for example, 'speed' is comparable to 'distance' divided by 'time'. (See [17] for a discussion of this question).

5.2 Entity Domains. The concept of 'entity' has been the subject of considerable discussion in the literature ([24], [1]), often in contrast with the concept of 'link' or 'association'. A 'person', a 'part' are examples of entities, the relationship of a father to his son is an example of an association.

However, these concepts are not exclusive of each other. Any association can be considered as an entity, perhaps more abstract, (of higher type), than the entities it is linking. This is reflected in the way in which these concepts are expressed in natural language : 'entities' are often expressed by nouns and 'associations' by verbs. However, many verbs have a noun-form (e.g. to 'ship', 'shipment'), and, if they do not, the action they represent can always be transformed into a noun expression, by prefixing the verb phrase by 'the fact that...' (e.g.'the fact that John is the father of Paul'). This mechanism of abstraction can be interpreted as making an 'entity' out of an 'association'.

It seems very important to have a means of uniquely identifying the entities about which the data base is dealing : one of the purposes is to be able to reference these entities across relations, or across attributes within a relation. This is essential for queries on the data base, but also in all the other data base operations, and for enforcing integrity constraints.

If no other information is provided than commonality of domains, joining two columns merely indicates that the values in the columns are equal. If we want to conclude from that equality of values the fact that two entities are identical, we need more semantic information: we first need to know that the values in the common domain are unique identifiers for a data base entity and furthermore we need to know that the identifying code is the same. The second kind of information will be discussed in section 5.6 . We propose that the first kind of information be conveyed by designating the corresponding domain as an <u>entity-domain</u>. The data base designer selects the entities which need to be uniquely identified for cross-reference purposes, chooses a unique identifier for them and declares the corresponding domain an entity-domain.

For example, in a personnel data base, the employee-serial-number domain would presumably be selected as an entity-domain. Whether or not departments would have an entity-domain depends on the need for uniquely identifying them across relations.

As another example,consider the relations :

SUPPLIER(S#,SNAME,SLOC)
PROJECT(J#,JNAME,JLOC)

where the domains of S# and J# are the only entity-domains, and SLOC, JLOC are on a common domain, city-names. A join of the two relations on SLOC and JLOC links those suppliers and projects which are located in cities with the same name. They may or may not be the same city, but the point is that there is no way of knowing that from the present information in the data base. However, if it is important to be able to recognize those cases where suppliers and projects are located in the same city, the data base designer needs to make sure that the values in the common domain of SLOC and JLOC are unique identifiers for cities. Declaring that domain an entity-domain is a way of telling the data base users that this has been done.

The concept of entity-domain provides, in many cases, the same information about the meaning of joins as does the concept of foreign key (Codd [6]) . There are a few differences, however.

A foreign key has to be on the same domain as the primary key of some relation : this would prevent JLOC and SLOC to be foreign keys in the previous example, even if they were unique identifiers for cities, since there is no relation with a primary key on that domain.

Also, a foreign key cannot be the primary key of the relation in which it is an attribute : this would prevent S# to be a foreign key in either of the two relations of the schema :

STUDENT(S#,NAME,ADDRESS)
TUITION(S#,TOTAL,AMT_PAID)

5.3 Overlapping Entities. In the real world, 'entities' have a complex structure : some are subentities of others ('man','woman' are subconcepts of 'person') and some entities more generally overlap with others (members of the board of directors of a corporation may be employees of the company, but they are not always).

There are different ways of dealing with this problem. We will discuss two possibilities in the following example . Suppose we have a university situation in which there are students and faculty members with some overlap. That is, there are some students teaching courses, and some faculty members taking courses. All those teaching courses (including students) have an employee-number (EMP#) and receive a salary, all those taking courses (including faculty members) have a student-number (STUDENT#) and pay a tuition. Finally, everybody has a name and address.

One way to deal with the problem is to have two distinct entity-domains for EMP# and STUDENT# . We can have two relations :

FACULTY(EMP#,NAME,ADDRESS,SAL)
STUDENT(STUDENT#,NAME,ADDRESS,TUITION)

However, we are in trouble if want the salary of a teaching student, or the tuition paid by a studying faculty member. One cannot in general use the pair NAME,ADDRESS to provide a reliable link, although, in this particular case, it is probably unlikely that a faculty member and a student with the same name live at the same address. Anyway, addresses are difficult to represent uniquely and there is no guarantee that changes of addresses will be reflected appropriately in both relations. Of course, in general there might not be such a combination of attributes.

We therefore need to add a cross-reference relation to the data base, such as :

CORRESP(EMP#,STUDENT#) ,

for the overlapping entities.

Notice that the NAME and ADDRESS of those people who are in the CORRESP relation will appear in the two relations FACULTY and STUDENT. This necessitates integrity checks on insertions, deletions and updates.

If, instead of two overlapping entities, we had three (like PRESIDENTS, VICE-PRESIDENTS and LOSERS in a U.S. presidential election data base), and if we adopted this technique of distinct entity domains for overlapping entities, we would need four relations to express all the possible combinations of overlaps. While it is certainly logically possible to record all the necessary information and to perform the necessary checks this way,it seems to be a complicated way of doing it.

Another technique to handle this problem is to adopt a single entity-domain for the union of the overlapping entities. In the university example, we might have an entity-domain for 'Academic-Persons', uniquely identifying both students and faculty members.

The data base schema might look like :

ACAD_PERS(ACAD_ID,NAME,ADDRESS)
FACULTY(ACAD_ID,SAL)
STUDENT(ACAD_ID,TUITION)

This design appears to have several advantages over the previous one. NAME and ADDRESS are now stored only in one place, regardless of 'overlap', and no integrity check is necessary. There is no need to store cross-references explicitly, and the number of relations will probably be much smaller if there are many overlapping entities.Only one tuple in one relation has to be modified if a faculty ceases to be a student or conversely.

Of course the fact that the entities overlap may become apparent only after the data base has been in existence for some time, in which case the first solution may be easier to implement.

5.4 Aggregated Entities. Some of the data base entities may actually be 'aggregated entities' rather than individual objects. For example,in a relation PART(PART_SERIAL_NUMBER,NAME,QINV), the entities denoted by the PART_SERIAL_NUMBER domain are not the individual parts themselves, but collections of indistinguishable parts. The attributes appearing are properties of the aggregates: a tuple ⟨p,n,q⟩ in that relation means that parts with serial number p are named n, and that there are q of them in stock. How much aggregation has to take place depends on the data base and its purposes. In fact, it is entirely possible that the same data base contains information at several levels of aggregation. For example a data base on airplanes might contain information on individual airplanes (date of purchase, hours of flight,...), on types of airplanes, such as 707,747(speed,capacity,...), and also on classes of airplanes, such as supersonic,subsonic jet,... (regulations,...) :

INDIVPLANE(PLANE#,PURCH_DATE,FLIGHT_HRS,PTYPE#)
PLANETYPE(PTYPE#,SPEED,CAPACITY,PCLASS#)
PLANECLASS(PCLASS#,REGULATION_CODE)

In this case, we have three entity-domains: planes, types and classes. Each of the relations contains an attribute belonging to the higher level entity-domain, indicating to which of the higher level the present one belongs (level here means level of aggregation).

5.5 Higher-Type Entities. Schmid and Swenson[24] suggested naming groups of attributes within a relation: for example, one might want to group attributes MONTH,DAY,YEAR into a DATE group, or STREET_NUMBER,STREET_NAME,CITY into an ADDRESS,etc... Groups need not be disjoint. Attributes which are grouped may be addressed individually, or as a group. Such groups have domains which can be designated entity-domains: if some component domain of the group is itself an entity-domain, then the group domain is a higher-type entity-domain.

Let us illustrate such a situation by augmenting the Supplier-Project example of Section 5.2 with the relations:

SHIPT(S#,J#,SDATE,QSHIP)
ORDER(S#,J#,ODATE,QORDER)
SHIPORDER(S1,J1,SDATE,S2,J2,ODATE)

The SHIPT relation has the group SHIPID(S#,J#,SDATE), which is the primary key of the relation. Similarly, the ORDER relation has the group ORDERID(S#,J#,ODATE) as primary key. SHIPID uniquely denotes a shipment, ORDERID uniquely denotes an order. SHIPORDER has the two groups SHIPID(S1,J1,SDATE) and ORDERID(S2,J2,ODATE). A tuple in that relation indicates that the shipment was made in response to the order (there may be several shipments for one order and vice versa).

The cross-referencing from SHIPORDER to SHIPT and ORDER can be done once the group domains of SHIPID and ORDERID have been designated as distinct entity-domains.

5.6 The ISSAME Relation. In many cases, the mapping between the values in an entity-domain and the actual entities (entity-code) will be the same throughout the data base. However, this is not necessarily true in general.

If we take for example a situation where there has been a change in the serial-numbering of employees, we might have a relation:

EMP(NEWEMP#,OLDEMP#,NAME,MANAGER#)

where NEWEMP# is the new employee-code, OLDEMP# is the old employee-code and MANAGER# is the new employee-code of the manager of the employee.

We certainly want the NEWEMP# domain to be an entity-domain. Suppose we place NEWEMP# and OLDEMP# in different domains: then, we cannot join the two columns, which forbids a query on employees whose old code is equal to their new code.

If we place them in the same domain, since NEWEMP# is on an entity-domain, so is OLDEMP#. But then the meaning of a join on the two columns is that the corresponding domains denote the same entity!

Therefore, in general, we need an equivalence relation between attributes on a common entity-domain to tell us whether their entity-denoting code is the same or not. We call that relation ISSAME. To solve the previous example, we would place the two employee-codes in the same domain, and then define ISSAME so that NEWEMP# and MANAGER# are in the same equivalence class, but OLDEMP# is in a different one.

We can actually extend ISSAME to groups of attributes: if, for instance, we wanted to be able to do group-comparisons of SHIPIDs and ORDERIDs in the example of Section 5.5 and still be able to do the cross-referencing adequately, we can simply do the following: make the SHIPID domain and the ORDERID domain the same (this is possible since the underlying component domains are the same), and place SHIPID and ORDERID into different equivalence classes of ISSAME.

7.Conclusion

In summary, we have described how some important semantic properties of relational data bases can be expressed in terms of the relations of the data base, at the schema level.

We see the need for future work in this area in several directions:

a) gain a better understanding of the decomposition process of a relation into 4NF, particularly when weak and strong dependencies are present;

b) obtain a formalization of a wider class of interrelational knowledge, (especially redundancy);

c) investigate how the relational model can be used as a general tool for representing knowledge about data, and its relationship with other forms of knowledge representation, such as semantic nets.

Acknowledgements

The author particularly wishes to thank E.F.Codd, of the IBM San Jose Research Laboratory, for introducing him to the relational model of data, and for many pleasant and illuminating discussions; he, R.Fagin and S.N.Zilles, of the same Laboratory, read and commented on early drafts of this paper and their help is gratefully acknowledged.

References

(For a Comprehensive Source of References on Relational Data Bases, see [14])

[1] J.R.Abrial, 'Data Semantics' in J.W.Klimbie (ed.), 'Data Base Management', North Holland, 1974

[2] W.W.Armstrong, 'Dependency Structures of Data Base Relationships', Proc. IFIP Congress, Stockholm, Aug 5-10 1974

[3] P.A.Bernstein, J.R.Swenson, D.Tsichritzis, 'A Unified Approach to Functional Dependencies and Relations', Proc. ACM-SIGMOD Conference, San Jose, Calif.,May 14-16, 1975

[4] D.D.Chamberlin, R.F.Boyce, 'SEQUEL: A Structured English Query Language' , Proc. ACM-SIGMOD on Data Description, Access and Control, Ann Arbor, Mich., May 1-3, 1974

[5] C.L.Chang, 'DEDUCE, A Deductive Query Language for Relational Data Bases', Proc. IEEE Joint Workshop on P. Recognition and Artificial Intelligence, Hyannis, Mass., June 1-3, 1976

[6] E.F.Codd, 'A Relational Model of Data for Large Shared Data Banks', CACM, 13(6), June 1970, pp 377-387

[7] E.F.Codd, 'Further Normalization of the Data Base Relational Model', Courant Computer Science Symposia Vol.6, 'Data Base Systems', New York City, May 24-25 1971, Prentice-Hall, pp 33-64

[8] E.F.Codd, 'Relational Completeness of Data Base Sublanguages', id. pp 65-98

[9] E.F.Codd, 'Normalized Data Base Structure: A Brief Tutorial', Proc. 1971 ACM-SIGFIDET Workshop on Data Definition, Access and Control, San Diego, Calif., Nov 11-12 1971

[10] E.F.Codd, 'A Data Base Sublanguage founded on the Relational Calculus', id.

[11] E.F.Codd, 'Understanding Relations', continuing series of articles published in FDT, the quarterly bulletin of ACM-SIGMOD, beginning with Vol 5, No 1, June 1973

[12] E.F.Codd, 'Seven Steps to Rendezvous with the Casual User', Proc. IFIP TC-2 Working Conference on Data Base Management Systems, Cargese, Corsica, April 1-5, 1974, North-Holland

[13] E.F.Codd, 'Recent Investigations in Relational Data Base Systems', IFIP 74, Stockholm, Aug 5-10 1974,North-Holland

[14] E.F.Codd, 'A List of References Pertaining to Relational Data Base Management', IBM Research Laboratory, San Jose, Calif., Aug 19 1975

[15] C.J.Date, 'An Introduction to Data Base Systems', Addison-Wesley 1975

[16] C.Delobel, R.G.Casey, 'Decomposition of a Data Base and the Theory of Boolean Switching Functions', IBM Journal of Research and Development, Vol 17, No 5, Sept 1973

[17] K.P.Eswaran, D.D.Chamberlin, 'Functional Specifications of a Subsystem for Data Base Integrity', Proc. International Conference on Very Large Data Bases, Framingham, Mass., Sept 22-24, 1975

[18] R.Fagin, 'Relational Data Base Decomposition and Propositional Logic', IBM Reseach Report, San Jose, Calif., June 1976

[19] R.Fagin, 'Weak Dependencies in a Relational Data Base', IBM Research Report, San Jose, Calif., July-August 1976

[20] R.Fagin, J.Howard, 'A Complete Axiomatization for Weak Dependencies in a Relational Data Base', IBM Research Report, San Jose, Calif.,(to appear)

[21] I.J.Heath 'Unacceptable File Operations in a Relational Data Base', Proc. 1971 ACM-SIGFIDET Workshop, San Diego (see Ref[9])

[22] J.Mylopoulos et al., 'TORUS- A Natural Language Understanding System for Data Management', Proc. 4th International Joint Conference on Artificial Intelligence, Tbilisi, Georgia, USSR, 3-8 Sept 1975

[23] J.Mylopoulos et al., 'Semantic Networks and the Generation of Context', id.

[24] H.A.Schmid, J.P. Swenson, 'On the Semantics of the Relational Data Model', Proc. ACM-SIGMOD Conference, San Jose, Calif., May 14-16, 1975

[25] M.M.Zloof, 'Query by Example', Proc. National Computer Conf., Anaheim, Calif., May 19-22, 1975

[26] M.M.Zloof, 'Query by Example: Operation on the Transitive Closure', IBM Research Report RC 5526, July 1975

THE EFFECTIVE ARRANGEMENT OF LOGICAL SYSTEMS

Edsger W.Dijkstra
Burroughs
Plataanstraat 5
NL-4565 NUENEN
The Netherlands

We all know that when we have to design something "large" or difficult", we have to apply in one way or another the old adagium "Divide and Rule". Our machines are made from components, our programs are made from modules and they should fit together via interfaces. That is fine, but it raises, of course, the questions how to choose the modules and how to formulate the interfaces. This paper explores the main goals of modularization; being aware of them should assist us in evaluating the quality of proposed modularization.

* * *

An inspiring example of modularization outside our own field is the way in which human knowledge is divided over the different scientific disciplines. Why do we teach different disciplines at our Universities? Why don't we teach all our students just "knowledge"? The answer is simple: our human skulls are too small and our days are too short. The amount of knowledge needed for each discipline must fit into a human head. Besides knowledge there are abilities, and human abilities have two characteristics: they take a lot of training before they are mastered, and thereafter the maintenance of their mastery requires that they are nearly daily exercised, for without such daily exercise they fade away. (This, by the way, is one of the explanations why the capable are always so busy.) In this sense, rather quantitative human characteristics impose a set of equally quantitative limitations on what we are willing to consider as a single scientific discipline.

But there are also internal, more structural constraints. I mean that just an arbitrary collection of scraps of knowledge of the right total amount does not constitute a scientific discipline! It must be sufficiently coherent and self-supporting: it must be possible to study the subject matter of a scientific discipline in isolation (or nearly so), largely independent of what is happening or known in other scientific fields. And the increased insight should enhance our abilities, our enhanced abilities should assist us in improving our insight.

The above very rough sketch of how mankind as a whole has parcelled out its knowledge has been included because it also provides a model of how, on a microscopic scale, a single scientist works when he focusses his attention on an aspect of his problem. For every problem too large to be solved at a single stroke of the pen we try to apply a similar technique. We try to isolate various aspects of the problem and to deal with them in turn by "concentrating our attention" on them. (The latter does not mean that we study them in complete isolation: through the corners of our eyes we usually still look at all we are temporarily ignoring!)

The usual catchphrase for this technique is "separation of concerns". Although very adequate from a descriptive point of view, it raises of course the same sort of questions as we raised initially about modules and interfaces, such as "Which concerns should be separated?" and perhaps "After separation, how do they combine again?". This similarity is a rather clear hint that the successful "modularization" of a large information processing system is <u>not</u> a trivial matter.

* * *

The discovery that from a "larger" concern, a few "smaller" concerns can be successfully extracted usually ranks as a scientific discovery. Let me mention a few of them from our own field, so that we know, what we are talking about.

a) The isolation of the definition of the syntax in the task of defining programming languages. (John Backus, 1959; as BNF immediately used in the definition of ALGOL 60.)

b) The isolation of logical aspects of operating systems via the model of cooperating sequential processes. (Edsger W.Dijkstra, 1961; quickly thereafter used in the design of the THE Multiprogramming System.)

c) The isolation of programming language semantics computational histories. (C.A. R.Hoare, 1968; immediately used in the axiomatic definition of semantics.)

I think that the above three examples are fairly typical: all three "separations" (or "isolations" or "extractions") have been highly rewarding. Firstly it was quite clear that the people responsible were not just playing a game, they extracted what seemed a very relevant and possibly manageable aspect from a large and burning problem. Secondly they created a real of thought rich enough to have many thoughts in!

Example (a) opened the way for parsing theory, example (b) for the theory of synchronization, deadlock prevention etc., and example (c) has opened the way for practicable techniques for proving the correctness of programs. In all three cases the problems addressed can now be dealt with quite professionally. All three are easily "rich" enough to be the subject of a one-semester course in a University curriculum, and all three are so well separated from other concerns that such a one-semester course could be fairly self-contained.

Yet another observation should be made. By ignoring, abstracting, generalizing (or whatever verb you wish to use to indicate the not taking into account of some facts) a dual goal has been achieved: thanks to it the theories are of a wide applicability and at the same time of an internal simplicity. (Think of the tremendous simplification of the theory of cooperating sequential processes that was made possible by <u>not</u> dragging speed ratios into the picture! If knowledge about speed ratios had been essential, the correctness arguments would have been an awful mixture of discrete and continuous arguments, and it would all have become very complicated.) It has been said that "everything can be regarded as a special instance of something more general", but I would like to add that there is only a point in doing so, provided that the general view <u>simplifies</u> our arguments. This condition is certainly not met when the more general something can only be understood via a case analysis ranging over the different special instances.

* * *

Another inspiring example is provided by the arrangement of mathematical arguments.

Of our various thinking activities I shall reserve the term "reasoning" for all manipulations that are formalized --or could readily be so-- by techniques such as arithmetic, formula manipulation or symbolic logic. These techniques have a few common characteristics.

First of all, their application is straightforward in the sense that as soon as it has been decided in sufficient detail, <u>what</u> has to be achieved by them, there is no question anymore <u>how</u> to achieve it. And whenever such a technique has been applied, the question whether this has been done correctly is undebatable.

Secondly --and this is not independent of the first characteristic-- we know how to teach these techniques: arithmetic is taught at the primary school, formula manipulation at the secondary school, and symbolic logic at the university.

Thirdly, we are very good at doing modest amounts of reasoning. When large amounts of it are needed, however, we are powerless without mechanical aids. To multiply two two-digit numbers is something we all can do; for the multiplication of two five-digit numbers, most of us would prefer the assistance of pencil and paper; the multiplication of two hundred-digit numbers is a task that, even with the aid of pencil and paper, most of us would not care to undertake.

In order to reach a conclusion the amount of reasoning needed is often the stumbling block, and I have yielded to the temptation to relate the effectiveness with which we have arranged our thoughts to the degree in which we have reduced the amount of reasoning needed. A recent experience has confirmed that this seems sensible. I was compiling a collection of what I thought to be impressively elegant solutions. The first thing that struck me was the surprising degree of consensus among my mathematical colleagues: when I asked them for suggestions they often came with the same examples. The second thing that struck me was that, when I showed any of them a solution from the collection that happened to be new for him, I evoked uniformly the same reaction: laughter! The thrid thing that struck me, however, is in this context the most important one: all the impressively elegant solutions were very short. I therefore ask you to subscribe --at least until the discussion after this talk-- my thesis that the effectiveness with which we think is closely related to the reduction of the amount of reasoning needed, because, as soon as you have subscribed that thesis, you will agree with me that it is a good thing to know by what methods we can reduce that amount and by what methods we can increase it: those of the former category are the ones to be applied, those of the latter category are the ones to be avoided.

* * *

An obvious method is avoiding repetition. When multiplying two ten-digit numbers with pencil and paper we constantly appeal to the 10 by 10 multiplication table of the products of one-digit factors. Whether or not we know the multiplication table by heart or have it written out in front of us for quick reference is unimportant for the purpose of this discussion. What is important is that while multiplying those two ten-digit numbers, we have 100 <u>theorems</u> at our disposal, of which $7 * 8 = 56$ is an instance. If we <u>know</u> how to count, or <u>know</u> how to add, we can <u>prove</u> that the product $7 * 8$ equals 56, but that proof requires a certain amount of reasoning, so much as a matter of fact that we would not like to do it over and over again, everytime we need the product $7 * 8$. Hence the knowledge that that product equals 56 is cast into a theorem; together with the other 99 theorems it forms what is known as the multiplication table.

Another remark of a directly quantitative nature is that we would not expect much use for a theorem whose statement is longer than its proof: instead of appealing to the theorem it would be simpler --at least "shorter"-- to mention directly its proof.

The quantitative remarks in the two previous paragraphs, although of some relevance, do, however, not tell the complete story: if they did, there would be no point in stating and proving a lemma that is used only once, and there <u>is</u> a point in doing so.

Suppose that the total proof of a Theorem consists of two parts:
A: a proof of the Theorem based on the validity of a Lemma, and
B: a proof of aforementioned Lemma.
If both proofs are correct, the Theorem has been established, but suppose that part B is shown to contain a flaw. If we cannot correct the flaw, or perhaps even discover that the Lemma does not hold, we are in bad shape. If, however, we can correct the flaw in part B , its correction is the only thing that needs to be done: part A survives unchanged and unattended. Thinking about the last scenario I have come to the conclusion that its likelyhood is, all by itself, a sufficient justification for splitting up the total proof --straight from the axioms, so to speak-- in part A relying on a Lemma and a part B establishing that Lemma, even if part A refers only once to it. The conclusion seems to be that we not only seek to reduce the amount of reasoning eventually needed when all would have gone well, but also the amount of reasoning to be expected in view of our fallibility.

But, again, there is more to it. Splitting the total proof into parts A and B , connected by a Lemma used in A and proved in B means
1) that we can study B ignoring A, i.e. ignoring the way in which the Lemma is used: we only need to consider what the Lemma asserts
2) that we can study A ignoring B , i.e. ignoring the way in which the Lemma is proved: again we only need to consider what the Lemma asserts. Because the statement of the Lemma can be expected --see above-- to be shorter than its proof, also here we have to take less into account, and that is nice in view of another human limitation, i.e. the limited span of our attention.

Such a separation of concerns is, however, not only nice in view of our limited span of attention, it has a much profounder consequence. It gives us the freedom of replacing part B by a shorter or nicer proof of the Lemma as soon as we find one, it gives us the freedomg of replacing part A by a nicer or shorter proof of the Theorem as soon as we find one. As long as the Lemma remains the same, changing one part does not invalidate the other. This observation makes it abundantly clear --at least in my mind-- that we should not regard the appeal to the Lemma as it occurs in part A as an abbreviation of its proof as described in part B . The appeal to a lemma is to what the lemma states, and *not* to its proof: the main purpose of the introduction of the explicitly stated Lemma was precisely to make part A a *consistent* whole that is *independent* of the particular shape of B .

* * *

The above must sound very familiar to every mathematician that has been trained always to try consciously to present his proofs both as concise and as clear as possible. (That not all mathematicians have been trained that way, is another matter that need not concern us now.) Computing scientists --the other designers of what I called in my title: "logical systems"-- seem, amazingly enough, to be in general less aware of it. They are in general aware of the circumstance that what on one level of detail can be regarded as an unanalysed whole, can be regarded at a next level of greater detail as a composite object, they are often not fully aware of its implications. The analogy with mathematical proofs tells us that whenever we regard a whole as composed of parts, the way of composition must define how the relevant properties of the whole depend functionally on the *properties* of the parts, without the need of taking their internal structure into account.

Let me give you one of my cherished examples. We consider a program part S for the computation of the remainder, more precisely, a program part S satisfying for constant c and d :

$$(c \geq 0 \ \underline{\text{and}}\ d > 0) \Rightarrow wp(S,\ r = c\ \underline{\text{mod}}\ d) \tag{1}$$

(in words: $c \geq 0$ *and* $d > 0$ implies the weakest pre-condition for the initial state such that activation of S is certain to establish a final state satisfying the post-condition $r = c$ *mod* d). Consider for S the following program part:

```
{c ≥ 0 and d > 0} r, dd := c, d;                                    (2)
                  do r > dd → dd:= 2 * dd od;
                  do dd ≠ d → dd:= dd / 2;
                              if r ≥ dd → r:= r - dd
                              ▯ r < dd → skip
                              fi
                  od {r = c mod d}
```

Many programmers, I have discovered, don't hesitate to consider this program part S as composed (primarily) of three parts, viz. of the form

"S" = "S0; S1; S2"

i.e. the outermost syntactical decomposition. The point, however, is that nowhere the properties of these parts S0, S1, and S2 have been stated, on account of which we can conclude that S satisfies (1). This point becomes a problem as soon as it is discovered that program (2) is wrong. It contains a well-engineered bug: in those cases where c divided by d leaves a remainder = 0 and, in addition, the quotient is a power of 2 , the final state satisfies $r = d$ instead of $r = 0$. As it stands we can only conclude that program (2) as a whole is wrong; we cannot --although regarding it as a concatenation of three statements-- decide which of these statements is in error. That question is void.

And, as a matter of fact, we can repair it in different ways. Either we replace S1 by

"do r ≥ dd → dd:= 2 * dd od"

or replace S2 by

"do r ≥ d → dd:= dd / 2;
        do r ≥ dd → r:= r - dd od
od"

If we had chosen the properties

$$P0 \Rightarrow wp(S0, P1) , \quad P1 \Rightarrow wp(S1, P2) , \quad \text{and} \quad P2 \Rightarrow wp(S2, P3) \qquad (3)$$

with P0: $c \geq 0$ and $d > 0$

P1: r mod $d = c$ mod d and ($\underline{E}$ i: $i \geq 0$: $dd = d * 2^i$) and $0 \leq r$

P2: P1 and $r < dd$

P3: $r = c$ mod d

then the bug would have been localized in S1 as it may fail to establish P2 .

Note. On account of the semantic definition of the semicolon

$$wp(\text{"S1; S2"}, R) = wp(S1, wp(S2, R))$$

we derive

$$wp(\text{"S0; S1; S2"}, R) = wp(S0, wp(S1, wp(S2, R)))$$

and conclude that (3) indeed allows us to derive

$$P0 \Rightarrow wp(\text{"S0; S1; S2"}, P3)$$ (End of Note.)

The moral of the story is that we can only claim that a whole has been properly composed of parts provided the necessary properties of the parts have been decided. Without that specification it is, as if we are trying to build up a mathematical theory while giving only the proofs of our theorems and lemmata, but not the theorems and lemmata themselves! I have, therefore, decided for myself that such specification of the parts is an absolutely essential constituent of the whole design. After all I have said, this decision may strike you as obvious, as nearly trivial. I am unhappy to report that it is not generally accepted. Quite regularly I see texts arguing that "we cannot impose upon the poor programmer the additional burden of also supplying the assertions that correctness proofs (still) need". Depending on the attitude of the writer, either today's proving techniques are blamed for "still" needing such assertions --in that case the author usually does not mention what alternative proving techniques he has in mind-- or the author now proposes to apply Artificial Intelligence techniques for deriving such assertions mechanically. I hope to have made clear why I regard the latter as a somewhat nonsensical activity; the assertions reflect an explicit choice of the designer, a responsibility that certainly cannot be delegated to a guessing AI-system. (For instance: in the above example we could have replaced in P1 and in P2 , or in P1 only, the term r <u>mod</u> d = c <u>mod</u> d by the more stringent r = c .) An "automatic specification guesser" that is only fed with a single instance of each part is almost certainly bound to be overspecific, and the whole activity strikes me as putting the cart before the horse.

<u>Example</u>. Given the following proof:

"The theorem is obvious, because

$$(x1 - x0)(x2 - x3) + (x2 - x0)(x3 - x1) + (x3 - x0)(x1 - x2) = 0 \quad " \quad ,$$

can you guess the theorem? It is --this is a hint-- a very well-known theorem that is usually proved in a rather indirect way. (End of example.)

* * *

I have shown you a small example, specially manufactured to illustrate the nature of the dilemma. Let me now turn to a more grandiose example that has been provided by "the real world". The original design of the IBM650 had the very special feature that the attempted execution of a special little program loop blew one of the fuses of the machine. Needless to say, this very special feature was not mentioned in the manual, but, programmers being as they are, they not only discovered it, they also used it in at least one organization, where reservations of machine time were extended with the down-time, when the machine broke down during your period of reservation. Programmers who had a one-hour reservation for a debugging session used the little loop when, after ten minutes of testing, they discovered a bug whose patching required some peaceful thinking!

The decomposition into the two parts "hardware" and "software" is certainly a time-honoured one, but in this case it was defective. As soon as the aggregate whole was required not to blow fuses while yet it did, <u>none</u> of the two parts could be proved to be wrong or to be correct. The maintenance engineer could argue that all programmers knew that the machine was such that that little loop would blow a fuse and that, therefore, they should not include it in their programs. The programmers, from their side, could argue that the manual nowhere stated that upon the attempted execution of that little loop the machine had to blow one of its fuses! They could throw the blame on the other party indefinitely, and the only way to end this ping-pong game is by <u>choosing</u> a well-defined interface. Either it is decided that the fuse should not be blown --which means a change in the hardware design-- , or it is decided that the fuse should be blown, and then all programmers have the obligation to program around it.

I definitely prefer the first alternative, not so much because I am more of a programmer than of a circuit designer, but because in the interplay between hardware and software we have the greatest variability at the software side. It is therefore simpler to propagate the obligation of fixing the bug through the limited number of machines than through all the programs that are or will be made for that type of machine. I have the sad impression that in user communities, management often takes the undesirable decision and obliges its programmers to program around such deficiencies.

The story about the fuse is old and nearly forgotten. We should, however, remember it as a paradigm for the sad situation in which the majority of today's programmers are supposed to do their work. I know of a respectable colleague who, in the year of the Lord 1976, is developing the basic software for a machine of a less respectable design: its hardware specifications are so obscure that quite regularly he has to get access to the prototype in order to discover experimentally what some commands are supposed to achieve! He has to do so under the assumption that the prototype is in perfect working condition, the trouble, of course, being that, logically speaking, that "perfect working condition" is, as yet, undefined. Together with the hardware designers he has to decide "after the fact", which machine they should have had in mind to build. I like to believe that this is an extreme case, but have no grounds for doing so.....

The complete functional specification of a machine must be given without any reference to its internal structure if, in the whole system, the machine is to be recognized as a part of a composite whole. This, however, does not only apply to hardware --"concrete machines", if you like-- , it is equally applicable to the abstract machines known as higher-level programming languages. Only when their semantics are fully defined without any reference to implementation details such as compilers, binders, interrupts and what have you, only then has the separation of concerns been effectuated that makes any progress possible. It is in this respect disheartening to observe that many a modern high-level language user is much worse off than the average programmer a quarter of a century ago. In the old days programmers used to have a complete functional description of their machine at their disposal and, as a result, they could know exactly what they were doing. This is in sharp contrast to the majority of the so-called high-level programming languages, the semantics of which are only so loosely indicated that most young programmers have lost the sense of complete control that we used to have. They live in a woolly environment in which the notion that a program is either correct or not is, by definition, not applicable.

A politically complicating factor is that the world's largest computer manufacturer has probably not the slightest incentive to change this state of woollyness of the programming languages it supports, because this woollyness only acts at its advantage as long as its products are accepted as what are euphemistically called "de facto standards". In the case of a well-defined programming language, it would have the obligation to implement that correctly and would run the risk of a competitor providing a better implementation; as things are its implementations are taken as "the definition". Such political considerations make its unwillingness to support such well-defined languages as, say, ALGOL 60 only too understandable.

So much for the ill effects of lacking specifications.

* * *

I hope that in the above I have convinced you that, in the invention of the complex composite systems we are considering, a rigorous definition of the essential properties of the parts is not a luxury but a necessity. In the final part of my talk I would like to tackle the more elusive question "By virtue of what type of properties can parts be nice or ugly?" It is the question what interfaces to invent. I called this question "elusive" because it is as impossible to give a final answer to it is impossible to teach young mathematicians how to discover beautiful theorems. What we can do --and, in fact, do while teaching mathematics-- is explaining why we think that some theorems are beautiful. In a similar vein we should be able to explain to young computer scientists what virtues to look for when they are evaluating or considering a proposed set of interfaces. It is in this connection a good thing to remember that one of the main roles of the decomposition of a whole into parts was the localization of the bug when something went wrong.

Again, let me start with a very simple example. Suppose that we have to control a printing device that accepts 27 different commands --say the printing of the 26 letters of the alphabet and the blank-- . If we control this device with a ternary machine, each command could be specified with three ternary digits because $3^3=27$. But suppose now that we are to control such a device with a binary machine. We would then need five bits for a command. Immediately the question arises what to do with the nonsensical remaining $32 - 27 = 5$ possible "commands". One answer would be that it does not matter because no correct program would ever send any of these five nonsensical commands to the device. But this would be a very silly choice, for it would give the designer of the device the licence to make it in such a way that a nonsensical command could cause a jam in the printing mechanism, and as soon as he has done that it is possible to write erroneous programs that, besides not producing the right results, may wreck the installation. Such a silly interface would cause the ill effects of an erroneous program to spread. Another possibility would be to postulate that such nonsensical commands are ignored by the device. That is safe as far as the working condition of the device is concerned but it is still silly: presumably it was not the programmer's intention to send such silly skip commands to the printing device and, if such a command is sent to the device, we may assume that something in the execution of his program has gone wrong. The sensible reaction is, on the one hand to protect the device from being wrecked and on the other hand to signal an error, thus giving the programmer another way of protecting himself. An alternative way of doing away with the problem would be to extend the character set of the printing device with another five characters.

This, again, was a simple example, specially manufactured to illustrate the problem; but it we look for it, we can find the silly choice made many times, and on a much larger scale. A famous example is the coupling to a general purpose computer of peripherals that may signal to the central processor that they require a certain service from it within a given number of milliseconds; in the worst situation the irrecoverable malfunctioning that results when the central processor fails to meet its real-time obligation is not even signalled! In any case the real-time obligation of the central processor with respect to such a peripheral places a heavy and ugly burden upon the system designer who, for instance, must guarantee that the interrupt is never disabled for too long a period of time.

We find the same flaw when compilers accept syntactically incorrect programs without warning or when system integrity relies on the correctness of the compilers used.

The quoted examples are instances of a general case. We are dealing with classes of strings: strings of characters representing source program, strings of words representing object programs, strings of commands controlling a device, etc. Either such a class of strings contains all the strings that are physically possible, as in the case of coding the 27 commands to the printer with three ternary digits. In this case there is no redundancy, and we note in passing that under many circumstances such an absence of redundancy is undesirable. Or --and this seems to be the much more common case-- the class of intended strings does not contain all the ones that are physically possible, i.e. our intended strings are represented by the physically ones with a certain redundancy. Using the terms "legal" and "illegal" for strings within and beyond the intended class respectively, we can formulate the following conclusions.

1) The class of legal strings must be defined precisely. If this already presents serious problems, this is a warning not to be ignored.

2) Any part processing such a string should establish whether the string is legal or not. If this presents serious problems, this is a warning not to be ignored.

3) Any part processing such a string should not react upon an illegal string as if it were a legal one.

4) Processing an illegal string may not wreck the part: none of the relations which are carefully kept invariant during the processing of legal strings may be destroyed by the processing of an illegal string.

Note. If program component B processes a string produced by program component A without satisfying the above conditions 2 through 4 --for instance because it is felt to be too expensive to make component B that way-- , we should regard components A and B as belonging to the same part. (End of Note.)

* * *

To wind up I would like to make two suggestions: I would like to suggest to programmers that they have a closer look at mathematics, and to mathematicians that they have a closer look at programming. By virtue of their tradition mathematicians have a more explicit appreciation for what it means to be rigorous, as a result of the power of currently available machines programmers are more aware of the problems created by sheer size.

I do not suggest that programmers should stuff their heads with mathematical results, but I would like them to get a better appreciation for how and how effectively mathematics are organized. If they do so I expect them to discover that many current topics in computing science are in a sense null-problems as they address problems that should never have been there to start with. I expect them to discover that if they are problems now, we are suffering from the pains of a hell into which our own sins have sent us. I also expect them to discover that these problems are only soluble by starting over again, and that the perpetuation of some old mistakes is the worst mistake we can make now. As very likely candidates for null-problems I mention those associated with compatability, portability and protection.

I also feel that many a mathematician could profit from the exposure to programming. I have that feeling because, while studying mathematical texts, I now very often observe as my reaction towards the author "He must be a very poor programmer!". We, as programmers, have, for instance, been so trained to avoid case-analysis like the plague that it is not unusual at all to encounter a mathematical argument, the length of which can be halved, perhaps even be halved a number of times.

While preparing this invited speech I had to guess what type of audience I would eventually address. The title of the Symposium's subject "Mathematical Foundations of Computing Science" was my only indication. If I have the privilege of addressing a primarily mathematically interested audience, it is clear how my ending note should sound, for in that case I can only urge you, Mathematicians, <u>not</u> to confine with respect to Computing Science your interest to its foundations! The praxis of computer programming needs you as much as you needs it challenge, if Mathematics is to remain the Queen of Sciences.

May 1976 | prof.dr.Edsger W.Dijkstra
NUENEN, The Netherlands | Burroughs Research Fellow

RECURSIVITY, SEQUENCE RECURSIVITY, STACK RECURSIVITY AND SEMANTICS OF PROGRAMS

G.Germano and A.Maggiolo-Schettini

Laboratorio di Cibernetica, 80072 Arco Felice, Italy

Ist.di Scienze dell'Informazione dell'Università, 84100 Salerno, Italy

The present paper introduces p.r. (partial recursive) stack functions and gives some characterizations of them. After a brief summary of results on sequence functions (see [1-8]) and their relationship to traditional p.r.functions, the relationship of stack functions to p.r.sequence functions is investigated.

The meaning of a program for a register machine can be described by a p.r.function $f:N^r \to N^s$ (p.r.sequence-to-sequence or simply sequence function) insofar as the program causes the content of the r registers, to which values have been assigned before execution, to be transformed into the content of the s registers which have a defined value after execution. On the other hand, consider a machine having a stack as storage (stack machine). The meaning of a program for a stack machine can be described by a p.r.function $f:N^* \to N^*$ (p.r.stack function) insofar as the program causes the content of the stack before execution to be transformed into the content of the stack after execution and the stack may contain a number sequence of indeterminate length.

The first section of the paper concerns p.r.sequence functions. The second section investigates the relationship between such functions and traditional p.r.functions. The third section introduces p.r.stack functions via normal form theorems for p.r.sequence functions. The fourth section compares different characterizations of p.r.stack functions. The fifth section gives the main theorems on the relationship between p.r.stack functions and p.r.sequence functions. Finally the sixth section illustrates, by means of an example concerning the Ackermann function, how stack functions express the meaning of programs for stack machines, while giving also a simple and natural method for proving the recursivity of the Ackermann function.

1.Sequence recursivity.

We consider the usual initial functions of traditional recursivity: O(zero of zero arguments),S(successor),P(predecessor)plus the deletion function $\Pi:N\to N^{o}$.

We define now the following operators on functions($t_1 \simeq t_2$ holds iff t_1 and t_2 are both defined and $t_1=t_2$ or t_1 and t_2 are both undefined): for $f:N^r\to N^s$, $m\in N$ and $\bar{m}\in N^r$, the left cylindrification operator $\lambda f\, {}^c f$ such that ${}^c f(m\bar{m})\simeq mf(\bar{m})$ and the right cylindrification operator $\lambda f\, f^c$ such that $f^c(\bar{m}m)\simeq f(\bar{m})m$;

for $f:N^r\to N^s$, $g:N^s\to N^t$ and $\bar{m}\in N^r$, the composition operator $\lambda f\lambda g(f\circ g)$ such that $(f\circ g)\bar{m}\simeq g(f(\bar{m}))$;

for $f:N^r\to N^r$ and $\bar{m}\in N^r$, the repetition operators(1)$\lambda f\, f^{\circ}$ such that $f^{\circ}(\bar{m})\simeq(\overbrace{f\circ\ldots\circ f}^{k})(\bar{m})$ where k is the smallest number for which there is a sequence of numbers $\bar{n}$ with $(\overbrace{f\circ\ldots\circ f}^{k})(\bar{m})=0\bar{n}$ and $f^{\circ}(\bar{m})$ is undefined if no such k exists,(2)$\lambda f\, f^{=}$ such that $f^{=}(\bar{m})\simeq(\overbrace{f\circ\ldots\circ f}^{k})(\bar{m})$ where k is the smallest number for which there is a sequence of numbers $\bar{n}$ and a m with $(\overbrace{f\circ\ldots\circ f}^{k})(\bar{m})=mm\bar{n}$ and $f^{=}(\bar{m})$ is undefined if no such k exists,(3)$\lambda f\, f^{\nabla}$ such that $f^{\nabla}(\bar{m})=\bar{n}$ iff $f^{\circ}(\bar{m})=0\bar{n}$,(4)$\lambda f\, f^{\square}(\bar{m})=\bar{n}$ iff $f^{=}(\bar{m})=mm\bar{n}$ for some m.

As to the computational counterpart of the operators above see for example [7].

Let

$$C_1:=\{0,S,P,\Pi\},C_2:=\{0,S,\Pi\},C_3:=\{0,S,P\},C_4:=\{0,S\}$$

and let $C_i(X)$ be the closure of the set X with respect to the left and right cylindrification operators,the composition operator and the repetition operator (i).

Set $S_i:=C_i(C_i)$ .From [7] we know the following

<u>Theorem 1</u>.The classes S_i(for i=1,2,3,4) meet.

So we can set $S:=S_i$.The class S is the class of partial recursive <u>sequence</u> functions.

2.Recursivity and sequence recursivity.

Let R be the class of traditional partial recursive functions.
The relationships between the class R and the class S are expressed by the following theorems.

Theorem 2. $R \subseteq S$.

For the proof see [5] noting that $L={}^{C}\Pi$.

Theorem 3. $(\forall f:N^r \to N \in S)\ f \in R$.

Proof.Even if the theorem is a consequence of the Church thesis,owing to the fact that functions in S are obviously computable,we give here a simple mathematical proof of the theorem.

Let

$$I_1^1 := S \circ P$$

$$I_1^r := {}^{c}\Pi^{c^{r-2}} \circ {}^{c}\Pi^{c^{r-3}} \circ \ldots \circ {}^{c}\Pi \qquad 1<r$$

$$I_i^r := \Pi^{c^{r-1}} \circ \ldots \circ \Pi^{c^{r-i+1}} \circ {}^{c}\Pi^{c^{r-i-1}} \circ \ldots \circ {}^{c}\Pi \qquad 1<i<r$$

$$I_r^r := \Pi^{c^{r-1}} \circ \Pi^{c^{r-2}} \circ \ldots \circ \Pi^{c} \qquad 1<r$$

It holds that

$$I_i^r(m_1 \ldots m_i \ldots m_r) = m_i$$

We prove first the following

Lemma 1. $(\forall f:N^r \to N^s \in S)\ (\forall i:1 \le i \le s)\ f \circ I_i^s \in R$.

Proof.It is obtained by induction on S characterized as $C_1(C_1)$.

The lemma is obvious for the initial functions.

Induction steps.

For $f:N^r \to N^s \in S$ satisfying the induction hypothesis it holds that

$$({}^{c}f \circ I_i^{s+1})(\bar{m}) = \begin{cases} I_1^{r+1}(\bar{m}) & \text{if } i=1 \\ (f \circ I_{i-1}^{s})(I_2^{r+1}(\bar{m}) \ldots I_{r+1}^{r+1}(\bar{m})) & \text{if } 1<i \le s+1 \end{cases}$$

The induction step for the right cylindrification operator is analogous.

For $f_1:N^{r_1} \to N^{s_1} \in S$ and $f_2:N^{r_2} \to N^{s_2} \in S$ satisfying the induction hypothesis it holds that

$$((f_1 \circ f_2) \circ I_i^{s_2})(\bar{m}) = (f_1 \circ (f_2 \circ I_i^{s_2}))(\bar{m})$$
$$= (f_2 \circ I_i^{s_2})((f_1 \circ I_1^{s_1})(\bar{m}) \ \ldots \ (f_1 \circ I_{s_1}^{s_1})(\bar{m}))$$

For $f:N^r \to N^r \in S$ satisfying the induction hypothesis we define by simultaneous recursion the functions $f_1,\dots,f_r : N^{r+1} \to N$

$$f_i(0\bar{m}) := I_i^r(\bar{m})$$
$$f_i(S(x)\bar{m}) := (f \circ I_i^r)(f_1(x\bar{m}) \dots f_r(x\bar{m}))$$

Each f_i results to belong to R.On the other hand it holds that

$$((\overbrace{f\circ \dots \circ f}^{k}) \circ I_i^r)(\bar{m}) = f_i(k\bar{m})$$

and as

$$(f^{\circ} \circ I_i^r)(\bar{m}) = f_i((\mu x\ f_1(x\bar{m})=0)\bar{m})$$

also $f^{\circ} \circ I_i^r$ belongs to R.This completes the proof of the lemma.

Now for $f:N^r \to N^s$ it holds that $f = f \circ I_i^s$ and therefore f belongs to R.

From theorem 2 and theorem 3 we obtain

Theorem 4. $(\forall f:N^r \to N)\ (f \in R \Leftrightarrow f \in S)$.

This theorem states that the class of traditional partial recursive functions coincides with the class of p.r.sequence functions with codomain N.

3.From sequence recursivity to stack recursivity.

Let $\bar{C}_i(X)$ be the closure of the set X with respect to the left cylindrification operator(only),the composition operator and the repetition operator (i).

We can now show the following normal form theorem for the classes $C_i(C_i)$.

<u>Theorem</u> <u>5</u>. $S_i = \bar{C}_i(\{f^{c^r} \mid f \in C_i, r \in N\})$.

Proof .It suffices to show that $S_i \subseteq \bar{C}_i(\{f^{c^r} \mid f \in C_i, r \in N\})$,which can be done by induction on S_i.The theorem is obvious for the initial functions. For the induction steps note that for f, f_1, f_2 in the classes considered

$$({}^{c}f)^{c^r} = {}^{c}(f^{c^r})$$
$$(f^{c})^{c^r} = f^{c^{r+1}}$$
$$(f_1 \circ f_2)^{c^r} = f_1^{c^r} \circ f_2^{c^r}$$
$$(f^{\circ})^{c^r} = (f^{c^r})^{\circ}$$
$$(f^{=})^{c^r} = (f^{c^r})^{=}$$

Theorem 5 says that we can limit ourselves to using cylindrification only at maximal depth,that is limiting ourselves to using $O^{c^r}, S^{c^r}, P^{c^r}, \Pi^{c^r}$ as initial functions and to working only with left cylindrification, composition and repetition.Each of such functions works on some items at the left of the sequence to which it is applied while leaving the next r items to the right unchanged. This reminds us of how one normally works on stacks and suggests the consideration of functions which work in the same way on some top items of a stack while leaving the next (undefinitely many) items unchanged.

To introduce functions which work on stacks as sketched above we have to consider first "indefinite right cylindrifications" of the initial functions: $O^{C^\infty}, S^{C^\infty}, P^{C^\infty}, \Pi^{C^\infty}$, where $O^{C^\infty} := \bigcup_{i=o}^{\infty} O^{C^i}$, $S^{C^\infty} := 1_N O \cup \bigcup_{i=o}^{\infty} S^{C^i}$, etc. (we will write simply "f" instead of "f^{C^∞}" when the context suggests that "indefinitely right cylindrificated functions" are concerned).

Then we have to introduce the following new operators analogous to those for sequence functions (but we will use the same symbols): a left cylindrification operator $\lambda f\ {}^{c}f$ for $f:N^* \to N^*$, a composition operator $\lambda f \lambda g (f \circ g)$ for $f,g:N^* \to N^*$ and repetition operators (1) $\lambda f\ f^{\circ}$, (2) $\lambda f\ f^{=}$, (3) $\lambda f\ f^{\nabla}$, (4) $\lambda f\ f^{\square}$ for $f:N^* \to N^*$.

Let $\overline{C}_i(X)$ be the closure of the set X with respect to the new left cylindrification operator, composition operator and repetition operator (i).

Paraphrasing theorem 5 set now $T_i := \overline{C}_i(\{f^{C^\infty} \mid f \in C_i\})$.

4. Stack recursivity.

As concerns the classes just introduced we can state the following

<u>Theorem 6</u>. The classes T_i (for i=1,2,3,4) meet.

Proof. We will use the following functions:

$$\Delta := {}^{c}O \circ {}^{cc}O \circ (P \circ {}^{c}S \circ {}^{cc}S)^{\nabla}$$

$$= {}^{c}O \circ {}^{cc}O \circ {}^{ccc}O \circ ({}^{c}S \circ {}^{cc}S \circ {}^{ccc}S)^{\square}$$

$$\Theta := {}^{cc}O \circ (P \circ {}^{cc}S)^{\nabla}$$

$$= O \circ {}^{ccc}O \circ (S \circ {}^{ccc}S)^{\square}$$

$$\Delta^2 := \Delta \circ {}^{cc}\Delta \circ {}^{c}\Theta$$

$$D := \Delta^2 \circ (P \circ {}^{c}P)^{\nabla} \circ {}^{c}\Theta \circ {}^{c}(P \circ {}^{c}P)^{\nabla} \circ (P \circ {}^{c}S)^{\nabla}$$

for which it holds that

$$\Delta(m\bar{\bar{m}}) = mm\bar{\bar{m}}$$

$$\Theta(mn\bar{\bar{m}}) = n\bar{\bar{m}}$$

$$\Delta^2(mn\bar{m}) = mnmn\bar{m}$$

$$D(mn\bar{m}) = |m-n|\bar{m}$$

where $m,n \in N$ and $m \in N^*$.

Now it holds that

a) $T_1 \subseteq T_3$, because $\Pi = P^{\nabla}$ and $f^{\circ} = f^{\nabla} \circ O$;

b) $T_1 \supseteq T_3$, because $f^{\nabla} := f^{\circ} \circ \Pi$;

c) $T_2 \subseteq T_4$, because $\Pi = O \circ ({}^{c}P)^{\square}$ and $f^{=} = \Delta^2 \circ (\Pi \circ \Pi \circ f \circ \Delta^2)^{\square}$;

d) $T_2 \supseteq T_4$, because $f^{\square} = f^{=} \circ \Pi \circ \Pi$

e) $T_3 \subseteq T_4$, because $P = {}^{c}O \circ {}^{cc}O \circ ({}^{cc}\Pi \circ {}^{c}\Delta \circ {}^{c}S)^{\square}$ and $f^{\nabla} = O \circ ({}^{c}f)^{\square}$;

f) $T_3 \supseteq T_4$, because $\Pi = P^{\nabla}$ and $f^{\square} = \Delta^2 \circ D \circ (\Pi \circ f \circ \Delta^2 \circ D)^{\nabla} \circ \Pi \circ \Pi$.

Having proved that the classes T_i meet, we can set $T := T_i$. The class T is the class of p.r. stack functions.

5. Sequence recursivity and stack recursivity.

The relationships between the class S and the class T are expressed by the following theorems.

Theorem 7. $(\forall f: N^r \to N^s \in S)\ (\exists g \in T)\ (\forall i)\ f^{c^i} = N^{r+i} \upharpoonleft g$.

Proof. It is obtained by induction on S characterized as $C_1(C_1)$.

As concerns the initial functions it holds that

$$O^{c^k} = N^k \upharpoonleft O^{c^\infty}$$

$$S^{c^k} = N^{1+k} \upharpoonleft S^{c^\infty}$$

$$P^{c^k} = N^{1+k} \upharpoonleft P^{c^\infty}$$

$$\Pi^{c^k} = N^{1+k} \upharpoonleft \Pi^{c^\infty}$$

Induction steps.

For $f: N^r \to N^s \in S$ satisfying the induction hypothesis it holds that there is a $g \in T$ such that

$$({}^{c}f)^{c^i} = {}^{c}(f^{c^i}) = {}^{c}(N^{r+i} \upharpoonleft g) = N^{r+1+i} \upharpoonleft {}^{c}g .$$

For $f_1: N^{r_1} \to N^{s_1} \in S$ and $f_2: N^{r_2} \to N^{s_2} \in S$ satisfying the induction hypothesis it holds that there are $g_1, g_2 \in T$ such that

$$(f_1 \circ f_2)^{c^i} = f_1^{c^i} \circ f_2^{c^i} = (N^{r_1+i} \upharpoonleft g_1) \circ (N^{s_1+i} \upharpoonleft g_2) = N^{r_1+i} \upharpoonleft (g_1 \circ g_2) .$$

For $f: N^r \to N^r \in S$ satisfying the induction hypothesis it holds that there is a $g \in T$ such that

$$(f^{\circ})^{c^i} = (f \circ \ldots \circ f)^{c^i} = N^{r+i} \upharpoonleft (g \circ \ldots \circ g) = N^{r+i} \upharpoonleft g^{\circ} .$$

To investigate the relationship between the class S and the class T in the opposite direction we introduce first some number theoretic functions to construct a codification $N^* \to N$.

Set (see [10])

$$a(0):=0$$

$$a(S(x)):=a(x)+S(x)$$

It holds that

$$a(x)=\sum_{i\leq x} i=(x\cdot(x+1))/2$$

Set $\quad A(xy):=a(x+y)+y$

A belongs to R and is bijective.

Set

$$\alpha(0):=0$$

$$\alpha(S(x)):=\alpha(x)+sg_1|a(S(\alpha(x)))\dot{-}S(x)|$$

It holds that

$$\alpha(A(xy))=x+y$$

Set

$$A_2(z):=z\dot{-}a(\alpha(z))$$

$$A_1(z):=\alpha(z)\dot{-}A_2(z)$$

It holds that

$$A_1(A(xy))=x$$

$$A_2(A(xy))=y$$

A_1 and A_2 belong to R.

Set

$$A^r(x_1\ldots x_r):=A(x_1A(x_2\ldots A(x_{r-1}x_r)\ldots)) \quad \text{for } r\geq 2 \ .$$

The A^r belong to R and are bijective.

Set

$$b(0):=1$$

$$b(S(x)):=b(x)+x$$

It holds that

$$b(x+1)=(\sum_{0\leq i\leq x} i)+1=(x\cdot(x+1))/2+1$$

Set

$$B(xy):=b(x+y)+y$$

B belongs to R.

Set

$$\beta(0):=0$$

$$\beta(S(x)):=\beta(x)+sg_1|b(S(\beta(x)))\dot{-}S(x)|$$

It holds that

$$\beta(B(xy))=x+y$$

Set

$$B_2(z):=z\dot{-}b(\beta(z))$$

$$B_1(z):=\beta(z)\dot{-}B_2(z)$$

It holds that

$$B_1(B(xy))=x$$

$$B_2(B(xy))=y$$

B_1 and B_2 belong to R.

Note that $B:N\times N\to N$ surjectively but not injectively, whereas it holds that $((N-\{0\})\times N)\upharpoonright B : (N-\{0\})\times N \to N-\{0\}$ bijectively.

Set

$$J^0(\Lambda):=0$$

$$J^1(x):=B(1x)$$

$$J^r(x_1\ldots x_r):=B(rA^r(x_1\ldots x_r)) \qquad \text{for } r\geq 2$$

It holds that

$$J^0 : N^0 \to \{0\} \quad \text{bijectively}$$

$$J^1 : N \to B(\{1\}\times N) \quad \text{bijectively}$$

$$J^r : N^r \to B(\{r\}\times N) \quad \text{bijectively} \qquad \text{for } r\geq 2$$

From being bijective J^0, J^1, J^r $(r\geq 2)$ and $((N-\{0\})\times N)\upharpoonright B$, it follows that

$$J^0 \cup J^1 \cup \bigcup_{r\geq 2} J^r : N^* \to N \quad \text{bijectively} .$$

For $1\leq i\leq r$ set

$$J_i^r(z):=\begin{cases} A_1(A_2^{i-1}(B_2(z))) & \text{if } i<r \\ A_2^{i-1}(B_2(z)) & \text{if } i=r \end{cases}$$

It holds that

$$J_i^r(J^r(x_1\ldots x_i\ldots x_r))=x_i \quad .$$

For every function $f\in T$ we define now the "codified function" f_J, i.e. the function which takes from the codification of a stack $\bar{m}$ to the codification of a stack $\bar{n}$ in the same way as f takes from $\bar{m}$ to $\bar{n}$.

The definition is given by induction on T characterized as $\bar{C}_1(\{f^{C^\infty} | f\in C_1\})$.

$$O_J^{C^\infty}(z) := \begin{cases} B(1\ 0) & \text{if } z=0 \\ B(S(B_1(z))\ A(OB_2(z))) & \text{otherwise} \end{cases}$$

$$S_J^{C^\infty}(z) := \begin{cases} z & \text{if } B_1(z)=0 \\ B(B_1(z)\ S(B_2(z))) & \text{if } B_1(z)=1 \\ B(B_1(z)\ A(S(A_1(B_2(z)))\ A_2(B_2(z))) & \text{otherwise} \end{cases}$$

$$P_J^{C^\infty}(z) := \begin{cases} z & \text{if } B_1(z)=0 \\ B(B_1(z)\ P(B_2(z))) & \text{if } B_1(z)=1 \\ B(B_1(z)\ A(P(A_1(B_2(z)))\ A_2(B_2(z))) & \text{otherwise} \end{cases}$$

$$\Pi_J^{C^\infty}(z) := \begin{cases} z & \text{if } B_1(z)=0 \\ 0 & \text{if } B_1(z)=1 \\ B(P(B_1(z))\ \ A_2(B_2(z)) & \text{otherwise} \end{cases}$$

$$({}^{c}f)_J(z) := \begin{cases} z & \text{if } B_1(z)=0 \\ B(S(B_1(f_J(0)))\ A(B_2(z)\ f_J(0))) & \text{if } B_1(z)=1 \\ B(S(B_1(f_J(A_2(B_2(z)))))\ A(A_1(B_2(z))\ f_J(A_2(B_2(z))))) & \text{otherwise} \end{cases}$$

$$(f\circ g)_J(z) := g_J(f_J(z))$$

$$(f^\circ)_J(z) := F(h(z)\ z)$$

where $F(0z) := z$

$F(S(i)\ z) := f_J(F(i\ z)$

and $h(z) := \mu x[F(xz)=1 \vee (B_1(F(xz))>1 \wedge A_1(B_2(F(xz)))=0)]$

Note that for every $g\in T$ the codified function g_J belongs to R and it holds the following

<u>Lemma 2</u>. $(\forall g\in T)\ (\forall \overline{m}\in N^r)\ \ (g(\overline{m})\in N^s \Rightarrow g_J(J^r(\overline{m}))=J^s(g(\overline{m})))$.

We can state now the following

<u>Theorem 8</u>. $(\forall f:N^r\to N^s)\ \ ((\exists g\in T)\, f=N^r\upharpoonright g \Rightarrow f\in S)$.

Proof.

Now J^r and J_i^s belong to R.

Set

$$(J^s)^{-1} := \Delta\circ{}^c\Delta\circ\ldots\circ{}^{c^{s-2}}\Delta\circ(J_1^s)^{c^{s-1}}\circ{}^c(J_2^s)^{c^{s-2}}\circ\ldots\circ{}^{c^{s-1}}(J_s^s)$$

It holds that $(J^s)^{-1}(J^s(x_1\ldots x_s))=x_1\ldots x_s$ and $(J^s))^{-1}$ belongs to S.

Consider now functions f and g such that $f:N^r\to N^s$, $g\in T$ and $f=N^r\upharpoonright g$.

For $\overline{m}\in N^r$ it holds that

$$(J^r\circ g_J\circ(J^s)^{-1})(\overline{m}) = (g_J\circ(J^s)^{-1})(J^r(\overline{m})) = (J^s)^{-1}(g_J(J^r(\overline{m}))) = (J^s)^{-1}(J^s(g(\overline{m})))$$
$$= g(\overline{m}) = f(\overline{m})$$

which means that $f=J^r\circ g_J\circ(J^s)^{-1}$.

As J^r and g_J belong to $R\subset S$ and $(J^s)^{-1}$ belong to S, also f belongs to S.

From theorem 7 and theorem 8 we obtain the following

Theorem 9. $(\forall f:N^r\to N^s)\ (f\in S \Leftrightarrow (\exists g\in T)(\forall i)\, f^{c^i} = N^{r+i}\restriction g)$.

This theorem states that the class of p.r. sequence functions coincides with the class of the limitations of those p.r. stack functions which transform only a fixed number of items on the top of the stack while leaving the others unchanged. It is important to note that not every p. r. stack function works in this way (see for example Π°) so that the class T is by no means a trivial extension of the class S.

6. Programming the Ackermann function as a stack function.

We consider the Ackermann function in the form

$$F(x0)=S(x)$$
$$F(0S(y))=F(1y)$$
$$F(S(x)S(y))=F(F(xS(y))y)$$

Following an idea of Hermes in [9], we note that the Ackermann function can be computed by repeatedly applying the following function on a stack which contains initially the two arguments m and n:

$$F^{c^\infty}(m0\overline{m})=S(m)\overline{m}$$
$$F^{c^\infty}(0S(n)\overline{m})=1n\overline{m}$$
$$F^{c^\infty}(S(m)S(n)\overline{m})=mS(n)\overline{m}$$

where $\overline{m}\in N^*$.

We will use a hypothetical programming language whose operations are intended to work on a stack. In this language a "shifted" operation is supposed to work on the items immediately below the one on the top which remains unchanged on the top of the new stack.

Assume the instructions f_1, f_2, f_3 compute the following functions F_1, F_2, F_3:

$$F_1(mn\overline{m}):=S(m)\overline{m}$$
$$F_2(mn\overline{m}):=S(m)P(n)\overline{m}$$
$$F_3(mn\overline{m}):=P(m)nP(n)\overline{m}$$

The Ackermann function can now be computed by repeatedly applying the following procedure on a stack (which contains initially two items) until only one item remains in the stack:

```
if ⟨stack⟩₂=0 then f₁
          else if ⟨stack⟩₁=0 then f₂
                             else f₃
```

The following picture shows how the procedure above modifies the stack step by step when we start with a stack containing the numbers 2 and 1 (the last element introduced into the stack is the leftmost one):

```
2 1
1 1 0
0 1 0 0
1 0 0 0
2 0 0
3 0
4
```

In order to record how many items are in the stack, so that we can stop the repetition of the procedure when only one item remains, we introduce a counter which has initially value 1, which has the value r-1 at each step of the computation if the items stacked are r and which eventually has value 0 when the procedure has reached the result.

The complete program for the computation of the Ackermann function on a stack is then the following:

```
push 1;
while ⟨stack⟩₁≠ 0 do
if ⟨stack⟩₃=0 then begin decrement;
                         shifted f₁ end
          else if ⟨stack⟩₂=0 then shifted f₂
                                   else begin increment;
                                              shifted f₃ end;
pop
```

The picture of the evolution of the stack in the previous example becomes

```
2 1
1 2 1
2 1 1 0
3 0 1 0 0
3 1 0 0 0
2 2 0 0
1 3 0
0 4
4
```

We want now to express the meaning of the program above using stack functions of the class T.

Set first

$$sg_o := {}^{c}O\circ(P\circ{}^{c}\Pi\circ{}^{c}O\circ{}^{c}S)^{\circ}\circ\Pi$$

$$sg_1 := {}^{c}O\circ{}^{c}S\circ(P\circ{}^{c}\Pi\circ{}^{c}O)^{\circ}\circ\Pi$$

$$\Theta_i := {}^{c^{i-2}}\Theta\circ{}^{c^{i-3}}\Theta\circ\ldots\circ{}^{c}\Theta\circ\Theta \qquad i\geq 2$$

It holds that

$$sg_o(m\bar{m}) = \begin{cases} O\bar{m} & \text{if } m=O \\ 1\bar{m} & \text{otherwise} \end{cases}$$

$$sg_1(m\bar{m}) = \begin{cases} 1\bar{m} & \text{if } m=O \\ O\bar{m} & \text{otherwise} \end{cases}$$

$$\Theta_i(m_1\ldots m_{i-1}m_i\bar{m}) = m_i m_1\ldots m_{i-1}\bar{m}$$

For $f,g\in T$ set

$$[f,g] := \Delta\circ sg_1\circ(P\circ{}^{cc}f)^{\circ}\circ\Pi\circ sg_o\circ(P\circ{}^{c}g)^{\circ}\circ\Pi$$

It holds that

$$[f,g](m\bar{m}) = \begin{cases} f(\bar{m}) & \text{if } m=O \\ g(\bar{m}) & \text{if } m\neq O \end{cases}$$

Set then

$$IF_i(f,g) := {}^{c^{i-1}}\Delta\circ\Theta_i\circ[f,g] \qquad i\geq 1$$

where Θ_1 is intended to be the identity function.

It holds that

$$(IF_i(f,g))(m_1\ldots m_i\bar{m}) = \begin{cases} f(m_1\ldots m_i\bar{m}) & \text{if } m_i=O \\ g(m_1\ldots m_i\bar{m}) & \text{if } m_i\neq O \end{cases}$$

The program above can now be expressed by the following function of the class T

$$G := O\circ S\circ(IF_3(P\circ{}^{c}F_1, IF_2({}^{c}F_2, S\circ{}^{c}F_3)))^{\circ}\circ\Pi$$

where $F_1 = S\circ{}^{c}\Pi$, $F_2 = S\circ{}^{c}P$, $F_3 = P\circ{}^{c}\Delta\circ{}^{cc}P$.

Note that

$$F = N^2 \upharpoonleft G$$

so that by theorem 8 we obtain that F belongs to S and by theorem 3 that F belongs to R.

This seems to be a particularly simple and natural way to show the recursivity of the Ackermann function.

References

1. S.Eilenberg and C.C.Elgot,Iteration and Recursion,Proc.Nat.Acad.Sci. U.S.A. 61(1968),378-379.
2. —— and ——,Recursiveness,New York 1970.
3. G.Germano and A.Maggiolo-Schettini,Markov's Normal Algorithms without Concluding Formulas,IV Congress for Logic,Methodology and Philosophy of Science,Bucharest,August 29-September 3,1971,Centre of Information and Documentation in Social and Political Sciences.
4. —— and ——,A Characterization of Partial Recursive Functions via Sequence Functions,Notices Amer.Math.Soc. 19(1972),332.
5. —— and ——,Quelques caractérisations des fonctions récursives partielles,C.R.Acad.Sci.Paris,Sér.A 276(1973),1325-1327.
6. —— and ——,Proving a Compiler Correct:A Simple Approach,J.Comput. System Sci. 10(1975),370-383.
7. —— and ——,Sequence-to-Sequence Recursiveness,Information Processing Lett. 4(1975),1-6.
8. —— and ——,Sequence-to-Sequence Partial Recursive Functions,V International Congress of Logic,Methodology and Philosophy of Science, London-Ontario-Canada,August 27-September 2,III-3,III-4.
9. H.Hermes,Enumerability·Decidability·Computability,Berlin 1965.
10. H.E.Rose,Ternary Recursive Arithmetic,Math.Scand. 10(1962),201-216.

DESCRIPTIONAL COMPLEXITY (OF LANGUAGES)

A SHORT SURVEY

Jozef Gruska
Computing Research Centre
Dúbravska 3, 885 31 Bratislava, Czechoslovakia

ABSTRACT

The paper attempts (i) to present descriptional complexity as an identifiable part of the theory of complexity incorporating many diverse areas of research, (ii) to formulate basic problems and to survey some results (especially those concerning languages) in descriptional complexity, (iii) to discuss relation between descriptional and computational complexity.

1. INTRODUCTION

There is a growing evidence that the study of complexity plays a very important role in theoretical computer science. It has identified some very central problems, unifying concepts and it has yielded insights into the nature of theoretical computer science. (HARTMANIS & SIMON [22]). The study of complexity has improved our intuition concerning descriptive power of languages, computational power of computers and intrinsic complexity of algorithmic problems. It has resulted in many new and useful algorithms, techniques and devices and it has already brought concepts and results of importance outside the computer science.

Main attention has been devoted to computational complexity. Among the most important problems we must include problems dealing with:

(i) The investigation of computational power of machines with and without restriction on computational resources (time and space).

(ii) The computation speed gained by adding new operations to machines.

(iii) The intrinsic computational complexity of specific problems with respect to specific models of computation.

(iv) The trade-offs among computation resources. (Time and space, determinism and nondeterminism and so on).

In descriptional complexity quite different types of problems are investigated. Many objects we deal with, for example languages, functions, are either infinite or finite but very large. Therefore, the existence of a finite and simple (in a reasonable way) description or realization is of prime importance. To describe objects a variety of descriptive languages (systems) is used: languages of formulas, expressions, schemes; languages of generative systems (grammars, deductive systems) and languages of algorithms (acceptors, transducers, programming languages). The description of an object, especially if it is an infinite one, can be viewed as a theory of that object, by which one is able to understand and to deal with the object. Naturally, we are looking for the most understandable and the most easy to deal with theory. Among the most important problems in descriptional complexity we must include problems dealing with:

(i) The investigation of descriptive power of languages, with and without restrictions on language resources.

(ii) The descriptive power gained by adding new language features.

(iii) The intrinsic descriptional complexity of specific objects with respect to a specific descriptive language.

(iv) The trade-offs between description resources. (Size and structure, determinism and nondeterminism.)

One can see an analogy between these main problems of computational and descriptional complexity. This is quite natural since in both cases the underlying goal is to capture some important features of the intuitive notion "difficult". The analogy is further extended in attempts to make precise the intuitive notion "feasible" (computation, description, realization), (HARTMANIS & SIMON [22], STOCKMEYER [38], ZASLAVSKIĬ [41]).

There are also results showing deep connections between computational and descriptional complexity. We mention here only two of them. Non-linear lower bounds on Turing machine time complexity has been derived from lower bounds on descriptional (combinational) complexity of Boolean functions (FISCHER [8]). The deterministic and nondeterministic linear bounded automata (LBA) describe the same class of languages iff the deterministic and nondeterministic (log n)-tape bounded languages over one-letter alphabets are the same [21]. In general, the study of relations and trade-offs between computational and descriptional complexity is of great importance in complexity theory. (The trade-off between program size and time is the closest to the original intuitive meaning of the time-space trade-off [10]).

To finish this introduction a few words should be said about the chosen name. Computational complexity is already well established and within it one can identify several subareas: abstract complexity, complexity of machine models, algebraic or combinatorial complexity, complexity of paralel computations and so on. On the other hand, descriptional complexity, despite its longer history, is only slowly emerging, as a specific area, from results in diverse areas of research and that is why no common name was as yet generally accepted. Information-theoretic or definitional complexity [4], static complexity [2], structural complexity [2,10], combinational or network complexity [8]-these are some of the names being used to identify specific subareas in what we call descriptional complexity.

This paper tries to bring into a broader context research in descriptional complexity of languages. It is only a preliminary version of an intended paper.

2. DESCRIPTIVE LANGUAGES (SYSTEMS) - EXAMPLES

Informally, by a descriptive language we mean a (formal) language of well-formed descriptions of certain objects from a universal class of objects, together with a measure of complexity of descriptions. In many cases, the objects themselves are formal languages and therefore we prefer to use the term descriptive system, instead of descriptive language, in order to avoid ambiguities or a need for a more formal treatment.

The concept of a descriptive system is introduced here in order to unify the presentation of descriptional complexity. No general theory of descriptive systems is developed in this paper.

Formally, a descriptive system is a quintuple $\mathcal{D}=\langle\Sigma,W,\mathcal{S},\mathcal{O},K\rangle$, where Σ is an alphabet, $W\subset\Sigma^*$ is a set of well-formed descriptions, (formulas, expressions), $\mathcal{O}$ is a class of objects, $\mathcal{S}:W\to\mathcal{O}(\mathcal{S}:W\to 2^{\mathcal{O}})$ is a semantics of descriptions and $K:W\to N$ is a measure of complexity of descriptions. (N denotes nonnegative integers).

If $d\in W$, then $\mathcal{S}(d)$ denotes the object described by d and if $\sigma\in\mathcal{O}$, then

$$\mathcal{S}^{-1}(\sigma)=\{d,\ d\in W,\mathcal{S}(d)=\sigma\}$$

is the set of all descriptions of the object σ in W. Complexity K of description in W induces in a natural way complexity K of objects from $\mathcal{S}(W)$. For $\sigma\in\mathcal{O}$ let

$$K(\sigma) = \min\ \{K(d);\ d\in \mathcal{S}^{-1}(\sigma)\}$$

In the rest of this section, for several classes of objects, some of the known descriptive systems are described in an informal way. They are chosen in such a way as to show the variety of descriptive systems and complexity measures and to serve, in the rest of the paper, to illustrate the main problems, issues and results in descriptional complexity.

1. Binary strings - information theoretic complexity. A very general approach to complexity of strings has been worked out by KOLMOGOROV and CHAITIN [4]. Let $\mathcal{U}$ be a universal computer with binary input-output alphabet $\{0,1\}$. For a string d let $\mathcal{U}(d)$ be the result of the halting computation of $\mathcal{U}$ on the input d. If $x\in\{0,1\}^*$ and $\mathcal{U}(d)=x$, then d is said to be a description of x (with respect to $\mathcal{U}$) and the length of d ($IT_{\mathcal{U}}(d)$) is said to be information-theoretic complexity measure of d ($IT_{\mathcal{U}}$-complexity).

Informally, the description of a string x is any "program" d which makes U compute x and IT $_U(x)$ is the length of the shortest description (program) which makes U to output x. (Or the information needed to define x). It can be shown that this notion of string complexity is (fairly) machine independent since there is a universal computer $\overline{U}$ such that for any other computer C there is a constant c such that $IT_{\overline{U}}(x) \leq IT_C(x)+c$ for all binary x. This approach to string complexity has several modifications (GEWIRTZ [12]) and can be extended to study IT-complexity of recursively enumerable sets and infinite strings.

2. Partial recursive functions - size and loop complexity. Axiomatic approach to the so-called size complexity of programs (partial recursive functions) is due to BLUM [1] . Let $\Phi = \{ p_i \}_{i=1}^{\infty}$ be an addmisible system of programs for partial recursive functions. Size complexity is any recursive function SIZE: $\Phi \to N$ satisfying the following Blum's axiom: For any integer k the set $\{p_i ;\ SIZE(p_i) = k\}$ is finite and can be determined effectively . (Note that the concept of SIZE-complexity applies to any descriptive system).

On the other hand, the so called LOOP-complexity of programs has been defined for several subrecursive programming languages - for example, the one with the statements: $X_i \leftarrow X_j , X_i \leftarrow X_j+1$, DO X_i-END [10] - to be the depth of nesting of loop instructions [6,31].

3. To describe Boolean functions a large variety of descriptive systems can be used (ZASLAVSKIĬ [41]): various types of Boolean formulas (expressions) with different base functions, logical networks (describing sets of Boolean functions), formulas of formal arithmetic and equational systems for subclasses of partial recursive functions.

Complexity measures: formulas - the length of formula or the number of occurences of literals (SIZE-complexity), the number of non-equivalent subformulas; logical networks - number of nodes (NET-complexity); equational systems - the length of the system.

4. Regular languages are usually described by different kinds of automata (namely) finite automata (FA) , grammars and regular expressions. If $\alpha \subset \{ \cup , \cdot , * , \cap , \neg , ^2 \}$ is a set of language operations with ^{2} standing for square and a regular expression may contain only operations from α, then we refer to it as an α - regular expression. Complexity measures: expressions - the length or the number of occurences of literals (SIZE-complexity), star - height and other graph - theoretical characteristics of the corresponding computation graph [7] , automata - the number of states (STATE-complexity), the size (SIZE-complexity), state-symbol product and so on.

5. Context-free languages can be described by grammars (especially context-free grammars (CFG)), automata (especially push-down automata (PDA)), context-free expressions and so on.

In the case of context-free expressions the length, the number of auxiliary symbols, context-free star height and other graph - theoretical characteristics of the corresponding computation graph can be taken as complexity measures [17] . A large number of complexity measures is defined for CFG's. To every CFG $G = \langle V, \Sigma, P, S \rangle$ a graph $\Gamma_G = \langle V-\Sigma, \Delta \rangle$ of nonterminals can be associated where $\Delta \subset (V-\Sigma) \times (V-\Sigma)$ and $(A,B) \in \Delta$ iff $(\exists x)(\exists y)\ (A \to xBy \in P)$. Graph - theoretical characteristics of Γ_G can be taken as complexity measures of G [17] : the number of nodes - VAR, the number of nodes of maximal strongly connected subgraphs - DEPTH and so on. Moreover, if $K: P \to N$ is a mapping, then one can define $K(G) = \sum_{p \in P} K(p)$. Several measures of this kind are investigated in [3, 17] : SIZE - total number of symbols in productions, PROD - the number of productions.

We have presented complexity measures of a variety of descriptive systems for several classes of objects. Each of these measures captures in a way one special aspect of the intuitive notion "difficult", for example size or structural complexity. Given two "natural" complexity measures K_1 and K_2 on the same set of descriptions, it may be useful, in some cases, to investigate a new measure $K(d) = f(K_1(d), K_2(d))$ where f is a function. (It has been done for complexity measures of CFG's in [3]).

3. BASIC PROBLEMS

In the previous section descriptive systems for several classes of objects have been described. For each of these classes descriptional complexity has its own set of well - motivated issues and problems and it would be hopeless to attempt a survey all of these issues. In this and the next sections we shall rely on examples from these areas, but our goal is different. We shall try to formulate the most basic problems in descriptional complexity and to survey some important, typical and/or interesting results, showing how these basic problems are attacked in specific areas of descriptional complexity. We want to show similarities and differences among various areas of descriptional complexity. They should confirm the possibility of and the need for a more systematic approach in descriptional complexity and they should indicate that research in specific areas of descriptional complexity can benefit from what is being done in other areas.

In this section six problems are stated and discussed. In doing so an underlying descriptive system $\mathcal{D} = \langle \Sigma, W, \mathcal{S}, \mathcal{O}, K \rangle$ is assumed.

(1) Characterization. Give a $\mathcal{D}$ - independent characterization of the objects being described by descriptions from W and determine basic properties of these objects.

Characterization problem is of importance, especially if the set W of descriptions is defined by imposing additional (by easing) syntactical restrictions on the original set of descriptions. Typical examples are definitions of different classes of grammars, automata and expressions for the description of languages. The advantage of having various descriptive systems for the same class of objects has been well demonstrated by descriptive systems for (subclasses) of partial recursive functions. It also seems to be generally accepted that once a class of languages is described in terms of grammars or automata or expressions, then it is generally useful to have all these three descriptive systems for this class of languages. Of special importance seems to be the search for descriptive systems for classes of functions and languages which are defined in terms of computational complexity and vice-versa. Typical examples are "machine-independent" descriptions of functions computable in polynomial time or logarithmic space [27] on Turing machines and the equality of classes of languages described-accepted-by two-way multihead PDA (FA) with classes of languages accepted in polynomial time (logarithmic space) on Turing machines [21] .

There are many important open characterization problems. Descriptive power of non-deterministic automata, with respect to deterministic, is one such major problem with the famous LBA problem as a special case [21] .

(2) Identification. Is there an effective way to idenify objects and decide equivalence of descriptions? [Are there predicates $S(d) = o$, with $o \varepsilon O$ fixed, and $S(d_1) = S(d_2)$ decidable on W?]

Interesting results have been obtained for the case that CFL´s and regular languages are described by CFG´s and regular expressions, resp. In general both problems are undecidable for CFG´s. The class of CFL´s L´ with L(G)= L´ decidable has been investigeted in [23] . By [24] , for any regular language R, the predicat L(G)=R is decidable in polynomial time for several classes of CFG´s : LL(1) grammars, subclasses of precedence grammars and so on. On the other hand, if $R \subset \{0,1\}^*$ is a regular language, then the language L = {E; E is $(\cup, \cdot, *)$ - regular expression over {0,1} , $S(E) \neq R$} is in P, (i.e. recognizable in polynomial time), if R is finite; NP-complete if R is infinite but bounded and PSPACE-complete if R is unbounded [24] .

(3) Complexity of descriptions. Can complexity of descriptions be determined effectively? [Is K( )effective on W?]

Depending on the answer there are several subproblems to be investigated. (i) No: What is the undecidability degree of K? For which n is predicate K(d)= n decidable? On which subclasses of W is K effective? (ii) Yes: Determine computational complexity of K on W or on some subclasses of W.(In the rest of the paper several other decision problems are presented, but only in the basic form, all such subproblems being implicit).

Complexity of descriptions can be determined effectively for IT-complexity of strings, SIZE-complexity of programs, LOOP-complexity of programs and for basic complexity measures for Boolean functions, regular and context-free languages as defined in previous section. However, if K(G)= the index of G, then for all k is K(G)= k undecidable on CFG´s [17] . If, for a CFG G,

K (G): = if G is not LR-grammar then 0 else (1+min {k;G is LR(k) –grammar }) then K is not effective on CFG´s. However, if $k \geq 0$ is fixed, then the predicate K(G)= k is decidable in time $O_T(n^{k+1})$ with n being the size of CFG´s. On the other hand, with $k>0$ being a parameter expressed in unary (binary) LR(k) testing is NP-complete (NEXPTIME-complete) [26].

(4) Complexity of objects. Can one determine effectively the complexity of objects? [Is $K(S(\ ))$ effective on W?]

This problem is unsolvable for: IT-complexity of strings [4], Blum´s SIZE-complexity of programs [1], LOOP-complexity of subrecursive programs and for many complexity measures of CFG´s [3,17] (However, restricting to subclasses of CFL´s with decidable equivalence problem (i.e. bounded or parenthesis languages), complexity of CFL´s can be effectively determined for complexity measures satisfying "Blum´s axiom".)

If complexity of objects cannot be determined easily enough, then it is natural to search for good lower and upper bounds for complexity of specific objects. It has been shown by SHANNON and LUPANOV that

$$\mathrm{SIZE}\ (f) \sim \frac{2^n}{\log n}\ ,\ \mathrm{NET}(f) \sim \frac{2^n}{n}\ .$$

for most of n-ary Boolean functions f. Important examples of sets of Boolean functions encoding finite portions of decision problems from logic and automata theory with large (at least exponential) lower bounds have been shown by MEYER, STOCKMEYER [38], ZASLAVSKIĬ [41] and others. Particular examples of Boolean functions with small but non-trivial lower bound on SIZE-complexity (NET-complexity) are given in [9] ([19]) In [19], it has been shown, for n-ary Boolean functions f_n with the property that there are at least 5 different functions which are obtainable from each way of restricting f_n to a subset of n-3 variables that

$$(7n-4)/6 \le \mathrm{NET}(f_n) \le (20n-1)/17.$$

Complexity of regular languages R_n, describing sets of all paths in complete and half-complete graphs (with edges (i,j), $i \le j$) of n nodes $\{1,2, \ldots, n\}$, has been studied in [7], for four measures of complexity of regular expressions. It has been shown, for example, for half-complete graphs, that

$$n^{2/3(\log(2/3\log n)-1)} \le \mathrm{SIZE}(R_n) \le 2n^{\log n+2}\ .$$

If FA (nondeterministic FA) [incompletely specified FA] M are used to describe regular languages, then the function SIZE (S(M)) [the predicate SIZE (S(M)) = k] can be computed in O(nlogn) time (cannot be computed in polynomial time if there is a context-sensitive language not in P [38]) [is NP-complete].

(5) Hierarchy. Is there an infinite hierarchy of complexity classes (with no gaps)? [$(\forall n)\ (\exists \sigma)\ (K(\sigma) \geq n)$?, $(\forall n)\ (\exists \sigma)\ (K(\sigma) = n)$?]

Infinite hierarchy with no gaps has been established in many cases; for example, for partial recursive functions with respect to STATE-complexity of Turing machines with fixed alphabet [37], for primitive recursive functions with respect to LOOP-complexity [31], for languages described by two-way multihead FA with respect to number of heads [33]; for subclasses of CFL's with respect to various complexity measures [3,17].

On the other hand, LR-complexity of CFL's gives only two complexity classes, in comparison with LL-complexity inducing infinite hierarchy with no gaps.

(6) Complexity classes. What are the properties of complexity classes $\overline{K}^{-1}(n) = \{\sigma; \sigma \varepsilon\ \mathcal{O},\ K(\sigma) = n\}$ and $K^{-1}(n) = \{\sigma; \sigma\ \varepsilon\ \mathcal{O}, K(\sigma) \leq n\}$?

For Turing machines and fixed alphabet X, STATE-complexity classes of recursively enumerable subsets of X^* are finite. Moreover, if $\mathcal{C}$ denotes regular or context-free or context-sensitive languages, then $(\exists n_o)\ (\overline{K}^{-1}(n) \cap \mathcal{C} \neq \theta$ iff $n \geq n_o)$ [37]. LOOP-complexity classes of primitive recursive functions are identical, for $n \geq 4$, with complexity classes of Axt and Grzegorczyk hierarchies [3] and with some computational complexity classes [28]. For complexity classes of languages closure properties are of special importance. Many complexity classes have been shown to be (full) [principal] AFL.

4. MINIMAL DESCRIPTIONS

Problems relating to the simplest or minimal descriptions belong to the most exciting and important problems in descriptional complexity from theoretical as well as practical point of view. While discussing the complexity of objects we have already touched this area and we shall continue to do it in this section where three main problems are treated.

(7) Construction of minimal descriptions. Is there an effective way to construct minimal descriptions? [Is there an effective maping $m: W \rightarrow W$ such that $\mathcal{S}(d) = \mathcal{S}(m(d))$ and $K(m(d)) = K(\mathcal{S}(d))$?]

(8) Identification of minimal descriptions. Is it decidable whether a given description is minimal? [$K(d) = K(\mathcal{S}(d))$?]

There are many relations among the decision problems (3), (4), (7) and (8). For example, solvability of (7) and (3) implies solvability of (4).
For complexity measures of CFG's the relation between problems (3),(3n), (4), (4n), (7) and (8) have been studied in [3]. ((3n) [(4n)] stands for $K(d) = n$? [$K(\mathcal{S}(d)) = n$?] with n fixed). For all but one combination of decidability and undecidability of these problems it has been shown, taht either the combination is impossible, or there exists a measure with such decidability properties.

Undecidability of (7) and (8) has been shown for STATE-complexity (of Turing machines) and Blum´s SIZE-complexity of partial recursive functions [1,37] and also for most of the naturally defined complexity measures of CFG´s [3,17]. Both problems are decidable for SIZE-complexity of CFG´s generating bounded or parenthesis languages. However, decidability for VAR-complexity of CFG´s generating bounded or parenthesis languages is open. Decidability of (6) and (7) has been shown for VAR-complexity of CFG´s generaling single-letter languages (ČERNÝ - personal communication). The case of PROD-complexity of CFG´s for single-letter languages is open. However, decidability of (7) and (8) for PROD-complexity of OL-systems for single-letter languages has been shown (KRAMOLIŠ - personal communication).

In some cases, for example for FA or Boolean formulas, the minimization problem is of such practical importance, that its computational complexity is of special significance. It is known that the problem to find minimal FA (Boolean formula), with respect to STATE-complexity (SIZE-complexity), can be solved in $O_R(n \log n)$ time (is NP-complete). Unfeasibility of minimization problem (for Boolean formulas) forces us to search for fast approximation algorithms [40].

(9) Properties of minimal descriptions. What are the properties of the set $M_{\mathcal{D}}$ of minimal descriptions of a descriptive system $\mathcal{D}$?

The set of minimal programs, of an admissible system of programs, with respect to SIZE-complexity, is immune [1]. However, restricting to subrecursive programming languages for total functions, the set $M_{\mathcal{D}}$ is recursively enumerable. Similarly, if $\mathcal{U}$ is a universal computer, then the set of minimal descriptions of binary strings, with respect to $IT_{\mathcal{U}}$-complexity, is immune. However, if $\mathcal{U}$ is a "universal computer for a fixed level of Grzegorczyk hierarchy" [12], then the set $M_{\mathcal{D}}$ is recursive.

In some cases it is of importance to determine the number of minimal descriptions. This problem has been thoroughly investigated for Boolean formulas [40].

There are descriptive systems, for example programs, automata or grammars, in which one can naturally define for every description (program), its time or space complexity. In such cases trade-offs between descriptional and computational complexity are of importance. These problems have been investigated in [29,39] for SIZE-complexity of programs (for computing finite functions).

To conclude this section, two properties of minimal descriptions are presented from the area of CFG´s: (i) If complexity of a context-free grammar form (CFGF) is defined to be the number of productions of the form grammar, then every two "fight-symbol" CFGF´s are either "pseudo-isomorphic" or they are not strongly equivalent (i.e. they define different classes of CFG´s) [14].(ii) It has been shown for several complexity measures of CFG´s that there are unambiguous CFL´s for which every minimal grammar is ambiguous [15].

5. RELATIVE DESCRIPTIONAL COMPLEXITY

Let $\mathcal{D} = \langle\Sigma,W,\mathcal{S},\mathcal{O},K\rangle$ be a descriptive system and $R \subset W$ be a set of "restricted" descriptions. If $\sigma \in \mathcal{S}(R)$, then

$$K_R(\sigma) = \min\{K(d);\ d \in R,\ \mathcal{S}(d) = \sigma\}$$

is said to be a relative complexity (K_R-complexity) of σ. Let us denote

$$M_{\mathcal{D},R} = \{d; d \in R,\ K(d) = K_R(\mathcal{S}(d))\}$$

the set of R-minimal descriptions.

There is also another way to define relative complexity. Let $\mathcal{D} = \langle\Sigma,R,\mathcal{S}',\mathcal{O},K'\rangle$ be a new descriptive system where $\mathcal{S}' = \mathcal{S}|R$, $K' = K|R$ are restrictions of $\mathcal{S}$ and K to R. It is now clear that $K'(\sigma) = K_R(\sigma)$ for any $\sigma \in \mathcal{S}'(R)$. This implies that for relative complexity all of the problems (1) to (9) are to be investigated. Of course, the results may be quite different. It may happen [17] that whereas K-complexity does not induce, K_R-complexity induces infinite hierarchy of complexity classes.

If $\mathcal{S}(W) = \mathcal{S}(R)$ and $K(\sigma) = K_R(\sigma)$ for any $\sigma \in \mathcal{S}(W)$, then the set R is said to be K-dense. For example CFG's in Greibach normal form are SP-dense in the class of all CFG's, with respect to complexity measure SP(G) = the maximal number of elements in equivalence classes of strict partitions [20].

There are two special problems for relative complexity.

(10) Determine good lower and upper bounds on $GAP_{\mathcal{D},R}(\sigma) = K_R(\sigma)/K(\sigma)$

(11) What are the relations between sets $M_{\mathcal{D}}$ and $M_{\mathcal{D},R}$ of minimal and R-minimal descriptions?

The function $GAP_{\mathcal{D},R}$ specifies how much one can gain in economy of descriptions by admitting unrestricted descriptions. This is an important problem and it will be treated in a more general way in the next section.

We are now ready to discuss the importance of the relative complexity. Quite often we are faced with the situation that it is difficult to determine good lower bounds on complexity of objects. However, if we are restricting descriptive language in the right way, we may be able to determine the relative complexity of objects, or at least to obtain good lower bounds. See discussion of network complexity below and in [8]. If, moreover, good upper bounds on the GAP function could be obtained, they would enable lower bounds on K-complexity to be concluded from lower bounds on K_R-complexity giving a technique for obtaining lower bounds on K-complexity.

In the rest of this section several results on relative complexity are presented.

Since there are no good techniques to determine the network complexity of (sets of) Boolean functions, attention has been directed tovard investigating the so-called negation-restricted complexity (FISCHER [8]). Let us denote R_k logical networks over the base $\Delta = \{\wedge,\vee,\neg\}$ which do not have more than k negations. (If k=0, we get the so-called monotone networks.) A survey of results on NET_{R_k}-complexity is given in [8]. We mention here only two of them. Let MP_n be the set of n-ary Boolean functions for Boolean product of two n×n matrices. Then $NET_{R_0}(MP_n) = 2n^3-n^2$ and $NET(MP_n) = O(n^{\log_2 7}(\log_2 n)^{1+\varepsilon})$ for any $\varepsilon>0$. It is an open problem to determine good upper bounds on $GAP_{NET,R_k}(F)$, if F is a set of n-ary functions. It is only known that if $k = \lceil \log_2(n+1) \rceil$, then $GAP_{NET,R_k}(F) = O(n \log^2 n)$ for any set R of n-ary Boolean functions.

If Boolean formulas are used to describe Boolean functions, then the relative SIZE-complexity, (with respect to (special kinds of) Boolean formulas in conjunctive (disjunctive) normal forms) and the GAP functions have been studied very intensively [40].

For a $(\cup,\cdot,*,\neg)$ - regular expression E let CD(E) be the concatenation depth of E. CD_R-complexity has been studied in [5] with respect to the set R of $(\cup,\cdot,\neg)$ - regular expressions. It is an open problem whether this relative complexity induces infinite hierarchy of complexity classes.

In all previous cases the set of restricted descriptions was recursive and was defined by syntactical restrictions on the original set of descriptions. This is not the case if R consists of unambiguous CFG's. In [15] K_R-complexities have been investigated for several complexity measures of CFG's.

Finally, we shall mention one special case of relative complexity. Let $\mathcal{D}_1 = \langle\Sigma,W,S,O,K_1\rangle$ and $\mathcal{D}_2 = \langle\Sigma,W,S,O,K_2\rangle$ be two descriptive systems which differ only in complexity measures. Denote $R = M_{\mathcal{D}_2}$ and let us denote $K_{1,2} = K_{\mathcal{D}_1,R}$. Obviously

$$K_{1,2}(\sigma) = \min \{K_1(d);\ S(d) = \sigma, K_2(d) = K_2(S(d))\}$$

for $\sigma \in S(W)$. Relative complexity defined in this way have been investigated for several pairs of complexity measures of CFG's [17].

6. ECONOMY OF DESCRIPTIONS

In this section we shall discuss the problem how much we can gain in economy of descriptions by using different descriptive systems.

Let $\mathcal{D}_1 = \langle\Sigma_1,W_1,S_1,O_1,K_1\rangle$, $\mathcal{D}_2 = \langle\Sigma_2,W_2,S_2,O_2,K_2\rangle$ be two descriptive systems with $S_1(W_1) \subseteq S_2(W_2)$. Let us define the function

$$E(\mathcal{D}_1\mathcal{D}_2,n) = \max \{K_2(\sigma); \sigma\in S_1(W_1), K_1(\sigma) \le n\}$$

which gives maximal K_2-complexity of objects having K_1-complexity $\le$ n. Two descriptive systems $\mathcal{D}_1, \mathcal{D}_2$ are said to be linearly (polynomially) related if both functions $E(\mathcal{D}_1,\mathcal{D}_2,n)$ and $E(\mathcal{D}_2,\mathcal{D}_1,n)$ are linearly (polynomially) bounded.

If $\mathcal{D}_1$ is an admissible system of programs with Blum´s SIZE-complexity and $\mathcal{D}_2$ is an enumerable subsystem of programs in $\mathcal{D}_1$, (for example programs in a subrecursive programming language), then, by BLUM [1], there is no recursive upper bound on $E(\mathcal{D}_1,\mathcal{D}_2,n)$. (However, it is interesting to note [6] that from computational complexity point of view both systems are linearly related). This result has been strenghtened to held as soon as the system $\mathcal{D}_1$ is "universal" with respect to $\mathcal{D}_2$,[29].

From this and from the results in [30] it follows that there is no recursive upper bound on economy of description that could be gained if context-sensitive (context-free) grammars in comparison to CFG´s (FA) describe CFL´s (regular languages).

Several other results on economy of descriptions by FA and PDA with respect to STATE-complexity have been obtained by MEYER & FISCHER [30]. For example, if $\mathcal{D}_1(\mathcal{D}_2)$ stands for the class of two-way (one-way) FA, then

$$(0.2n-1)^{(0.2n-1)} \le E(\mathcal{D}_1,\mathcal{D}_2,n) \le (n+2)^{(n+1)}$$

Moreover, it is well-known that $E(\mathcal{D}_1,\mathcal{D}_2,n) = 2^n$ if $\mathcal{D}_1(\mathcal{D}_2)$ denotes nondeterministic (deterministic) FA.

Economy of descriptions of deterministic CFL´s by parser´s, deterministic PDA and PDA is investigated in [11].

Several results on economy of descriptions of CFL´s using the whole class of CFG´s and CFG´s in a normal form have been obtained by PIRICKÁ [34,35] and in [18]. For example - personal communication - if $\mathcal{D}_1(\mathcal{D}_2)$ is a descriptive system of CFG´s (in Greibach normal form) with SIZE-complexity, then there are constants c_1 and c_2 such that

$$c_2 n^3 \le E(\mathcal{D}_1,\mathcal{D}_2,n) \le c_1 n^3$$

GINSBURG & LYNCH [13] have investigated the case that $\mathcal{D}_1$ and $\mathcal{D}_2$ are two descriptive systems of CFG´s of two grammar forms which generate exactly all regular (linear) languages. They have shown, for complexity measures SIZE, VAR and PROD, that systems $\mathcal{D}_1$ and $\mathcal{D}_2$ are polynomially related and, moreover, for every k, there are $\mathcal{D}_1$ and $\mathcal{D}_2$ such that $cn^k \le E(\mathcal{D}_1,\mathcal{D}_2,n)$ for a constant $c>0$.

A survey of results on economy of descriptions of Boolean functions has been given by ZASLAVSKIĬ [41] for a large variety of descriptive systems. We mention here only the recent result of PRATT [36].

Let $\mathcal{D}_1,\mathcal{D}_2$ be two descriptive systems of Boolean formulas, with operators from two complete bases B_1,B_2 of binary functions and with SIZE-complexity. In [36], it has been shown that $E(\mathcal{D}_1,\mathcal{D}_2,n) \le O(n^{\log_3 10})$, i.e. $\mathcal{D}_1$ and $\mathcal{D}_2$ are polynomially related.

Moreover, PRATT has shown that complete binary Boolean bases can be partitioned into two classes B_1, B_2 in such a way, that if B_1 and B_2 are in the same class, then $\mathcal{D}_1$ and $\mathcal{D}_2$ are linearly related.

The function E reflects only the worst-case situation. In some cases the study of the average case would also be of interest. Moreover, given two descriptive systems, one would like to know for which objects little can be gained by using one system instead of another. This can be made precise as follows: Let $g(n) < E(\mathcal{D}_1, \mathcal{D}_2, n)$ for all n. Determine $\{\sigma; \sigma \varepsilon \mathcal{O}, K_2(\sigma) \leq g(K_1(\sigma))\}$. What is cardinality of this set?

Several results along these lines are in [16] for three descriptive systems for finite languages: enumeration, CFG's generating languages and CFG's approximating languages. A CFG G is said to approximate a finite language L if $L = \{x; x \varepsilon L(G); |x| \leq \max \{|y|; y \varepsilon L\}\}$.

7. SPEED-UP AND DESCRIPTIONS

It has been found out that computational complexity of algorithmic problems may very much depend on the way the input data are described. For example, planarity of graphs with n edges can be recognized in linear time if graphs are described by lists; but it requires $0_R(n^2)$ time, if graphs are described by matrices. Recognition of primes can be done in $0_T(\log n)$ space (and therefore in polynomial time) in the case of unary notation; but if binary notation is used, it is known to be recognizable in polynomial time but only with the assumption that the Generalized Riemann's Hypothesis holds [32].

Several important results, showing to what extent computational complexity may depend on the descriptive system which is being used to describe objects, have been obtained by MEYER, STOCKMEYER [38] and others. Some of them are now stated in terms of Turing machine computational complexity.

Let us consider the language

$L = \{(E_1, E_2); \; E_1, E_2$ are α-regular expressions over $\{0,1\}$, $S(E_1) \neq S(E_2)\}$ where $\alpha \subset \{\cup, \cdot, *, \cap, \neg, ^2\}$. This language has been shown to be [38,24]:

(1) Nonelementary recursive if $\alpha = \{\cup, \cdot, \neg\}$.

(2) EXPNTIME - complete if $\alpha = \{\cup, \cdot, ^2\}$.

(3) Requiring space $2^{\sqrt{n}}$ if $\alpha = \{\cup, \cdot, *, \cap\}$.

(4) PSPACE - complete if $\alpha = \{\cup, \cdot, *\}$.

(5) NP - complete if $\alpha = \{\cup, \cdot\}$.

(6) In P if $\alpha = \{\cup, \neg\}$.

The case $\alpha = \{\cdot, \neg\}$ is open.

In the previous case one special predicate was considered. Similar results for a large class of predicates have been obtained in [24,25].

The results on computational complexity of nonequivalence of regular expressions were used to derive large lower bounds for decision problems of some decidable logical theories [22,38]. The basic idea behind these results has been stated by HARTMANIS & SIMON [22] as

Heuristic principle. If in some descriptive system one can describe with descriptions of length n or less Turing machine computations using tape up to length L(n), then the decision problem for equality of these expressions must be of at least tape complexity L(n).

8. CONCLUSIONS

Several descriptional complexity problems could not be treated here at all or they have been only touched because of the lack of space. For example, trade-offs between descriptional and computational complexity [4,6,10,39] descriptional complexity of approximations [16], synthesis and analysis. There are also specific areas of descriptional complexity not mentioned here: for example, complexity of arithmetic functions, special kinds of grammars, automata and formal systems.

The axiomatic approach to computational complexity has been profitable, same as the axiomatic approach to size complexity. So far a similar approach to structural complexity remains a pending research problem.

REFERENCES

1. BLUM, M., On the size of machines. Information and Control, 11 (1967), 257-265.
2. BORODIN, A., Computational Complexity: Theory and Practice. In "Currents in the Theory of Computing. Ed. A.V. Aho , Prentice-Hall, (1973), 35-89.
3. ČERNÝ, A., Complexity and minimality of context-free languages and grammars. University of Bratislava, (1976), 1-64.
4. CHAITIN, G.J., Information-theoretic limitations of formal systems. J. Assoc. Comput. Mach. 21 (1974), 403-424.
5. COHEN, R.S, BRZOZOWSKI, J.A., Dot-depth of star-free events. J. Comput. System Sci. 5 (1971), 1-16.
6. CONSTABLE, R.L., BORODIN, A.B., Subrecursive programming languages Part I: Efficiency and program structure, J. Assoc. Comput. Mach. 19 (1972), 526-568.
7. EHRENFEUCHT, A., ZEIGER, P., Complexity measures for regular expressions. Proc. ACM Symposium on Theory of Computing, (1974), 75-79.

8. FISCHER, M.J., The complexity of negation-limited networks - a brief survey Proc. 2nd GI Conference Automata Theory and Formal Languages. Lecture Notes in Computer Science 33, (1975), 71-82.

9. FISCHER,M.J., MEYER, A.R., PATERSON, M.S., Lower Bounds on the Size of Boolean formulas. Proc. ACM Symposium on Theory of Computing, (1975), 37-44.

10. FISCHER, P.C., Trends in computational complexity. In "Computational Complexity". Ed. R. Rustin, Algorithmics Press, (1973), 1-22.

11. GELLER, M.M., HUNT III, H.B., SZYMANSKI, T.G., ULLMAN, J.D., Economy of description by parsers, DPDA´s and PDA´s, Proc. Symposium on Foundations of Computer Science, (1975), 122-127.

12. GEWIRTZ, W.L., Investigations in the theory of descriptive complexity. RN NSO-5, Courant Institute of Mathematical Sciences, (1974), 1-60.

13. GINSBURG, S., LYNCH, N., Comparative complexity of grammar forms. Proc. Symposium on Theory of Computing, (1975), 153-158.

14. GINSBURG, S., MAURER, H.A., On strongly equivalent context-free grammar forms. Computing, 16, (1976), 281-290.

15. GRUSKA, J., Complexity and unambiguity of context-free grammars and languages. Information and Control, 18, (1971), 502-519.

16. GRUSKA, J., Generation and approximation of finite and infinite languages. Proc. MFCS´72, Warsaw, (1972), 1-7.

17. GRUSKA, J., Descriptional complexity of context-free languages. Proceedings of MFCS´73, High Tatras, 71-83.

18. GRUSKA, J., A note on ε-rules in context-free grammars. Kybernetika, 11, (1975), 26-31.

19. HARPER, L.H., NSIEH, W.N., SAVAGE, J.E., A class of Boolean functions with linear combinational complexity. Theoret. Comput. Sc. 1 (1975), 161-184.

20. HARRISON, M.A., HAVEL, I.M., Strict deterministic grammars. J. Comput. System Sci. 7 (1973), 237-277.

21. HARTMANIS, J., HUNT III, H.B., The LBA Problem and its importance in the theory of computing. SIAM-AMS Proc. 7, (1974), 1-26.

22. HARTMANIS, J., SIMON, J., On the structure of feasible computations. In Advances in Computers. V 14, Academic Press, New York, 1976.

23. HUNT III, H.B., RANGEL, J.L., Decidability of Equivalence, Containment, Intersection, and Separability of Context-Free Languages. Proc. Symposium on Foundations of Computer Science, (1975), 144-150.

24. HUNT III, H.B., ROSENKRANTZ, D.J., Computational Parallels between the Regular

and Context-free Languages. Proc. ACM Symposium on Theory of Computing. (1974), 64-74.

25. HUNT, III, H.B., SZYMANSKI, T.G., On the complexity of grammar and related problems. Proc. ACM Symposium on Theory of Computing, (1975), 54-65.

26. HUNT III, H.B., SZYMANSKI, T.G., ULLMAN, J.D., On the complexity of LR(k) testing. Proc. Conf. on Principles of Computer Languages. Palo Alto, (1975), 130-136.

27. LIND, J.C., Computing in Logarithmic space. MAC MEM. 52, MIT, 1974.

28. McCREIGHT, E.M., MEYER, A.R., Classes of computable functions defined by bounds on computation. Proc. ACM Symposium on Theory of Computing, (1969), 79-88.

29. MEYER, A.R., BAGCHI, A., Program size and economy of descriptions. Proc. ACM Symposium on Theory of Computing, (1972), 183-186.

30. MEYER, A.R., FISCHER, M.J., Economy of description by automata, grammars, and formal systems. Proc. Symposium on Switching and Automata Theory, (1971), 188-191.

31. MEYER, A.R., RITCHIE, D.M., The complexity of loop programs. Proc. 22nd National ACM Conference, (1967), 465-470.

32. MILLER, G.L., Riemann´s hypothesis and tests for primality. Proc. ACM Symposium on Theory of Computing, (1975), 234-239.

33. MONIEN, B., Transformational methods and their application to complexity problems. Universität Hamburg, (1975), 1-16.

34. PIRICKÁ, A., Complexity and normal forms of context-free languages. Proc. MFCS ´74. Lecture Notes in Computer Science. 28, (1975), 292-297.

35. PIRICKÁ, A., Greibach normal form complexity. Proc. of MFCS´75, Lecture Notes in Computer Science, 32, (1975), 344-350.

36. PRATT, W.R., The effect of basis on size of Boolean expressions. Proc. Symposium on Foundations of Computer Science, (1975), 119-121.

37. SCHMITT, A.A., The state complexity of Turing machines. Information and Control, 17, (1970), 217-225.

38. STOCKMEYER, L.J., The complexity of decision problems in automata theory and logic. Project MAC TR 133, 1974.

39. SYMES, D.M., The computation of finite functions. Proc. ACM Symposium on Theory of Computing, (1972), 177-182.

40. VASILIEV, Ju.L., GLAGOLEV, V.V., KOROBKOV, V.K., Metric investigations in discrete analysis. Problemy Kibernet., No 27 (1973), 63-74.

41. ZASLAVSKIĬ, J.D., On some models of computability of Boolean functions. Proc. MFCS´75. Lecture Notes in Computer Science, 32, (1975), 153-159.

ON THE BRANCHING STRUCTURE OF LANGUAGES

Ivan M. Havel
Institute of Information Theory and Automation
Czechoslovak Academy of Sciences
180 76 Prague, Czechoslovakia

This essay is dedicated to Professor Jiří Bečvář
on the occasion of his fiftieth birthday

By its purely mathematical essence the theory of formal languages is a study of sets of strings /finite sequences of abstract symbols/ – or, in algebraic terms, a study of subsets of a free semigroup. Despite this rather general subject area the mainstream of activity in language theory has been directed towards posing and answering questions related to its two leading motivational sources: linguistics and computing. Correspondingly the most favored approaches rest on formal grammars and abstract automata, and typical theoretical results concern the question how /a string in/ a language can be generated or recognized. The original intuition for a language is given by the term itself: a language as a set of all expressions /sentences, programs/ formed according to some well-defined rules. In current theoretical computer science formal languages serve as a uniform way of representing the computational capability of various mathematical models of computation /the role of language theory in theoretical computer science is nicely surveyed by Book [1] /.

In the present paper I discuss an approach that is in many respects unconventional. The related intuition can be roughly explained by viewing a language as the set of all potential realizations of some discrete-time terminating process, or perhaps as the set of all paths through a fixed flow diagram of a certain generalized type. This approach was originally motivated by a research in problem solving in the context of artificial intelligence /cf. [2]/. A solution to a problem is a plan how to achieve a goal and mathematically can be expressed as a string, or in general case of conditionally branching plans as a language over an alphabet with symbols representing actions /for more about this motivation see [3] /.

Our primary concern is how such a language branches – something which we may consider as an example of a "structural" property of a language. It is noticeable how little attention has been paid in the past to the structural properties of languages in general /among the few results of this type are the pumping or iteration theorems and results on certain subfamilies of regular languages/. The exception is the analytic approach in algebraic linguistics /cf. Marcus [4] / where the structural properties are essential. With the last mentioned approach we share also the interest in general languages, without restricting ourselves to the universe of recursively enumerable languages. This fact, as well as our concern with whole families of languages /with a common "structure"/ yields quite a few nonstandard mathematical features. This may be exemplified by our treatment of languages as points in a metric space in Section 2.[1]

Yet there is a point in which we comply with the convention: we utilize a special finite-state acceptor /the finite branching automaton of [3] and [6]/. It will serve, however, as a tool for defining whole families of languages rather than single languages.

1. What branching is

Among the structural properties of languages viewed as processes the phenomenon of branching seems to be particularly attractive. Let L be a language over an alphabet[2] Σ , i.e., $L \subseteq \Sigma^*$. One may say that L properly branches at $u \in \Sigma^*$ iff u is the longest common prefix of at least two distinct strings in L . Thus, e.g., the language

$$L_1 = (abc)^* c(ba)^* = \{c, cba, abcc, cbaba, abccba, \ldots\}$$

properly branches at any $u \in (abc)^*$ as well as at any $u \in L_1$. We can easily visualize it graphically:

---

1 Some other unconventional aspects of the discussed approach are exposed by Benda and Bendová [5] in this volume.

2 We fix throughout this paper the alphabet Σ – a finite nonempty set of abstract symbols – and denote by Σ^* the free monoid of strings over Σ with the empty string denoted by Λ . We define $\Sigma_\Lambda := \Sigma \cup \{\Lambda\}$. For $u \in \Sigma^*$ we denote by lg(u) the length of u .

$$
\Lambda \left\{
\begin{array}{l}
abc \left\{
\begin{array}{l}
abc\ldots \\
c \left\{
\begin{array}{l}
\Lambda \\
ba \left\{
\begin{array}{l}
\Lambda \\
ba\ldots
\end{array}
\right.
\end{array}
\right.
\end{array}
\right. \\
c \left\{
\begin{array}{l}
\Lambda \\
ba \left\{
\begin{array}{l}
\Lambda \\
ba\ldots
\end{array}
\right.
\end{array}
\right.
\end{array}
\right.
$$

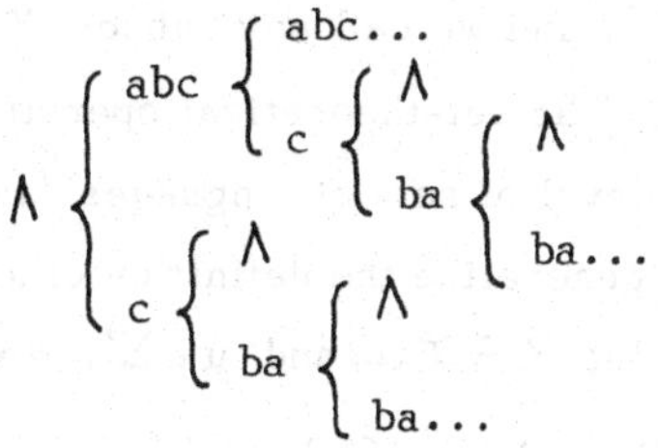

/For the purposes of the present paper the reader is suggested to view languages as branching trees of the above form rather than merely as sets./ For any language L one can specify the furcation at a given string $u \in \Sigma^*$ by the set $\Delta_L(u) \subseteq \Sigma_\Lambda$ of all symbols that immediately follow u in strings of L, including also Λ whenever $u \in L$. In our example, for instance, $\Delta_{L_1}(abc) = \{a, c\}$, $\Delta_{L_1}(c) = \{\Lambda, b\}$, and by definition also $\Delta_{L_1}(ab) = \{c\}$, $\Delta_{L_1}(b) = \emptyset$ etc.

Two operations will be very useful for our study. The first associates with a language L the set of all its prefixes,

$$\text{Pref } L := \{u \in \Sigma^* \mid \exists v \in \Sigma^*,\ uv \in L\}\ ,$$

the second cuts out "subtrees" of L : for any $u \in \Sigma^*$, the derivative of L /with respect to u / is the language

$$\partial_u L := \{v \mid uv \in L\}\ .$$

Now we can express the furcation formally as

$$\Delta_L(u) := (\text{Pref } \partial_u L \cap \Sigma) \cup (\partial_u L \cap \{\Lambda\})\ ,$$

i.e. $\Lambda \in \Delta_L(u)$ iff $u \in L$, and for $a \in \Sigma$, $a \in \Delta_L(u)$ iff $ua \in \text{Pref } L$. Note that

$$\Delta_L(u) = \Delta_{\partial_u L}(\Lambda)\ .$$

We propose to study languages in terms of the function $\Delta_L : \Sigma^* \to \mathcal{P}(\Sigma_\Lambda)$ which represents completely the branching structure of L ; otherwise, of course, the knowledge of Δ_L is equivalent to the knowledge of L.

It is obvious that branching is a property of languages and not of single strings. Where conventional language theory introduces languages as sets of strings with a certain common property /as, e.g., the palindromes/, we have to pay more attention to whole families of languages.

It is a formal advantage in excluding once for all the empty language from our consideration. We denote by $\mathcal{L}(\Sigma)$ the collection of all nonempty languages over

Σ, i.e., $\mathcal{L}(\Sigma) := \mathcal{P}(\Sigma^*) - \{\emptyset\}$, and we call any subset $X \subseteq \mathcal{L}(\Sigma)$ a family of languages /over Σ, by default/. The set-theoretical operations when applied to families are naturally meant on the level of sets of languages /and not on the level of languages/. On the other hand, we generalize the definition of a derivative from languages to families "internally": let $X \subseteq \mathcal{L}(\Sigma)$ and $u \in \Sigma^*$. We define

$$\partial_u X := \{\partial_u L \mid L \in X\} - \{\emptyset\}$$

/this operation will be important for our considerations/.

2. The Metric Space of Languages

It is natural to consider two languages similar if they have the same branching structure /represented by the furcation function/ for all prefixes up to certain length. This will enable us to treat $\mathcal{L}(\Sigma)$ as a metric /or topological/ space helpful for handling less tractable languages in terms of "simpler" languages in their neighborhood.

Let $L_1, L_2 \in \mathcal{L}(\Sigma)$, $L_1 \neq L_2$. We define the similarity of L_1 and L_2, denoted by $s(L_1, L_2)$, as the length of a shortest string $u \in \Sigma^*$ such that

$$\Delta_{L_1}(u) \neq \Delta_{L_2}(u) .$$

Thus $0 \leqslant s(L_1, L_2) < \infty$. We introduce a distance function d on $\mathcal{L}(\Sigma)$, $d : \mathcal{L}(\Sigma) \times \mathcal{L}(\Sigma) \to [0,1]$, as follows. For any $L_1, L_2 \in \mathcal{L}(\Sigma)$

$$d(L_1, L_2) := \begin{cases} 2^{-s(L_1, L_2)} & \text{if } L_1 \neq L_2 \\ 0 & \text{if } L_1 = L_2 . \end{cases} \qquad (1)$$

One can easily verify that for any L_1, L_2, L_3

$$d(L_1, L_3) \leqslant d(L_1, L_2) + d(L_2, L_3)$$

and thus $\mathcal{L}(\Sigma)$ together with the distance d is a metric space /in fact, it is an ultrametric space/.

Remark. A different metric space of languages /including $\emptyset$ / was defined by Bodnarčuk [7] on the basis of a similarity $s'(L_1, L_2)$ given by the length of a shortest string in the symmetrical difference of L_1 and L_2. His definition does not take into account the branching structure; the similarity is then, e.g., invariant under reversal. Note that our similarity measure can be obtained on the basis of s' as follows: $s(L_1, L_2) = \min\left(s'(L_1, L_2),\ s'(\mathrm{Pref}\, L_1, \mathrm{Pref}\, L_2)\right)$.

In the following by the metric space $\mathcal{L}(\Sigma)$ we always mean $\mathcal{L}(\Sigma)$ together with the distance d according to (1). Of course, any family $X \subseteq \mathcal{L}(\Sigma)$ can be viewed also as a metric space with the distance d restricted to $X \times X$. We can use the standard concepts and results of the theory of metric spaces /cf., e.g., [8] /. Even if for the purposes of our study the only important concept is that of a closed set, in the present section we rewiew the properties of $\mathcal{L}(\Sigma)$ as a metric space.

The closure $\bar{X}$ of a family $X \subseteq \mathcal{L}(\Sigma)$ is defined as

$$\begin{aligned} \bar{X} &:= \{ L \in \mathcal{L}(\Sigma) \mid \forall \varepsilon > 0 \ \ \exists L' \in X,\ d(L, L') < \varepsilon \} \\ &= X \cup \{ L \in \mathcal{L}(\Sigma) \mid \forall n \geqslant 0 \ \ \exists L' \in X,\ s(L, L') > n \} \end{aligned} \qquad (2)$$

A family X is a <u>closed subset</u> of $\mathcal{L}(\Sigma)$ iff $X = \bar{X}$, i.e., iff it contains limits of all convergent /in $\mathcal{L}(\Sigma)$/ sequences of languages from X . An example of a closed set is the family

$$X_{inf} := \{ L \mid L \text{ is an infinite language} \}$$

/indeed, no sequence of infinite languages can converge to a finite language/. A family X is an <u>open subset</u> of $\mathcal{L}(\Sigma)$ iff $\mathcal{L}(\Sigma) - X$ is closed, i.e., iff with every L X contains also all languages of certain degree of similarity to L . An example of an open set is the family

$$X_{fin} := \{ L \mid L \text{ is a finite nonempty language} \}$$

as well as any its subfamily.

It can be easily seen that X_{fin} is dense in $\mathcal{L}(\Sigma)$ and thus $\mathcal{L}(\Sigma)$ is a separable metric space. In fact, it is a precompact /or totally bounded/ space since for any $\varepsilon > 0$ the set of all languages with strings of length at most ε^{-1} forms a finite ε-net in $\mathcal{L}(\Sigma)$. On the other hand, $\mathcal{L}(\Sigma)$ is not a complete space: the sequence of singletons $\{a\}, \{aa\}, \ldots, \{a^n\}, \ldots$ / $a \in \Sigma$ / is clearly a Cauchy sequence but has no limit in $\mathcal{L}(\Sigma)$ /it tends to a single infinite string aaa... /. Let us note by passing that the Bodnarčuk metric space of languages is complete /[7] , Theorem 2/.

Our next observation concerns connectedness. A singleton $\{L\}$ is open iff L is finite. On the other hand, any singleton is always closed and thus we have families that are both open and closed. Therefore $\mathcal{L}(\Sigma)$ is not connected.

Let us summarize the mentioned properties of $\mathcal{L}(\Sigma)$:

Theorem 1. $\mathcal{L}(\Sigma)$ together with the distance d is a precompact /and hence separable/ metric space. It is neither complete /hence not compact/ nor connected.

Since the precompactness is shared by subspaces, any family of languages is compact iff it is complete. An example of a compact family is the set $\{L \mid L = \text{Pref } L\}$. It is interesting to note that the finite languages are all and the only isolated points in $\mathcal{L}(\Sigma)$. Any neighborhood of an infinite language is uncountable and contains an infinite number of finite languages.

3. The Replacement and Compatibility

There is a canonical way of partitioning an arbitrary language L into a finite number of disjoint sublanguages $a\partial_a L$ $/a \in \Sigma/$ and also $\{\Lambda\}$ if $\Lambda \in L$. We introduce an operation that replaces a sublanguage of one language by the corresponding sublanguage of another language. For $a \in \Sigma$ and $L_1, L_2 \in \mathcal{L}(\Sigma)$ we define

$$\text{Rep}_a(L_1, L_2) \quad := \quad (L_1 - a\partial_a L_1) \cup a\partial_a L_2 \ .$$

The operator Rep_a is called a simple replacement. It can be easily extended to a replacement[3],

$$\text{Rep}_u(L_1, L_2) \quad := \quad (L_1 - u\partial_u L_1) \cup u\partial_u L_2 \tag{3}$$

for any $u \in \Sigma^*$. In particular, $\text{Rep}_\Lambda(L_1, L_2) = L_2$.

Let X be a family of languages, $X \subseteq \mathcal{L}(\Sigma)$. We say that X has the simple replacement property iff for any $L_1, L_2 \in X$ and any $a \in \text{Pref } L_1 \cap \text{Pref } L_2 \cap \Sigma$ $\text{Rep}_a(L_1, L_2) \in X$; if also $\text{Rep}_u(L_1, L_2) \in X$ for all $u \in \text{Pref } L_1 \cap \text{Pref } L_2$ then X has the replacement property. Note that X has the replacement property iff each family $\partial_u X$ $/u \in \Sigma^*/$ has the simple replacement property.

Our next definition concerns a property of families of languages which is already connected to branching. Let $X \subseteq \mathcal{L}(\Sigma)$. We say that a language $L \in \mathcal{L}(\Sigma)$ is compatible with X iff for each $u \in \Sigma^*$ there is a language $L_u \in X$ such that

$$\Delta_L(u) \quad = \quad \Delta_{L_u}(u)$$

Intuitively the compatibility of L with X means that the branching structure of L

[3] The replacement operator R_u of [6] is defined in a different way.

is in a certain sense inherent to X – but may be distributed among various members of X . We define the C-closure of X as

$$C(X) \; := \; \{ L \in \mathcal{L}(\Sigma) \mid L \text{ compatible with } X \}$$

and say that X is self-compatible iff $C(X) = X$.

It was shown in [6] that self-compatibility implies the replacement property and that the converse is true for finite families. The general relationship is established by the following theorem.

Theorem 2. A family of languages is self-compatible iff it has the replacement property and is closed in the metric space $\mathcal{L}(\Sigma)$.

Proof. Let $X \subseteq \mathcal{L}(\Sigma)$, $X \neq \emptyset$ /avoiding the trivial case of $X = \emptyset$ /.

I. Assume X self-compatible, i.e. $X = C(X)$. We already know that then it has the replacement property. To show that it is closed it is enough to verify $\overline{X} \subseteq C(X)$. For this consider any $L_0 \in \overline{X}$ and assume $L_0 \notin C(X)$, i.e., there is $u \in \Sigma^*$ such that for all $L \in X$, $\Delta_L(u) \neq \Delta_{L_0}(u)$. Thus for all $L \in X$, $s(L_0, L) \leqslant lg(u)$ contrary to (2). Hence $L_0 \in C(X)$. We conclude that $\overline{X} = X$.

II. Now let us assume that X is closed and has the replacement property. To prove that X is self-compatible consider any $L_0 \in C(X)$. Since X is closed it is enough to show that $L_0 \in \overline{X}$. Assume the contrary: $L_0 \notin X$ and there exists a minimal number $n \geqslant 0$ such that

$$\forall L \in X, \qquad s(L_0, L) \leqslant n \tag{4}$$

/cf. (1)/. By the minimality of n the family

$$X_n := \{ L \in X \mid s(L_0, L) = n \}$$

is nonempty /by assumption $X \neq \emptyset$ /. For each $L \in X_n$ define

$$M_L := \{ u \in \Sigma^n \mid \Delta_L(u) \neq \Delta_{L_0}(u) \}$$

and let L_1 have this set minimal, i.e.,

$$\forall L \in X_n, \qquad 0 < \text{card } M_{L_1} \leqslant \text{card } M_L \; . \tag{5}$$

Choose $u \in M_{L_1}$ and define

$$L_2 := Rep_u(L_1, L_u)$$

where $L_u \in X$ and satisfies $\Delta_{L_u}(u) = \Delta_{L_0}(u)$; the existence of such L_u follows from the assumption $L_0 \in C(X)$. Since X is assumed to have the replacement property, $L_2 \in X$. By the definition of the replacement (3), if $M_{L_1} = \{u\}$ then $s(L_0, L_2) > n$ contrary to (4). If, on the other hand, $\mathrm{card}\, M_{L_1} > 1$ then $L_2 \in X_n$ and $\mathrm{card}\, M_{L_2} < \mathrm{card}\, M_{L_1}$ contrary to (5). We conclude that $L_0 \in \overline{X}$, i.e., $L_0 \in X$. Hence $X = C(X)$. □

The reader will find some examples of families with the mentioned properties at the end of the next section.

4. Finite Branching Automata: the Deterministic Case

We have proposed to study properties of languages related to branching extensionally, in terms of corresponding families of languages. However, we did not yet exhibit any uniform way of defining such families. One may inquire, e.g., about a suitable general class of finite mathematical structures, each representing in a well-defined way exactly one family of languages from certain interesting class of families. On the basis of our preceding considerations we stipulate that such an "interesting class" contains only self-compatible families. There is a quantitative argument that it cannot be the class of all self-compatible families: the latter appears to be uncountable /cf. [12] /, while any finitary approach may yield at most countably many distinct families.

One of the simplest structures that theoretical computer science can offer is the finite automaton. Its modification, suitable for our purposes, was introduced in [6] under the name of a finite branching automaton.

Let $\mathcal{A} = \langle Q, \delta, q_0 \rangle$ be an ordinary deterministic finite automaton over Σ without final states; Q is a finite set of states, $\delta : Q \times \Sigma \to Q$ a /total/ transition function and $q_0 \in Q$. We extend δ in the usual way to $\delta : Q \times \Sigma^* \to Q$ and for $u \in \Sigma^*$ we write qu instead of $\delta(q, u)$. Let $B \subseteq Q \times \mathcal{P}(\Sigma_\Lambda)$. The quadruple $\mathcal{B} = \langle Q, \delta, q_0, B \rangle$ is called the finite branching automaton /shortly fb-automaton and, by default, considered over Σ /; B is the branching relation of $\mathcal{B}$. We say that a language $L \in \mathcal{L}(\Sigma)$ is accepted by $\mathcal{B}$ iff

$$(q_0 u, \Delta_L(u)) \in B$$

for any $u \in \mathrm{Pref}\, L$. A family of languages $X \subseteq \mathcal{L}(\Sigma)$ is recognized by $\mathcal{B}$ iff

$$X = \{ L \mid L \text{ is accepted by } \mathcal{B} \};$$

X is <u>recognizable</u> iff it is recognized by some fb-automaton. We denote by $\mathrm{Rec}_{fb}\Sigma$ the class of all recognizable families over Σ. Note the distinction we put between the terms "accept" and "recognize". As recognizers the fb-automata do not represent languages but families of languages.

A well-known result in automata theory states that a language $L \subseteq \Sigma^*$ is regular, i.e. recognizable by a "classical" finite automaton, iff the set $\{\partial_u L \mid u \in \Sigma^*\}$ is finite. Analogously it can be shown that if a family X is recognizable / $X \in \mathrm{Rec}_{fb}\Sigma$ / then the set $\{\partial_u X \mid u \in \Sigma^*\}$ is finite /we say that X is <u>finitely derivable</u>/. However, the equivalence in this case does not hold: finite derivability is by no means a sufficient condition for recognizability by fb-automata /again we can use the cardinality argument, cf. [5] /.

One of the main results of [6] is the characterization of recognizable families:

<u>Theorem 3</u> /The Characterization Theorem for $\mathrm{Rec}_{fb}\Sigma$ /. A family $X \subseteq \mathcal{L}(\Sigma)$ is recognizable iff it is finitely derivable and self-compatible.

In view of Theorem 2 we have also another characterization of $\mathrm{Rec}_{fb}\Sigma$:

<u>Theorem 3a</u>. A family $X \subseteq \mathcal{L}(\Sigma)$ is recognizable iff it is (1) finitely derivable, (2) closed in /the metric space/ $\mathcal{L}(\Sigma)$, and (3) has the replacement property.

From the point of view of the theory of branching Theorem 3 justifies utilizing fb-automata for representation of families of languages: the stipulation of self-compatibility is satisfied and the finite derivability is a natural compensation for using only finite-state devices.

Let us complete this section with a few examples. The following families are recognizable /we assume $L \neq \emptyset$ /: $\emptyset$, $\mathcal{L}(\Sigma)$, $\{L \mid \mathrm{Pref}\, L = \Sigma^*\}$ /the complete languages/, $\{L \mid \mathrm{Pref}\, L = L\}$ /the prefix-closed languages/, $\{L \mid uv \in L$ and $u \in L$ imply $v = \Lambda\}$ /the prefix-free languages/; if L is regular then also: $\{L\}$ /a singleton/, $\{\{u\} \mid u \in L\}$, $\{L' \mid \emptyset \neq L' \subseteq L\}$, $\{L' \mid L \subseteq L'\}$.

On the other hand, X_{fin} and X_{inf} are not recognizable, even if both are finitely derivable – X_{fin} has the replacement property but is not closed, while for X_{inf} holds the converse. Note that any singleton $\{L\}$ is trivially self-compatible but for a nonregular L it is not finitely derivable. Except for $\mathcal{L}(\Sigma)$ any family containing all finite languages is not recognizable: bad news for the Chomsky hierarchy.

5. Finite Branching Automata: the Nondeterministic Case

A perpetual question in automata theory concerns the relative power of the deterministic versus nondeterministic variants of one or the other type of device. Nondeterministic branching automata were introduced in [9] and [10]. It was shown first, that their behavior properly extends the behavior of their deterministic siblings, and second, that there exists an interesting relationship of these new devices to classical nondeterministic finite automata with a generalized /in a certain natural way/ behavior.

There is no difficulty in introducing nondeterminism into the definition of finite branching automaton from the previous section: one just uses a set $I \subseteq Q$ of initial states and a nondeterministic transition function $\delta : Q \times \Sigma \rightarrow \mathcal{P}(Q)$. We call the resulting quadruple $\mathcal{B} = \langle Q, \delta, I, B \rangle$ the nondeterministic finite branching automaton /nfb-automaton; by default considered over Σ /.

To define an acceptance by an nfb-automaton $\mathcal{B}$ we have first to introduce the concept of a run in $\mathcal{B}$ as a partial function $f : \Sigma^* \dot{\rightarrow} Q$ such that

(i) if $I \neq \emptyset$ then $f(\Lambda) \in I$;

(ii) for any $u \in \Sigma^*$ and $a \in \Sigma$, if $f(u)$ is defined and $f(u)a :=$ $\delta(f(u), a) \neq \emptyset$ then $f(ua) \in f(u)a$;

(iii) f remains undefined in all other cases.

A language $L \in \mathcal{L}(\Sigma)$ is accepted by an nfb-automaton $\mathcal{B}$ iff there exists a run f in $\mathcal{B}$ such that $\mathrm{Pref}\, L \subseteq \mathrm{Dom}\, f$ and for any $u \in \mathrm{Pref}\, L$

$$(f(u),\ \Delta_L(u)) \in B \quad .$$

$\mathcal{B}$ recognizes the family of all languages it accepts. A family $X \subseteq \mathcal{L}(\Sigma)$ recognized by some nfb-automaton is nondeterministically recognizable. We denote by $\mathrm{Rec}_{nfb}\Sigma$ the class of all nondeterministically recognizable families over Σ .

Let us note that /deterministic/ fb-automata can be viewed also as a special case of nfb-automata with a unique run given by the transition function δ .

We shall now prove the following important result.

Theorem 4. Each family in $\mathrm{Rec}_{nfb}\Sigma$ is closed in the metric space $\mathcal{L}(\Sigma)$.

Proof[4]. Let X be recognized by an nfb-automaton $\mathcal{B} = \langle Q, \delta, I, B \rangle$. We shall show that $\bar{X} \subseteq X$. Let $L \in \mathcal{L}(\Sigma)$ be such that

$$\forall n \geqslant 0, \ \exists L_n \in X, \qquad s(L, L_n) > n \ . \tag{6}$$

For every such L_n there exists a run f_n, such that $\mathrm{Pref}\, L_n \subseteq \mathrm{Dom}\, f_n$ and

$$\forall u \in \mathrm{Pref}\, L_n, \qquad (f_n(u), \Delta_{L_n}(u)) \in B \ . \tag{7}$$

For our proof we need to define certain subsequences of the sequence (f_n). For any $f : \Sigma^* \dot{\to} Q$ and any $k \geqslant 0$ we use the notation

$$f/k := f \restriction \bigcup_{i=0}^{k} \Sigma^i$$

/the restriction of f to strings of length at most k /. For each $k \geqslant 0$ we shall construct a subsequence $(g_n^{(k)})$ of (f_n) as follows.

Step 0. Let $k = 0$. Since Q is finite there is at least one infinite subsequence of (f_n) with a common value $f_n(\Lambda)$. Define $(g_n^{(0)})$ as one of such infinite subsequences.

Step k+1. Assume that $(g_n^{(k)})$ have been already constructed for some $k \geqslant 0$. There is at least one infinite subsequence of $(g_n^{(k)})$ with a common restriction $g_n^{(k)} \restriction \Sigma^{k+1}$. Define $(g_n^{(k+1)})$ as one of such infinite subsequences.

It can be easily seen directly from the construction that for $k, n \geqslant 0$

$$g_n^{(k)}/k = g_{n+1}^{(k)}/k = g_{n+1}^{(k+1)}/k \ .$$

Let us now define $f : \Sigma^* \dot{\to} Q$ by

$$f(u) := g_n^{(n)}(u)$$

for $u \in \Sigma^*$ and $n = \lg(u)$.

Claim 1. f is a run in $\mathcal{B}$.

Indeed, since every $g_n^{(k)}$ is a run in $\mathcal{B}$,

$$f(\Lambda) = g_0^{(0)}(\Lambda) \ \dot{\in} \ I \ .$$

Also for any $n \geqslant 0$, $u \in \Sigma^n$, and $a \in \Sigma$

$$f(ua) = g_{n+1}^{(n+1)}(ua) \ \dot{\in} \ (g_{n+1}^{(n+1)}(u))a = (g_n^{(n)}(u))a = f(u)a \ .$$

---

4 In this and the subsequent proofs we use the following notation: $\dot{\to}$ in $f : A \dot{\to} B$ indicates that f is a partial function. The expression $\alpha \dot{\in} \beta$ has the meaning "α is defined and $\alpha \in \beta$" if β is defined and denotes a nonempty set; otherwise it means "α undefined" /thus f is a run iff $f(\Lambda) \dot{\in} I$ and $f(ua) \dot{\in} f(u)a$ /.

Claim 2. $\forall n \geq 0$, $\forall u \in \mathrm{Pref}\, L \cap \Sigma^n$, $\quad (f(u),\ \Delta_L(u)) \in B$.

We have, by the construction, $f(u) = g_n^{(n)}(u) = f_m(u)$ for some $m \geq n$. By (6) $s(L, L_m) > m \geq n$, hence $\Delta_L(u) = \Delta_{L_m}(u)$. Therefore,

$$(f(u),\ \Delta_L(u)) = (f_m(u),\ \Delta_{L_m}(u))$$

and Claim 2 follows from (7).

Now, as a direct consequence of Claim 1 and 2, we can conclude that $L \in X$. Hence $\overline{X} = X$. □

6. Characterization of Nondeterministically Recognizable Families

Let us set ourselves the task to characterize the class $\mathrm{Rec}_{nfb}\Sigma$ in a similar manner as Theorem 3 or 3a did for the case of $\mathrm{Rec}_{fb}\Sigma$. According to Theorem 4 the topological property of being closed is shared by families in $\mathrm{Rec}_{fb}\Sigma$ and in $\mathrm{Rec}_{nfb}\Sigma$. The same holds, as we shall see later, for the finite derivability – which is hardly suprising as this property is connected with the finiteness of recognizing devices. It appears that the main difference between $\mathrm{Rec}_{nf}\Sigma$ and $\mathrm{Rec}_{nfb}\Sigma$ is rooted in the replacement property.

Let $\mathcal{Y} \subseteq \mathcal{P}(\mathcal{L}(\Sigma))$ be a class of families of languages. Let us say that $\mathcal{Y}$ is locked under derivatives iff for each $Y \in \mathcal{Y}$ and each $a \in \Sigma$, $\partial_a Y$ is a union of some elements of $\mathcal{Y}$. Note that this property is preserved by union and intersection of classes.

Theorem 5. /The Characterization Theorem for $\mathrm{Rec}_{nfb}\Sigma$ /. A family $X \subseteq \mathcal{L}(\Sigma)$ is nondeterministically recognizable iff it is closed in /the metric space/ $\mathcal{L}(\Sigma)$ and is a union of some elements of a class $\mathcal{Y}$ which is finite, locked under derivatives, and consists of families with the simple replacement property.

Proof. Let us first prove the $\Leftarrow$ direction. Let $\mathcal{Y}$ be a class of families which satisfies the properties from the theorem and let X be a union of some elements of $\mathcal{Y}$. We shall construct an nfb-automaton $\mathcal{B} := \langle Q, \delta, I, B\rangle$ over Σ as follows:

$$Q := \mathcal{Y}\ ;$$

$$Ya = \delta(Y, a) := \{Y' \in \mathcal{Y} \mid Y' \subseteq \partial_a Y\}\ ;$$

$$I := \{Y \in \mathcal{Y} \mid Y \subseteq X\}\ ;$$

$$B := \{(Y, \Delta_L(\Lambda)) \mid L \in Y \in \mathcal{Y}\} .$$

Denote $X_{\mathcal{B}}$ the family recognized by $\mathcal{B}$. We shall show that $X = X_{\mathcal{B}}$.

I. $/ X_{\mathcal{B}} \subseteq X /$. Let $L_0 \in X_{\mathcal{B}}$, i.e., there is a run f in $\mathcal{B}$, such that $(f(u), \Delta_{L_0}(u)) \in B$ for each $u \in \text{Pref } L_0$. By definition of B then $\Delta_{L_0}(u) = \Delta_L(u)$ for some $L \in f(u) \in \mathcal{Y}$. Thus

$$\forall u \in \text{Pref } L,\ \exists L_u \in f(u),\qquad \Delta_{L_u}(\Lambda) = \Delta_{L_0}(u) . \tag{11}$$

Since f is a run, $f(\Lambda) \in I$, i.e., $f(\Lambda) \subseteq X$. Moreover, if $ua \in \text{Pref } L_0$ then $f(ua) \in f(u)a$ and by definition of δ, $f(ua) \subseteq \partial_a f(u)$. Thus

$$\forall ua \in \text{Pref } L_0,\ \forall L \in f(ua),\ \exists L' \in f(u),\quad \partial_a L' = L . \tag{12}$$

Claim 1. Let $n, k \geq 0$. If for each $u \in \text{Pref } L_0 \cap \Sigma^n$ there exists $L_u \in f(u)$ such that $s(L_u, \partial_u L_0) > k$ then there exists $L \in f(\Lambda)$ such that $s(L, L_0) > n{+}k$.

To show this we proceed by induction on n. If $n = 0$ then $u = \Lambda$ and we set $L := L_u$. For the inductive step assume the claim proved for some $n \geq 0$ and consider the case of $n + 1$. Let $k \geq 0$ and let for any $ua \in \text{Pref } L_0 \cap \Sigma^{n+1}$ there is $L_{ua} \in f(ua)$ such that $s(L_{ua}, L_0) > k$. By (8) also $\Delta_{L_u}(\Lambda) = \Delta_{L_0}(u)$ for some $L_u \in f(u)$ and by (9) for any $a \in \Delta_{L_0}(u)$ there is $L'_{ua} \in f(u)$ such that $L_{ua} = \partial_a L'_{ua}$. Recall that $f(u) \in \mathcal{Y}$ and thus by the assumption has the simple replacement property. Using this property /perhaps several times/ we can construct trom L_u and L'_{ua} $/ a \in \Delta_{L_0}(u) /$ a language $L'_u \in f(u)$ such that $s(L'_u, \partial_u L_0) > k + 1$. Now by the induction hypothesis there is $L \in f(\Lambda)$ such that $s(L, L_0) > n + k + 1$.

Claim 2. $\forall n \geq 0,\ \exists L'_n \in f(\Lambda),\quad s(L'_n, L_0) > n$.

Indeed, by (8) for each $u \in \text{Pref } L_0 \cap \Sigma^n$ there is $L_u \in f(u)$ such that $\Delta_{L_u}(\Lambda) = \Delta_{L_0}(u) = \Delta_{\partial_u L_0}(\Lambda)$. Thus $s(L_u, \partial_u L_0) > 0$ and using Claim 1 for $k = 0$ we obtain $L'_n \in f(\Lambda)$ such that $s(L'_n, L_0) > n$.

Now, since in Claim 2 all $L'_n \in f(\Lambda) \subseteq X$, we can use the assumption that X is closed and conclude that $L_0 \in X$.

II. $/ X \subseteq X_{\mathcal{B}} /$. Let $L_0 \in X$. To show that $\mathcal{B}$ accepts L_0 we define a run f in $\mathcal{B}$ inductively as follows.

Step 0. Since $L_0 \in X$ there is at least one element of $\mathcal{Y}$, say Y_0, such that $L_0 \in Y_0 \in I$. Define $f(\Lambda) := Y_0$.

Step n+1. Case 1. Let $ua \in \text{Pref } L_0$ and assume that $f(u)$ is defined, $f(u) = Y \in \mathcal{Y}$, and $\partial_u L_0 \in Y$. There is at least one element of $\mathcal{Y}$, say Y_1, such that $\partial_{ua} L_0 \in Y_1 \subseteq \partial_a Y$. Define $f(ua) := Y_1$.

Case 2. If $ua \notin \mathrm{Pref}\, L_0$ or the assumption does not hold then leave $f(ua)$ undefined.

A trivial inductive argument shows that $f(u)$ is defined iff $u \in \mathrm{Pref}\, L_0$. Since $f(\Lambda) \in I$ and for any $ua \in \mathrm{Pref}\, L_0$, $f(ua) \subseteq \partial_a Y$, i.e., $f(ua) \in Ya$, f is indeed a run. Now let $u \in \mathrm{Pref}\, L_0$. Since $\Delta_{L_0}(u) = \Delta_{\partial_u L_0}(\Lambda)$ and using the fact that, by the definition of f, $\partial_u L_0 \in f(u) \in \mathcal{Y}$, we have

$$(f(u), \Delta_{L_0}(u)) = (f(u), \Delta_{\partial_u L_0}(\Lambda)) \in B .$$

Hence $L_0 \in X_{\mathcal{B}}$.

Let us prove now the $\Rightarrow$ direction of the theorem. Let $\mathcal{B} = \langle Q, \delta, I, B\rangle$ be an nfb-automaton over Σ and let X be the family recognized by $\mathcal{B}$. By Theorem 4, X is closed in $\mathcal{L}(\Sigma)$. For each $q \in Q$ define a new nfb-automaton $\mathcal{B}_q :=$ $\langle Q, \delta, \{q\}, B\rangle$ and denote by Y_q the family recognized by $\mathcal{B}_q$. We claim that the set $\mathcal{Y} := \{Y_q \mid q \in Q\}$ has the properties from Theorem 5. Clearly $\mathcal{Y}$ is finite and X is a union of some elements of $\mathcal{Y}$, viz. $X = \bigcup_{q \in I} Y_q$. Moreover, for each $q \in Q$ and $a \in \Sigma$,

$$\partial_a Y_q = \bigcup_{p \in qa} Y_p .$$

Thus $\mathcal{Y}$ is locked under derivatives. It remains to show that each Y_q has the simple replacement property. Let $L_1, L_2 \in Y_q$ and $a \in \mathrm{Pref}\, L_1 \cap \mathrm{Pref}\, L_2$. There are runs f_1, f_2 in $\mathcal{B}_q$ such that $f_1(\Lambda) = f_2(\Lambda) = q$ and both $f_1(a)$, $f_2(a)$ are defined. It can be easily observed that the partial function $f : \Sigma^* \dashrightarrow Q$, defined as

$$f(u) := \begin{cases} f_1(u) & \text{if } u \notin a\Sigma^* \\ f_2(u) & \text{if } u \in a\Sigma^* \end{cases}$$

is also a run in $\mathcal{B}_q$, and that for $L := \mathrm{Rep}_a(L_1, L_2)$ and any $u \in \mathrm{Pref}\, L$ we have $(f(u), \Delta_L(u)) \in B$. Thus $L \in Y_q$. □

As an immediate consequence of the fact that the class $\mathcal{Y}$ in Theorem 5 is finite and locked under derivatives we obtain

Corollary. Each family $X \in \mathrm{Rec}_{nfb}\Sigma$ is finitely derivable.

Note that the characterization for $\mathrm{Rec}_{fb}\Sigma$ from Theorem 3a can now be obtained easily by observing that for $X \in \mathrm{Rec}_{fb}\Sigma$ we can use as $\mathcal{Y}$ just the class

$$\mathcal{Y} = \{\partial_u X \mid u \in \Sigma^*\} .$$

7. Boolean Operations and a Hierarchy of Families[5]

As an application of the characterization theorem let us show that the family X_{inf} of all infinite languages belongs to $\mathrm{Rec}_{nfb}\Sigma$. As we shall see this example is nontrivial and theoretically important.

Recall that X_{inf} was mentioned in Section 2 as an example of a closed family. Let us define for each $a \in \Sigma$ the family $Y_a := \{L \mid \partial_a L \in X_{inf}\}$ and consider the finite class

$$\mathcal{Y} := \{Y_a \mid a \in \Sigma\} \cup \{\mathcal{L}(\Sigma)\} .$$

Clearly $X_{inf} = \bigcup_{a\in\Sigma} Y_a$. Moreover, for $a, b \in \Sigma$,

$$\partial_a Y_b = \begin{cases} X_{inf} & \text{if } a = b \\ \mathcal{L}(\Sigma) & \text{if } a \neq b \end{cases}$$

and, of course, $\partial_a \mathcal{L}(\Sigma) = \mathcal{L}(\Sigma)$. It remains to show that each Y_a has the simple replacement property. But this is obvious since for any $L_1, L_2 \in Y_a$, $\partial_a \mathrm{Rep}_b(L_1, L_2)$ is either $\partial_a L_1$ if $a \neq b$, or $\partial_a L_2$ if $a = b$. We conclude by Theorem 5 that $X_{inf} \in \mathrm{Rec}_{nfb}\Sigma$.

The construction used in the proof of Theorem 5 can be used for finding the corresponding nfb-automaton. For instance, in the case $\Sigma = \{0, 1\}$ we have

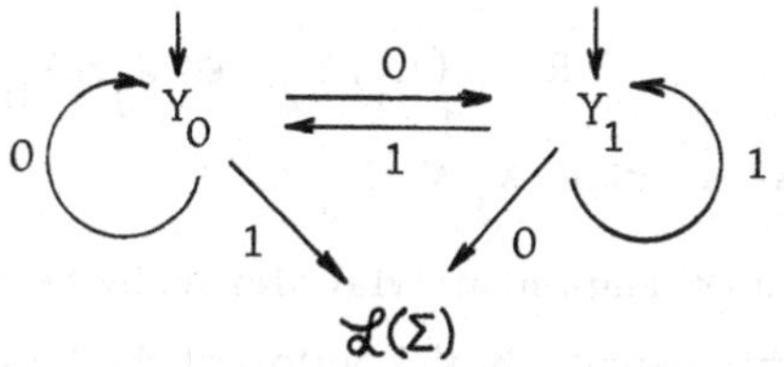

with the branching relation $B = \{(Y_a, \Gamma) \mid \Gamma \subseteq \Sigma_\Lambda, a \in \Gamma \cap \Sigma\}$.

<u>Theorem 6.</u> The class $\mathrm{Rec}_{nfb}\Sigma$ is not closed under complementation /of families of languages/.

---

[5] Some of the material in this section was contributed by V. Benda.

Proof. As we have just shown $X_{inf} \in Rec_{nfb}\Sigma$. But $X_{fin} = \mathcal{L}(\Sigma) - X_{inf}$ is not closed in the metric space $\mathcal{L}(\Sigma)$. □

Thus the Boolean closure of $Rec_{nfb}\Sigma$ contains families that are not closed in $\mathcal{L}(\Sigma)$. In fact, the same holds for the Boolean closure of $Rec_{fb}\Sigma$: for any infinite regular language L the family $\mathcal{L}(\Sigma) - \{L\}$ is not closed while $\{L\} \in Rec_{fb}\Sigma$.

It was shown in [6] that $Rec_{nf}\Sigma$ is closed under intersection but not under union. In [9] it was shown that $Rec_{nfb}\Sigma$ is closed under both union and intersection. One may ask about the position of the class $URec_{fb}\Sigma$ of all finite unions of recognizable families.

Theorem 7. $$Rec_{fb}\Sigma \subsetneq URec_{fb}\Sigma \subsetneq Rec_{nfb}\Sigma \quad .$$

Proof. In view of the above discussion the only case that remains to prove is that $URec_{fb}\Sigma \neq Rec_{nfb}\Sigma$. For this we use our favorite family X_{inf} and show that $X_{inf} \notin URec_{fb}\Sigma$. Suppose for contradiction that for some $n \geq 1$

$$X_{inf} = \bigcup_{i=1}^{n} X_i$$

where $X_i \in Rec_{fb}\Sigma$. Let L be a finite prefix-free language of n+1 strings, $L = \{w_1, \ldots, w_{n+1}\}$. Construct a family of n+1 infinite languages $L_k = L \cup w_k^*$, $k = 1, \ldots, n+1$. Then necessarily two of them, say L_1 and L_2 , belong to the same family, say X_j . But then

$$Rep_{w_1}(L_1, L_2) \in X_j \cap X_{fin} \neq \emptyset ,$$

which contradicts the assumption $X_j \subseteq X_{inf}$. □

Theorem 7 suggests a certain nontrivial hierarchy of families of languages as studied by methods of this paper. On the bottom of the hierarchy we may add the class $WRec_{fb}\Sigma$ of the so called well-recognizable families, introduced and studied by Benda and Bendová / [11] , [12] /. /A family X is well-recognizable iff both X and its complement $\mathcal{L}(\Sigma) - X$ are recognizable./ On the other end of the hierarchy we may place the class $FDC\Sigma$ of all finitely derivable families closed in the metric space $\mathcal{L}(\Sigma)$. We already know /Theorem 4 and Corollary to Theorem 5/ that $Rec_{nfb}\Sigma \subsetneq FDC\Sigma$. A cardinality argument shows that this inclusion is proper: FDC includes an uncountable set of families of the form $\{L \mid \Lambda \notin L\} \cup \{L'\}$ for L' such that $\Lambda \in L'$.

The obtained hierarchy is displayed on the next page.

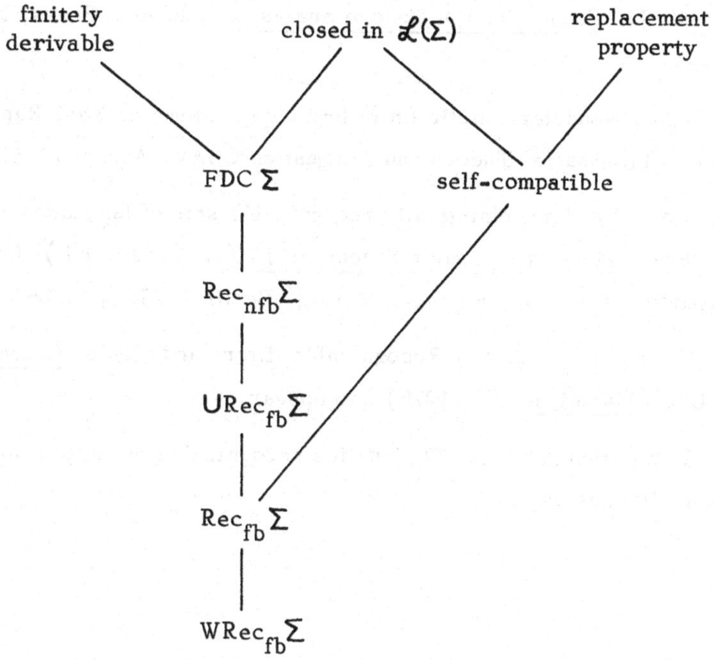

REFERENCES

1. Book, R. V., Formal language theory and theoretical computer science. In: Automata Theory and Formal Languages, Proc. 2nd GI Conf., Lecture Notes in Computer Science 33, Springer Verlag, Berlin 1975, pp. 1–15.

2. Štěpánková, O. and Havel, I. M., A logical theory of robot problem solving. Artificial Intelligence 7 (1976), 165–197.

3. Havel, I. M., Finite branching automata: automata theory motivated by problem solving. In: Mathematical Foundations of Computer Science (A. Blikle, Ed.) Lecture Notes in Computer Science 28, Springer-Verlag, Berlin 1975, pp. 53–61.

4. Marcus, S., Algebraic Linguistics: Analytical Models, New York 1967.

5. Benda V. and Bendová, K., On specific features of recognizable families of languages. This volume

6. Havel, I. M., Finite branching automata. Kybernetika 10 (1974), pp. 281–302.

7. Bodnarčuk, V. G., Metričeskoe prostranstvo sobytij I. /The metric space of events I./ Kibernetika /Kiev/, (1965) No. 1, pp. 24–27 /In Russian/.

8. Dieudonné, J., Foundations of Modern Analysis, Academic Press, New York 1960.

9. Havel, I. M., Nondeterministic finite branching automata. Res. Report 623/75 Institute of Information Theory and Automation ČSAV, August 1975.

10. Havel, I. M., Nondeterministically recognizable sets of languages. In: Mathematical Foundations of Computer Science 1975 (J. Bečvář, Ed.) Lecture Notes in Computer Science 32, Springer-Verlag, Berlin 1975, pp. 252–257.

11. Benda, V. and Bendová, K., Recognizable filters and ideals. Commentationes Math. Univ. Carolinae 17 (1976) , to appear.

12. Benda, V. and Bendová, K., On families recognizable by finite branching automata. /Manuscript/.

ALGORITHMS AND REAL NUMBERS

N.M. Nagorny
Computing Center, Academy of
Sciences of the USSR
II7333, Moscow, Vavilova 40, USSR

At the present time we clearly realize the fact that the mathematical standardization of the rather vague general idea of algorithm made by A.Church, S.C.Kleene and A.M.Turing was found to be an event of outstanding importance in mathematics. On the one hand, the algorithm theory based on an exact concept of algorithm (such as the partial recursive function, the Turing machine or the Markov normal algorithm) allowed to establish the unsolvability of a series of famous algorithmical problems such as the identity problem for semigroups (A.A.Markov, E.L.Post - I947) and groups (P.S.Novikov - I952), the homeomorphy problem (A.A.Markov - I958), Hilbert's tenth problem (Yu.V. Matijasevič - I970). On the other hand, has arisen the possibility of giving exact constructive variants to the most important mathematical concepts of real number and real function. In the following (section I) we shall give the exact formulations of these definitions.

In connection with the concepts of constructive real number and constructive real function the constructive mathematical analysis has developed (see, for instance, [I] , [2] , [II] , [I2]). The constructive mathematical analysis is engaged in the study of some natural algorithmical problems dictated by our wish to understand which initial data are sufficient to carry out certain calculations and which are not. The impossibility of the algorithmical realization of some operation over the constructive numbers and functions we could interpret as a hint of insufficiency of the initial data. In section 2 we shall dwell in more details upon this problem and consider some explanatory examples.

The establishment of the unsolvability of any algorithmical problem is usually a very difficult mathematical task. Thus the discovery of the general cause determining the unsolvability of some algorithmical problems is always considered to be an important mathematical achievement. A very interesting approach to this problem area based on the concept of the algorithm complexity was elaborated by A.A.Markov [3] . In section 3 we shall consider in more details this approach which gives some interesting results in many discret cases. However it must be pointed out that application of this approach to problems dealing with continuity is not found to be very efficient. Unfortunately, we are forced to acknowledge that till now there is no satisfactory explanation about reasons responsible for the unsolvability of some algorithmical problems concerning constructive real numbers and functions. In a number of papers the complexity approach was also applied to analyse the Specker's sequences (section 4) and in other situations (see section 5).

The author of the present survey is trying to draw the attention of the experts in computer science to the problems discussed here. The main attention is drawn to the quantitative consideration of the situation. Details, often very exotic, are ignored because (on the author's opinion) the finding of new conceptions and problem formulations is more important here than the perfection of results early obtained. The survey does not lay claim to be perfectly complete. The choice of the reviewed papers is determinated by the author's personal taste.

I. In this paper the notations m,n stand for natural numbers, ε stands for positive rational numbers.

<u>A constructive real number</u> (see, for instance, [I] , [2]) is either a rational number or a pair (A,B) where A and B are algorithms such that

for each n $A(n)$ is a rational number,

for each ε $B(\varepsilon)$ is a natural number,

for each m,n,ε if $m,n \geqslant B(\varepsilon)$ then $|A(m) - A(n)| < \varepsilon$.

We will use x and y as notations for constructive real numbers.

For x,y the following relations can be naturally defined: $x = y$, $x \neq y$, $x \geqslant y$, $x > y$.

Also $|x|$, $x + y$, $x - y$, $x \cdot y$, $x:y$ (if $y \neq 0$) can be defined. The results of these operations themselves are constructive real numbers. $\min(x,y)$ is defined as follows

$$\min(x,y) = \frac{x + y - |x - y|}{2} .$$

By <u>constructive real function</u> (see, for instance, [I] , [2]) we understand an algorithm F satisfying for each x,y the condition if: I) $F(x)$ is defined and 2) $x = y$

then: I') $F(y)$ is also defined and 2') $F(x)$ and $F(y)$ are equal constructive real numbers.

A constructive real function F is said to be <u>continuous at point y</u> iff there exists an algorithm A such that

for each ε $A(\varepsilon)$ is a positive rational number,

for each x, ε if $|x - y| < A(\varepsilon)$ then $|F(x) - F(y)| < \varepsilon$.

(See, for instance, [I], [2]).

2. Let's consider the following example (historically one of the first in this field; see [4], [I3]).

Let F be a constructive real function continuous on $[0,I]$. Let $F(0) \cdot F(I) < 0$. One wonders whether the equation $F(x) = 0$ could not have a constructive real number as a solution in $(0,I)$. It happens that this is impossible. There is no algorithm however, that using F would produce an x satisfying $F(x) = 0$. So, the information contained in F is not sufficient to find the root of the equation $F(x) = 0$. The couple (F, ε) supplies yet enough information for finding a constructive real number y for which $|F(y)| < \varepsilon$. The algorithm is easily provided by the well known dichotomy procedure.

A similar situation takes place in the travelling salesman problem [5]. Let G be a complete finite graph having edges of constructive real length. Let us consider the Hamiltonian cycles in G. For every such graph G the minimum of lengths of the Hamiltonian cycles may be found algorithmically. Let us denote it by x. We wonder whether the graph G could not have a Hamiltonian cycle with the length equal to x. It happens that this is impossible. There is no algorithm however that using G would provide such a cycle. The couple (G, ε) may be nevertheless worked out algorithmically into a Hamiltonian cycle in G with length y such that $|y - x| < \varepsilon$. On the MFCS-75 the author recalled a similar result concerning linear programming problem [5].

In the examples considered "approximated" ε-variants of unsolvable "exact" algorithmical problems happened to be solvable. However it would be wrong thinking that it is always so. The ε-variants of certain known unsolvable problems came out to be also unsolvable (as, for example, in the computing of the Riemannian integral of an integrable constructive real function; see [6]).

3. The complexity approach turned out to be very fruitful in many branches of the algorithm theory. Methods that now would be classi-

fied as related to complexity have been sometimes used since the fifties (see, for example, [7] , theorem 3.I). Nevertheless only in I964 a complexity approach to investigations about the solvability of algorithmical problems was suggested by A.A.Markov [3], shedding light on the nature of unsolvability of a wide class of such problems. This was a pioneer and stimulating work.

A.A.Markov proposed to "approximate" the given problem P by a sequence of "restricted" problems P_n such that: I) each of problems P_n can not be unsolvable and 2) an algorithm solves the problem P if and only if it solves each of the problems P_n. Let us suppose that the general recursive function l(n) is a lower bound of complexity of algorithms solving P_n and that l(n) is unbounded. In this case the problem P is unsolvable. Indeed, the complexity of an algorithm solving P would be greater than all l(n) i.e. would be "infinite".

In such a method much depend on how the given problem is approximated by the "restricted" problems. For instance, if P consists in deciding whether any word belongs to a given recursively enumerable set of words, for P_n it would be natural to choose the problem of deciding whether any word bounded in length by n belongs to the same set. Such an approximation of this problem have been well studied.

Unfortunately, it came out, that under natural approximations the most important algorithmical problems in constructive mathematical analysis give rise to such "restricted" problems that have only bounded general recursive lower bounds of complexity. A very general theorem proved by B.A.Kušner (see [8], theorem I) implies that it must be so in problems such as the simulation of the signum function, solution of systems of the linear algebraic equations, integration of the polygonal functions. As it is very well known all these algorithmical problems are unsolvable.

4. A famous example due to E.Specker [I4] consists of a bounded monotonic algorithmical sequence of rational numbers having no constructive limit. Such constructions because of their importance have been studied subsequently from different standpoints. M.I.Kanovič [9] investigated these sequences from the complexity point of view. By combining the ε- and the complexity approaches Kanovič found that the complexity of the ε-limit of a Specker sequence grows unboundedly as ε decreases.

Similar questions in relation to the least upper bounds of bounded constructive real functions were also studied [9]. As it is very well known there exist functions for which the least upper bound is attained at no constructive point.

5. Let's note finally B.A.Kušner's work [IO] on the computational complexity of constructive real numbers. By computation of a number x Kušner calls an algorithmical sequence of rational numbers converging quickly enough to x. Computation resource functions satisfying M.A.Blum's axioms [I5] are considered. It is shown, in particular, that the set C_h of constructive real numbers which allow computations with resource functions having a given bound h in infinitely many points has its constructive measure equal to zero. Thus the complement of C_h is a set of full costructive measure.

References

I. Шанин Н.А. Конструктивные вещественные числа и конструктивные функциональные пространства. Труды Матем. инст. им. В.А.Стеклова АН СССР, 67 (I962), I5 - 294.

2. Кушнер Б.А. Лекции по конструктивному математическому анализу. Физматгиз, Москва, I973.

3. Марков А.А. О нормальных алгорифмах, вычисляющих булевы функции. Доклады АН СССР, I57 № 2 (I964), 262 - 264.

4. Цейтин Г.С. Теоремы о среднем значении в конструктивном анализе. Труды Матем. инст. им. В.А.Стеклова АН СССР, 67 (I962), 362 - 384.

5. Нагорный Н.М. Об алгорифмах для решения некоторых оптимизационных задач. Материалы к конфер. по опыту и персп. применения матем. методов и электр. вычисл. машин в планировании. Новосибирск, I962, 3 - 5.

6. Кушнер Б.А. Некоторые массовые проблемы, связанные с интегрированием конструктивных функций. Труды Матем. инст. им. В.А.Стеклова АН СССР, II3 (I970), 39 - 72.

7. Нагорный Н.М. О минимальном алфавите алгорифмов над данным алфавитом. Труды Матем. инст. им. В.А.Стеклова АН СССР, 52 (I958), 66 - 74.

8. Канович М.И., Кушнер Б.А. Об оценке сложности некоторых массовых проблем анализа. Зап. научн. семинаров Ленингр. отд. Матем. инст. им. В.А.Стеклова АН СССР, I6 (I969), 8I - 90.

9. Канович М.И. Сложность предела шпекеровых последовательностей. Доклады АН СССР, 2I4 № 5 (I974), I020 - I023.

IO. Кушнер Б.А. Сложно-вычислимые действительные числа. Zeitschr. f. math. Logik und Grundlagen d. Math., I9 (I973), 447 - 452.

II. Bishop E. Foundations of constructive analysis. New York, I967.

I2. Martin-Löf P. Notes on constructive mathematics. Almqvist & Wiskell, Stockholm, I970.

I3. Kreisel G. Analysis of the Cantor - Bendixon theorem by means of analytic hierarchy. Bull. Acad. Polon. Sci., 7 (I959), 62I - 626.

I4. Specker E. Nicht konstruktiv beweisbare Sätze der Analysis. Journ. Symbolic Logic, I4 No 3 (I949), I45 - I58.

I5. Blum M.A. A machine-independent theory of the complexity of recursive functions. Journ. Ass. Comp. Mach., I4 No 2 (I967), 322 - 336.

ON MAPPINGS OF MACHINES

Miroslav Novotný

Mathematical Institute of the Czechoslovak Academy of Sciences

Branch Brno, Czechoslovakia

0. Introduction

Let c be a set, o a partial mapping of c into itself and r a subset of c - dom o. Then the ordered triple A = (c,o,r) is called a <u>machine</u>. For a machine A = (c,o,r), we put $c_A = c$, $o_A = o$, $r_A = r$. This notion includes some important special cases, e.g. machines of Pawlak (1) and autonomous automata (2).

If A is a machine, we put $o_A^0 = id_A$. Let $n \geq 0$ be an integer and suppose that the partial mapping o_A^n of c_A into c_A has been defined. If $x \in c_A$ is such that $o_A^n(x)$ is defined and $o_A^n(x) \in \text{dom } o_A$, then we put $o_A^{n+1}(x) = o_A(o_A^n(x))$. By induction, we define o_A^m for any nonnegative integer m.

Thus, for any $x \in c_A$, the value $o_A^0(x)$ is defined. Two cases can occur:

a) $o_A^i(x)$ is defined for any nonnegative integer i. Then we put $\delta_A(x) = \omega$ where ω is the least infinite ordinal.

b) There exists $n \geq 1$ such that $o_A^i(x)$ is defined for any i, $0 \leq i < n$, and $o_A^{n-1}(x) \notin \text{dom } o_A$. Then we put $\delta_A(x) = n$.

Let A, B be machines, $m: c_A \longrightarrow c_B$ a mapping. It is said to be an <u>s-mapping</u> of A into B if the following conditions are satisfied:

(i) For any $x \in \text{dom } o_A$, there exists an integer $i(x) \geq 1$ such that $m(x) \in \text{dom } o_B^{i(x)}$ and $m(o_A(x)) = o_B^{i(x)}(m(x))$.

(ii) $m[r_A] \subseteq r_B$.

An s-mapping m is said to be an <u>h-mapping</u> if $i(x) = 1$ for any $x \in \text{dom } o_A$. An injective h-mapping is said to be an <u>i-mapping</u>.

In (3), (4), all h-mappings (homomorphisms) of a complete unary algebra with one operation were constructed. Bartol (5) studied some properties of h-mappings of machines in the sense of Pawlak. Injective homomorphisms (i-mappings) of autonomous automata were investigated by Stucky and Walter (2) and Kopeček (6), (7) used the methods of (3) and (4) for the construction of all h-mappings of a Pawlak machine and for the construction of all i-mappings of a partial unary algebra with one operation. The notion of an s-mapping (simulation) for a Pawlak machine is due to Pawlak (8). The construction of all simulations of a Pawlak machine into another was described by Novotný (9).

In this lecture, we give a method of describing all j-mappings of a machine into another machine for $j \in \{s,h\}$. It is sufficient to describe all j-mappings of a connected machine into a connected machine; the general problem reduces to this special case.

The method consists in assigning a characteristic to any element of the machine. On the basis of these characteristics, an initial j-mapping of a submachine of the first machine into the second can be constructed. By extending these initial j-mappings by means of the characteristics, we obtain exactly all j-mappings of the first machine into the second.

1. Submachines

Let A be a machine and $c \subsetneq c_A$. Then the machine $(c, o_A \cap (c \times c), r_A \cap c) = C$ is said to be a submachine of A on the set c. Clearly, a submachine C of A is uniquely determined by the set c_C. Hence, we shall not distinguish between submachines of A and subsets of c_A. If C is a submachine of A, we write $C \leq A$. A submachine C of A is said to be trivial if c_C has exactly one element.

Let C be a submachine of A; we put $\hat{c} = c_C \cup o_A^{-1}[c_C]$. The submachine $\hat{C}$ of A such that $c_{\hat{C}} = \hat{c}$ is said to be the successor of the submachine C. A nonempty submachine C of A is said to be closed if $o_A[c_C \cap \operatorname{dom} o_A] \leq c_C$. We put $[x]_A = \{o_A^i(x);\ 0 \leq i < \delta(x)\}$ for any $x \in c_A$; clearly, $[x]_A$ is a closed submachine of A.

1. If $C \leq A$ is closed, then so is $\hat{C}$.

Proof. Clearly, $o_A[c_{\hat{C}} \cap \operatorname{dom} o_A] = o_A[(c_C \cup o_A^{-1}[c_C]) \cap \operatorname{dom} o_A] =$

$o_A[c_C \cap \mathrm{dom}\, o_A] \cup o_A[o_A^{-1}[c_C] \cap \mathrm{dom}\, o_A] \subseteq c_C \subseteq c_{\hat{C}}$. □

For a machine A, we put

$$\varrho_A = \{(x,y) \in c_A \times c_A;\ \text{there exist } m \geq 0,\ n \geq 0 \text{ such that } x \in \mathrm{dom}\, o_A^m,\ y \in \mathrm{dom}\, o_A^n,\ o_A^m(x) = o_A^n(y)\}.$$

Clearly, ϱ_A is an equivalence on c_A and its blocks are closed submachines of A; these submachines are called <u>components</u> of A. A machine is said to be <u>connected</u> if it has exactly one component. We denote by U the class of all connected machines.

The following lemma can be easily proved.

<u>2. If $A \in U$ and $C \subseteq A$ is closed, then $C \in U$.</u> □

<u>3. Let $A \in U$ and $C \subseteq A$ be closed. We put $C_0 = C$, $C_{n+1} = \hat{C}_n$ for any nonnegative integer n. Then</u>

$$c_A = \bigcup_{0 \leq n < \omega} c_{C_n}, \qquad o_A = \bigcup_{0 \leq n < \omega} o_{C_n}, \qquad r_A = \bigcup_{0 \leq n < \omega} r_{C_n}.$$

Proof. If $x \in c_A$, $y \in c_C$, then there exist $m \geq 0$, $n \geq 0$ such that $o_A^m(x) = o_A^n(y) \in c_C$ where we have used the fact that C is closed. By an easy induction, we obtain that $x \in c_{C_m}$. Hence, $c_A \subseteq \bigcup_{0 \leq n < \omega} c_{C_n}$. Since the reverse inclusion is clear, we obtain the first assertion. The second and the third assertion are consequences of the first. □

Let $A \in U$; we define $D_A = c_A - \mathrm{dom}\, o_A$. Clearly, D_A contains at most one element. If $D_A \neq \emptyset$, we denote by d_A its only element. Further, for $A \in U$, we define

$$Z_A = \{x \in c_A;\ \text{there exists } n(x) > 0 \text{ such that } x \in \mathrm{dom}\, o_A^{n(x)} \text{ and } o_A^{n(x)}(x) = x\}.$$

It is easy to see

<u>4. Let $A \in U$. Then the following assertions hold.</u>

<u>(i) If $D_A \neq \emptyset$, then $Z_A = \emptyset$.</u>

<u>(ii) If $Z_A \neq \emptyset$, then $D_A = \emptyset$.</u>

<u>(iii) If $Z_A \neq \emptyset$, then it is finite.</u> □

We denote by R_A the cardinal of Z_A.

<u>5. Let $A \in U$ and $Z_A \neq \emptyset$, $x \in Z_A$. Then $Z_A = \{o_A^i(x);\ 0 \leq i < R_A\}$.</u> □

2. s-mappings and h-mappings

In what follows, we suppose that $j \in \{s,h\}$.

It is easy to see

1. Let A, B be machines, C a submachine of A, m a j-mapping of A into B. Then $m \cap (c_C \times c_B)$ is a j-mapping of C into B. □

Let A be a machine and C its submachine. We put $u_A(C) = \{t \in c_C;\ o_A^{-1}(t) \nsubseteq c_C\}$.

2. Let A, B $\in$ U be machines, C a submachine of A, m a j-mapping of C into B. For any $t \in u_A(C)$ let m_t be a j-mapping of $c_C \cup o_A^{-1}(t)$ into B which is an extension of m. Then $\bar{m} = m \cup \bigcup_{t \in u_A(C)} m_t$ is a j-mapping of $\hat{C}$ into B.

Proof. If j = s and $z \in c_{\hat{C}} - c_C$, then $t = o_A(z) \in c_C$. Hence, $\bar{m}(o_A(z)) = m_t(o_A(z)) = o_B^{i(z)}(m_t(z)) = o_B^{i(z)}(\bar{m}(z))$ for some $i(z) \geq 1$ because m_t is an s-mapping. The case j = h is included when putting $i(z) = 1$. □

3. Let A, B $\in$ U be machines, C a closed submachine of A, $C_0 = C$, $C_{n+1} = \hat{C}_n$ for any $n \geq 0$, m_n a j-mapping of C_n into B for any $n \geq 0$, m_{n+1} being an extension of m_n for any $n \geq 0$. Then $\bigcup_{0 \leq n < \omega} m_n$ is a j-mapping of A into B.

Proof. By 1.3, $\bar{m} = \bigcup_{0 \leq n < \omega} m_n$ is defined on $\bigcup_{0 \leq n < \omega} c_{C_n} = c_A$. If $t \in \operatorname{dom} o_A$, then there exists n, $0 \leq n < \omega$, such that $t \in c_{C_n}$. Since C_n is closed by 1.1, we have $o_A(t) \in c_{C_n}$.

For j = s, we obtain the existence of $i(t) \geq 1$ such that $m_n(o_A(t)) = o_B^{i(t)}(m_n(t))$ because m_n is an s-mapping. Thus, $\bar{m}(o_A(t)) = o_B^{i(t)}(\bar{m}(t))$. The case j = h is included if putting $i(t) = 1$. □

3. Construction of all s-mappings and h-mappings

Let A $\in$ U. An element $x \in c_A$ is said to have the property (1) if there exists a sequence $(x_i)_{0 \leq i < \omega}$ such that $x_0 = x$ and $o_A(x_{i+1}) = x_i$ for any $i \geq 0$. We denote by L_A the set of all elements in c_A such that they have the property (1). Clearly, $Z_A \subseteq L_A$.

1. If A $\in$ U and $x \in L_A$, then there exists $t \in o_A^{-1}(x)$ such that

$t \in L_A$. □

We put $S_A^0 = \{t \in c_A;\ o_A^{-1}(t) = \emptyset\}$,

$S_A^\alpha = \{t \in c_A - \bigcup_{\lambda<\alpha} S_A^\lambda,\ o_A^{-1}(t) \subseteq \bigcup_{\lambda<\alpha} S_A^\lambda\}$ for any ordinal $\alpha > 0$.

Clearly, $S_A^\lambda \cap S_A^\mu = \emptyset$ for any ordinals $0 \leq \lambda < \mu$ and $S_A^\lambda \subseteq c_A$ for any ordinal λ. It follows that there exists the least ordinal ϑ_A such that $S_A^{\vartheta_A} = \emptyset$.

Let $\infty \notin$ Ord be a new symbol. We suppose that $\alpha < \infty$ for any $\alpha \in$ Ord and we put $S_A^\infty = L_A$.

2. If $A \in U$, then $c_A = \bigcup_{\lambda \in W(\vartheta_A) \cup \{\infty\}} S_A^\lambda$ with disjoint summands.

For the proof see (3) Lemma 3 or (4) 2.3. □

Let $A \in U$; for any $t \in c_A$, we put $g_A(t) = \alpha$ if $t \in S_A^\alpha$ for some $\alpha \in W(\vartheta_A) \cup \{\infty\}$.

3. Let $A \in U$, $x \in c_A$. If $g_A(x) \neq \infty$, then $g_A(o_A(x)) > g_A(x)$; if $g_A(x) = \infty$, then $g_A(o_A(x)) = \infty$.

For the proof see (3) Lemma 4 or (4) 2.4. □

In what follows, suppose $j \in \{s,h\}$.

4. Let $A, B \in U$, let m be a j-mapping of A into B. Then $g_A(t) \leq g_B(m(t))$ for any $t \in c_A$.

For the proof see (3) Lemma 7 or (4) 2.8. □

Let C be a submachine of $A \in U$ and m a mapping of C into $B \in U$. Then m is said to be bounded if $g_A(t) \leq g_B(m(t))$ for any $t \in c_C$. If A, B are connected machines, then a j-mapping of a trivial submachine $C \subseteq A$ into B is said to be trivial.

5. Let A, B be connected machines, $t \in c_A$, $z \in o_A^{-1}(t)$, m a trivial j-mapping of $\{t\}$ into c_B. Then the following assertions are equivalent.

(i) There exists an extension $\bar{m}$ of m where $\bar{m}$ is a bounded j-mapping on $\{z,t\}$.

(ii) m is bounded.

Proof. Clearly, (i) implies (ii).

Let (ii) hold. We put $m(t) = t'$.

If $g_B(t') = \infty$, then there exists at least one $z' \in o_B^{-1}(t')$ such that $g_B(z') = \infty$ by 1. Thus, we can find $z' \in o_B^{-1}(t')$ such that $g_A(z) \le g_B(z')$. Similarly, we can find z' such that $o_B^{i(z')}(z') = t'$ for some $i(z') \ge 1$ and $g_A(z) \le g_B(z')$.

Let us have $g_B(t') < \infty$; hence, $g_A(t) \le g_B(t') < \infty$. If $g_B(z') < g_A(z)$ for any $z' \in o_B^{-1}(t')$, then $g_B(z') < g_A(z) < g_A(t) \le g_B(t') < \infty$, by 3, whence $g_B(t') \le g_A(z) < g_B(t')$ which is impossible. Thus, there exists $z' \in o_B^{-1}(t')$ such that $g_A(z) < g_B(z')$. Similarly, we can find z' such that $o_B^{i(z')}(z') = t'$ for some $i(z') \ge 1$ and $g_A(z) \le g_B(z')$.

We put $\bar{m}(z) = z'$, $\bar{m}(t) = t'$. Then $\bar{m}$ is an extension of m and is a bounded j-mapping of $\{z,t\}$ into c_B. Hence, (ii) implies (i). □

6. Let A, B ∈ U, let C be a closed submachine of A, m a j-mapping of C into B, $t \in u_A(C)$. Then the following assertions are equivalent.

(i) There exists an extension $\bar{m}$ of m where $\bar{m}$ is a bounded j-mapping on $c_C \cup o_A^{-1}(t)$.

(ii) m is bounded.

Proof. Clearly, (i) implies (ii).

Let (ii) hold. Then $m_0 = m \cap (\{t\} \times c_B)$ is a bounded trivial j-mapping by 2.1. For any $z \in o_A^{-1}(t)$, there exists an extension m_z of m_0 and it is a bounded j-mapping on $\{z,t\}$, by 5. We put $\bar{m} = m \cup \bigcup_{z \in o_A^{-1}(t) - c_C} m_z$; it is easy to see that $\bar{m}$ is a bounded j-mapping on $c_C \cup o_A^{-1}(t)$ and that it is an extension of m. □

Let A, B be connected machines, C a closed submachine of A, m a bounded j-mapping of C into B, $t \in u_A(C)$, let m_t be an extension of m where m_t is a bounded j-mapping on $c_C \cup o_A^{-1}(t)$. Then m_t is said to be a *j-elementary extension* of m. Further $m \cup \bigcup_{t \in u_A(C)} m_t$ is a mapping of $\hat{C}$ into B which is said to be a *j-direct extension* of m.

7. Let A, B be connected machines, C a submachine of A, m a bounded j-mapping of C into B, $\bar{m}$ a mapping of $\hat{C}$ into B where $\bar{m}$ is an extension of m. Then the following assertions are equivalent.

(i) $\bar{m}$ is a j-direct extension of m.

(ii) $\bar{m}$ is a bounded j-mapping.

Proof. If (i) holds, then $\bar{m} = m \cup \bigcup_{t \in u_A(C)} m_t$ where m_t are j-elementary extensions of m, i.e. bounded j-mappings. By 2.2, $\bar{m}$ is a j-mapping which is, clearly, bounded. Thus, (ii) holds.

If (ii) holds, then, for any $t \in u_A(C)$, we put $m_t = \bar{m} \cap ((c_C \cup o_A^{-1}(t)) \times c_B)$. By 2.1, m_t is a bounded j-mapping on $c_C \cup o_A^{-1}(t)$ and is an extension of m, i.e., is a j-elementary extension of m. Since $\bar{m} = m \cup \bigcup_{t \in u_A(C)} m_t$, (i) holds. □

Suppose that A, B are connected machines, let C be a closed submachine of A, m a bounded j-mapping of C into B. We put $m_0 = m$, $C_0 = C$, $C_{n+1} = \hat{C}_n$ for any $n \geq 0$. From 7, we obtain by an easy induction, that, for any $n \geq 0$, there exists a bounded j-mapping m_n of C_n into B such that m_{n+1} is a j-direct extension of m_n for any $n \geq 0$. By 1.3, $\bigcup_{0 \leq n < \omega} m_n$ is a mapping of A into B. It is said to be a <u>j-extension</u> of m.

<u>8. Let A, B be connected machines, let C be a closed submachine of A, m a bounded j-mapping of C into B. Let $\bar{m}$ be a mapping of A into B which is an extension of m. Then the following assertions are equivalent.</u>

<u>(i) $\bar{m}$ is a j-extension of m.</u>

<u>(ii) $\bar{m}$ is a j-mapping.</u>

Proof. If (i) holds, then $\bar{m} = \bigcup_{0 \leq n < \omega} m_n$, any m_n is a j-mapping and m_{n+1} is an extension of m_n for $n \geq 0$; it implies (ii) by 2.3.

If (ii) holds, then $\bar{m} \cap (c_{C_{n+1}} \times c_B)$ is a j-direct extension of $\bar{m} \cap (c_{C_n} \times c_B)$ by 7 and 4. It follows that $\bar{m} = \bigcup_{0 \leq n < \omega} \bar{m} \cap (c_{C_n} \times c_B)$ is a j-extension of m. Thus, (i) holds. □

Hence, we are interested to know whether there exists a closed submachine C of A and a bounded j-mapping of C into B. The existence is guaranteed by the following definitions.

A strictly increasing sequence $(i_n)_{0 \leq n < \omega}$ of nonnegative integers is said to be <u>marked</u> if $i_0 = 0$.

Let $A \in U$, $B \in U$, $x \in c_A$, $x' \in c_B$. The ordered pair (x,x') is said to be an <u>s-pair</u> for (A,B) if exactly one of the following cases occurs.

(sA) $Z_A \neq \emptyset \neq Z_B$, $x \in Z_A$, $x' \in Z_B$.

(sB) $D_A \neq \emptyset$, $x = d_A$, $g_A(x) \leq g_B(x')$; if $x \in r_A$, then $x' \in r_B$.

(sC) $Z_A = \emptyset = D_A = D_B$ and there exists a marked sequence $(i_n)_{0 \leq n < \omega}$ such that $g_A(o_A^n(x)) \leq g_B(o_B^{i_n}(x'))$ for $0 \leq n < \omega$.

We denote by sAD the class of all ordered pairs $(A,B) \in U \times U$ such that there exists at least one s-pair for (A,B). If $(A,B) \in$ sAD and (x,x') is an s-pair for (A,B), then we define an <u>s-initial</u> mapping m of $[x]_A$ as follows.

If (sA) holds, then m is an arbitrary mapping of Z_A into Z_B such that $m(x) = x'$.

If (sB) holds, then we put $m(x) = x'$.

If (sC) holds, then we define $m(o_A^n(x)) = o_B^{i_n}(x')$ for any n, $0 \leq n < \omega$.

We denote by (hA) the conjunction of (sA) with the following condition: R_B divides R_A. Further, we denote by (hC) the special case of (sC) where $i_n = n$ for any n, $0 \leq n < \omega$. Finally, we put (hB) = (sB).

Let $A \in U$, $B \in U$, $x \in c_A$, $x' \in c_B$. The ordered pair (x,x') is said to be an <u>h-pair</u> for (A,B) if exactly one of the conditions (hA), (hB), (hC) is satisfied.

We denote by hAD the class of all ordered pairs $(A,B) \in U \times U$ such that there exists at least one h-pair for (A,B). If $(A,B) \in$ hAD and (x,x') is an h-pair for (A,B), then we define an <u>h-initial</u> mapping m of $[x]_A$ by putting $m(o_A^n(x)) = o_B^n(x')$ for any n, $0 \leq n < \delta_A(x)$.

<u>9. Let $(A,B) \in$ jAD, let (x,x') be a j-pair for (A,B), m a mapping of $[x]_A$ into c_B such that $m(x) = x'$. Then the following assertions are equivalent.</u>

<u>(i) m is a j-initial mapping.</u>

<u>(ii) m is a bounded j-mapping of $[x]_A$ into c_B.</u>

Proof. If (ii) holds, then (i) follows directly from definitions.

Let (i) hold. Clearly, m is a j-mapping of $[x]_A$ into c_B. If either (jB) or (jC) holds, m is bounded. Let (jA) be satisfied. Then $g_A(o_A^n(x)) = \infty = g_B(o_B^n(x'))$ for any n, $0 \leq n < \omega$ which implies the boundedness of m. □

<u>10. Let (A,B) ∈ jAD, let m be a mapping of A into B. Then the following assertions are equivalent.</u>

<u>(i) m is a j-mapping.</u>

<u>(ii) m is a j-extension of a j-initial mapping.</u>

Proof. If (i) holds and (x,x′) is an arbitrary j-pair for (A,B), then $n = m \cap ([x]_A \times c_B)$ is a j-initial mapping by 9 and 4 and m is a j-extension of n by 8. Thus, (ii) holds.

If (ii) holds, then m is a j-extension of a bounded j-mapping defined on a closed submachine of A by 9. Then (i) follows by 8. □

<u>11. Let A, B be connected machines, m a mapping of A into B. Then the following assertions are equivalent.</u>

<u>(i) m is a j-mapping.</u>

<u>(ii) (A,B) ∈ jAD and m is a j-extension of a j-initial mapping.</u>

Proof. Clearly, (ii) implies (i) by 10. Let (i) hold. If $D_A \neq \emptyset$, we put $x = d_A$. If $Z_A \neq \emptyset$, we take an arbitrary $x \in Z_A$. If $D_A = \emptyset = Z_A$, we take an arbitrary $x \in c_A$. By 1.4, these cases exclude each other. We put $x' = m(x)$. By 4, we obtain exactly one of the cases (jA), (jB), (jC). Thus, (A,B) ∈ jAD and (i) implies (ii) by 10. □

<u>4. The general case</u>

The general case reduces to the case of connected machines.

<u>1. Let $j \in \{s,h\}$, let A, B be machines, m a mapping of A into B. Then the following assertions are equivalent.</u>

<u>(i) m is a j-mapping.</u>

<u>(ii) For any component C of A, there exists a component D of B and a j-mapping m_C of C into D such that $m = \bigcup_{C \in A/\varrho_A} m_C$.</u>

Proof. If (i) holds, we put $m_C = m \cap (c_C \times c_B)$ for any $C \in A/\varrho_A$. By 2.1, m_C is a j-mapping of C into B. It is easy to see that $(x,y) \in \varrho_A$

implies $(m(x),m(y)) \in \varrho_B$. Hence, there exists $D \in B/\varrho_B$ such that m_C is a mapping of C into D. Clearly, $m = \bigcup_{C \in A/\varrho_A} m_C$. Thus, (i) implies (ii). The reverse implication is obvious. □

References

(1) Pawlak, Z., Maszyny programowane. Algorytmy 10 (1969), 7-22.

(2) Stucky, W. and Walter, H., Minimal linear realizations of autonomous automata. Information and Control 16 (1970), 66-84.

(3) Novotný, M., O jednom problému z teorie zobrazení. Spisy vyd. Přír. Fak. Univ. Masaryk Brno, No 344 (1953), 53-64.

(4) Novotný, M., Über Abbildungen von Mengen. Pac. J. Math. 13 (1963), 1347-1359.

(5) Bartol, W., Programy dynamiczne obliczeń. Państwowe wydawnictwo naukowe, Warszawa 1974.

(6) Kopeček, O., Homomorphisms of machines. To appear.

(7) Kopeček, O., Monomorphisms of partial unary algebras. Unpublished manuscript.

(8) Pawlak, Z., oral communication, June 1975.

(9) Novotný, M., On simulations of machines. Lecture held at the 4th Symposium on Mathematical Foundations of Computer Science 1975, Mariánské Lázně, Sept. 1-5, 1975. This lecture is not included in the Proceedings of the Symposium.

RECENT RESULTS ON L SYSTEMS

Arto Salomaa
Mathematics Department
University of Turku, Finland

The purpose of this paper is to discuss certain recent aspects in the theory of L systems. Here "recent" means "after the 4th MFCS Symposium". We focus attention on three aspects only. Some other results are covered in [13]. We assume the reader to be familiar with basic L systems theory to the extent of one of the references [4], [5], [8] or [9]. (References [4] and [9] are general expositions. The former is much more comprehensive but the latter contains some more recent results. References [5] and [8] are collections of articles. The former contains also the most up-to-date bibliography available on L systems.)

1. Growth

Growth functions, i.e., functions indicating the growth in word length, are a special case of Z-rational formal power series. We begin with some problems discussed in [11] but we consider now L systems with tables. From the power series point of view this means series with several variables.

Consider a Z-rational formal power series

$$r = \sum_{w} (r,w)w$$

over an alphabet $X = \{x_1,\dots,x_n\}$. Thus, there are square matrices $M_1,\dots,M_n$, a row vector π and a column vector η, all of the same dimension and with integer entries, such that for each $w = x_{i_1}\dots x_{i_t}$ the coefficient of w in r satisfies

$$(r,w) = \pi M_{i_1}\dots M_{i_t}\eta .$$

The series is N-rational iff all entries in π, η and each M_i are nonnegative. An N-rational series is termed DT0L iff all entries in η

equal 1. A DT0L series is termed PDT0L iff every row in each of the matrices $M_1,\ldots,M_n$ contains at least one element greater than zero. In the special case of a one-letter alphabet, $n=1$, DT0L (resp. PDT0L) series are referred to as D0L (resp. PD0L) series. Note that n equals the number of tables, whereas the dimension of the matrices gives the cardinality of the alphabet of the L system involved.

In [11], several interconnections between the different types of series were discussed in case of a one-letter alphabet, and the results were applied to problems concerning merging and decidability. Similar interconnections can be obtained also in the general case. The proofs of our first two theorems run very much along the lines of the proofs of Theorems 1 and 2 in [11]. The proofs are carried out in detail in [12].

Theorem 1. Every Z-rational series can be represented as the difference of two DT0L series.

Theorem 2. For every Z-rational series r, there is a number u_o such that, for all integers $u \geq u_o$, the series r_1 defined by

$$(r_1,w) = u^{lg(w)+1} + (r,w)$$

is PDT0L.

Thus, we can always go from a Z-rational series to a PDT0L series by taking a big enough dominant term. By Theorem 2, we obtain now immediately the following stronger version of Theorem 1.

Theorem 3. Every Z-rational series can be represented as the difference of two PDT0L series.

The following theorem constitutes a basic lemma for proving undecidability results for DT0L and PDT0L series. The argument used in the proof of the theorem, due to M. Soittola, is an interesting application of Hilbert's Tenth Problem. More details along these lines will appear in [14].

Theorem 4. The following problems are undecidable for Z-rational series s over an alphabet X with two letters, $X = \{x,y\}$:

(i) Does s have at least one coefficient equal to 0?

(ii) Are all coefficients of s nonnegative?

Proof. We show that if we could decide (i), we would be solving Hilbert's Tenth Problem. For this purpose we construct, for a given integer polynomial P with u variables, a Z-rational series r over $\{x,y\}$ satisfying for all $n_i \geq 0$:

$$(r,x^{n_1}yx^{n_2}y\ldots x^{n_u}y) = P(n_1,\ldots,n_u).$$

For $i = 1,\ldots,u$, let r_i be the N-rational series defined by the following (i+1)-dimensional vectors and matrices:

$$\pi_i = (1\,0\,\ldots\,0) \quad , \quad \eta_i = (0\,\ldots\,0\,1)^T ,$$

$$M_i(x) = \left(\begin{array}{cccc|cc} 1 & & & & & \\ & 1 & 0 & & 0 & \\ 0 & & & 1 & & \\ \hline & & 0 & & 1 & 1 \\ & & & & 0 & 1 \end{array}\right) , \quad M_i(y) = \left(\begin{array}{cccc|cc} 0 & 1 & & 0 & & \\ & 0 & 1 & & 0 & \\ & 0 & & 1 & & \\ & & & 0 & 1 & \\ \hline & & 0 & & 0 & 0 \\ & & & & 0 & 1 \end{array}\right) .$$

It is easy to see that r_i satisfies

$$(r_i, x^{n_1}y\ldots x^{n_u}y) = n_i .$$

The series r can now be constructed from the series r_i by the rational operations used in the definition of the polynomial P.

Let now L_u be the complement of the (regular) language $x^*(yx^*)^{u-1}$ and s_u the (Z-rational) characteristic series of L_u. If we add the Hadamard square of r to s_u, we obtain a Z-rational series s which has at least one coefficient equal to 0 iff

$$P(n_1,\ldots,n_u) = 0$$

has a solution in nonnegative integers n_i.

Because all coefficients of the series $s-1$ are nonnegative iff no coefficient of s equals 0, we see that also (ii) is undecidable.

The next theorem deals with "merging" considered in [11]. We state only a weak version sufficient for our purposes but a stronger version, corresponding exactly to Theorem 7 in [11] is valid. The operator ODD is defined for words of odd length by

$$\mathrm{ODD}(b_1b_2\ldots b_{2n+1}) = b_1b_3\ldots b_{2n+1} .$$

For words w of even length, ODD(w) is undefined.

Theorem 5. For any Z-rational series r, there is a number u_o such that, for any integer $u \geq u_o$, the series s defined in the following way is DT0L:

$$(s,w) = u^{n+1} \quad \text{for} \quad \lg(w) = 2n,$$

$$(s,w) = u^{n+1} + (r,ODD(w)) \quad \text{for} \quad lg(w) = 2n+1.$$

Consider now the following four decision problems. In the statement of the problems r (resp. r_P) is a DTOL (resp. PDTOL) series, s is a PDOL series, all series being over the alphabet $\{x,y\} = X$ and PDOL series over the alphabet $\{x\}$. w is always a word over X, and b one of the two letters of X.

(1) Given s and r_P, decide whether $(s,x^n) \leq (r_P,w)$ holds for all n and w with $lg(w) = n$.

(2) Given r, decide whether $(r,w) \leq (r,wb)$ holds always.

(3) Given s and r_P, decide whether there exist n and w with $lg(w) = n$ such that $(s,x^n) = (r_P,w)$.

(4) Given r of which it is known that always $(r,w) \leq (r,wb)$, decide whether there exist w and b such that $(r,w) = (r,wb)$.

The intuitive meaning of these problems from the L systems point of view should be obvious. For instance, as regards problem (4), the meaning is the following. We are given a DTOL system with two tables. We know that no step in any derivation according to the system decreases the length of the string. We want to decide whether or not there is a sequence of tables w and a table b (i.e., one of the two in the system) such that the length of the string obtained by applying w equals that obtained by applying wb.

The following theorem is an almost immediate consequence of Theorems 2, 4 and 5. Although problems (1)-(4) are very "innocent looking", they turn out to be undecidable and are perhaps the simplest problems about L systems known to be undecidable. (There are even simpler problems whose decidability status is open.) The reader is referred also to [12], where some other problems of similar nature are considered.

Theorem 6. Each of the problems (1)-(4) is undecidable.

The work of Soittola, [15] and [16], cf. also [14] gives a complete characterization of PDOL, DOL and N-rational series over a one-letter alphabet. It is decidable whether a Z-rational series is of one of the three types mentioned, and whether an N-rational series is DOL, as well as whether a DOL series is PDOL. The condition characterizing N-rational series is the well known "Berstel condition" concerning the poles of minimal modulus of the generating function. The condition characteristic for DOL growth sequences is that such a sequence is not mergeable of parts with different growth orders. Finally, a growth sequence r_n is PDOL iff the sequence $r_{n+1} - r_n$ is N-rational. Using these results, a number of open problems can be solved. Of these we mention the DOL (growth) synthesis problem, the problem of constructing a strictly increasing DOL growth sequence which is not a PDOL growth sequence, and the problem of (considered in [11]) whether or not the quotient of two DOL series, provided it has integral coefficients, is always a DOL series. The answer to the last problem is "yes".

An eventually interesting notion might be that of a "differentiation function" introduced in [3]. For a DTOL system G, $d_G(n)$ equals the number of words derivable in exactly n steps. The functions d_G are somewhat related to growth functions but a more detailed specification is so far missing.

2. Forms

The notion of a grammar form was introduced in [1] as an attempt to define families of structurally similar grammars by means of one underlying grammar called a "grammar form" and an "interpretation" mechanism defining a family of grammars related to the given grammar form. The notion of a grammar form can be introduced for L systems as well. This seems to be well motivated because it will certainly aid to the understanding of the structure of "L grammars" (as regards problems such as what types of EOL systems suffice to generate all EOL languages). Furthermore, from a biological point of view, a family of related L systems can be interpreted as a "family" or "species" of organisms.

The study of L forms has been initiated in [6]. The results in [6] deal with EOL forms only. However, work concerning other types of forms, in particular ETOL forms, is in progress.

By definition, an EOL form F is just an EOL system, $F = (\Sigma,P,S,\Delta)$. (Here Σ is the total alphabet, Δ the terminal alphabet, P the production set, and S the initial letter.) An EOL system $F = (\Sigma',P',S',\Delta')$ is called an interpretation of F, in symbols F' int F iff there is a substitution μ defined on Σ such that the following conditions are satisfied:

(i) $\mu(A)$ is a subset of $\Sigma' - \Delta'$ for each A in $\Sigma - \Delta$.

(ii) $\mu(a)$ is a subset of Δ' for each a in Δ.

(iii) $\mu(\alpha)$ and $\mu(\beta)$ are disjoint for all $\alpha \neq \beta$.

(iv) P' is a subset of $\mu(P)$ (where $\mu(P)$ is defined in the obvious fashion).

(v) S' is in $\mu(S)$.

The family $Gr(F) = \{F' \mid F' \text{ int } F\}$ is referred to as the grammar family of F, and the family $La(F) = \{L(F') \mid F' \text{ int } F\}$ as the language family generated by F. Two EOL forms F_1 and F_2 are termed equivalent (resp. strictly equivalent) iff $La(F_1) = La(F_2)$ (resp. $Gr(F_1) = Gr(F_2)$). (We make the convention that languages differing by the empty word only are considered to be equal.)

For readers familiar with the theory of (ordinary) grammar forms, we would like to point out that our definition of interpretation differs from the one in [1] with respect to terminals: terminals are interpreted in the same way as nonterminals. Besides being more natural mathematically, our definition has also several advantages from the point of view of L systems. They are explained in [6]. Moreover the reason for the exceptional definition of interpretation of terminals in [1] (the obtained language families become semi-AFL's) is not an important issue in L systems theory.

It is clear that known decidability results concerning ordinary grammar forms carry over to the family $Gr(F)$. As regards the family $La(F)$, the situation is quite different. The basic lemma concerning ordinary grammar forms, according to which $La(F)$ is contained in $La(F')$, provided every production $A \rightarrow x$ in F can be simulated by a derivation $A \Rightarrow^* x$ according to F', is not valid for EOL forms. For the latter, the situation is much more complicated. Some substitutes for this basic lemma have been established in [6].

Theorem 7. For every EOL form an equivalent EOL form can be constructed such that the productions in the latter are of the types

$$A \rightarrow a, \quad A \rightarrow BC, \quad A \rightarrow B, \quad a \rightarrow A,$$

where A, B, C are nonterminals (not necessarily distinct and a is terminal.

An EOL form is termed complete iff its language family equals the whole family of EOL languages. No exhaustive characterization for completeness is known, although a number of necessary, as well as a number of sufficient conditions have been established in [6]. Rather than going into them explicitly, we mention below some typical examples F_1-F_3 (resp. H_1-H_3) of complete EOL forms (resp. of non-complete EOL forms). In each case, only the productions are listed.

F_1: $S \to a$, $S \to S$, $S \to SS$, $a \to S$

F_2: $S \to a$, $S \to S$, $S \to Sa$, $a \to S$

F_3: $S \to A$, $A \to S$, $A \to SS$, $A \to a$, $a \to A$

H_1: $S \to a$, $S \to S$, $S \to aa$, $a \to S$

H_2: $S \to a$, $S \to S$, $a \to S$, $S \to SSS$

H_3: $S \to A$, $A \to S$, $S \to SS$, $A \to a$, $a \to A$

Note the similarity between F_3 and H_3. However, F_3 is complete and H_3 is not complete.

In addition to EOL forms, one can consider also so-called pure forms having just one alphabet (as OL systems have). The distinction between terminals and nonterminals will be made in interpretations only.

It is well known that some L families have very weak, and some others strong closure properties. Therefore, it is not surprising that, for EOL forms F, the family La(F) is sometimes an AFL, sometimes an anti-AFL.

3. Squeezing

The basic language definition mechanism for rewriting systems is the exhaustive one: one accepts to the language all words generated according to the productions. One can also consider various selective mechanisms. In case of sequential rewriting, the only widely studied selective mechanism is to intersect the language obtained by the set of words of a terminal alphabet, i.e., to accept only those generated words which are over a specific terminal alphabet. In L systems theory quite a number of different selective definition mechanisms (ways of "squeezing" a language out of a system) have been investigated. As typical examples we mention references [2] and [7].

We discuss now briefly new definitional mechanisms introduced in [10]. Consider an L system G defining its language in the exhaustive way, such as a OL, TOL, DOL or DTOL system. Fix a subset of the production set of G (whose elements are referred to as "good" productions). In case of systems with tables, the set of good productions may be different for each table. In the production-universal (resp. production-existential) definition of the language, only those words in L(G) are accepted which possess a derivation such that at the last step every production (resp. at least one production) applied is good. These two definition mechanisms are denoted by $\forall_p$ and $\exists_p$. Thus, we may speak of $\forall_p$ 0L or $\exists_p$ DT0L languages, etc. From a biological point of view, one is led naturally to these definitions if one wants to consider only certain stages in the development.

Similarly, one may specify a subset of the alphabet of G (consisting of letters referred to as "good"). In the letter-existential definition of the language, only those words in L(G) are accepted which contain at least one good letter. The notation for letter-existential definition is $\exists_l$. (Clearly, the analogous letter-universal definition mechanism coincides with the familiar E-mechanism.)

As a sample result, we mention the following theorems about mutual relations among the language families thus obtained. In general, if the underlying L structure is strong enough (such as a table structure) then the different definitional mechanisms coincide in generative capacity, whereas strict inclusion and incomparability results are obtained for weaker underlying L structures.

Theorem 8. $\exists_l$ D0L $\subsetneq$ $\exists_p$ D0L $\subsetneq$ CD0L. $\forall_p$ D0L = ED0L and the family is incomparable with both of the existential families.

Theorem 9. $\exists_l$ 0L $\subsetneq$ $\exists_p$ 0L $\subsetneq$ $\forall_p$ 0L = E0L,

$\exists_l$ T0L = $\exists_p$ T0L = $\forall_p$ T0L = ET0L,

$\exists_l$ DT0L = $\exists_p$ DT0L = $\forall_p$ DT0L = EDT0L.

References

1 A. Cremers and S. Ginsburg: Context-free grammar forms. JCSS 11 (1975) 86-117.

2 K. Culik II and J. Opatrny: Context in parallel rewriting. Contained in [8].

3 J. Dassow: Eine neue Funktion von DT0L-Systemen. EIK, to appear.

4 G. Herman and G. Rozenberg: Developmental Systems and Languages. North-Holland (1975).

5 A. Lindenmayer and G. Rozenberg (ed.): Automata, Languages, Development. At the Crossroads of Biology, Mathematics and Computer Science. North-Holland (1976).

6 H. Maurer, A. Salomaa and D. Wood: E0L forms. Technical Report, Inst. f. Angew. Informatik und Formale Beschreibungsverfahren, Univ. Karlsruhe (1976).

7 G. Rozenberg, K. Ruohonen and A. Salomaa: Developmental systems with fragmentation. Int. J. Comp. Math., to appear.

8 G. Rozenberg and A. Salomaa (ed.): L Systems. Springer Lecture

Notes in Computer Science 15 (1974).

9 G. Rozenberg and A. Salomaa: The mathematical theory of L systems. To appear in J. Tou (ed.), Advances in Information Systems Science, Vol. 6.

10 G. Rozenberg and A. Salomaa: New squeezing mechanisms for L systems. UIA, Antwerpen, Publ. 76-06 (1976).

11 A. Salomaa: Formal power series and growth functions of Lindenmayer systems. Springer Lecture Notes in Computer Science 32 (1975) 101-113.

12 A. Salomaa: Undecidable problems concerning growth in informationless Lindenmayer systems. EIK, to appear.

13 A. Salomaa: L systems: a parallel way of looking at formal languages. Lecture notes for the 2nd Advanced Course on Foundations of Computer Science, Amsterdam (1976).

14 A. Salomaa and M. Soittola: Automata-Theoretic Aspects of Formal Power Series. Springer Verlag, in preparation.

15 M. Soittola: Remarks on DOL growth sequences. Revue Francaise Informatique Theoretique, to appear.

16 M. Soittola: Positive rational sequences. Theoretical Computer Science, to appear.

DECISION PROBLEMS FOR MULTI-TAPE AUTOMATA

Peter H. Starke
Sektion Mathematik
der Humboldt-Universität zu Berlin
DDR-1086 Berlin, PSF 1297

Abstract

The paper reviews the solvability resp. unsolvability of decision problems for the relations represented by deterministic and nondeterministic multi-tape automata with or without endmarker on the one hand and the solvability resp. unsolvability of decision problems for the languages defined by the same types of automata on the other hand. The first section presents results on the inclusions between the different classes of relations and languages under consideration. The second section deals with decision problems for relations. The main new result here is that all the considered problems are decidable for autonomous relations. The last section contains the results on the solvability resp. unsolvability of decision problems for languages. These results are sharpenings of known ones, some of them are entirely new.

1. Inclusions

We here make use of the definitions and notations introduced in the paper [10]. Moreover, for $n \geq 2$ and a fixed finite nonempty alphabet X not containing the symbol + (which is used as an endmarker) let be $\mathcal{R}_d^{(n)}$ (resp. $\mathcal{R}_{nd}^{(n)}$) the class of all n-ary relations $R \subseteq \bigtimes_n W(X)$ such that there exists a finite deterministic (resp. nondeterministic) n-tape automaton $\underline{B}$ with $R = R(\underline{B})$, and, $\mathcal{R}_{d,+}^{(n)}$ (resp. $\mathcal{R}_{nd,+}^{(n)}$) the set of all n-ary relations $R \subseteq \bigtimes_n W(X)$ such that there exists a finite deterministic (resp. nondeterministic) n-tape automaton $\underline{B}$ with the input alphabet $X \cup \{+\}$ such that

$$R = R_+(\underline{B}) = \{ q \mid q \in \bigtimes_n W(X) \wedge q\vec{+}^n \in R(\underline{B})\},$$

where $\vec{p}^n = [p,p,\ldots,p] \in \bigtimes_n W(X\cup\{+\})$ for every $p \in W(X\cup\{+\})$. Finally let be $\mathcal{R}_o^{(n)}$ the class of all regular languages R over the alphabet $\bigtimes_n X$ considered as relations over W(X).

The sets just defined are related as follows

Theorem 1. $\mathcal{R}_o^{(n)} \subset \mathcal{R}_d^{(n)} \subset \mathcal{R}_{d,+}^{(n)} \subset \mathcal{R}_{nd}^{(n)} = \mathcal{R}_{nd,+}^{(n)}$.

The equality $\mathcal{R}_{nd}^{(n)} = \mathcal{R}_{nd,+}^{(n)}$ is nearly obvious. We remark that the set $\mathcal{R}_{nd}^{(n)}$ is the set of all n-regular relations over W(X) (cf. [10]) which in the case that n = 2 coincides with the set of all rational transductions (cf. [1]). Mirkin [5] has shown that a relation $R \subseteq W(\bigtimes_n X)$ is an element of $\mathcal{R}_o^{(n)}$ iff R is in $\mathcal{R}_{nd}^{(n)}$, and that $R \in \mathcal{R}_{nd}^{(n)}$ iff $R \in \mathcal{R}_d^{(n)}$, which makes the first proper inclusion obvious. To see that the remaining two inclusions are proper we recall that $\mathcal{R}_{d,+}^{(n)}$ is closed under complementation and that $\mathcal{R}_{nd}^{(n)}$ is not closed under complementation (cf. [2],[14]).

For finite ND-n-TA $\underline{B}$ (resp. $\underline{B}_+$) with the input alphabet X (resp. $X\cup\{+\}$) we define the language

$$L(\underline{B}) = \{p \mid p \in W(X) \wedge \vec{p}^n \in R(\underline{B})\} \; (L_+(\underline{B}_+) = \{p \mid p \in W(X) \wedge \vec{p}^n \in R_+(\underline{B}_+)\})$$

so that $L(\underline{B})$ (resp. $L_+(\underline{B}_+)$ is the diagonal $D(R) = \{p \mid \vec{p}^n \in R\}$ of the relation $R = R(\underline{B})$ (resp. $R_+(\underline{B}_+)$). Moreover, let be

$$\mathcal{L}_d^{(n)} = \{D(R) \mid R \in \mathcal{R}_d^{(n)}\},\quad \mathcal{L}_{d,+}^{(n)} = \{D(R) \mid R \in \mathcal{R}_{d,+}^{(n)}\} \text{ and}$$

$$\mathcal{L}_{nd}^{(n)} = \{D(R) \mid R \in \mathcal{R}_{nd}^{(n)}\}.$$

As usual we denote by $\mathcal{L}_1$ (resp. $\mathcal{L}_3$) the set of all context-sensitive (resp. regular) languages over X.

Theorem 2. If $\mathrm{card}(X) \geq 2$ then $\mathcal{L}_3 \subset \mathcal{L}_d^{(n)} \subset \mathcal{L}_{d,+}^{(n)} \subset \mathcal{L}_{nd}^{(n)} \subset \mathcal{L}_1$.

The inclusions $\subseteq$ obviously follow from Theorem 1 above and from

Theorem 1 in [13] which says that all the diagonals of n_regular relations are context-sensitive languages. Since $\mathcal{L}_3$ and $\mathcal{L}_{d,+}^{(n)}$ are closed under complementation (cf. [8], Th. 4) from the following Lemma 1.1 we obtain that the first two inclusions are proper.

Lemma 1.1. $\mathcal{L}_d^{(n)}$ is not closed under complementation.

Proof. Consider for $a,b \in X$ the language

$$L = \{a^k b^k \mid k \geq 1\}.$$

A deterministic 2-TA $\underline{A}$ with $L(\underline{A}) = L$ is given by the deterministic regular expression (cf. [10], [11])

$$T = \langle [a,1] \rangle [b,1] [a,2] \langle [a,2] [b,1] \rangle [b,2] \langle [b,2] \rangle,$$

thus $L \in \mathcal{L}_d^{(2)}$. Since for $R \in \mathcal{R}_d^{(i)}$, $j > 0$ the relation

$$R^{*j} = \{[p_1,\dots,p_i,\underbrace{p_i,\dots,p_i}_{j \text{ times}}] \mid [p_1,\dots,p_i] \in R\}$$

is an element of $\mathcal{R}_d^{(i+j)}$, we obtain $\mathcal{L}_d^{(2)} \subseteq \mathcal{L}_d^{(n)}$ for all $n \geq 2$, and consequently, $L \in \mathcal{L}_d^{(n)}$.

Now assume that $\bar{L} = \{p \mid p \in W(\{a,b\}) \wedge p \notin L\} \in \mathcal{L}_d^{(n)}$. Since $\mathcal{L}_d^{(n)}$ is obviously closed under intersection with regular languages we obtain

$$L' = \bar{L} \cap \langle\{a\}\rangle\langle\{b\}\rangle = \{e\} \cup \{a^k b^l \mid k,l \geq 0 \wedge k \neq l\} \in \mathcal{L}_d^{(n)}.$$

Let $\underline{A}' = (n,\{a,b\},Z,\tau,\delta,z_1,M)$ be a finite deterministic n-TA with $L' = L(\underline{A}')$. Since for all $k \geq 0$ we have $a^k \in L'$, for all $k \geq 0$ the state $\bar{\delta}(z_1,\overrightarrow{(a^k)}^n)$ is defined and an element of M. From the finiteness of M it follows that there exist numbers i and j with $i \neq j$ and $\bar{\delta}(z_1,\overrightarrow{(a^i)}^n) = \bar{\delta}(z_1,\overrightarrow{(a^j)}^n)$. By $a^i b^j \in L'$, $\bar{\delta}(z_1,\overrightarrow{(a^i b^j)}^n)$ is defined and an element of M. Now we obtain the contradiction

$$\bar{\delta}(z_1,\overrightarrow{(a^i b^j)}^n) = \bar{\delta}(\bar{\delta}(z_1,\overrightarrow{(a^i)}^n),\overrightarrow{(b^j)}^n)$$

$$= \bar{\delta}(\bar{\delta}(z_1,\overrightarrow{(a^j)}^n),\overrightarrow{(b^j)}^n) = \bar{\delta}(z_1,\overrightarrow{(a^j b^j)}^n) \notin M.$$

This proves Lemma 1.1.

The proper inclusion $\mathcal{L}_{d,+}^{(n)} \subset \mathcal{L}_{nd}^{(n)}$ is a consequence of the

Lemma 1.2. $\mathcal{L}_{nd}^{(n)}$ is not closed under complementation.

This proposition follows from the closedness of $\mathcal{L}_{nd}^{(n)}$ under union, the De Morgan's law and the

Lemma 1.3. $\mathcal{L}_{nd}^{(n)}$ is not closed under intersection.

Proof. Let be $t = \frac{n}{2}(n-1)+1$ and

$$L_n = \left\{ a^{m_1}ba^{m_2}b\ldots a^{m_t}bba^{m_t}ba^{m_{t-1}}b\ldots a^{m_2}ba^{m_1} \mid \bigwedge_{i=1}^{t} m_i \geq 1 \right\}.$$

In the paper [8], Rosenberg proves that $L_n \notin \mathcal{L}_{d,+}^{(n)}$. The same argument shows that $L_n \notin \mathcal{L}_{nd}^{(n)}$. Now consider for $j = 1,\ldots,t$ the language

$$L_n^{(j)} = \left\{ a^{m_1}ba^{m_2}b\ldots a^{m_t}bba^{m_{t+1}}b\ldots a^{m_{2t-1}}ba^{m_{2t}} \mid \bigwedge_{i=1}^{2t} m_i \geq 1 \wedge m_j = m_{2t-j+1} \right\}.$$

Clearly, $L_n^{(j)} \in \mathcal{L}_d^{(n)} \subseteq \mathcal{L}_{nd}^{(n)}$ and

$$L_n = \bigcap_{j=1}^{t} L_n^{(j)},$$

which proves Lemma 1.3.

Finally, the proper inclusion $\mathcal{L}_{nd}^{(n)} \subset \mathcal{L}_1$ follows from the fact that the context-free language $L = \{ paa\overleftarrow{p} \mid p \in W(\{a,b\}) \setminus W(\{a,b\})\{aa\}W(\{a,b\}) \}$ is in $\mathcal{L}_{nd}^{(n)}$ for no integer n (cf. [8], Th. 5), where $\overleftarrow{p}$ denotes the mirror image of p.

The assumption that X contains at least two letters is essential since we have (cf. [13], Th. 3):

Theorem 3. If card(X) = 1 then $\mathcal{L}_3 = \mathcal{L}_{nd}^{(n)}$.

Finally let us remark that the classes of languages under consideration form three hierarchies:

Theorem 4. If card(X) ≥ 2 then $\mathcal{L}_d^{(n)} \subset \mathcal{L}_d^{(n+1)}$, $\mathcal{L}_{d,+}^{(n)} \subset \mathcal{L}_{d,+}^{(n+1)}$ and $\mathcal{L}_{nd}^{(n)} \subset \mathcal{L}_{nd}^{(n+1)}$.

This follows from the fact that, if $R \in \mathcal{R}_{d}^{(n)}$ resp. $\mathcal{R}_{d,+}^{(n)}$ resp. $\mathcal{R}_{nd}^{(n)}$, then $R^{\times 1} \in \mathcal{R}_{d}^{(n+1)}$ resp. $\mathcal{R}_{d,+}^{(n+1)}$ resp. $\mathcal{R}_{nd}^{(n+1)}$ on the one hand and from the proof of Theorem 3 in [8], which shows that the language L_n defined above is an element of $\mathcal{L}_{d}^{(n+1)} \setminus \mathcal{L}_{nd}^{(n)}$.

Considering the languages L_n, L' defined above and the language

$$L'' = \{psp \mid p,s \in W(\{a,b\}) \wedge p \neq e\} \in \mathcal{L}_{nd}^{(2)}$$

one can see that the three hierarchies of Theorem 4 are pairwise incomparable.

2. Decision problems concerning relations

In this section we give a review of the solvability resp. unsolvability of decision problems for finite multi-tape automata with respect to the relations represented by them. The results are presented by the following Table 1 (see next page). Thereby the entry "n" (resp. "a") indicates that the property in question is never (resp. always) fullfilled and the entry "s" or "S" (resp."u" or "U") indicates that the corresponding problem is solvable (resp. unsolvable). The solvability (resp. unsolvability) of a problem marked by a capital letter implies the solvability (resp. unsolvability) of the problems in the same row marked by the same lower case letter. The problems marked by "?" are open.

To prove Theorem 5 below we need some preliminary considerations relating n-regular relations over a one-letter alphabet with semilinear sets.

Definition. Let be $n \geq 2$ fixed. A set $S \subseteq \times_n nz$ is said to be linear if there exist an integer $k \geq 0$ and vectors $v_o,\ldots,v_k \in \times_n nz$ such that $S = \{v_o + \bigwedge_{i=1}^{k} a_i v_i \mid a_i \in nz\}$. The (k+1)-tuple $V = [v_o,\ldots,v_k]$ is called

Table 1

$R_1, R_2 \in$	card(X) = 1 $\mathcal{R}_d^{(n)}$	$\mathcal{R}_{d,+}^{(n)}$	$\mathcal{R}_{nd}^{(n)}$	card(X) ≥ 2 $\mathcal{R}_d^{(n)}$	$\mathcal{R}_{d,+}^{(n)}$	$\mathcal{R}_{nd}^{(n)}$	Reference
1. Emptiness $R_1 = \emptyset$?	s	s	s	s	s	S	[2], Th. 5
2. Universe $R_1 = \times_n W(X)$?	n	s'	S'	n	S"	U	S': Th.5 below S": [2], Th. 5 U : [2], Th. 8
3. Finiteness R_1 finite ?	s	s	s	s	s	s	[2], Th. 5
4. Cofiniteness $\bar{R}_1$ finite ?	n	s'	S'	n	S"	U	S': Th.5 below S": [2], Th. 5 U : [2], Th. 8
5. Disjointness $R_1 \cap R_2 = \emptyset$?	s	s	S	U	u	u	S: Th. 5 below U: [14], Th. 2
6. Containment $R_1 \subseteq R_2$?	s	s	S	U	u	u	S: Th. 5 below U: [14], Th. 2
7. Equivalence $R_1 = R_2$?	s	s	S	?	?	U	S: Th. 5 below U: [2], Th. 8
8. $R_1 \in \mathcal{R}_d^{(n)}$?	a	s	S	a	?	U	S: [12], Th. 7 U: [14], Th. 2
9. $R_1 \in \mathcal{R}_{d,+}^{(n)}$	a	a	S	a	a	U	S: Corr.6 below U: [2], Th. 9

a representation of S. A set $S \subseteq \times_n nz$ is called semilinear if there exist a number $l \geq 0$ of linear sets $S_1, \dots, S_l$ (with representations $V_1, \dots, V_l$) such that $S = \bigcup_{i=1}^{l} S_i$; $\{V_1, \dots, V_l\}$ then is a representation of S.

For $x \in X$, $v = [i_1, \dots, i_n] \in \times_n nz$ let be $x^v = [x^{i_1}, \dots, x^{i_n}]$.

Lemma 2.1. For every finite autonomous ND-n-TA $\underline{B}$ with the input alphabet $X = \{x\}$ the set

$$S(\underline{B}) = \{v \mid v \in \times_n nz \wedge x^v \in R(\underline{B})\}$$

is semilinear and a representation of $S(\underline{B})$ can be constructed effectively.

Proof. By Theorem 19 in [11] we can construct a regular expression T over $Y_n = \{x\}\times\{1,\ldots,n\}$ such that $\underline{\text{Wert}}_n(T) = R(\underline{B})$. We consider the Parikh-mapping ψ_n over $W(Y_n)$ defined by the equations

$$\psi_n(e) = [0,\ldots,0] \in \times_n nz, \quad \psi_n([x,i]) = [0,\ldots,0,\underset{i}{1},0,\ldots,0],$$
$$\psi_n(qy) = \psi_n(q) + \psi_n(y) \qquad (1 \leq i \leq n,\ q \in W(Y_n),\ y \in Y_n).$$

Next we show by induction on q that for all $q \in W(Y_n)$ it holds

$$p_n(q) = x^{\psi_n(q)}.$$

For $q = e$ we have $p_n(e) = [e,\ldots,e] = x^{[0,\ldots,0]} = x^{\psi_n(e)}$. For $y = [x,i] \in Y_n$ it holds $p_n(y) = [e,\ldots,e,\underset{i}{x},e,\ldots,e] = x^{\psi_n(y)}$, thus

$$p_n(qy) = p_n(q)\,p_n(y) = x^{\psi_n(q)}x^{\psi_n(y)} = x^{\psi_n(q)+\psi_n(y)} = x^{\psi_n(qy)}.$$

Now we have for $v \in \times_n nz$

$$\begin{aligned} v \in S(\underline{B}) \text{ iff } & x^v \in R(\underline{B}) \\ \text{iff } & \exists q(\, q \in \text{Wert}(T) \wedge p_n(q) = x^v\,) \\ \text{iff } & \exists q(\, q \in \text{Wert}(T) \wedge \psi_n(q) = v\,) \\ \text{iff } & v \in \psi_n(\text{Wert}(T)). \end{aligned}$$

Since Wert(T) is a regular language, $S(\underline{B}) = \psi_n(\text{Wert}(T))$ is semilinear and a representation of $S(\underline{B})$ can be constructed effectively (cf. [6]).

The converse of Lemma 2.1 holds true too

Lemma 2.2. For every semilinear set S the relation $R(S) = \{x^v \mid v \in S\}$ is representable by a finite autonomous nondeterministic multitape automaton.

Since $\mathcal{R}_{nd}^{(n)}$ is closed under union it suffices to prove the assertion for linear sets. Let be $S \subseteq \times_n nz$ a linear set with the representation $V = [v_0,\dots,v_1]$. Then $R(S) = x^{v_0} \cdot \langle\{x^{v_1},\dots,x^{v_1}\}\rangle$ is obviously n-regular.

Theorem 5

1. There are algorithms which for autonomous finite ND-n-TA $\underline{B}$, $\underline{B}'$ with the input alphabet $\{x\}$ construct autonomous finite ND-n-TA $\underline{B}_1$, $\underline{B}_2$ with $R(\underline{B}_1) = R(\underline{B}) \cap R(\underline{B}')$, $R(\underline{B}_2) = \overline{R(\underline{B})}$, hence, $\mathcal{L}^{(n)}_{nd}(\{x\})$ is a Boolean algebra of sets.
2. The universe problem, the cofiniteness problem, the disjointness problem, the containment problem and the equivalence problem are solvable for finite autonomous ND-n-TA.

Proof. By Lemma 2.1 and Lemma 2.2 all the assertions and problems of Theorem 5 are carried over to assertions and problems for semilinear sets which are positively solved in the paper [3].

Corollary 6. For n-regular relations R over $W(\{x\})$ one can decide effectively whether $R \in \mathcal{R}^{(n)}_{d,+}$.

Proof. Let be $\underline{B}_+$ a finite ND-n-TA with the input alphabet $\{x,+\}$ such that $R = R_+(\underline{B}_+)$. There exists a deterministic n-TA $\underline{A}_+$ with the input alphabet $\{x,+\}$ and $R = R_+(\underline{A}_+)$ iff there is such an automaton $\underline{A}_+$ having at most as much states as $\underline{B}_+$. Since there are only finitely many deterministic n-TA-s with at most as much states as $\underline{B}_+$ by the solvability of the equivalence problem the assertion follows.

3. Decision problems concerning languages

The last portion of the present paper is devoted to an investigation of decision problems for finite multi-tape automata with respect to the languages defined by them. The results given by Table 2 below are mainly sharpenings of results by Rosenberg [8] .

Table 2

	L, L' ∈	$\mathcal{L}_{d}^{(n)}$	$\mathcal{L}_{d,+}^{(n)}$	$\mathcal{L}_{nd}^{(n)}$	Reference
1. Emptiness	$L = \emptyset$?	U	u	u	Lemma 3.1
2. Universe	$L = W(X)$?	?	U	u	[8], Th. 8
3. Finiteness	L finite ?	U	u	u	Lemma 3.1
4. Cofiniteness	$\bar{L}$ finite ?	?	U	u	[8], Th. 8
5. Disjointness	$L \cap L' = \emptyset$?	U	u	u	Lemma 3.2
6. Containment	$L \subseteq L'$?	U	u	u	Lemma 3.2
7. Equivalence	$L = L'$?	U	u	u	Lemma 3.2
8.	$L \in \mathcal{L}_{d}^{(n)}$?	a	U	u	Lemma 3.3
9.	$L \in \mathcal{L}_{d,+}^{(n)}$?	a	a	U	Lemma 3.4
10.	$\bar{L} \in \mathcal{L}_{d}^{(n)}$?	U	u	u	Lemma 3.5
11.	$\bar{L} \in \mathcal{L}_{d,+}^{(n)}$?	a	a	U	Lemma 3.4
12.	$\bar{L} \in \mathcal{L}_{nd}^{(n)}$?	a	a	U	Lemma 3.6
13.	$L \in \mathcal{L}_{3}$?	U	u	u	Lemma 3.7
14.	$L \in \mathcal{L}_{2}$?	U	u	u	Lemma 3.7

In Table 2 the case that X is a singleton is not contained since in that case all the problems of Table 2 are solvable or trivial. This follows from the proof of Theorem 3 in [13] which supplies us with an algorithm constructing a type-3-grammar $\underline{G}$ with $L(\underline{G}) = L(\underline{B})$ for every finite autonomous ND-n-TA $\underline{\underline{B}}$.

In the sequel we prove a collection of Lemma's justifying Table 2. First we note that from Theorem 2 above it follows that it is sufficient to prove the first 7 undecidability results in the case that n = 2.

Lemma 3.1. Emptiness and finiteness are undecidable for $L \in \mathcal{L}_d^{(n)}$.

Proof. Let be Y a nonempty finite set and $\varphi, \psi : X \to W(Y)$ homomorphisms, moreover put

$$L_{\varphi,\psi} = \{p \mid p \in W(X) \setminus \{e\} \wedge \varphi(p) = \psi(p)\}.$$

Thus $L_{\varphi,\psi}$ is the set of solutions of the Post Correspondence Problem (PCP) (φ, ψ) over (X,Y). Now we have $L_{\varphi,\psi} = D(R_{\varphi,\psi})$, where

$$R_{\varphi,\psi} = \{[p,r] \mid p,r \in W(X) \setminus \{e\} \wedge \varphi(p) = \psi(r)\}.$$

One proves without difficulties that $R_{\varphi,\psi} \in \mathcal{R}_d^{(2)}$, hence $L_{\varphi,\psi} \in \mathcal{L}_d^{(2)}$. From the undecidability of the PCP which in fact is the question " $L_{\varphi,\psi} = \emptyset$?" the unsolvability of the emptiness problem follows. Since $L_{\varphi,\psi}$ is finite iff it is empty, we obtain the undecidability of the finiteness problem.

Lemma 3.2. Disjointness, Containment and Equivalence are undecidable for $L, L' \in \mathcal{L}_d^{(n)}$.

Obviously $\emptyset$, $W(X) \in \mathcal{L}_d^{(2)}$ and

$$L \cap W(X) = \emptyset \text{ iff } L \subseteq \emptyset \text{ iff } L = \emptyset,$$

so that Lemma 3.2 is an immediate consequence of Lemma 3.1.

Lemma 3.3. The question "$L \in \mathcal{L}_d^{(n)}$?" is undecidable for $L \in \mathcal{L}_{d,+}^{(n)}$.

Proof. Let be $a,b \notin X'$, $X = X' \cup \{a,b\}$, $X' \neq \emptyset$ and

$$L' = \{e\} \cup \{a^k b^l \mid k,l \geq 0 \wedge k \neq l\}.$$

Obviously, $L' \in \mathcal{L}_{d,+}^{(n)}$ for every $n \geq 2$. It is easy to see that for every

PCP (φ,ψ) over (X',Y) it holds

$$L_{\varphi,\psi}\cdot L' \in \mathcal{L}_{d,+}^{(n)} .$$

Next we show that

$$L_{\varphi,\psi}\cdot L' \in \mathcal{L}_{d}^{(n)} \text{ iff } L_{\varphi,\psi} = \emptyset,$$

from which our proposition follows.

Clearly, if $L_{\varphi,\psi} = \emptyset$, then $L_{\varphi,\psi}\cdot L' = \emptyset \in \mathcal{L}_{d}^{(n)}$. If $L_{\varphi,\psi} \neq \emptyset$ let be $p \in L_{\varphi,\psi}$ fixed. Assume for contradiction that $L_{\varphi,\psi}\cdot L' \in \mathcal{L}_{d}^{(n)}$. The closedness of $\mathcal{L}_{d}^{(n)}$ under forming of left-derivatives implies that

$$\partial_p(L_{\varphi,\psi}\cdot L') \in \mathcal{L}_{d}^{(n)}.$$ Since $\mathcal{L}_{d}^{(n)}$ is closed under intersection with regular languages we obtain

$$L' = \partial_p(L_{\varphi,\psi}\cdot L') \cap W(X')\cdot W(\{a,b\}) \in \mathcal{L}_{d}^{(n)}$$

which is in contradiction with a result achieved in the proof of Lemma 1.1.

Lemma 3.4. The question "$L \in \mathcal{L}_{d,+}^{(n)}$?" and "$\bar{L} \in \mathcal{L}_{d,+}^{(n)}$?" are undecidable for $L \in \mathcal{L}_{nd}^{(n)}$.

Consider the languages $L_n^{(j)} \subseteq W(\{a,b\})$, $j = 1,\dots,t$, defined in the proof of Lemma 1.3. We have $L_n^{(j)} \in \mathcal{L}_{d}^{(n)} \subseteq \mathcal{L}_{d,+}^{(n)}$, thus $\overline{L_n^{(j)}} \in \mathcal{L}_{d,+}^{(n)}$ and

$$\bar{L}_n = \bigcup_{j=1}^{t} \overline{L_n^{(j)}} \in \mathcal{L}_{nd}^{(n)},$$

therefore,

$$L_n' = L_{\varphi,\psi}\cdot \bar{L}_n \in \mathcal{L}_{nd}^{(n)},$$

where (φ,ψ) is as above. Since $\mathcal{L}_{d,+}^{(n)}$ is closed under forming of left-derivatives and under intersection with regular languages one can show in the same way as above (using $\bar{L}_n \notin \mathcal{L}_{d,+}^{(n)}$) that

$$L_n' \in \mathcal{L}_{d,+}^{(n)} \text{ iff } L_{\varphi,\psi} = \emptyset.$$

This proves Lemma 3.4.

Lemma 3.5. The question "$\bar{L} \in \mathcal{L}_{d}^{(n)}$?" is undecidable for $L \in \mathcal{L}_{d}^{(n)}$.

Proof. Let be $X = X' \cup \{a,b,c\}$, $a,b,c \notin X' \neq \emptyset$ and (φ,ψ) a PCP over (X',Y). Then $L_{\varphi,\psi} \in \mathcal{L}_d^{(n)}$, hence $\overline{L_{\varphi,\psi}}\cdot\{c\} \in \mathcal{L}_d^{(n)}$ and

$$L_{oo} = \overline{L_{\varphi,\psi}}\cdot\{c\}\cdot\{a^k b^k \mid k \geq 1\} \in \mathcal{L}_d^{(n)}.$$

One proves that

$$\overline{L_{oo}} \in \mathcal{L}_d^{(n)} \text{ iff } L_{\varphi,\psi} = \emptyset.$$

Lemma 3.6. The question "$\overline{L} \in \mathcal{L}_{nd}^{(n)}$?" is undecidable for $L \in \mathcal{L}_{nd}^{(n)}$.

To prove Lemma 3.6 one shows that

$$\overline{L_n'} \in \mathcal{L}_{nd}^{(n)} \text{ iff } L_{\varphi,\psi} = \emptyset.$$

Lemma 3.7. The questions "$L \in \mathcal{L}_3$?" and "$L \in \mathcal{L}_2$?" are undecidable for $L \in \mathcal{L}_d^{(n)}$.

This becomes obvious from the facts that

$$L_{\varphi,\psi}\cdot\{a^k ba^k ba^k \mid k \geq 1\} \in \mathcal{L}_d^{(n)},$$

$$L_{\varphi,\psi}\cdot\{a^k ba^k ba^k \mid k \geq 1\} \in \mathcal{L}_2 \text{ iff } L_{\varphi,\psi} = \emptyset \text{ and}$$

$$L_{\varphi,\psi}\cdot\{a^k ba^k ba^k \mid k \geq 1\} \in \mathcal{L}_3 \text{ iff } L_{\varphi,\psi} = \emptyset.$$

Thus all the assertions contained in Table 2 are proved. Using the methods applied in theese proofs one can show that it is undecidable whether a language defined by a n-tape automaton is definable by a (n-1)-tape automaton, i.e. the tape-number reduction problem is unsolvable.

References

[1] Berstel, J.: Memento sur les transductions rationelles. Inst. de Programmation, Univ. de Paris VI, N°IP 74-23 (1974).

[2] Fischer, P.C.; Rosenberg, A.L.: Multitape one-way nonwriting automata. J.Comp.Syst.Sci. 2 (1968), 88 - 101.

[3] Ginsburg, S.; Spanier, E.H.: Bounded ALGOL-like languages. Trans. Amer.Math.Soc. 113 (1964), 333 - 368.

[4] Makarevski, A.; Stotskaya, E.V.: Representability in deterministic multitape automata. Kibernetika (Kiev) 1969, No. 4 (in russian).

[5] Mirkin, B.G.: On the theory of multitape automata. Kibernetika (Kiev) 1966, No. 5, 12 - 18 (in russian).

[6] Parikh, J.R.: Language generating devices. MIT Res.Lab. of Electronics Quarterly Progress Rep., No. 60, 199 - 212 (1961).

[7] Rabin, M.O.; Scott, D.: Finite automata and their decision problems. IBM J. Res. Develop. 3 (1959) 125 - 144.

[8] Rosenberg, A.L.: On multi-head finite automata. IBM J. Res. Develop. 10 (1966) 2, 61 - 75.

[9] Salomaa, A.: Formal Languages. Academic Press, New York 1973.

[10] Starke, P.H.: On the representability of relations by deterministic and nondeterministic multi-tape automata. Lecture Notes in Comp. Sci. 32 (1975) 114 - 124.

[11] Starke, P.H.: Über die Darstellbarkeit von Relationen in Mehrbandautomaten. Elektron. Informationsverarb. u. Kybernetik (EIK) 12 (1976) 1/2, 61 - 81.

[12] Starke, P.H.: Entscheidungsprobleme für autonome Mehrbandautomaten. Z.Math.Logik Grundl.Math. 22 (1976) No.1 .

[13] Starke, P.H.: On the diagonals of n-regular relations. EIK 12 (1976) 6, 281 - 288.

[14] Starke, P.H.: Closedness properties and decision problems for finite multi-tape automata. Kybernetika (Praha) 12 (1976) 2, 61 - 75.

[15] Stotskaya, E.V.: On deterministic multitape automata without endmarker. Avtomatika i Telemehanika 9 (1971) 105 - 110 (in russian).

RECURSIVE PROGRAM SCHEMES AND COMPUTABLE FUNCTIONALS

B.A.Trakhtenbrot

Institute of Mathematics, Siberian Branch of
the USSR Academy of Sciences, Novosibirsk 630090

§0. Introduction

Modern high level programming languages have a broad assortment of modes, including procedures of high types; clearly this stimulates interest to computable functionals of high type. However, attention to them is also paid in the investigation of more elementary languages, that are oriented on functions of lower type. Thus in schematology, the important problem arises how to compare the power of different scheme languages: flow-charts, recursive schemes, schemes with counters, etc. In specifying a concrete programming language from a given scheme language concrete interpretations to the domain D, to the functions and the predicates, which are named in the scheme-signature, must be given. In summary any given particular program scheme in signature $\langle f_1,\dots,P_1,\dots,x_1,\dots,x_k\rangle$ can be interpreted as functional $F(f_1,\dots,P_1,\dots,x_1,\dots,x_k)$, which depends on functional (f_i), predicate (P_j) and individual (x_s) arguments, and yields only a single output value of the domain D. In our classification rank 2 is assigned (cf.§1) to such functionals; generally there exist functionals of arbitrary high ranks. Therefore, the hierarchy of scheme languages, which mirrors their expressing power is related to a hierarchy of functionals of rank 2. Hence, the important question arising in schematology, whether a well defined notion of universal computing scheme is possible , demands a preliminary formalization of the general notion of a computable functional and of those classes of computable functionals we are interested in. Approaches to such a formalization have been developed yet in the well known works of Gödel and Kleene. By this time definitions of high-typed computable functionals are elaborated that are worthy a status which is similar to that prescribed by the Church-thesis to the well known definition of lower type computable functions

We give some superficial explanations on this subject in §1; for more details the reader is refered to primary sources, e.g. to [3].

Besides computability other features of functionals must be mentioned which haven't yet got a definitive and universally accepted formalization. One of these features is connected with the fact that not every functional $F(f_1,\dots,P_1,\dots,x_k)$ - and even of rank 2 - may be considered as the behaviour of some program scheme. That is because such behaviour don't actually deal with the concrete character of the individuals in the basic domain D. E.g. the related functional may acquire the following form :

$$F(f_1,f_2,P,x,y) = \begin{cases} f_2(y,y) & \text{if } P(f_1(x,y)) \\ w \text{ (i.e. undefined)} & \text{otherwise} \end{cases}$$

Note that even if D is supposed to be the set of natural numbers, the numerical values of the individuals are not mirrored in the value the functional yields. Usually this phenomenon is refered to as a functional in an uninterpreted domain. In §1 and §4 we formalize it in terms of invariance and termality of functionals.

Also the parallelism phenomenon must be considered, which may be illustrated by well known function OR, a parallel variant of the logical disjunction. Namely, OR(x,y) is true if at least one of its argument is true, even if the other one is undefined (equals w). Here parallelism means rather some kind of inherent nondeterminism in the order the computations are to be implemented, than simultaneous implementation of computations. E.g. which argument of OR(x,y) should be computed firstly? The deterministic strategy starting with the computation of x(y) may fail when x(y) is the output of a nonterminating procedure ; but the computation of the alternative argument might happen to be resultative. The difference between sequential and parallel functionals seems to be evident on the intuitive level; nevertheless, a generally accepted formalization of these notions (by the way, computability must not be supposed) is not straightforward. In §5 we discuss some possible approaches to such a formalization and to the problem of supplying programming languages with some basic parallel functionals.

In this paper we summarize and systematize a certain material which deals with the relation between computability, invariance and parallelism on the one hand and language features which are able to express them on the other hand. As a main language model, typed recursive schemes are choosed; their semantics and implementation are considered in §§ 2-3. Interest to these topics was stimulated by the well known papers of D.Scott, M.Paterson, H.Strong, Z.Manna, R.Constable, J.Vuillemin. Mainly, results of V.Yu.Sazonov, M.B.Trakhtenbrot and of the author himself are surveyed.

§1 Functionals

Types. Let $D_\alpha, D_\beta, \ldots$ be sets, partially ordered by $\sqsubseteq_\alpha$, $\sqsubseteq_\beta, \ldots$ and containing a least undefined element w_α, $w_\beta, \ldots$ Total and continuous mappings from $D_\alpha \times \ldots \times D_\beta$ into D_γ, are briefly named functionals. The set of all such functionals is designated $D_{\alpha,\ldots,\beta\to\gamma}$; it is partially ordered by $f \sqsubseteq g =_{def} \forall x \in D_\alpha \ldots \forall y \in D_\beta (f(x,\ldots y) \sqsubseteq_\gamma g(x,\ldots,y))$ and has a least element $w_{\alpha,\ldots,\beta\to\gamma}$. Usually one-argument functionals are defined starting from a basic domain D_0, whose elements are said to be functionals of type o. Further by induction, given sets D_α and D_β of functionals of type α and type β, $D_{\alpha\to\beta}$ is the set of functionals of type $(\alpha\to\beta)$. And now - two remarks :

a) Literally - our definition assignes no types to many-argument functionals, e.g. to the two-argument functionals from $D_{\alpha,\beta\to\gamma}$. But really the well known technique is applicable, which eliminates special notations for many-argument functionals, e.g. in our considerations the identification of $D_{\alpha,\beta\to\gamma}$ with $D_{\alpha\to(\beta\to\gamma)}$ is allowed. Thus each many-argument functional of type $(\alpha_1, \alpha_2, \ldots, \alpha_k \to \beta)$ is uniquely represented by a functional of type $(\alpha_1 \to (\alpha_2 \to \ldots (\alpha_k \to \beta)\ldots))$. Hence, in addition to usual notations for application of functionals to their arguments - e.g. f(x), g(x,y,z) - also notations are used - e.g.(fx), (((gx)y)z) -which mirror the representation of many-argument functionals by one-argument functionals. Furthermore, current omitting parantheses is practised, e.g. we write $A_1 A_2 A_3 \ldots A_n$ instead of $(((A_1 A_2) A_3)\ldots A_n)$

b) Let us call <u>full functionals</u> those many-argument functionals of type $(\alpha_1, \alpha_2, \ldots, \alpha_k \to o)$ which yields a value from the basic domain D_0. Taking account of remark a) identification of each type with the associated full type is allowed. To full types ranks are assigned : the rank of type o is o ; the rank of type $\alpha \equiv (\alpha_1, \ldots, \alpha_k \to o)$ is n iff to all α_i rank $\leqslant$ n-1 is assigned and at least to one of them - rank n-1.

Computable functionals. Further the elements of D_0 are assumed to be constructive objects, and all of them except w are $\sqsubseteq$ incomparable with each other. Firstly, by induction, for each α the subset $D'_\alpha \subseteq D_\alpha$ of finite functionals of type α is defined : (1) $f \in D'_0 =_{def} f \in D_0$; $f \in D'_{\alpha\to\beta} =_{def} \exists a_1 \ldots a_n \in D'_\alpha \quad \exists b_1 \ldots b_n \in D'_\beta$ such that

$$\forall i(f(a_i) \equiv b_i) \text{ and } \forall x \in D_\alpha (f(x) \equiv \bigsqcup_{a_i \sqsubseteq x} f(a_i))$$

Thus finite functionals are constructive objects and hence recursive enumerable sets of finite functionals may be considered. At last, by definition functional g is computable iff it is effectively approximable by finite functionals, e.g.

$$\{f \mid f \text{ is finite and } f \sqsubseteq g\} \text{ is recursively enumerable}$$

Invariance. of a functional F means that it doesn't change while renaming elements in D_0 escept w. Given a 1-1 - mapping f of D_0 on D_0 and the inverse mapping $\bar{f}$ that preserve $\sqsubseteq$, for each functional $F \in D_\alpha$ F^f and $F^{\bar{f}}$ are defined by induction. For $F \in D_0$, $F^f =_{def} fF$, $F^{\bar{f}} =_{def} \bar{f}F$. For $\alpha \equiv (\beta \to \gamma)$ F^f (and by the analogy $F^{\bar{f}}$) are characterized by the condition:

$$\forall x \in D_\beta \ (F^f x \equiv (F x^{\bar{f}})^f) \tag{1}$$

At last, F is said to be invariant iff

$$\forall f \ (F^f \equiv F) \tag{2}$$

Usually in the basic domain some constants $a_0, \ldots, a_k$ are considered and in accordance with them, condition (2) is to be replaced by

$$\forall f \text{ preserving } a_0, \ldots a_k \ (F^f \equiv F) \tag{2'}$$

We confine oneself to two basic constants, designated by 0,1, that eventually may be interpreted as boolean values false and true

Examples of invariant computable functionals.

Rank 1. There are only a few invariant one-argument functionals and all of them are computable : the identity function f $-\forall x(fx = x)$, the constant functions g,h $-\forall x\,(gx \equiv 0)$, $\forall x(hx \equiv 1)$ and some other insignificant modifications of them. Among many-argument functionals monotonic equality = , parallel disjunction OR, conditional functions if, IF and "voting" functions Γ, Γ' are worthy of noting (don't confuse equality relation = defined below with ordinary ≡ which is not monotonic; also remenber, that in our definitions cases are omitted, when the value of the functional is undefined, i.e.it equals w).

a) x=y≡1 if x≡y≢w; x=y≡0 if w≢x≢y≢w

b) OR(x,y)≡1 if x≡1 $\vee$ y≡1; OR(x,y)≡0 if x≡0 and y≡0

c) if1yz≡IF1yz≡y; if0yz≡IF0yz≡z; IFxyy≡y

d) Γxxy≡ Γxyx≡ Γyxx≡x;

e) Γ'11x≡1; Γ'xoo≡o; Γ'xyx≡x if x≢o and x≢1

Rank 2. We define below full functionals F_1, F_2, F_3, F_4, F_5 where f,g denote arguments of type (o→o) and x,y,z - of type o:

F_1fg≡o if fw≡o; F_1fg≡1 if for k times g f(g(...g(1)...))≡1 k=1,2,3,...

F_2fxyz= Γ(fx)(fy)(fz); F fxyz= Γ'(fx)(fy)(fz)

F_4fx≡fx if fw≢w; F_4fx≡fx if for k times f f(f(...(fx)...))≡1 k=1,2,3,...

F_5fx≡x if for some y fy≡x

High type functionals. First of all we mention for each α the fix-point functional Y_α:

$\forall x \in D_{(\alpha\to\alpha)}(Y_\alpha x$ ≡ the least $y \in D_\alpha$ such that xy≡y

Furthermore, description of functionals by means of typed terms, which are built from the arguments, is obvious. Especially in such manner for each α, β, γ combinators S,K are defined;

Sxyz≡(xz)(yz); Kuz≡u;

where to z,u,x,y the types α, γ, $(\alpha\to\beta)$ and $(\alpha\to(\beta\to\gamma))$ are assigned.

§2. Recursive schemes. Semantics.

To express functionals of arbitrary finite types the language of recursive schemes (briefly - R-schemes) will be used. Following two features of R-schemes schould be mentioned though they are not usually kept in mind.

Firstly, an R-scheme must not be a finite set of recursive definitions ; an infinite enumerable set of definitions is allowed as well, since the mutual description of an infinite set of functionals is intended. Let $\phi = \{F_i\}$ be the set of typed symbols for the functionals to be defined by the scheme.

Secondely, in a given R-scheme for each F many definitions are allowed. If the type of F is associated with the full type ($\alpha_1, \dots, \alpha_k \rightarrow o$), each of its corresponding definitions is of the form

$$Fx_1x_2\dots x_k \Leftarrow t \qquad (1)$$

Here x_i are variables of type α_i, and the term t of type 0 is well formed from symbols in $\{x_1, \dots, x_k\} \cup \phi \cup \{if, =, 0, 1, w\}$

The R-scheme $\mathfrak{M}$ is <u>determinate</u> (Rdet - scheme), if to each F a unique definition exists; $\mathfrak{M}$ is <u>computable</u> if the set of all its definitions is recursively enumerable; $\mathfrak{M}$ is of rank $\leqslant$ n if all F_i have rank $\leqslant$ n. At last the R-scheme $\mathfrak{M}$ is <u>semantically consistent</u> if to the symbols F_i functionals of corresponding types can be assigned such that simultaneously the following statements hold

$$\forall x_1 \in D_{\alpha_1} \dots \forall x_k \in D_{\alpha_k} \; (Fx_1 \dots x_k \sqsupseteq \underline{t}); \qquad (2)$$

where in $\underline{t}$ symbols if, =,0,1 are interpreted as in §1. In the alternative case $\mathfrak{M}$ is semantically inconsistent.

Let $\mathfrak{M}$ be semantically consistent; then a unique least solution $\{F_i\}$ of the system (2) exists and each of these F_i is said to be expressed by $\mathfrak{M}$. Determinate R-scheme are always semantically consistent and functionals which are expressible by them can be defined as solution not only of (2) but also of

$$\forall x_1 \in D_{\alpha_1} \dots \forall x_k \in D_{\alpha_k} \; (Fx_1 \dots x_k \equiv \underline{t}) \qquad (2')$$

However in the general case one can not substitue (2') for (2).

<u>Theorem 1.</u> If a functional F of rank n is expressed by a (computable) R-scheme, then F is is invariant (and computable)and a (computable) R-scheme of rank n, expressing F, exists as well.

<u>Remark.</u> Mind you that functional F_5 from §1, though invariant and computable is expressible by no R-scheme.

<u>Theorem 2.</u> Among the functionals that are expressible by computable R-scheme : a) such exist that are expressible by no computable Rdet-schemes, though expressible by noncomputable Rdet-schemes

b) such exist that are inherently nondeterministic, i.e. that are expressible by no Rdet schemes (noncomputable ones included).

Theorem 2b is illustrated by the well known rank 1 functionals OR, IF and also by the voting function Γ which was defined for the first time in [12] and used there in describing all the inherently nondeterministic functionals of rank 1 (ref. Theorem 7 below).

Theorem 2a and the corresponding example appear firstly in [11].

Let the elements of D_0(except w) be named by the natural numbers 0,1,2,...; then one can consider the computable function of type $(o \to o)$ σ-the successor function, which of course isn't invariant. Furthermore, R(σ), Rdet(σ)-schemes and their semantics are defined like R and Rdet, whith difference only that in addition to if,=,0 symbol σ is allowed.

Theorem 3. The class of (computable) functionals coincides with the class of functionals, which are expressible by (computable) R(σ)-schemes.

This theorem is a straightforward modification of a statement, established in other terms in [6].

§3. Implementation.

Let $\{F_i\}$ be the set of invariant functionals, which are mutually expressed by an R-scheme $\mathfrak{M}$. Consider a constant typed term τ of type 0,i.e. a term that is well formed from if,=,0,1 and some of the F_i. According to the admited semantics the value of the term - denoted by val(r)-belongs to D_0. How may it be computed from $\mathfrak{M}$? I.e. what is the correct implementation of the language of R-schemes? In [13] this question is investigated by Vuillemin in connection with a particular case of rank 2 R-schemes. In [6] V.Yu.Sazonov stated a general theorem (the homomorphism theorem), which allows to extend the results from [13] on R-schemes of arbitrary rank (ref.Theorem 4 below). As in [13] we consider two transformation rules for constant term r :

1) Simplification rule. While it is possible, substitute for each subterm of the form a=b (where a,b=0,1,w) or of the form ifaAB its value. E.g. substitute 1 for 0=0 and B for if0AB.

2) Leftmost call rule: let r be of the form $Fr_1 \ldots r_k$,

where r_i are subterms and the head F is one of the functional symbols in $\{F_i\}$. If $Fx_1...x_k \leftarrow t$ is one of the corresponding definitions, the occurences of x_i in t are substituted by r_i and such transformed t is the needed result. Now let us suppose that the head of r is not in $\{F_i\}$, but nevertheless some F occurs in r . Then subterms r' of type 0 exist with the head in $\{F_i\}$ and among such subterms the leftmost must be transformed as above. Note that unlike simplification leftmost call must be realized in different ways, when $\mathfrak{M}$ is an undeterminate scheme.

The sequence $r^1, r^2, \ldots r^n, \ldots$ is said to be a computation generated by the constant term r if r^1 is r and each r^{i+1} is the result of simplification or leftmost call of r^i , assumed that always when simplification is possible, leftmost call is used only after accomplishing simplification. The computation is said to be complete if it is finite and neither simplification no leftmost call are applicable to its last member. Clearly, if $\mathfrak{M}$ is determinate each constant term r generates a unique computation; if in addition $\mathfrak{M}$ is computable so is the procedure generating the members of the computation.

The extension of all the notions and remarks pointed above on R(σ)-schemes and Rdet(σ)-schemes is obvious; the simplification rule must include supplemental cases concerning terms $\sigma(\sigma(\ldots\sigma(o)\ldots))$ interpreted as corresponding natural numbers.

It is easy to see, that given an R-scheme each complete computation may terminate only with one of the symbols 0,1,w and we shall say (confusion of semantical and syntactical notions is avoided by context) that the computation elaborates the corresponding value 0,1,w. By the analogy if $\mathfrak{M}$ is an R(σ)-scheme, complete computations elaborate w or natural numbers.

Theorem 4. For R-scheme val(r) can equal (semantically!) only w,0,1 and for $R(\sigma)$ -schemes - w,0,1,2,3,...; in any case each complete computation generated by r elaborates val(r) or w. If val(r)$\neq$w, there exists a computation, elaborating val(r).

§4. Rank 2.

In the introduction we have already mentioned the reason for special investigating rank 2 functionals. We describe below the language model of Strong-schemes (briefly - S-schemes) which is intended for expressing such functionals. As a matter of fact the version we consider here is not identical with Strong's one; some features from [10] are taken into account as well. Our main goal is to compare S-schemes with R-schemes (Theorem 5)in connection with some classification of important classes of rank 2 functionals (Theorem 6).

An S-scheme in a given signature $\langle f_1,\dots f_m, x_1,\dots,x_k\rangle$ is a sequence of constructions

$$k_1 \to t_1 \quad k_2 \to t_2 ;\dots \tag{1}$$

named S-computations, by means of which a functional of arguments $(f_1,\dots,f_m,x_1,\dots,x_k)$ is given. E.g. for the functional F defined by recursion

$$F(s,f,x) \Leftarrow \text{ if } \quad sx=0 \text{ then } x \text{ else } F(s,f,fx)$$

the corresponding S-scheme in the signature s,f,x is

$$sx=0 \to x; \qquad sx\neq 0,\ s(fx)=0 \to fx;$$

$$sx\neq 0,\ s(fx)\neq 0,\ s(f(fx))=0 \to f(fx);\dots$$

Now we pass to more accurate definitions. Terms of type 0 which are built from w,0,1 and signature symbols are said to be signature terms (briefly S-terms). In an S-computation $k\to t$, t is an S-term and k is a finite (or empty) sequence of premises of two kinds : equalities of S-terms, e.g. r=q and unequalities - e.g. $r\neq q$.

The S-scheme is said to be computable if the sequence (1) is computable. The following semantics is intended. Given a fixed interpretation $J\equiv\langle f_1^o,\dots,f_m^o,x_1^o,\dots,x_k^o\rangle$ of the signature all the S-terms get values in D_0; these values form a subset $D_0(J)$ of D_0. If in such case all the premises of a computation $k\to t$ are defined and true, the corresponding value of t should be declared as value of $Ff_1^o\dots,f_m^o x_1^o\dots,x_k^o$. It may however happen that in a given interpretation two S-computations $k_i\to t_i$ and $k_j\to t_j$ are suitable and moreover that the value of t_i and t_j are different from w and from each other. If so, the scheme is said to be <u>semantically inconsistent</u>; only semantically consistent S-schemes are to be considered and they express in a natural way functionals of rank 2.

It is easy to understand that a functional F expressed by an S-scheme, in addition to invariance have also the following "termality" property. Given an interpretation $J=\langle f_1^o,\dots,f_m^o,x_1^o,\dots,x_k^o\rangle$ let $f_1',\dots,f_m'$ coincide with $f_1^o,\dots,f_m^o$,on $D_0(J)$ and equal w otherwise; then the equality $F(f_1',\dots f_m',x_1^o,\dots,x_k^o)\equiv F(f_1^o,\dots,x_k^o)$ holds.

<u>Theorem 5.</u> In the class of rank 2 functionals the following characteristics are equivalent: (I) expressibility by (computable)

R-schemes, (II) expressibility by (computable) S-schemes, (III) termal invariance (and computability).

Formalizing in syntactical terms the notion of semantical consistency of S-schemes is actually a particular case of the analogous, but more general problem for R-schemes. We focus attention only on rank 2 functionals and S-schemes; the facts observed here suggest how to treat the general situation.

Given equalities of S-terms $q_1=r_1, q_2=r_2, \ldots, q_n=r_n$, $q=r$ we say that $q=r$ is a formal consequence of $\{q_i=r_i\}$

$$q_1=r_1, \ldots, q_n=r_n \models q=r$$

iff $q=r$ may be obtained from $\{q_i=r_i\}$ by the following rules :

1). Transivity : $q_i=q_j, q_j=q_k \models q_i=q_k$; 2). Symmetry : $q_i=q_j \models q_j=q_i$; 3). Substitution : $q=q' \models t=t'$, where t' is obtained from t by substituting q' for the subterm q of t. Given a set $\{q_i \approx r_i\}$ where $\approx$ means = either $\neq$, $q=r$ is said to be a formal consequence of $\{q_i \approx r_i\}$ if it is a formal consequence of its subset including only equalities. $\{q_i \approx r_i\}$ is formal inconsistent if it includes some $q_i \neq r_i$ such that $q_i=r_i$ is a formal consequence of $\{q_i \approx r_i\}$. Given an S-scheme M the following properties may be considered :

a) M is formal consistent $=_{def}$ for each computations $k_i \to t_i$ and $k_j \to t_j$ the implication holds : ($k_i \cup k_j$ formal consistent) $\longrightarrow$ $k_i \cup k_j \models t_i=t_j$

b) M is single-valued $=_{def}$ for arbitrary computations $k_i \to t_i$ and $k_j \to t_j (k_i \cup k_j)$ is formal inconsistent.

Consider a binary tree (perhaps infinite) whose leaves are labelled by S-terms but other vertices - by equalities $q_i=t_i$. To each path leading from the root to some leaf a computation is associated in a natural way.

c) S-scheme M is (effectively) tree-like if the set of its computations is generated by a (computable) tree.

Let S be the class of all the functionals expressible by computable S-schemes, Scons, Ssing, Stree its subclasses consisting of functionals expressible by computable S-schemes, that are correspondingly formal consistent, single-valued, effectively tree-like. Let Rdetcomp denotes the class of rank 2 functionals expressible by computable Rdet-schemes.

Theorem 6 (I) S $\supsetneqq$ Scons $\supsetneqq$ Ssing $\supsetneqq$ Stree;
(II) Rdetcomp $\supsetneqq$ Stree; Rdetcomp - Ssing $\not\equiv \emptyset$; Ssing - Rdetcomp $\equiv \emptyset$.

The theorem is illustrated by the functionals F_1, F_2, F_3, F_4 from §1 and namely :

$F_1 \in$ S-Scons; $F_2 \in$ Scons-Ssing; $F_3 \in$ Ssing-Stree;
$F_4 \in$ Rdetcomp-Ssing, and hence $F_4 \in$ Rdetcomp-Stree.

Remark. Statement a) of Theorem 2 may be strengthened as follows : there exists a functional in S-Rdetcomp which is expressible by a tree-like (but noncomputable!) S-scheme.

§5. Parallelism

Specifying the terminology. Contrast between parallel and sequential functionals was primary observed only in regard to functionals of rank $\leqslant 2$ ([4], [8], [9]). However, Theorem 6 points that even in such restriction some lack of coordination is to be emphasized in the previous approaches. On the one hand according to [4] parallelism is treated as inherent undeterminism, i.e. as nonexpressibility by Rdet - schemes; as a matter of fact the cited examples (e.g. OR, IF) are all like that. On the other hand only such examples of sequential functionals were considered for which representation by tree-like S-schemes is possible; moreover in [9] this property was identified by definition with sequentiality. Note that for rank 1 functionals determinism is actually equivalent to tree-likehood and hence for them no collision arises. But what about the rank 2 functional F_4, which is not tree-like? On the face of it and on the intuitive level the impression arises, that F_4 is parallel: you see that F_4 yields a value different from w iff :

$$fw \not\equiv w \quad \text{OR} \quad \exists k(\underbrace{f(\ldots(fx)\ldots)}_{k\ \text{times}\ f} \equiv x \not\equiv w),$$

where OR (in infix notation) is the parallel disjunction (§1). Nevertheless, we prefer the approach which identifies always (for functionals of arbitrary ranks and types) sequentiallity with determinism. Just this standpoint is adopted in [7], where though rather in other form functionals of arbitrary finite types are considered. In connection with that, notice once again Theorem 2a and remark to Theorem 6; they give evidence of the fact that if a computable functional F is sequential it must not be effective-sequential, i.e. expressible by a computable Rdet-scheme.

Supplying deterministic languages with parallelism - devices.

Theorem 6 points the difficulties which occur in picking out semantically consistent schemes by syntactical means only. An alternative possible approach is the following. Let us consider such extentions of computable Rdet-schemes or Rdet(σ)-schemes, in which symbols $f_1, \ldots f_k$ interpreted by fixed parallel functionals are allowed; the corresponding notations are Rdet($f_1, \ldots, f_k$), Rdet(σ ;$f_1, \ldots, f_k$). Clearly, schemes of this kind are semantically consistent. The question arises whether by means of some few functionals f_i-(it is desirable - the ones simplest possible) expressibility of all functionals which we are interested in, is achievable. Also care for correct implementation, including convenient manipulation technique with the added f_i is required. From this standpoint in [4] and [8] the parallel functionals of rank 1 IF and OR are discussed; In a similar way the question is put in [9] about rank 2 functionals. Theorem 5 of [9] deals with the effect of joining of some concrete functional designated g; unfortunately, we could not well understand neither the definition of g, nor the theorem itself.

Essential progress of the considered approach concerning rank 1 functionals is in 11 and its further developpment - in [7]. In assertions we formulate below the following parallel functionals occur: rank 1 functionals Γ , OR and rank 2 functional $\exists$ defined by

$$\exists f =_{\mathrm{def}} F_1(f,\sigma) \quad \text{(ref. §1).}$$

Theorem 7. (1) All invariant functionals of rank 1 are expressible in Rdet(Γ), and all computable ones - in Rdet(σ,OR); (II) but Γ is not expressible in Rdet(OR); (III) all computable functionals of arbitrary ranks are expressible in Rdet(σ,OR,$\exists$); (IV) OR is not expressible in Rdet(σ,$\exists$), $\exists$ is not expressible in Rdet(σ,OR).

Assertions (I)-(II) in some stronger form are in [11]; in fact schemes in Rdet(Γ) and in Rdet(OR) may be replaced by suitable superpositions. Statements (III)-(IV) are insignificant modifications of a theorem in [7].

Degrees of parallelism. It is natural to interpret assertions (II) and (IV) of theorem 7 as the existence of different parallelism degrees with respect to sequential reduction. The investigation of parallelism degrees for rank 1 functionals is started in [11], and subsequently its author succeeded in obtaining a quite fine picture of the related upper semilattice of degrees. This investigation is proceeded with in [7], where parallelism degrees are considered of high type functionals. The readers are refered to [11] and [7].

§6. Discussion. Problems.

I. Finite R-schemes. A computable R-scheme is in general infinite, though it may happen to be finite. Is it possible to manage without infinite schemes? The negative answer is suggested perhaps by the example considered in [4] of a special rank 2 functional F expressed by a finite nondeterminate scheme. Obviously, deterministic (i.e. expressible by Rdet-schemes) functionals, which coincide with F on each total interpretation exist. However, it follows from [4], that none of them is expressible by a finite Rdet-scheme of rank 2. Is it true for Rdet-schemes of higher rank as well? In connection with Theorem 2 another question arises : do any functionals exist which are expressible by infinite computable Rdet-schemes, as well as by finite R-schemes, but by no finite Rdet-scheme?

II. Separation of data structure and control mechanism.

In schematology counters, arrays and other devices use natural numbers in the control mechanism; but these numbers have nothing to do with the elements of the basic domain. Naturally, this approach allows also to manage without infinite R-schemes if in addition to the basic domain D_0 with uninterpreted elements, an auxiliary set $\tilde{D}_0 = \{w, 0, 1, \dots\}$ of natural numbers is considered. Thus for instance instead of applying one place functionals $T_1, T_2, \dots$ to argument x, the application $T i x$ of a unique two-argument functional T may be considered, where $i \in \tilde{D}_0$; from T by suitable fixation of parameter i each of the mutually described T_i may be obtained. If it turns out that from the very beginning D_0 coincides itself with the set of natural numbers, the idea arises that the auxiliary domain $\tilde{D}_0$ is superfluous.

III. Scott's language LCF [8]. This language actually converts into a fact the reason we alluded to above. Here is a slight modification of Scott's original definition : symbols designating combinators S,K fix-point operators Y and if,=,w,0, (ref. §1) are said to be atoms of the language. Typed terms built from atoms are formulas of LCF with the obvious interpretation. In [6] V.Yu.Sazonov stated (in somewhat other form) that expressibility by computable (but in general infinite!) Rdet(σ)-schemes is equivalent to expressibility by

LCF formulas and hence to expressibility by finite Rdet(σ) formulas. In connection with Theorem 7 this result clears the way to explicit finite expression for each computable functional supplying LCF with some suitable assortment of parallel atomary functionals.

Among the atoms of LCF only the noninvariant function σ assumes numerical interpretation of the basic domain D_0. Hence the language LCF' which results in deleting σ from LCF expresses only invariant and computable functionals, perhaps all of those expressible by finite Rdet-schemes. To cover all computable functionals expressible by Rdet-schemes, the use of auxiliary domain $\widetilde{D}_0$ as explained above is sufficient. Practically it signifies that atoms are to be added to LCF', which are of the type of $\widetilde{D}_0$ and of mixed types arising in simultaneous consideration of D_0 and $\widetilde{D}_0$. The question is open how to achieve one's object by more ingenious way.

IV. On the basic domain D_0. Up to now according to the partial order of D_0 all the elements except w were supposed to be incomparable with each other. For what other partial orders in the basic domain, a satisfactory recursive description of functionals (including convenient implementation) is still possible? Suppose, for instance, that as before a unique least element w and at least two maximal elements 0,1 exist, i.e.

$$\forall x(x \sqsupseteq 0 \rightarrow x \equiv 0), \quad \forall x(x \sqsupseteq 1 \rightarrow x \equiv 1).$$

Let us define:

$$s{=}t =_{def} \begin{cases} 1 & \text{if } s \equiv t \text{ and } s,t \text{ are maximal} \\ 0 & \text{if } \neg\exists x(x \sqsupseteq s \text{ and } x \sqsupseteq t) \\ w & \text{- otherwise} \end{cases}$$

Then, as before R-schemes will express only invariant functionals. For sufficiently good partial orders, such defined equality together with the conditional if or eventually with some other primitives may suit.

V. Rank 2 versus high ranks. What are the suitable extensions of S-schemes and termal invariance, that should permit an analogue of Theorem 5 to functionals of arbitrary high ranks? For instance, one might attempt to extend the notion of S-scheme with the allowance for S-terms to be built from signature symbols and symbols for undefined elements w_α of high type α. However, this doesn't suffice. Note also, that for all invariant functionals of rank 2 (termality not supposed) a simple scheme characterization like R-schemes is possible. For this it suffices to use recursive definitions of the kind

$Fx_1 \ldots x_k \Leftarrow t$, where in t besides $x_1 \ldots x_k$ also extra-argument variables are permitted. Accordingly, in defining semantics (ref.(2) in §2) all the argument variables (not only $x_1, \ldots x_k$) are to be quantified.

VI. Is there an advantage in using high types and parallelism? According to theorem 1 no scheme of rank > n is needed to express functionals of rank n. However it is not excluded that for some functional F of rank n a concrete scheme of rank > n may happen to be better than an arbitrary scheme of rank n. In analogy, for some deterministic functionals, perhaps nondeterminate schemes turn out to be more convenient (comp.theorem 2a and other remarks in this §). In both cases different optimum criteria may be considered as size of the scheme, speed of implementation etc. And hence - the question in the headline.

REFERENCES

1. Chandra, A.K., Z.Manna, Program schemes with equality, Stanford Artifitial Intelligence Project Memo AIM-158, Stanford, 1971.

2. Constable,R.L., D.Gries, On classes of program schemes, Conf. Record, 12 Symposium on switching and automata theory, 1971.

3. Ershov,Yu.L., Computable functionals of finite types, Algebra and Logic, 11, no.4 (1972), pp.367-437.

4. Paterson,M.S., C.E.Hewitt, Comparative schematology, Conf. Record of Project MAC, Conference on Concurrent Systems and Parallel Computation, ACM, no.9, 1970.

5. Sazonov, V.Yu., On expressibility and computability of objects in Scott's LCF. In Proceedings of the Third All-Union Conference on Mathematical Logic, pp.191-194, Novosibirsk, 1974 (in Russian).

6. Sazonov,V.Yu., Sequentiallity and parallely computable functionals (extended abstract), in Proceedings of the Symposium on - Calculus and Computer Science Theory, Roma, 1975, Lecture Notes in Computer Science, 37, pp.312-318.

7. Sazonov, V.Yu., Degrees of parallelism in computations, in these Proceedings.

8. Scott, D., A type-theoretical alternative to ISWIM, CUCH,OWHY, Oxford University, 1969.

9. Strong, H.R., High level languages of maximum power, Conf. Record 12 Symposium on switching and automata theory, 1971.

10. Trakhtenbrot, B.A., On universal class of program schemes, Lecture Notes in Computer Science, 5, 1973.

11. Trakhtenbrot,M.B., On representation of sequential and parallel functions, in Proceedings of 4th Symposium on Mathematical Fundations of Computer Science, Lecture Notes in Computer Science, no.32, pp.411-417, 1975.

12. Trakhtenbrot,M.B., On interpreted functions in program schemes, in System and Theoretical Programming, Novosibirsk, 1973.

I3. Vuillemin,J., Proof technique for recursive programs, Ph.D.Thesis, Computer Science Dept. Stanford University, Stanford, I973.

SOME FUNDAMENTALS OF ORDER-ALGEBRAIC SEMANTICS

E.G.Wagner, J.B.Wright, J.A.Goguen[†] and J.W.Thatcher[††]
Mathematical Sciences Department
IBM Thomas J. Watson Research Center
Yorktown Heights, New York 10598

ABSTRACT: The order-theoretic enrichment of the algebraic approach to theoretical computer science, and to the theory of programming in particular, can be accomplished rather directly and elegantly, and appears to have a wide range of applications. This paper presents mathematical fundamentals of order-algebraic semantics. The principal new results concern free continuous algebraic theories and minimal conditions for solving general "systems of (recursive) equations" in algebraic theories.

1. Introduction

Order-theoretic and algebraic methods have played a major role in theoretical computer science. Particularly in the theory of programming, there has been a steadily increasing flow of papers which combine the two approaches. We believe this literature deserves, indeed requires, a mathematics in which the order-theoretic and algebraic approaches are truly joined. This paper presents a basis for such a development.

This material grew out of work on inital algebra semantics reported in ADJ (1975). For ease of access, that paper used only universal algebra, and in particular, no category theory despite the authors' general advocacy of that approach (ADJ (1976)). However, proofs of some results in the first versions of ADJ (1975), which were quite unwieldy in the universal algebra framework, are much simpler in a categorical framework.

Fortunately the essential concept of algebraic theory (Lawvere (1963)) requires very little category theory. Thus, this paper assumes familiarity only with the notions of category and functor; it doesn't require or explicitly employ, any further basic categorical concepts.

Ordered algebraic theories result from wedding algebraic theories to order-theoretic concepts. This permits considerable refinement of results in ADJ (1975) about solving equations and leads naturally to the construction of free continuous algebraic theories (via infinite trees).

Much has been omitted, particularly many sorted theories. These correspond to many-sorted algebras of ADJ (1975) and are needed for the full treatment of recursive equations and flow diagrams. The decision to minimize the number of categorical concepts has again had its effect; had we decided to include coproducts of algebraic theories, we could have given an even more unified treatment of solving equations.

---

† Currently: Computer Science Department, UCLA, Los Angeles, California 90024 Partial support received from the University of Colorado and Naropa Institute, both of Boulder, Colorado 80302.

†† This <u>set</u> of authors is herein, and we hope subsequently will be, referred to by the symbols ADJ.

2. Preliminaries

We use standard set theoretic notation: $\cup$, $\bigcup$, $\cap$, $\bigcap$ (union and intersection); $\times$ (cartesian product); p (power set or set of subsets); and $\subseteq$, $\supseteq$ (for set inclusion). Function composition is written in diagramatic order: given $f:A \to B$ and $g:B \to C$, then $fg:A \to C$. Consistent with this, function application is (usually) written with the arguments to the function on the left. Thus, for example, $a(fg) = (af)g$.

ω denotes the set $\{0,1,2,\ldots\}$ of natural numbers, and for $n \in \omega$, $[n] = \{1,2,\ldots,n\}$; also $[\omega] = \{1,2,3,\ldots\}$. For any set X, X^* denotes the set of strings (or words) over X, including the empty word, λ. For $w \in X^*$, $(w)\ell g$ is the length of w and $(\lambda)\ell g = 0$.

We assume familiarity with the concepts, category, subcategory and functor. See ADJ (1976) for a leisurely treatment; for more detail consult Mac Lane (1971), Mitchell (1957), Pareigis (1970) or Herrlich and Strecker (1973). Our double underline as in $\underline{\underline{C}}$ or $\underline{\underline{Set}}$ indicates a category and $\underline{\underline{C}}$ is ambiguously used to denote the class of morphisms of $\underline{\underline{C}}$ while its objects are denoted $|\underline{\underline{C}}|$. $\underline{\underline{C}}(A,B)$ denotes the class of morphisms from A to B. We try to use $\circ$ to denote composition in a category and we write that composition in diagramatic order: $f:A \to B$ and $g:B \to C$ gives $f \circ g:A \to C$. As mentioned above, we omit the circle with function composition (i.e., in the category $\underline{\underline{Set}}$ of sets and functions). The identity for an object $A \in |\underline{\underline{C}}|$ is denoted 1_A and is in $\underline{\underline{C}}(A,A)$.

Definition 2.1. An algebraic theory $\underline{\underline{T}}$ is a category $\underline{\underline{T}}$ (called the underlying category of the algebraic theory) with objects the non-negative integers ($|\underline{\underline{T}}| = \omega$); with a family $\langle x_i^n \mid i \in [n]\rangle$ of distinguished morphisms in $\underline{\underline{T}}(1,n)$ for each $n \in \omega$ (these are called injections); and with an operation $(\ ,\ldots,\ )_{n,p}:\underline{\underline{T}}(1,p)^n \to \underline{\underline{T}}(n,p)$, called source-tupling for each $n,p \in \omega$. The case $n = 0$ yields a (unique) morphism, denoted $0_p:0 \to p$. (We immediately drop the subscripts from the tupling operations as they are retrievable from context.) The injections and tupling operations are required to satisfy the following two conditions:

(2.1.1) For all $n,p \in \omega$ and all families $\langle \beta_i \mid i \in [n]\rangle$ in $\underline{\underline{T}}(1,p)$ and for all $i \in [n]$,

$$x_i^n \circ (\beta_1,\ldots,\beta_n) = \beta_i.$$

(2.1.2) For all $n,p \in \omega$ and $\beta \in \underline{\underline{T}}(n,p)$

$$(x_1^n \circ \beta,\ldots,x_n^n \circ \beta) = \beta.$$

A morphism $H:\underline{\underline{T}} \to \underline{\underline{T}}'$ of algebraic theories is a functor from $\underline{\underline{T}}$ to $\underline{\underline{T}}'$ which is the identity on objects, and which preserves the distinguished morphisms: $x_i^n H = x_i^n$. (It follows from functionality and (2.1.1,2) that such morphisms preserve tupling.) □

We remove the restriction that the source of morphisms being tupled is 1, with the notion of source pairing: Given $\alpha:n \to q$ and $\beta:p \to q$, the source pair $(\alpha,\beta):n+p \to q$ is defined in terms of the original tupling operation by $(\alpha,\beta) = (x_1^n \circ \alpha,\ldots,x_n^n \circ \alpha, x_1^p \circ \beta,\ldots,x_p^p \circ \beta)$ and there are corresponding generalizations of the distinguished morphisms: $x_{(1)}^{n+p} = (x_1^{n+p},\ldots,x_n^{n+p})$; and $x_{(2)}^{n+p} = (x_{n+1}^{n+p},\ldots,x_{n+p}^{n+p})$.

Corresponding to the "tupling equations" of Definition 2.1 we have:

(2.1.1') $x^{n+p}_{(1)} \circ (\alpha,\beta) = \alpha$; $x^{n+p}_{(2)} \circ (\alpha,\beta) = \beta$

(2.1.2') For $\gamma: n+p \to q$, $(x^{n+p}_{(1)} \circ \gamma,\ x^{n+p}_{(2)} \circ \gamma) = \gamma$.

Any n-tuple of distinguished morphism is called a mapping because in any (non-degenerate) algebraic theory $\underline{\underline{T}}$, These mappings form a subcategory (also a theory) isomorphic to the category $\underline{\underline{N}}$ which has objects [n] for $n \in \omega$ and morphisms $\underline{\underline{N}}(n,p)$, all functions from [n] to [p]. The isomorphism sends [n] to n and $f:[n] \to [p]$ to $(x^p_{1f},\ldots,x^p_{nf})$.

"Variables" are a key to algebraic theories (see Section 4 and the discussion of parameters in Section 5). At first the notation for distinguished morphisms may seem awkward; but it has rewards. The reader might think of x^n_i as the "variable x_i"; $x^{n+p}_{(1)}$ as the "first n variables, $\{x_1,\ldots,x_n\}$;" $x^{n+p}_{(2)}$ as the "last p variables, $\{x_{n+1},\ldots,x_{n+p}\}$; and, even more generally, $x^{n+p+q+r}_{(1,3)}$ as the "first n and middle q variables, $\{x_1,\ldots,x_n, x_{n+p+1},\ldots,x_{n+p+q}\}$."

Equations 2.1.1' and 2.1.2' imply that the pair of morphisms, $\langle x^{n_1+n_2}_{(i)} : n_i \to n_1+n_2\rangle$, is a coproduct in any algebraic theory $\underline{\underline{T}}$. There is a corresponding coproduct for morphisms: given $\alpha_i : n_i \to p_i$ (for i=1,2), we can view $\alpha_1+\alpha_2 : n_1+n_2 \to p_1+p_2$ as an abbreviation for $(\alpha_1 \circ x^{p_1+p_2}_{(1)},\ \alpha_2 \circ x^{p_1+p_2}_{(2)})$. Equations 2.1.1' and 2.1.2' give $(\alpha_1+\alpha_2)\circ\beta = (\alpha_1\circ\beta,\ \alpha_2\circ\beta)$, for morphisms in $\underline{\underline{T}}$ with appropriate sources and targets.

A poset is a set with a partial order. We follow Scott's (1970) notation for arbitrary posets ($\sqsubseteq, \sqcup, \bigsqcup, \perp$) and think of "$\alpha \sqsubseteq \beta$" as "$\beta$ is at least as defined as α"; $\perp$, the minimum element, means "totally undefined," and we assume all posets are strict i.e., have a minimum element. A poset P is ω-complete iff all ω-chains in P have least upper bounds. A function f from a poset P to a poset Q is strict iff it preserves $\perp$, $\perp_P f = \perp_Q$ (it is sometimes convenient to distinguish minimum elements in different posets, but certainly not always); f is monotonic iff $p \sqsubseteq q$ in P implies $pf \sqsubseteq qf$ in Q and ω-continuous iff for all ω-chains $\langle p_i \mid i \in \omega\rangle$ in P, if $\bigsqcup p_i$ exists in P then $\bigsqcup (p_i f)$ exists in Q and $(\bigsqcup p_i)f = \bigsqcup (p_i f)$.

3. Ordered Categories and Theories

Definition 3.1. An ordered category is a category in which each $\underline{\underline{C}}(A,B)$ is a poset with partial order $\sqsubseteq_{A,B}$, and composition is monotonic (for $f,f' \in \underline{\underline{C}}(A,B)$ and $g,g' \in \underline{\underline{C}}(B,D)$, $f \sqsubseteq f'$ and $g \sqsubseteq g'$ implies $f\circ g \sqsubseteq f'\circ g'$). $\underline{\underline{C}}$ is left-strict if, in addition to the above, each $\underline{\underline{C}}(A,B)$ has a minimum element $\perp_{A,B}$ and composition is left-strict (for $f \in \underline{\underline{C}}(B,D)$, $\perp_{A,B}\circ f = \perp_{A,C}$). $\underline{\underline{C}}$ is ω-continuous iff it is ordered and each $\underline{\underline{C}}(A,B)$ is ω-complete and composition is ω-continuous.

A morphism $F:\underline{\underline{C}} \to \underline{\underline{C}}'$ of ordered categories is a monotonic functor. A morphism of left-strict [ω-continuous] categories is, in addition, strict [ω-continuous]. □

The idea of order-enriched algebraic structure is not new. A one-object category is just a monoid and ordered monoids have been around for a long time (c.f. Birkhoff (1967) and references there). Closer to our objectives, every quasinet (Blikle (1974)) is a one-object, left-strict, ω-continuous category (but not conversely).

The general concept of ordered category is important. But in this paper only left-strict ordered categories will be used. Therefore, in the rest of this paper, "ordered category" will mean "left strict ordered category."

Now we combine Definition 2.1 and 3.1 to get the principal concept amalgamating the algebraic and order-theoretic approaches:

Definition 3.2. An ordered algebraic theory $\underline{\underline{T}}$ is an algebraic theory whose underlying category is ordered and whose tupling operations are monotonic: for all $n,p \in \omega$ and families $\langle \beta_i \mid i \in [n] \rangle$ and $\langle \beta_i' \mid i \in [n] \rangle$ in $\underline{\underline{T}}(1,p)$, if $\beta_i \sqsubseteq \beta_i'$ for $i \in [n]$, then $(\beta_1,\ldots,\beta_n) \sqsubseteq (\beta_1',\ldots,\beta_n')$. $\underline{\underline{T}}$ is ω-continuous iff its underlying category is ω-continuous. (Note no additional conditions are required on tupling; ω-continuity of tupling follows from that of composition and equations 2.1.1, 2.1.2.). A morphism $H:\underline{\underline{T}} \to \underline{\underline{T}}'$ of ordered algebraic theories is simply a morphism of the underlying ordered categories (i.e., a strict monotonic functor) which is also an algebraic theory morphism. □

Some examples of ω-continuous algebraic theories, which will be useful in the sequel, will give some hints as to how these ideas are applied.

Let S be a set (think of a set of states) and let $\underline{\underline{Pf}}_S$ be the category with objects ω and homsets $\underline{\underline{Pf}}_S(n,p)$ consisting of all partial functions from $[n] \times S$ to $[p] \times S$ under function composition. The set $[n] \times S$ should be thought of as "n-disjoint copies of S." The distinguished morphism, $x_i^n:[1] \times S \to [n] \times S$, is the injection of S into the ith copy, sending $\langle 1,s \rangle$ to $\langle i,s \rangle$. The tupling of n given partial functions, $f_i:[1] \times S \to [n] \times S$ for $i=1,\ldots,n$, lets each function work on "its copy" in the source; that is, $(f_1,\ldots,f_n)$ sends $\langle i,s \rangle$ to $\langle 1,s \rangle f_i$.

The order theoretic properties of $\underline{\underline{Pf}}_S$ are inherited from the category $\underline{\underline{Pfn}}$ of sets and partial functions; so $\underline{\underline{Pf}}_S$ is an ω-continuous algebraic theory. The minimum element in $\underline{\underline{Pf}}_S(n,p)$ is the totally undefined function; thus composition is both left and right strict.

The importance of this algebraic theory, without its order-theoretic properties, was first recognized by Elgot (1970, 1973). The crucial point concerns (monadic) conditionals. Looking at partial function interpretations of computation, one may be struck (or even perplexed) by the fact that the conditional, if p then x else y, determined by a predicate p, is not a partial function (of its two arguments). But these conditionals do behave properly and neatly in $\underline{\underline{Pf}}_S$: For a predicate p on S, define $\hat{p}:1 \to 2$ in $\underline{\underline{Pf}}_S$ by

$$\langle 1,s \rangle \hat{p} = \begin{cases} \langle 1,s \rangle & \text{if } p \text{ is true of } s \\ \langle 2,s \rangle & \text{if } p \text{ is false of } s \\ \text{undefined} & \text{if } p \text{ is undefined on } s. \end{cases}$$

Now for any pair of partial functions $f_1, f_2 : S \to S$ (we identify $[1] \times S$ with S), the tuple $(f_1, f_2) : [2] \times S \to S$ has f_i operating on "its copy of S," and $\langle 1,s\rangle(\hat{p} \circ (f_1, f_2))$ has value $(s)f_1$ if p is true, $(s)f_2$ if p is false, and is undefined if p is undefined.

This coincides with the partial-identity-function interpretation of Karp (1959): if $p_1 : S \to S$ is the partial identity defined when p is true and $p_2 : S \to S$ is defined when p is false, then $\hat{p} \circ (f_1, f_2) : S \to S$ is $p_1 f_1 \cup p_2 f_2$ (or $p_1 ; f_1 \cup p_2 ; f_2$ in notation of de Roever (1974)).

$\underline{\underline{\mathrm{Pf}}}_S$ generalizes to $\underline{\underline{\mathrm{Re}}}_S$ with $\underline{\underline{\mathrm{Re}}}_S(n,p)$ all relations from $[n] \times S$ to $[p] \times S$. $\underline{\underline{\mathrm{Re}}}_S$ is also an ω-continuous theory, and has (monadic) nondeterministic interpretations analogous to those in $\underline{\underline{\mathrm{Pf}}}_S$.

$\underline{\underline{\mathrm{Pf}}}_S$ can be generalized to the case where the "state set" is partially ordered as in Bekić (1969), Scott and deBakker (1969), Scott (1970) and others. Let P be an ω-complete poset with $\perp$, and let $[n] \cdot P$, be n disjoint copies of P with all their minimum elements identified: $[n] \cdot P = \{\langle i,p\rangle \mid i \in [n] \text{ and } \perp \neq p \in P\} \cup \{\perp\}$, with the obvious ordering; this is a "coalesced sum." The poset $[n] \cdot P$ is ω-complete (since all chains are in some "copy" of P); and so is the partially ordered set of all <u>strict</u> ω-continuous functions from $[n] \cdot P$ to $[q] \cdot P$. (ω-continuous functions between ω-complete posets form an ω-complete poset and composition is ω-continuous). Let $\underline{\underline{\mathrm{Sm}}}_P$ be the algebraic theory with $\underline{\underline{\mathrm{Sm}}}_P(n,q)$ all strict ω-continuous functions from $[n] \cdot P$ to $[q] \cdot P$. Distinguished morphism and tupling (retrievable from $\underline{\underline{\mathrm{Pf}}}_S$ above) work (i.e., satisfy 2.1.1 and 2.1.2) because of strictness. $\underline{\underline{\mathrm{Sm}}}_P$ is an ω-continuous theory. If a minimum element is adjoined to a set S to get a "flat poset" $S_\perp$ with the trivial ordering, then $S_\perp$ is trivially ω-complete; moreover; all monotonic functions from $[n] \cdot S_\perp$ to $[q] \cdot S_\perp$ are ω-continuous, since chains are finite. The reader can check that there is a bijection between partial functions $f : S \to [n] \times S$ and ω-continuous (monotonic) functions from $S_\perp$ to $[n] \cdot S_\perp$; thus $\underline{\underline{\mathrm{Pf}}}_S$ and $\underline{\underline{\mathrm{Sm}}}_{S_\perp}$ are isomorphic. (The notation $\underline{\underline{\mathrm{Sm}}}_P$ is intended to suggest <u>Sums</u> of P with (strict) functions between sums having the continuity property corresponding to the completeness properties of P. And below, $\underline{\underline{\mathrm{Px}}}_P$ has ω-continuous functions between <u>powers</u> of an ω-complete poset, P.)

Again let P be an ω-complete poset with $\perp$. Define $\underline{\underline{\mathrm{Px}}}_P$ to be the ω-continuous algebraic theory with homsets, $\underline{\underline{\mathrm{Px}}}_P(n,q)$, all ω-continuous functions from $P^q \to P^n$. (Note the reversal!) Composition is reversed function composition: for $f \in \underline{\underline{\mathrm{Px}}}_P(n,q)$ and $g \in \underline{\underline{\mathrm{Px}}}_P(q,r)$, $f \circ g = gf$. For the same reasons indicated above, $\underline{\underline{\mathrm{Px}}}_P(n,p)$ is ω-complete and (even though reversed) composition is ω-continuous. Composition is left, but not necessarily right strict. The injection $x_i^n : P^n \to P$ is actually a projection, $\langle p_1, \ldots, p_n\rangle x_i^n = p_i$ and given $f_i : P^n \to P$, $(f_1, \ldots, f_q)$ sends $\langle p_1, \ldots, p_n\rangle$ to $\langle (p_1, \ldots, p_n)f_1, \ldots, (p_1, \ldots, p_n)f_q\rangle$. The reader may check the tupling equations.

4. Free Theories

The non-algebraist might question our interest in free objects, we hope this will become more apparent in what follows. For one thing, "syntactic specifications" occur in free objects. This is argued for algebras in ADJ (1975), and for (ordered) (ω-continuous) theories here. When a syntactic specification is interpreted (i.e., meanings assigned to primitives) in some semantic target, the interpretation (meaning, semantics) of the entire specification is uniquely determined. Using ordered algebraic theories, one meaning (semantics) for the syntactic specification is the "solution" (Section 5) within the free-theory (strong behavior or free interpretation); and if two specifications have the same semantics (are identical) in the free theory, then so do they in any semantic target.

To get started, we need the notion of a partial p-ary Σ-tree, where Σ is a ranked alphabet, i.e. a family of sets (operator symbols) $\Sigma = \langle \Sigma_i \mid i \in \omega \rangle$ with $\Sigma_i \cap \Sigma_j = \emptyset$ for $i \neq j$. (The disjointness is a technical convenience; we ambiguously write Σ for $\bigcup_i \Sigma_i$.)

Definition 4.1. (ADJ (1975)) Let Σ be a ranked alphabet and $X_p = \{x_1,\ldots,x_p\}$ a set of p variables disjoint from Σ. The set $CT_\Sigma(X_p)$ of partial p-ary Σ-trees is the set of all partial functions, $t:[\omega]^* \to X_p \cup \Sigma$ satisfying the following condition.

(4.1.1) For all $v \in [\omega]^*$, $k \in [\omega]$ and $\xi \in X_p \cup \Sigma$, if $\langle vk,\xi\rangle \in t$, then there exist $j \geq k$ and $\sigma \in \Sigma_j$ such that $\langle v,\sigma\rangle \in t$.

The set $TT_\Sigma(X_p)$ of total p-ary Σ-trees, is that subset of $CT_\Sigma(X_p)$ satisfying the additional condition:

(4.1.2) For all $v \in [\omega]^*$, $k > 0$ and $\sigma \in \Sigma_k$, if $\langle v,\sigma\rangle \in t$ then there exist $\xi_1,\ldots,\xi_k \in X_p \cup \Sigma$ with $\langle vi,\xi_i\rangle \in t$ for $i \in [k]$.

The set $FT_\Sigma(X_p)$, of finite partial p-ary Σ-trees, is that subset of $CT_\Sigma(X_p)$ consisting of partial functions with finite domains of definition.

$T_\Sigma(X_p) = TT_\Sigma(X_p) \cap FT_\Sigma(X_p)$ is the set of p-ary Σ-trees (both finite and total). □

One visualizes a Σ-labeled tree as a partial function on $[\omega]^*$ in the following way: $\lambda \in [\omega]^*$ is the root; and for any node $v \in [\omega]^*$ its successors are $v1, v2, v3, \ldots$. If t is the empty partial function then t is the "empty tree" which we denote $\perp$. If $\langle v,\sigma\rangle \in t$, then node v is labeled σ and the reader can check that condition (4.4.1) ensures that all of v's predecessors are also labeled. The trees are partial because if, say, $\sigma \in \Sigma_2$ and $\langle v,\sigma\rangle \in t$, then only $v1$ and $v2$ can be labeled; but they don't have to be. Infinite trees are included; for example, if $\sigma \in \Sigma_1$, then $\{\langle w,\sigma\rangle \mid w \in [1]^*\}$ is the infinite tree (sequence) of σ's and if $\sigma \in \Sigma_2$ then the same partial function is the infinite partial tree of σ's with the first argument of σ always "defined" and the second argument always "not defined."

The finite total trees coincide with the usual Σ-expressions or terms built up from the operator symbols Σ and variables X_p. For informal discussion, we identify the finite total trees with expressions. It is also helpful to identify $FT_\Sigma(X_p)$

with expressions having one additional symbol of rank 0, say $\perp$. For example, if $\Sigma = \langle\{a\},\{b\},\{c\}, \emptyset,\ldots\rangle$ the expression $c(b(b(\perp))c(\perp a))$ is identified with the partial function $\{\langle\lambda,c\rangle, \langle 1,b\rangle, \langle 2,c\rangle, \langle 11,b\rangle, \langle 22,a\rangle\}$.

Proposition 4.2. $CT_\Sigma(X_p)$ is a strict ω-complete poset under the ordering of inclusion of (graphs of) the partial functions, and with the empty function $\perp$ as minimum element □

The ordered algebraic theory $\underline{\underline{CT}}_\Sigma$ is now obtained by taking n-tuples of partial p-ary Σ-trees as its morphisms from n to p, $\underline{\underline{CT}}_\Sigma(n,p) = CT_\Sigma(X_p)^n$, with the component-wise ordering. Composition is <u>substitution</u>, defined set theoretically as follows (in ADJ (1975) substitution was defined viewing $CT_\Sigma(X_p)$ as a free Σ-algebra on n generators): Given $(t_1,\ldots,t_n) \in \underline{\underline{CT}}_\Sigma(n,p)$ and $(t_1',\ldots,t_p') \in \underline{\underline{CT}}_\Sigma(p,q)$, the composite is $(t_1'',\ldots,t_n'') \in \underline{\underline{CT}}_\Sigma(n,q)$ where,

$$t_i'' = \{\langle u,\sigma\rangle \mid \langle u,\sigma\rangle \in t_i \text{ and } \sigma \in \Sigma_k \text{ for some } k\} \cup \bigcup_{j\in[p]}\{\langle uv,\xi\rangle \mid \langle u,x_j\rangle \in t_i \text{ and } \langle v,\xi\rangle \in t_j'\}$$

Composition (substitution) is associative, monotonic, ω-continuous (Propositions 2.4, 4.14, ADJ (1975)), and left-strict. The minimum element in $\underline{\underline{CT}}(n,p)$ is the n-tuple of empty partial functions. Tupling is tupling (after identifying $CT_\Sigma(X_p)$ with $(CT_\Sigma(X_p))^1$). (But composition is <u>not</u> right-strict: if $t:2 \to 2$ is $\langle c(xa), c(b(x_2)\perp)\rangle$ then $t \circ \perp_{2,0}:2 \to 0$ is $\langle c(\perp a), c(b(\perp)\perp))\rangle$.) The distinguished morphism $x_i^p:1 \to p$ is $\{\langle\lambda,x_i\rangle\}$, which we have identified with the expression $x_i \in X_p$. The tupling equations are easily checked.

So $\underline{\underline{CT}}_\Sigma$ is an ω-continuous algebraic theory and Theorem 4.5 below says it is <u>freely generated by</u> Σ. There is a ranked alphabet map $\iota_\Sigma:\Sigma \to \underline{\underline{CT}}_\Sigma$ (a ranked alphabet map $H:\Sigma \to \underline{\underline{T}}$ with an algebraic theory $\underline{\underline{T}}$ as target, is actually a family of functions $\langle H_n:\Sigma_n \to \underline{\underline{T}}(1,n) \mid n\in\omega\rangle$) which sends $\sigma \in \Sigma_n$ to the (total) n-ary Σ-tree $\sigma(x_1,\ldots,x_n)$ (which is actually the 1-tuple $\langle\{\langle\lambda,\sigma\rangle,\langle 1,x_1\rangle,\ldots,\langle n,x_n\rangle\}\rangle$). For notational convenience we identify the operator symbol $\sigma \in \Sigma_n$ with its image index ι_Σ, i.e., σ and $\sigma(x_1,\ldots,x_n)$ are the same.

The families $TT_\Sigma(X_p)$, $FT_\Sigma(X_p)$ and $T_\Sigma(X_p)$ are closed under substitution (composition); the distinguished morphisms x_i are in the smallest, $T_\Sigma(X_p)$; and we have subtheories $\underline{\underline{TT}}_\Sigma$, $\underline{\underline{FT}}_\Sigma$ and $\underline{\underline{T}}_\Sigma$ of $\underline{\underline{CT}}_\Sigma$.

Theorem 4.3. $\underline{\underline{T}}_\Sigma$ is the algebraic theory freely generated by Σ: if $\underline{\underline{T}}$ is any algebraic theory and $H:\Sigma \to \underline{\underline{T}}$ any ranked alphabet map, then there is a unique theory morphism $\overline{H}:\underline{\underline{T}}_\Sigma \to \underline{\underline{T}}$ which extends H. □

Theorem 4.3 says that if we have interpretations for the operator symbols, then we get interpretations for all tuples of expressions, uniquely determined by preservation properties of theory morphisms.

Let $\Sigma(\perp)$ be the ranked alphabet Σ with a single zero-ary symbol $\perp$ adjoined. As algebraic theories, $\underline{\underline{FT}}_\Sigma$ and $\underline{\underline{T}}_{\Sigma(\perp)}$ are isomorphic; this is an identification indicated earlier. Given an ordered theory $\underline{\underline{T}}$ and a ranked alphabet map $H:\Sigma \to \underline{\underline{T}}$, extend H to $H_\perp:\Sigma(\perp) \to \underline{\underline{T}}$ by sending $\perp \in \Sigma(\perp)_0$ to $\perp_{1,0} \in \underline{\underline{T}}(1,0)$; now apply Theorem 4.3 to get $\overline{H}_\perp:\underline{\underline{T}}_{\Sigma(\perp)} \to \underline{\underline{T}}$, viewing $\underline{\underline{T}}$ as an (unordered) algebraic theory. Since $\overline{H}_\perp$ extends H, and is strict by construction, the proof of the following theorem is mainly a proof that $\overline{H}_\perp$ is monotonic. (This follows the proof of the initiality of the ordered algebra FT_Σ in ADJ (1975), Proposition 4.7.)

Theorem 4.4. $\underline{\underline{FT}}_\Sigma$ is the ordered theory freely generated by Σ: that is, if $\underline{\underline{T}}$ is any ordered theory and $H:\Sigma \to \underline{\underline{T}}$ is any ranked alphabet map, then there is a unique ordered theory morphism $\overline{H}:\underline{\underline{FT}}_\Sigma \to \underline{\underline{T}}$ which extends H. □

Now let $\underline{\underline{T}}$ be an ω-continuous ordered theory and $H:\Sigma \to \underline{\underline{T}}$ a ranked alphabet map. Since $\underline{\underline{T}}$ is ordered, we can apply Theorem 4.4 to obtain a unique ordered theory morphism $\overline{H}:\underline{\underline{FT}}_\Sigma \to \underline{\underline{T}}$, and by uniqueness any ω-continuous extension of H must agree with $\overline{H}$ on $\underline{\underline{FT}}_\Sigma$. Consider an infinite tree t in $\underline{\underline{CT}}_\Sigma(1,n)$ and let $t^{(n)}$ be its restriction to words in $[\omega]^*$ of length at most n; obviously $t = \bigsqcup t^{(n)}$. Now each $t^{(n)}$ is in $\underline{\underline{FT}}_\Sigma(1,n)$ and its image is determined by $\overline{H}$. Therefore any ω-continuous G extending H satisfies $tG = (\bigsqcup t^{(n)})G = \bigsqcup(t^{(n)}G) = \bigsqcup t^{(n)}\overline{H}$. This is the crux of the proof of:

Theorem 4.5. $\underline{\underline{CT}}_\Sigma$ is the ω-continuous theory freely generated by Σ; that is, if $\underline{\underline{T}}$ is any ω-continuous theory and if $H:\Sigma \to \underline{\underline{T}}$ is any ranked alphabet map, then there is a unique ω-continuous theory morphism, $\overline{H}:\underline{\underline{CT}}_\Sigma \to T$, extending H. □

Not only do infinite trees in $\underline{\underline{CT}}_\Sigma$ hold fascinating prospects for syntactic specifications, but we also find the representation of prototypical flow charts in $\underline{\underline{CT}}_\Sigma$ (actually in $\underline{\underline{FT}}_\Sigma$). As in Elgot (1970), we shall consider flow charts with n entries and p exits. We let the nodes of such an object be $\{x_1,\ldots,x_q x_{q+1},\ldots,x_{q+p},\}$, partitioned into q internal nodes, $\{x_1,\ldots,x_q\}$, which are labeled by $\Sigma(\perp)$, and p exit nodes, $\{x_{q+1},\ldots,x_{q+p}\}$ which are not labeled. If $\perp$ labels node x_i (for $i\in[q]$) then x_i is a loop node and has no successors. If $\sigma \in \Sigma_0$ labels x_i then x_i is a halt node and also has no successors. If $\sigma \in \Sigma_1$ labels x_i then x_i is a (standard) operation node and must have one successor. If $\sigma \in \Sigma_k$ (for $k \geq 2$) labels x_i then x_i is a test (with possible "side effects") node and x_i must have k successors. This much information is just a q-tuple $\alpha = (\alpha_1,\ldots,\alpha_q)$ from q to $q+p$ in $\underline{\underline{FT}}_\Sigma$ where: $\alpha_i = \perp$ if x_i is a loop node; $\alpha_i = \sigma$ if x_i is a halt node; and $\alpha_i = \sigma(x_{i_1},\ldots,x_{i_k})$ if x_i is a test or operation node with successors $x_{i_1},\ldots,x_{i_k}$ (in that order). The n entries to the flowchart are given to us by an n-tuple, $b = (x_{i_1},\ldots,x_{i_n})$, of its nodes ($i_n \in [q+p]$), but under identifications we are using this as just a mapping (n-tuple of distinguished morphisms) in $\underline{\underline{FT}}_\Sigma(n,q+p)$. Motivated by this informal discussion, we define a Σ-flow chart from n to p of weight q to be a pair $\langle b,\alpha\rangle$, where $b:n \to q+p$ is the entry map, a tuple of distinguished morphisms, and $\alpha:q \to q+p$ is in $\underline{\underline{FT}}_\Sigma$. This generalizes our discussion above in which each $\alpha_i:1 \to q+p$ was "primitive;" more general α_i's (which are just expressions built up from $\Sigma(\perp)$) can be thought of as cycle free blocks.

As usual, an interpretation of a Σ-flow chart is (uniquely) determined by specifying interpretations for the primitives: An interpretation of a Σ-flow chart is a ranked alphabet map $I:\Sigma \to \underline{\underline{T}}$ where $\underline{\underline{T}}$ is an ω-continuous theory. The examples at the end of Section 3 show us that these "interpretations" include at least the standard ones. Given I, Theorem 4.5 guarantees a unique extension $\overline{I}:\underline{\underline{CT}}_\Sigma \to \underline{\underline{T}}$ and gives us an interpreted flow chart, $\langle b,\alpha\overline{I}\rangle$ in $\underline{\underline{T}}$ (with $b\overline{I} = b$).

We now provide some motivation for the discussion of the (terminal) behavior of an interpreted flowchart, which is discussed in more detail in the next section.

The terminal behavior of an interpreted flow chart will be the same kind of object as was used to interpret the primitives; e.g., a flow chart from 1 to k interpreted in $\underline{\underline{Sm}}_S$ will have a behavior which is a partial function from S to $[k] \times S$, sending s to $\langle j,s'\rangle$, when x_j is the exit node reached with initial state s, and s' is the final state. This can be found by first finding the behavior for every (internal) node x_i, $i \in [q]$ and later selecting out the behavior specified by the entry nodes. Consider $\alpha\overline{I}:q \to q+p$, in $\underline{\underline{Sm}}_S$. The (terminal) behavior of $\alpha\overline{I}$ is a morphism $\beta:q \to p$ in $\underline{\underline{Sm}}_S$) i.e., a partial function $\beta:[q] \times S \to [p] \times S$; and the ith component, $\beta_i:S \to [p] \times S$ $(= x_i^q \circ \beta)$, is the behavior relative to start node x_i. Now β is uniquely characterized by being the smallest (least defined) partial function such that if node x_j $(j \in [q])$ is labeled $\sigma \in \Sigma_k$ and has successors $x_{j_1},\ldots,x_{j_k}$, then $(\sigma\overline{I})\circ(\beta_{j_1},\ldots,\beta_{j_k}) = \beta_j$. Put in the preceeding formalism, β is the least partial function ξ satisfying the equation $\xi = (\alpha\overline{I})\circ(\xi,1_p)$; thus β is the minimum solution for $\alpha\overline{I}$ in $\underline{\underline{Sm}}_S$, denoted $(\alpha\overline{I})^\dagger$. Moreover the behavior of the interpreted flow chart $\langle b,\alpha\overline{I}\rangle$ is just the composite $b\circ((\alpha\overline{I})^\dagger,1_p):n \to p$ in $\underline{\underline{Sm}}_S$.

The "free interpretation" amounts to finding the behavior of $\langle b,\alpha\rangle$ in $\underline{\underline{CT}}_\Sigma$ (the interpretation of σ is $\sigma(x_1,\ldots,x_n)$ in $\underline{\underline{CT}}_\Sigma(1,n)$), i.e., to solving $\xi = \alpha\circ(\xi,1_p)$ in $\underline{\underline{CT}}_\Sigma$. The solution $\alpha^\dagger:n \to p$ is an n-tuple of (possibly infinite) p-ary Σ-trees, the ith one being the tree which is obtained by "unfolding" the flow chart beginning at node x_i. (Compare this with an alternative approach to "unfoldments" in Goguen (1974).)

5. Solving Equations

Ever since Arden (1961) used equations to describe regular sets ($X = aX \cup b$ with solution $X = a^*b$), solving equations has been important in theoretical computer science. Equational theory had a local climax with Mezei and Wright's (1967) theory of equational sets in arbitrary algebras. The order-theoretic (or fixed-point) approach now widely used in the theory of programming is an extension of the basic Mezei-Wright ideas (c.f. Blikle (1971, 1973, 1974), Engelfriet (1974), Engelfriet and Schmidt (1975), and Wagner (1971, 1971a)). We believe that the rational algebraic theories defined here unify the notion (and process) of "solving equations," with theoretical work on iterative and recursive program schemes (see, e.g., de Bakker and Scott (1969), Park (1969), deRoever (1974) and Berry (1975)). Algebraic theories were introduced into the subject by Eilenberg and Wright (1969) and Wagner (1971), while Elgot (1970) was the first to see the importance of solving equations within algebraic theories. Burstall and Thatcher (1974) have pointed out the connection between ordered theories and recursion.

The approach is to view a system of n "equations" in n "unknowns" and p "parameters" as a morphism $\alpha : n \to n+p$ in an algebraic theory $\underline{\underline{T}}$: the ith component of α is interpreted as describing the ith unknown in terms of all the other unknowns and the parameters. Note, however, that neither this interpretation nor the process of solution depends on the "type" of the unknowns or parameters. Depending on the theory, we may be talking about iteration, or recursion, or a fixed-point definition of context-free sets (among many other possibilities).

The latter example is classical and may help to motivate and exemplify the material to follow. If T is a set (of <u>terminal</u> symbols), define the category $\underline{\underline{Sub}}_T$ to have objects ω, and as morphisms from n to p, n-tuples of subsets of $(T \cup X_p)^*$, where X_p is a set of p <u>nonterminal</u> symbols, or <u>variables</u>. Composition in $\underline{\underline{Sub}}_T$ is substitution: given $(U_1,\ldots,U_n):n \to p$ and $(V_1,\ldots,V_p):p \to q$, the composite $(U_1,\ldots,U_n)\circ(V_1,\ldots,V_p)$ is the n-tuple $(W_1,\ldots,W_n)$ where W_i is the set of all words obtained by taking $u \in U_i$ and for each occurrence in u of an $x_j \in X_p$ substituting some $v_j \in V_j$ for x_j. One can check that this composition is associative and that $(\{x_1\},\ldots,\{x_n\})$ is the identity for n. Moreover, with $\{x_i\}:1 \to n$ as the injection x_i^n, and with set inclusion as the ordering, $\underline{\underline{Sub}}_T$ is an ω-continuous algebraic theory with $\perp_{n,p} = \underbrace{(\emptyset,\ldots,\emptyset)}_{n}$.

A morphism $U = (U_1,\ldots,U_n):n \to n$ corresponds to a context-free grammar (assuming U_i infinite); the nonterminals are the "variables" $\{x_1,\ldots,x_p\}$ and the productions are $x_i \to u_i$ for all $u_i \in U_i$. (E.g., take $T = \{0,1\}$ with productions $x_1 \Rightarrow 1$ and $x_1 \Rightarrow 0x_10$; the corresponding morphism is $\langle\{1,0x_10\}\rangle$ in $\underline{\underline{Sub}}_T(1,1)$.) We solve U by finding the least fixed-point; for $k=0$ define $U^{(k)} = U^k \circ \perp_{n,0}$. The family $\langle U^{(k)} | k \in w\rangle$ is an ω-chain in $\underline{\underline{Sub}}_T$ and $U^\dagger = \bigsqcup U^{(i)}$ is the least fixed-point of U in the sense that $U \circ U^\dagger = U^\dagger$ and if $U \circ V = V$ then $U^\dagger \sqsubseteq V$. $(U^\dagger)_i$ (for $i \in [n]$) is the context-free set determined by U with "start symbol" x_i. Similarly, to solve $U:n \to n+p$ we view the p "extra" nonterminals as parameters, and obtain $U^\dagger : n \to p$; with $U_i^\dagger$ a set of strings containing nonterminals $\{x_1,\ldots,x_p\}$. This is done by forming a new system, $(U_1,\ldots,U_n,\{x_{n+1}\},\ldots,\{x_{n+p}\}) = (U,x_{(2)}^{n+p})$ from $n+p$ to $n+p$ which is solved by substituting $\{\emptyset\} = \perp_{1,0}$ for the nonterminals $x_1,\ldots,x_n$ and the "first available" nonterminal for each parameter. I.e.,

$$U^{(0)} = (\underbrace{\{\emptyset\},\ldots,\{\emptyset\}}_{n},\{x_1\},\ldots,\{x_p\}) = (\perp_{n,p},1_p) \quad \text{and} \quad U^{(k)} = (U,x_{(s)}^{n+p})^k \circ (\perp_{n,p},1_p).$$

The family $\langle U^{(k)} | k \in \omega\rangle$ is an ω-chain in $\underline{\underline{Sub}}_T$ and its least upper bound, $U^\nabla = \bigsqcup (U,x_{(2)}^{n+p})^k \circ (\perp_{n,p},1_p)$ is an $(n+p)$-tuple of subsets of $(T \cup X_p)^*$; $(U^\nabla)_i$, for $i \in [n]$ is the context free set for start symbol x_i (involving parameters X_p), and it turns out $(U^\nabla)_j$, for $j \in n+[p]$ is just $\{x_p\}$. Our desired "solution" is $U^\dagger = x^{n+p}_{(1)} \circ U^\nabla$ which is the minimum fixed-point of the "equation" $\xi = U \circ (\xi, 1_p)$ (c.f. Elgot (1973)) in the sense that $U \circ (U^\dagger, 1_p) = U \circ U^\nabla = U^\dagger$ and if $U \circ (V, 1_p) = V$ then $U^\dagger \sqsubseteq V$. This is the concept of solution in Definition 5.1 below, as well as the basis for our definition of rational theories (Definition 5.3).

One more comment before proceeding with those definitions. At first confusing, it is really one of the beauties of algebraic theories, that "variables" are "canonicalized." We started the parameterized case with $U: n \to n+p$; the parameters occurred as nonterminals (variables) $x_{n+1}, \ldots, x_{n+p}$. But in the solution $U^\dagger: n \to p$ these parameters have been "translated" to $x_1, \ldots, x_p$. If $V: p \to p$ yields a context-free p-tuple of sets $V^\dagger: p \to 0$, the composite $U^\dagger \circ V^{\dagger p}$ is "substitution" of $(V^\dagger)_i$ for parameter x_i and the substitution theorem (c.f. Ginsburg (1966)) says the composite is context-free. This result, for rational theories in general, is (5.6.3) below and applies uniformly for context-free sets, copy rule semantics of monadic recursive program schemes (Burstall and Thatcher (1975)) and behaviors of monadic flow diagram schemes (Elgot (1973)) among many other things. The important generalization to the case of $p \neq 0$ parameters was first systematically treated in Wagner (1971).

Definition 5.1. In an ordered algebraic theory $\underline{\underline{T}}$, a morphism $\alpha^\dagger: n \to p$ is the (minimum) solution for $\alpha: n \to n+p$ iff $\alpha \circ (\alpha^\dagger, 1_p) = \alpha^\dagger$ and for any $\eta: n \to p$ in $\underline{\underline{T}}$ if $\alpha \circ (\eta, 1_p) = \eta$ then $\alpha^\dagger \sqsubseteq \eta$. An ordered algebraic theory is rationally closed iff every morphism $\alpha: n \to n+p$ has a solution. □

The minimum solution $\alpha^\dagger$ for $\alpha: n \to n+p$ is in fact the minimum solution for ξ in the equation

$$(*) \qquad \xi = \alpha \circ (\xi, 1_p).$$

Elgot's approach does not use a partial ordering, but requires solutions for (*) to be unique, provided α is ideal (no α_i is distinguished ($i \in [n]$)). We shall use $\alpha^\dagger$ to denote the minimum solution of (*) (if it exists), and speak of "the solution" with "minimum" being understood.

Most examples of rationally closed ordered theories (we've seen $\underline{\underline{CT}}_\Sigma$ and $\underline{\underline{Sub}}_T$) are (at least) ω-continuous. However, there are important ordered theories which are not ω-continuous, yet rationally closed. The concept of rational theory results from seeking minimum conditions on an ordered theory which ensure that solutions always exist (rational closure) and that these solutions behave properly with respect to composition, tupling and iteration as expressed in Theorems 5.6 and 5.8 below.

Definition 5.2. Let $\underline{\underline{T}}$ be an ordered theory and let $\alpha: n \to n+p$ be any morphism in $\underline{\underline{T}}$. Define the ω-sequence $\langle \alpha^{(k)} | k \in \omega \rangle$ by:

(5.2.1) $\alpha^{(k)} = (\alpha, x^{n+p}_{(2)})^k \circ (\perp_{n,p}, 1_p)$.

Then $\underline{\underline{T}}$ is rational iff for each $n, p \in \omega$ and $\alpha \in \underline{\underline{T}}(n, n+p)$, we have:

(5.2.2) (Completeness) $\alpha^\nabla = \bigsqcup \alpha^{(k)}$ exists;

(5.2.3) (Right continuity) $\tau \circ \alpha^\nabla = \bigsqcup (\tau \circ \alpha^{(k)})$ for all $\tau \in \underline{\underline{T}}(m, n+p)$ and $m \in \omega$;

(5.2.4) (Left continuity) $\alpha^{\nabla} \circ \tau = \bigsqcup (\alpha^{(k)} \circ \tau)$ for all $\tau \in \underline{T}(p,q)$ and $q \in \omega$.

A morphism of rational theories is an ordered theory morphism that preserves , i.e., $(\alpha^{\nabla})H = (\alpha H)^{\nabla}$, for all $\alpha : n \to n+p$ in $\underline{T}$. □

Connecting the principal definition (5.2) with solutions (5.1) we have

Theorem 5.3. If $\underline{T}$ is a rational theory then $\underline{T}$ is rationally closed; in particular, for all $\alpha : n \to n+p$ in $\underline{T}$, $\alpha^{\dagger} = x_{(1)}^{n+p} \circ \alpha^{\nabla} = \bigsqcup \alpha \circ \alpha^{(k)}$. □

By induction and properties of tupling we can prove that the sequence $\langle \alpha^{(k)} | k \in \omega \rangle$ can be written $\alpha^{(0)} = (\bot_{n,p}, 1_p)$ and $\alpha^{(k+1)} = (\alpha \circ \alpha^{(k)}, 1_p)$, from which it follows that $\alpha^{(k)}$ is a chain with least upper bound $\alpha^{\nabla} = \bigsqcup \alpha^{(k)}$ in any ω-continuous theory, $\underline{T}$. Continuity properties of $\underline{T}$ gives us (5.2.3) and (5.2.4) so we have,

Proposition 5.4. If $\underline{T}$ is ω-continuous then $\underline{T}$ is rational and hence rationally closed. □

The fundamental fact underlying what Engelfreit and Schmidt (1975) call "Mezei-Wright-like results" is that morphisms of rational theories preserve solutions. If $H : \underline{T} \to \underline{T}'$ is a morphism of ordered theories and if $\alpha : n \to n+p$ in $\underline{T}$ has a minimum solution $\alpha^{\dagger} : n \to p$, then $\alpha^{\dagger} H$ is always a solution for αH: $\alpha H \circ (\alpha^{\dagger} H, 1_p) = (\alpha \circ (\alpha^{\dagger}, 1_p))H = \alpha^{\dagger} H$, because H preserves tupling, composition and identities. Requiring H to preserve $^{\nabla}$ insures that $\alpha^{\dagger} H$ is the minimum solution for α.

Proposition 5.5. If $H : \underline{T} \to \underline{T}'$ is a morphism of rational theories, and $\alpha : n \to n+p$ in $\underline{T}$, then $\alpha^{\dagger} H = (\alpha H)^{\dagger}$. □

The existence and preservation of solutions involves neither left continuity nor the full power of right continuity. These latter conditions relate to the well behavedness of solutions we've mentioned before. The following theorem collects the most important identities holding for rational theories. We give informal (or computational) interpretations of some of these below.

Theorem 5.6. Let $\underline{T}$ be a rational theory and let $\alpha : n \to n+p$, $\tau : p \to q$ and $\beta : p \to p+q$ in $\underline{T}$. Then

(5.6.1) $\alpha^{\nabla} = (\alpha + 1_p)^{\dagger}$

(5.6.2) $\alpha^{\dagger} \circ \tau = (\alpha \circ (1_n + \tau))^{\dagger}$

(5.6.3) $\alpha^{\dagger} \circ \beta^{\dagger} = x_{(1)}^{n+p} \circ ((\alpha + \beta) \circ (x_{(1,2)}^{n+p+q}, x_{(2,3)}^{n+p+q}))^{\dagger}$

If $\alpha : n \to n+p+q$ and $\beta : p \to n+p+q$, then

(5.6.4) $(\alpha, \beta)^{\dagger} = (\alpha^{\dagger} \circ (\beta \circ \alpha^{\nabla})^{\nabla}, (\beta \circ \alpha^{\nabla})^{\dagger})$.

Finally, if $\alpha_i : m_i \to n_i$ and $\beta_i : n_i \to n_i + p$, for $i=1,2$, then

(5.6.5) $(\alpha_1 \circ \beta_1^{\dagger}, \alpha_2 \circ \beta_2^{\dagger}) = (\alpha_1 + \alpha_2) \circ ((\beta_1 + \beta_2) \circ (x_{(1,3)}^{n_1+n_2+p}, x_{(2,3)}^{n_1+n_2+p}))^{\dagger}$. □

Theorem 5.3 expresses "$\dagger$" in terms of "∇", and (5.6.1) does the opposite. Given $\alpha : n \to n+p$, then $\alpha \circ (1_n + \tau)$ is the result of substituting τ for the p parameters of α; and (5.6.2) says that substituting and then solving gives the same result as solving and then substituting. The composite of solutions comes from "placing" α and β side by side while identifying the parameters of α with the unknowns of β; this is (5.6.3). Given $\gamma:s \to s+q$ we can split off one or more of the equations, say $(\gamma_1,\ldots,\gamma_n) = \alpha:n \to n+p+q$ $(s=n+p)$; solve these with the discarded unknowns (p) as parameters $(\alpha^\nabla:n+p+q \to p+q)$; then substitute the result into the remaining equations, $(\gamma_{n+1},\ldots,\gamma_{n+p}) = \beta:p \to n+p+q$, getting $\beta\circ\alpha^\nabla$; and, finally, solve the resulting system $(\beta\circ\alpha^\nabla)^\dagger$. This process should be essentially the same as solving γ in the first place; that's what (5.6.4) says. The last identity is related to, and really simpler than, (5.6.3). Look at the case $\alpha_i = 1_{n_i}$. Then $(\beta_1{}^\dagger,\beta_2{}^\dagger)$ is the result of solving the systems obtained by placing β_1 and β_2 side by side and identifying the parameters of β_1 with those of β_2.

For the main theorem of this section (paralleling Elgot's (1973) main theorem for iterative theories) we derive mathematically more convenient, though less perspicuous, identities:

Proposition 5.7. For any rational theory $\underline{\underline{T}}$, the following identities hold.

(5.7.1) $(0_p)^\nabla = 1_p$.

(5.7.2) For $\alpha:n \to n+p$ and $\tau:p \to q$, $\alpha^\nabla\circ\tau = (\alpha+\tau)^\dagger$.

(5.7.3) For $\alpha_i:m_i \to n_i$ and $\beta_i:n_i \to n_i+p$, $i \in [2]$,

$$(\alpha_1\circ\beta_1{}^\nabla,\ \alpha_2\circ\beta_2{}^\nabla) = (\alpha_1+\beta_2)\circ f\circ((\beta_1+\beta_2)\circ f)^\nabla$$

when $f = (x^{(n_1+n_2+p)}_{(1,3)},\ x^{(n_1+n_2+p)}_{(2,3)})$ as in 5.6.5.

(5.7.4) For $\alpha:x \to s+n+p$ and $\beta:s \to s+n+p$, $(\alpha\circ\beta^\nabla)^\nabla = x^{s+n+n}_{(2,3)}\circ(\beta,\alpha)^\nabla$. □

Theorem 5.8. Let $\underline{\underline{F}}$ be a subtheory of a rational theory $\underline{\underline{T}}$ and define $\underline{\underline{R}}(n,p)$ to be the set of all $\alpha\circ\beta^\nabla$ such that for some $s \in \omega$, $\alpha:n \to s+p$ and $\beta:s \to s+p$ in F. Then $\underline{\underline{R}}$ is a subtheory of $\underline{\underline{T}}$ which is rational and it is the smallest such containing $\underline{\underline{F}}$. Call this the rational closure of $\underline{\underline{F}}$. □

We sketch the proof of 5.8: $\underline{\underline{F}}$ is contained in $\underline{\underline{R}}$ because $\alpha\circ(0_p^\nabla) = \alpha\circ 1_p = \alpha$ (5.7.1). $\underline{\underline{R}}$ is closed under tupling (5.7.3), $^\nabla$ (5.7.4), and composition, since $(\alpha_1\circ\beta_1{}^\nabla)\circ(\alpha_2\circ\beta_2{}^\nabla) = (\alpha_1\circ(\beta_1+\alpha_2)^\dagger\circ(\beta_2+1_q)^\dagger)$ by (5.7.2) and (5.6.1). Then (5.6.3) and Theorem 5.4 give the desired form $\gamma\circ\eta^\nabla$ for rather complicated γ and η in $\underline{\underline{F}}$.

Taking $\underline{\underline{T}}$ to be $\underline{\underline{CT}}_\Sigma$ and $\underline{\underline{F}}$ to be in $\underline{\underline{FT}}_\Sigma$ we obtain a rational theory $\underline{\underline{RT}}_\Sigma$ which in ADJ (1976a) is shown to be the rational theory freely generated by Σ.

It is an ordered version of the free iterative theory (Bloom and Elgot (1974)) which is given a concrete construction in Ginali (1976).

We conclude the technical results on rational theories stating a stronger version of Theorem 5.8 from which one can glean a generalized "Chomsky Normal Form" Theorem for rational theories. The proof of Corollary 5.9 comes from a careful analysis of that of Theorem 5.8.

Corollary 5.9. Let $\underline{\underline{T}}$ be a rational theory and let $F = \langle F_n | F_n \subseteq \underline{\underline{T}}(1,n),\ n\in\omega\rangle$ be a subfamily of $\langle\underline{\underline{T}}(1,n)|n\in\omega\rangle$. Let F^+ be the closure of F under +. Define

$\underline{\underline{R}}(n,p)$ to be the set of all $a\circ\beta^{\nabla}$ such that $a:n \to s+p$ is a mapping and $\beta = \beta'\circ b:s \to s+p$ where $\beta' \in F^{+} \cup \{0_k | k\in\omega\}$ and b is a mapping. Then $\underline{\underline{R}}$ is a subtheory of $\underline{\underline{T}}$ which is rational and it is the smallest such containing F (i.e. $F_n \subseteq \underline{\underline{R}}(1,n)$.)

We can now apply the "theory of rational theories" to flowcharts. Recall (or see Section 4) that a Σ-flowchart from n to p of weight q, is a pair $\langle b,\alpha\rangle$, where b is an n-tuple of distinguished morphisms from $\underline{\underline{FT}}_{\Sigma}(1,q+p)$ and $\alpha \in \underline{\underline{FT}}_{\Sigma}(q,q+p)$. Let I be an interpretation to an ω-continuous (thus rational) theory $\underline{\underline{T}}$; e.g., to $\underline{\underline{Sm}}_S$, $\underline{\underline{Px}}_P$ or even $\underline{\underline{CT}}_{\Sigma'}$, or $\underline{\underline{Sub}}_T$ (for S a set, P an ω-complete poset, Σ' a ranked alphabet, T a set of "terminal" symbols). We argued at the end of Section 4 that the interpreted behavior of $\langle b,\alpha\rangle$ was $b\circ((\alpha\bar{I})^{\dagger}, 1_p) = b\circ(\alpha\bar{I})^{\nabla}$. But morphisms of rational theories preserve $^{\nabla}$, so $b\circ(\alpha\bar{I})^{\nabla} = (b\circ\alpha^{\nabla})\bar{I}$. Thus the behavior of the interpreted flowchart is the same as the interpretation of the (free or strong) behavior in $\underline{\underline{CT}}_{\Sigma}$. If two flowcharts have the same strong behavior (i.e., if $b_1\circ\alpha_1{}^{\nabla} = b_2\circ\alpha_2{}^{\nabla}$), then they have the same behavior under all interpretations (to ω-continuous, thus rational, theories) because $\bar{I}$ preserves composition and $^{\nabla}$.

The main theorem (5.8) (and its proof) can be interpreted for flowcharts: $\underline{\underline{RT}}_{\Sigma}$ is the rational theory of strong behaviors of flowcharts; the composite of behaviors of flowcharts is the behavior of a flowchart and the same is true for tupling. These are all familiar facts, but rational theories give us a single framework and a single proof.

6. Conclusion

We have introduced the concept of rational algebraic theory and presented some simple applications and important results. It is obvious that the usefulness of such a new concept depends on its simplicity, manipulability and breadth of application. On the first score, one just has to gain some experience with algebraic theories, i.e., with the injections and the way composition and tupling work. Once gained, that experience leads to direct equational-type proofs (algebraic "line-by-line" proofs) of properties like those stated in Theorems 5.6 and 5.7. Choosing (monadic) flowcharts with partial function interpretations as on principal example, we may not have been convincing about the breadth of application of rational theories. But we have suggested, and want to emphasize now, that those canonicalized flowcharts (which might better be called "finite control schemes") can be interpreted in <u>any</u> rational theory leading to useful and perspicuous treatments of fixed-point (generalized) language definition and of recursion. Some of these applications, however, require extension of the ideas to many-sorted (rational) algebraic theories, paralleling the treatment of many-sorted algebras in ADJ (1975). This is a step best postponed until the efficacy of the one-sorted case is appreciated.

In summary, the fundamentals in this paper provide a basis for a uniform approach to recursive definitions in general with, we believe, exciting potential for teaching, for further research, and for practical applications.

Bibliography

ADJ (Coauthored by J.A. Goguen, J.W. Thatcher, E.G. Wagner and J.B. Wright.)

(1975) "Initial algebra semantics and continuous algebras," IBM Research Report RC 5701, November 3, 1975. To appear, JACM.

(1976) "A junction between computer science and category theory: I, Basic definitions and examples," Part 1, IBM Research Report RC 4526 (September 1973); Part 2, IBM Research Report 5908 (March 1976); Part 3 to appear.

(1976a) "Rational algebraic theories and fixed-point solutions," submitted for presentation; IBM Research Report to appear.

Arden, D.N.

(1961) "Delayed-logic and finite-state machines," Course Notes 6.531, E.E.Dept., MIT, Summer, 1961.

Bekic, H.

(1969) "Definable operations in general algebra, and the theory of automata and flowcharts," Report IBM Laboratory Vienna, (1969).

Berry, G.

(1975) "Bottom up computation of recursive programs," IRIA Research Report 133, September 1975.

Birkhoff, G.

(1967) Lattice Theory, Amer. Math. Soc. Colloq. Pub. 25 New York (1948). (revised edition) (1967).

Blikle, A.

(1971) "Nets, complete lattices with a composition," Bulletin de l'Academie Polonaise des Sciences, Serie des Sciences Math. Astr., et Phys. 19 (1971) 1123-1127.

(1973) "Equations in nets, complete oriented lattices," CCPAS Report No. 99, Warsaw (1973).

(1974) "An extended approach to mathematical analysis of programs," CCPAS Report No. 169, Warsaw (1974).

Bloom, S.L. and Elgot, C.C.

(1974) "The existence and construction of free iterative theories," IBM Research Report RC-4937 (1974). To appear JCSS.

Burstall, R.M. and Thatcher, J.W.

"The algebraic theory of recursive program schemes," Proceedings AAAS Symposium on Category Theory Applied to Computation and Control, Univ. of Mass. Press, Amherst (1974); Lecture Notes in Computer Science 25 (1975) 126-131.

de Bakker, J.W. and Scott, D.

(1969) "A theory of programs," unpublished notes, IBM Seminar, Vienna (1969).

de Roever, W.P.

(1974) "Operational, mathematical and axiomatized semantics for recursive procedures and data structures," Mathematical Centre Report ID 1/74 (1974).

Eilenberg, S. and Wright, J.

(1967) "Automata in general algebras," Information and Control 11 (1967) 52-70.

Elgot, C.C.

(1970) "The common algebraic structure of exit-automata and machines," Computing 6 (1970) 349-370.

(1971) "Algebraic theories and program schemes," Symp. on Semantics of Algorithmic Languages, (Ed. E.Engeler), Springer-Verlag (1971) 71-88.

(1972) "Remarks on one-argument program schemes," Formal Semantics of Programming Languages,(Ed.R.Rustin), Prentice-Hall, N.J. (1972) 59-64.

(1973) "Monadic computation and iterative algebraic theories," IBM Research Report RC 4564, October 1973. Proceedings, Logic Colloquium '73, North Holland Publishing Company (1975) 175-230.

(1974) See Bloom and Elgot (1974).

(1975) "Structured programming with and without GO TO statements," IBM Research Report RC 5626 (1975). IEEE Trans.on Software Eng. SE-2 (1976) 41-54.

Englefriet, J.
(1974) "Simple program schemes and formal languages," Lecture Notes in Computer Science 20, Springer-Verlag (1974).

Engelfriet, J. and Schmidt, E.M.
(1975) "IO and OI," Datalogisk Afdeling Report DAIMI PB-417, Aarhus University, Denmark, July, 1975.

Ginsburg, S.
(1966) The Mathematical Theory of Context-Free Languages, McGraw-Hill, N.Y.(1966).

Ginali, S.
(1976) Ph.D. Dissertation, University of Chicago, forthcoming.

Goguen, J.A.
(1974) "On homomorphisms, correctness, termination, unfoldments, and equivalence of flow diagram programs," J. of Comp. and Sys. Sci. 8 (1974) 333-365.

Herrlich, H. and Strecker, C.E.
(1973) Category Theory, Allyn and Bacon (1973)

Karp, R.M.
(1959) "Some applications of logical syntax to digital computer programming," Harvard University Thesis (1959).

Lawvere, F.W.
(1963) "Functional semantics of algebraic theories," Proceedings, Nat'l Acad. Sci. 50 (1963) 869-872.

Mac Lane, S.
(1971a) Category Theory for the Working Mathematician, Springer-Verlag (1971).

Mezei, J. and Wright, J.B.
(1967) "Algebraic automata and context-free sets," Information and Control 11 (1967) 3-29.

Mitchell, B.
(1965) Theory of Categories, Academic Press, New York (1965).

Pareigis, B.
(1970) Categories and Functors, Academic Press, New York (1970).

Park, D.M.R.
(1969) "Fixpoint induction and proofs of program properties," Machine Intelligence 5 (Eds. B.Meltzer and D.Michie) Edinburgh Univ.Press (1969) 59-78.

Scott, D.
(1970) "Outline of a mathematical theory of computation," Proceedings, 4th Princeton Conf. on Inform. Science and Systems (1970).

Wagner, E.G.
(1971) "Languages for defining sets in arbitrary algebras," Proceedings, 12th IEEE Symp. on Switching and Automata Th., E.Lansing, Mich. (1971).

(1971a) "An algebraic theory of recursive definitions and recursive languages," Proceedings, 3rd ACM Symp. on Theory of Comp., Shaker Hghts,Ohio (1971).

ON ATTRIBUTE GRAMMARS

V.N.Agafonov
Institute of mathematics,
Novosibirsk 90, USSR

A common mechanism for specifying a programming language L can be viewed as consisting of two components. The first one is a context free (CF) grammar G which generates a broader language $L(G) \supset L$. The second one contains more or less formal rules which take into account so called context conditions and select from language L(G) strings of language L. In the recent literature on formal languages much attention is paid to the following way of specifying languages which are not context free. A CF grammar G is supplied with some type of device which controls applications of production rules in the course of derivations. This control device C picks out, from the set of all derivations, a subset called control set. A control device grammar G'=(G,C) defines language $L(G') \subset L(G)$ in such a way that a string $\varphi \in L(G)$ belongs to L(G') iff its derivation is contained in the control set. Such grammars include, among others, matrix, programmed and conditional grammars (see the survey [9]). Restrictions which are imposed on derivations in these grammars are but poorly related to semantics of programming languages and corresponding context conditions. In this paper a method for specifying languages which are not CF is suggested and investigated in which restrictions are computed in such a way that was previously used for defining semantics of programming languages [5, 6]. This method is based on the notion of attribute CF grammar introduced by Knuth [6] for specifying semantics of CF languages. In [7] Knuth's notion was transformed into the concept of attributed translation (AT) grammar adapted for specifying translations of CF languages whose terminal strings are supplied with attributes.

I. An <u>attribute generative (AG) grammar</u> G is a pair (G',C) where G' is a CF grammar (called the <u>base</u> of the grammar G) and C is a control device. The grammar G'= (N,T,R,S) is supposed to be reduced, the start nonterminal $S \in N$ does not appear on the right-hand side of any production rule $r \in R$, and for any nonterminal $A \in N$ there does not exist a nontrivial derivation $A \overset{+}{\Rightarrow} A$. The control device $C = (A, V, F, \sigma)$ is defined as follows. I) A is a function which associates a finite set $A(X)$ of attributes to each nonterminal $X \in N$. Each $A(X)$ is partitioned into two disjoint sets, the synthesized attributes $A_{syn}(X)$ and the inherited attributes $A_{inh}(X)$. It is supposed that $A_{inh}(S) = \emptyset$. A set $A' = \bigcup_{X \in N} A(X)$ will be called attribute alphabet. 2) V is a function which associates a set of values to each attribute $\alpha \in A$. Let the set $\bigcup_{\alpha \in A'} V(\alpha)$ be set of strings in a finite alphabet. 3) F is a finite set of <u>control functions</u> which is defined in the following way. Let the r-th production of the set R $(I \leq r \leq m)$ be $X_0 \rightarrow \varphi_0 X_I \varphi_1 X_2 \ldots X_{m_r} \varphi_{m_r}$ where $\varphi_i \in T$, $X_i \in N$. Then a control function set $F_r = \{ f_{rj\alpha} \mid I \leq j \leq m_r$ and $\alpha \in A_{syn}(X_j)$ if $j = 0$, $\alpha \in A_{inh}(X_j)$ if $j > 0 \}$ corresponds to this production and $F = \bigcup_{I \leq r \leq m} F_r$. The function $f_{rj\alpha}$ is a recursive mapping of $V(\alpha_1) \times \ldots \times V(\alpha_t)$ into $V(\alpha)$, for some $t = t(r,j,\alpha) \geq 0$, where each $\alpha_i = \alpha_i(r,j,\alpha)$ is an attribute of some X_k , for $0 \leq k_i = k_i(r,j,\alpha) \leq m_r$, $I \leq i \leq t$. 4) $\sigma \in A_{syn}(S)$ is a special attribute for which $V(\sigma) = \{0, I\}$ and $\sigma \notin \bigcup_{X \neq S} A(X)$. A language $L(G) \subseteq L(G')$ generated by the AG grammar G is defined as follows. Let $\varphi \in L(G')$ and t be a derivation tree of φ in the CF grammar G'. If each node of the tree labeled by a nonterminal X is labeled also by attributes of the set A(X) then we obtain the corresponding attributed tree. Now, by means of control functions $f_{rj\alpha}$ the computation of the value of each attribute in the tree should be attempted. If this can be done and the value of the attribute σ is I then the tree t is accepted. The string φ belongs to L(G) iff φ has an accepted tree.

In the sequel AG grammars are supposed to be well defined (G is <u>well defined</u> [6] if for any attributed tree values of all atributes at all nodes can be defined).

The difference between AG grammars and Knuth grammars is that in an AG grammar I) terminals have no attributes (or if you like the terminal itself is its only own attribute) and 2) there is a special attribute whose value at the root of a given tree tells us whether this tree is accepted or not. These differences reflect different viewpoints. An AG grammar is intended for generating a language which is not CF and so satisfies some context conditions whereas a Knuth grammar is intended for assigning values (meanings) to strings of a CF language. It should also to be noted that in the definition of AG grammar values of attributes are only strings in a finite alphabet.

2. Some types of grammars which were previously introduced to handle programming languages may be interpreted as AG grammars, i.e. corresponding control device may be naturally expressed in terms of attributes and control functions. They are: a) grammars with a mechanism of identification [4,I] which generate exactly the class of extended definable Algol-like languages [8], b) indexed grammars [2], c) grammars with context conditions [3].

3. In [6] and [7] the order of computing values of attributes in attributed trees was considered. But no attention was paid to the nature of control functions ("semantic rules"). We, however, are interested in the relation between complexity of control functions and complexity of the corresponding class of AG languages. The situation here can be outlined by the following theorems.

a) If control functions are not made to meet additional restrictions then AG grammars generate all recursive languages and only these.

b) If all control functions are finite then only CF languages can be obtained.

Note that the mechanism of recognizing derivation trees by a finite tree automaton is a particular case of AG grammars with finite control functions.

Statements (a) and (b) establish upper and lower bounds for complexity of AG languages. In common cases control functions are expected to be not too complex but not necessarily finite. A control function $f(x_I,\dots,x_k)$ is <u>computable in linear time</u> if there are a random access machine M and a costant c such that for all strings $\varphi_1,\dots,\varphi_k$ the value $f(\varphi_1,\dots,\varphi_k)$ is computable by the machine M in time (number of steps) $\leq c\cdot\max_{1\leq i\leq k}|\varphi_i|$. An AG grammar G = (G',C) is <u>linear bounded</u> if there exists a constant c such that for any string $\varphi \in L(G')$ and for any its attributed tree t values of all attributes in t have lengths $\leq c\cdot|\varphi|$, where $|\varphi|$ is the length of the string φ.

c) If G is a linear bounded AG grammar with an unambiguous base and control functions which are computable in linear time then the language L(G) is recognized by a random access machine in time proportional to n^2, where n is the length of the input string.

The linear computation time of control functions seems to be too restrictive for checking context conditions in programming languages. If in the theorem (c) we replace linear time by time proportional to m^2, where m is the maximal length of argument values, then the conclusion of (c) is to be replaced by the following:

c') language L(G) is recognized by a random access machine in time proportional to n^3.

The statements (c) and (c') may be interpreted in the sense that AG grammars of practical interest generate not too complex languages.

4. In [7] a classification of AT grammars was given which depends on the order in which the values of attributes in attributed trees are computed and a hierarchy of corresponding classes of translations was established. A similar classification is possible for AG grammars (in particular a SAG grammar is such a grammar that all attributes are synthesized, i.e. the computation of their values is performed bottom up) but corresponding classes of AG languages are identical. Besides, in [7] the notion of attributed push down (ATPD) machine was introduced and it was shown that for a given LAT grammar an ATPD machine can be constructed which performs the same translation and vice versa. A similar notion and relation holds for LAG grammars (an attributed push down machine recognizes the corresponding language).

References.

I. V.N.Agafonov, On grammars with a mechanism of identification, System and theoretical programming, vol. 2, Kishinev, I974. (in Russian).
2. A.V. Aho, Indexed grammars - an extention of context-free grammars, J.Assoc.Comput.Mach. I5 (I968), N 4.
3. I.L.Bratčikov, Teurig, H.I., On a formalization of some context conditios in programming languages, Z.Vycisl.Mat. i Mat. Fiz. I4 (I974), N 4. (in Russian)
4. A.P.Eršov, G.I.Kožuxin, Ju. M.Vološin, Input language for automatic programming systems, Novosibirsk, I964, (in Russian)
5. E.T.Irons, A syntax-directed compiler for Algol 60, Comm. Assoc.Comput.Mach. I5 (I968), N I.
6. D.E.Knuth, Semantics of context-free languages, Math. System theory 2 (I968), N 2.
7. P.M.Lewis, D.J.Rosenkrantz, R.E.Stearns, Attributed translations, J.Comput.System Sci. 9 (I974), N 3.
8. G.F.Rose, An extention of Algol-like languages, Comm.Assoc. Comput.Mach. 7 (I964), N 2.
9. E.D.Stockij, Control of derivations in formal grammars, Problemy Peredači Informacii 7 (I97I), N 3. (in Russian)

FORMAL DEFINITION OF SEMANTICS OF GENERALIZED CONTROL REGIMES

L. Aiello °

M. Aiello, G. Attardi, P. Cavallari, G. Prini °°

In order to give a formal semantics to programming languages, a model of computation has been axiomatized in a typed logic. Such a model allows to associate with any program the function it denotes, as a mapping from stores into stores. A store is considered as an association of values with names and is structured into frames, to take into account the change of environment due to a transfer of control in the program. Any control regime, such as procedure call or coroutine activation, may be represented in our axiomatization by specifying how a new environment is created and how it is related to the previous ones. With this notion of store we give a formal semantics to the ALGOL-like procedure activation, the coroutine activation and backtracking. The semantics of a programming language is defined by interpreting each primitive with a function in the logic and providing for any construct of the language the corresponding term in the logic (which represents a transformation from stores into stores). It is then defined how such terms are combined, according to the syntactic structure of any given program, to obtain the function which constitutes its meaning. The logic we use to represent functions is LCF, a typed λ-calculus augmented with some constructs (such as conditional expressions) to increase its expressive power (Sco69,Mil72,Aie75). Our model of computation is based on the frame structure as defined in (Bob73): the set of information contained in a frame includes a binding link (it specifies where parameters are bound), an access link (it points to the environment where free variables are bound), a control link (it specifies in which

---

° **IEI del CNR - Via S. Maria 46 - I-56100 PISA (Italy)**

°° ISI - Università di Pisa - Corso Italia 40 - I-56100 PISA (Italy)

environment the process continues in the case of a normal exit) and a process state (i.e. a continuation point and the value of temporary variables). This last information is stored when control is transferred to another frame; it specifies how to continue the process in the present frame.

In our axiomatization stores are represented by conditional expressions as mappings from names of frames into frames:

$$
\begin{aligned}
[\lambda\, \mathrm{framename.framename}&=\langle \mathrm{framename1}\rangle \rightarrow \langle \mathrm{frame1}\rangle,\\
&\ \vdots\\
\mathrm{framename}&=\langle \mathrm{framenamen}\rangle \rightarrow \langle \mathrm{framen}\rangle, \mathrm{EOS}]
\end{aligned}
$$

Note that identifiers included in angle brackets are metavariables. Each <framei> maps location names into values:

$$
\begin{aligned}
[\lambda\, \mathrm{locationname.locationname}&=\langle \mathrm{locationname1}\rangle \rightarrow \langle \mathrm{value1}\rangle,\\
&\ \vdots\\
\mathrm{locationname}&=\langle \mathrm{locationnamem}\rangle \rightarrow \langle \mathrm{valuem}\rangle, \mathrm{EOF}]
\end{aligned}
$$

In the above formulas the constants EOS (End Of Store) and EOF (End Of Frame) allow to decide whether or not a frame with a given name is present in a store and a location with a given name is present in a frame.

Frames are added to a store by the function MAKEFRAME:

$$\mathrm{MAKEFRAME}=[\lambda\, \mathrm{fn}\ \mathrm{s}.[\lambda\, \mathrm{fl.fl}=\mathrm{fn}\rightarrow[\lambda\, \mathrm{loc.EOF}],\mathrm{s(fl)}]]$$

Locations are added to a frame by the function MODFRAME:

$$\mathrm{MODFRAME}=[\lambda\, \mathrm{fn}\ \mathrm{n}\ \mathrm{v}\ \mathrm{s}.[\lambda\, \mathrm{fl.fl}=\mathrm{fn}\rightarrow[\lambda\, \mathrm{loc.loc}=\mathrm{n}\rightarrow \mathrm{v},\mathrm{s(fn,loc)}],\mathrm{s(fl)}]]$$

The semantics of a program in a given environment (°) is a mapping

---

° The referencing environment in the sense of ALGOL, i.e. all the active bindings between identifiers and values.

from stores into stores. It is defined by the function EVAL reported in Appendix. In the following we present comments on its behaviour as well as some of the auxiliary functions it uses.

The semantics of the assignment is defined by the function ASSIGN.

```
ASSIGN=[λfn vr v s.
          ISLOCAL(fn,vr,s)→
            ISADMISVAL(vr,v,fn,s)→
              MODFRAME(fn,vr,v,s),UU,
            ISTOPF(fn)→UU,
              ISLOCAL(s(fn,blink),vr,s)→
                ISADMISVAL(vr,v,s(fn,blink),s)→
                  MODFRAME(s(fn,blink),vr,v,s),UU,
                s(s(fn,blink),bindloc(n))≠EOF→
                  ASSIGN(father(fn),s(s(fn,blink),bindloc(n)),v,s),
                  ASSIGN(s(fn,alink),vr,v,s)]
```

In the environment accessible from fn, the value of the variable represented by vr (°) is set to v. Type checkings are performed by ISADMISVAL. If the variable represented by vr has not been declared in the environment accessible from fn the result of ASSIGN is the undefined store.

The semantics of procedure statements may be informally explained as follows: in the current frame the continuation point, c-point, is set to the tail of the currently evaluated text. A new frame (the basic frame for this procedure activation (Bob73)) is created which contains all parameter bindings. ENVEVAL then creates another frame in which the called procedure is interpreted. Appropriate a-link, b-link and c-link are set up for this frame. The function ACCESSENV returns a pointer to the frame where the called routine has been declared.

° vr itself or the variable bound to it if vr is a variable parameter.

```
ENVEVAL=[λfn form f1 f2 f3 s.
          MAKEFRAME(fn,s) ∘ MODFRAME(fn,alink,f1,s) ∘
          MODFRAME(fn,clink,f2,s) ∘ MODFRAME(fn,blink,f3,s) ∘
          EVALDECL(fn,declof(form),s) ∘ EVAL(fn,statmof(form),s)]
```

The operator ∘ denotes functional composition.

The meaning of a coroutine system call is quite similar to the meaning of a procedure call. In this case the basic frame (°) contains also a set of global information necessary to pass control among the various routines of the system (it includes the list of names of all routines of the system, the name of the currently active one and some control information for each suspended routine (°°)). After creating the basic frame the first routine of the system is activated.

The meaning of an operation of <u>resume</u> is defined by the function RESUME applied to current frame f, the name of the called routine n, the pointer f1 to the first control frame (°) met in the c-link chain starting from f.

```
RESUME=[λn f f1 s.
         nεs(f1,funsloc)→
           ACCESSIBLE(f,s(f1,accesloc),s)→
             MODFRAME(f1,s(f1,activloc),f,s) ∘
             MODFRAME(f1,activloc,n,s) ∘
             ACTIVATE(n,f1,s),
             ISTOPF(father(f1))→UU,
               RESUME(n,f,CONTROLF(father(f1),s),s),
           ISTOPF(father(f1))→UU,
             RESUME(n,f,CONTROLF(father(f1),s),s)]

ACTIVATE=[λn f s.s(f,n)=EOF→
```

° In the following we refer to such a frame as the control frame for coroutine systems.

°° It consists of the name of the frame where each routine has been suspended.

```
          EVAL(s(f,n),s(s(f,n),cpoint),s),
          ENVEVAL(NEWSON(father(f,s),
                   TEXT(n,s(f,accesloc),s),
                   s(f,accesloc),
                   father(f),
                   f,
                   MAKENEWSON(father(f),s))]
```

RESUME tests if n belongs to the routines of the system activated in f1 and if this system has been declared in the environment of f. If so, the global information is updated in f1 (i.e. the control information for the actual active routine is set to f and n is set as the currently active routine), then the called procedure is activated. Otherwise, a previously activated system is searched for.

Backtracking has been represented in our axiomatization by means of two statements: a <u>select</u> statement (whose syntax is:

<u>select</u>(<text1>, ... ,<textn>)

where each <texti> is one of the alternative texts) and a <u>fail</u> statement.

```
    FAILSET=[λf lt s.
             MODFRAME(f,alternativesloc,cdr(lt),s) ∘
             MODFRAME(TOPFRAME,
                      failistloc,
                      cons(cons(f,CODESTORE(s)),
                           s(TOPFRAME,failistloc)),
                      s)]

   SELECT=[λf s.
           iseof(ALTERNATIVES(f,s))→
             s(TOPFRAME,failistloc)=EOF→UU,
               SELECT(LASTCHOICEF(s),LASTCHOICES(s)),
             EVAL(f,
                  car(ALTERNATIVES(f,s)),
                  FAILSET(f,ALTERNATIVES(f,s),s))]
```

The function FAILSET stores in the special location failistloc in the TOPFRAME the encoding of the actual store so that, if a failure occurs, it is possible to restore the state of the computation at the time the last choice point occurred. The function SELECT forces the evaluation of the text associated with the first unexplored alternative in the appropriate frame and store.

We stress the relevance of our formal treatment of the semantics of programming languages, which allows to study features of classes of programs, not only of single programs. Furthermore, different definitions of the semantics for a programming language may be given, and then their equivalence proved. As an example, the equivalence between two different semantic definitions for backtracking (the previously described one and another one which uses a context mechanism like in some existing very high level programming languages) has been proved with the aid of PPC (Aie75). This proof ensures that a semantic definition which models an actual implementation is equivalent to a conceptually clearer one, which conversely is very far from any reasonable implementation.

Due to the lack of space, our presentation is necessarily incomplete. We refer to (Aie74) for the definition of some semantic functions appearing in EVAL, and, mostly, to a forthcoming memo where the treatment of coroutines and backtracking is described in full detail.

REFERENCES

(Aie74) Aiello,L.,Aiello,M.,Weyhrauch,R.W., The semantics of PASCAL in LCF, AIM 221, Stanford University, 1974

(Aie75) Aiello,L.,Aiello,M.,Attardi,G.,Prini,G., Informal proofs formally checked by machine, Annals of the Logic International Summer Seminar, Clermont-Ferrand, 1975

(Bob73) Bobrow,D.,Wegbreit,B., A model and stack implementation of multiple environments, Comm. ACM, 591-603, 1973

(Mil72) Milner,R., Logic for computable functions: description of a machine implementation, AIM 169, Stanford University, 1972

(Sco69) Scott,D., A type theoretical alternative to CUCH, ISWIM, OWHY, Unpublished Paper, 1969

APPENDIX

```
EVAL=[λf st s.
        iseof(st)→s,
          iscompound(st)→
            isconditional(car(st))→
              MBEXPR(f,testof(car(st)),s)→
                EVAL(f,append(thenof(car(st)),cdr(st)),s),
                  EVAL(f,append(elseof(car(st)),cdr(st)),s),
            isreturn(car(st))→
              EVAL(s(f,clink),s(s(f,clink),cpoint),s),
            isgoto(car(st))→
              EVAL(FETCH(f,labloc(namof(car(st))),s),
                   FETCHV(f,labloc(namof(car(st))),s),
                   s),
            isprocall(car(st))→
              MODFRAME(f,cpoint,cdr(st),s) ∘
              MAKEBASICFORPROCALL(NEWSON(f,s),
                                  car(st),
                                  MAKENEWSON(f,s)) ∘
              ENVEVAL(NEWSON(f,s),
                      TEXT(f,namof(car(st)),s),
                      ACCESSENV(f,namof(car(st)),s),
                      f,
                      SON(f,s),
                      MAKENEWSON(f,s)),
            iscorcall(car(st))→
              MODFRAME(f,cpoint,cdr(st),s) ∘
              MAKEBASICFORCORCALL(NEWSON(f,s),
                                  car(st),
                                  MAKENEWSON(f,s)) ∘

              ENVEVAL(NEWSON(f,s),
                      TEXT(ACCESSENV(f,namof(car(st)),s),
                           car(FUNS(f,namof(car(st)),s)),
                           s),
                      ACCESSENV(f,namof(car(st)),s),
                      f,
                      SON(f,s),
                      MAKENEWSON(f,s)),
            isresume(car(st))→
              MODFRAME(f,cpoint,cdr(st),s) ∘
              RESUME(namof(car(st)),f,CONTROLF(f,s)),
            isselect(car(st))→
              EVAL(f,
                   car(alternativesof(car(st))),
                   FAILSET(f,alternativesof(car(st)),s)),
            isfail(car(st))→
              s(TOPFRAME,failistloc)=EOF→UU,
                SELECT(LASTCHOICE(s),LASTCHOICES(s)),
            isassign(car(st))→
              EVAL(f,
                   cdr(st),
                   ASSIGN(f,leftof(car(st)),
                               MEXPR(f,rightof(car(st)),s),s)),
            UU,UU]
```

MINIMAL WHILE PROGRAMS *

E. S. Bainbridge
Mathematics Department
University of Ottawa
Ottawa, Ontario, Canada

Let F be a fixed set of function symbols, and let P be a fixed set of predicate symbols. Two WHILE programs over (F,P) are strongly equivalent if their flowcharts, as automata, determine the same regular subset of $(F \cup P)^*$. The major result described here is that, relative to a certain class of size measures, there is, among all WHILE programs strongly equivalent to a given WHILE program W , a unique program of minimal size. Moreover, this minimal WHILE program is the same regardless of the choice of size measure within the class. It is a consequence that among all WHILE programs strongly equivalent to W , the minimal one has simultaneously the fewest number of occurrences of each function symbol $f \in F$, of branches involving any particular predicate symbol $p \in P$, and of loops involving any particular $p \in P$.

There is a simple procedure to construct from a WHILE program W the minimal WHILE program strongly equivalent to it. Also, there is a simple algebraic procedure to determine if a given flowchart is strongly equivalent to a WHILE program, and, if so, to construct such a program, and hence the minimal one. This last procedure follows directly without appeal to Kasai's (1974) graph-theoretic characterization of flowcharts which are strongly equivalent to WHILE programs. Indeed, one can deduce Kasai's result from the procedure given here.

Let P be equipped with a function $p \mapsto \overline{p}: P \to P$ such that $\overline{p} \neq P$ and $\overline{\overline{p}} = p$. Let $1 \in (F \cup P)^*$ denote the empty string.

The set $\mathbf{W}$ of WHILE terms over (F,P) is defined inductively by: (i) $1 \in \mathbf{W}$; (ii) if $X, Y, Z \in \mathbf{W}$, $f \in F$, $p \in P$, then fZ , $(pX + \overline{p}Y)Z = (\overline{p}Y + pX)Z$, $(pX)^*\overline{p}Z$ are in $\mathbf{W}$.

* Research supported by NSF grant DCR 72-03703 A01 at Columbia Univ.

A WHILE term $W \in \mathbf{W}$ is, on the one hand, an abbreviated notation for the WHILE program $[W]$ defined by: (i) $[1]$ = NULL; (ii) $[fZ] = f[Z]$, $[(pX + \overline{p}Y)Z]$ = (IF p THEN $[X]$ ELSE $[Y]$)$[Z]$, $[(pX)*\overline{p}Z]$ = (WHILE p DO $[X]$)$[Z]$.

On the other hand, $W \in \mathbf{W}$ as a regular expression denotes the set $|W| \subset (F \cup P)^*$ of traces of the corresponding program, that is: (i) $|1| = \{1\}$; (ii) $|fZ| = f|Z|$, $|(pX + \overline{p}Y)Z| = (p|X| \cup \overline{p}|Y|)|Z|$, $|(pX)*\overline{p}Z| = (p|X|)*\overline{p}\,|Z|$.

The size $\#W$ of $W \in \mathbf{W}$ is defined by: (i) $\#1 = 0$; (ii) $\#(fZ) = K_f + \#Z$, $\#((pX + \overline{p}Y)Z) = K_p + \#X + \#Y + \#Z$, $\#((pX)*\overline{p}Z) = K^*_p + \#X + \#Z$; where K_f , $K_p = K_{\overline{p}}$, K^*_p are positive integers which we shall leave unspecified.

A WHILE term W is minimal if for all $U \in \mathbf{W}$ $|W| = |U|$ implies $\#W \leq \#U$. Since there are only a finite number of $U \in \mathbf{W}$ with a given size, it follows that for every $V \in \mathbf{W}$ there is at least one minimal $W \in \mathbf{W}$ such that $|W| = |V|$.

The product $UV \in \mathbf{W}$ of WHILE terms U, V is defined by induction on U for fixed V by: (i) $1V = V$; (ii) $(fZ)V = f(ZV)$, $((pX + \overline{p}Y)Z)V = (pX + \overline{p}Y)(ZV)$, $((pX)*\overline{p}Z)V = (pX)*\overline{p}(ZV)$. It follows immediately that $|UV| = |U|\,|V|$ and $\#(UV) = \#U + \#V$.

Let $a \in (F \cup P)$. The derivative $a^{-1}W$ of $W \in \mathbf{W}$ with respect to a is defined by: (i) $a^{-1}1 = \emptyset$; (ii) $a^{-1}(fZ)$ equals Z if $a = f$ and $\emptyset$ otherwise, $a^{-1}((pX + \overline{p}Y)Z)$ equals XZ if $a = p$ and YZ if $a = \overline{p}$ and $\emptyset$ otherwise, $a^{-1}((pX)*\overline{p}Z)$ equals $X(pX)*\overline{p}Z$ if $a = p$ and Z if $a = \overline{p}$ and $\emptyset$ otherwise. Evidently $|a^{-1}W| = a^{-1}|W|$, where $|\emptyset| = \emptyset$ and for $A \subset (F \cup P)^*$, $a^{-1}A = \{x \in (F \cup P)^* \mid ax \in A\}$. For $x \in (F \cup P)^*$ we define $x^{-1}W$ to be W if $x = 1$ and $y^{-1}(a^{-1}W)$ if $x = ay$.

A WHILE term W is locally minimal if $W = 1$ or $W = VZ$ where Z is locally minimal and V is minimal and either of the form f , or $(pX + \overline{p}Y)$, or $(pX)*\overline{p}$. It follows immediately that if W is minimal then W is locally minimal; and that if U, V are locally minimal, then UV is locally minimal. The central theorem, whose rather intricate proof will appear elsewhere, is the following.

<u>Theorem</u>: If U is minimal and V is locally minimal, then $|U| = |V|$ implies $U = V$.

<u>Corollary</u>: If W is locally minimal then W is minimal.

<u>Corollary</u>: If U, V are minimal, then UV is minimal.

Somewhat less directly we have

<u>Corollary</u>: If W is minimal and $x^{-1}W \neq \emptyset$, then $x^{-1}W$ is minimal.

<u>Proof</u>: By induction on $x \in (F \cup P)^*$ it is sufficient to show that W minimal implies $a^{-1}W$ minimal, for $a \in F \cup P$. The result follows by induction on W by showing that if W is minimal its constituents are minimal, and using the previous corollary.

<u>Corollary</u>: If $W = (pX + \overline{p}Y)Z$ is minimal and $|W| = |U|$, then U is of the form $(pR + \overline{p}S)T$.

<u>Proof</u>: $|W| = |U|$ implies $p^{-1}U \neq \emptyset$, so U must be either of the form $(pR + \overline{p}S)T$, or $(pR)^*\overline{p}T$, or $(\overline{p}R)^*pT$. If $U = (pR)^*\overline{p}T$, then $|XZ| = |p^{-1}W| = |p^{-1}U| = |RU| = |RW| = |QW|$, where Q is minimal and $|Q| = |R|$. Then $XZ = p^{-1}W$ is minimal, QW is a product of minimal terms and hence is minimal, so $XZ = QW$ which is absurd. Thus $U \neq (pR)^*\overline{p}T$, and similarly $U \neq (pR)^*\overline{p}T$.

<u>Corollary</u>: If W is minimal and $|W| = |(pX)^*\overline{p}Z|$, then W is of the form $(pR)^*\overline{p}T$.

Proof: By the previous corollary, we cannot have $W = (pR + \overline{p}S)T$. Thus, since $p^{-1}W \neq \emptyset$ we must have $W = (pR)^*\overline{p}T$ or $W = (\overline{p}R)^*pT$. The latter yields $|Z| = |\overline{p}^{-1}W| = |RW| = |R(pX)^*\overline{p}||Z|$ which can be satisfied only if $|Z| = \emptyset$, which is impossible. Thus W has the form $(pR)^*\overline{p}T$.

We can now establish a simple procedure for minimizing any $W \in \mathbf{W}$.

<u>Lemma</u>: If $|UW| = |VW|$ then $|U| = |V|$.

<u>Proof</u>: If $|U| \neq |V|$, let x be a shortest element of $(|U| - |V|) \cup (|V| - |U|)$. Without loss of generality we may assume that $x \in |U| - |V|$. Since $|W| \neq \emptyset$, let w be a shortest

element of $|W|$. Thus $xw \in |UW| = |VW|$, so $xw = yw'$ where $y \in |V|$, $w' \in |W|$. By choice of w, we must have $w' = zw$. We cannot have $z = 1$, since then $x = x' \in |V|$, a contradiction. Thus $x = yz$, $z \neq 1$. We must have $y \in |U|$, otherwise $y \in |V| - |U|$, contradicting minimality of x. However, $y \in |U|$ implies $1 \in y^{-1}|U| = |y^{-1}U|$; and in general, $1 \in |X|$ implies $|X| = 1$. Thus $y^{-1}U = 1$. But $z \in y^{-1}|U|$ since $yz = x \in |U|$. Thus $z = 1$, a contradiction.

<u>Theorem</u>: If Z is minimal then fZ is minimal. If $(pX + \bar{p}Y)Z$ is not minimal then either one of X, Y, Z is not minimal; or $X = UT$, $Y = VT$, $T \neq 1$; or $Y = 1$ and $X = S(pS)^*\bar{p}$. If X, Z are minimal then $(pX)^*\bar{p}Z$ is minimal.

<u>Proof</u>: f is minimal, so fZ is minimal if Z is minimal.

Suppose that X, Y, Z are minimal but $(pX + \bar{p}Y)Z$ is not minimal. Then $pX + \bar{p}Y$ is not minimal. Let W be minimal and satisfy $|W| = |pX + \bar{p}Y|$. If $W = (pU + \bar{p}V)T$, then $|UT| = |X|$ and $|VT| = |Y|$. By minimality of X, Y, W, we have $X = UT$, $Y = VT$. Moreover, $T \neq 1$ otherwise $pX + \bar{p}Y$ equals W and is minimal. If $W = (pS)^*\bar{p}T$ then $|SW| = |X|$, $|T| = |Y|$ and so $X = S(pS)^*\bar{p}T$, $Y = T$ which gives one desired form if $T \neq 1$ and the other if $T = 1$. If $W = (\bar{p}S)^*\bar{p}T$ we have the desired forms by writing $(pX + \bar{p}Y)Z = (qX' + \bar{q}Y')Z$ where $q = \bar{p}$, $X' = Y$, $Y' = X$.

Suppose that X, Z are minimal. Then if W is minimal and $|W| = |(pX)^*\bar{p}Z|$ we must have $W = (pS)^*\bar{p}T$, $|T| = |\bar{p}^{-1}W| = |Z|$ and by minimality, $T = Z$. Thus $|(pX)^*\bar{p}Z| = |(pS)^*\bar{p}Z|$ so by the lemma, $|(pX)^*\bar{p}| = |(pS)^*\bar{p}|$. Taking derivatives with respect to p we have $|X(pX)^*\bar{p}Z| = |S(pS)^*\bar{p}Z| = |S(pS)^*\bar{p}Z| = |S(pX)^*\bar{p}Z|$, so $|X| = |S|$. By minimality $X = S$, so $(pX)^*\bar{p}Z$ equals W and is minimal.

<u>Corollary</u>: If no constituent of W can be simplified by either of the rules

1. if $T \neq 1$ then $(pUT + \bar{p}VT) \to (pU + \bar{p}V)T$
2. $(pS(pS)^*\bar{p} + \bar{p}) \to (pS)^*\bar{p}$

then W is minimal.

Proof: This follows immediately by induction using the preceding theorem and the obvious inductive definition of constituents.

Procedure: To minimize W apply rules 1 and 2 until no further application is possible.

Proof: The rules can be applied only a finite number of times, since each application strictly reduces the size. The result is minimal.

Corollary: Minimality is independent of the constants K_f, K_p, K_p^*.

Observe that we may choose a particular K_{f_o} arbitrarily large, and $K_f = 1$ if $f \neq f_o$, $K_p = K_p^* = 1$. Then minimality implies fewest occurances of that f_o. Likewise other constants can be made large to establish the other properties of minimal forms stated earlier.

A flowchart is a deterministic automaton (in the sense of Eilenberg (1973)) $\mathbf{F} = (Q,i,t)$ over $F \cup P$ such that for each $q \in Q$ either $q = t$ and there is no edge from q, or $q \neq t$ and there is just one edge from q and its label is in F, or $q \neq t$ and there are just two edges from q and their labels are respectively $p, \bar{p}$ for some $p \in P$.

The behavior $|\mathbf{F}| \subset (F \cup P)^*$ of a flowchart $\mathbf{F} = (Q,i,t)$ is the set of all labels of paths in $\mathbf{F}$ from i to t.

If $W \in \mathbf{W}$, the derived flowchart $\mathbf{F}(W) = (DW, W, 1)$ has states $DW = \{x^{-1}W \mid x \in (F \cup P)^*\}$, initial state W, final state 1, and next state function $a: U \mapsto a^{-1}U$ for $a \in F \cup P$, $U \in DW$. Note that $W \in DW$, and that $1 \in DW$ since $|W| \neq \emptyset$ and $x^{-1}W = 1$ for $x \in |W|$. Moreover, DW is finite by a modification of Brzozowski's (1964) argument, and one readily checks that $\mathbf{F}(W)$ is a flowchart. Note, however, that $\mathbf{F}(W)$ is not the flowchart of the corresponding program $[W]$.

Proposition: $|\mathbf{F}(W)| = |W|$

Proof: Brzozowski (1964).

The flowchart $\mathbf{F}(W)$ is always reachable, and the subautomaton $\mathbf{F}(U)$ with initial state U has behavior $|U|$. Also, if W is minimal, then $x^{-1}W$ is minimal. Thus if $U, V \in DW$ satisfy

$|U| = |V|$, then $U = V$; that is, **F**(W) is a minimal automaton if W is minimal. Indeed, more is true.

Theorem: W is minimal if and only if **F**(W) is a minimal automaton.

This demonstrates more forcefully the invariant significance of minimality.

To each state j of a flowchart **F** assign an equation which is either (i) $j = 1$ if j is terminal, (ii) $j = fk$ if $j \xrightarrow{f} k$ is an edge of **F** , (iii) $j = pk + \overline{p}\ell$ if $k \xleftarrow{p} j \xrightarrow{\overline{p}} \ell$ are edges of **F** .

Consider the following rules for solving such equations, where X, Y ∈ **W** : (I) if $j = Xk$ or $j = X$, elmiminate j by substitution, (ii) if $j = pXk + \overline{p}Yk$, deduce $j = (pX + \overline{p}Y)k$, (III) if $j = pXj + \overline{p}Yk$ or $j = pXj + \overline{p}Y$, deduce respectively $j = (pX)^*\overline{p}Yk$, or $j = (pX)^*\overline{p}Y$.

If **F** = (Q,i,t) and these rules yield the equation $i = W$ from the equations of **F** , then we shall write **F** ⊢ W .

Proposition: If **F** ⊢ W then W ∈ **W** and |**F**| = |W| .

Proof: A straightforward induction on the number of applications of rules I, II, III.

Theorem: If W is minimal, then **F**(W) ⊢ W .

Proof: An induction of W using results about the form of minimal W ∈ **W** .

Procedure: Given a flowchart **F** , to determine if there is W ∈ **W** such that |**F**| = |W| , minimize **F** as an automaton and attempt a solution of the resulting equations by rules I, II, III.

Proof: By the form of the rules, eventually a point is reached at which none of the rules applies, so the procedure terminates. By the above proposition, if there is no W ∈ **W** such that |W| = |**F**| then no solution exists. If there is a W ∈ **W** such that |W| = |**F**| , then there is a minimal such W , and **F**(W) is the minimal automaton with behavior |**F**| . If $\overline{\mathbf{F}}$ is the minimized automaton, then $\overline{\mathbf{F}}$ ⊢ W by the above theorem, so a solution exists.

Example: Consider the flowchart specified by the equations

$$i = p_o q_1 + \bar{p}_o q_2 \qquad q_4 = f q_5$$

$$q_1 = p_1 q_4 + \bar{p}_1 q_5 \qquad q_5 = p_5 i + \bar{p}_5 q_1$$

$$q_2 = g q_3 \qquad q_6 = p_6 q_1 + \bar{p}_6 t$$

$$q_3 = p_3 q_5 + \bar{p}_3 q_6 \qquad t = 1$$

The flowchart is minimal. Eliminating q_4 gives $q_1 = p_1 f q_5 + \bar{p}_1 q_5$, hence $q_1 = (p_1 f + \bar{p}_1) q_5$ by II. Eliminating q_1, q_2 and t yields the equations

$$i = p_o(p_1 f + \bar{p}_1) q_5 + \bar{p}_o g q_3 \qquad q_5 = p_5 i + \bar{p}_5 (p_1 f + \bar{p}_1) q_5$$

$$q_3 = p_3 q_5 + \bar{p}_3 q_6 \qquad q_6 = p_6 (p_1 f + \bar{p}_1) q_5 + \bar{p}_6$$

Applying III gives $q_5 = (\bar{p}_5(p_1 f + \bar{p}_1))^* p_5 i = Xi$, say. Eliminating q_5 gives $i = p_o(p_1 f + \bar{p}_1) Xi + \bar{p}_o g q_3$ and so, by III, $i = (p_o(p_1 f + \bar{p}_1)X)^* \bar{p}_o g q_3 = Y q_3$, say. Eliminating i, we have the equations

$$q_3 = p_3 XY q_3 + \bar{p}_3 q_6 \qquad q_6 = p_6 (p_1 f + \bar{p}_1) XY q_3 + \bar{p}_6 \quad .$$

Thus by III, $q_3 = (p_3 XY)^* \bar{p}_3 q_6 = Z q_6$, say. This gives $q_6 = p_6 (p_1 f + \bar{p}_1) XYZ q_6 + \bar{p}_6$, hence $q_6 = (p_6 (p_1 f + \bar{p}_1) XYZ)^* \bar{p}_6 = W$, say. Therefore, $i = YZW$. Complicated as this may be, there is no shorter equivalent WHILE program, since YZW is minimal by our second theorem.

References

Brzozowski, J.A., "Derivatives of regular expressions", J.A.C.M. XI (1964), 481-94.

Eilenberg, S. Automata Languages and Machines, Academic Press, New York, 1973.

Kasai, T. , "Translatability of flowcharts into While programs", J. Comp. Syst. Sci. 9 (1974), 177-95.

ON SPECIFIC FEATURES OF RECOGNIZABLE FAMILIES OF LANGUAGES

Václav Benda
Railway Research Institute
118 00 Prague 1

and

Kamila Bendová
Mathematical Institute ČSAV
115 67 Prague 1
Czechoslovakia

/Dedicated to Professor Jiří Bečvář
on the occasion of his fiftieth birthday/

A study of families of languages recognizable by recently introduced finite branching automata /cf. [1] / leads to a variety of results reminding analogical results from "classical" theory of automata and formal languages, if the involved concepts have the same or similar meaning for families of languages as they have for languages /sets of strings/. Let us mention for instance the property of having a finite number of distinct derivatives and the related decomposition of families [1], [2]. There are, on the other hand, some old questions with different answers: the class of all recognizable families is not closed under union and complement and it is properly included in the class of nondeterministically recognizable families.

In the present paper we are concerned with some problems that are inherently specific to the new area and which often require using notions and approaches of certain other branches of mathematics, otherwise seldom used in computer science /as, e.g., infinite cardinalities and the notions of a filter and ultrafilter/.

1 We use the following notation and terminology. Σ is a finite alphabet, Σ^* the free monoid of strings over Σ /including the empty string Λ /, $\mathcal{L}(\Sigma)$ is the set of all nonempty subsets of Σ^*. $L \in \mathcal{L}(\Sigma)$ is called a <u>language</u>, $X \subseteq \mathcal{L}(\Sigma)$ a <u>family /of languages/</u>. $\partial_u L = \{v ;\ v \in \Sigma^* \ \&\ uv \in L\}$ is the <u>derivative of L with respect to</u> $u \in \Sigma^*$, Pref L is the set of all prefixes of L ; we define

$$\mathrm{Fst}_\Lambda L = (\mathrm{Pref}\, L \cap \Sigma) \cup (L \cap \{\Lambda\}) ,$$

i.e, using the notation of [3], $\mathrm{Fst}_\Lambda L = \Delta_L(\Lambda)$. Analogously to $\partial_u L$ we define the <u>derivative of a family</u> X with respect to $u \in \Sigma^*$ as the family

$$\partial_u X = \{\partial_u L ;\ L \in X\} - \{\emptyset\} .$$

We define the <u>C-closure of a family</u> X as the family

$$C(X) = \{L ;\ (\forall u \in \Sigma^*)(\exists L_u \in X)\ [\mathrm{Fst}_\Lambda\ \partial_u L = \mathrm{Fst}_\Lambda\ \partial_u L_u]\}.$$

We say that a family X is <u>finitely derivable</u> if the set $D(X) = \{\partial_u X ;\ u \in \Sigma^*\}$ is finite. X is <u>self-compatible</u> if $C(X) = X$.

When defining the recognizability of families we shall bypass the definition of a /deterministic/ finite branching automaton /c.f., e.g. [3] / by using the characterization theorem from [1] :

<u>Characterization Theorem.</u> A family of languages is recognizable /by a finite branching automaton/ iff it is finitely derivable and self-compatible.

<u>2</u> Our first observation concerns the cardinalities. Even if the set of all recognizable families – being associated with automata, i.e. finitary objects – is countable / $\aleph_0$/, it is obtained by intersecting two relatively "large" sets /of cardinalities $\aleph_1$ and $\aleph_2$; we tacitly use the continuum hypothesis/.

<u>Theorem 1.</u> The cardinality of the set of all self-compatible families is $\aleph_1$. The cardinality of the set of all finitely derivable families is $\aleph_2$.

<u>Outline of the proof</u>[1]. Every singleton $\{L\}$ is clearly self-compatible and thus the number of all self-compatible families is larger or equal to $\mathrm{card}(\mathcal{L}(\Sigma)) = \aleph_1$. On the other hand, every self-compatible family is fully specified by a countable set of pairs $\langle u, \Gamma \rangle$ where $\Gamma = \mathrm{Fst}_\Lambda\ \partial_u L$ for any $L \in X$. Thus, in fact, the equality holds.

Let $Y = \{L ;\ \Lambda \notin L\}$ and for every $X \subseteq Y$ define $X' = X \cup (\mathcal{L}(\Sigma) - Y)$. Then for any $u \neq \Lambda$, $\partial_u X' = \mathcal{L}(\Sigma)$; thus the family X' is finitely derivable and the set of such families is clearly uncountable with the cardinality $\aleph_2$. Q. e. d.

<u>3</u> Let us now consider the family W of all <u>complete languages</u> /using the terminology of [4] /:

---

[1] Detailed and rigorous proofs of theorems 1–5 /as well as some other results/ will be included in [2] .

$$W = \{L ; (\forall u \in \Sigma^*)[\Sigma \subseteq \mathrm{Fst}_\Lambda \partial_u L]\} .$$

W is clearly an uncountable family and one can easily show that it is recognizable.

Theorem 2. If L_1 and L_2 are two disjoint complete languages such that $L_1 \cup L_2 = \Sigma^*$ then $C(L_1, L_2) = W$.

Outline of the proof. By the definition of W and from the assumption on L_1 and L_2 it can be shown that for any $L \in W$ and any $u \in \Sigma^*$, $\mathrm{Fst}_\Lambda \partial_u L$ equals either $\mathrm{Fst}_\Lambda \partial_u L_1$ or $\mathrm{Fst}_\Lambda \partial_u L_2$ /note that $\mathrm{Fst}_\Lambda \partial_u L$ is either Σ or $\Sigma \cup \{\Lambda\}$/. Thus $L \in C(L_1, L_2)$. Q.e.d.

Thus an uncountable family W can be characterized by just two languages /in fact, they may be chosen regular/. It is natural to ask whether, in general, any recognizable family can be characterized in this way by a finite number of languages. We shall return to this question soon.

Let us call a family X strong if it is not recognizable and the only recognizable family containing X is the whole $\mathcal{L}(\Sigma)$. The following theorem gives a negative answer to a problem posed in [1].

Theorem 3. There is no finite strong family.

Outline of the proof. Let $X = \{L_1, \ldots, L_n\}$ be a finite family of languages. Let us take any $w \in \Sigma^*$ of length greater than n. For each $L_i \in X$ at most one prefix v of w can exist such that $\partial_v L_i = \{\Lambda\}$. Hence there exists a prefix u of w such that $X \subseteq \{L ; \partial_u L \neq \{\Lambda\}\} = Y \neq \mathcal{L}(\Sigma)$. It is easy to show that Y is recognizable. Q. e. d.

Theorem 3 gives also a negative answer to our earlier question: $\mathcal{L}(\Sigma)$ is an example of a family that cannot be characterized in the above sense by a finite set of languages. Let us note, however, that, as shown in [2], there exists another way of characterizing recognizable families by means of a finite number of regular languages. Moreover, this number is bounded and depends only on card(Σ).

4 It is known that the complement $\sim X = \mathcal{L}(\Sigma) - X$ of a recognizable family X may not be recognizable [1]. One may be interested in the restricted class of so called well-recognizable families: recognizable families with recognizable comple-

ments. An example of a well-recognizable family is any family $\{L \,;\, \partial_u L = \{\Lambda\}\}$ where $u \in \Sigma^*$.

First of all we have the following interesting characterization theorem.

Theorem 4. A family X is well-recognizable iff both X and $\sim X$ are self-compatible.

Outline of the proof. The $\Rightarrow$ direction is immediate. The proof of the $\Leftarrow$ direction is much harder and is based on an auxiliary lemma according to which if X and $\sim X$ are self-compatible then for any $u \in \Sigma^*$ the family $\partial_u X \cap \partial_u \sim X$ is either empty or $\mathcal{L}(\Sigma)$. To show that both X and $\sim X$ are finitely derivable one may use König's theorem to refute the assumption that the language $\{u \in \Sigma^* \,;\, \emptyset \neq \partial_u X \neq \mathcal{L}(\Sigma)\}$ is infinite. Q. e. d.

Theorem 4 indicates, incidentally, that the properties of being self-compatible and finitely derivable are not as independent as one would expect from their definitions: by strengthening the former /by requiring it also from the complement/ one obtains the latter. /Compare also the "quantitative" relationship of these two properties in Theorem 1 above./

Let us call a family of languages nontrivial if it is neither empty nor $\mathcal{L}(\Sigma)$. The following theorem shows an interesting structural property of well-recognizable families.

Theorem 5. Let X be a nontrivial well-recognizable family. Then there exists exactly one string $u_X \in \Sigma^*$ such that for every $v \in \Sigma^*$, $\partial_v X$ is nontrivial iff v is a prefix of u_X.

Outline of the proof. Obviously, if $\partial_u X$ is nontrivial than for any prefix v of u, $\partial_v X$ is also nontrivial. Using Theorem 4 one can show that, for a well-recognizable X, the set $\{u \,;\, \partial_u X \text{ is nontrivial}\}$ is finite and linearly ordered with respect to the prefix relation. Q. e. d.

Let us call the string u_X from Theorem 5 the characteristic string of X. In a certain sense the characteristic string determines the degree of complexity of X: its length gives the number of derivatives of X, i.e., the number of states of a minimal branching automaton recognizing X.

Furthermore, there exists a finite set of special unary operations which generate exactly all the well-recognizable families from a certain finite class of "simple" well-recognizable families /cf. [2] for details/. It appears that the number of applications of these unary operations needed for obtaining a particular well-recognizable family X equals the length of the characteristic string of X .

5 Finally we mention several interesting facts concerning the relationship of filters and ultrafilters over Σ^* to the recognizable and well-recognizable families of languages.

In general, a filter F over a set M is a collection of nonempty subsets of M closed under intersection and such that $A \in F$ and $A \subseteq A' \subseteq M$ implies $A' \in F$. If, moreover, F is not contained in any other filter over M it is called an ultrafilter. A filter over Σ^* is a family of languages since it does not contain /by definition/ the empty set. A filter of the form $\{L' ; L \subseteq L'\}$ for some $L \in \mathcal{L}(\Sigma)$ is a principal filter /we denote it by F_L /. It is known that a principal filter F_L is an ultrafilter iff $L = \{u\}$ for some $u \in \Sigma^*$. /For the background of filters and ultrafilters cf., e.g., [5]./

We call a filter over Σ^* a recognizable /well-recognizable/ filter if it is a recognizable /well-recognizable/ family of languages.

Theorem 6. A filter over Σ^* is recognizable iff it is a principal filter of the form F_L where L is a regular language.

Outline of the proof[2]. The harder part of the proof is to show that a filter F is self-compatible iff it is a principal filter /i.e., iff $\bigcap F \in F$; cf. [5] /. One can show that for each $L \in W$ /the family of complete languages from Theorem 2/, if $\bigcap F \subseteq L$ then $L \in F$. For properly chosen L_1 and L_2 in F we obtain $L_1 \cap L_2 = \bigcap F$, hence F is a principal filter. Conversely, every principal filter is clearly self-compatible. Now, for a principal filter F_L we have

$$\partial_u F_L = \begin{cases} F_{\partial_u L} & \text{if } u \in \operatorname{Pref} L \\ \mathcal{L}(\Sigma) & \text{if } u \notin \operatorname{Pref} L \end{cases}$$

and thus F_L is finitely derivable /hence recognizable/ iff L is regular. Q. e. d.

---

[2] Details of proofs of theorems 6 and 7 will appear in [6] .

The expressions for $\partial_u F_L$ from this proof suggest, moreover, a direct correspondence between the complexity of a recognizable filter F_L /in terms of a minimal finite branching automaton for F_L/ and the complexity of the regular language L /in terms of a minimal finite automaton for L /.

Our last theorem concerns well-recognizable filters.

Theorem 7. A recognizable filter is well-recognizable iff it is an ultrafilter /and thus of the form $F_{\{u\}}$, for some $u \in \Sigma^*$ /.

Outline of the proof. One can easily show that, for any $u \in \Sigma^*$, both $F_{\{u\}}$ and $\sim F_{\{u\}}$ are self-compatible and thus, by Theorem 4, well-recognizable. Conversely, $\partial_u F_L$ is nontrivial iff $u \in \text{Pref}\, L$. Thus necessarily /cf. Theorem 5/ $u_{F_L} \in L$. We claim that $L = \{u_{F_L}\}$. To show this assume the converse, $L \neq \{u_{F_L}\}$. Then $\{u_{F_L}\} \in \sim F_L$ and thus the derivatives with respect to u_{F_L} have a nontrivial intersection, which contradicts to the lemma quoted in the proof of Theorem 4.

Q. e. d.

This proof reveals an interesting observation that the characteristic string of any ultrafilter $F_{\{u\}}$ is just the string u itself.

The above theorems establish a deeper connection between the recognizable families and two concepts of general mathematical interest: that of a filter and an ultrafilter /about their role in the study of plans of behavior cf. also [7] /. Especially Theorem 7 may stimulate an independent research of well-recognizable families /one can for instance show that no recognizable family can be obtained as a union of two distinct recognizable ultrafilters/. A result analogous to Theorem 6 holds also for a dual notion of an ideal /cf. [6] /.

REFERENCES

1. Havel, I. M., Finite Branching Automata. Kybernetika 10 1974, 281–302.

2. Benda, V. and Bendová, K., On Families Recognizable by Finite Branching Automata /in preparation/.

3. Havel, I. M., On the Branching Structure of Languages. This volume, pp.

4. Eilenberg, S., Automata, Languages, and Machines. Volume A. Academic Press, New York 1974.

5. Cohn, P. M., Universal Algebra. Harper and Row, New York 1965.

6. Benda V. and Bendová K., Recognizable Filters and Ideals. Commentationes Math. Univ. Carolinae /to appear/.

7. Katětov, M., O základech matematického vyjadřování plánu /On the basis of mathematical expression of a plan/. Mimeographed notes, Faculty of Mathematics and Physics, Charles University.

ON THE TERMINATION OF SIMPLE COMPUTER PROGRAMS

Eberhard Bergmann

Technische Universität Berlin

Informatik-Forschungsgruppe Programmiersprachen und Compiler I

Abstract

In the area of semantics of programming languages the problem of calculating the termination domain (the set of inputs for which a program terminates) is considered: For simple non-nested loop-programs compile-time testable conditions are given such that the resp. programs are total (terminate for all inputs). Auxiliary tool is a global (=mathematical) semantics for infinite loop-programs whose properties are studied in detail. An application yields a proof that the well-known termination proof technique of Floyd cannot be generalized, i.e. you only have to look for statements of the form y:=y+k and a suitable condition controlling the loop and not for more complicated ones.

This paper is an overview on a part of the author's doct. dissertation.

1. Introduction

1.1 Among the problems in the area of semantics of programming languages and programs there is the problem of calculating the termination domain of programs which we will study in this paper.

Beyond the termination proof technique of Floyd (where you have to look for a variable within the loop which will be counted up or down during program execution and will finally be bounded by the condition controlling the loop) there is little known on how to get termination proofs for programs. Strictly speaking, even simplest programs have surprising and not predictable properties with respect to termination, f.e.

π_0 = (x:=x_0;y:=y_0; <u>while</u> <u>not</u> x+y ⩾ 0 <u>do</u> x:=-x+5·y; y:=3·x-16·y <u>od</u>)

π_1 = (x:=x_0;y:=y_0; <u>while</u> <u>not</u> x+y ⩾ 0 <u>do</u> x:= x+5·y; y:=3·x-16·y <u>od</u>)

We claim that π_0 is a total program whereas the termination domain of π_1 is the set $\{(x,y) | x+y \geq 0\}$,i.e. the change of a minus sign in π_0 into a plus sign in π_1 has changed the property of always leaving the loop if entered into the property of never leaving the loop if entered. We call programs with the property of π_1 <u>distotal</u>; for details cf. /Be/

1.2 In a situation where little is known on a certain problem it seems to be necessary not to hope for instant strong results but to search for singulary and isolated ones at first in order to collect facts for a final systematic knowledge. In this way we want to attack the termination problem and therefore restrict ourselves to a specific class of programs, namely programs without loop-nesting such that the variables used range over the real numbers and the loop only contains two assignment statements of a simple form. Because of these restrictions we can get positive results in spite of the well-known undecidability of this question for each sufficiently rich class of algorithmic bases, cf. /LPP 67/

1.3 The results we are interested in should be obtainable by the static data of the programs, f.e.

Proposition 1.1: The following program

$(x:=x_0; y:=y_0;$ while not $\alpha\cdot x+\beta\cdot y+\gamma$ $\underline{ch0}^*$ 0 do $x:=a\cdot x+b\cdot y;\ y:=c\cdot x+d\cdot y$ od$)$

is total for each real $\alpha,\beta,\gamma,a,b,c,d$ such that $a+bc+d \leq 0$, $ad \geq 0$ and γ $\underline{ch0}^*$ 0 where $\underline{ch0}^*$ is a variable ranging over $\{\leq,\geq\}$.

This proposition shows that it is possible to test for totality during compile-time since only static data of the program are to be tested. For a proof of Prop.1.1 cf. section 4

2. Definitions

2.1 Let $a,b,c,d,\alpha,\beta,\gamma,\xi,\eta,x_0,y_0$ be real constants, i,j,m,n positive integers and chi, CHi variables $(i \geq 0)$ ranging over $\{-1,+1\}$ with the convention that chi = CHi holds. We define predicate symbols for the values of these variables by

$\underline{chi}^* =$ if chi=+1 then $\geq$ else $\leq$ fi

$\underline{CHi}^* =$ if CHi=+1 then $>$ else $<$ fi

If products occur like $\underline{ch1}\cdot\ldots\cdot\underline{chN}$ or $-\underline{chi}$, then it is assumed that they are uniquely named by a $\underline{chj}$ for some $j>0$.

Simple properties: (i) not$(t_1\ \underline{chi}^*\ t_2)$ iff $t_1(-\underline{CHi})^*t_2$

(ii) if $t_i\ \underline{chi}^*\ 0$ $(i=1,2)$, then $t_1\cdot t_2(\underline{ch1}\cdot\underline{ch2})^*\ 0$

2.2 Let $Ak = (x:=a\cdot x+b\cdot y+\xi;\ y:=c\cdot x+d\cdot y+\eta)$ be a list of assignment statements which we will call an action. Further let B be a boolean condition $(\alpha\cdot x+\beta\cdot y+\gamma\ \underline{ch0}^*\ 0)$ with real variables x and y such that $\gamma\ \underline{ch0}^*\ 0$ Then we consider all programs of the form

$$\Pi^{B}_{Ak} = (x:=x_0; y:=y_0;\ \text{while not } B \text{ do } Ak \text{ od})$$

We abbreviate $Ak = \binom{a\ b\ \xi}{c\ d\ \eta}$ and $A = \binom{a\ b\ 0}{c\ d\ 0}$ where we omit the zeros. We denote by x_n and y_n the values of the variables x and y resp. after $n \geq 0$ executions of Ak, further let be $\alpha_n = \alpha \cdot x_n + \beta \cdot y_n$

3. Global (=mathematical) semantics of infinite loops

3.1 In this section we develop the tools for obtaining the desired termination results. The quantities which occurred in Prop.1.1 play an important rôle to get these tools. We define

$$P = a + b \cdot c + d \quad \text{and} \quad Q = a \cdot d$$

Further let be $K_{n+1} = P \cdot K_n - Q \cdot K_{n-1}$ for $n \geq 0$ where $K_{-1}=0$ and $K_o=1$

$$X_n = \sum_{i=o}^{n} K_i \quad \text{for } n \geq 0 \text{ and } X_{-i}=0 \quad (i=1,2)$$

We call $P, Q, (K_n)_{n=o}^{\infty}$ and $(X_n)_{n=o}^{\infty}$ characteristics of Ak

Proposition 3.1: $X_{n+1} = P \cdot X_n - Q \cdot X_{n-1} + 1$ for $n \geq 0$

Proof: induction on n

3.2 Now we are able to describe the global semantics of the following (infinite) loop-program

$$\mathbf{L} = (x{:=}x_o;\ y{:=}y_o;\ \text{label: Ak};\ \underline{\text{goto}}\ \text{label})$$

by regarding that the execution of $\mathbf{L}$ is equivalent to a system of finite difference equations

$$x_{n+1} = a \cdot x_n + b \cdot y_n + \xi \qquad y_{n+1} = c \cdot x_{n+1} + d \cdot y_n + \eta$$

The classical solutions, cf. /LL/, give no hint for a global semantics, but by the K_n and X_n we obtain a closed expression for x_n and y_n in terms of the initial values x_o and y_o

Theorem 3.1: For $n \geq 0$ holds

$$\begin{aligned} x_n &= (K_n-(bc+d)K_{n-1})x_o + b \cdot K_{n-1} \cdot y_o + \xi \cdot X_{n-1} + (b\eta - d\xi)X_{n-2} \\ y_n &= ac \cdot K_{n-1} \cdot x_o + (K_n - aK_{n-1})y_o + (c\xi+\eta)X_{n-1} - a\eta \cdot X_{n-2} \end{aligned} \qquad (*)$$

If for some $n \geq 2$ holds $K_{n-1}=0$, then $(*)$ simplifies to

Theorem 3.2:

$$K_{n-1} = 0 \quad \text{iff} \quad \begin{aligned} x_n &= K_n \cdot x_o + (\xi + b\eta - d\xi) \cdot X_{n-2} \\ y_n &= K_n \cdot y_o + (c\xi + \eta - a\eta) \cdot X_{n-2} \end{aligned}$$

<u>Proof of Th.3.1:</u> induction on n (n=0,1 are obvious)

$$\begin{aligned}
x_n &= a\cdot x_{n-1} + b\cdot y_{n-1} + \xi \\
&= a\Big((K_{n-1}-(bc+d)K_{n-2})x_o + bK_{n-2}y_o+\xi X_{n-2}+(b\eta-d\xi)X_{n-3}\Big)+ \\
&\quad\; b\Big(acK_{n-2}x_o+(K_{n-1}-aK_{n-2})y_o+(c\xi+\eta)X_{n-2}-a\eta X_{n-3}\Big) + \xi \\
&= (aK_{n-1}-adK_{n-2})x_o+bK_{n-1}y_o+((a+bc)X_{n-2}-adX_{n-3}+1)\xi+b\eta X_{n-2} \\
&= \big((PK_{n-1}-QK_{n-2})-(bc+d)K_{n-1}\big)x_o+bK_{n-1}y_o+(PX_{n-2}-QX_{n-3}+1)\xi+(b\eta-d\xi)X_{n-2} \\
&= (K_n-(bc+d)K_{n-1})x_o + bK_{n-1}y_o + \xi X_{n-1} + (b\eta-d\xi)X_{n-2}
\end{aligned}$$

The induction step for y_n is similar.

The global semantics (*) enables us to get the values of x and y after n executions of Ak by using the static daty only without applying any of the operations prescribed by the program L.

3.3 Note that the K_n and the X_n do not depend on the realizing a,b,c, and d but only on P and Q, so that each of these characteristics describe an infinite class of Ak's

<u>Example:</u> Let A be an action such that P=1 and Q=-1. Then $(K_n)_{n=o}^{\infty}$ is the sequence of Fibonacci numbers, in the nomenclature of /Kn/: $K_n = F_{n+1}$. By Theorem 3.1 we get $x_n = K_n$ if $x_o=1$ and $y_o=(bc+d)/b$ where $b\neq 0$. Hence the following program π_2 generates the Fibonacci numbers for each (!) action A such that P=1,Q=-1

π_2 = (x:=1; y:=(b·c+d)/b; <u>while</u> <u>not</u> x≥maxno <u>do</u> print(x); A <u>od</u>

In this class of actions you will find the good old $A_1=\begin{pmatrix}1 & 1\\ 1 & -1\end{pmatrix}$ but also the weird $A_2=\begin{pmatrix}-5 & 2.9\\ 2 & 0.2\end{pmatrix}$ The reader may try an operational approach in order to verify that A_2 really generates the Fibonacci numbers. Note that there is nevertheless no correctness proof necessary because of Th.3.1. You may look at this example as a case of "automatic" programming.

3.4 We now list properties of K_n and X_n

<u>Theorem 3.3 (Partition Lemma):</u> For $n\geq 1$ and $0\leq j\leq n$ holds

(1) $K_n = K_j\cdot K_{n-j} - Q\cdot K_{j-1}\cdot K_{n-j-1}$

(2) $X_n = K_j\cdot X_{n-j} - Q\cdot K_{j-1}\cdot X_{n-j-1} + X_{j-1}$

<u>Proof</u> with induction on j

<u>Proposition 3.2:</u> Let be $n\geq 2$ and $K_{n-1}=0$. Then $K_{m\cdot n-1}=0$ for each $m\geq 0$

<u>Proof</u> with induction on m and Partition Lemma

Proposition 3.3: Let be $n \geqslant 2$ and $K_{n-1}=0$, then holds for each $m \geqslant 0$

$$(1) \quad K_{m\cdot n} = K_n^m \qquad (2) \quad X_{m\cdot n-2} = X_{n-2}\cdot\sum_{i=0}^{m-1} K_n^i$$

Proof with induction on m and Partition Lemma

Theorem 3.4: Let be $n \geqslant 2$ and $K_{n-1}=0$, then holds for each $m \geqslant 0$

$$x_{m\cdot n} = K_n^m\cdot x_o + X_{n-2}\cdot(\xi - d\xi + b\eta)\cdot\sum_{i=0}^{m-1} K_n^i$$

$$y_{m\cdot n} = K_n^m\cdot y_o + X_{n-2}\cdot(c\xi + \eta - a\eta)\cdot\sum_{i=0}^{m-1} K_n^i$$

Proof: Th.3.2, Prop.3.2,3.3

Example: $A_3=\begin{pmatrix}3 & -2\\ 0.5 & 1\end{pmatrix}$ and $A_4=\begin{pmatrix}6 & -7\\ 0.5 & 0.5\end{pmatrix}$ have the same P and Q, further $K_5=0$ and $K_6=-27$. Thus it holds for both and for each $m \geqslant 0$

$$x_{6\cdot m} = (-1)^m\cdot 27^m\cdot x_o \quad \text{and} \quad y_{6\cdot m} = (-1)^m\cdot 27^m\cdot y_o$$

Proposition 3.4: Let be $n \geqslant 0$, then holds

$$(1) \quad K_n = \sum_{i=0}^{\lfloor \frac{n}{2} \rfloor}(-1)^i\binom{n-i}{i} P^{n-2i}\, Q^i \qquad (2) \quad X_n = \sum_{i=0}^{\lfloor \frac{n}{2} \rfloor}(-1)^i Q^i\Big(\sum_{j=2i}^{n}\binom{j-i}{i}P^{j-2i}\Big)$$

where $\binom{r}{k}$ is the binomial coefficient of row r and column k and $\lfloor m \rfloor$ is the greatest integer less than or equal to a real m.

Proof: (1) by induction on n, (2) is an immediate consequence of (1)

Theorem 3.5: Let be $n \geqslant 2$ and $K_{n-1}=0$. Then holds for each $m \geqslant 1$

$$(a) \quad K_{m\cdot n} = \pm Q^{\frac{m\cdot n}{2}} \qquad (b) \quad K_{m\cdot n-2} = \pm Q^{\frac{m\cdot n}{2}-1}$$

If n is even: $\quad (c) \quad K_{m\cdot n} = (-1)^m Q^{\frac{m\cdot n}{2}} \qquad (d) \quad K_{m\cdot n-2} = (-1)^{m+1} Q^{\frac{m\cdot n}{2}-1}$

Proof: cf. /Be/

Theorem 3.6: Let be $P^2 = m\cdot Q$ for a real m, then we get

$$K_n = C_n(m)\cdot P^{n-2\cdot\lfloor\frac{n}{2}\rfloor} Q^{\lfloor\frac{n}{2}\rfloor} \quad \text{where} \quad C_n(m) = \sum_{j=0}^{\lfloor\frac{n}{2}\rfloor}(-1)^j\binom{n-j}{j}\, m^{\lfloor\frac{n}{2}\rfloor-j}$$

This theorem shows how to find for a given action Ak some positive integer $n \geqslant 1$ such that $K_n=0$, namely test if $P^2=mQ$ for some m and $C_n(m)=0$ for some n. A proof of Th.3.6 is in /Be/.

3.5 Remarks:

(i) $P^2=0\cdot Q$ yields $K_1=0$, $P^2=1\cdot Q$ yields $K_2=0$, $P^2=2\cdot Q$ yields $K_3=0$, and $P^2=3\cdot Q$ yields $K_5=0$.

(ii) We can show that $C_n(m)\neq 0$ for $m<0$ for each $n \geqslant 0$, cf. /Be/, §6.2;

It is not known whether there are other positive integers m for which $C_n(m)=0$ holds for some $n \geq 0$, f.e $C_{2k}(4)=2k+1$, $C_{2k+1}(4)=k+1$

(iii) For the polynomials $(C_n(m))_{n=0}^{\infty}$ a Partition Lemma holds, cf. /Be/

(iv) It is possible to obtain a global semantics for actions with three assignment statements (even for each positive integer $N \geq 2$)

$$Ak = (x:=a\cdot x+b\cdot y+r\cdot z+\xi;\ y:=c\cdot x+d\cdot y+s\cdot z+\eta;\ z:=u\cdot x+v\cdot y+w\cdot z+\zeta)$$

But this case seems not to be of practical interest, therefore we omit it. The resp. characteristics of these Ak's are

$P=a+bc+d+r(u+cv)+sv+w$, $-Q=bsu-asv-dru-bcw-ad-aw-dw$, and $S=adw$

For details cf. /Be/

4. Total programs

Based on Theorems 3.2 and 3.5 we can establish a termination result:

Proposition 4.1: Let A be an action such that $K_{n-1}=0$ for some $n \geq 2$,

if n is divisible by 4 or
if n is even and $Q \geq 0$ } then Π_A^B is a total program for all B

Proof: (i) $\alpha_n = K_n \cdot \alpha_o$ since $K_{n-1}=0$. Suppose Π_A^B has not terminated after zero executions of A, i.e. $\alpha_o(-\underline{CHO})^* 0$ holds. We get $\alpha_n\ \underline{ch0}^*\ 0$, if $K_n \leq 0$. Hence $\alpha_n + \gamma\ \underline{ch0}^*\ 0$, i.e. the given program terminates after n steps, if $K_n \leq 0$. (ii) if n is divisible by 4, then $K_n=K_{4k}=-Q^{2k}$ (Th.3.5), therefore $K_n \leq 0$. (iii) if n is divisible by 2, then $K_n=K_{2k}=-Q^k$ (Th.3.5). Since $Q \geq 0$ we have $K_n \leq 0$.

A characterization of α_n yields another termination result:

Proposition 4.2: Let Ak be an action. Then holds for each $n \geq 0$

(1) $\alpha_n = K_{n-j} \cdot \alpha_j - Q \cdot K_{n-j-1} \cdot \alpha_{j-1} - X_{n-j-1} \cdot Z$ for $0 < j \leq n$

(2) $\alpha_n = K_n \cdot \alpha_o + K_{n-1} \cdot R + X_{n-2} \cdot Z + K_{n-1} \cdot C$

where $Z=\alpha((1-d)\xi+b\eta)+\beta(c\xi+(1-a)\eta)$, $R=(\beta ac-\alpha(bc+d))x_o+(\alpha b-\beta a)y_o$ and $C=\alpha\xi+\beta(c\xi+\eta)$

Proof: (1) induction on j (2) Th.3.1

Proposition 4.3: Let A be an action such that $K_{n-1} \leq 0$ for some $n \geq 2$ if $Q\ \underline{ch1}^*\ 0$ and $K_{n-2}\ \underline{ch1}^*\ 0$, then Π_A^B is total for each B

Proof: (i) put j=1 in Prop.4.2.1, i.e. $\alpha_n = K_{n-1} \cdot \alpha_1 - Q \cdot K_{n-2} \cdot \alpha_o$

(ii) suppose Π_A^B has not yet terminated after one execution of A, i.e. α_i ($-\underline{CHO}$)* 0 for i=0,1. It follows from the assumptions that holds $K_{n-1}\cdot\alpha_1$ $\underline{chO}^*$ 0 and $-Q\cdot K_{n-2}\cdot\alpha_0$ $\underline{chO}^*$ 0, hence termination after n steps.

Remark: the case n=2 is a proof of Prop.1.1

Example: $A_5=\begin{pmatrix} 2 & 14 \\ -0.5 & 9 \end{pmatrix}$ yields $P\geqslant 0$, $Q\geqslant 0$, $P^2 < Q$, i.e. $K_2<0$, $K_1\cdot Q\geqslant 0$ Therefore each $\Pi_{A_3}^B$ terminates after at most three executions of A_3

Proposition 4.4: Let A be an action such that $P\geqslant 0$, $Q\geqslant 0$ and $K_n\leqslant 0$ for some $n\geqslant 1$, then Π_A^B is a total program for each B

Proof: cf. /Be/

To treat Ak rather than A is difficult but necessary from a practical point of view:

Proposition 4.5: Let Ak be an action such that $P\geqslant 0$, $Q\geqslant 0$, $K_n\leqslant 0$, and $K_{n-1}\geqslant 0$ for some $n\geqslant 1$. Further let be 1-d=b and 1-a=c. Let B be a boolean condition such that $X_{n-2}\cdot(\alpha b+\beta c)(\xi+\eta)$ $\underline{chO}^*$ 0 and $\alpha\xi+\beta(c\xi+\eta)$ $\underline{chO}^*$ 0

Then Π_{Ak}^B is a total program

For a proof and similar results cf. /Be/

5. A note on the Floyd termination proof technique

It is obvious that programs like

Π_3 = (x:=x_o; y:=y_o; while not y $\leqslant$0 do x:=a·x+b·y+ξ; y:=y-1 od)

are total ones. We ask whether it is possible to generalize this method by looking for a statement with the effect of y:=y-1 in Π_3 but more complicated. We exclude the case when the variable x is an auxiliary one for y, f.e. in Ak=(x:=b·y+ξ; y:=c·x+d·y+η), and vice versa. Furthermore we suppose that after each execution of the loop the value of the variable under consideration increases (or decreases) by a constant amount, i.e. $y_n - y_{n-1}$ = const for each $n\geqslant 1$. By these assumptions we can show that there is no other form of statements than y:=y+k which can be utilized for this termination proof technique.

Proposition 5.1: Let Ak be an action, then we have

(1)	$x_n - x_{n-1}$ = const for each $n\geqslant 1$ and y is not an auxiliary variable for x	iff	a = 1 and b = 0 i.e. x:=x+ξ

(2)	$y_n - y_{n-1}$ = const for each $n \geq 1$ and x is not an auxiliary variable for y	iff	c = 0 and d = 1 i.e. $y := y + \eta$

Remark: $x_n - x_{n-1} = \xi$ and $y_n - y_{n-1} = c\xi + \eta$

The proof utilizes methods of the theory of finite difference equations. The idea is that $(K_n)_{n=o}^{\infty}$ has to satisfy the equation $X \cdot K_n - Y \cdot K_{n-1} - X = 0$ with $X = c\xi + \eta$ and $Y = a\eta$. From the solution we can yield the consequences expressed in Prop.5.1. For a proof cf. /Be/

6. Conclusions

There is a strong connection between the algorithmic basis chosen and the results obtained because it is obvious that the easiness we do calculations with real numbers has supported most the establishing of the presented results. There seems to be no hope to generalize these results immediately to strings, algorithmic basis: free half group (which would be necessary from the point of view of computer science) because we know too few a things to do easy calculations with strings.

I think that these singulary results have their merits in demonstrating what kind of termination results we should think of and what aims we should try to reach.

Among many open problems the important ones: to widen these results to interesting and relevant cases, f.e. loop-nesting, much more complicated assignments (with function procedures) and so forth

The author would like to thank B. Eggers for helpful suggestions.

7. References

/Be/ E. Bergmann: Über das Terminationsverhalten von einfachen Computer-Programmen. Dissertation Technische Universität Berlin 1975

/Kn/ D. Knuth: The Art of Computer Programming. Vol 1: Fundamental Algorithms. Reading(Mass) 1968

/LL/ H. Levy and F. Lessman: Finite Difference Equations. London 1959

/LLP 67/ D. Luckham, D. Park, and M. Paterson: On formalised computer programs. Programming Research Group Oxford University, Aug. 1967

REDUCTION OF PETRI-NETS

by

G. BERTHELOT and G. ROUCAIROL
INSTITUT DE PROGRAMMATION
4, Place JUSSIEU
75005 Paris, FRANCE

1. INTRODUCTION

Among the different formalizations of parallel processing (5), (8), Petri-nets provide a useful tool in order to represent and analyse the flow of control in concurrent systems (9). Properties of Petri-nets, like liveness and boundedness, well characterize absence of deadlock in a set of cooperating processes and finitness of resources needed by those processes. But the number of operations involved in algorithms of detection of such properties grows fast with the number of places of a net (6), (2). So in order to reduce the number of places of a net we define three rules of reduction, one of them being, for Petri-nets, an extension of the substitution rule introduced in (3) in order to check"proper termination" of UCLA graphs. We state that the three rules conserve initial properties of a net in regard to liveness and boundedness and we point out an important property of those reductions : if the initial net is live and bounded, the application of the three rules in any order, as long as possible, leads to irreducible nets which have an identical structure (Church-Rosser property). Note that the experiments related in (1), show that a large class of nets may be reduced. Especially the nets corresponding to the solutions of the well-known "five philosophers" problem and "producer-consumer" problem, are reducible to nets with only one transition and one place, the later of them being obviously live and bounded. In this last case, the reduction process provides the fastest proof of correctness we know (7).

2. BASIC DEFINITIONS

A Petri-net is usually defined (4) as a 5-tuple $N = (P,T,F,B,M_0)$ where P is finite set of places, T is finite set of transitions, $F : P \times T \rightarrow \mathbb{N}$ a forward function, $B : T \times P \rightarrow \mathbb{N}$ a backward function, M_0 an initial marking, a mapping : $P \rightarrow \mathbb{N}$

A transition t is called *fireable* under a marking M iff : $\forall p \in P \;\; M(p) \geq F(p,t)$. The *firing* of a transition t, fireable under a marking M, is defined as a mapping $M \xrightarrow{t} M'$ where $\forall p \;\; M'(p) = M(p) - F(p,t) + B(t,p)$. Consider two markings M and M', M' is said to be *reachable* from M if there exist a sequence of transitions $t_a, t_b, \ldots, t_m$ and sequence of markings $M_a, M_b, \ldots, M_n$ such that $M = M_a \xrightarrow{t_a} M_b \xrightarrow{t_b} \ldots \xrightarrow{t_m} M_n = M'$. The word over T^* $\sigma = t_a t_b \ldots t_m$ is called a *firing sequence* and we write $M \xrightarrow{\sigma} M'$. The set of markings which are reachable from a given marking M (including M) is denoted by $[M\rangle$.

A Petri-net N is called *live* iff $\forall t \in T \;\; \forall M \in [M_0\rangle \;\; \exists M' \in [M\rangle$ such that t is fireable under M'.

A Petri-net N is called *bounded* iff $\exists b \in \mathbb{N}, \forall p \in P \;\; \forall M \in [M_0\rangle \;\; M(p) \leq b$.

Because in the reduction process it may appear a net with several initial markings we define a multi-net as $MN = (P,T,F,B,\mathcal{M})$ where $\mathcal{M}$ is a finite set of initial markings. Then a multi-net is said live (resp. bounded) iff each represented net is live (resp.bounded).

For more convenient definition and application of reduction rules we introduce a *grammatical representation* of a multi-net.

The grammatical representation of a multi-net MN is a triple $\widetilde{MN} = (P,S,E)$ where P is the set of places of $\widetilde{MN}$, S an initial symbol, E a finite set of *firing expressions* (f.e.) of the form $L \rightarrow R$ $(L \in P^* \cup S,\ R \in P^*)$ such that :

- a f.e. $S \rightarrow R \in E$ iff $\exists M_0 \in \mathcal{M}, \forall p \in P \;\; |R|_p = M_0(p)$ ($|R|_p$ denotes the number of occurrences of p in the word R)
- a f.e. $L \rightarrow R \in E$ $(|L|_S = 0)$ iff $\exists t \in T, \;\; \forall p \in P \;\; |L|_p = F(p,t)$ and $|R|_p = B(t,p)$.

Remark

In $\widetilde{MN}$, one f.e. may represent a subset of transitions $T' \subset T$ such that : $\forall p \in P \;\; \forall t,t' \in T' \;\; F(p,t) = F(p,t')$ and $B(t,p) = B(t',p)$. Thus $\widetilde{MN}$ represents a *class of multi-nets* (c.m.n) which are obviously equivalent in regard to liveness and boundedness.

3. REDUCTION RULES ON $\widetilde{MN} = (P,S,E)$

3.1 Relation and operations on $V = P^* \cup S$, notations

- $\forall u,v,w \in V$

$$u = v \Leftrightarrow \forall q \in P \cup S \qquad |u|_q = |v|_q$$

$u \leq v \Leftrightarrow \quad q \in P \cup S \quad |u|_q \leq |v|_q$

$w = u - v \Leftrightarrow \quad q \in P \cup S \quad |w|_q = |w|_q = |u|_q - |v|_q$ *if* $v \leq u$ undefined otherwise

$w = u + v \Leftrightarrow \forall q \in P \cup S \quad |u|_q = |u|_q + |v|_q$

$w = u \wedge v \Leftrightarrow \forall q \in P \cup S \quad |u|_q = min\ (|u|_q, |v|_q)$

- $\forall k \in \mathbb{N}\ w = k.u \Leftrightarrow \forall q \in P \cup S \quad |w|_q = k|u|_q$
- Let f be a *f.e.*, L_f denotes the left part of f and R_f its right part.
- $\mathcal{S}$ is a subset of E such that $f \in \mathcal{S}$ iff $L_f = S$.
- λ denotes the empty string.
- $\hat{P}$ is the set of places referenced in *f.e* – *i.e* – $\hat{P} = \{p \in P / \exists f \in E, |L_f|_p + |R_f|_p > 0\}$

3.2 Substitution rule (R1)

- Let G, H be non-empty subsets of E :
  - $H \not\subseteq \mathcal{S}$
  - $\forall g \in G \quad L_g \neq \lambda$ and $R_g \neq \lambda$ and $L_g \wedge R_g = \lambda$
  - $\forall g, g' \in G \quad L_g = L_{g'}$
  - $\forall h \in H \quad \forall g \in G$ – $\exists k_h \in \mathbb{N}, k_h.L_g \leq R_h$ and $(R_h - k_h.L_g) \wedge L_g = \lambda$.
    – $L_h \wedge L_g = \lambda$
  - $\forall f \in E - (G \cup H)\ \forall_g \in G \quad L_f \wedge L_g = \lambda$ and $R_g \wedge L_g = \lambda$
- Let h be any *f.e.* of H and g be any one of G

  Q [h/G] is the set of *f.e.* in which sub-words of right part of h are substituted by right parts of elements of G *i.e* $Q[h/G] = \{L_h \rightarrow R_h - k_h.L_g + \sum_{g \in G} m_g.R_g \ / \sum_{g \in G} m_g = k_h\}$.

The result of the substitution rule is

$\widetilde{MN}' = (P, S, E[H/G])$ with $E[H/G] = (E - (G \cup H)) \cup (\bigcup_{h \in H} Q[h/G])$

Note that the number of places referenced in E [H/G] is inferior to the one of E.

3.3 Elimination of a redundant place (R2)

A place $p \in \hat{P}$ is called redundant iff there exist a subset A_p of $\hat{P}$ and a mapping φ : $A_p \cup \{p\} \rightarrow \mathbb{N}$ such that :

- $\forall g \in \mathcal{S}\ \exists b_g \in \mathbb{N},\ \varphi(p)\ |R_g|_p - \sum_{q \in A_p} \varphi(q)\ |R_g|_q = b_g$
- $\forall f \in E - \mathcal{S}\ \exists c_f \in \mathbb{N},\ \varphi(p)\ (|R_f|_p - |L_f|_p) - \sum_{q \in A_p} \varphi\ (q)\ (|R_f|_q - |L_f|_q) = c_f$
- $\forall f \in E - \mathcal{S}\ \varphi(p)\ |L_f|_p - \sum_{q \in A_p} \varphi(q)\ |L_f|_q \leq min\ (\{b_g / g \in \mathcal{S}\})$

The result of partial elimination of occurrences of p in *f.e.* is

$\widetilde{MN}' = (P, S, E' = E_1 \cup E_2)$

where $E_1 = \{S \to L_g - |L_g|_p.p/g \in \mathcal{G}\}$

$E_2 = \{L_f - |L_f|_p.p \to R_f - |R_f|_p.p + c_f.p \;/\; f \in E - \mathcal{G}\}$

3.4 Elimination of irrelevant f.e.

A *f.e.* $f \in E$ is *irrelevant* iff :

- $L_f = R_f$
- $\exists g \in E - \mathcal{G},\ L_f \leq R_g$

The result of elimination of f is $\widetilde{MN} = (P,S,E')$ with $E' = E - \{f\}$.

4. RESULTS

4.A. Conservation of liveness and boundedness

Let $\widetilde{MN} = (P,S,E)$ be a c.m.n, we call $\widetilde{MN}_R = (P,S,E_R)$ with $R \in \{R_1,R_2,R_3\}$ the c.m.n resulting from $\widetilde{MN}$ applying R_1 or R_2 or R_3 .

Property

Any multi-net represented by $\widetilde{MN}$ is live (resp.bounded) iff anyone represented by $\widetilde{MN}_R$ is live (resp.bounded)

Sketch of a proof.

If $R = R_1$ this property is based upon the fact that the result of the firing of any transition t_f represented by f.e. f in $\widetilde{MN}_R$ is :

- either identical to the result of the firing of a transition represented by the same f.e. f in $\widetilde{MN}$
- or identical to the result of a firing sequence $t_h\, t_{g_1} \ldots t_{g_{k_h}}$ where t_h and t_{g_i} are transitions represented by f.e h and g_i in $\widetilde{MN}$ $(h \in H, g_i \in G)$

If $R = R_2$ it is sufficient to verify that for any initial marking M_0 of a net represented by $\widetilde{MN}$ we have $M_0 \overset{\sigma}{\to} M$ iff we have $M'_0 \overset{\sigma}{\to} M'$ for net represented by $\widetilde{MN}_R$, where M'_0 is an initial marking and $\forall q \neq p$ $M'_0(q) = M_0(q)$, $M'(q) = M(q)$ and $M'(p) = M(p) - \frac{1}{\varphi(p)} \sum_{q \in A_p} \varphi(q)\, M(q) - \frac{b}{\varphi(p)}$ with $b = min\,(\{b_g/g \in \mathcal{G}\})$, $M'_0(p) = 0$.

If $R = R_3$ the preceding property is trivially deduced from the definition of R_3.

4.2 Church-Rosser property

Using the terminology given in (12), we consider the replacement system $(\mathcal{N}, \Rightarrow, \equiv)$ where $\mathcal{N}$ is the set of c.m.n such that the represented multi-nets are *live* and *bounded*, $\Rightarrow$ is the relation linking one c.m.n and the resulting one applying any rule R_1, R_2 or R_3, $\equiv$ is the equivalence relation between c.m.n defined below.

Définition

Two c.m.n $M\tilde{N} = (P,S,E)$ and $\tilde{M}N' = (P',S,E')$ are structurally equivalent ($M\tilde{N} \equiv M\tilde{N}'$) iff there exist two one-one mappings $\gamma : \hat{P} \cup S \rightarrow \hat{P}' \cup S$ and $\xi : E \rightarrow E'$ and a mapping $\delta : \hat{P} \rightarrow Q^+$ such that

- $\gamma(S) = S$
- $\forall e \in E \ \forall p \in \hat{P} \cup S \qquad \delta(p)|L_e|_p = |L_{\xi(e)}|_{\gamma(p)}$

  and $\quad \delta(p)|R_e|_p = |R_{\xi(e)}|_{\gamma(p)}$

Theorem

The replacement system $(\mathcal{N}, \Rightarrow, \equiv)$ is finite Church-Rosser -i.e. the reduction process is finite, and given any two equivalent c.m.n of $\mathcal{N}$, any irreducible c.m.n derived from the first is equivalent to any irreducible one derived from the second.

Sketch of the proof

The finitness of the reduction process is directly deduced from the definition of the reduction rules which application decreases the number of places referenced in f.e.. Moreover, from the definition of equivalence, it is straightforward that :

for all m,n and x in $\mathcal{N}$, $m \equiv n$ and $m \Rightarrow x$ imply that there exists y such that $n \Rightarrow y$ and $x \equiv y$ (this satifies property P_1 in (12)).

In order to achieve the proof of the theorem the replacement system must also have (according to the theorem 2.2 in (12)) the following property:
for all m, n and ℓ in $\mathcal{N}$, $m \Rightarrow n$ and $m \Rightarrow \ell$ imply that there exist x and y such that $n \overset{*}{\Rightarrow} x$, $\ell \overset{*}{\Rightarrow} y$ and $x \equiv y$. ($\overset{*}{\Rightarrow}$ denotes the reflexive and transitive closure of $\Rightarrow$).

For this purpose we use the following lemmas.
Let $M\tilde{N} = (P,S,E)$ be a c.m.n belonging to $\mathcal{N}$

Lemma 1

Let H_1, G_1 and H_2, G_2 be two pairs of subsets of f.e as defined in 3.2
If $H_1 \cap G_2 \neq \emptyset$ and $H_2 \cap G_1 \neq \emptyset$ then :

$\forall g \in H_1 \cap G_2, \ \forall f \in H_2 \cap G_1 \quad L_g = R_f$ and $L_f = R_g$

Lemma 2

For any redundant place, for each f.e. f $c_f = 0$ (where cf is the integer defined in 3.3).

Lemma 3

A place p is a redundant place in regard to a subset of place A_p iff there exists a mapping $\varphi : A_p \cup \{p\} \rightarrow \mathbb{N}^+$ such that :

- for any initial marking M_0^i represented in $\widetilde{MN}$, for any M belonging to $[M_0^i>$ there exists $b_i \in N$ such that $\varphi(p)\ M(p) - \sum_{q \in A_p} \varphi(q)\ M(q) = b_i$
- for each f.e. f $\varphi(p) |L_f|_p - \sum_{q \in A_p} \varphi(q) |L_f|_q \leq \min_i (b_i)$

In order to prove the preceding property holds for the replacement system we consider, six cases have to be investigated ; for the three most important ones we have

\- 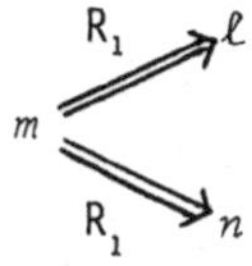

imply : . there exist x,y s.t. 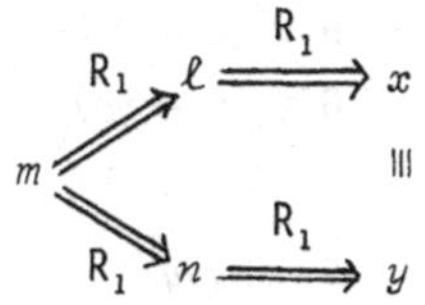

• or there exist x,x',y,y' s.t. 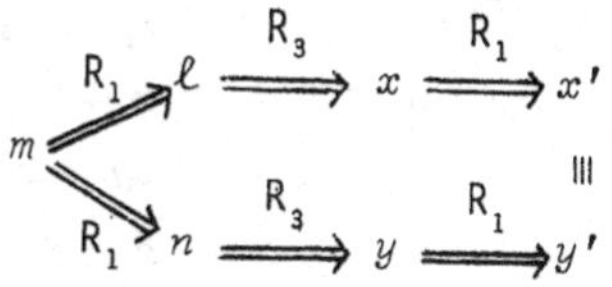

\- 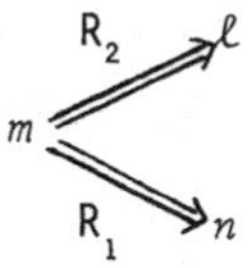

imply : • there exist x,y s.t. 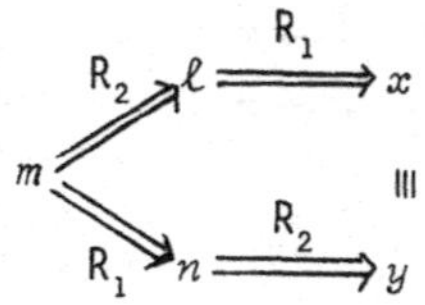

• or there exists x s.t. 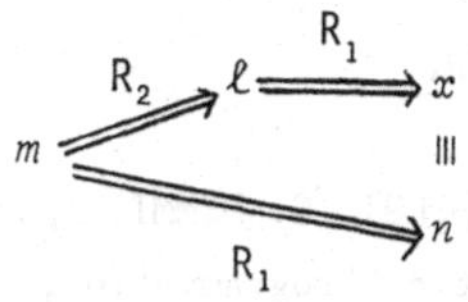

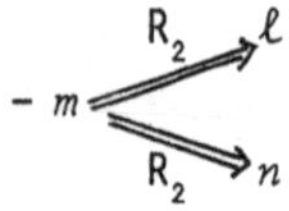

$- m \begin{smallmatrix} R_2 \nearrow \ell \\ R_2 \searrow n \end{smallmatrix}$ imply : • there exist s, y s.t. $m \begin{smallmatrix} R_2 \nearrow \ell \xRightarrow{R_2} x \\ R_2 \searrow n \xRightarrow{R_2} y \end{smallmatrix}$

• or $m \begin{smallmatrix} R_2 \nearrow \ell \\ \| \\ R_2 \searrow n \end{smallmatrix}$

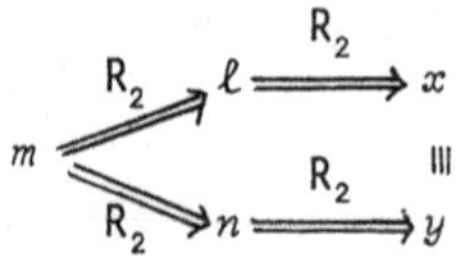

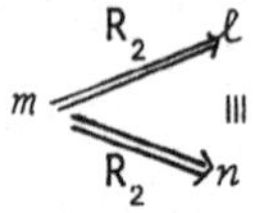

5. EXAMPLE

$S \to adgxyyy$		$S \to gxyyy$		$S \to gxyyy$
$ax \to b$		$x \to b$		$x \to b$
$by \to cz$		$by \to cz$		$by \to xz$
$c \to ax$		$c \to x$		$x \to e$
$dx \to e$	$\xRightarrow{R_2, R_2, R_1}$	$x \to e$	$\xRightarrow{R_1, R_1, R_1}$	$ey \to xz$
$ey \to fz$		$ey \to fz$		$zg \to yg$
$f \to dx$	$A_a = \{x, e, f\}$	$f \to x$		
$zg \to h$	$A_d = \{x, b, c\}$	$zg \to h$		
$h \to i$	$H = \{h \to i\}$	$h \to yg$		
$i \to yg$	$G = \{i \to yg\}$			

	$S \to xyyy$		$S \to xyyy$		$S \to x$
$\xRightarrow{R_2}$	$x \to b$	$\xRightarrow{R_1}$	$x \to b$	$\xRightarrow{R_2}$	$x \to b$
	$by \to xz$		$by \to xy$		$b \to x$
$A_g = \emptyset$	$x \to e$		$x \to e$	$A_y = \emptyset$	$x \to e$
	$ey \to x z$		$ey \to xy$		$e \to x$
	$z \to y$				

$\xRightarrow{R_1, R_3 , R_1}$ $\begin{aligned} S &\to x \\ x &\to x \end{aligned}$ $\xRightarrow{R_2}$ $\begin{aligned} S &\to \lambda \\ \lambda &\to \lambda \end{aligned}$

$A_x = \emptyset$

BIBLIOGRAPHY

1. G. BERTHELOT, G. MEMMI. Analyse et réductions de réseaux de Petri. Rapport de DEA Institut de Programmation, Juin 1975.

2. E. BEST, H.A. SCHMID. Systems of open paths in Petri-nets. Proc. of the Symp. on MFCS 75, Lect. notes in Comp. Sc. n°32, Springer-Verlag ed.

3. K. GOSTELOW, et al... Proper termination of flow of control in programs involving concurrent processes. SIGPLAN Notices, 7, 11, 1972.

4. M.H. HACK. Analysis of production schemata by Petri nets. TR 94, Project MAC, M.I.T 1972.

5. R.M. KARP, R.E. MILLER. Parallel program schemata. JCSS 3,2 1969

6. R.M. KELLER. Vector replacement systems. Tech. Rept. 117, Computer Science Laboratory Princeton University, 1974.

7. K. LAUTENBACH, H.A. SCHMID. Use of Petri-nets for proving correctness of concurrent process systems. IFIP 1974, North-Holland Publ. Comp. 1974.

8. A. MAZURKIEWICZ. Parallel recursive program schemes. Proc. of the Symp. on MFCS 75, Lect. notes in Comp. Sc n°32, Springer-Verlag ed.

9. C.A. PETRI. Concepts of net theory. Proc. of the Symp. on MFCS 73, High-Tatras, 1973.

10. G. ROUCAIROL. Une transformation de programmes séquentiels en programmes parallèles. Symp. on Programming, Paris, Lect. in Comp. Sc. n°19, Springer-Verlag ed.

11. G. ROUCAIROL. Two transformations of single-assignment programs. Communication to the 2° Conference on Petri-nets and their related methods, M.I.T, July 1975.

12. R. SETHI. Testing for the Church-Rosser property. JACM Vol. 21, n°4, Oct. 1974.

ON BEHAVIOUR OF R-FUZZY AUTOMATA

Jürgen Brunner and Wolfgang Wechler
Department of Mathematics
Technical University of Dresden
8027 Dresden, German Democratic Republic

The present paper deals with cut-point languages accepted by so-called R-fuzzy automata. In this notion R denotes an arbitrary partially ordered semiring which determines the special kind of fuzzy dynamics. Since the concept of R-fuzzy automaton is a generalization of the previously proposed notions of deterministic as well as stochastic automaton it seems advisable to classify the partially ordered semirings R in such a way that the appropiate R-fuzzy automata can be compared with that of deterministic or stochastic automata.

1. Introduction

A semiring R (cf. [1]) is said to be partially ordered (hereafter abbreviated po-semiring) if R is a partially ordered set and the two binary operations + and $\circ$ are consistent with the ordering. An R-fuzzy subset of a set M is a mapping from M into R.

Definition 1 (cf. [5]). Let R be a po-semiring. An R-fuzzy automaton over a (finite) alphabet X is a system $\mathfrak{A} = (S, S_o, S_f, d)$, where S is the set of internal states, S_o and S_f are R-fuzzy subsets of S (subset of initial and final states respectively), and the transition function d is a mapping from $S \times X$ into the set of all R-fuzzy subsets of S.

Every R-fuzzy automaton can be represented in matrix-form. Let S be a set of n elements then S_o and S_f are n-dimensional row and column vectors with coefficients in R respectively. The transitions can be described by a set of matrices $d(x)$, $x \in X$, from the semiring $(R)_n$ of all $n \times n$ matrices with coefficients in R.
If we use special po-semirings then it is easily to show that the concept of R-fuzzy automaton includes deterministic, non-deterministic, stochastic, fuzzy and other kinds of automata.
For describing the behaviour of an R-fuzzy automaton the transition function d must be extended to a monoid homomorphismus $\underline{d}$ from the free

monoid X^* generated by X into the multiplicative monoid of $(R)_n$. Therefore, to every R-fuzzy automaton $\mathfrak{A}$ over X an R-fuzzy subset $A = [\mathfrak{A}]$ of X^* can be associated by setting $A(w) = S_o \cdot \underline{d}(w) \cdot S_f$ for all $w \in X^*$.

Definition 2. Let R be a po-semiring and $\mathfrak{A}$ be an R-fuzzy automaton over X. Then the set $L(\mathfrak{A}, r) = \{w \in X^* \mid A(w) > r\}$ is said to be the language accepted by $\mathfrak{A}$ with respect to the cut-point $r \in R$. $L \subseteq X^*$ is called an R-fuzzy language if an R-fuzzy automaton $\mathfrak{A}$ and a cut-point $r \in R$ exist such that $L = L(\mathfrak{A}, r)$ holds. The set of all R-fuzzy languages over X is denoted by $\mathcal{L}_R$.

2. Regularity of R-Fuzzy Languages

In this section we intend to compare the behaviour of R-fuzzy automata for different kinds of po-semirings R by means of the related families $\mathcal{L}_R$. It is well-known that the set $\mathcal{L}_{reg}$ of all regular languages is equal to $\mathcal{L}_2$, where $2 = \{0,1\}$ is the Boolean semiring. Now, the problem arises to classify all po-semirings R for which $\mathcal{L}_R = \mathcal{L}_{reg}$ is valid. In the cases R is being one of the following po-semirings $\mathbb{Z}$ (set of integers), $\mathbb{Q}$ (set of rational numbers), or $\mathbb{R}$ (set of real numbers), $\mathcal{L}_{reg}$ is properly included in $\mathcal{L}_R$ (cf. [3]). Especially, $\mathcal{L}_{\mathbb{R}}$ coincides with the family $\mathcal{L}_{stoch}$ of all stochastic languages. Moreover, $\mathcal{L}_{\mathbb{Z}}$ is equal to $\mathcal{L}_{\mathbb{Q}}$. A language belonging to $\mathcal{L}_{\mathbb{Q}}$ is called rational. The family $\mathcal{L}_{rat}$ of all rational languages is a proper subfamily of $\mathcal{L}_{stoch}$.
Our first theorem, due to M. Karpinski, shows that every language is a R-fuzzy language for a suitable po-semiring R.

Theorem 1. For every language L over X there exists a po-semiring R such that L belongs to $\mathcal{L}_R$.

Proof. Let $\partial(L) = \{w^{-1}L \mid w \in X^*\}$ denotes the set of all (left) derivatives of $L \subseteq X^*$. Then we construct the following po-semiring R:
R is the disjoint union $\{0,1,\omega\} \dot\cup X^* \dot\cup \partial(L)$ equipped with two operations and a partial order defined as follows

(i) $r + 0 = 0 + r = r$ for $r \in R$

(ii) $r + r' = \omega$ elsewhere

(iii) $r \cdot 1 = 1 \cdot r = r$ for $r \in R$

(iv) $r \cdot 0 = 0 \cdot r = 0$ for $r \in R$

(v) concatenation in X^*

(vi) $v^{-1}L\cdot w = (vw)^{-1}L$ for $v,w \in X^*$
(vii) $r\cdot r' = \omega$ elsewhere
(viii) $0 < w^{-1}L$ if $w \in L$
It is easily to see that R is a po-semiring.

With $S = \{s_0,s_1\}$, $S_0 = (1,0)$, $S_f = \begin{cases}(0,1)^T \text{ if } e \notin L \\ (1,1)^T \text{ if } e \in L\end{cases}$, $d(x) = \begin{vmatrix} 0 & x^{-1}L \\ 0 & x \end{vmatrix}$

for $x \in X$, $\mathcal{A} = (S, S_0, S_f, d)$ yields to $L(\mathcal{A},0) = L$.

Observe that this construction is similar to that one of a deterministic (possibly infinite) automaton accepting a given language (cf. [1]). Now we shall be concerned with po-semirings R satisfying the identity $\mathcal{L}_R = \mathcal{L}_{reg}$.

Theorem 2. Assume that R is a po-semiring such that every finitely generated subsemiring is finite. Then all R-fuzzy languages are regular.

Proof. Let D be the set of all coefficients in the transition matrices of a given R-fuzzy automaton $\mathcal{A}$. Then $\mathcal{A}$ can also be regarded as an $R_{\mathcal{A}}$-fuzzy automaton, whereby $R_{\mathcal{A}}$ is the subsemiring generated by D. By assumption $R_{\mathcal{A}}$ is finite. In analogy to the subset construction for the non-deterministic case, to every $R_{\mathcal{A}}$-fuzzy automaton a deterministic one can be associated. Hence the assertion holds.

Corollary. The premise of Theorem 2 is valid for any complete distributive lattice.

Given two po-semirings R, R' a cut-point morphism φ_c from R into R', $c \in R$, is a semiring morphism (cf. [1]) which the condition $c < r$ iff $\varphi_c(c) < \varphi_c(r)$ fulfils for all $r \in R$.

Theorem 3. Let $\mathcal{A}$ be an R-fuzzy automaton. A language accepted by $\mathcal{A}$ with respect to the cut-point $c \in R$ is regular if there exists a cut-point morphism φ_c such that the image $\varphi_c(R)$ is finite.

Proof. The required property of a cut-point morphism yields to
$L(\mathcal{A},c) = \{w \in X^* \mid A(w) > c\} = \{w \in X^* \mid \varphi_c(A(w)) > \varphi_c(c)\}$.
Since a $\varphi_c(R)$-fuzzy automaton $\mathcal{B}$ with $L(\mathcal{A},c) = L(\mathcal{B},\varphi_c(c))$ exists, by Theorem 2, $L(\mathcal{A},c)$ is regular under the assumption.

Theorem 4. Let R be a po-semiring with monotonous operations (i. e., $r \leq r + r'$ and $r \leq r \cdot r'$, $r' \neq 0$, $r, r' \in R$) and $\mathcal{A}$ be an R-fuzzy automaton. If the set $N(R_{\mathcal{A}}, c) = \{r \in R_{\mathcal{A}} | r \not> c\}$ is finite for an element c of R then $L(\mathcal{A}, c)$ is a regular language.

Proof. Since the operations of R are monotonous a cut-point morphism $\varphi_c : R_{\mathcal{A}} \longrightarrow R^c_{\mathcal{A}}$ can be defined, where $R^c_{\mathcal{A}}$ is the disjoint union of $N(R_{\mathcal{A}}, c)$ and $\{\omega\}$. The sum and the product of two elements r and r' of $N(R_{\mathcal{A}}, c)$ coincide with $r+r'$ and $r \cdot r'$ in R if $r+r' \not> c$ and $r \cdot r' \not> c$ hold, respectively. Elsewhere, the results of addition and multiplication of two elements from $R^c_{\mathcal{A}}$ are always equal to ω. The partial order in $R^c_{\mathcal{A}}$ is given by that one in R and, additionally, ω is the top element. In order to prove $R^c_{\mathcal{A}}$ being a po-semiring the assumed monotony of operations in R is used. Obviously, $\varphi_c : R_{\mathcal{A}} \longrightarrow R^c_{\mathcal{A}}$ with $\varphi_c(r) = r$ if $r > c$ and $\varphi_c(r) = \omega$ otherwise is a cut-point morphism. By Theorem 3, $L(\mathcal{A}, c)$ is a regular language.

Corollary. (i) Every $\mathbb{N}$-fuzzy language is regular (cf. [1]), where $\mathbb{N}$ denotes the po-semiring of natural numbers.
(ii) If $R = \{r \in \mathbb{Q} \mid r \geq 1\} \cup \{0\}$, then every R-fuzzy language is regular. The same is true for the analogous case of real numbers.

In many important examples of po-semirings R, the sum of two elements coincides with their suprema (last upper bound with respect to the partial order on R). A monoid R is called semilattice ordered monoid (hereafter abbreviated slo-monoid [2]) if R is a po-set having binary suprema and the multiplication is distributive connected with the suprema operation. Moreover, a slo-monoid R with a special element 0, which is a multiplicative zero of R as well as being the bottom element of the partial order on R can already be regarded as a po-semiring. A slo-monoid R with zero is said to be integral if the unit of R is the top element of the partial order. For instance, the closed real interval [0,1] under customary order forms an integral slo-monoid with zero by defining $r \cdot r' = rr'$ (usual product of real numbers) or $r \cdot r' = \max(r+r'-1, 0)$.

Theorem 5. Assume that R is an integral slo-monoid with zero such that $r^n > r'$ for all $n > 0$ implies $r = 1$ for any $r, r' \in R$. Then every R-fuzzy language is regular.

Proof. Theorem 5 will be proved by means of Theorem 3. Therefore, for any R-fuzzy automaton $\mathcal{A}$ and any $c \in R$ a cut-point morphism φ_c from

$R_{\mathfrak{A}}$ into $R_{\mathfrak{A}}^c$ must be constructed. This construction is analogous to that one of Theorem 4, whereby instead of $N(R_{\mathfrak{A}},c)$ the set $P(R_{\mathfrak{A}},c) = \{r \in R_{\mathfrak{A}} | r > c\}$ is used. The required feature of R yields to the finiteness of any $\varphi_c(R_{\mathfrak{A}})$. Hence, the assertion is valid.

By the product $R = R' \times R''$ of two po-semirings R' and R'' is meant this po-semiring whose operations and partial order are defined component-wise.

Theorem 6 (cf. [7]). Let R' and R'' are po-semirings then the family of all $(R' \times R'')$-fuzzy languages is characterized as follows $\mathcal{L}_{R' \times R''} = \{L | L = L' \cap L'' \text{ for some } L' \in \mathcal{L}_{R'} \text{ and } L'' \in \mathcal{L}_{R''}\}$.

Corollary. Let R be a product $R = R_1 \times R_2 \times \ldots \times R_k$ of po-semirings $R_1, R_2, \ldots, R_k$, then every R-fuzzy language is regular if and only if every R_i-fuzzy language is regular for all $i = 1,2,\ldots,k$.

3. A Hierarchy of R-Fuzzy Languages

Considering the multiplicative structure of a po-semiring an interesting hierarchy of special R-fuzzy languages can be introduced [7].

Theorem 7. The family of all R-fuzzy languages properly includes all regular languages if the multiplicative monoid of R contains a non-trivial subgroup.

Proof. Assuming the po-semiring has the required feature and $r > 1$ be an arbitrary element of R belonging to the mentioned subgroup then the following R-fuzzy automaton $\mathfrak{A} = (S, S_o, S_f, d)$ over $X = \{x,y\}$ with $S = \{s_1, s_2\}$, $S_o = (1,0)$, $S_f = (0,1)^T$,

$d(x) = \begin{vmatrix} r & r \\ 0 & 0 \end{vmatrix}$ and $d(y) = \begin{vmatrix} 0 & 0 \\ 0 & r^{-1} \end{vmatrix}$ accepts the context-free language

$L = \{x^m y^n | m > n \geq 1\}$ with respect to the cut-point 1, because

$$A(w) = \begin{cases} r^{m-n} & \text{if } w = x^m y^n \text{ for } m,n = 1,2,\ldots \\ 0 & \text{otherwise.} \end{cases}$$

Hereby, the addition of R is not used. Therefore, the assertion of Theorem 7 is valid.

Corollary. For every slo-group R with zero the family of R-fuzzy languages properly includes $\mathcal{L}_{reg}$.

At the end of our paper we focus our attention to the multiplicative structure of the po-semirings $\mathbb{Q}^n$, whereby $\mathbb{Q}^n$ denotes the n-times product of $\mathbb{Q}$.

Definition 3. A language belonging to $\mathcal{L}_{\mathbb{Q}^n}$ is called n-rational. The set of all n-rational languages shall be abbreviated as $\mathcal{L}_{n\text{-rat}}$.

Theorem 8 (cf. [7]). The n-rational language families form an infinite hierarchy $\mathcal{L}_{rat} = \mathcal{L}_{1\text{-rat}} \subset \mathcal{L}_{2\text{-rat}} \subset \dots \subset \mathcal{L}_{n\text{-rat}} \subset \dots$.

Sketch of the proof. By means of Theorem 6 it follows that every n-rational language is also (n + 1)-rational. $\mathcal{L}_{2\text{-rat}}$ properly contains $\mathcal{L}_{1\text{-rat}}$, since the language $L = \bigcup_{k \geq 1} x^k y X^* y x^k y X^*$ over $X = \{x,y\}$ is 2-rational but not stochastic, hence L is not rational.
Based on this fact the proper inclusion $\mathcal{L}_{n\text{-rat}} \subset \mathcal{L}_{(n+1)\text{-rat}}$, $n \geqq 2$, can be proved now.

Corollary. $\mathcal{L}_{n\text{-rat}}$ is not closed under intersection.

References

[1] S. Eilenberg, Automata, Languages, and Machines, Vol. A, Academic Press, New York and London, 1974

[2] J. A. Goguen, L-fuzzy sets, J. of Math. Anal. and Appl., 18, 145 - 174, 1967

[3] P. Turakainen, On languages representable in rational probabilistic automata, Ann. Sci. Fennicae, Ser. A, I 439, 1969

[4] P. Turakainen, Generalized automata and stochastic languages, Proc. Amer. Math. Soc. 21, 303 - 309, 1969

[5] W. Wechler and V. Dimitrov, R-fuzzy automata, Inform. Processing 74, North-Holland Publ. Company, 657-660, 1974

[6] W. Wechler, The concept of fuzziness in the theory of automata, in Modern Trends in Cybernetics and Systems, Editura tehnica, Bucharest 1976

[7] W. Wechler, A hierarchy of n-rational languages, TU-Preprint 1976

CANNONIZING REDUCIBILITY METHOD
IN THE THEORY OF PROGRAM SCHEMATA

A.O.Buda
Institute of Mathematics and Mechanics
Bulgarian Academy of Sciences,Sofia 13

The problem of finding a decidable equivalence relation of program schemata, allowing a broad system of equivalent transformations, is formulated in the paper [1].Investigations in this field demand examination of a number of equivalence relations,defined on the subclasses of program schemata. In other words, pairs (K',E) are studied, whereK' is a subclass of schemata, and E is an equivalence relation given on $K' \subseteq K$ (K denotes the class of all program schemata). We are interested both in the decidability problem E in K', and in comparing different pairs (K',E) in their "computing power".For this purpose we describe the procedure of reducing the problem (K',E) to the decidability problem of the termal equivalence of program schemata. The procedure is determined by means of the concept of termalizator.

A program schema is depicted on figure 1. The initial vertex is denoted by 1, the final one - by 7; 2,4,5,6 are statement vertices to which correspond the assignment statements (4,5) or the transition statements (2,6); 3 is the logic vertex to which corresponds the recognizer. To the final vertex corresponds the final statement; x^* is the exit variable; the variables x_1, x_2in the right side of the final statement are final variables;f^* is the final functional symbol. The finite sets X,F,P of variables, functional and predicate symbols with K class schemata built on,are supposed to be fixed.

Functional equivalence of two program schemata means that for all recursive interpretations of F,P symbols and arbitrary initial values of variables from X, both schemata either diverge or converge with equal values of the exit variable x^*,received in result.

Let us fix some schema path from the initial to the final vertex (be-path) and consider the functional term of the exit variable x^*, obtained by formal execution of the schema along this path.This term be called termal value of the path.Two schemata are termal (T)equival-

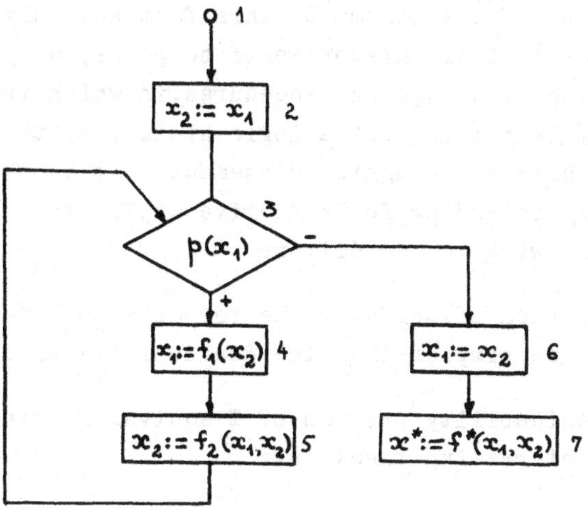

Fig.1

ent, if the sets of all termal values of their be-paths are equal.

Example 1. The termal value of the path L

1 2 (3,+) 4 5 (3,-) 6 7

of the schema depicted on figure 1 is equal to

$$t^* = f^*(f_2(f_1(x_1),x_1),f_2(f_1(x_1),x_1)).$$

It should be noted that functional equivalence is the weakest in the set of interpretive equivalences [1,2], and so is the termal one in the set of formal equivalences. Moreover, T-equivalence coincides with the functional one for schemata without logic vertices [3,4]. The concept of termal value is introduced in [5]. In that paper it is called S-representation of exit values of the variables.

By a termalizator of the pair (K',E) we mean a transformation φ defined on the subclass K' and for any schemata $D,D' \in K'$ satisfying the relation

$$D(E)D' \Longleftrightarrow \varphi D(T)\varphi D'.$$

Taking into account the utmost simplicity of termal equivalence, it may be expected that the whole logic nature of difference of E - equivalence from the termal one will be revealed by the structure of the termalizator. At that, information chains will appear in the termal values of the schema φD, coding the logic connections between transformations of the schema D. This fact not only leads us to a certain unification of the histories of be-paths, but proves to be as well a formalization of debugging procedures, in which tracing [1,2], as it is clear now, is nothing but a logic history of the path, coded by the information chain of debugging statements. It should be noted that all termalizators, pretending for effective application, should satisfy at least the following two conditions.

1. The problem of building the termalizator φ of the pair (K',E) is in some sense simpler than the decidability problem of E in K'.

2. The decidability problem of T-equivalence in the subclass $\varphi K'$ allows some interesting treatment.

In this paper, the application of the cannonizing reducibility method is illustrated by a proof of the decidability of logic-termal (LT) equivalence of program schemata [1,2], having an important applied significance. Decidability of LT-equivalence was first established in the paper [6], but all proofs of this fact, received by now, used the trace method and therefore contained the algorithm, which enumerates all schema paths whose length is less than some large constant fixed a priori. The proof using the cannonizing reducibility method proposes a more effective for practical applications algorithm, it reveals a new aspect of LT-equivalence nature. Besides, the idea, used in it, allows to establish new connections between the problems of the theory of program schemata and the actual problems of the theory of automata.

Two schemata be called <u>logic-termal equivalent</u>, if the sets of all logic-termal histories of their be-paths are equal. Unstrictly speaking, the LT-history of the given be-path L of some schema is a sequence of formulae for formal execution of the values of recognizers met at travelling along the path L. The termal value of the path L uses to be set at the end of the sequence. A strict definition of LT-history can be found in the paper [6].

<u>Example 2.</u> The LT-history of the path from example 1 is equal to

$$p^{+}(x_1)p^{-}(f_1(x_1))t^{*}.$$

<u>Lemma 1.</u> There exists a termalizator φ_1 of the pair (K,LT). The transformation φ_1 is built as follows.

a. The auxilliary variable y is fixed.

b. Let p be an arbitrary predicate symbol; $w \in \{+,-\}$.

To every pair (p,w) corresponds the auxiliary functional k+1-arity symbol f_p^w, where k is the arity of the symbol p.

c .The schema $\varphi_1 D$ is obtained from D by adding the variable y to the final variables and applying to every logic vertex transformations of the sort of those depicted on figure 2.

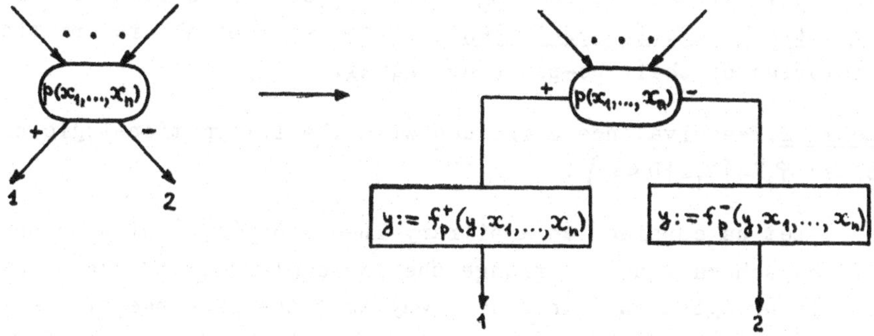

Fig.2

The termal value of some be-path L can be represented as a tree. <u>The information chain</u> of the path L is a path in the tree of its termal value. The information chain is represented as a word beginning with a variable, all the other elements of which are pairs of the type (f,i), where f is a functional symbol and i is an entry number of the symbol f (a positive integer number not greater than the arity of the symbol f). <u>The logic chain</u> of the path L is the sequence of pairs of the type (p,w), where p is a predicate symbol, which one meets at travelling along the path L and passing a logic vertex; $w \in \{+,-\}$ is a sign, labelling the arc, one passes in order to leave the logic vertex for further movement along the path L. There is the automation which accepts exactly the set of logic chains of all be-paths of some schema D. The graph of this automation be called <u>the logic graph</u> of the schema D.

<u>Example 3</u>. Let us consider the logic chain l of the path L from example 1

$$(p,+)(p,-).$$

Let L' be the path of the schema $\varphi_1 D$, whose logic chain is equal to l. The paths, leading from the hanging vertices to f^* in the tree of the termal value of the path L', are the information chains of the path L'. Besides, the information chain

$$y(f_p^+,1)(f_p^-,1)(f^*,1)$$

codes the logic chain l.

By s we denote an arbitrary information chain of the be-path and by l - the logic chain of this path. The pair (s,l) be called <u>information-logic history</u> of the path. It should be noted that one path may have several information-logic histories. Two schemata be called <u>information-logic(IL) equivalent</u>, if the sets of all information-logic histories of their be-paths are equal.

<u>Lemma 2</u>. T-equivalence coincides with the information-logic one in the class $\varphi_1 K=\{\varphi_1 D \mid D \in K\}$.

Let us consider an arbitrary IL-history(s,l) of some be-path L of the schema D and rearrange the logic elements of the word sl with the information ones in such a way that the sequence of the elements would coincide with the sequence of vertices of the path L forming those elements. The sequence obtained be called <u>trajectory</u> of the schema D.

<u>Example 4</u>. Let us consider the path L from example 1 and its information chain

$$x_1(f_1,1)(f_2,1)(f^*,1).$$

This chain coincides with the trajectory

$$x_1(p,+)(f_1,1)(f_2,1)(p,-)(f^*,1).$$

<u>Lemma 3.</u> The set of all trajectories of an arbitrary program schema is a regular set.

For any schema D there can be effectively built a finite automation, accepting exactly the set of all trajectories of the schema D. The graph of this automation be called <u>T-graph</u>. The T-graph proves to be an important information-logic invariant of program schema.

<u>Example 5</u>. On figure 3 there is depicted the T-graph of the schema from the figure 1. q_0 is the initial, q_1-the final state. The other states are either of the type (p,w,x) or (b,i). An arbitrary state of the first type is intuitively treated as an arc of the logic graph with the variable x "joined" it, and a state of the second type- as a statement vertex with i-th entry of the functional symbol, corres - ponding to this vertex.

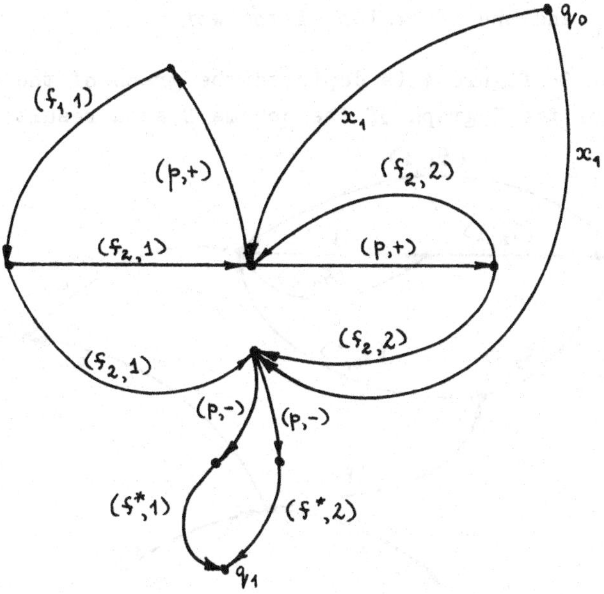

Fig.3

Let

$$M_1=\{(p,w)\}\cup a_0$$
$$M_2=\{(f,i)\}\cup X,$$

where a_0 is a symbol of the initial arc of any logic graph. We define the class $\{A(D)|D\in K\}$ of two-tapes nondeterministic automata, identifying the graph of the automation A(D) with the T-graph of the schema D (the symbols of the alphabet M_1 correspond to the first tape, and those of M_2 - to the second one).

<u>Lemma 4</u>. For any schema D the automation A(D) accepts exactly the set of all information-logic histories of the schema D.

We have proved the following assertion.

<u>Lemma 5.</u> There exists a transformation F satisfying the following two relations for any automata A,A' belonging to the class $\{A(D)|D\in K\}$.

1. FA,FA' are deterministic two-tapes automata

2. $A\sim A' \Longleftrightarrow FA\sim FA'$

The two-tapes deterministic automata obtained, accept exactly the sets of IL-histories of the initial schemata with an accuracy of the element a_0 and the inversion of the words.

Example 6. On figure 4 is depicted the graph of the automation FA(D),obtained from the T-graph of the schema D as a result of the transformation F.

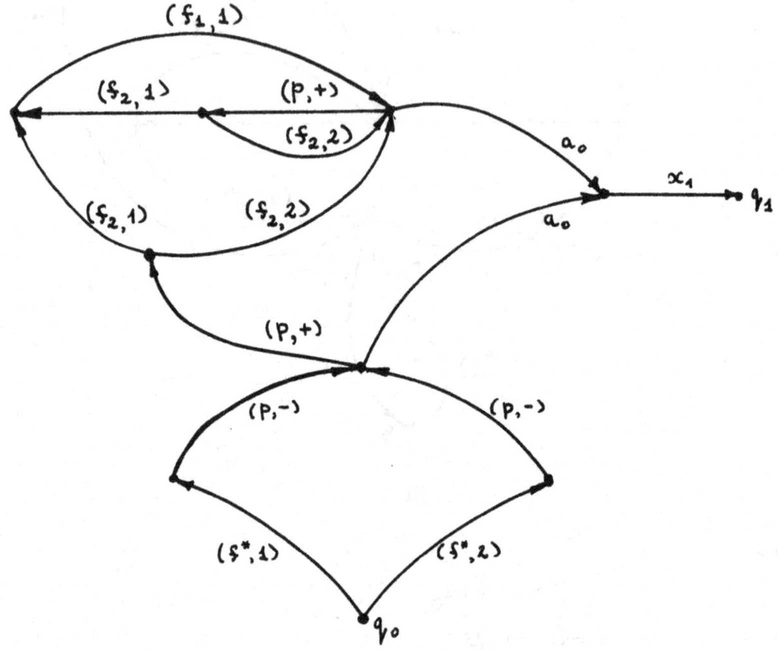

Fig.4

Now the decidability of LT-equivalence problem follows from lemmas 1-5 and Bird's result [7] about the decidability of the equivalence problem of two-tapes deterministic automata.

Theorem 1. There exists an algorithm for the recognition of logic-termal equivalence in the class of all program schemata K.

This result strengthens Itkin's and the author's result published in the paper [8]. Other results concerning the termal equivalence and the termalization can be found in [8,9].

References

1. Ershov,A.P., Theory of Program Schemata, Proc.Congress IFIP 71,invited papers(1972) Ljubljana.
2. Ershov,A.P.,The modern state of the theory of program schemata,Problems of Cybernetics,27 (1973),Nauka,Moscow(in Russian)
3. Luckham,D.C.,Park,D.M.R.,Paterson,M.S.,On Formalized Computer Prog-

rams,JCSS,4,3(1970).

4.Letichevsky,A.A., The functional equivalence of discrete processors I, Cybernetics, 2(1969),Kiev (in Russian).

5.Ershov,A.P.,Denotion of the based programming constructions,Problems of Cybernetics, 8 (1962),Nauka,Moscow (in Russian).

6.Itkin,V.I., Logic-termal equivalence of program schemata,Cybernetics, 1(1972),Kiev (in Russian).

7.Bird,M., The Equivalence Problem for Deterministic Two-Tapes Automata, JCSS,7, 2 (1973).

8.Buda, A.O.,Itkin,V.I., Termal equivalence of program schemata,Theoretical and System Programming,4 (1974), Computer centre SOAN SSSR, Novosibirsk (in Russian).

9.Buda,A.O., The equivalence relations on the classes of program schemata, Kandidatskaya dissertatsiya(1975),Computer centre SOAN SSSR,Novosibirsk(in Russian).

STRONGLY CONNECTED G-S-M MAPPINGS PRESERVING CONJUGATION

C. Choffrut
Université Paris VII
Département de Mathématiques
T. 45-55, 2, place Jussieu - 75221 PARIS CEDEX 05

INTRODUCTION

gsm mappings of a free monoid X^* into another Y^* are defined as rational transductions realized in a certain way, by finite automata provided with an output. They play an important role in the theory of rational transductions. In particular every rational transduction which is a function can be obtained by composition of two gsm mappings (see for ex. [3], [6] and [7]).

We study in this paper to what extent gsm mappings preserve such basic notions as imprimitivity and conjugation in free monoids.

Our main result concerns gsm mappings θ of X^* into Y^* whose underlying automaton is strongly connected. We show that if θ preserves conjugation, it does it in a trivial manner. More precisely we prove that if θ is not a morphism and if for all $f,h \in X^*$ there exist $u,v \in Y^*$ such that $\theta(fh) = uv$ and $\theta(hf) = vu$, then there exists a word $w \in Y^*$ such that for all $f \in X^*$, $\theta(f)$ is a left factor of a power of w .

The proof of this result is not given and will appear in a next publication. We just state the three technical lemmas which are used in the proof and show how they are utilized.

FREE MONOID

Given any finite, non empty set X, X^* shall denote the free monoid generated by X and 1 the unit element of X^*. Elements of X and X^* are respectively called *letters* and *words* and 1 is called the *empty* word.

For each word $f \in X^*$ and each letter $x \in X$, $|f|_x$ shall denote the number of occurrences of x in f and $|f| = \sum_{x\in X} |f|_x$ the *length* of f .

A word $h \in X^*$ is a *left factor* of $f \in X^*$ if there exists a word $f' \in X^*$ such that : $f = hf'$.

Words $f,h \in X^*$ are *conjugate* (resp. *properly conjugate*) if there exist $u,v \in X^*$ (resp. $u,v \in XX^*$) such that : $f = uv$ and $h = vu$.

Let us recall [5] that $f,h \in X^*$ commute (i.e. $fh = hf$) iff f and h are powers of a same word.

A word $f \in X^*$ is *primitive*, if for each $h \in X^*$ and each integer $n > 0$, $f = h^n$

implies $n = 1$. If f is not primitive, it is *imprimitive*. Thus 1 is imprimitive. Notice that f is imprimitive iff it is properly conjugate with itself.

GSM MAPPING

A *generalized sequential machine* T [4], abbreviated gsm , is defined by :

- three finite non empty sets Q, X, Y, respectively called set of *states*, *input alphabet* and *output alphabet*.
- an element $q_o \in Q$, called *initial state*.
- two functions $\mu : Q \times X \to Q$ and $\bar{\theta} : Q \times X \to Y^*$ which are extended to $Q \times X^*$ by induction on the length of the words :

i) $\forall q \in Q,\ \mu(q,1) = q$ and $\bar{\theta}(q,1) = 1$

ii) $\forall q \in Q,\ \forall x \in X,\ \forall f \in X^*,\ \mu(q,fx) = \mu(\mu(q,f),x)$ and $\bar{\theta}(q,fx) = \bar{\theta}(q,f)\ \bar{\theta}(\mu(q,f),x)$

μ and $\bar{\theta}$ are respectively called *transition* and *output* function. As usual we shall write $q.f$ instead of $\mu(q,f)$.

A gsm T is *minimal* if it verifies the two conditions :

$\mathcal{U}_a$: $\forall q \in Q,\quad f \in X^*,\quad q_o f = q.$

$\mathcal{U}_r$: $\forall q, q' \in Q,\ q \neq q' \Longrightarrow \exists\, f \in X^*,\ \bar{\theta}\,(q,f) \neq \bar{\theta}\,(q',f).$

Each gsm T defines a mapping θ_T of X^* into Y^* by : $\forall f \in X^*,\ \theta_T(f) = \bar{\theta}(q_o,f)$. We shall say that T *realizes* θ_T . Conversely we shall say that a mapping θ of X^* into Y^* is a *gsm mapping* if it can be realized by a gsm T, i.e. : $\theta = \theta_T$. Notice that every morphism can be realized by a gsm whose set of states is reduced to the initial state.

It can be shown [3], that for each gsm mapping θ there exists a minimal gsm T_θ, unique up to an isomorphism, which realizes θ.

A gsm mapping θ is *strongly connected* if the transition function of T_θ verifies: $\forall q \in Q,\quad \exists\, f \in X^*,\ q.f = q_o$.

In all our examples we shall consider gsm mappings θ of X^* into Y^* where $X = \{x,y\}$ and $Y = \{z,t\}$.

Example 1. Let $\theta : X^* \to Y^*$ be defined for all $f \in X^*$ by :

$$\begin{cases} \theta(f) = (zt)^{|f|_x + 3/2\,|f|_y} & \text{if } |f|_y \equiv 0\ [2] \\ \text{and} & \\ \theta(f) = (zt)z^{|f|_x + 3/2\,(|f|_y - 1)} & \text{if } |f|_y \equiv 1\ [2]. \end{cases}$$

Then θ is realized by the minimal gsm which is represented in the usual way :

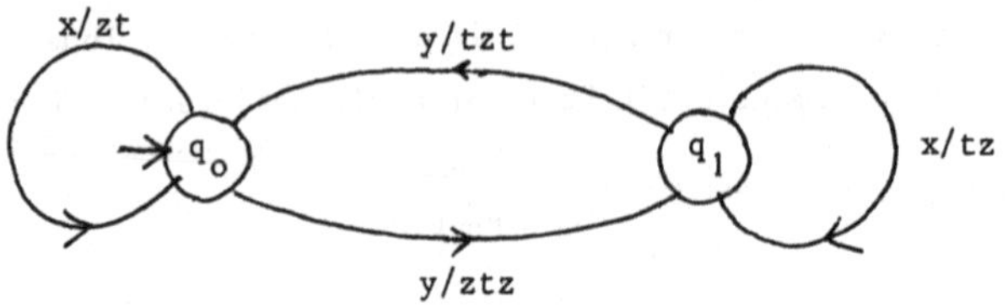

Clearly, θ is strongly connected.

Example 2. Let $\alpha : X^* \to Y^*$ be the morphism defined by : $\alpha(x) = z^2$ and $\alpha(y) = t$. Let us define $\theta : X^* \to Y^*$ by :

$$\begin{cases} \forall f \in X^* \setminus \{x\}^* & \theta(f) = \alpha(f) \\ \text{and} & \\ \forall n \geq 0 \quad \theta(x^{2n}) = z^{4n} & \text{and} \quad \theta(x^{2n+1}) = z^{4n+1} \end{cases}$$

One easily verifies that θ is realized by the following gsm :

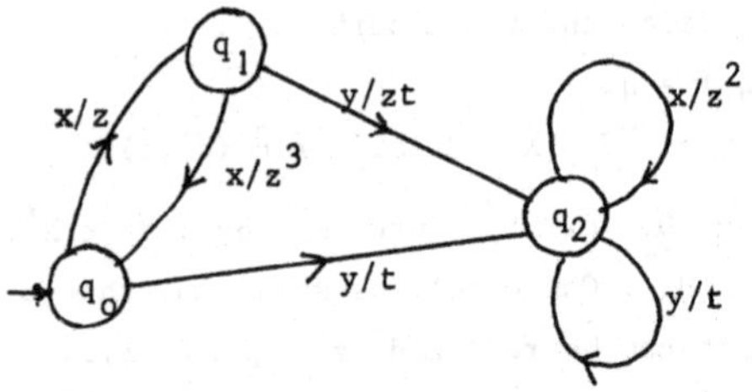

Then θ is not strongly connected because for all $f \in X^*$: $q_2.f = q_2$.

A gsm mapping θ is *trivial*, if for all $f \in X^*$, $\theta(f) = 1$. It possesses a *pit* if it is not trivial and if there exists a word $f \in X^*$ such that for all $h \in X^*$, $\theta(fh) = \theta(f)$. Notice that if θ possesses a pit then it is certainly not strongly connected.

A gsm mapping θ is *narrow* (resp. *thin*) if there exists a word $u \in Y^*$ such that the image by θ of each word $f \in X^*$, is a left factor of a power of u (resp. is a power of u).

Example 3. Let θ be defined for all $f \in XX^*$ by : $\theta(f) = (z^2t)^{|f|+1}$. Then θ is thin, and thus narrow.

Example 4. The gsm mapping defined in Ex. 1 is narrow but not thin.

PRESERVATION OF IMPRIMITIVITY AND CONJUGATION

A gsm mapping $\theta : X^* \to Y^*$ preserves *imprimitivity* if the image of each imprimitive word of X^* is an imprimitive word of Y^* . Equivalently, for all $f \in X^*$,

$n > 1$, there exist $u \in Y^*$ and $p > 1$ such that $\theta(f^n) = u^p$.

Example 5. Any morphism $\alpha : X^* \to Y^*$ preserves imprimitivity because of : $\alpha(f^n) = \alpha(f)^n$.

Example 6. Let α_1, α_2 be the two morphisms of X^* into Y^* defined by : $\alpha_1(x) = \alpha_2(x) = z$, $\alpha_1(y) = t$ and $\alpha_2(y) = t^2$. Define $\theta: X^* \to Y^*$ by : $\theta(xf) = \alpha_1(xf)$ and $\theta(yf) = \alpha_2(yf)$ for all $f \in X^*$. Then θ preserves imprimitivity.

A gsm mapping $\theta : X^* \to Y^*$ preserves *conjugation* (resp. *proper conjugation*) if the images of any two conjugate (resp. properly conjugate) words of X^*, are conjugate (resp. properly conjugate) words of Y^*. Notice that any morphism $\alpha: X^* \to Y^*$ preserves conjugation and that it preserves proper conjugation iff it is continuous i.e. for all $x \in X$, $\alpha(x)$ is different from the empty word.

Example 7. Let θ be defined by $\theta(f) = zt^{|f|}$ for all $f \in XX^*$. Any two conjugate words of X^* have the same image by θ . Thus θ preserves conjugation, but not proper conjugation.

Example 8. The gsm mapping of Ex. 2 preserves proper conjugation.

We study in the sequel the relationship between the different notions which have been introduced. We first have the following result, which the reader can easily verify :

Proposition. Let $\theta : X^* \to Y^*$ be a gsm mapping which preserves proper conjugation. Then it preserves conjugation and imprimitivity.

It is not true in general that if θ preserves imprimitivity then it preserves conjugation, neither that if it preserves conjugation then it preserves imprimitivity as it is respectively shown by examples 6 and 7. Nevertheless, if θ is strongly connected and not thin, the first implication is true :

Théorem 1 [2] *: Let $\theta : X^* \to Y^*$ be a strongly connected gsm mapping which is not thin. Then θ preserves imprimitivity iff it is a morphism.*

The principal result of this paper concerns the second implication :

Theorem 2 : Let $\theta : X^* \to Y^*$ be a strongly connected gsm mapping which is not narrow. Then it preserves conjugation iff it is a morphism.

The hypothesis that θ is not narrow is necessary. Indeed we defined in example 1 a strongly gsm mapping which preserves conjugation, which is not a morphism but which is narrow.

We now state the three technical lemmas which are used in the proof of theorem 2.

Lemma 1. Let a, b, c *be three words in X^* verifying the two conditions :*

i) $2|c| \geq |a| > |b| + |c| > |c| > 2|b|$.

ii) *there exist two integers* $p, q > 6$ *and* a', c' *in* X^* *such that* $a = a'^p$ *and* $c = c'^q$.

If for some value $n > 2$ $a^n bc$ *and* $a^n cb$ *are conjugate words, then two of the three words* a, b, c *are powers of a same word.*

Lemma 2. Let a, b, c *be three words in* X^* *and suppose that* $a^n b$ *and* $c^n b$ *are conjugate words for all* n *. Then* a, b, c *satisfy one of the following conditions:*

i) $a = c$

ii) *there exist* u, v *in* X^* *and* $r, s, t \geq 0$ *such that :*

$$b = ((uv)^r u)^t \text{ and } \begin{cases} a = ((uv)^r u)^s uv \text{ and } c = vu\,((uv)^r u)^s. \\ \text{or} \\ a = vu\,((uv)^r u)^s \text{ and } c = ((uv)^r u)^t uv. \end{cases}$$

Lemma 3 [1]. *Let* θ *be a g-s-m mapping of* X^* *into* Y^**, without pit. Then* θ *is a morphism iff for each* f *in* X^* *there exists* u *in* Y^* *such that for each* h *in* X^* *there exists a power* u^p *of* u *such that :* $\theta(hf) = \theta(h)u^p$.

Let $\theta : X^* \to Y^*$ be a strongly connected gsm mapping which preserves conjugation and T_θ its minimal gsm . To every $f \in X^*$, the transition function of T_θ associates a mapping of the set Q into itself. Let us say that f is idempotent if this mapping is idempotent i.e. if for every $q \in Q$, $qf = qf^2$. Three cases have to be considered.

1) There exists an idempotent $f \in X^*$ such that $\theta(f)$ and $\theta(f^2)$ are not powers of a same word. Then one applies lemme 1, and proves that θ is narrow.

2) For all idempotent $f \in X^*$, $\theta(f)$ and $\theta(f^2)$ are powers of a same word, but there exist an idempotent $f_1 \in X^*$, a word $g \in X^*$ and a word $u \in Y^*$ such that $\theta(gf_1^2) = \theta(gf_1)u$, where u and $\theta(f_1)$ are not powers of a same word. Then one applies lemme 2 and proves that θ is narrow.

3) For all idempotent $f \in X^*$ and all $g \in X^*$, there exists a word $u \in Y^*$ such that $\theta(gf^2) = \theta(gf)u$ where $\theta(f)$ and u are powers of a same word. Then, one proves that for every idempotent f, there exists a word $v \in Y^*$ such that for every $g \in X^*$, $\theta(gf) = \theta(g)u$ where u is a power of v . Lemma 3 implies that θ is a morphism.

REFERENCES

[1] C. CHOFFRUT - *Transducteurs unilatères et morphismes*, Thèse de 3ème cycle, Université Paris VI, 1972.

[2] C. CHOFFRUT - *Transducteurs conservant l'imprimitivité, in "Automata, Languages and Programming"*, (M. Nivat, Ed.), North-Holland, Amsterdam.

[3] S. EILENBERG - *"Automata, Languages and Machines"*, Vol. A, Academic Press, New-York.

[4] S. GINSBURG - *"The Mathematical Theory of Context-free Languages"*, Mc Graw-Hill New-York.

[5] A. LENTIN - *"Equations dans les monoïdes libres"*, Gauthier-Villars, 1972.

[6] M. NIVAT - *Transductions des langages de Chomsky*, Ann. Inst. Fourier 18, 339-455

[7] M.P. SCHUTZENBERGER - *Sur les relations rationnelles fonctionnelles entre monoïdes libres*, Theoretical Computer Science, to appear.

ANALYSIS OF THE NON-CONTEXT-FREE COMPONENT OF FORMAL LANGUAGES

Michal P. Chytil
Charles University
Malostranské nám. 25
118 00 Prague 1 - M. Strana

Dedicated to my teacher, Professor Jiří Bečvář on the occasion of his fiftieth birthday.

Introduction

G. Wechsung has recently introduced a new complexity measure for Turing machine computations [1]. In [2] he has proved that the class of context-free languages forms a complexity class wrt. this measure. Namely: a language is context-free iff it is recognized by a nondeterministic Turing machine with the Wechsung's measure bounded by a constant.

Since recognition of context-free languages is almost "free of cost" if measured by the Wechsung's measure, a question arises, whether the "price" of a computation can be characterized as a non-context-free component of the recognized language.

We shall introduce a measure of context-sensitivity as the complexity of computations of Turing machines which can use an auxiliary gratuitous information supplied by an arbitrary context-free language. For computations of at least linear complexity, this measure and the Wechsung's measure coincide.

From that fact several consequences are obtained. For example:

- complements of context-sensitive languages have in general the same context complexity as context-sensitive languages;
- the language $\{wcw \; ; \; w \in \{a,b\}^*\}$ is "essentially context-sensitive";
- linear speed-up result for the Wechsung's measure;
- space restrictions imposed upon computations by the restrictions of context-sensitivity;

etc.

Wechsung's measure of active visits

In [1] G. Wechsung has introduced a complexity measure for the computations of 1-tape, 1-head Turing machines, which can be described as follows.

In every computation of a machine, the history of every tape square can be divided into two periods: the active one and the passive one. The active history of a square is all the period after the visit of the head during which the content of the square was rewrited for the first time. The passive history is the period preceding the active history (i.e. it includes the first-rewriting visit, too).

The number of active visits is the number of visits payed by the head to the square during its active history.

The maximal number of active visits corresponding to a given computation determines the measure of active visits of the computation.

$V_M(w) = n \quad \Longleftrightarrow_{df}$ 1) there is a computation of the nondeterministic machine M accepting w with the measure of active visits equal to n,
2) there is no computation of M accepting w with a lower measure of active visits.

$V(f) =_{df}$ the class of languages which can be recognized by nondeterministic Turing machines with the measure of active visits bounded by the function f.

Remark. The above defined measure is called "return complexity measure" in [1] . We use different name throughout this paper to get an abbreviation different from R, which is used for the reversal measure.

Wechsung has proved [2] that

V(0) = REG (the class of regular languages),

V(1) = LIN (the class of linear languages) ,

$V(4) = \bigcup_{k=0}^{\infty} V(k)$ = CFL (the class of context-free languages).

It could be interesting to know whether also CSL (the class of context-sensitive languages can be characterized as a complexity class V(f) for some f. In that case, the V-measure would characterize all the Chomsky hierarchy in terms of complexity classes.

Recall that for the nondeterministic space measure (denote S), the nondeterministic crossing measure C (given by the maximal length of crossing sequence) and the nondeterministic reversal measure R (number of reversals of the head) , the class CSL forms a complexity class (cf. [3]):

CSL = S(id) = C(id) = R(id), where id is the identity function, i.e. id(n) = n.

The question whether V(id) = CSL is still open. The following two theorems, however, give an insight into the question.

Theorem 1. Let CSL and CCSL denote the class of context-sensitive languages and the class of complements of context-sensitive languages. Then

$$CSL \cup CCSL \subsetneq V(id).$$

Theorem 2. Let $L = \{wcw \; ; \; w \in \{a,b\}^*\}$ and let $\inf_{n \to \infty} \frac{f(n)}{n} = 0$. Then $L \notin V(f)$.

Apparently, if V(f) = CSL for some f, then f = id. But if V(id) were equal to CSL then CSL would obviously be closed under complements. And the latter is a very long opened problem.

We close this section by a generalization of Theorem 1.

Theorem 3. For any $f: N \longrightarrow N$ is

$S(f) \cup$ complements of $S(f) \subsetneq V(f)$.

Measure of context-sensitivity

For arbitrary disjoint alphabets A, A_1 the homomorphism $h_A: (A \cup A_1)^* \longrightarrow A^*$ will be defined as follows:

$$h_A(a) = \begin{cases} a \; , & \text{for } a \in A \\ \text{empty}, & \text{for } a \in A_1. \end{cases}$$

DC(f) will denote the class of languages recognizable by deterministic Turing machines with the crossing measure (determined by the maximal length of crossing sequence) bounded by the function f.

Definition 1. Let $A \subset B$ be finite alphabets, $L_o \subseteq B^*$. The class $DC_A(f,L_o)$ of languages (in the alphabet A) recognizable with the DC-measure f and the auxiliary language L_o will be defined as follows:

$L \in DC_A(f,L_o) \iff_{df}$ there is a deterministic M and a language $L_1 \subseteq B^*$ such that

1) M recognizes L_1

2) for every $w \in L_1$ is $DC_M(w) \leq f(|h_A(w)|)$

3) $L = h_A(L_1 \cap L_o)$.

We shall write $L \in DC(f,L_o)$ iff $L \in DC_A(f,L_o)$ for some A.

Let us recall the conditions 1) - 3) informally: symbols of the input word w can be sandwiched by strings of auxiliary symbols from B - A so that the resulting word w' is from L_o. Then M computes over the word w' with the complexity bound $f(|w|)$. The word w belongs to L iff any such computation over any such w' is accepting. (The computation is uniquely determined by w', of course.)

<u>Example</u>. Let

$L =_{df} \{x_1 x_2 \ldots x_n c y_1 y_2 \ldots y_n \; ; \; x_i, y_i \in \{a,b\} \;\&\; x_i \neq y_i$ for at least $\lceil \log n + 1 \rceil$ different indeces $i\}$.

Then $L \in DC_A(\log n, L_o)$ for $A = \{a,b,c\}$ and

$L_o = \{u_1 d u_2 d \ldots u_{r-1} d u_r c v_r d v_{r-1} \ldots d v_2 d v_1 \; ; \; u_i, v_i \in \{a,b\}^+ \;\&\; |u_i| = |v_i|$ for every $i\}$.

(L_o is apparently context-free.)

Proof. Let $w \in L_o$, $n = |h_A(w)|$. A computation (of an M recognizing an L_1) with the length of crossing sequences bounded by log n is sufficient to verify whether

i) c divides w into two words of equal length

ii) the number od symbols d in w is equal to $\lceil \log n \rceil$

iii) the last symbol of u_i is different from the first symbol of v_i, for every i.

w is accepted iff all three conditions hold, i.e. $w \in L_1 \cap L_o$.

Apparently, $L = h_A(L_1 \cap L_o)$.

<u>Definition 2</u>. Let CFL denote the class of context-free languages. We define CTX(f), the class of <u>languages with the measure of context-sensitivity bounded by f</u> as follows:

$$CTX(f) = \bigcup_{L \in CFL} DC(f,L) .$$

Remark. Using slightly modified techniques from [3] and [4], we can prove that the same measure CTX is obtained if the DC-measure is replaced by the deterministic space measure (for on-line Turing machines) or by the deterministic reversal measure in Definition 1 and Definition 2.

The intuitive feeling that the Wechsung's measure describes a non-context-free component of languages is reflected by the following theorem.

Theorem 4. 1) $V(f) \subseteq CTX(f)$ for every f.
2) If $f(n) \geq n$ for all n, then $V(f) = CTX(f)$.

We give here only a very brief outline of the proof.

1) Let $L \in V(f)$. A word $w = ¢u_1^R a_1 v_1 ¢u_2^R a_2 v_2 ¢ \ldots ¢u_n^R a_n v_n ¢$ will be called a (full) history of a computation of a machine M over the tape segment $a_1 \ldots a_n$, if there is a computation of M over $a_1 \ldots a_n$ such that for every a_i, u_i and v_i are the left and the right crossing sequence adjacent to a_i, respectively. Every such a history is characterized by two conditions:

a) u_i and v_i are consistent with the fact that the tape square initially contained the symbol a_i (for more details cf. [3])

b) $v_i = u_{i+1}$.

Consider the active history of a computation instead of the full history, now. Then u_i and v_i are the (final) segments of crossing sequences corresponding to the active history of the square a_i.

The condition a) must hold for them as well. The condition b), however, does not hold in general, as in a moment when a_i has been active for a long time, a_{i+1} might be still passive. v_i then corresponds with some u_{i+p}, $p > 1$.

But for every M there is a context-free language L_0 such that the condition b) can be replaced by the following condition, in this case:

b') $w \in L_0$.

The condition a) characterizes a language L_1. Every word $w \in L_1$ can be recognized with DC-bound equal to $\max_i (|u_i|, |v_i|)$. (cf. [3])

w is apparently an active history of a computation iff $w \in L_1 \cap L_0$.

A homomorphism h_A can be used to erase everything but the input word. Then $L = h_A(L_1 \cap L_o)$.
2) follows from 1) and the fact [2] that CFL = V(const).

We close the paper by three results based on the relation between V and CTX measures.

Theorem 5. (linear speed-up result) Let $f(n) \geq n$ for all n and let $c > 0$. Then

$$V(f) = V(c.f).$$

The following result estimates space restrictions imposed upon a computation by the V-restrictions.

Theorem 6. Let $L \in V(f)$. Then there is a nondeterministic Turing machine and a constant $c > 0$ such that

1) M recognizes L
2) $V_M(w) \leq f(|w|)$ for all $w \in L$
3) $S_M(w) \leq 2^{c^{f(|w|)}}$ for all $w \in L$.

Corollary. The measure V is a complexity measure in the sense of Blum's axioms [5].

An open question is whether the space bounds given by Theorem 6 can be improved. For the special case of CS-languages and their complements it is so, as the following theorem shows. The upper bound 2^{c^n} given by theorems 1 and 6 is replaced by the bound c^n.

Theorem 7. Let L be a CS-language or a complement of a CS-language. Then there is a nondeterministic Turing machine M and a constant $c > 0$ such that

1) M recognizes L
2) $V_M(w) \leq |w|$ for all $w \in L$
3) $S_M(w) \leq c^{|w|}$ for all $w \in L$.

References

1. Wechsung G., Characterization of some classes of context-free languages in terms of complexity classes. In Proceedings of MFCS 1975, Lecture Notes in Computer Science 32, p. 457-461.

2. Wechsung G., Kompliziertheitstheoretische Characterisierung der kontext-freien und linearen Sprachen, preprint.

3. Chytil M. P., On complexity of nondeterministic Turing machine computations. In Proceedings of MFCS 1975, Lecture Notes in Computer Science 32, p. 199-205.

4. Chytil M. P., Crossing-bounded computations and their relation to the LBA-problem, Kybernetika 12 (1976).

5. Blum M., A machine-independent theory of the complexity of recursive functions, JACM 14 (1967), 322-336.

PROGRAMS , COMPUTATIONS AND TEMPORAL FEATURES

BY Marco Colombetti° and Enrico Pagello°°

°MP-AI PROJECT, Politecnico di Milano, Italy
°°LADSEB-CNR, Area della Ricerca, Padova, Italy

ABSTRACT

Predicate Logic is a natural support to computing systems:computation and deduction are closely related. The way to describe proof strategies can clarify the theoretical soundness of programming. This description involves the clarification of the role of control statements.
A semantic analysis of program statements can suggest useful restrictions to the interpreter. These find a natural representation in a temporal framework.

KEY WORDS: Predicate-Logic-like Programming Language, Control Structures Temporal Features, Restrictions

1. INTRODUCTION

An approach to automatic theorem proving research has been pointed out by R. Kowalski [1] , who proposed Predicate Logic as a natural support to computing systems.

As remarked by P. Hayes [2] , computation and deduction are closely related in the way that computation is best regarded as a process of controlled deduction: the interpreter can be considered to generate proofs of statements, while the theorem prover's behaviour may be assimilated to a programmable device whose computations are controlled by its input language.

The description of the search strategy in a theorem prover leads, under the procedural interpretation, to the possibility of syntetically describing traditional control structures for functional computation. While under the problem reduction interpretation,the search strategy, often suggested by semantic analysis of problem, may involve a drastic increase in efficency of the solution process.

Experience in programming suggests a number of tricks, closely related to the non deterministic nature of the language, which should eventually be generalized to an autonomous system for the description of search strategy[6].

As it will be argued, it seems convenient to have a declarative control language distinct from representation language.

As well noted in [2] , "we would need a language which controls the deployment of resources and defines the mood of statements" and possibly these "control statements should be able to be posed as goals, proved as theorems and take part in proof construction"; still we could "give the user access to a meaningful set of primitive control abilities in an explicit representation scheme concerned with deductive control" and among them should be evidenced "primitives which describe temporal relation between events such as the achievement of a goal, e.g. the construction of a proof" [3] .

Unluckily many problems arise in the attempt of really constructing this control language and its temporal framework. However, if a programming point of view is a real improvement of the old problem solving paradigm, the way to describe proof strategy can be viewed as a temptative way to make the formal system closer to users' needs and contemporarly to best clarify the theoretical soundness of programming.

In section 2 we will illustrate with some examples how control ordering over the clausal statements of programs resolves the problem to express conditionals and we will give prominence to the power of non deterministic computation.
In section 3 we will show some programs from an artificial intelligence approach and we will try to understand the connection between the construction of their solution and the theory of programming; moreover we will evidence the importance of expressing temporal relations between events in the processes.

2. CLAUSAL FORMS AND CONDITIONAL EXPRESSIONS

The Predicate Logic counterpart of a computation process is the proof of a theorem.
Let us consider the following simple function definition:

$$f(x) \Leftarrow= g(h(x))$$

where g and h are supposed to be known.
Using the Horn clause formalism, as presented in [1], we can translate it into:

$$F(x,y) \leftarrow H(x,z), G(z,y)$$

where F(x,y) means that the value of f(x) is y.
A function call like f(0) corresponds to the goal of proving the theorem $(\exists y)F(0,y)$, or $\leftarrow F(0,y)$ in clausal form.
The theorem prover will compute **y** by proving the theorem and outputting "the" $\bar{y}$ such that $F(0,\bar{y})$ is provable.

It must be noted that an essential role is played by the way in which the proof is built.
Let us consider for instance a top-down Horn-clause theorem prover following a depth-first search strategy (exiting at the first success).
The function definition in the following:
$f(x) \Leftarrow=$ <u>if</u> x=0 <u>then</u> 1 <u>else</u> 2

can be translated into

A1. $F(0,1) \leftarrow$

A2. $F(x,2) \leftarrow$

If the theorem prover is submitted the goal

G: $\leftarrow F(0,y)$

the output is y:=1 ; with such an activation, the value y:=2 is never yelded, although F(0,2) is provable.
In fact the result is y:=2 if and only if the first argument of F is different from 0 .
In this way the <u>if</u>-<u>then</u>-<u>else</u> control structure is obtained.

If numbers are represented by 0 and the successor function s the same program can be written:

A1'. $F(0,s(0)) \leftarrow$
A2'. $F(s(x),s(s(0))) \leftarrow$

In such case, any complete search strategy will yield the desired result, as the sets of variable-free terms unifying with the first argument of F in A1' and A2' are disjoint (so that any theorem of type

$\leftarrow F(s^n(0),y)$

can be proved in only one way ; this implies that the control structure is now completely characterized by the program P: (A1',A2') , while before it was characterized by the pair < P:<A1,A2 > ; depth first strategy >) .

Let us now consider the following definition:

g(x) <== <u>if</u> f(x) <u>then</u> 1 <u>else</u> 0

f(x) <== <u>if</u> x=0 <u>then</u> T <u>else</u> p(x)=q(x)

where p and q are known, and truth values are considered as possible arguments and values of functions.

An obvious translation is:

```
B1.    G(x,1) ← F(x,T)
B2.    G(x,0) ← F(x,F)
B3.    F(0,T) ←
B4.    F(x,u) ← EQ(x,0,F),P(x,y),Q(x,z),EQ(y,z,u)
```

with the auxiliary axioms:

```
B5.    EQ(x,x,T) ←
B6.    EQ(0,s(x),F) ←
B7.    EQ( s(x),0,F) ←
B8.    EQ(s(x),s(y),u) ← EQ(x,y,u)
```

If we use a depth-first search strategy, a different translation is possible:

```
B1'.   G(x,1) ← F(x)
B2'.   G(x,0) ←
B3'.   F(0) ←
B4'.   F(x) ← P(x,y),Q(x,y)
```

This definition is more efficient and does not need the axioms for EQ, but in fact it has a different flavour.

In the first case, the output is 1 or 0 depending on the fact that either F(x,T) or F(x,F) is proved (meaning f(x) has value true or false).

In the second case, the output depends on the fact that 'it is' or 'it isnot' possible to prove F(x) (meaning that truth and falsity of f(x) correspond here to the metalogical concepts of provability and non provability).

The latter approach is typical of various programming languages based on predicate logic and its extension like MICROPLANNER [4] , and PROLOG [5] .

The power of such an implicit characterization of conditional expressions joined with the non deterministic features of logical languages is pointed out by the elegant program, resolving the sorting of list of a fixed number of elements (three in the case), given through the following set of axioms in clausal form:

```
C1.  SORT(x,y,z,x',y',z') ← GEQ(x,y,T),SORT(y,x,z,x',y',z')
C2.  SORT(x,y,z,x',y',z') ← GEQ(y,z,T),SORT(x,z,y,x',y',z')
C3.  SORT(x,y,z,x',y',z') ← GEQ(x,y,F),GEQ(y,z,F)
```

activated by a goal of the type

G: $\leftarrow SORT(s^n(0),s^m(0),s^p(0),x,y,z)$

where the predicate GEQ calls the following subprogram:

C4. GEQ(x,0,T) ←
C5. GEQ(0,s(x),F) ←
C6. GEQ(s(x),s(y),u) ← GEQ(x,y,u)

3. CONTROL STRUCTURES IN A TEMPORAL FRAMEWORK

Let us consider the problem of determining the sequence of steps needed by a robot to walk from block A to block B in the world of fig 1.

The problem may be represented by the following set of axioms:

1. $On(A,S_o) \leftarrow$
2. $On(x,goup(x,s)) \leftarrow Near(x,s)$
3. $Near(x,go(y,x,s)) \leftarrow Near(y,s)$
4. $Near(x,godown(x,s)) \leftarrow On(x,s)$

to be activated by the goal statement

5. $\leftarrow On(B,u)$

It is trivial that a depth first strategy will never guide to the solution, because it corresponds to a nonterminating search for the source block A; changing the order of clauses 3. and 4. , the same strategy, applied to the new program, would correspond to a nonterminating moving up and down the same block B.

From a semantic analysis of the problem we can abstract the advice "don't indefinitely search for the source block".

To transform this advice into a control statement, we should be able to supply to the interpreter the temporal restriction:

"if clause 3. has been activated at time t,
it cannot be activated at time t+1"

Therefore we need to superimpose a control to the interpreter, while the active process is carried out by the deduction.

From this point of view, a process can be defined the sequence of single steps each one being the combination of the action of calling clauses to match and the action of keeping the result of the unification performed between the matched clauses, when the unification secceeds.

Such a definition implies the choice of some suitable primitives involved in the description of process' activity and their organization in a system acting as the interpreter for input programs.

A control language then could be a tool to describe the behaviour of such a process and to pass advices and restrictions to the interpreter during the process performance.

The features of such a language consequently should respect the suggestions exposed in the sequent.

We must name the single subjects of the unification steps and distinguish between literals and clauses and their activation subprocesses which constitute the program execution steps;

we may think about activations with "call by name" («activate the named element at time t: $Act_t(y)$», where y is a clause u or a literal x inside a clause u), with "call by property" («activate an x such that A(x) at time t: $Act_t(y) \leftarrow A_t(y)$»), with "restrictions" (don't activate at time t any x such that A(x) at time t : $Act_t(x) \quad A_t(x)$) and their combination ;

it is clear the role played by the possibility to manipulate time instants and temporal relations;

the general framework could be a non deterministic one to which restrictions are passed little by little, possibly suggested by experience, learning or similar tricks.

From these remarks a declarative high level language, coherent with the program's language and the more as possible "natural", i.e. nearer to the common think than to the machine structure, enriched by temporal features treating facilities becomes the candidate for being the control language.

Following such an approach a temptative representation of the conditions passed to the interpreter from the program in the previous robot walking example can be expressed by the following restriction:

$$\text{R.}\quad \overline{\mathrm{Called}_{t+1}(3., x)} \leftarrow \mathrm{Called}_{t}(3., y)$$

meaning that if clause 3. was called at time t by a literal y processed at time t to unify with another matched clause, it cannot be called at time t+1 .

Then the advice has become a control statement preventing the interpreter to fall into an infinite loop when following the depth first strategy.

As illustrated before the execution of a program is based on the coordinate activation of subprocesses managed by the control. Very notable are programs in which the order of process' scheduling is deliberately left undetermined or such that the resulting values depend on respective speed of various subprocesses.

Those problems traditionally arise in the field of artificial intelligence and problem solving, but they present many features usual to the problems of topics like system programming and so on, so that it is worthy to care for the possible implications in the field of the theory of programming.

Let us consider two independent sequential prrocedures P1 and P2, each one working on the same area as in fig. 2.

The problem here is to schedule correctly the procedures to protect the buffer from a simultaneous transformation by P1 and P2 ; i.e. if we suppose that P1 write in T a word and P2 read the same word, we have to avoid that P1 write a new word before than P2 have read and that P2 read twice the same word.

The problem has a good solution by the well known Dijkstra's semaphores, but it is interesting to express it by a clausal form program,whose activation needs restrictions, to better understand the connection between the control structures and the logical programs.

Let us consider the following program segment in clausal form:

1. $P \leftarrow P1,\ P2$
2. $P1 \leftarrow <B>,\ <WRITE>,\ P1$
3. $P1 \leftarrow <\sim B>,\ R$
4. $P2 \leftarrow <B>,\ <READ>,\ P2$
5. $P2 \leftarrow <\sim B>,\ Q$
6. $R \leftarrow \cdots$
7. $Q \leftarrow \cdots$

where $<B>$, $<\sim B>$, $<WRITE>$, $<READ>$, are valuable predicates which encode tests and procedures.

The two procedures are correctely scheduled if we suppose to have the following restrictions, expressed by suitable primitives:

$$\text{R1.}\quad \overline{\mathrm{Act}}_{t+\tau}(<WRITE>) \leftarrow \mathrm{Act}_{t}(<WRITE>), \mathrm{Lastact}_{\varepsilon}(<READ>), U(\varepsilon,t)$$

$$\text{R2.}\quad \overline{\mathrm{Act}}_{t+\tau}(<READ>) \leftarrow \mathrm{Act}_{t}(<READ>), \mathrm{Lastact}_{\varepsilon}(<WRITE>), U(\varepsilon,t)$$

where $Act_t(x)$ means that the clause x was the subject of some unification to carry out at time t, $Lastact_t(x)$ means that the literal x has last been activated at time t and $U(\varepsilon,t)$ predicates that ε is a time instant precedent to t .

This approach allows the programmer to write two independent procedures for P1 and P2 withouth caring about the mutual interaction, leaving to the clausal statements 1.&2.&3. joined with the control restrictions R1 & R2 the task of scheduling the process.

We have tried to abstract some features of the usual control structures and to express restrictions in an effective way.

We believe that a deeper understanding of these concepts and a better clarification of their role will give many suggestions to treat logical systems as programming tools.

We hope that the efforts in this direction will be next improved.

REFERENCES

[1] R. Kowalski, Predicate Logic as a Programming Language
IFIP 74, Stockolm, 1974

[2] P. Hayes, Computation and Deduction
Proc. of MFCS Symposium, Czech. Academy of Sciences, 1973

[3] P. Hayes, Some problems and non problems in Representation Theory
Proc. of AISB Summer Conference, Brighton, 1974

[4] G. Sussman & T. Winograd, Microplanner reference manual
Project MAC, AI Memo n° 203, M.I.T., Cambridge, Mass, 1970

[5] P. Roussel, PROLOG, Manuel de reference et d'utilization, U.E.R. de Marseille, Groupe d'Intelligence Artificielle, Luminy, 1975

[6] M. Colombetti & E. Pagello, A Logical Framework for Robot Programming ; Proc. of the 2° CISM-IFToMM International Symposium on Theory and Practice of Robots and Manipulators, Warsaw, 1976

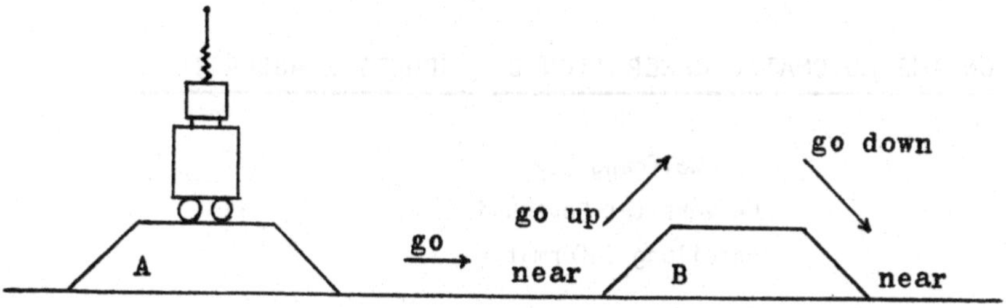

Fig. 1. Robot walking example

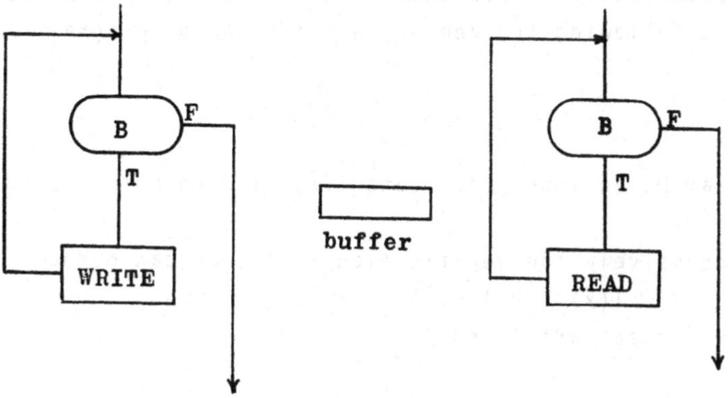

Fig. 2. Process scheduling example

A NOTE ON THE AUTOMATIC GENERATION OF INDUCTIVE ASSERTIONS

Wolfgang Coy
Universität Dortmund
Abteilung Informatik

INTRODUCTION

HOARE's while-rule [1] which is based on the inductive assertion approach by FLOYD [2] demands in general the manual insertion of an appropriately chosen inductive assertion; this process is the basis for the following theorem on verification of programs (cp. MANNA [3]):

THEOREM

Given a while-program P, an input predicate $I(\bar{x})$, and an output predicate $\Omega(\bar{x})$.
If, by applying successively the verification rules, we can deduce

$$I(\bar{x}) \ \{ \ P \ \} \ \Omega(\bar{x})$$

then P is partially correct wrt I and Ω.

The if-then reflects two difficulties within this approach, a theoretical and a practical one.

- We do not know whether the method is complete, i.e. we are not sure that a loop assertion exists for every loop. (This is not to be confused with "logical completeness" which depends on underlying logical calculi , used for the verification process.)
- We do not know of a simple and general algorithm for the detection of loop assertions (but cp. ELSPAS [4], WEGBREIT [5] a.o.).

We will investigate in this short note the first question for a large class of programming languages, demonstrating completeness of the inductive assertion method in the above sense, i.e. we will show that incompleteness problems in verification are an intrinsic feature of logical basis but not of FLOYD's method.

BASIC NOTIONS

We investigate programming languages with variables and constants over a countably large domain Δ (for simplicity the natural numbers). We assume these languages to possess the following program constructs (cp. DAHL, DIJKSTRA and HOARE [8]):

- assignments : $\bar{x} \leftarrow f_i(\bar{x})$,
- conditionals : <u>if</u> $t(\bar{x})$ <u>then</u> π <u>else</u> μ <u>fi</u> ,
- do-loops : <u>do</u> n : π <u>end</u> ,
- while-loops : <u>while</u> t(x) <u>do</u> π <u>end</u> ,

where $\bar{x}$ denotes a vector of variables of natural numbers, n is a natural number and π,μ denote admissible program constructs. (do-loops are, of course, only a specialization of while loops; we do not allow n to be changed within π , so termination is assured for do-loops, but in general not for while-loops). In addition to the above constructs the language uses

- concatenation : $\pi;\mu$

of constructs. Languages with these features shall be called numerical programming languages.

The process of verification demands the description of the relation (I,Ω) between the input predicate $I(\bar{x})$ and the output predicate $\Omega(\bar{x})$ to be expressed in some adequately chosen logical calculus. We use as such a calculus the Formal Number Theory as defined in KLEENE [9] (other calculi may be used as well, of course). Because of the well-known incompleteness of formalized arithmetic it is obvious that there exist correctness relations (I,Ω) which may not be provable for a given calculus though they may hold for the program to be verified. On the other hand it might be realistic to expect the programmer to state relations which are not too artificial to be provable.

AXIOMATIZATION OF THE FUNCTIONAL BEHAVIOUR OF PROGRAMS

There are many ways to describe the logical content of program constructs. HOARE and MANNA establish relations between predicates which are to be fulfilled by the execution of the construct. Another way would be to associate with every program construct a function $f:\bar{x} \rightarrow \bar{x}$, which is computed over the variables of the construct. As a first example we show this functional description for assignments:

(A) (Axiom-scheme of assignment)

$$p(f(\bar{x})) \; \{ \; \bar{x} \leftarrow f(\bar{x}) \; \} \; p(\bar{x})$$

It is recognized that in this case functional description and HOARE's axiom-scheme of assignment are close related.

Next, we describe concatenation by the functional approach. Let h,g be the functions defined by the constructs π, μ respectively; then:

(R_1) (rule of concatenation)

$$\frac{\begin{array}{l} p(h(\bar{x}))\ \{\ \pi\ \}\ p(\bar{x}) \\ p(g(\bar{x}))\ \{\ \mu\ \}\ p(\bar{x}) \end{array}}{p(h(g(\bar{x}))\ \{\ \pi;\mu\ \}\ \ p(\bar{x})}$$

The rule states that the concatenation of a construct π representing the function $h:\bar{x} \rightarrow \bar{x}$ with a construct μ representing the function $g:\bar{x} \rightarrow \bar{x}$ leads simply to the concatenation of the respective functions for all predicates p.

Conditionals shall be described by:

(R_2) (rule of conditionals)

$$\frac{\begin{array}{l} t(\bar{x}) \wedge p(h(\bar{x}))\ \{\ \pi\ \}\ p(\bar{x}) \\ \sim t(\bar{x}) \wedge p(g(\bar{x}))\ \{\ \mu\ \}\ p(\bar{x}) \end{array}}{t(\bar{x}) \wedge p(h(\bar{x})) \vee \sim t(\bar{x}) \wedge p(g(\bar{x}))\ \{\ \underline{\text{if}}\ t(\bar{x})\ \underline{\text{then}}\ \pi\ \underline{\text{else}}\ \mu\ \underline{\text{fi}}\ \}\ p(\bar{x})}$$

The left side constitutes really a function, which is proved in the theory of recursive functions. We will not insist on this point and take a look at do-loops. By definition, a do-loop will execute the loop-body π n times and terminate then. Let $f:\bar{x} \rightarrow \bar{x}$ be the function computed by the body π of the loop {do n: π. end}; then the loop computes successively $f(\bar{x}), f(f(\bar{x})), f(f(f(\bar{x}))), \ldots$ or in shorthand $f^1(\bar{x}), f^2(\bar{x}), \ldots, f^n(\bar{x})$. In addition, we set $f^0(\bar{x})=\bar{x}$, for the case n=0, where the loop body should not be executed. Then we propose the following rule:

(R_3) (rule of do-loops)

$$\frac{p(f(\bar{x}))\ \{\ \pi\ \}\ p(\bar{x})}{p(f^n(\bar{x}))\ \{\ \underline{\text{do}}\ n:\ \pi\ \underline{\text{end}}\ \}\ p(\bar{x})}$$

This rule is only a proposal as long as we do not prove that $p(f^n(\bar{x}))$ may be expressed in terms of Formal Number Theory resp. the chosen logical calculus. We will come back to this point after we have stated a rule for while-loops.

Only partial correctness will be investigated throughout this note; hence we assume that a proof of termination for every while-loop has been achieved seperately to the verification process. That means, that we know for a given $\bar{x}$ of the existence of some n, such that the while-condition $t(\bar{x})$ becomes false for $t(f^n(\bar{x}))$

after n executions of the body π with the function $f:\bar{x} \to \bar{x}$. We propose in analogy to R_3:

(R_4) (rule of while-loops)

$$\frac{t(\bar{x}) \to p(f(\bar{x}))\ \{\pi\}\ p(\bar{x})}{\exists n\ (\ p(f^n(\bar{x}))\ )\ \{\ \underline{\text{while}}\ t(\bar{x})\ \underline{\text{do}}\ \pi\ \underline{\text{end}}\ \}\ p(\bar{x}) \wedge \sim t(\bar{x})}$$

Rules R_3 and R_4 hold for all p; hence all p are loop assertions; i.e. they are true after every instance of the loop (when $t(\bar{x})$ true), if they have been true after the first allowed instance of the loop. They are not necessarily loop invariants, because this property demands the validity of $p(f(\bar{x})) \longleftrightarrow p(\bar{x})$.

Now we will demonstrate that the proposed rules R_3 and R_4 are meaningful in Formal Number Theory [9], i.e. that $p(f^n(x))$ may be represented in that theory. This representability problem is analogeous to the translation of primitive recursion into elementary arithmetic, as demonstrated by Gödel in [10]. The following lemma holds:

<u>LEMMA</u>

Let $f:\bar{x} \to \bar{x}$, where $\bar{x} = x_1,\ldots,x_k$. Then $p(f^n(\bar{x})) = p(\bar{w})$ may be described by the arithmetical predicate (in Formal Number Theory)

$$\exists\bar{w}\exists c\exists d\,(\beta(c,d,0)=\bar{x} \wedge \forall i\{i<n \to \beta(c,d,i+1)=f(\beta(c,d,i))\wedge\beta(c,d,n)=\bar{w}\} \wedge p(\bar{w}))$$

where $\beta(c,d,i) = rem(c,1+(k\cdot i+1)d),\ldots,rem(c,1+(k\cdot i+k)d)$.

The proof of the lemma is based on the chinese remainder theorem (which may be expressed in FNT); it is a generalisation of GÖDEL's lemma on the translation of primitive recursion into elementary arithmetic [10]. A proof of a similiar lemma may be found in [7].

By the lemma we know, that programs of numerical programming languages (with assignments, conditionals and loops) are completely representable in Formal Number Theory. Every output predicate $\Omega(\bar{x})$ which should be fulfilled by a program P may be transformed into some initial predicate $\Omega'(\bar{x})$, which must be a logical consequence of the given input predicate $I(\bar{x})$ iff the program is partially correct wrt (I,Ω). It should be noted that P is always partially correct wrt (Ω, Ω') for all $\Omega(\bar{x})$. Hence, the completeness of the inductive assertion method depends only on the provability of $I(\bar{x}) \to \Omega(\bar{x})$ (namely the completeness of the deduction rules). Of course, the result is primarily of theoretical interest, because the proof of $I(\bar{x}) \to \Omega'(\bar{x})$ may be quite tedious in some cases. Anyway,we have shown that a true logical formula stating the correctness of the program is always derivable in the underlying logical calculus. Another practical trade-off is in the fact, that the relation between the n (which must exist by proof of termination) and $\bar{x}$ is not necessarily simply derivable for while-loops (though all information that is necessary to establish a simple relation depends on t and f).

Besides all practical problems that still exist, we have shown the following theorem:

THEOREM

Given a program P in some numerical programming language and some input predicate $I(\bar{x})$, and some output predicate $\Omega(\bar{x})$. P is partially correct wrt (I,Ω) if and only if by successively application of the axiom-scheme A and the rules R_1-R_4

$$\Omega'(x) \; \{ \; P \; \} \; \Omega(x)$$

is derived and $I(x) \rightarrow \Omega'(x)$ is true.

The theorem is an expansion of the theorem given in the beginning. It states the completeness of the inductive assertion method wrt to a given program and a given output predicate. As long as the implication between the given input predicate and the derived initial predicate is provable, the method is also complete wrt provability. This situation reflects the fact that a program is a scheme which may be applied to quite different input predicates. We have furthermore shown, that any incompleteness results on partial correctness of numerical programming languages is absolutely due to the incompleteness of the proof rules, but not to the method of inductive assertions.

DISCUSSION

It was shown that the method of inductive assertions as a verification tool is as complete as it can be in the case of numerical programming languages with countably large data domains. The result is primarily of theoretical interest. The following points indicate further theoretical and practical problems:

- It is an interesting question whether the same result holds if countability of the domain (and hence some type of gödelization that was used in the proof of the lemma) is no longer given.
- Only the completeness of partial correctness verification was investigated. Termination is essentially an undecidable property for languages with infinite domains of the test variables. On the other hand,

with actual programs, it is usually relatively easy to prove termination (easier than the proof of partial correctness).

- The rules used for the proof of completeness yield only inductive assertions, not the much more seeked loop invariants. Inductive assertions which are no invariants may demand difficult verification proofs by induction. On the other hand, it is questionable whether there are sufficently strong loop invariants for every loop and every predicate to be verified.

REFERENCES

[1] HOARE,C.A.R., An axiomatic basis for computer programming, CACM 12, Oct. 1969, pp. 576-580, 583.

[2] FLOYD,R.W., Assigning meaning to programs, in Proc. of a Symp. in Appl. Math., Vol. 19, J.T.Schwartz (ed.), AMS, Providence Island, 1967, pp. 19-32.

[3] MANNA,Z., Mathematical Theory of Computation, McGraw-Hill, New York, 1974.

[4] ELSPAS,B., The semi-automatic generation of inductive assertions for program correctness proofs, GMD-Bericht Nr.55, St.Augustin (W.Germany), 1972.

[5] WEGBREIT,B., The synthesis of loop predicates, CACM 17, No. 2, Feb. 1974, pp. 1o2-112.

[6] MANNA,Z. and PNUELI,A., Axiomatic approach to total correctness of programs, Acta informatica 3, 1974, pp. 243-263.

[7] COY,W., Inductive assertions in subrecursive programming languages, Information Proc. Letters, Vol. 4, No. 5, 1976, pp. 121-126.

[8] DAHL,O.-J., DIJKSTRA,E.W., and HOARE,C.A.R., Structered programming, Academic Press, London, 1972.

[9] KLEENE,S.C., Introduction to metamathematics, North Holland Publ., Amsterdam, 1971.

[10] GÖDEL,K., Über formal unentscheidbare Sätze der Principia Mathematica und verwandter Systeme 1, Monatshefte für Mathematik und Physik 38, 1931, pp. 173-198.

ON THE RELATIONSHIP BETWEEN A PROCEDURE AND ITS DATA

(Extended Abstract)

Armin Cremers and Thomas N. Hibbard
University of Southern California, Los Angeles, California

The motivation for our current work on data spaces [1], of which the present paper is a part, is to provide a theoretical framework for programming methodology. We do not mean by this a theoretical framework which contains all of programming methodology, for programming, like number theory, must by its nature escape the bounds of any formal system. On the other hand, a methodology of anything must not be ambiguous, and it seems that certain of the principles of programming methodology are susceptible to more precise formulation than they have heretofore had.

Programming consists largely of implementing a given data space in another. (The notion of a data space will be given a precise formulation in the sequel.) The first of these two data spaces represents the "problem," and the second is typically defined by the manual of some programming language. It is a well-known principle of programming methodology that careless description of the problem data space eventually leads to enormous complications in producing the program.

To enunciate this principle precisely we must first say what a data space is, and then what it is we mean by an implementation. In this paper we study one aspect of the nature of data spaces, and, briefly, some implementation considerations which arise from it.

First of all, it is clear that included in the notion of data space are a set X of states and a processor p (possibly nondeterministic) which provides transitions from one state to another. We also know that these states have some kind of structure: there is some coherent way to describe them. This we state formally, at least in part, by saying that a data space includes a set $\mathcal{F}$ of functions defined on X.

We can notice at once that $\mathcal{F}$ should provide a complete and nonredundant description for each state, and this is easily stated formally:

Definition: A set $\mathcal{F}$ of functions defined on X is complete for X if, for all x, y in X, $f(x) = f(y)$ for all f in $\mathcal{F}$ implies $x = y$. $\mathcal{F}$ is orthogonal for X if for every function η: $\mathcal{F} \to X$ there exists z in X such that for all f in $\mathcal{F}$ we have $f(z) = f(\eta(f))$.

The definition of orthogonality captures the desired nonredundancy of the functions for describing the states. Using this definition, we can now state formally what we mean by a data space:

Definition: A (deterministic) data space is a triple $\mathcal{D} = (X, \mathcal{F}, p)$ where X is a set, the set of states, p is a partial function $X \to X$, called the processor, and $\mathcal{F}$ is a complete and orthogonal set of functions $f: X \to \mathcal{T}_f$, each $\mathcal{T}_f$ a data type.

We note here that part of our subsequent work on data spaces [2] concerns the nondeterministic case in which p is a relation, $p \subseteq X \times X$. However, in the present paper we shall focus on deterministic data spaces.

Also note that, for a data space as defined above, notions such as "computation sequence," "halting of p," "result function," and finally "computability" can be defined in the conventional way.

We would expect that there would be an intimate relation between p and $\mathcal{F}$. E.g., it would be entirely unsuitable that the states be numbered arbitrarily from 0 to (say) 10^6-1 and $\mathcal{F}$ be defined as the set $\{f_0, \ldots, f_5\}$ where f_i is the i-th digit of the state's number.

The expected "reasonable" relationship between p and $\mathcal{F}$ is very difficult to describe formally, since it has to do with our intuitive notions of structure and coherence. It is precisely these notions, of course, which are the central issue in programming methodology.

It is the purpose of this paper to suggest what we think may be one of the more important notions about the formal nature of $\mathcal{F}$ and p. This basically is the concept of the "data region" and its companion, the "result region," first introduced by Kwasowiec [4] in the context of Pawlak's computer model [7], and developed independently by the authors for general data spaces $(X, \mathcal{F}, p)$. (Similar, but different approaches have been studied in [3, 6, 8].)

In particular, we address ourselves to the question as to how the set $\mathcal{F}$ of descriptors can be used to define and interpret a state transformation p(x). Intuitively, it is clear that for any given state x the action of p depends on the current values f(x) for certain of the functions in $\mathcal{F}$, and also that, as a result of applying p to x, certain functions g in $\mathcal{F}$ get changed. More formally, we would expect the "data set" $K(x) \subseteq \mathcal{F}$ of x to have the property that if a state y "agrees" with x on K(x), i.e., $f(x) = f(y)$ for all f in K(x), then any function of $\mathcal{F}$ that changes its value under p will assume the same value for both p(x) and p(y). In Kwasowiec's terms, agreement of x and y on K(x) implies that every f in $\mathcal{F}$ is either "unevaluated" $[f(p(y)) = f(y)]$ or "constant valued" $[f(p(y)) = f(p(x))]$. Similarly, a "result region" $R(x) \subseteq \mathcal{F}$ of x would include a function of f in $\mathcal{F}$ if there exists a data set K(x) and a state y which agrees with x on K(x) such that $f(p(y)) \neq f(y)$.

From a practical point of view it seems natural to look for the "smallest" among the data sets K(x) defined above, i.e., the "smallest" amount of information necessary to determine the move of p under a given state x.

So the question arises as to whether there are data spaces for which

(a) there exists a unique minimal data set (i.e. least K(x)) for each state,

(b) there exists a minimal data set for each state, but some states have more than one minimal data set,

(c) some states have no minimal data sets.

Although it is possible to find examples for (c) there is reason to label this case pathological and therefore exclude it from our further considerations. Kwasowiec, in his work on Pawlak's computer model, concentrated on machines with property (a) above. (Our present work contains an analysis of both type (a) and type (b) data spaces, the latter being of highest relevance to practical computer science.)

In particular, Kwasowiec considered the question as to how to "build up" the "data region" D(x) (i.e. the least data set for x) by means of an "indirect-addressing" hierarchy of lower-level data regions. To this end, he constructed the "smallest" set of functions $D^2(x)$ with the property that agreement of a state y with x on $D^2(x)$ implies that D(x) = D(y). Given $D^2(x)$, he defined a "smallest" set $D^3(x)$ which completely determines $D^2(x)$, and so on. Now if

(A1) the $D^n(x)$ exist and are unique,

and if

(A2) for some integer m, $D^m(x)$ becomes empty for all states x,

then, since this D-hierarchy is decreasing, one can conclude that, among the functions in D(x) which p needs to determine the next state, p would first inspect the functions in $D^{m-1}(x)$ and then successively "recover" $D^{m-2}(x), \ldots, D^2(x)$, and finally all of D(x). Thus, speaking in terms of conventional computer architecture, the role of the "ground level" data set $D^{m-1}(x)$ can be compared to that of a location counter or instruction register. The very desirable property of being able to prove the existence of something like an instruction register suggested to Kwasowiec to postulate (A1) and (A2) above as axioms. (The resulting machine was called "address computer" [5].)

Unfortunately, there is probably no data space in use which is an address computer. The reason for this assertion can be seen in the following simple example: Consider any machine which has a location counter and an instruction pointed to by the location counter, which instruction may or may not contain a reference to data memory. If the instruction is a "GO TO," then the data region is just the location counter and the corresponding instruction, and D^3 will be empty. If the instruction has a memory reference, then D^3 will not be empty.

This, in all but name, is "variable-depth indirect addressing." The Kwasowiec hierarchy models only fixed-depth indirect addressing.

So the question arises as to how to define a variable-depth indirect addressing data hierarchy which still has the desirable property that it leads to the empty set. We attack the problem from two sides. First we introduce the decreasing hierarchy of sets $E^n(x)$ which, for a given state x, starts with the data region D(x) and, for all but pathological cases, leads to a "basic" set of functions before becoming the empty set. The basic set is interpreted as the minimal amount of information from which the full data region can be recovered. Also we show that this basic set is present in the intersection of all data regions taken over all states, and thus is part of some kind of instruction register for p.

Here is the basic definition for the E-hierarchy:

Definition: For a state x with data region D(x), let $E^1(x) = D(x)$, and let $E^{n+1}(x)$ be the least set $K \subseteq \mathcal{F}$ such that, for any state y with data region D(y), if y agrees with x on K then $E^n(x) \subseteq D(y)$.

An alternative way to tackle the problem is to define an increasing hierarchy $H^n(x)$ which might be considered "dual" to the E-hierarchy:

Definition: For a state x, let $H^0(x) = \emptyset$ and $H^{n+1}(x) = \cap D(y)$, the intersection being taken over all y which agree with x on $H^n(x)$.

The "dual" nature of the H-hierarchy with respect to the E-hierarchy is expressed in the following fact. Suppose that for a state x and some n and m,

$$E^n(x) \subseteq H^m(x) .$$

Then

$$E^{n-i}(x) \subseteq H^{m-i}(x)$$

for all i, $-m \leq i < n$. Furthermore,

$$H^{m+n-1}(x) = D(x) .$$

Thus,

$$E^m(x) = \emptyset \text{ for some m if and only if } H^n(x) = D(x) \text{ for some n} .$$

All practical data spaces that we have studied have the property that if only the data regions D(x) exist then the $E^n(x)$ exist and are unique for each x and n, and $E^m(x) = \emptyset$ for some m. Data spaces with this property are said to be sequentially resolved.

In the last part of this paper we turn to the problem of data spaces with non-unique minimal data sets. These data sets arise when p interprets an algorithm containing e.g. OR's, AND's, or multiplication. (One easily admits that these are probably the most "practical" kinds of data spaces!)

In fact, all of the deterministic data spaces one sees in use have the following property: each of them can be simulated by a sequentially resolved data space in which all data regions are finite. The resulting class of formal data spaces has some interesting properties.

Definition: A macro space of a data space $(X, \mathcal{F}, p)$ is a data space $(X', \mathcal{F}', p')$ satisfying the following conditions:

(i) $X' \subseteq X$,

(ii) $\mathcal{F}' \subseteq \mathcal{F}$,

(iii) $p'(x)$ is defined only if $p^k(x)$ is in X' for some $k > 0$, and in that case is equal to $p^k(x)$ for the least such k,

(iv) if x, y are in X' and y agrees with x on $\mathcal{F}'$ then $p'(x)$ being defined implies $p'(y)$ is defined and, in that case, $p'(x)$ agrees with $p'(y)$ on $\mathcal{F}'$.

Definition: A data space is sequentially resolvable if it is the macro space of a sequentially resolved space.

The sequentially resolvable spaces can be given a remarkably simple structure. In fact, we can prove that every sequentially resolvable data space is a macro space of a data space whose Kwasowiec (D-) hierarchy becomes empty at level 3. This particular theorem is first proved for sequentially resolved spaces and then follows after proving the technical lemma that the "macro" relation is transitive.

We can give examples to show that the sequentially resolvable data spaces can exhibit pathological behavior in spite of this simple structure. These examples seem to suggest that the critical property is that each data set have a minimal subset which is a data set. (A natural way to ensure this is to insist that all data sets be finite.)

REFERENCES

1. Cremers, A. and Hibbard, T. N., "The Semantical Definition of Programming Languages in Terms of their Data Spaces," in Programmiersprachen, Informatik-Fachberichte, vol. 1, Springer-Verlag, 1976.

2. Cremers, A. and Hibbard, T. N., "An Algebraic Approach to Concurrent Programming Control and Related Complexity Problems," Symposium on Algorithms and Complexity, Pittsburgh, Pennsylvania, 1976.

3. Elgot, C. C. and Robinson, A., "Random-Access Stored-Program Machines, an Approach to Programming Languages," JACM 11, 365-399, 1964.

4. Kwasowiec, W., "Data Regions in Computers," Bull. Acad. Polon. Sci., Ser. Sci. Math. Astronom. Phy. 21, 1153-1158, 1973.

5. Kwasowiec, W., "Address Computer Properties Concerned with Data Regions," ibid, 1159-1162, 1973.

6. Maurer, W. D., "On the Definition of the Variables Used and Set by a Computation," Math. Syst. Theory 6, 86-89, 1972.

7. Pawlak, Z., "On the Notion of a Computer," Logic, Math. and Phil. Sci. 3, 255-267, 1968.

8. Wagner, E. G., "Bounded Action Machines: Toward an Abstract Theory of Computer Structure," J. Comp. Syst. Sci. 2, 13-75, 1968.

ON THE RELATIVIZATION OF DETERMINISTIC AND NONDETERMINISTIC COMPLEXITY CLASSES

M.I. Dekhtyar
Institute of Mathematics, Siberian Branch of the USSR Academy of Sciences, Novosibirsk

Introduction

There are some open questions on the relations between the complexity classes in the machine-dependent theory of computational complexity. A lot of them are closely related to the existence of essentially trial problems or to the trade off between time and space of computations. Most of the known results of comparing complexity classes have been gathered in the work of Book [I]. Trakhtenbrot in his work [2] have defined some new classes. From the table in the work [I] one can see that the results of comparing of complexity classes are absent in most nontrivial cases and the proofs of inequalities $\mathcal{A} \neq \mathcal{B}$ for some classes $\mathcal{A}$ and $\mathcal{B}$ don't, however, allow us to know which of two differences $\mathcal{A} \setminus \mathcal{B}$ or $\mathcal{B} \setminus \mathcal{A}$ is nonempty.

In this work we consider the containment relations between some relativized complexity classes, i.e. between complexity classes of deterministic and nondeterministic computations with oracles. As noted in [3], Gill and Baker the existence such oracles A and B that $P^A = NP^A$ and $P^B \neq NP^B$. Therefore the answer to the question "$P^A = NP^A$?" essentially depends on the particular choice of oracle A in the relativized theory. Below we show that for a number of complexity classes in [I] and [2] answers to the questions on their equalities in the relativized theory essentially depend on oracles. For some pairs $(\mathcal{A}_1, \mathcal{B}_1)$ and $(\mathcal{A}_2, \mathcal{B}_2)$ of complexity classes we obtain that truthness of the implication "$\mathcal{A}_1^A = \mathcal{B}_1^A \Longrightarrow \mathcal{A}_2^A = \mathcal{B}_2^A$" also essentialy depends on the choice of A. At the same time in all known cases when for complexity classes $\mathcal{A}_1, \mathcal{B}_1, \mathcal{A}_2, \mathcal{B}_2$ the relation $\mathcal{A}_1 = \mathcal{B}_1$ ($\mathcal{A}_1 \neq \mathcal{B}_1$) or the implication "$\mathcal{A}_1 = \mathcal{B}_1 \Longrightarrow \mathcal{A}_2 = \mathcal{B}_2$" has been obtained, it remained true for the relativized classes $\mathcal{A}_1^A, \mathcal{B}_1^A, \mathcal{A}_2^A, \mathcal{B}_2^A$ irrespective of A, i.e. $\forall A [\mathcal{A}_1^A = \mathcal{B}_1^A]$ ($\forall A [\mathcal{A}_1^A \neq \mathcal{B}_1^A]$) or $\forall A [\mathcal{A}_1^A = \mathcal{B}_1^A \Longrightarrow \Rightarrow \mathcal{A}_2^A = \mathcal{B}_2^A]$. Therefore, the clearing up of the containment relations between the complexity classes, for which relativized analogs essentially depend on oracles, needs apparently new methods. Such methods may be easier to discover in some mentioned cases than for the question " P = NP ? "

Relativized complexity classes

We consider the usual concepts of recognition (acception) of sets by deterministic (nondeterministic) oracle Turing machines (T.m.). Deterministic T.m. $D^{(A)}$ (A - an oracle) recognizes a set B if it computes the characteristic function of B. Following [2] we assume that every course of computation of nondeterministic T.m. $N^{(A)}$ with input x is determined by some binary word - guess $p = p(1)p(2)\dots$ $\dots p(t)$ ($p(i) \in \{0,1\}$) and we write $N^{(A)}(x|p) < \infty$, if this course of computation results in the stop-state. We write $N^{(A)}(x) < \infty$ if there exists guess p such that $N^{(A)}(x|p) < \infty$. Nondeterministic T.m. $N^{(A)}$ accepts a set B if $B = \{ x \mid N^{(A)}(x) < \infty \}$. We define time complexity $t_N^{(A)}(x)$ as the length of the shortest guess p for which $N^{(A)}(x|p) < \infty$ (if for all p $N^{(A)}(x|p) = \infty$ then $t_N^{(A)}(x) = \infty$).

For every oracle A we let P^A, EL^A, EP^A denote the classes of sets recognized by deterministic T.m. with oracle A in time bounded by polynomials $\{|x|^k\}$, linear exponents $\{ 2^{k|x|} \}$ and correspondingly polynomial exponents $\{ 2^{|x|^k} \}$ (here $|x|$ is the length of input x). We let NP^A, NEL^A and NEP^A denote the corresponding classes of sets accepted by nondeterministic T.m. with oracle A. $SpaceP^A$ is the class of sets recognized by deterministic T.m. with oracle A within polynomial space complexity. It follows from the work of Savitch [4] that this class coincides with the corresponding nondeterministic one. We define also the next relativized complexity classes :

$$P^A_{un} = \{ B \mid B \in P^A \ \& \ B \subseteq \{2^K \mid K \geq 1\} \} \ ; \ NP^A_{un} = \{ B \mid B \in NP^A \ \& \ B \subseteq \{2^K \mid K \geq 1\} \} \ ; \ NPP^A = \{ B \mid B \in NP^A \ \& \ \bar{B} \in NP^A \} \ ;$$

$N^1P^A = \{ B \mid$ there exists a nondeterministic T.m. $N^{(A)}$ which accepts B within polynomial time and for every $x \in B$ there exists the only one guess p such that $N^{(A)}(x|p) < \infty \}$.

If $A = \emptyset$ we say that the computations are made without oracle and we abbreviate denotation of complexity class $\mathcal{C}^{\emptyset}$ as $\mathcal{C}$.

Using the definitions and the relativizations of the results of Book [1] , Savitch [4] , Cook [5] it can be shown that the next inclusions are true for all A :

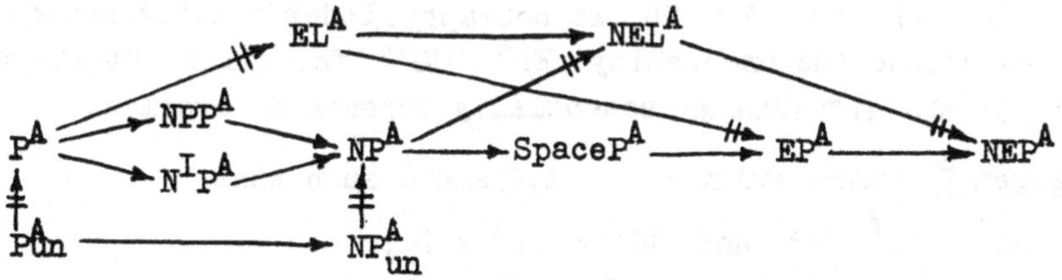

(I)

here $\mathfrak{A}^A \longrightarrow \mathfrak{B}^A$ means $\mathfrak{A}^A \subseteq \mathfrak{B}^A$ and $\mathfrak{A}^A \nrightarrow \mathfrak{B}^A$ means $\mathfrak{A}^A \subsetneq \mathfrak{B}^A$.

The relationships dependent on oracles

Our goal is to find out what relationships between the classes of diagram (I) depend on the oracle choice. At first we consider the chain of inclusions :

$$P^A \longrightarrow NP^A \longrightarrow SpaceP^A \longrightarrow EP^A \longrightarrow NEP^A \qquad (2)$$

Theorem I. (a) There exist recursive sets (r.s.) A_1, A_2 and A_3 such that $P^{A_1} = NP^{A_1} = \text{Space } P^{A_1}$; $NP^{A_2} = SpaceP^{A_2} = EP^{A_2}$ and $SpaceP^{A_3} = EP^{A_3} = NEP^{A_3}$.

(b) There exist r.s. B_1, B_2, B_3 and B_4 such that $P^{B_1} \neq NP^{B_1}$, $NP^{B_2} \neq SpaceP^{B_2}$, $SpaceP^{B_3} \neq EP^{B_3}$, $EP^{B_4} \neq NEP^{B_4}$.

Remark. From (I) follows that $P^A \subsetneq EP^A$ and $NP^A \subsetneq NEP^A$ for all A. Therefore the chains of equalities for oracles A_1 and A_2 can't be continued correspondingly by the classes EP^{A_1} and NEP^{A_2}.

By relativization of some results of Book [I] the truth of following implications is established for all A :

$$P^A = NP^A \Longrightarrow P^A_{un} = NP^A_{un} \Longleftrightarrow EL^A = NEL^A \Longrightarrow EP^A = NEP^A \qquad (3)$$

Then from the theorem I (a) and (3) we obtain

Corollary I. For any pair of classes $\mathfrak{A}^A$, $\mathfrak{B}^A$ such that $\mathfrak{A}^A \longrightarrow \mathfrak{B}^A \in$ (I) there exists a r.s. B such that $\mathfrak{A}^B = \mathfrak{B}^B$.

The following theorem shows that the conversions of implications (3) are true not for all oracles

Theorem 2. There exist r.s. A and B such that

I) $EP^A = NEP^A$ and $P^A_{un} \neq NP^A_{un}$ (therefore $EL^A \neq NEL^A$ and $P^A \neq NP^A$) ;

2) $P^B_{un} = NP^B_{un}$ ($EL^B = NEL^B$) and $P^B \neq NP^B$.

We take the pair NP, EL as an example of noncoincided classes. From (I) follows that EL $\neq$ NP but it is unknown what of two differences EL ∖ NP or NP ∖ EL is nonempty. Under relativization we can also establish the unequality $EL^A \neq NP^A$ for all A but the nonemptiness of the differences essentially depends on oracles.

Theorem 3. There exist r.s. A,B and C such that

I) $EL^A \setminus NP^A \neq \emptyset$ and $NP^A \setminus EL^A \neq \emptyset$;

2) $EL^B \setminus NP^B = \emptyset$ and $NP^B \setminus EL^B \neq \emptyset$;

3) $EL^C \setminus NP^C \neq \emptyset$ and $NP^C \setminus EL^C = \emptyset$.

We consider now the subclasses NPP and N^IP of the class NP which have been studied in the works [2,6] .

If $P^A = NP^A$ then it's clear that $P^A = NPP^A$, $NP^A = NPP^A$ (or $\exists^A = \forall^A$ in the notations of [2]) and $P^A = N^IP^A$, $NP^A = N^IP^A$ (i.e. a projection of any plane set from P^A coinsides with the projection of some one-valued set from P^A). All converse statements hold not for all oracles.

Theorem 4. There exist r.s. A,B,C and D such that

I) $P^A = NPP^A$ and $P^A \neq NP^A$;

2) $NP^B = NPP^B$ and $P^B \neq NP^B$;

3) $P^C = N^IP^C$ and $P^C \neq NP^C$;

4) $NP^D = N^IP^D$ and $P^D \neq NP^D$.

Corollary I shows that any arrow $\longrightarrow$ in (I) can't be replaced by proper inclusion $\not\twoheadrightarrow$. Using the theorems I, 2 and 4 we can show that any arrow $\longrightarrow$ in (I) can't be replaced by the equality.

Corollary 2. For any pair of classes $\mathfrak{A}^A, \mathfrak{B}^A$ such that $\mathfrak{A}^A \longrightarrow \mathfrak{B}^A \in$ (I) there exists a r.s. C such that $\mathfrak{A}^C \neq \mathfrak{B}^C$.

All the oracles of theorems I - 4 and corollaries I,2 are built by the straight diagonalizations. Their absolute complexity exeeds a little the complexity of classes which take part in their constructions. In particular all of them are elementary by Kalmar.

The next lemma on the uniform comleteness for relativized complexity classes is helpful to simplify some constructions. Completeness is meant in sense of Karp [7] .

Lemma. There exist nondeterministic T.m. N_I, N_2, N_3 and constant c such that for all A :

I) the set $U_I^A = \{ x \mid N_I^{(A)}(x) < \infty \}$ is complete in the class

THE METRIC PROPERTIES ON THE SEMIGROUPS AND THE LANGUAGES

Alexandru Dincă
University of Craiova
Romania

1. The Metric Properties of the Algebraic Semigroups

Let S be a set on which was defined an associative algebraic operation and let e be the unity of S. We say that S is a semigroup with unity. If $x, y \in S$, then we note the composition result of x and y by xy. Let M be a nonempty subset of S. With respect to M we define on the set S an equivalence and we give a distance on the set of equivalence classes. Let $\varphi_M : S \longrightarrow \mathcal{P}(S \times S)$ be the function defined by:

(1) $\varphi_M(x) = \{ (u,v) \in S \times S \mid uxv \in M \}$

To function φ_M one associates the following equivalence:

(2) $x \underset{M}{\sim} y$ if and only if $\varphi_M(x) = \varphi_M(y)$

We note the equivalence class of x (with respect to $\underset{M}{\sim}$) by $\hat{x}$ and the set of all equivalence classes by $S/\underset{M}{\sim}$. We define, in the same way, the function $\psi_M : S \times S \longrightarrow \mathcal{P}(S)$:i.e.

(3) $\psi_M(u,v) = \{ x \in S \mid uxv \in M \}$

and the equivalence:

(4) $(u,v) \underset{M}{\approx} (z,t)$ if and only if $\psi_M(u,v) = \psi_M(z,t)$

One notes the equivalence class of (u,v) by $\widehat{(u,v)}$ and the set of all equivalence classes by $S \times S/\underset{M}{\approx}$.

Theorem 1. Either $\varphi_M(x) = \emptyset$, or $\varphi_M(x)$ is a reunion of $\underset{M}{\approx}$ equivalence classes, for each $x \in S$.

The proof is immediately.
This result allows us to built the set $\varphi_M(x)/\underset{M}{\approx}$. In continuation we'll consider only those subsets M of the semigroup S having the property:

(5) the set $\varphi_M(x)/\underset{M}{\approx}$ is finite, for each $x \in S$.

NP^A and $\forall x \in U_I^A \left[t_{N_I}^{(A)}(x) \leq |x|^c \right]$;

2) the set $U_2^A = \{ x \mid N_2^{(A)}(x) < \infty \}$ is complete in the class NEP^A and $\forall x \in U_2^A \left[t_{N_2}^{(A)}(x) \leq 2^{|x|^c} \right]$;

3) the set $U_3^A = \{ x \mid N_3^{(A)}(x) < \infty \}$ is complete in the class NP_{un}^A and $\forall x \in U_3^A \left[t_{N_3}^{(A)}(x) \leq |x|^c \right]$.

References

I. Book R., Comparing complexity classes, J. Comp. and Syst. Sci., I974, 9, 2I3-229.
2. Trakhtenbrot B.A., On problems solvable by successive trials, Lect. Notes in Computer Sci., 32, I975, I25-I37.
3. Ladner R., Lynch N., Selman A.L., Comparison of polynomial-time reducibilities, Sixth ACM Symp. on Thery of Computing, I974, II0-I2I.
4. Savitch W.J., Relationships between nondeterministic and deterministic tape complexities, J.Comp. and Syst. Sci., I970, 4 , I77-I92.
5. Cook S.A., A hierachy for nondeterministic time complexity, J.Comp. and Syst. Sci., I973, 7, 343-352.
6. Valiant L.G., Relate complexity as checing and evaluating, Center of Comput. Studies, University of Lids, I974.
7. Karp R.M., Reducibility among combinatorial problems, in Complexity of Computer Computations, Miller and Thatcher (eds.), Plenum Press, I973, 85-I03.

Such a subset is called local finite. If there is a natural number m so that:

(6) $\operatorname{card} \varphi_M(x)/\approx_M \le m$, for each $x \in S$

then M is called local bounded. Refering to the local finite and local bounded parts class we shall demonstrate the following:

<u>Theorem 2</u>. If M_2 and M_1 are two local finite (local bounded) parts of S and $M_1 \cap M_2 \neq \emptyset$, then $M_1 \cap M_2$ is a local finite (local bounded) part of S .

<u>Proof</u>. Let be $x \in S$. We note $A = \varphi_{M_1 \cap M_2}(x)/\approx_{M_1 \cap M_2}$, $A_1 = \varphi_{M_1}(x)/\approx_{M_1}$, $A_2 = \varphi_{M_2}(x)/\approx_{M_2}$. Let $(u,v)_C$ be a fixed pair in C, for each $C \in A$. We define a function $f : A \longrightarrow A_1 \times A_2$ by $f(C) = (C_1, C_2)$ where $C_i = \{ (z,t) \mid (u,v)_C \approx_{M_i} (z,t) \}$, $i=1,2$. From $f(C) = f(C')$ results $C_1 = C_1'$ and $C_2 = C_2'$. Because $C \supset C_1 \cap C_2 \neq \emptyset$ and $C' \supset C_1' \cap C_2' \neq \emptyset$ results $C \cap C' \neq \emptyset$ and thus $C = C'$. We deduce $\operatorname{card} A \le \operatorname{card} A_1 \cdot \operatorname{card} A_2$ and the theorem results from this inequality.

<u>Theorem 3</u>. There are two local bounded parts of S , M_1 and M_2 , so $M_1 \cup M_2$ isn't a local finite part of S .

<u>Proof</u>. Let be $M_1 = \{ a^{3n} \mid n \in N \}$ and $M_2 = \{ a^n b^n \mid n \in N \}$. M_1 and M_2 are the local bounded parts of $S = \{a,b\}^*$. For $x = a \in S$, $\varphi_{M_1 \cup M_2}(x) \supset \{ (a^{3n-1}, e) \mid n \in N$ and $\widehat{(a^{3n-1}, e)} \neq \widehat{(a^{3m-1}, e)}$ if $m \neq n$.

<u>Theorem 4</u>. Let M be a local finite (local bounded) part of S . The following statements are equivalent:

a) $S \setminus M$ is a local finite (local bounded) part of S

b) $S/\sim_M$ is a finite set

c) $S \times S/\approx_M$ is a finite set.

<u>Proof</u>. Let be $S/\sim_M = \{ c_1, c_2, \dots, c_m \}$. We define the function $f : S \times S/\approx_M \longrightarrow \{0, 1\}^m$ so: $f(C) = (i_1, i_2, \dots, i_m)$ where $i_k = 1$ if $\varphi_M(c_k) \supset C$ and $i_k = 0$ otherwise $(k=1,2, \dots, m)$, for each $C \in S \times S/\approx_M$. From $f(C) = f(D)$ results $C = D$. Results that the set $S \times S/\approx_M$ is finite and $\operatorname{card} S \times S/\approx_M \le 2^m$. Thus b) $\Rightarrow$ c). In the same way we prove that c) $\Rightarrow$ b). From 1) results $\varphi_{S \setminus M}(x) = S \times S \setminus \varphi_M(x)$. Thus $\varphi_{S \setminus M}(x) = \varphi_{S \setminus M}(y)$ if and only if $\varphi_M(x) = \varphi_M(y)$. Results $S/\sim_M = S/\sim_{S \setminus M}$ and $S \times S/\approx_M = S \times S/\approx_{S \setminus M}$. Let be $S/\sim_M$ a finite set. Thus $S/\approx_{S \setminus M}$ is a finite set and $S \setminus M$ is a local bounded part of S . Therefore b) $\Rightarrow$ a). We have $S \times S/\approx_M = \varphi_M(x)/\approx_M \cup \varphi_{S \setminus M}(x)/\approx_M$ for each $x \in S$ and we deduce that a) $\Rightarrow$ b).

If M is a local finite part of S we'll introduce a distance on the set $S/\underset{M}{\sim}$ so: let be $D = \{(x,y) \in S \times S \mid \varphi_M(x) \cap \varphi_M(y) \neq \emptyset\}$. We define

$$d_M(x,y) = 1 - \frac{card(\varphi_M(x) \cap \varphi_M(y))/\underset{M}{\approx}}{card(\varphi_M(x) \cup \varphi_M(y))/\underset{M}{\approx}} \text{, for each } (x,y) \in D$$

The function d_M doesn't represent a distance on S, because $d_M(x,y)=o$ doesn't imply $x = y$. Therefore we define a distance on the set $S/\underset{M}{\approx}$. We'll call a chain from x to y a sequence L_{xy} : $x = x_o, x_1, \ldots, x_n=y$ where $n \in N$, $x_i \in S$ $(i=o, \ldots, n)$ and $(x_i,x_{i+1}) \in D$. The expression $l(x,y) = \sum_{i=o}^{n-1} d_M(x_i,x_{i+1})$ is called the length of the chain. Let be $\hat{x}, \hat{y} \in S/\underset{M}{\sim}$.

If $\hat{x} = \hat{y}$ then we define $\delta_M(\hat{x},\hat{y}) = o$.

If $\hat{x} \neq \hat{y}$ and there is no chain from x to y then we define $\delta_M(\hat{x},\hat{y}) = +\infty$

If $\hat{x} \neq \hat{y}$ and there is at least a chain from x to y then we define $\delta_M(\hat{x},\hat{y}) = \inf_{L_{xy}} l(L_{xy})$.

We prove that δ_M is a distance on $S/\underset{M}{\sim}$ and we establish any properties of metric space $S/\underset{M}{\approx}$. If we replace the string x by the pairs (u,v) and the function φ_M by function ψ_M in the above definitions then we get a distance δ'_M on $S \times S/\underset{M}{\approx}$.

<u>Theorem 5</u>. If the semigroup S is commutative then the diameter of $S/\underset{M}{\sim}$ with respect to δ_M is equal to the diameter of $S \times S/\underset{M}{\approx}$ with respect to δ'_M.

<u>Proof.</u> To prove this, we establish first: $(u,v) \underset{M}{\approx} (z,t)$ if and only if $uv \underset{M}{\sim} zt$. One deduces that for each chain in the set $S/\underset{M}{\sim}$ there is a chain in $S \times S/\underset{M}{\approx}$ with the same length.

2. The Applications to the Formal Languages

Let Σ be a finite set and Σ^* the free semigroup generated by Σ. If in the preceded paragraph we take $S = \Sigma^*$ and $M = L$ then we get the following interpretations:

- Σ is an alphabet af a language
- L is a language on Σ
- $\varphi_L(x)$ is the set of all contexts admiting x
- $\psi_L(u,v)$ is the set of all strings appearing in the context (u,v).

If the language L satisfies the condition (5) then it is called local finite. If L satisfies the condition (6) then it is called local bounded. The following properties establish the relation between the two language classes and the languages from the Chomsky hierarchy.

Theorem 6. Any regular set is local bounded.

Proof. If $L \subset \Sigma^*$ is a regular set, then $\Sigma^*/_{\widetilde{L}}$ is a finite set. Let m be the cardinal number of $\Sigma^*/_L$. Results that card $\varphi_M(x)/_{\widetilde{L}} \leq m$ for each $x \in \Sigma^*$.

Theorem 7. There is a local bounded language which is context free and not regular.

Proof. The language $L = \{ a^n b^n \mid n \in N \}$ satisfies the conditions of the theorem.

Theorem 8. There is a context free language which isn't local finite.

Proof. Let be $L_1 = \{ a^{3n} \mid n \in N \}$. L_1 is a regular set. Let be $L_2 = \{ a^n b^n \mid n \in N \}$. L_2 is a context free language. Thus $L_1 \cup L_2$ is a context free language but $L_1 \cup L_2$ isn't a local finite language (see proof T3).

Theorem 9. There is a local bounded language which is contextsensitive and not context free.

Proof. The language $L = \{a^n b^n c^n \mid n \in N$ satisfies the conditions of the theorem.

The theorem 3 gets the following form:

Theorem 3! Let L be a local finite (local bounded) language. The language $\Sigma^* \setminus L$ is local finite (local bounded) if and only if L is a regular set.

The distance δ_M defined in the general case of a semigroup becomes the distance between the distributional classes (with respect to the language $L = M$) and shows the difference of contextual behaviour of of strings x and y.

Theorem lo . For any rational number $\frac{p}{q}$ there is an alphabet Σ and a language $L \subset \Sigma^*$ so the sets diameter $\Sigma^*/_{\widetilde{L}}$ and $L/_{\widetilde{L}}$ is equal to $\frac{p}{q}$.

Proof. Let be $\Sigma = \{a\}$, $S = \Sigma^*$ and $L = \{ a^{2nq+i}$ $n=o,1,2, \ldots ; i = 1,2, \ldots ,2q-p \}$. We have:

$$S/_{\widetilde{L}} = \{c_o, c_1, \ldots, c_{2q-1}\}$$

$$c_k = \{a^i \mid i=2qn+k,\ n=o,1, \ldots\}; \quad k=o,1, \ldots, 2q-1$$

$$S \times S/_{\approx L} = \{C_o, C_1, \ldots, C_{2q-1}\}$$

$$C_k = \{(a^i, a^j) \mid i+j=2qn+k, n=o,1, \ldots \}; \ k=o,1, \ldots ,2q-1.$$

$$\delta(c_i, c_j) \leq \frac{p}{q} \quad \text{for each } i,j;\ o \leq i,j \leq 2q-1$$

$$\delta(c_1, c_{p+1}) = \frac{p}{q}$$

Results that the diameters of the set $\Sigma^*/_{\widetilde{L}}$ and $L/_{\widetilde{L}}$ are equal to $\frac{p}{q}$.

Theorem 11. If the set $\Psi_M(u,v)/\widetilde{\widetilde{M}}$ is finite for each $(u,v) \in S \times S$ then the topology induced by δ_M on $S/\widetilde{M}$ is the discreet topology.

Proof. Let be $x \in S$ and $\varphi_M(x)/\widetilde{\widetilde{M}} = \{C_1, \ldots, C_p\}$. Let be $C_i = \widehat{(u_i,v_i)}$. One notes $A_i = \Psi_M(u_i,v_i)/\widetilde{\widetilde{M}}$. From the hypotesis results that A_i is a finite set for each i. Thus there is $m_i = \max_{\hat{y} \in A_i} \text{card}\, \varphi_M(y)/\widetilde{\widetilde{M}}$

Let be $m = \max_i m_i$ and $r = \frac{1}{m+p-1}$. One proves:

$$\mathfrak{S}(\hat{x},r) = \{\hat{y} \in S/\widetilde{M} \mid \delta(\hat{x},\hat{y}) < r\} = \{\hat{x}\}.$$

Abstract - In this paper a way to define a distance on a semigroup (with respect to a nonempty subset of S) one gives. We establish any properties of build metric space. When S is the free semigroup generated by a finite set Σ we obtain the distances on the languages. Two new language classes one defines: local finite and local bounded and the conections between the two language classes and languages from the Chomsky hierarchy are establish.

REFERENCES

1. A.Dincă, Sur queques problêmes d'analyse contextuelle métrique. Rev.roum.math.,Tom13,nr.1,pp.65-7o, Bucarest.

2. A.Dincă, Distanţe contextuale în lingvistica algebrică. St.cerc. mat.Tom25,nr.2,p.223-265,1973,Bucureşti.

3. A.Dincă, Distanţe şi diametre într-un semigrup(cu aplicaţii la teoria limbajelor). St.cerc.mat.Tom25,Nr.3,p.359-378,Bucureşti,1973.

4. M.Gross,A.Lentin, Notions sur les grammaire formelles, Gauthier-Villars, Paris, 1967.

5. S.Ginsburg, The mathematical theory of context-free languages. McGraw-Hill, New York,1966.

6. M.Ito, Quelques remarques sur l'espace contextuel. Mathematical Linguistics, nr.57,1971,pp.18-28.

7. S.Marcus, Analyse contextuelle. Zeitschrift fur Phonetik, Sprachwissesschaft und Kommunikationsforshung,3,1965,pp.3o1-313, Berlin.

8. S.Marcus, Algebraic Linguistics, Analytical Models. New York, London Academic Press, 1967.

A LOWER BOUND OF $\frac{1}{2}n^2$ ON LINEAR SEARCH PROGRAMS FOR THE KNAPSACK PROBLEM

David Dobkin and Richard J. Lipton
Department of Computer Science
Yale University
New Haven, CT 06520/USA

1. Introduction

The purpose of this paper is to establish the following theorem:

Theorem: For each n, any linear search tree that solves the n-dimensional knapsack problem requires at least $\frac{1}{2}n^2$ comparisons for almost all inputs.

Previously the best known lower bound on this problem was nlogn [1]. The result presented here is the first lower bound of better than nlogn given for an NP-complete problem for a model that is actually used in practice. Previous non-linear lower bounds have been for computations involving only monotone circuits [8] or fanout limited to one. Our theorem is derived by combining results on linear search tree complexity [4] with results from threshold logic [11]. In section 2, we begin by presenting the results on linear search trees and threshold logic. Section 3 is devoted to using these results to obtain our main theorem.

2. Basic Concepts

In this section we introduce the basic concepts necessary to the understanding of our main theorem. To begin, we present the model for which our bounds hold. It has been previously studied in [6, 7, 10].

Definition. A linear search tree program is a program consisting of statements of one of the forms:

(a) L_i: if $f(x) > 0$ then goto L_j else go to L_k;

(b) L_i: halt and accept input x;

(c) L_j: halt and reject input x.

In (a) f(x) is an affine function (i.e., $f(x) = \sum_{i=1}^{n} a_i x_i + a_0$ for some $a_0, a_1, \ldots, a_n$) of the input $x = (x_1, \ldots, x_n)$ which is assumed to be from some eucildean space E^n. Moreover the program is assumed to be loop free.

In a natural way each linear search tree program computes some predicate on E^n. The complexity of such a program on a given input is the number of statements executed on this input. The complexity of such a program is defined as the maximum complexity over all inputs.

---

*Portions of this research were supported by the Office of Naval Research under grant N00014-75-C-0450 to the first author and the National Science Foundation under grant DCR-74-12870 to the second author.

Theorem [4]: Any linear search tree program that determines membership in the set

$$\bigcup_{i\in I} A_i$$

where the A_i are pairwise disjoint nonempty open subsets of E^n requires at at least $\log_2|I|$ queries for almost all inputs.

In this paper we shall study the complexity of linear search trees for the n-dimensional knapsack problem, which we state as a geometric problem. It should be noted however that our methods can be applied to many other problems. We may state two equivalent versions of this problem.

Knapsack Problem (KSn):

i) Given a point $(x_1,\ldots, x_n) \in E^n$, does there exist a subset I such that

$$\sum_{i\in I} x_i = 1.$$

ii) Given the hyperplanes $H_{\underline{\alpha}}$, $\alpha \in \{0,1\}^n$ where

$$H_\alpha \triangleq \{(y_1,\ldots,y_n) \in E^n | \sum_{i=1}^{n} \alpha_i y_i = 1\}$$

does $(x_1,\ldots,x_n)$ lie on some hyperplane.

Clearly these two formulations are equivalent and they both correspond to the usual knapsack problem which is NP-complete [5].

The lower bound established here is proved by appealing to results from threshold logic. Before defining the necessary terms from this field, we demonstrate our method and the chief obstacle in applying it.

Let $\Gamma = \{0, 1\}^n - \{0^n\}$. Say a point x is above (below) the hyperplane H_α with $\alpha \in \Gamma$ provided

$$\sum_{i=1}^{n} \alpha_i x_i - 1$$

is positive (negative). Also let R_I for $I \subseteq \Gamma$ be the set

$$\{x \in E^n | \text{ x is above } H_\alpha \text{ with } \alpha \in I \text{ and below } H_\alpha \text{ with } \alpha \notin I\}.$$

Intuitively R_I is one of the regions formed by the hyperplanes. There are 2^{2^n-1} possible such regions; however, many of these regions are empty. For example,

$$x_1 + x_2 > 1,\ x_3 + x_4 > 1,\ x_1 + x_3 < 1,\ x_2 + x_4 < 1$$

is empty. This example shows that the key problem is to determine how many regions are formed by the hyperplanes $\{H_\alpha\}\alpha \in \Gamma$.

The answer to this problem lies in threshold logic. We will now sketch the relevant results. Further details appear in [9].

Definition. Let A be a subset of $\{0, 1\}^n$. Then the partition of $\{0, 1\}^n$ into A and $\{0, 1\}^n - A$ corresponds to a threshold function provided there exist weights $w_1, \ldots, w_n$ such that

(1) $x_1 \ldots x_n \in A$ iff $w_1x_1 + \ldots + w_nx_n > 1$.

(2) $x_1 \ldots x_n \notin A$ iff $w_1x_1 + \ldots + w_nx_n < 1$.

Note that (2) does not follow from (1).

Let N(n) be the number of such threshold functions, then [11] shows that

$$2^{1/2n^2} \leq N(n) \leq 2^{n^2}.$$

In the next section we use this result to obtain our lower bound.

3. Main Result

In this section we prove our main result, i.e., that any linear search tree for KS_n requires at least $\frac{1}{2}n^2$ comparisons. We first state a technical lemma:

Lemma: (1) R_I is an open set.

(2) $R_{I_1} = R_{I_2}$ implies that $I_1 = I_2$.

The proof of this is elementary and is omitted. This lemma shows (part (2)) that we need only prove that R_I is nonempty for many sets I in order to prove our theorem. The next lemma does this.

Lemma: Suppose that A partitions $\{0, 1\}^n$ and gives rise to a threshold function. Then R_A is nonempty.

Proof: Let $w_1, \ldots, w_n$ be weights for A. Now we claim that $w = (w_1, \ldots, w_n) \in R_A$.

(a) Let α be in A. Then w is above H_α since

$$\sum_{i=1}^{n} \alpha_i w_i > 1$$

by the definition of threshold function.

(b) Let α be in $\{0, 1\}^n - A$. Then w is below H_α since

$$\sum_{i=1}^{n} \alpha_i w_i < 1$$

and again this follows by the definition of threshold function.

Thus we have shown that $w \in R_A$. □

In summary we have shown that there are at least $2^{1/2n^2}$ distinct open sets R_I's. An appeal to our earlier theorem [4] yields the claimed lower bound.

Finding an upper bound on the linear search tree complexity of knapsack problem appears to be a non-trivial problem. Two possible methods of attack are available. In the first, an algorithm is sought that works uniformly in n. That is, we seek a single method of solving knapsack problems of all dimensions. The existence of such an algorithm that runs in polynomial time is unlikely because this would imply that P = NP. But, for each n, it may be possible to construct a linear search tree that solves all n-dimensional knapsack problems. To construct such a tree, it is necessary to study partitions of the set of knapsack regions by new hyperplanes in order to determine appropriate tests at each stage of the algorithm. Based on considerations of the structure of the regions of the knapsack problem, we conjecture that a polynomial-time algorithm does exist for this problem. The existence of such an algorithm would resolve an open question posed in [3] but would not show that P and NP are equal for the reason given there.

References

[1] D. Dobkin.
A non-linear lower bound on linear search tree programs for solving knapsack problems.
Yale Computer Science Research Report #52, 1975.

[2] D. Dobkin and R. Lipton.
The complexity of searching lines in the plane.
Submitted for publication.

[3] D. Dobkin and R. Lipton.
On some generalizations of binary search.
ACM Symposium on the Theory of Computing, Seattle, Washington, May 1974.

[4] D. Dobkin and R. Lipton.
On the complexity of computations under varying sets of primitive operations.
Automata Theory and Formal Languages, Springer-Verlag Lecture Notes in Computer Science #33.

[5] R. Karp.
Reducibilities among combinatiral problems.
In R. Miller and J. Thatcher, editors, Complexity of Computer Computations, 85-104, Plenum Press, 1972.

[6] M. Rabin.
Proving the simultaneous positivity of linear forms.
JCSS, 6, 1972.

[7] E. Reingold.
Computing the maximum and the median.
Twelfth Annual Symposium on Switching and Automata Theory, 1971.

[8] C. Schnorr.
A lower bound on the number of additions in monotone computations of monotone rational polynomials.
Unpublished manuscript.

[9] E. L. Sheng.
Threshold Logic.
Academic Press, 1969.

[10] P. Spira.
Complete linear proofs of systems of linear inequalities.
JCSS, 6, pp. 205-216, 1972.

[11] S. Yajima and T. Ibaraki.
A lower bound on the number of threshold functions.
IEEE EC14:926-929, 1965.

THE DIRECT PRODUCT OF AUTOMATA AND QUASI-AUTOMATA

W. Dörfler
Klagenfurt, Austria

There are several possible ways for defining a product-automaton of two given automata which as its state-set has the cartesian product of the state-sets of the given automata. We refer the reader to [1] and [6]. In the case of the homogeneous direct product both factors have the same input-set which will be also the input-set of the product. This product has been studied extensively, compare [5,6,7,8]. In contrast to that the inhomogeneous direct product where the input-set of the product is the cartesian product of the input-sets of the factors until now has not been studied in detail. The subject of this paper will be the inhomogeneous product. For concepts not defined here we refer to [6].

Definition 1. An automaton A is a triple A = (S,I,M) where S is the set of states, I is the set of inputs and M is a mapping $M: S \times I \to S$.

The automata are supposed to be finite, i.e. S and I are finite sets. We extend M to a mapping $M: S \times I^* \to S$ by

$$M(s,xy) = M(M(s,x),y) \qquad s \in S,\ x,y \in I$$

Definition 2. A quasi-automaton Q is a triple Q = (S,H,M) where S is the set of states, H is the input-semigroup and $M: S \times H \to S$ is a mapping which fulfills $M(s,xy) = M(M(s,x),y)$ for all $s \in S$ and $x,y \in H$.

An automaton A = (S,I,M) can therefore be considered as the quasi-automaton (S,I*,M) but at some places there will be essential differences between these two points of view. Those definitions where no difference between automata and quasi-automata exist will be given only for quasi-automata.

Definition 3. A quasi-automaton Q = (S,H,M) is strongly connected if for any $s_1,s_2 \in S$ there exists $x \in H$ with $M(s_1,x) = s_2$.

The concept of a connected automaton and quasi-automaton is a weaker one than the strong connectivity and has been used in [2].

Definition 4. A quasi-automaton Q = (S,H,M) is state independent if from $M(\bar{s},x_1) = M(\bar{s},x_2)$ for a state $\bar{s} \in S$ and $x_1,x_2 \in H$ follows $M(s,x_1) = M(s,x_2)$ for all $s \in S$.

The terms homomorphism, endomorphism, isomorphism and automorphism of automata and quasi-automata will be used in their usual sense. By E(A)(E(G)) we denote the endomorphism monoid of A(Q) and by G(A)(G(Q)) the automorphism group of A(Q).

Definition 5. The characteristic semigroup S(Q) of a quasi-automaton (S,H,M) is defined as the semigroup of mappings α from S to S under composition given by

$$S(Q) = \{\alpha \in S^S \mid \exists x \in H,\ \alpha(s) = M(s,x) \text{ for all } s \in S\}.$$

The mention that S(Q) is anti-isomorphic to the quotient-semigroup H/R where R is the congruence relation on H defined by

$$xRy \text{ iff } M(s,x) = M(s,y) \text{ for all } s \in S.$$

Definition 6. The direct product $A_1 x A_2$ of two automata $A_1 = (S_1, I_1, M_1)$ and $A_2 = (S_2, I_2, M_2)$ is the automaton $(S_1 x S_2,\ I_1 x I_2,\ M_1 x M_2)$ with

$$(M_1 x M_2)(s_1,s_2),(x_1,x_2)) = (M_1(s_1,x_1), M_2(s_2,x_2))$$

The direct product $A_1 x A_2$ of two quasi-automata $Q_1 = (S_1, H_1, M_1)$ and $Q_2 = (S_1, H_2, M_2)$ is the quasi-automaton $(S_1 x S_2, H_1 x H_2, M_1 x M_2)$ with

$$(M_1 x M_2)((s_1,s_2),(x_1,x_2)) = (M_1(s_1,x_1), M_2(s_2,x_2))$$

Here by $H_1 x H_2$ is understood the usual direct product of semigroups.

This inhomogeneous direct product can always be represented as the homogeneous direct product of two suitably chosen automata (quasi-automata). Let for instance A_1, A_2 be as above and define $\tilde{A}_i = (S_i, I_1 x I_2, \tilde{M}_i)$ by

$$\tilde{M}_1(s,(x,y)) = M_1(s,x) \text{ for all } s \in S_1, (x,y) \in I_1 x I_2$$

and

$$\tilde{M}_2(t,(x,y)) = M_2(t,y) \text{ for all } t \in S_2, (x,y) \in I_1 x I_2$$

Then it is clear that the direct product $A_1 x A_2$ as given by Definition 6 is isomorphic with the homogeneous direct product of $\tilde{A}_1$ and $\tilde{A}_2$.

We emphasize that one has to distinguish precisely between the direct product of automata and of quasi-automata. The quasi-automaton defined by the direct product of two automata is in general not the quasi-automaton as obtained by forming the direct product of the quasi-automata belonging to the factor-automata. First we note some simple properties.

Property 1. The direct product of automata (quasi-qutomata) is associative and commutative (up to isomorphism).

Property 2. The direct product of two connected quasi-automata is again a connected quasi-automaton.

The analogous property does not hold for automata and there is no convenient characterization of those automata having a connected direct product. Even the direct product of two strongly connected automata may be a disconnected automaton.

Property 3. The direct product of two strongly connected quasi-automata is strongly connected. The direct product of two cyclic quasi-automata is a cyclic quasi-automaton.

Again the situation is much more difficult for the direct product of automata.

Theorem 1. The direct product $A_1 x A_2$ of two automata $A_1 = (S_1,I_1,M_1)$ and $A_2=(S_2,I_2,M_2)$ is strongly connected iff both A_1,A_2 are strongly connected and if for any states $s_1,s_1' \in S_1$ and $s_2,s_2' \in S_2$ there exist words $w_1 \in I_1^*$ and $w_2 \in I_2^*$ of the same length such that $M_1(s_1,w_1) = s_1'$ and $M_2(s_2,w_2) = s_2'$.

The proof is immediate from the definitions. We can give a structural characterization by using the concept of a circuit in a automaton.

Definition 7. Let $A=(S,I,M)$ be an automaton. The sequence of states $s_1,s_2,\dots,s_n$ is called a circuit of length n, $n \geq 1$, if there are inputs $x_i \in I$, $i=1,\dots,n$, with $M(s_i,x_i)=s_{i+1}, 1 \leq i \leq n-1$ and $M(s_n,x_n)=s_1$. By $L(A)$ we denote the greatest common divisor of the lengths of all circuits in A.

Theorem 2. The direct product $A_1 x A_2$ of two strongly connected automata is strongly connected iff $L(A_1)$ and $L(A_2)$ are relatively prime.

Intuitively the condition of Theorem 2 is equivalent to the condition of Theorem 1 but the exact proof is too lengthy to be encluded. An easy consequence of Theorem 2 is that $A_1 x A_2$ is strongly connected if A_1,A_2 are strongly connected and in both automata exists a circuit of lenght one. For determining $L(A)$ one only needs to consider finitely many circuits of A which could be characterized explicitly.

A condition similar to that in Theorem 1 has to be imposed on the automata A_1,A_2 to assure that the direct product of two cyclic automata is again a cyclic automaton. Using Properties 2 and 3 and Theorem 1 one can state results on the components and strong components of the direct product of quasi-automata and automata.

Property 4. The direct product of two quasi-automata (of two automata) is abelian iff both factors abelian. The direct product of two perfect (i.e. abelian and strongly connected) quasi-automata is a perfect quasi-automaton.

Property 5. The direct product of two quasi-automata (of two automata) is state-independent iff both factors are state independent.

The characteristic semigroup $S(A_1 x A_2)$ of the direct product of two automata is a subdirect product of $S(A_1)$ and $S(A_2)$, see [6].

Theorem 3. If Q_1, Q_2 are two strongly connected quasi-automata then $S(Q_1 x Q_2)$ is isomorphic to the direct product of $S(Q_1)$ and $S(Q_2)$.

Proof. Since $S(Q_1 x Q_2)$ is isomorphic with a sub-semigroup of $S(Q_1) x S(Q_1)$ it remains to show that $S(Q_1) x S(Q_2) \subset S(Q_1 x Q_2)$. Let $(f,g) \in S(Q_1) x S(Q_2)$, i.e. $f \in S(Q_1), g \in S(Q_2)$. Then there exist $x \in H_1$ and $y \in H_2$ with $f(s) = M_1(s,x), s \in S_1$ and $g(t) = M_2(t,y), t \in S_2$, such that $(M_1 x M_2)((s,t),(x,y)) = (f,g)(s,t)$ for all $(s,t) \in S_1 x S_2$. But this means $(f,g) \in S(Q_1 x Q_2)$.

It should be mentioned that Theorem 3 holds actually not only for the abstract semigroups but for the characteristic semigroups as semigroups of transformations.

The automorphism group $G(A_1 x A_2)$ of the direct product of two automata contains the direct product $G(A_1) x G(A_2)$ as a subgroup and in general may be different from it. A similar remark holds for the endomorphism monoid.

Theorem 4. Let Q_1 and Q_2 be strongly connected quasi-automata. Then the endomorphism monoid $E(Q_1 x Q_2)$ is isomorphic with direct product $E(A_1) x E(A_2)$.

Theorem 5. Let Q_1, Q_2 be as in Theorem 4. Then for the automorphism group holds $G(Q_1 x Q_2) \cong G(Q_1) x G(Q_2)$.

Proof of Theorems 4 and 5. At first we show that for any endomorphism φ of $Q_1 x Q_2$ there exist $\varphi_i \in E(Q_i)$, $i = 1,2$ with $\varphi(s,t) = (\varphi_1(s), \varphi_2(t))$ for all $(s,t) \in S_1 x S_2$. Consider $L_{\bar{s}} = \{(\bar{s},t) | t \in S_2\}$ for an arbitrary but fixed $\bar{s} \in S_1$. Choose some state (s_o,t_o) with $s_o \neq \bar{s}$ and $\bar{x} \in H_1$ with $M_1(s_o,\bar{x}) = \bar{s}$. Then for any $y \in H_2$ we have $(M_1 x M_2)((s_o,t_o), (\bar{x},y)) \in L_{\bar{s}}$ and therefore also

$\varphi(M_1 x M_2)((s_o,t_o),(\bar{x},y)) = (M_1 x M_2)\ (\varphi(s_o,t_o), (\bar{x},y)) \in \varphi L_{\bar{s}}$.

Denoting $\varphi(s_o,t_o)$ by (s_1,t_1) and $M_1(s_1,\bar{x})$ by $\bar{s}_1$ from this follows that $\varphi L_{\bar{s}} \subset L_{\bar{s}_1}$. In this way a mapping $\varphi_1: S_1 \to S_1$ is defined for which holds $\varphi L_s \subset L_{\varphi_1 s}$ for all $s \in S_1$. If L_t is defined similarly for $t \in S_2$ we can define a mapping $\varphi_2 : S_2 \to S_2$ with $\varphi L_t \subset L_{\varphi_2 t}$ for all $t \in S_2$. From the construction of φ_1 and φ_2 it is clear that $\varphi = (\varphi_1,\varphi_2)$ and we only have to show $\varphi_i \in E(Q_i)$. Let $(s,t) \in S_1 x S_2$, $(x,y) \in H_1 x H_2$ be arbitrary, $(s_1,t_1) = (M_1(s,x),M_2(t,y))$. Then $(s,t) \in L_s \cap L_t$, $(s_1,t_1) \in L_{s_1} \cap L_{t_1}$, $\varphi(s,t) = (\varphi_1 s,\varphi_2 t) \in L_{\varphi_1 s} \cap L_{\varphi_2 t}$ and $\varphi(s_1,t_1) = (\varphi_1 s_1,\varphi_2 t_1) \in L\varphi_1 s_1 \cap L\varphi_2 s_2$ from which follows $(M_1(\varphi_1 s,x),M_2(\varphi_2 t,y)) = (M_1 x M_2)((\varphi_1 s,\varphi_2 t),(x,y)) =$
$= (M_1 x M_2)(\varphi(s,t),(x,y)) = \varphi(M_1 x M_2)((s,t),x,y)) = \varphi(s_1,t_1) = (\varphi_1 M_1(s,x),$ $\varphi_2 M_2(t,y))$. This proves Theorem 4. Theorem 5 is now an immediate consequence.

In the following we make the general assumption that all automata and quasi-automata are strongly connected.

Definition 8. A congruence of the quasi-automaton $Q = (S,H,M)$ is an equivalence relation R on the state-set S such that holds

$$s_1 R s_2 \Rightarrow M(s_1,x) R M(s_2,x) \text{ for all } x \in H.$$

Definition 9. If R_1,R_2 are equivalence relations on the sets S and T, resp., then the direct product $R_1 x R_2$ is the equivalence relation on SxT defined by

$$(s_1,t_1) R_1 x R_2 (s_2,t_2) \Leftrightarrow s_1 R_1 s_2 \text{ and } t_1 R_2 t_2.$$

Theorem 6. If R_i is a congruence of the quasi-automaton $Q_i = (S_i,H_i,M_i)$ for $i=1,2$, then $R_1 x R_2$ is a congruence of the direct product $Q_1 x Q_2$.

The converse of Theorem 6 is not true and there may exist congruences of $Q_1 x Q_2$ which are not the direct product of congruences of Q_1 and Q_2.

The following two lemmas are the main tool for describing the general case.

The results only have been established under an additional assumption: we consider quasi-automata $Q=(S,H,M)$ where exists $e \in H$ with $M(s,e) = s$ for all $s \in S$. In other words $S(Q)$ contains the identity.

Lemma 1. Let R be a congruence of $Q_1 x Q_2$ and $K_1, K_2 \subset S_1 x S_2$ two R-classes. If π_1 denotes the projection onto S_1 then from $\pi_1 K_1 \cap \pi_1 K_2 \neq \emptyset$ follows $\pi_1 K_1 = \pi_1 K_2$. Similarly for the projection π_2 onto S_2.

Proof. Let $\pi_1 K_1 \cap \pi_1 K_2 \neq \emptyset$ and $\pi_1 K_2 - \pi_1 K_1 \neq \emptyset$. Choose $s_1 \in \pi_1 K_1 \cap \pi_1 K_2$, $s_2 \in \pi_1 K_2 - \pi_1 K_1$ and $t_1, t_2, t_3 \in S_2$ with $(s_1,t_1) \in K_1$, $(s_1,t_2) \in K_2$ and $(s_2,t_3) \in K_2$, further $e_1 \in H_1$ with $M_1(s,e_1) = s$ for all $s \in S$, and $y \in H_2$ with $M_2(t_2,y) = t_1$. Then $(M_1 x M_2)((s_1,t_2), (e_1,y)) = (s_1,t_1) \in K_1$ but $(M_1 x M_2)((s_2,t_3),(e_1,y)) \notin K_1$ what contradicts $(s_1,t_2)R(s_2,t_3)$.

Lemma 2. Let R be a congruence of $Q_1 x Q_2$ and $(s_1,t_1),(s_1,t_2),(s_2,t_1)$ three different states which belong to the same R-class K. Then K contains (s_2,t_2) too.

The proof proceeds along similar lines as for Lemma 1. From Lemma 1 one easily deduces the next theorem.

Theorem 7. If R is a congruence of $Q_1 x Q_2$ then the projections $\pi_1 K_1, \ldots, \pi_1 K_m$ of the R-classes K_i, $1 \le i \le m$, are the classes of a congruence R_1 of Q_1.

Similarly a congruence R_2 of Q_2 is induced but in general we have $R \neq R_1 x R_2$. If $R \neq R_1 x R_2$ then a class of $R_1 x R_2$ contains several R-classes. This situation can be described in the following way.

Theorem 8. Let R be a congruence of $Q_1 x Q_2$ and R_1, R_2 be the induced congruences of Q_1 and of Q_2, resp., with congruence classes $K_1^{(1)}, \ldots, K_m^{(1)}$ and $K_1^{(2)}, \ldots, K_n^{(2)}$ resp. Then there exist congruences P_1 and P_2 of Q_1 and Q_2, resp., the classes of which can be numbered as $L_{ik}^{(1)}$, $1 \le i \le m$, $1 \le k \le r$, and $L_{jk}^{(2)}$, $1 \le j \le n$, $1 \le k \le r$, resp., such that holds:

(i) $K_i^{(1)}$ is the union of the $L_{ik}^{(1)}$ over $k=1,\ldots,r$, and

$K_j^{(2)}$ is the union of the $L_{jk}^{(2)}$ over $k=1,\ldots,r$.

(ii) If the R-class K is contained in $K_i^{(1)} \times K_j^{(2)}$ then for an appropriate permutation p of {1,...,r} holds

$$K = \bigcup_{k=1}^{r} (L_{ik}^{(1)} \times L_{j,pk}^{(2)})$$

The proof is based on the lemmas but though not difficult is too lengthy to be encluded here.

References

[1] Birkhoff, G. and J.D. Lipson. Heterogeneous algebras. J. Combinatorial Theory 8(1970), 115-133

[2] Dörfler, W. Halbgruppen und Automaten. Rend. Sem. Mat. Univ. Padova 50(1973), 1-18

[3] Eilenberg, S. Automata, Languages and Machines. Academic Press, 1974

[4] Fleck, A.C. Isomorphism groups of automata. J. Assoc. Comp. Machinery 9(1962), 469-476

[5] Fleck, A.C. On the automorphism group of an automaton. J. Assoc. Comp. Machinery 12(1965), 566-569

[6] Gecseg, F. and I. Peak. Algebraic theory of automata. Akadêmiai Kiado, Budapest 1972

[7] Trauth, Ch.A. Group-Type Automata. J. Assoc. Comp. Machinery 13(1966), 160-175

[8] Weeg, G.P. The automorphism group of the direct product of strongly related automata. J. Assoc. Comp. Machinery 12(1965), 187-195

AN AXIOMATIC APPROACH TO INFORMATION STRUCTURES

H.-D. Ehrich

Abteilung Informatik, Universität Dortmund
46oo Dortmund 5o / Fed. Rep. of Germany

1. Introduction

Information structures are viewed here as formal objects on which certain operations can take place. Three operations are considered basic: selection of parts, construction of new objects by "naming" given ones, and addition of objects, modelling the integration or merging of information structures.

Concrete examples of the sort of objects we have in mind are Vienna objects [6,7] as well as their generalizations and modifications [3,4]. Axiomatic foundations of Vienna objects have been given previously by Ollongren [7] and by the author [3]. Being broader in perspective, however, this paper gives a general axiomatic basis for the type of algebraic structures developed in [4].

2. Basic Operations

Let D be a set, + be a binary operation on D, and O be a special object in D. The elements of D will be called (structured) objects. Here is our first axiom:

Addition: $D \times D \rightarrow D$

Ax(A) $(D,+,O)$ is a commutative monoid.

We adopt the intuition that objects carry information, and that the addition of objects forms in some sense the union of their information contents. The null object O carries empty information.

Selection and construction are accomplished by means of "names" or "access paths", represented by the set of words S^* over a finite alphabet S of selectors. The empty word will be denoted by 1 .

In the sequel, we will maintain the following notational conventions: $a,b,c,\ldots \in D$; $s,t,\ldots \in S$; $x,y,\ldots \in S^*$. Specifications "$\in D$" etc. will be omitted whenever possible. Similarly, if quantification is omitted in subsequent formulas, universal quantification for each free variable occuring should be inserted. In what follows, index i runs over an index set $I \subset \mathbb{N}$.

<u>Selection</u>: $D \times S^* \to D$

Ax(S1) $a1 = a$

Ax(S2) $a(xy) = (ax)y$

Ax(S3) $(\sum a_i)x = \sum(a_i x)$

<u>Construction</u>: $S^* \times D \to D$

Ax(C1) $1a = a$

Ax(C2) $(xy)a = x(ya)$

Ax(C3) $x(\sum a_i) = \sum(xa_i)$

Construction xa may be interpreted as giving object a the name x; addition of differently named objects may be viewed as combining them into one composite object, and selection ax selects that part of a named x. The two last axioms require that addition and selection (resp. construction) be independent in the sense that they can be applied in either order.

Algebraically, D is a S^*-left(and right)-semimodule [2]. Right semimodules are called right transformation semigroups in [5].

An object $e \in D$ is called <u>elementary</u> iff, for each $x \neq 1$, we have $ex=0$. Let E be the set of all elementary objects. Its elements will be denoted by letters e,f,... , often omitting the specification "$\in E$". Obviously, E is a subsemigroup of D. Let x and y be called <u>independent</u>, $x \not\sim y$, iff neither is x a prefix of y nor vice versa.

<u>Interaction</u>

Ax(I1) $(xa)x = a$

Ax(I2) $x \not\sim y \Rightarrow (xa)y = 0$

Ax(I3) $\forall a \, \forall x \, \exists b : \; a = x(ax) + b \; \wedge \; bx = 0$

The third axiom claims that each object a can be subdivided into two parts: that part of a named x and the rest b having no x-part.

From these axioms, we can draw several conclusions. Let $A := D - E$. Obviously, $a \neq 0$ and $x \neq 1$ implies $xa \in A$ since $(xa)x = a \neq 0$. Furthermore, it is easy to prove the following: (i) $xa = xb \Rightarrow a = b$, (ii) $x0 = 0$, and (iii) $0x = 0$. As a consequence of (ii), E is a submonoid of D.

<u>Theorem 2.1</u> : $\forall a \, \exists e : \; a = \sum_{s \in S} s(as) + e$

<u>Proof</u>: We apply axiom (I3) repeatedly. Let $S = \{s_1, \ldots, s_n\}$. If $a = a_1$, we have for $i = 1, 2, \ldots, n$:

$$a_i = s_i(a_i s_i) + a_{i+1} = s_i(a s_i) + a_{i+1} \quad ,$$

where $a_{i+1}s_k = 0$, $a_{i+1}s_j = a s_j$ if $1 \le k \le i < j \le n$. This means that a_{n+1} is elementary . ///

<u>Definition 2.2</u> : $F(a) := \{ e \in E \mid a = \sum_{s \in S} s(as) + e \}$

The sets F(a) play an important role in the sequel. Evidently, $F(a) \neq \emptyset$ for each a, and for elementary objects we have $F(e) = \{e\}$.

<u>Theorem 2.3</u> : (i) $x \neq 1 \Rightarrow 0 \in F(xa)$

(ii) $F(a) + F(b) \subset F(a+b)$

<u>Proof</u>: (i) is evident from axioms (I1) and (I3). In order to prove (ii), let $e_a \in F(a)$ and $e_b \in F(b)$. Then we have

$$a + b = \sum_{s \in S} s(as) + e_a + \sum_{s \in S} s(as) + e_b$$

$$= \sum_{s \in S} s((a+b)s) + e_a + e_b \qquad ///$$

3. Equality

It is important to have a criterion for the equality of objects. A sufficient condition for finite objects to be equal will be axiomatically extended to arbitrary objects.

<u>Theorem 3.1</u> : $(\forall s : as = bs \wedge F(a) \cap F(b) \neq \emptyset) \Longrightarrow a = b$

<u>Proof</u>: $e \in F(a) \cap F(b) \Rightarrow a = \sum_{s \in S} s(as) + e = \sum_{s \in S} s(bs) + e = b$ ///

<u>Definition 3.2</u> : $a \sim b \;:\Longleftrightarrow\; \forall x : F(ax) \cap F(bx) \neq \emptyset$.

If $a \sim b$, a and b will be called <u>compatible</u> .

It is evident that $\sim$ is reflexive and symmetric, and it is an easy exercise to prove that $a \sim b$ implies (i) $a+c \sim b+c$, (ii) $ax \sim bx$, and (iii) $xa \sim xb$. Thus, the transitive closure of $\sim$ is a congruence relation on D.

An object a is called <u>finite</u> iff the set $\{x \mid ax \neq 0\}$ is finite.

<u>Theorem 3.3</u> : If a and b are finite objects, we have : $a \sim b \Rightarrow a = b$

<u>Proof</u>: Repeated application of theorem 3.1 . ///

These circumstances suggest the last axiom in our axiom system :

<u>Equality</u>

Ax(E) $a \sim b \Rightarrow a = b$

This axiom is related to the completeness of data spaces as defined in [1].

As a consequence, each object can be represented by a sum of the following form:

<u>Theorem 3.4</u> : For each x, let $e_x \in F(ax)$. Then we have

$$a = \sum_{x \in S^*} x\, e_x$$

<u>Proof</u>: Let $y \in S^*$. Since $(\sum_{x \in S^*} x e_x)y = \sum_{z \in S^*} z e_{yz} = e_y + \sum_{z \neq 1} z e_{yz} = e_y + \sum_{s \in S} s b_s$,

where $b_s = \sum_{w\in S^*} we_{ysw}$, we have $e_y \in F((\sum x e_x)y) \cap F(ay)$. ///

This theorem allows us to represent each object by a formal power series with coefficients in $\mathbb{P}(E)$, the power set of E:

$$a = \sum_{x\in S^*} x E^x \qquad , \text{ where } \quad E^x = F(ax) \subset E$$

A word x is called peripheral with respect to an object a iff ax is elementary, i.e. $axy=0$ for each $y \neq 1$. Since $F(e) = \{e\}$, the coefficients of peripheral words are singletons.

4. Orthogonality

The considerations made above show that each model of our axiom system can be represented by a set $D \subset \mathbb{P}(E)^{S^*}$ of formal power series, given E and S. The operations are defined in an obvious way, taking account of theorem 2.3 . Adopting the notion of orthogonality as introduced in [1], we define orthogonal sets of formal power series as follows. Here, a(x) denotes the coefficient of x, $a(x) \subset E$.

Definition 4.1 : A set $D \subset \mathbb{P}(E)^{S^*}$ is called orthogonal iff

$$\forall \beta \in D^{S^*} \exists c \in D \ \forall x \in S^* \ : \ c(x) = \beta(x)(x)$$

A model of our axiom system which is an orthogonal set will be called an orthogonal model.

Theorem 4.2 : If D is an orthogonal model, all coefficients are singletons.

Proof: Given a and x , let $\beta \in D^{S^*}$ be any function such that $\beta(x)=a$ and $\beta(xy)=0$ for each $y \neq 1$. By orthogonality, there is an object c such that $c(x)= a(x)$ and $c(xy)= 0$ if $y\neq 1$. Thus, cx is elementary, and we have $|a(x)| = |c(x)| = 1$. ///

As a consequence, each orthogonal model is represented by a subset of $\mathbb{D}=E^{S^*}$. Some of these have been considered in [4]. Vienna objects, however, do not form an orthogonal model: they correspond to the case where each coefficient of a non-peripheral word is the whole set E. Non-peripheral words will be called inner words in the sequel.Thus, in the case of Vienna objects, inner words are not able to carry distinctive information. In order to include this case, we generalize the notion of orthogonality slightly.

Definition 4.3 : A function $\beta \in D^{S^*}$ is called admissible iff

$$\forall x \ (\ (\forall s \ : \ \beta(xs)xs = 0 \ ) \Rightarrow |\beta(x)(x)| = 1 \ )$$

Let $\mathbb{B}$ be the set of admissible functions in D^{S^*}.

__Definition 4.4__ : A set $D \subset \mathbb{P}(E)^{S^*}$ is called __quasi-orthogonal__ iff

$$\forall \beta \in \mathbb{B} \; \exists c \in D \; \forall x \in S^* \; : \; c(x) = \beta(x)(x)$$

__Theorem 4.5__ : If D is a quasi-orthogonal model, the coefficients of inner words form a partition on E .

__Proof__: Let x,y be inner words wrt a resp. b . Let $a(x) \cap b(x) \neq \emptyset$, $e \in E$, $e \neq 0$, and $s \in S$. Due to quasi-orthogonality, objects $c_1 = se + a(x)$ and $c_2 = se + b(y)$ exist by the functions

$$\beta_1(z) = \begin{cases} ax & \text{if } z=1 \\ se & \text{if } z=s \\ 0 & \text{otherwise} \end{cases} \quad \text{and} \quad \beta_2(z) = \begin{cases} by & \text{if } z=1 \\ se & \text{if } z=s \\ 0 & \text{otherwise} \end{cases}$$

Evidently, β_1 and β_2 are admissible. By theorem 3.1 , we have $c_1 = c_2$ and thus $a(x) = b(y)$. To complete the proof we observe that, for each e, we have $e \in F(se+e)$ by theorem 2.3 . ///

This theorem shows that the set $C = \{ a(x) \mid a \in D \wedge x \in S^* \}$ of all coefficients in a quasi-orthogonal model is of the form $C = C_0 \cup C_1$, where C_0 is the set of all singletons, and C_1 is a partition on E. From theorem 2.3 (ii) we conclude that the equivalence relation $\equiv$ corresponding to C_1 is a congruence on the monoid (E,+,0). It is not difficult to see that each congruence on (E,+,0) is implied by some quasi-orthogonal model, and that among all quasi-orthogonal models implying a fixed congruence there is one comprehensive model including all others as subsets. This latter model is given by the set of all formal power series associating members of C_0 with peripheral words and members of C_1 with inner words. The subset of all finite objects is an example of another model implying the same equivalence relation.

It is shown in [4] that the set of Vienna objects is isomorphic to a quotient structure of the fundamental orthogonal model, provided that there are "no zero sums", i.e. a+b=0 implies a=b=0. This result is generalized in the next theorem.

__Theorem 4.6__ : Let D be a quasi-orthogonal model with no zero sums. Then there is an orthogonal model D' and a congruence relation $\equiv$ on D' such that

$$D \cong D'/\equiv \quad .$$

__Proof__: Let D' be the set of power series obtained from D by replacing each $a \in D$ by the set of all a' where a' is obtained from a by replacing all coefficients of inner words by arbitrary singletons. It is straightforward to prove that D' is an orthogonal model. Let $\equiv$ be the congruence relation on E implied by the quasi-orthogonality of D. We extend $\equiv$ to D' as follows: for $a,b \in D$, let

$a \equiv b$ iff $a(x) \equiv b(x)$ for all inner words x wrt a and b, and $a(x)=b(x)$ for all peripheral words x wrt a or b. In order to show that $\equiv$ is a congruence on D' , we must show that, for each c resp. x, we have $a+c \equiv b+c$, $ax \equiv bx$, and $xa \equiv xb$. The last two relationships are very easy to prove; so we drop it here. That $a+c \equiv b+c$ is seen as follows: the sets of inner resp. peripheral words of a and b are equal. Since there are no zero sums, the set of inner words of a+c is the union of the respective sets of a and c. The same holds true for b. Let x be an inner word wrt a+c. Then, if x is inner wrt a, we have $a(x) \equiv b(x)$; otherwise, we have $a(x)=b(x)$. In each case, we have by theorem 2.3 (ii) : $(a+c)(x)=a(x)+c(x) \equiv b(x)+c(x)=(b+c)(x)$. Now let x be a peripheral word wrt a+c. Then x is peripheral both wrt to a and c, and we have $(a+c)(x)= a(x)+c(x)=b(x)+c(x)=(b+c)(x)$. This shows that $a+c \equiv b+c$.

Now we consider the quotient structure $D'/\equiv$ which is, of course, a model of our axiom system when making the usual conventions about the operations. The isomorphism of $D'/\equiv$ and D is established by the 1-1-correspondence between congruence classes [a] on D' and objects $a' \in D$ given by

$$\forall x \quad : \quad F(a'x) = \bigcup_{b \equiv a} F(bx) \quad . \qquad ///$$

5. Conclusions

The axiom system given here evolved from a specific philosophy of how information is structured in order to be manipulated by computers. It leads to a general framework comprising a great variety of models, from which the Vienna objects and their derivatives considered so far are only special cases. The axiom system is consistent in the sense that there is a model for it. The problems of independence and completeness have not been considered. They lie outside the scope of this paper.

REFERENCES

1. Cremers,A.-Hibbard,T.N.: The semantic definition of programming languages in terms of their data spaces. Proc.4.Fachtagung der GI über Programmiersprachen.Fachberichte Informatik,Springer-Verlag,Berlin 1976, 1-11 .

2. Deussen,P.: Halbgruppen und Automaten. Heidelberger Taschenbücher, Springer-Verlag, Berlin 1971 .

3. Ehrich,H.-D.: Ein axiomatischer Ansatz für eine Algebra strukturierter Objekte. Bericht 5/74, Abteilung Informatik, Universität Dortmund 1974.

4. Ehrich,H.-D.: Outline of an algebraic theory of structured objects. Proc. 3rd International Colloquium on Automata, Languages and Programming, Edinburgh University Press, Edinburgh 1976 .

5. Goodwin,J.R.: The structure of finite right transformation semigroups. Ph.D.thesis, University of California, Berkeley 1969 .

6. Lucas,P.-Lauer,P.-Stigleitner,H.: Method and notation for the formal definition of programming languages. Tech. Report TR 25.087, IBM Lab. Vienna, 1968, rev. 1970 .

7. Ollongren,A.: Definition of programming languages by interpreting automata. Academic Press, London 1974 .

PARALLELISM OF MANIPULATIONS IN MULTIDIMENSIONAL INFORMATION STRUCTURES

Hartmut Ehrig
Hans-Jörg Kreowski
Technical University Berlin, FB 20 (ATFS)
1000 Berlin 10, Otto-Suhr-Allee 18-20 (West Germany)

Key Words: Multidimensional Information Structures, Graph Grammars, Parallelism, Church-Rosser-Properties, Canonical Derivation Sequences, Applications of Category Theory.

INTRODUCTION

The manipulation of information structures, like strings, trees, linked data structures, state vectors and files, is a basic problem in several fields of Computer Science, especially paralellism of manipulations in the case of multidimensional structures (for example asynchronous parallel updating of data bases, asynchronous parallel computing, and Church-Rosser-properties in operational semantics). In analogy to ALGOL 68 we use the notion "collateral" if two manipulations can be performed in parallel such that the resulting structure is the same as in the case of sequential application of the manipulations in arbitrary order. In this case the "parallel manipulation" is called equivalent to both of the sequential manipulation sequences.

In this paper the following problems are considered:

Problem 1: Are there necessary and sufficient conditions for two manipulations to be collateral?

Problem 2: Given a sequence of manipulations is there an algorithm to obtain an equivalent canonical sequence in which each manipulation is applied leftmost, with respect to the derivation sequence, and collateral manipulations are performed in parallel?

In most cases multidimensional information structures can be represented as graphs with suitable labels for nodes and edges. A manipulation is performed by relabeling, adding or deleting of nodes and edges. Such a manipulation can be formalized by a production and a direct derivation in a graph grammar, a generalization of Chomsky-Grammars to labelled graphs. We are using the algebraic approach to graph grammars as given in /Eh-Pf-Sch 73/ and /Ros 74/. In this terminology we will give solutions to the problems mentioned above. One basic step is a Church-Rosser-Theorem for Graph-Grammars stated first by B. Rosen in /Ros 75/. We are able to present a short algebraic proof of this theorem, called Church-Rosser-Theorem I in the following. Moreover we need a Church-Rosser-Theorem II to solve the necessity in problem 1 and part of problem 2. Using both theorems we are able to introduce parallel derivations for graph grammars, as well as equivalence of derivations and canonical forms in analogy to left- and rightmost derivations in the string case. Finally we give an algorithm to solve problem 2. But for the proof we refer to /Kr 76/. Especially the uniqueness of canonical derivation sequences is very hard to show because this is already difficult in the string case (cf. /Gri 68/). Details for the graph case are given in /Kr 76/.

Following /Eh-Pf-Sch 73/ and /Ros 74/ a "production" $p=(B_1 \xleftarrow{b_1} K \xrightarrow{b_2} B_2)$ consists of a pair of graphs (B_1, B_2), an auxiliary graph K (gluing points) and a pair of graph morphisms $b_1:K \longrightarrow B_1$ and $b_2:K \longrightarrow B_2$.

In this paper we assume for simplicity that all graphs are totally labelled and that the graph morphisms are label preserving.

Given a production $p=(B_1 \xleftarrow{b_1} K \xrightarrow{b_2} B_2)$ and an "enlargement" $d:K \longrightarrow D$ we obtain a direct derivation $G \overset{p}{\Longrightarrow} H$ where G and H are the pushout objects in the following diagrams

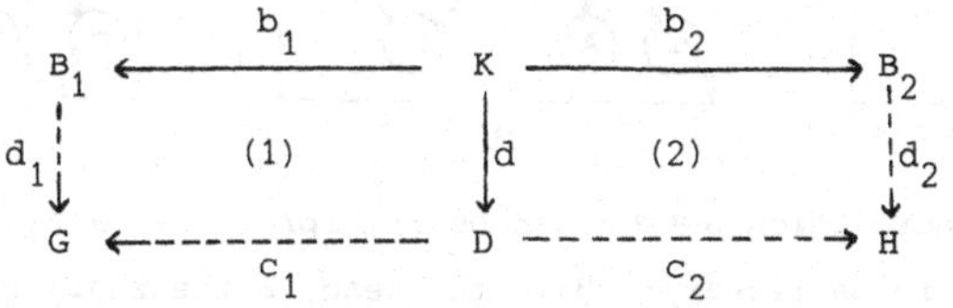

constructed in the category of graphs (cf. /MacL 72/).

The subgraphs $d_1(B_1)$ in G and $d_2(B_2)$ in H are called the "occurence of the production p" in G and H respectively.

The pushout constructions above have the following effects: The graph G becomes the gluing of B_1 and D glued together in the "gluing points" $b_1(k)$ in B_1 and $d(k)$ in D for all "gluing points" k in K. Similarily, H becomes the gluing of B_2 and D (along K) such that H is obtained from G by replacing B_1 by B_2, or more precisely the occurrence $d_1(B_1)$ of p in G by the occurrence $d_2(B_2)$ of p in H.

Vice versa, given a graph G and a production $p=(B_1 \xleftarrow{b_1} K \xrightarrow{b_2} B_2)$, where the occurrence of B_1 in G is specified by a graph morphism $d_1:B_1 \longrightarrow G$, we first have to find a suitable enlargement $d:K \longrightarrow D$ and a morphism $c_1:D \longrightarrow G$ such that diagram (1) becomes a pushout. In the second step (2) is constructed as pushout of d and b_2. In /Eh-Kr 75a/ we have given a "gluing condition" which is necessary and sufficient for a unique "pushout complement" D, together with d and <u>injective</u> c_1, such that (1) becomes a pushout. Hence, in the following we will only consider natural direct derivations, meaning that c_1 is injective.

EXAMPLE 1

The diagram below shows a direct derivation of graphs where corresponding gluing points have the same numbers.

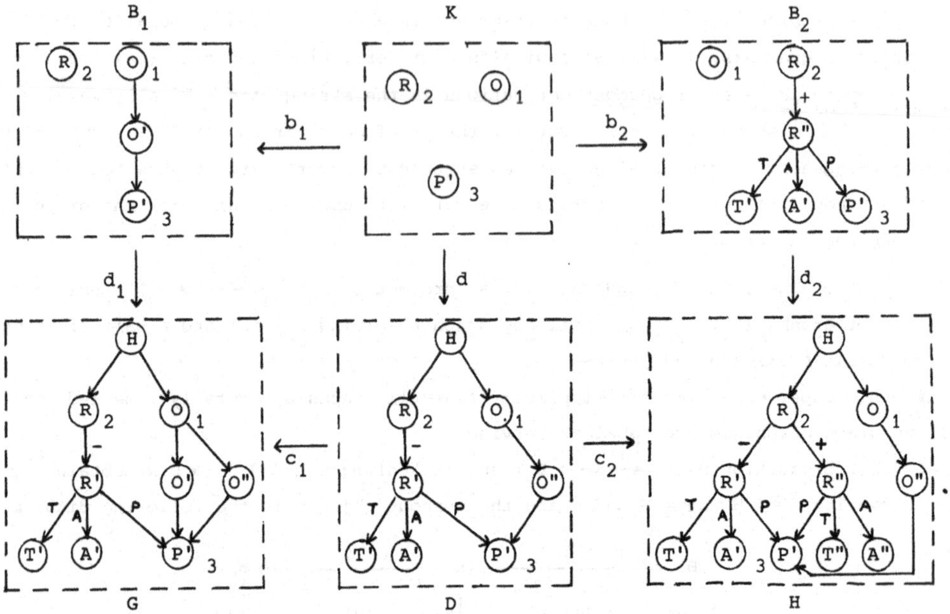

The resulting direct derivation $G \xrightarrow{p} H$ can be interpreted as a manipulation in a
very simple data base for a library: H is the head, R the registerlist with different register numbers R', R", ... for different books with titles T', T",..., authors
A', A",... and publishers P', P",... . O corresponds to the orderlist of books
with O', O",... for different order numbers of books from publishers P', P",... .
The production stands for registering a book which was already ordered with order O'
from publisher P'. Hence, starting with one book and two orders in G we obtain two
books and one remaining order in H.

Moreover ordering a new book might be given by a production

p' $\boxed{O_1 \quad P'_2} \longleftarrow \boxed{O_1 \quad P'_2} \longrightarrow \boxed{O_1 \rightarrow O" \rightarrow P'_2}$

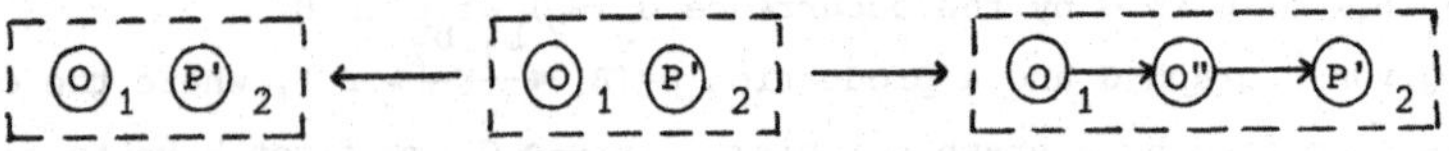

and lending a book by a production

p" $\boxed{R_1 \xrightarrow{+} R'_2} \longleftarrow \boxed{R_1 \quad R'_2} \longrightarrow \boxed{R_1 \xrightarrow{-} R'_2}$

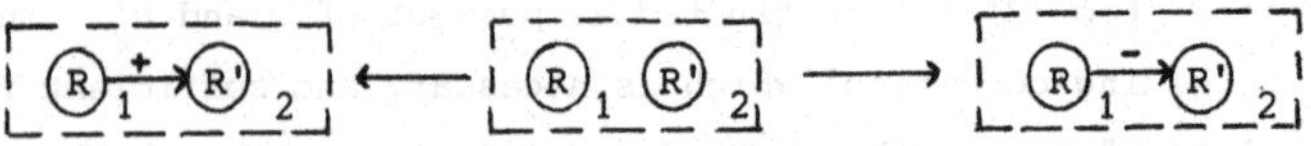

whereas cancelling an order or returning a book would correspond to the productions
in opposite order respectively. It is clear, that for different books our productions have to be used with different parameters indicated by R', R", etc.
In example 2 we will show that the manipulations of ordering one and registering another book are collateral, but not of course registering and cancelling.

In order to solve problem 1 we introduce the notions of parallel and sequential independence.

INDEPENDENCE OF DIRECT DERIVATIONS

Let $p:G \Longrightarrow H$, $p':G \Longrightarrow H'$ and $\bar{p}:H \Longrightarrow \bar{H}$ natural direct derivations with the following gluing diagrams

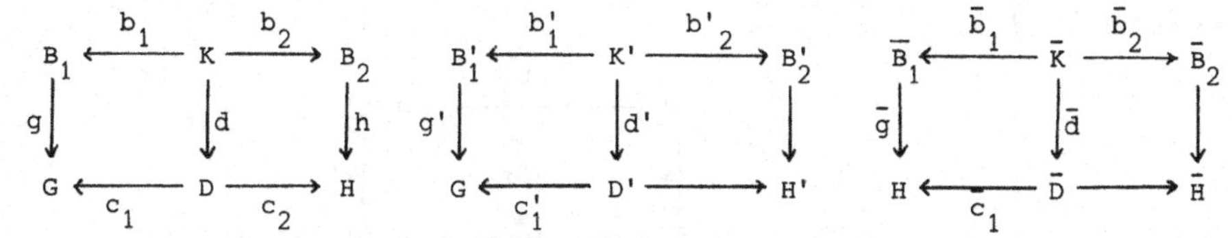

Then p and p' are called parallel independent, if there are graph morphisms $\tilde{g}$, $\tilde{g}'$ with $c_1' \circ \tilde{g}=g$ and $c_1 \circ \tilde{g}'=g'$. On the other hand p and $\bar{p}$ are called sequential independent, if there are graph morphisms $\tilde{h}$, $\tilde{\tilde{g}}$ with $\bar{c}_1 \circ \tilde{h}=h$ and $c_2 \circ \tilde{\tilde{g}}=\bar{g}$.

Interpretation: Independence means that one side of the first production (e.g. B_1) is included in the "restgraph" (e.g. D') of the second derivation up to homomorphism and vice versa, in other words the intersection of B_1 and B_1' in G (resp. B_2 and $\bar{B}_1$ in H) is not necessary empty, but must consists of the common gluing points.

CHURCH-ROSSER-THEOREM I

Let $p:G \Longrightarrow H$ and $p':G \Longrightarrow H'$ natural direct derivations which are parallel independent, then there is a graph $\tilde{H}$ and natural direct derivations $p':H \Longrightarrow \tilde{H}$ and $p:H' \Longrightarrow \tilde{H}$. Moreover p and p' as well as p' and p becomes sequential independent

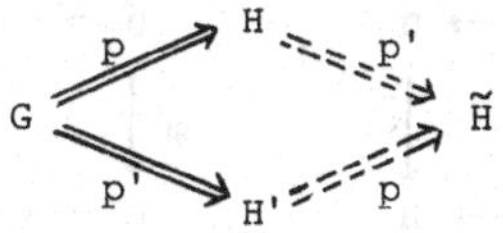

Proof: The main idea is to derive $\tilde{H}$ from G in parallel with the productions p and p'.

Consider the following first diagram which are the left hand sides of $G \underset{p}{\Longrightarrow} H$ and $G \underset{p'}{\Longrightarrow} H'$ using parallel independence.

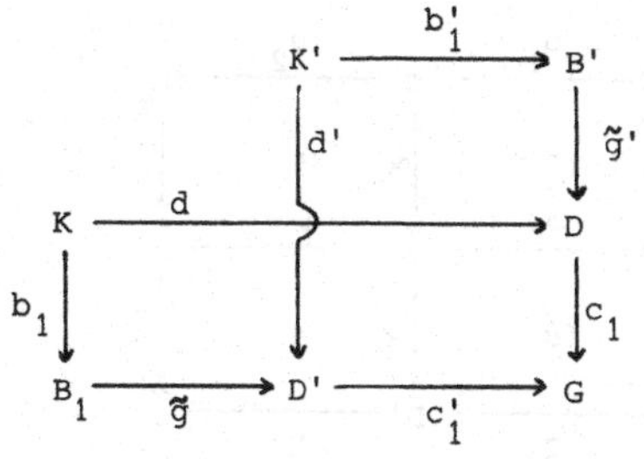

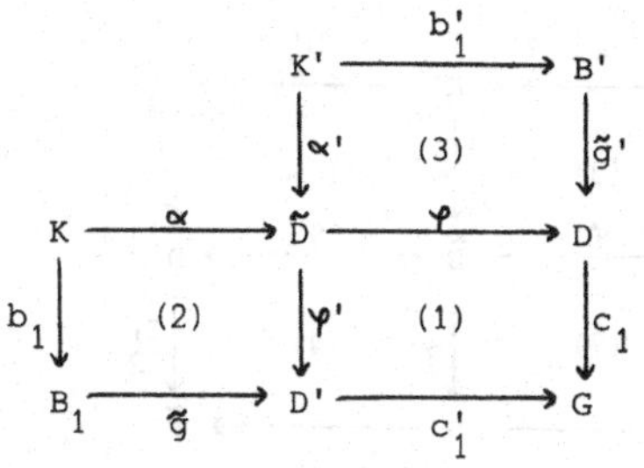

The second diagram is obtained by constructing the pullback $\tilde{D}$ of c_1' and c_1, meaning that $\tilde{D}$ is the intersection of D and D', such that d' and d are factored $d'=\varphi' \circ \alpha'$, $d=\varphi \circ \alpha$ where (1) is pullback by construction and (2) $\cup$ (1), (3) $\cup$ (1) are pushouts because they are left hand sides of productions.

Since the derivations are natural, we have c_1, c_1' injective and hence also φ, φ' injective and a generalization of the division lemma in /Eh-Kr 75a/ implies that also (2) and (3) and hence also (1) are pushouts.

Next we will construct $\tilde{H}$ as a parallel derivation from G using p, p' and identical productions for $\tilde{D}$

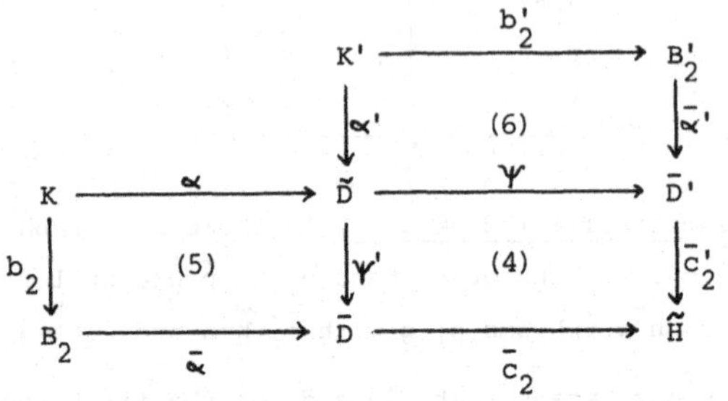

where b_2, α, α', b_2' are given and the pushouts (5), (6) and (4) are constructed one after another.

Next we observe that the pushouts for H and H', the right hand sides of the given derivations $G \overset{p}{\Longrightarrow} H$ and $G \overset{p'}{\Longrightarrow} H'$, can be decomposed using $d = \varphi \circ \alpha$, $d' = \varphi' \circ \alpha'$, and the pushouts (5) and (6) above

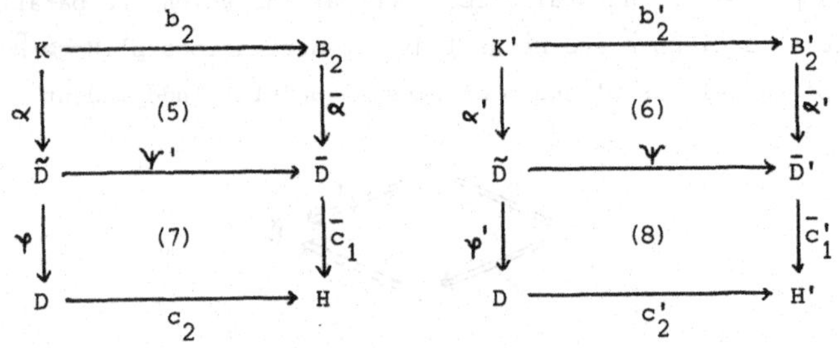

where (7) and (8) also become pushouts.

Note that φ , φ' injective implies $\bar{c}_1$, $\bar{c}_1'$ injective.

Finally we give the natural ($\bar{c}_1$, $\bar{c}_1'$ injective) direct derivations $H \underset{p'}{\Longrightarrow} \tilde{H}$ and $H' \underset{p}{\Longrightarrow} \tilde{H}$

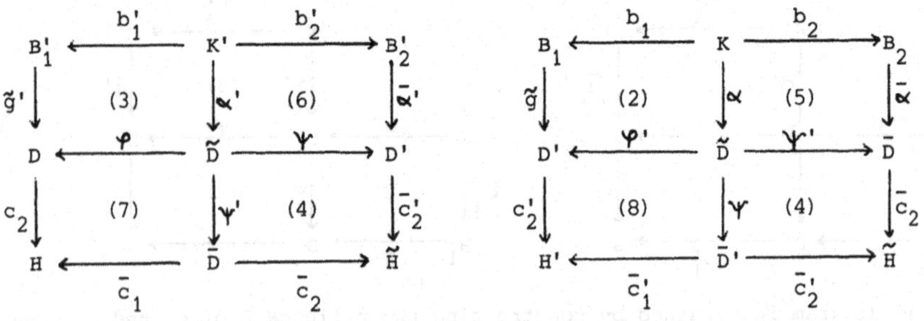

Combining diagrams (3), (5), and (7) (resp. (2), (6), (8)) we see that $p{:}G \Longrightarrow H$ and $p'{:}H \Longrightarrow \tilde{H}$ (resp. $p'{:}G \Longrightarrow H'$ and $p{:}H' \Longrightarrow \tilde{H}$) are sequential independent. □

In the Church-Rosser-Theorem I above we have started with two parallel independent direct derivations leading to two pairs of sequential independent ones. Now in

Church-Rosser-Theorem II we will start with sequential independent derivations leading to parallel independent ones, such that the notions parallel independent and sequential independent become equivalent and we are able to define a parallel direct derivation.

CHURCH-ROSSER-THEOREM II

Let $p:G \Longrightarrow H$ and $p':H \Longrightarrow \tilde{H}$ natural direct derivations which are sequential independent, then there is a graph H' and natural direct derivations $p':G \Longrightarrow H'$ and $p:H' \Longrightarrow \tilde{H}$ such that p' and p become sequential and parallel independent.

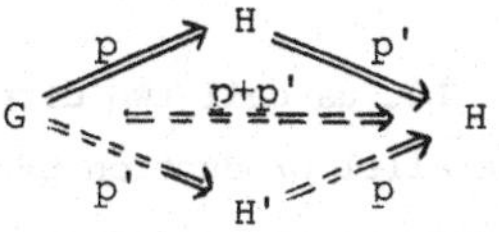

Moreover, there is a natural direct parallel derivation $p+p':G \Longrightarrow \tilde{H}$ using the production

$$p+p' = (B_1 \cup B_1' \xleftarrow{b_1 \cup b_1'} K \cup K' \xrightarrow{b_2 \cup b_2'} B_2 \cup B_2')$$

and as enlargement the intersection $\tilde{D}$ of the enlargements D and D' corresponding to $p:G \Longrightarrow H$ and $p':G \Longrightarrow H'$ respectively. Finally let us note, that this parallel derivation is a special case of direct derivations in the sense of parallel graph-grammars in /Eh-Kr 75b/.

Proof: Since the techniques of the proof are very similar to that above we only give the main steps using the same notation. Actually the same pushouts are constructed in a different order. Whereas before parallel independence allowed us to start with diagrams (1), (2), (3) we now start with (7), (5), (3) using sequential independence, where (7) is constructed from $\bar{c}_1$ and c_2 as pullback which also becomes a pushout similar to (1) in Church-Rosser-Theorem I .

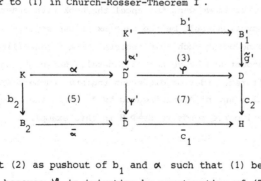

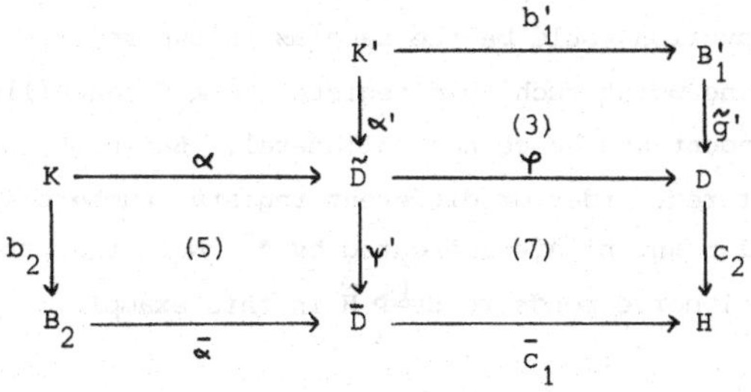

Next we construct (2) as pushout of b_1 and α such that (1) becomes a pushout and also a pullback, because ψ is injective by construction of (7), where $\bar{c}_1$ is injective by assumption. Thus, with c_1 by assumption also φ' and with ψ also c_1' are injective. Next we construct (6) and (8) as pushouts such that also (4) becomes pushout using $p':H \Longrightarrow \tilde{H}$. Now, combining (3), (1), (6) and (8) on one hand and (2), (8), (5) and (4) on the other hand we obtain natural direct derivations $p':G \Longrightarrow H'$

and $p:H' \Longrightarrow \tilde{H}$ respectively, and also the desired independence results.
Finally, the natural parallel direct derivation is given by the following diagrams (9) and (10) which

$$\begin{array}{ccccc}
B_1 \dot{\cup} B_1' & \xleftarrow{\;b_1 \dot{\cup} b_1'\;} & K \dot{\cup} K' & \xrightarrow{\;b_2 \dot{\cup} b_2'\;} & B_2 \dot{\cup} B_2' \\
\downarrow & (9) & \downarrow & (10) & \downarrow \\
G & \xleftarrow[\;c_1 \circ \varphi\;]{} & D & \xrightarrow[\;\bar{c}_2 \circ \varphi'\;]{} & \tilde{H}
\end{array}$$

are built up by the pushouts (1), (2), (3) and (4), (5), (6) respectively, and turn out to be also pushouts. □

Now we come back to problem 1. Let us call two direct derivations $p:G \Longrightarrow H$ and $p':G \Longrightarrow H'$ <u>collateral</u> if the parallel production $p+p'$ can be applied to G, p' to H and p to H' such that in all three cases we obtain the same graph $\tilde{H}$, i.e. $p+p':G \Longrightarrow \tilde{H}$, $p':H \Longrightarrow \tilde{H}$ and $p:H' \Longrightarrow \tilde{H}$.
Now problem 1 is solved by

<u>THEOREM FOR COLLATERAL DERIVATIONS</u>

Two natural direct derivations $p:G \Longrightarrow H$ and $p':G \Longrightarrow H'$ are collateral if and only if p and p' are parallel independent. Moreover, parallel independence implies sequential independence and vice versa.
Using the Church-Rosser-Theorems above it only remains to show that collateral derivations are parallel independent. This is shown in /Kr 76/.

<u>EXAMPLE 2</u>

Let p be the first production in example 1 (registering of a book) and p' the second production (ordering of a book). These manipulations are parallel independent and hence collateral. Actually, in the example below the intersection of the occurrences of the left hand sides, consists of the nodes labelled O and P' but these are common gluing points. But if we want to cancel the book with order number O' the occurrence of this production would be the same as in the registering case and O' would be no common gluing point such that registering and cancelling the same book is not parallel independent and hence not collateral. But note, that all manipulations concerning different order or different register numbers are independent. Common gluing points of p and p' are indicated by *. Note that the direct derivation $G \overset{p}{\Longrightarrow} H$ in example 1 corresponds to $H \overset{p}{\Longrightarrow} \tilde{H}$ in this example.

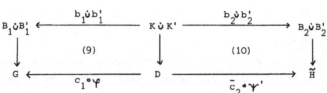

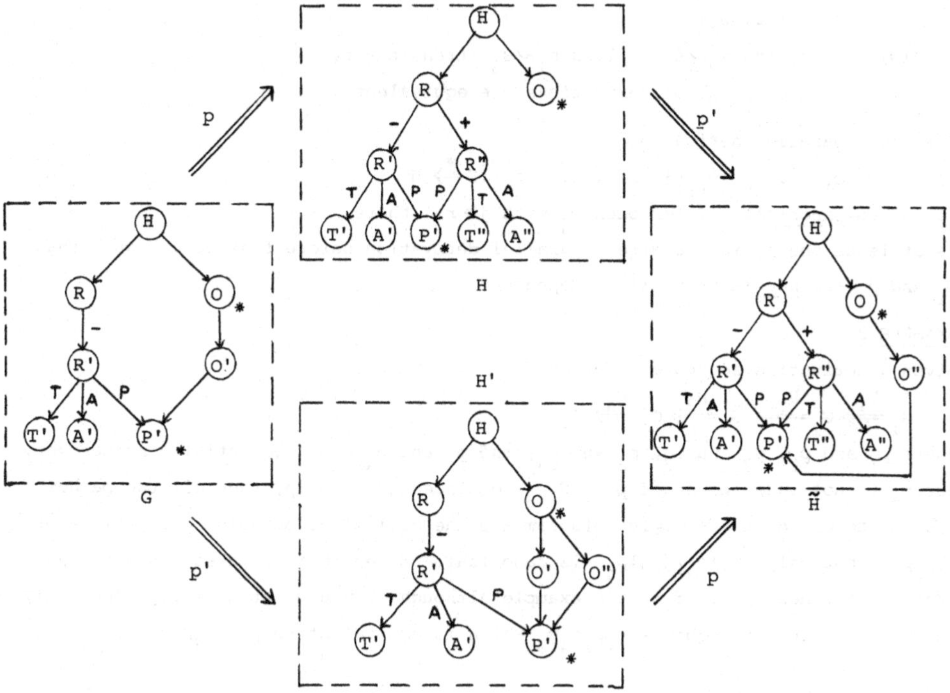

Now we consider problem 2.

In the following we only sketch the main ideas, more details and the complete proofs are given in our technical report /Kr 76/.

EQUIVALENCE AND CANONICAL DERIVATIONS

Direct parallel derivations are defined as above but generalized to several direct derivations

$$p_1 + p_2 + \ldots + p_r : G \Longrightarrow H$$

in the case that each of them is parallel independent of each other.

Parallel derivations (in the sense of sequential graph grammars) are sequences of direct parallel derivations

$$G \xrightarrow{p_1+\ldots+p_r} H_1 \xrightarrow{p_{r+1}+\ldots+p_s} H_2 \Longrightarrow \ldots \xrightarrow{\ldots+p_k} H_n$$

Now equivalence of parallel derivations, denoted by $\sim$, is defined recursively:

(i) If $p=p_1+\ldots+p_r:G\Longrightarrow G'$ and $p'=p_1'+\ldots+p_s':G'\Longrightarrow G''$ are pairwise sequential independent then:

$p\,p' \sim p+p' \sim p'\,p$

which is well-defined by Church-Rosser-Theorem II

(ii) $s_1 \sim s_2 : G \overset{*}{\Longrightarrow} H$ and $p:G'\Longrightarrow G$ (resp. $q:H\Longrightarrow H'$) direct parallel derivation implies

$p\,s_1 \sim p\,s_2$ resp. $s_1\,q \sim s_2\,q$

(iii) $s \sim s$ (reflexivity)

(iv) $s_1 \sim s_2$ and $s_2 \sim s_3$ implies $s_1 \sim s_3$ (transitivity)

(v) no other parallel derivations are equivalent

Finally a parallel derivation

$$(p_1+\ldots+p_r)(p_{r+1}+\ldots)\ldots(\ldots+p_k):G \overset{*}{\Longrightarrow} H$$

is called canonical, if for each p_j with $j \geq r+1$ there is at least one p_i in the direct parallel derivation before that of p_j, such that p_i and p_j are not (sequential) independent.

EXAMPLE 3

Given a derivation sequence of graphs

$$G_1 \overset{p_1}{\Longrightarrow} G_2 \overset{p_2}{\Longrightarrow} G_3 \overset{p_3}{\Longrightarrow} G_4 \overset{p_4}{\Longrightarrow} G_5$$

where p_1 and p_2, p_2 and p_3, p_3 and p_4, and p_1 and p_4 are (sequential) independent, but p_4 is not independent of p_2 and p_3 not independent of p_1 then all the pathes from G_1 to G_5 in the following diagram are the equivalent parallel derivations of $p_1p_2p_3p_4$ but only $(p_1+p_2)(p_3+p_4)$ is canonical. Note, that it makes sense to say that p_4 is independent of p_1 for example although they are not directly connected, but they are in the sequence $p_2p_1p_4p_3$ which is equivalent to $p_1p_2p_3p_4$.

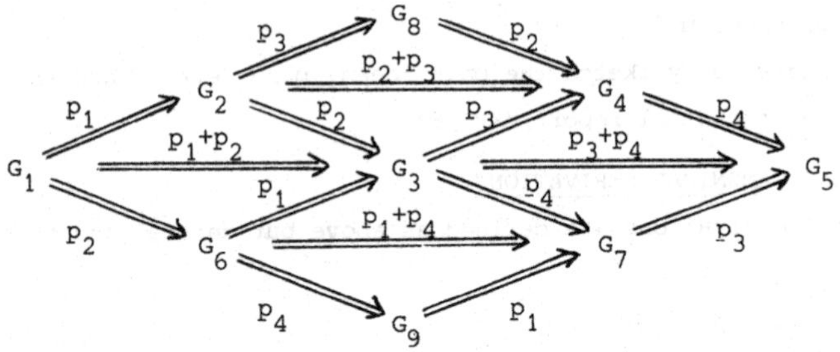

Thus, intuitively spoken, in a canonical parallel derivation the productions are applied leftmost with respect to the derivation sequence, whereas leftmost in the string case usually is meant with respect to the order in the word to be derived.

THEOREM: Uniqueness and Algorithm for Canonical Derivations

Equivalent canonical parallel derivations are equal and for each parallel derivation $(p_1+\ldots)\ldots p_r\ldots(\ldots+p_k)$ there is a unique equivalent canonical one which can be obtained by the following algorithm:

Beginning from left, each p_r in the sequence has to be shifted to the left as fas as p_r is independent from all the p_i's in the direct parallel derivation before p_r, or p_r is already in the first one.

In example 3 this algorithm applied to $p_1p_2p_3p_4$ would construct the following equivalent derivation sequences in each step, respectively.

$$p_1p_2p_3p_4,\ (p_1+p_2)\ p_3p_4,\ (p_1+p_2)\ p_3p_4,\ (p_1+p_2)\ (p_3+p_4)$$

If p_4 would also be independent of p_2 the last step of the algorithm would be $(p_1+p_2+p_4)\ p_3$.
The proof of this theorem is by far too long to be included in this paper. A first version will appear in our Technical Report /Kr 76/.

Now, we have a solution for problem 2 which seems to be most important for all fields of graph-grammar applications. Especially it seems to be a key for syntax-analysis of graph grammars (cf. /De-Fr-St 74/), for correctness of macro expansion of recursive computation (cf. /Eh-Ros 76/) and for asynchronous parallel updating of data bases as sketched in our very simple examples.

REFERENCES

/De-Fr-St 74/ Denert, E., Franck, R., Streng, W.: PLAN2D - towards a 2-dimensional programming language, in Lecture Nores in Comp. Sci. 26, 202-213 (1975)

/Eh-Kr 75a/ Ehrig, H., Kreowski, H.-J.: Categorical Approach to Graphic Systems and Graph Grammars, Proc. Symp. Algebraic System Theory, Udine 1975, to appear in Springer Lect.Notes in Math.

/Eh-Kr 75b/ --: Parallel Graph Grammars, in Proc.Conf. Formal Languages, Automata and Development, Noordwijkerhout 1975

/Eh-Pf-Sch 73/ Ehrig, H., Pfender, M., Schneider, H.J.: Graph Grammars: An Algebraic Approach, Proc. IEEE Conf. on Automata and Switching Theory, Iowa City 1973, 167-180

/Eh-Ros 76/ Ehrig, H., Rosen, B.: Commutativity of independent transformations of complex objects, to appear

/Gri 68/ Griffiths, T.V.: Some Remarks on Derivations in General Rewriting Systems, Information and Control 12, 27-54 (1968)

/Kr 76/ Kreowski, H.-J.: Kanonische Ableitungssequenzen für Graph-Grammatiken, to appear

/MacL 72/ MacLane, S.: Categories for the Working Mathematician, Springer Verlag 72

/Ros 74/ Rosen, B.: Deriving Graphs from Graphs by Applying a Production, Acta Informatica 4, 337-357 (1975)

/Ros 75/ --: A Church-Rosser-Theorem for Graph Grammars (announcement), SIGACT News (7,3), 26-31 (1975)

ON STRICT INTERPRETATIONS OF GRAMMAR FORMS

by

Seymour Ginsburg
University of Southern California, Los Angeles

and

Otto Mayer
University of Kaiserslautern, Germany

In [CG] the concept of a "(context-free) grammar form" was introduced in order to model the situation where all grammars "structurally close" to a given master grammar are of interest. A grammar form frequently provides a uniform way of treating all the grammars associated with the form. Each of the grammars in the associated family is obtained by an "interpretation", a notion which involves a substitution of the nonterminals and terminals by disjoint sets of nonterminals and (not necessarily disjoint) sets of terminal words respectively.
In two recent documents, [B] and [GS], dealing with parsing and the structure of "grammatical families" respectively, the identical notion of a "strict interpretation" was formulated. (A strict interpretation is an interpretation where different terminals are replaced by disjoint sets of terminals). It turns out that the "string homomorphism" as used for skeletal parsing in [D] is the inverse of a certain kind of strict interpretation. And the relation "G' is a restriction of G",G' and G grammars, which appeared in [H] and [N], implies that G' is a strict interpretation grammar of the form associated with G. This pervasiveness suggests that strict interpretations may play an important role in the development of grammar forms. As such, their properties should be carefully examined. The purpose of the present paper is to initiate that investigation.

Organisationalwise, our results fall into three categories:

(1) Decidability properties of strict interpretations of unambiguous grammar forms;

(2) Preservation of unambiguity by strict interpretations; and

(3) Parsing of strict interpretation grammars based on parsing methods for the master grammar.

In addition, there is an appendix which reviews the basic material about grammar forms and their interpretations.

Turning to decidability there are three results, the first two depending on the following:

Lemma: Let F be an unambiguous grammar form and let $I_1 = (\mu_1, G_{I_1})$ and $I_2 = (\mu_2, G_{I_2})$ be coextensive [(1)] strict interpretations. If a terminal word w is generated by a derivation tree τ_1 of G_{I_1} and τ_2 of G_{I_2}, then τ_2 and τ_2 are equally shaped [(2)].

Theorem 1: It is decidable to determine for an unambiguous grammar form and an arbitrary strict interpretation I, whether or not G_I is unambiguous.

The proof is based on the facts that (i) ambiguity of a word in $L(G_I)$ can only occur form equally shaped derivation trees and (ii) it suffices to check all derivation trees having a uniformly bounded maximum path length for two different ones which generate the same word.

Theorem 2: It is decidable to determine for an arbitrary unambiguous grammar form and each $l \geq 2$ coextensive strict interpretations $I_1, \ldots, I_l$, whether or not the intersection $\bigcap_{i=1}^{l} L(G_{I_i})$ is (a) empty, (b) nonempty finite, and (c) infinite.

The procedures consist of checking all derivation trees in $G_{I_1}, \ldots, G_{I_l}$, which have certain maximal path lengths, for common words generated.

Theorem 3: It is decidable to determine for an arbitrary unambiguous grammar form and all coextensive strict interpretations I_1 and I_2, whether or not $L(G_{I_1}) \subseteq L(G_{I_2})$.

The proof consists in showing that $L(G_{I_1}) \subseteq L(G_{I_2})$ if and only if $L(G_{P_1}) \subseteq L(G_{P_2})$, where G_{P_1} and G_{P_2} are the parenthesis grammars resulting from G_{I_1} and G_{I_2} respectively by enclosing the right sides of all productions in parentheses. The decidability of the latter inclusion follows form [McN].

Turning to the preservation of unambiguity by strict interpretations, we get the following result (which we consider the most interesting of the paper):

---

(1) By this is meant that $(\bigcup_{i=1}^{2} \mu_i(a)) \cap (\bigcup_{j=1}^{2} \mu_j(b)) = \emptyset$ for all elements $a \neq b$ in $\mathcal{S}$ where $F = (V, \Sigma, \mathcal{V}, \mathcal{S}, \mathcal{P}, \sigma)$.

(2) By this is meant that each of the two trees can be converted into the other by relabelling nonterminal nodes.

Theorem 4: For each unambiguous grammar form F and each strict interpretation I of F, $L(G_I)$ is an unambiguous language.

The proof consists in constructing a grammar $\bar{G}_I$ such that different, but equally shaped derivation trees for the same word in G_I, correspond to exactly one derivation tree in $\bar{G}_I$. In general $\bar{G}_I$ does not come from a strict interpretation of G. We do not know if there always exists an unambiguous strict interpretation I' of F such that $L(G_{I'})=L(G_I)$. However, there is a grammar form $\bar{F}$, closely related to F, such that for each strict interpretation grammar G_I of F, $\bar{G}_I$ comes from a strict interpretation of $\bar{F}$.

The last of the categories concerns parsing. Let M_F be a parsing procedure for the form grammar $G_F = (\mathcal{V},\mathcal{S},\mathcal{P},\sigma)$ of a grammar form F and let $I = (\mu,G_I)$ be a strict interpretation of F. Then a parsing method M_I for $G_I = (V_I,\Sigma_I,P_I,\sigma_I)$, depending on M_F, can be constructed. For a word w in Σ_I^*, M_I operates as follows:
First, M_I determines the unique word $\bar{w}$ in $\mathcal{S}^*$ for which w is in $\mu(\bar{w})$. Next, M_I parses $\bar{w}$ by M_F. Finally, M_I checks to see if there are G_F-derivations of $\bar{w}$ which give rise to G_I-derivations of w. We have two results in this area.

Theorem 5: Let F be an arbitrary grammar form with the property that there is a function p(n), $n \geq 0$, for which the number of leftmost G_F-derivations of an arbitrary word $\bar{w}$ in $L(G_F)$ is at most $p(|\bar{w}|)$. Suppose there is a function f(n), $n \geq 0$, and a parsing procedure M_F for G_F which, for each word $\bar{w}$ in $\mathcal{S}^*$, yields in $f(|\bar{w}|)$ time all leftmost G_F-derivations if $\bar{w}$ is in $L(G_F)$ and rejects if $\bar{w}$ is not in $L(G_F)$. Then there exists a constant c such that for each word w in Σ_I^*, M_I (as constructed above) yields in $f(|w|) + c\big(f(|w|)p(|w|) + |w|\ p(|w|) + |w|\big)$ time at least one leftmost G_I-derivation of w or rejects w.

We remark that in case G_F is unambiguous, then M_I has, up to a constant factor, the same time requirements as M_F. This is Bertsch's [B] result.

Theorem 6: Let F be an arbitrary grammar form. Suppose, there exist functions s(n) and l(n), $n \geq 0$, and a parsing procedure M_F for G_F with the following properties:

(1) For each word $\bar{w}$ in $\mathcal{S}^*$, M_F needs at most $s(|\bar{w}|)$ space to determine each leftmost G_F-derivation if $\bar{w}$ is in $L(G_F)$ and reject $\bar{w}$ if it is not in $L(G_F)$; and

(2) The length of each G_F-derivation of a word $\bar{w}$ in $L(G_F)$ is at most $l(|\bar{w}|)$.

Then there is a constant c such that for each word w in $\Sigma_I{}^*$, M_I (as constructed above), using at most $s(|w|) + |w| + cl(|w|)$ space, yields a leftmost derivation of w if it is in $L(G_I)$ and rejects w if it is not in $L(G_I)$.

<u>Appendix:</u> We here briefly recall some grammar form concepts from [CG], [B], and [CGS].

A <u>(context-free) grammar form</u> is 6-tuple $F = (V,\Sigma,\mathcal{V},\mathcal{S},\mathcal{P},\sigma)$ where

(i) V is an infinite set of abstract symbols,

(ii) Σ is an infinite subset of V such that $V - \Sigma$ is infinite,

and (iii) $G_F = (\mathcal{V},\mathcal{S},\mathcal{P},\sigma)$, called the <u>form grammar (of F)</u>, is a context-free grammar with $\mathcal{S} \subseteq \Sigma$ and $(\mathcal{V}-\mathcal{S}) \subseteq (V - \Sigma)$.

We assume throughout that V and Σ are fixed infinite sets satisfying (i) and (ii) above. All grammar forms discussed will be with respect to this V and Σ. The adjective phrase "context-free" in "context-free grammar form" and "context-free grammar" is usually omitted.

A grammar form determines a specific family of grammars, each "structurally close" to the form grammar, by means of the following concept: An <u>interpretation</u> of a <u>grammar form</u> $F = (V,\Sigma,\mathcal{V},\mathcal{S},\mathcal{P},\sigma)$ is a 5-tuple $I = (\mu,V_I,\Sigma_I,P_I,S_I)$, where

(1) μ is a substitution on $\mathcal{V}^*$ such that $\mu(a)$ is a finite subset of Σ^* for each element a in $\mathcal{S}$, $\mu(\xi)$ is a finite subset of $V - \Sigma$ for each ξ in $\mathcal{V}-\mathcal{S}$, and $\mu(\xi) \cap \mu(\eta) = \emptyset$ for each ξ and η, $\xi \neq \eta$, in $\mathcal{V}-\mathcal{S}$.

(2) P_I is a subset of $\mu(\mathcal{P}) = \bigcup_{\pi \text{ in } \mathcal{P}} \mu(\pi)$, where $\mu(\alpha \to \beta) = \{u \to v \mid u \text{ in } \mu(\alpha), v \text{ in } \mu(\beta)\}$,

(3) S_I is in $\mu(\sigma)$,

and (4) Σ_I (V_I) contains all symbols in $\Sigma(V)$ which occur in P_I (together with S_I).

$G_I = (V_I,\Sigma_I,P_I,S_I)$ is called the <u>grammar of I.</u>

For brevity, an interpretation I is frequently written as (μ,G_I).

Each production in G_I is "structurally close" to a particular production in G_F. Thus, G_F is a "master grammar" for the grammars of interpretations. The structural nearness is heightened if one imposes on the interpretation of terminals the same restriction as on the interpretation of nonterminals. This leads to the following definition (cf. [B], [CGS]:

Let $F = (V,\Sigma,\mathcal{V},\mathcal{S},\mathcal{P},\sigma)$ be a grammar form. A <u>strict interpretation of</u> F is an interpretation (μ,G_I) of F such that $\mu(x)$ is a subset of V for each x in $\mathcal{V}$, and $\mu(x) \cap \mu(y) = \emptyset$ for all $x \neq y$ in $\mathcal{V}$.

Thus a strict interpretation is an interpretation (μ,G_I) in which μ maps the different symbols of $\mathcal{S}$ into different subsets of Σ.

References

[B] E. Bertsch: "Analyzing Families of Grammars", 2nd Professional Conference on Formal Languages and Automata Theory", May 20-23, 1975, Kaiserslautern, Germany.

[CG] A.B.Cremers and S.Ginsburg: "Context-Free Grammar Forms", Journal of Computer and System Sciences, Vol. 11 (1975), pp. 86-117.

[CGS] A.B.Cremers, S.Ginsburg, and E.H.Spanier: "The Structure of Context-Free Grammatical Families", submitted for publication.

[D] A.J.Demers: "Skeletal LR Parsing", 15th Annual Symposium on Switching and Automata Theory, New Orleans, Louisiana, 1974.

[H] R. Haskell: "Formal languages: Structure preserving maps and decidability properties", Ph.D. Dissertation, Imperial College, London, 1970.

[McN] R. McNaughton: "Parenthesis Grammars", JACM, Vo. 14, (1967), pp. 490-500.

[N] M. Nivat: "Extensions et Restrictions de Grammaires Algebriques", University of Paris VII document, 1975.

A HIERARCHY OF CONTEXT-SENSITIVE LANGUAGES

By Irina Gorun in Bucharest (Romania)

1. Notation and preliminaries

a) We denote by $\mathcal{L}(i)$ the class of all languages of type i in the sense of [4], i = 0,1,2,3. We denote by $\mathcal{L}^k$ the set of all the intersections of k context-free languages. In [5] the proper inclusion $\mathcal{L}^{k-1} \subset \mathcal{L}^k$ is proved for each k. We denote by $\mathcal{L}^\infty$ the union of the classes $\mathcal{L}^k$. In [5] the proper inclusions $\mathcal{L}(2) \subset \mathcal{L}^\infty \subset \mathcal{L}(1)$ are proved. We denote by $\mathcal{L}(m)$ the class of languages accepted by the automata of type m. We denote by $\mathcal{M}$ the class of matrix languages.

b) We denote by T(M) the language accepted by the Turing machine M and by N(M) the language accepted by a push-down automaton (pda) M, which accepts by empty store (cf. [4]). We denote by $|x|$ the length of the word x. A move of a pda for which no input symbol is scanned is called an ε-move.

2. A description of the elements of $\mathcal{L}^\infty$

As the questions involving an intersection of context-free (cf) languages (is it empty ?, finite ?, infinite ?) are unsolvable, the representation of the elements of $\mathcal{L}^\infty$ as intersections of cf languages is not easy to handle.

Proposition 1. It is unsolvable whether: for arbitrary cf languages $L_1,\dots,L_k,L_1',\dots,L_n'$, is the intersections of the L_i's equal to the intersections of the L_i''s or not.

Proof. Suppose our question is solvable. Then, taking k = 1 and $L_1 = \emptyset$, it follows that it is solvable whether a finite intersection of cf languages is or is not empty. This contradicts [4], p. 220.

We exhibit a type of automata denoted by n-pda such that

$$\mathcal{L}^n = \mathcal{L}(\text{n-pda}).$$

Definition. A n-pda M is a system $(K,\Sigma,Z,(f_i)_1^n,q_o,z_o)$ describing a multi-head and multi-push-down tape automaton.

1. K is the set of states; a state q different from q_o is of the form $(q_1,\dots,q_n)$. The symbol placed on the i-th position denotes the state of the i-th head. We denote by K_i the set of the components of order i of the elements $q \neq q_o$ from K. The start state q_o is commonly used for the n heads.

2. Z is the set of the pushdown symbols; the elements of Z are n-uples $(z_1,\dots,z_n)$ where the i-th component is placed on the i-th pushdown tape; some z_i may be the empty word. We denote by Z_i the set

of the components of order i of the elements from Z.
The start pushdown symbol is denoted by $z_o = (z_1^o, \dots, z_n^o)$.

3. The function f_i describes the moves of the i-th head,

$$f_i: (K_i \cup \{q_o\}) \times (\Sigma \cup \{\varepsilon\}) \times Z_i \longrightarrow \mathcal{P}((K_i \cup \{q_o\}) \times Z_i^*).$$

A configuration of M is denoted by $((q_1,\dots,q_n),(x_1,\dots,x_n),(p_1,\dots,p_n))$ where q_i is the state of the i-th head, x_i the string of pushdown symbols on the i-th pushdown tape and p_i the position of the i-th head on the input. We denote the change of a configuration when the head reads a symbol "a" by $a: ((q_1,\dots,q_n),(x_1z_1,\dots,x_nz_n),(p_1,\dots,p_n)) \vdash ((q_1',\dots,q_n'),(x_1y_1,\dots,x_ny_n),(p_1',\dots,p_n'))$ where $(q_i',y_i) \in f_i(q_i,a,z_i)$ and $p_i' = p_i + 1$ if a was really scanned by f_i and $p_i' = p_i$ if f_i made an ε-move. A series of changes from a configuration c to another c' due to an input x is denoted by $x: c \overset{*}{\vdash} c'$. Finally we define the language accepted by M, denoted by N(M), as being the set of those words $w \in \Sigma^*$ such that $w: ((q_o,z_o,(0,\dots,0)) \overset{*}{\vdash} (q,(\varepsilon,\dots,\varepsilon),(m,\dots,m))$ where $m = |w|$.

Proposition 2. For any $L \in \mathcal{L}^\infty$ there exist $k \in N$ and a k-pda M such that L = N(M).

Proof. As $L \in \mathcal{L}^\infty$, there are $k \in N$ and $L_1,\dots,L_k \in \mathcal{L}(2)$ such that $L = \bigcap_{i=1}^k L_i$. As $\mathcal{L}(2) = \mathcal{L}(\text{pda})$ there are k pda $M_1,\dots,M_k$ such that $L_i = N(M_i)$. Let $M_i = (K_i,\Sigma,Z_i,f_i,q_o^i,z_o^i)$. We exhibit the k-pda $M = (K,\Sigma,Z,(f_i)_1^k,q_o,z_o)$ where $K = K_1 \times \dots \times K_k$, $Z = (Z_1 \cup \{\varepsilon\}) \times \dots \times (Z_k \cup \{\varepsilon\})$, $q_o = (q_o^1,\dots,q_o^k)$, $z_o = (z_o^1,\dots,z_o^k)$. It is obvious that L = N(M).

Proposition 3. Let M be a n-pda. Then $N(M) \in \mathcal{L}^n$.

Proof. We exhibit n pd automata $(M_i)_1^n$ such that $N(M) = \bigcap_1^n N(M_i)$. Let $M = (K,\Sigma,Z,(f_i)_1^n,q_o,z_o)$. Let us put $M_i = (K_i,\Sigma,Z_i,f_i,q_o,z_o^i)$, where Z_i, z_o^i are as in Definition and K_i is the set from the definition to which we added an element q_o. M_i will simulate the moves of the i-th head of M using only the i-th pushdown tape. Obviously $\bigcap_1^n N(M_i) \supseteq N(M)$. If a string of Σ^* is in $N(M_i)$ for each i, this means that each head of M beginning with the state q_o and the start symbol z_o^i will empty its corresponding pushdown tape when scanning the string. This means exactly that M accepts this input.

3. An hierarchy of context-sensitive languages

In [1] and [2] C. Caşlaru claims to prove that any matrix language is a finite union of finite intersections of cf languages, but the converse is not true. In our notation this gives the proper inclusion $\mathcal{M} \subset \mathcal{L}^\infty$. More precisely, $\mathcal{L}^\infty$ is the smallest class of languages containing $\mathcal{M}$ and closed under finite intersections.

It is known that $\mathcal{L}(1) = \mathcal{L}(\text{lba})$ where we denote by lba the class of linear bounded automata as defined in [4] . It is an open problem if the inclusion $\mathcal{L}$(det.lba)$\subset\mathcal{L}$(lba) is proper or not. Anyhow we prove that $\mathcal{L}^\infty$ is properly contained in $\mathcal{L}$(det.lba).

Lemma 1 (Exercise 8.3 in [4]). Every context-free language is accepted by a deterministic lba.

Lemma 2. $\mathcal{L}$ (det.lba) is closed under finite intersections.

Proof. Let L_1 and L_2 be the languages accepted by the det. lb automata M_1, M_2 respectively. Let $M_i = (K_i, \Sigma, V_i, f_i, q_o^i, F_i)$, $i = 1,2$. We may suppose that $K_1 \cap K_2 = \emptyset$. We exhibit $M = (K, \Sigma', V, f, q_o, F)$, where $K = K_1 \cup K_2$, $q_o = q_o^1$, $F = F_2$, $\Sigma' = \Sigma \times \{ƀ\}$ and $V = V_1 x V_2$. M has two tracks; on the first track is initially written the input. M starts in q_o by simulating M_1 on the second track. If M reaches the rightmost cell (the cell (ø,ƀ)) in a state of F_1 then M returns to the leftmost cell, enters the state q_o^2 and simulates M_2 on the first track. If M_2 enters finally a state of F_2, then M enters a state of F and accepts.

Corollary. $\mathcal{L}^\infty$ is contained in $\mathcal{L}$(det.lba).

Proof. Obviously follows from Lemmas 1 and 2.

Proposition 4. The language $L = \{a^{n^2} : n \geq 1\}$ is in $\mathcal{L}$(det.lba).

Proof. We find an algorithm for a deterministic lba using the identity $n^2 = 1 + 3 + 5 + \ldots + (2n-1)$. Let $M = (K, \quad , q_o, F, f)$ where $K = \quad e, p, s_o, s_1, \ldots, s_{10}, s_2', \ldots, s_9'$, $\Sigma = \{(a,X),(X,X),(X,ƀ),(ø,ƀ),$ $(ø,ƀ),(a,ƀ)\}$, $V \subset \Sigma$ is the input alphabet containing only (a,ƀ), F = $\{e\}$ and $q_o = s_o$. The action of f is given by the following list. We recall that f is defined on $K \times \Sigma$ and takes values in $K \times \Sigma \times \{-1,0,1\}$ where -1 signifies a left move of the head, 1 a right move and 0 an ε-move. The pairs of $K \times \Sigma$ which are not listed are supposed to go through f in (p,(X,X),1), where p is the passive state.

Nr.	State	Symbol	State	Symbol	Move
1	s_o	(ø,ƀ)	s_o	(ø,ƀ)	1
2	s_o	(ø,ƀ)	p	(ø,ƀ)	0
3	s_o	(a,ƀ)	s_1	(X,X)	1
4	s_1	(ø,ƀ)	e	(ø,ƀ)	0
5	s_1	(a,ƀ)	s_2'	(X,X)	1
6	s_2'	(ø,ƀ)	p	(ø,ƀ)	0
7	s_2'	(a,ƀ)	s_3'	(X,X)	1
8	s_3'	(ø,ƀ)	p	(ø,ƀ)	0
9	s_3'	(a,ƀ)	s_4'	(X,X)	1
10	s_4'	(ø,ƀ)	e	(ø,ƀ)	0
11	s_4'	(a,ƀ)	s_5'	(X,X)	1
12	s_5'	(a,ƀ)	s_6'	(X,ƀ)	1

Continuation:

Nr.	State	Symbol	State	Symbol	Move
13	s_6'	(a,b̸)	s_7'	(X,b̸)	1
14	s_7'	(a,b̸)	s_8'	(X,b̸)	1
15	s_8'	(a,b̸)	s_9'	(X,b̸)	1
16	s_9'	(¢,b̸)	e	(¢,b̸)	0
17	s_9'	(a,b̸)	s_8	(a,b̸)	-1
18	s_7	(X,X)	s_2	(X,X)	-1
19	s_2	(X,X)	s_2	(X,X)	-1
20	s_2	(¢,b̸)	s_3	(¢,b̸)	1
21	s_3	(X,X)	s_3	(a,X)	1
22	s_3	(X,b̸)	s_4	(X,b̸)	-1
23	s_4	(a,X)	s_4	(X,X)	1
24	s_4	(X,X)	s_4	(X,X)	1
25	s_4	(X,b̸)	s_4	(X,b̸)	1
26	s_4	(a,b̸)	s_5	(X,b̸)	-1
27	s_5	(X,X)	s_5	(X,X)	-1
28	s_5	(X,b̸)	s_5	(X,b̸)	-1
29	s_5	(a,X)	s_4	(a,X)	0
30	s_5	(¢,b̸)	s_6	(¢,b̸)	1
31	s_6	(X,X)	s_6	(X,X)	1
32	s_6	(X,b̸)	s_6	(X,b̸)	1
33	s_6	(¢,b̸)	e	(¢,b̸)	0
34	s_6	(a,b̸)	s_8	(a,b̸)	-1
35	s_8	(X,b̸)	s_8	(X,b̸)	-1
36	s_8	(X,X)	s_9	(X,X)	1
37	s_9	(X,b̸)	s_{10}	(X,X)	1
38	s_{10}	(X,b̸)	s_7	(X,X)	0
39	p	(¢,b̸)	p	(¢,b̸)	0 .

<u>Corollary</u>. $\mathcal{L}^\infty$ is properly contained in $\mathcal{L}$(det.lba).

<u>Proof</u>. It is enough to prove that the language L from Proposition 4 is not in $\mathcal{L}^\infty$. Suppose there are of languages $(L_i)_1^n$ such that their intersection equals L. Observe that a^* is a regular set containing L; we have $L = \bigcap_1^n(L_i \cap a^*)$ and $L_i \cap a^*$ is still a cf language. But each cf language contained in a^* is a regular set (cf. [3] ,Theorem 3.1.2) and regular sets are closed under intersection. It follows that L is a regular set, a contradiction.

Thus we have the following hierarchy:

$$\mathcal{L}(2) \subset \mathcal{M} \subset \mathcal{L}^\infty \subset \mathcal{L}(\text{det.lba}) \subseteq \mathcal{L}(1)$$

where the inclusions are proper, excepting the last one which is not known to be proper.

REFERENCES

[1] C. Câşlaru, On matrix languages, The 6-th International Symposium over the Informational Processes, Bled, 1970.

[2] C. Câşlaru, On intersections of context-free languages, Rev. Roum. Math. Pures et Appl., 18(1974), 755-760.

[3] S. Ginsburg, The Mathematical Theory of Context-Free Languages, McGraw-Hill, 1966.

[4] J. E. Hopcroft, J. D. Ullman, Forma Languages and Their Relations to Automata, Addison-Wesley, 1969.

[5] L. Y. Liu, P. Weiner, An infinite hierarchy of intersections of context-free languages, Math. Systems Theory, 7(1973), 187-192.

ON CONSECUTIVE STORAGE OF RECORDS

Janusz Górski
Instytut Informatyki, Politechnika Gdańska
Majakowskiego 11, 80-952 Gdańsk, POLAND

INTRODUCTION

Significant improvement of the retrieval efficiency can be obtained if records to be retrieved jointly are stored in consecutive memory locations. This kind of memory organization was investigated by Ghosh [3,4,5], Lipski and Marek [11] and Lipski [10]. Such a memory organization involves the following combinatorial problem. For a given set /of records/ X and a given $\mathcal{R} \subseteq \mathcal{P}(X)$ /each $R \in \mathcal{R}$ is a set of records to be retrieved jointly/, find a linear arrangement /without repetitions/ of X such that each $R \in \mathcal{R}$ is a segment, i.e. R is a set of consecutive elements of this arrangement. A family $\mathcal{R}$ which admits such an arrangement is called linear. Different algorithms which construct this arrangement /if one exists/ can be found in [2] and [10]. Since most families we encounter in practice are not linear, we must allow repetitions of records if we want all $R \in \mathcal{R}$ to be stored as segments. Although the problem of finding an arrangement with the minimal possible redundancy is computationally very hard /see Kou [8]/, nevertheless several algorithms producing suboptimal arrangements are known /see [1,5,10,11]/.

In the paper we make an additional assumption that every record $x \in X$ is characterized by its length $l(x)$ - the number of storage locations occupied by x . We look for a linear arrangement of records /with repetitions allowed/ which minimizes the total storage requirement. An algorithm which solves this problem for an arbitrary family of sets is presented along with some ways of its simplification. Finally, we define a class of suboptimal algorithms which allow us to store every set $R \in \mathcal{R}$ as a segment although the total storage requirement need not be minimal.

Throughout the text we use the standard mathematical notation such as $\mathcal{P}(X)$ /the power set of X/, $|X|$ /the cardinality of X/, $\bigcup \mathcal{R}$ /the union of sets of a family $\mathcal{R}$/. The end of a theorem is denoted by ∎ .

1. EXTENSIONS OF A FAMILY OF SETS

Let $\mathcal{R}\subseteq\mathcal{P}(X)$. An ordered pair $\langle x,R\rangle\in X\times\mathcal{R}$, $x\in R$ is the <u>appearance</u> of an element x in the family $\mathcal{R}$. We denote

$$\mathcal{T}(\mathcal{R})=\{\langle x,R\rangle :\ R\in\mathcal{R}\wedge x\in R\}\ . \qquad /1/$$

The number of different appearances of x in $\mathcal{R}$ is denoted by $n_{\mathcal{R}}(x)$. We are interested in equivalence relations γ on $\mathcal{T}(\mathcal{R})$ such that

$$\langle x,R\rangle\,\gamma\,\langle x',R'\rangle \Longrightarrow x=x'\ . \qquad /2/$$

The set of all equivalence relations on $\mathcal{T}(\mathcal{R})$ which satisfy /2/ is denoted by $\Gamma(\mathcal{R})$. Let $\gamma\in\Gamma(\mathcal{R})$. Each class $P\in\mathcal{T}(\mathcal{R})/_{\gamma}$ is composed of appearances of an element $E(P)$ called the <u>label</u> of P. Let $\mathcal{R}=\{R_1,R_2,\dots,R_m\}$. We define

$$R_i(\gamma)=\{P\in\mathcal{T}(\mathcal{R})/_{\gamma} :\ \exists(x\in X)\,\langle x,R_i\rangle\in P\}\ ,\ \text{for } i=1,2,\dots,m\ ,$$
$$\mathcal{R}(\gamma)=\{R_i(\gamma) :\ i=1,2,\dots,m\}\ . \qquad /3/$$

$\mathcal{R}(\gamma)$ is an <u>extension</u> of $\mathcal{R}$. The notion of an extension was introduced to consider as different records every two different occurences of the same record in our arrangement with repetitions. In the extreme case we can obtain such an extension of $\mathcal{R}$ that all sets $R_i(\gamma)\in\mathcal{R}(\gamma)$ are disjoint. Fig.1 shows an example of a family $\mathcal{R}$ and some its extensions. For sake of simplicity the equivalence classes of γ_1, γ_2 are denoted by their labels.

$\mathcal{R}=\{R_1,R_2,R_3\}$, $\mathcal{R}(\gamma_1)=\{R_1(\gamma_1),R_2(\gamma_1),R_3(\gamma_1)\}$, $\mathcal{R}(\gamma_2)=\{R_1(\gamma_2),R_2(\gamma_2),R_3(\gamma_2)\}$.

Fig.1 Family $\mathcal{R}$ and its extensions $\mathcal{R}(\gamma_1)$, $\mathcal{R}(\gamma_2)$.

It is easy to see that the family $\mathcal{R}$ in Fig.1 is not linear, but its extensions $\mathcal{R}(\gamma_1)$, $\mathcal{R}(\gamma_2)$ are linear.

For every $x\in X$ let $n_{\gamma}(x)$ denote the number of different classes of γ having x as a label, i.e. the number of repetitions of record x. If the extension $\mathcal{R}(\gamma)$ is linear, then the records can be arranged in such a way, that each $R\in\mathcal{R}$ is a segment and the total storage requirement is

$$l_{\gamma}=\sum_{x\in X} n_{\gamma}(x)\cdot l(x)\ . \qquad /4/$$

Since our goal is to minimize the storage requirement, we look for the relation $\gamma^{*}\in\Gamma(\mathcal{R})$ such that

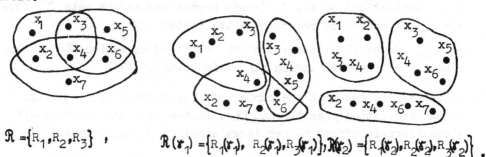

$$l_{\gamma^*} = \min_{\gamma \in \Gamma_L(\mathcal{R})} l_\gamma \quad , \qquad /5/$$

where $\Gamma_L(\mathcal{R}) \subseteq \Gamma(\mathcal{R})$ is the set of all relations $\gamma \in \Gamma(\mathcal{R})$ for which $\mathcal{R}(\gamma)$ is linear.

We can achieve our goal by applying the following algorithm.

Algorithm 1.

Step 1. Let $\mathcal{R} \subseteq \mathcal{P}(X)$, $X=\{x_1,x_2,\dots x_r\}$. For every element $x_i \in X$ determine the set $\mathcal{T}_i$ of appearances of x_i in $\mathcal{R}$ and put

$$\mathcal{T}(\mathcal{R}) = \bigcup_{i=1}^{r} \mathcal{T}_i \qquad /6/$$

Find numbers $n_{\mathcal{R}}(x_i) = |\mathcal{T}_i|$, for $i=1,2,\dots,r$.

Step 2. Generate consecutively the elements of the set $\mathcal{N}(\mathcal{R})=\{\langle n_1,n_2,\dots,n_r\rangle : 1 \leq n_i \leq n_{\mathcal{R}}(x_i)\}$. For every $\langle n_1,n_2,\dots,n_r\rangle \in \mathcal{N}(\mathcal{R})$ find all relations $\gamma \in \Gamma(\mathcal{R})$ such that

$$n_\gamma(x_i) = n_i \ , \text{ for } i=1,2,\dots,r \ . \qquad /7/$$

The set of all relations $\gamma \in \Gamma(\mathcal{R})$ which satisfy /7/ may be obtained using an algorithm for calculating all different partitions of the set of cardinality $n_{\mathcal{R}}(x_i)$ into n_i classes. Such an algorithm was presented in [6]. Combinations of all different partitions of the sets $\mathcal{T}_i$ form the set of all different relations which satisfy /7/.

Step 3. Check the linearity of the obtained extensions $\mathcal{R}(\gamma)$. Then choose the linear extension $\mathcal{R}(\gamma^*)$ which satisfy /5/.

It is easy to see that the number of operations of the Algorithm 1 grows exponentially as $|X|$ and $|\mathcal{R}|$. In the next section we shall make a considerable effort to get large simplify our algorithm.

2. DECOMPOSITION OF THE FAMILY $\mathcal{R}$.

In this section we shall show that using the concept of components /see [9]/ we can make Algorithm 1 dependent only on a number of non-empty components of the family $\mathcal{R}$ but independent of X . Then we shall formulate decomposition theorems which enable us to restrict ourselves to some subfamilies of $\mathcal{R}$. These theorems are based on some ideas of Fulkerson and Gross [2]. Detailed proofs of our theorems may be found in [7]. First we give some auxiliary definitions.

Definition 1. Let $\mathcal{R}=\{R_1,R_2,\dots,R_m\}$ X and let $\eta_1,\eta_2,\dots,\eta_m \in \{0,1\}$. Sets of the form $S_{\mathcal{R}}(\eta_1,\eta_2,\dots,\eta_m) = R_1^{\eta_1} \cap R_2^{\eta_2} \cap \dots \cap R_m^{\eta_m}$, where

$$R^{\eta} = \begin{cases} R & \text{if } \eta = 1 \\ X \setminus R & \text{if } \eta = 0 \end{cases}$$

are called <u>components</u> of the family $\mathcal{R}$.

<u>Definition 2.</u> Let $\mathcal{R} = \{R_1, R_2, \ldots, R_m\} \subseteq \mathcal{P}(X)$. We define for $i=1,2,\ldots,m$

$$Z(R_i) = \{ \langle \eta_1, \eta_2, \ldots, \eta_m \rangle \in \{0,1\}^m : \eta_i = 1 \wedge S_{\mathcal{R}}(\eta_1, \eta_2, \ldots, \eta_m) \neq \emptyset \},$$

$$\mathcal{Z}(\mathcal{R}) = \{ Z(R_i) : i=1,2,\ldots,m \} .$$

<u>Theorem 1.</u> Let $\mathcal{R} = \{R_1, R_2, \ldots, R_m\} \subseteq \mathcal{P}(X)$. For every element $\langle \eta_1, \eta_2, \ldots, \eta_m \rangle \in \bigcup \mathcal{Z}(\mathcal{R})$ we define its length as follows

$$l(\eta_1, \eta_2, \ldots, \eta_m) = \sum_{x \in S_{\mathcal{R}}(\eta_1, \eta_2, \ldots, \eta_m)} l(x) .$$

Then the optimal relation $\gamma^* \in \Gamma(\mathcal{R})$ may be obtained by applying Algorithm 1 to $\mathcal{Z}(\mathcal{R})$. First we find the optimal relation $\gamma_z^* \in \Gamma(\mathcal{Z}(\mathcal{R}))$ and then we obtain the classes of γ^* from classes of γ_z^* replacing every $\langle \langle \eta_1, \eta_2, \ldots, \eta_m \rangle , Z(R_i) \rangle$ by $\{ \langle x, R_i \rangle : x \in S_{\mathcal{R}}(\eta_1, \eta_2, \ldots, \eta_m) \}$. ∎

By Theorem 1 we may restrict ourselves to families with each nonempty component consisting of exactly one element.

<u>Definition 3.</u> Let $\mathcal{R} \subseteq \mathcal{P}(X)$.

/a/ The <u>intersection graph</u> $\mathcal{J}(\mathcal{R})$ is a nondirected graph with $\mathcal{R}$ as the set of vertices, two vertices $R, R' \in \mathcal{R}$ joined by an edge iff $R \cap R' \neq \emptyset$.

/b/ A family $\mathcal{B} \subseteq \mathcal{R}$ is an <u>intersection block</u> of $\mathcal{R}$ if $\mathcal{B}$ is a set of vertices of a component of $\mathcal{J}(\mathcal{R})$.

<u>Theorem 2.</u> Let $\mathcal{R} = \mathcal{B}_1 \cup \mathcal{B}_2 \cup \ldots \cup \mathcal{B}_k$ be a decomposition of $\mathcal{R}$ into intersection blocks. Then the optimal relation $\gamma^* \in \Gamma(\mathcal{R})$ may be obtained as the union

$$\gamma^* = \gamma_1^* \cup \gamma_2^* \cup \ldots \cup \gamma_k^* ,$$

where $\gamma_i^* \in \Gamma(\mathcal{B}_i)$ is the optimal relation for the family $\mathcal{B}_i$, $i=1,2,\ldots,k$.

From Theorem 2 it follows immediately that without loss of generality we may assume that $\mathcal{R}$ consist of only one intersection block.

<u>Definition 4.</u> Let $\mathcal{R} \subseteq \mathcal{P}(X)$.

/a/ The <u>overlap graph</u> $\mathcal{O}(\mathcal{R})$ is a nondirected graph with $\mathcal{R}$ as the set of vertices, two vertices $R, R' \in \mathcal{R}$ joined by an edge iff $R \cap R' \neq \emptyset$ $R \setminus R' \neq \emptyset$ $R' \setminus R \neq \emptyset$.

/b/ A family $\mathcal{W} \subseteq \mathcal{R}$ is an <u>overlap block</u> of $\mathcal{R}$ if $\mathcal{W}$ is a set of vertices of a component of $\mathcal{O}(\mathcal{R})$.

/c/ We define a partial ordering $\leqslant$ on the set of blocks of as follows

$$\mathcal{W}_1 \leqslant \mathcal{W}_2 \Longleftrightarrow (\exists R_1 \in \mathcal{W}_1)\ (\exists R_2 \in \mathcal{W}_2)\ R_1 \subseteq R_2 \ .$$

/d/ A block $\mathcal{W}$ of $\mathcal{R}$ is <u>minimal</u> if it is a minimal element in the ordering $\leqslant$.

Let there be given a decomposition of $\mathcal{R}$ into overlap blocks. Let $\mathcal{W}$ be the minimal overlap block of $\mathcal{R}$ and let $\mathcal{W}$ be linear. Let $\gamma^{*\prime} \in \Gamma(\mathcal{R}')$, where $\mathcal{R}' = \mathcal{R} \setminus \mathcal{W}$, be the optimal relation for the family $\mathcal{R}'$. We modify the relation $\gamma^{*\prime}$ as follows.

<u>Algorithm 2.</u>

We find some $R \in \mathcal{R}'$ such that $\bigcup \mathcal{W} \subseteq R$ and then for every $x \in \bigcup \mathcal{W}$ we find a class $P \in \mathcal{J}(\mathcal{R}')/_{\gamma^{*\prime}}$ such that $\langle x,R \rangle \in P$ and change P into $P \cup \{\langle x,R' \rangle : R' \in \mathcal{W}\}$.

This procedure results in a relation γ^* such that $\gamma^{*\prime} \subseteq \gamma^*$.

<u>Theorem 3.</u> $\gamma^* \in \Gamma(\mathcal{R})$, and if $\gamma^{*\prime}$ is optimal for $\mathcal{R}'$ then γ^* is optimal for $\mathcal{R}$.

By Theorem 3 the optimal relation γ^* for $\mathcal{R}$ may be obtained by the following procedure.

<u>Algorithm 3.</u>

First we find a family $\mathcal{R}'' \subseteq \mathcal{R}$ in the following way:

<u>Step 1.</u> We decompose $\mathcal{R}$ into overlap blocks.

<u>Step 2.</u> If $\mathcal{W}$ is a linear minimal block of $\mathcal{R}$ then we put $\mathcal{R}' = \mathcal{R} \setminus \mathcal{W}$.

<u>Step 3.</u> We continue Step 2 for fhe family $\mathcal{R}'$. We obtain the family $\mathcal{R}''$ all minimal blocks of which are nonlinear.

Then we determine the optimal relation $\gamma^{*\prime\prime}$ for $\mathcal{R}''$. The relation γ^* may be easily obtained from $\gamma^{*\prime\prime}$ by applying Algorithm 2.

The above results somewhat simplify the problem of determining the optimal extension of a given family of sets. However, in the case when, in spite of applying the decomposition theorems, we obtain families of large cardinality, the problem is still very complicated /cf.[8]/.

3. SUBOPTIMAL ALGORITHMS

In practice we often deal with a situation in which a family of sets to be stored in a computer memory is a very large one. In a such case it is imposible to determine the optimal extension of the family because of a very long time of computation. What we can do then is to decompose the family into subfamilies and store each of them separately. We shall define a class of such decomposition algorithms.

Let $\mathfrak{R} = \{R_1, R_2, \dots, R_m\} \subseteq \mathcal{P}(X)$ where m= k • n . Decomposition $\mathfrak{R} = \mathfrak{R}_1 \cup \mathfrak{R}_2 \cup \dots \cup \mathfrak{R}_n$ is of <u>order k</u> if for every i= 1,2,...,n $|\mathfrak{R}_i| = k$. The best decomposition of order k is the one maximizing the coefficient

$$r = \frac{\sum_{i=1}^{m} (l_i - l_{\gamma_i^*})}{l_o} \quad \text{, where}$$

$$l_i = \sum_{x \in \bigcup \mathfrak{R}_i} n_{\mathfrak{R}_i}(x) \cdot l(x) \quad \text{, for } i = 1,2,\dots,m \text{ ,}$$

$$l_o = \sum_{x \in X} n(x) \cdot l(x) \text{ ,}$$

$$l_{\gamma_i^*} = \sum_{x \in \bigcup \mathfrak{R}_i} n_{\mathfrak{R}_i}(x) \cdot l(x) \text{, for } i = 1,2,\dots,m$$ / γ_i^* is the optimal relation for $\mathfrak{R}_i$/.

Below we present a simple decomposition algorithm which, in general, produces suboptimal decomposition of order k of the family $\mathfrak{R}$. For k=2 an algorithm of this kind was presented in [11] .

<u>Algorithm 4.</u>

<u>Step 1.</u> Find a family $\mathfrak{R}_1 \subseteq \mathfrak{R}$ such that $|\mathfrak{R}_1| = k$ and it has the greatest coefficient $(l_1 - l_{\gamma_1^*})$ among all subfamilies of $\mathfrak{R}$ of cardinality k. Then find a family $\mathfrak{R}_2 \subseteq \mathfrak{R} \setminus \mathfrak{R}_1$ with the greatest coefficient $(l_2 - l_{\gamma_2^*})$ and continue this process until you obtain the decomposition $\mathfrak{R} = \mathfrak{R}_1 \cup \mathfrak{R}_2 \cup \dots \cup \mathfrak{R}_n$.

<u>Step 2.</u> Find the optimal extensions of the families $\mathfrak{R}_i$, i = 1,2,...,n.

CONCLUSIONS

The paper presents a method of a very efficient /in the sense of the access time/ organization of a computer memory. However, if we achieve better time parameters of a system, we have to pay for it by a greater redundancy in storage space. Moreover, a minimization of the redundancy is computionally very hard. We give some methods of decompositing the problem and then we define a class of suboptimal algorithms. These algorithms were tested on Elliott 905 computer for k=2,3 /see[7]/.

ACKNOWLEDGEMENTS

The author wish to thank Dr W. lipski from Polish Academy of Science for his remarkable discussion and suggestions in the paper.

REFERENCES

[1] Ehrich H.D., Lipski W. On the storage space requirement of consecutive retrieval with redundancy. Inf. Proc. Lett. 4, 1976, 101-104.

[2] Fulkerson D.S., Gross O.A. Incidence matrices and interval graphs. Pacif. Jour. Math. 15,1965, 835-855.

[3] Ghosh S.P. File organization. The consecutive retrieval property. Comm. ACM 15, 1972, 802-808.

[4] Ghosh S.P. On the theory of consecutive storage of relevant records. Inform. Sci. 6, 1973, 1-9.

[5] Ghosh S.P. Consecutive storage of relevant records with redundancy. Comm. ACM 18, 1975, 464-471.

[6] Górski J. An effective algorithm for finding partitions of a given set. To appear.

[7] Górski J. Memory organization for effective information retrieval. Doctoral thesis, CC PAS, 1976, Warsaw. In Polish.

[8] Kou L.T. Polynomial complete consecutive information retrieval problems. Technical Report TR74-193, Dept. of Comp. Sci.,Cornell University, Ithaca, NY, 1974.

[9] Kuratowski K., Mostowski A. Set Theory. North Holland, Amsterdam, 1967.

[10] Lipski W. Combinatorial aspects of information storage and retrieval. Proc. MFCS 74, Springer-Verlag, Berlin-Heidelberg-New York 1975, 270-279.

[11] Lipski W., Marek W. File organization, an application of graph theory. Proc. Collq. Automata, Languages and Progr., Saarbrücken, 1974, 270-279.

A REMARK ON EQUIVALENCE OF MAZURKIEWICZ'S FINITE - CONTROL ALGORITHMS OVER NETS

M. Grabowski
Warsaw Uniwersity

Introduction

The notion of a net introduced by A. Blikle in [2] is connected with the fixed-point approach to the theory of programs. /cf [2],[3]/

Definition 1 By a net we mean an ordered algebra $(S;\leqslant,\circ,0,e)$ such that

1^0 $(S;\leqslant)$ is a complete lattice with 0 as the least element

2^0 $(S;\circ,e,0)$ is a monoid with zero 0 and unit e and $\circ$ is the composition operation

3^0 The operation of composition $\circ$ is continuous, i.e. for every directed set $D\subseteq S$ and every element $a\in S$
$a\circ \cup D = \cup\{a\circ d \mid d\in D\}$ and $(\cup D)\circ a = \{d\circ a \mid d\in D\}$

4^0 The operation of composition $\circ$ is additive, i.e. for every $a,b,c\in S$ $a\circ(b\cup c) = a\circ b\cup a\circ c$ and $(b\cup c)\circ a = b\circ a\cup c\circ a$

Basic examples

1. Powerset net. Let $(P;\circ,e,0)$ be a monoid with unit e and zero 0. Now, let P(P) be the family of all nonempty subsets of the semigroup P; $(P(P);\subseteq,\circ,\{e\},\{0\})$ where $A_1\circ A_2 = \{a_1\circ a_2 \mid a_1\in A_1 \wedge a_2\in A_2\}$, is called the powerset net.

2. Net of languages. Let $(\Sigma^*;{}^\frown,\varepsilon,0)$ be a free semigroup over Σ with zero 0 and unit ε. By a net of languages $Lan(\Sigma)$ over the alphabet Σ we mean the powerset net $P(\Sigma^*)$.

3. Binary relations net. By a binary relations net over a set Ω we mean the algebra $(2^{\Omega\times\Omega};\subseteq,\circ,id,\emptyset)$ of all binary relations in the set Ω; $\circ$ is composition of relations.

I. Some algebraic properties of nets.

Definition 2 Let S_1,S_2 be the nets. A mapping $h:S_1\to S_2$ is said to be a homomorphism iff $h(0_{s1}) = 0_{s2}$, $h(e_{s1}) = e_{s2}$ and h preserves the composition and the least upper bounds.

<u>Th1</u>. There does not exist a net S and a set $X \subseteq S$ such that for every net S_1, every mapping $f: X \to S_1$ can be extended to a homomorphism $h_f: S \to S_1$ preserving the greatest lower bounds of finite sets.

We obtain the theorem1 as a direct corollary from the relevant theorem about non-existance of free complete lattices.

<u>Th2</u>. /Amalgamation property/ For every net N and every family of homomorphisms $\beta_i: N \to S_i$, $i \in I$, there exists a net S and a family of homomorphisms $\alpha_i: S_i \to S$ such that for every net S_1 and for every family of homomorphisms $h_i: S_i \to S_1$, $i \in I$, there exists exactly one homomorphism ξ such that the following diagram commutes

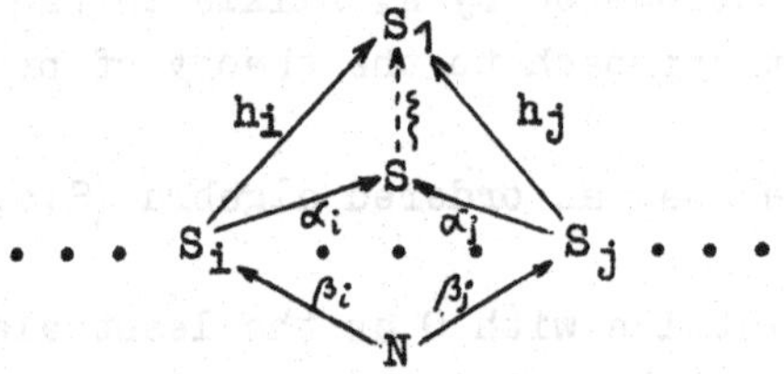

We obtain the proof of the theorem 2 by applying the standard algebraic technique.

Now we shall formulate the theorems needed in the next part of our paper.

Let S be a net and $a \in S$. By a^* we mean the least fixed-point of $\lambda x. a \cdot x \cup e$ /i.e. $\bigcup_{i \in \omega} a^i$/.

Let X be a nonempty set of variables.

The set of <u>regular expressions</u> over X it is the least set Reg such that

1° $X \subseteq Reg$, $0 \in Reg$, $e \in Reg$

2° if $R_1, R_2 \in Reg$, then $(R_1 \cdot R_2)$, $(R_1 \cup R_2)$, $R_1^* \in Reg$

We shall denote regular expressions by $R_1, R_2, \ldots$

By a <u>word-tem</u> we mean any regular expression R such that the symbols $\cup, {}^*$ do not appear in R.

By a equality over X we mean any atomic formula of the form $R_1 = R_2$ where R_1, R_2 are regular expressions over X. We omit the obvious definitions of satisfability and validity of equalities in nets.

We assume that every considered set of equalities contains the axioms of semigroups with zero and unit.

Let T be a finite set of equalities over X /X is considered to be finite/ such that if $t_1=t_2 \in T$, then t_1, t_2 are word-terms.

Let $X \subseteq \Sigma$ and let Σ^*/T be the quotient semigroup modulo congruence $\approx_T$ in Σ^* generated by equalities from T. The symbol $\|w\|_T$ denotes the equivalence class of element $w \in \Sigma^*$.

Example

Let $X = \{x_1, \dots, x_n\}$, $Y = \{y_1, \dots, y_m\}$, $X \cap Y = \emptyset$ and $T_{\|} = \{x_1 \circ y_1 = y_1 \circ x_1, \dots, x_i \circ y_j = y_j \circ x_i, \dots, x_n \circ y_m = y_m \circ x_n\}$.
The semigroup $(X \cup Y)^*/T$ is isomorphic to the semigroup $(X^* X \times Y^* Y; \circ, e, 0)$ where $\langle x,y\rangle \circ \langle x',y'\rangle \overset{df}{=} \langle x^\frown x', y^\frown y\rangle$, $\langle 0,y\rangle = \langle x,0\rangle = 0$, $e = \langle \varepsilon_{X^*}, \varepsilon_{Y^*}\rangle$

The net $P((X \cup Y)^*/T_{\|})$ is called paralel product of nets Lan(X), Lan(Y) and is denoted by the symbol Lan X $\|$ Lan Y . /It is possible to generalize the notion of paralel product to arbitrary nets/.

Likewise as in universal algebra, we can prove the following:

Th3. Let $\bigwedge_{t_1=t_2 \in T} t_1=t_2$ denote the coniunction of all formulas from T.

A formula of the form:

$$\bigwedge_{t_1=t_2 \in T} t_1=t_2 \Rightarrow R_1=R_2 \qquad /1/$$

is valid in every net iff the equality $R_1=R_2$ is satisfied in the net $P(\Sigma^*/T)$ by the valuation $v: x \to \{\|x\|_T\}$, $x \in X$.

It can be proved that the following theorem holds:

Th4. A formula of the form /1/ is valid in every net iff it is valid in every net of binary relations.

II. Equivalence of algorithms with actions fulfilling equational conditions.

By a finite-control algorithm A over a net S we mean a system $A = (V, \alpha_1, \varepsilon, \mathbb{P})$ where

$V = \{\alpha_1, \dots, \alpha_n\}$ is a finite set of labels,

$\alpha_1 \in V$ and α_1 is called the initial label,

$\varepsilon \in V^*$ is the empty word /plays the role of stop- label/,

$\mathbb{P}$ is a finite set of triples /called instructions/ (α, a, β) where $a \in S$, $\alpha \in V$, $\beta \in V \cup \{\varepsilon\}$. The element a is called action of algorithm.

Any sequence /finite or infinite/ of instructions

$$(\alpha_1, a_1, \alpha_{i_2}), (\alpha_{i_2}, a_2, \alpha_{i_3}), \dots, (\alpha_{i_m}, a_m, \alpha_{i_{m+1}}), \qquad m \leq \infty$$

is said to be a computation; a computation is finite iff $\alpha_{i_{m+1}} = \varepsilon$.

The sequence of actions $(a_1,a_2,\dots,a_m)$/for $m<\infty$/ is called a <u>trace</u> of A. The set of all traces of A is denoted by Tr(A).

We define the resulting element of A, ResA:

$$\mathrm{ResA} \overset{\mathrm{df}}{=} \bigcup_{a_1,\dots,a_m \in \mathrm{Tr}\,A} a_1 \circ a_2 \dots \circ a_m$$

/examples in Blikle [3]/.

Because of the well-known connection between finite-control algorithms and regular expressions we are interested in partial solvability of the set E of all valid sentences of the form considered in the theorem 3. We shall prove that the set E is not partially solvable. This result is the simple corollary from the essential Griffith's result on ε-free nondeterministic generalized machines /cf. Griffith[4]/.

Let X,Y be finite, disioint, at least two-elements alphabets; $X^+=X^*X$, $Y^+=Y^*Y$; let $P_{fin}(Y^+)$ be the family of all finite subsets of the set Y^+.

<u>Definition 3</u> A triple $(A,M,\bar{a})$ is said to be an <u>ε-free nondetemi-nistic generalized machine</u> /in abbreviation εngm/ over (X,Y) iff

1^0 A is a finite set /of states/,

2^0 M is a function from $A\times X\times A$ into $P_{fin}(Y^+)$,

3^0 $\bar{a}\in A$ /initial state/.

The function M can be extended to $A\times X^+\times A$ as follows: for $w\in X^+$, $x\in X$

$$M(p,w^\frown x,q) = \bigcup_{a\in A} M(p,w,a)^\frown M(a,x,q).$$

<u>A function M_T defined by a machine T</u> is the function from X^+ into $P_{fin}(Y^+)$

$$M_T\, w \overset{\mathrm{df}}{=} \bigcup_{a\in A} M(\bar{a},w,a)$$

Machines T_1,T_2 are <u>equivalent</u> iff $M_{T_1}=M_{T_2}$

<u>Th5</u>. The set E is not partially solvable.

Outline of proof.

Without loss of generality we can assume that for every $a_1,a_2\in A$, $x\in X$, the set $M(a_1,x,a_2)$ has at most one element.

To every εngm T we construct an algorithm A_T over Lan X ‖ Lan Y : the set A of states of T is the set of labels of A_T. Instructions are defined as follows: for $x\in X, a_1,a_2\in A$ if $M(a_1,x,a_2)=z\in Y^+$, then $(a_1,\{\langle x,z\rangle\},a_2)$, $(a_1,\{\langle x,z\rangle\},\varepsilon)$ are instructions of A_T; a is the initial label.

Next we prove that εngm T_1,T_2 are equivalent iff $ResA_{T_1}=ResA_{T_2}$. Hence, with regard to the connection between algorithms and regular expressions and to the theorem 3, the equivalance of T_1,T_2 can be reduced to the validity of the sentence of the following form:

$$x_1 \circ y_1 = y_1 \circ x_1 \wedge \ldots \wedge x_n \circ y_m = y_m \circ x_n \Rightarrow R_1 = R_2$$

where R_1,R_2 are appropriate regular expressions over $X \cup Y$.
Hence, it suffices to prove that the equivalence, Eqv, of εngm is not partially solvable. Let us suppose the contrary ($Eqv \in \Sigma_1^0$).
We define the predicate $K(.,.,.)$

$K(n,m,k)$ iff for a machine T_n of a Gödel number n and for a word z_m of a number m and for a finite set $Y_k \subseteq P_{fin}(Y^+)$ of a number k, $M_{T_n}(z_m)=Y_k$

The predicate K is decidable, so $Eqv \in \Pi_1^0$ - this contradicts the Griffith's result that $Eqv \notin \Sigma_0^0$

q.e.d

Theorems 4 and 5 imply the follwing

Corollary

The set of all valid assertions of the de Bakker-de Roever calculus which corespond to formulas of the form /1/ in the theorem 3 is not partially solvable.

We inform that the presentation of complete proofs treated here in the cursory way and the results of further investigations of Blikle's nets are prepared for a publication in Fundamenta Informaticae.

ACKNOWLEDGMENTS

I wish to thank dr A. Blikle for many stimulating remarks concerning the subject of the paper. I also wish to thank dr W. Rytter for turning my attention on Griffith's paper 4 .

REFERENCES

[1] de Bakker I.W. and de Roever W.P., A calculus for recursive program schemes, Proc.IRIA Symp. on Automata Formal Languages and Programming 1972, North-Holland, Amsterdam

[2] Blikle A.,Nets; complete lattices with a composition, Bull. Acad.Polon. Sci.,Sér.Sci.Math.Astr.Phys.19,859-863,1971

[3] Blikle A., An extended approach to mathematical analysis of programs, CC PAS Reports 169,1974

[4] Griffith T.V., The unsolvability of the equivalence problem for Λ-free nondeterministic generalized machines, Journal of ACM, vol15, No3,pp.409-413.

MICROPROGRAM - ORIENTED MODEL OF THE CONTROLLED STRUCTURE

I. Hansen
Institute of Computer Science, Warsaw Technical University
ul. Nowowiejska 15/19, 00-665 Warszawa, Poland

J. Leszczyłowski
Computation Centre, Polish Academy of Sciences
PKiN, P.O. Box 22, 00-901 Warszawa, Poland

1. STRUCTURE CONTEXT IN MICROPROGRAM ANALYSIS

The purpose of this paper is to introduce a certain approach to the formal analysis of microprograms. The specific character of this approach is determined by the fact that the structure, controlled by the microprogram analyzed, is taken under consideration and all occurences, taking place in microprograms, are studied in the context of this structure. It must be said, that in order to obtain a demonstrative and clear presentation some simplifications and shortcuts were made.

The controlled structure is understood as a set of somehow interconnected digital blocks. Each block is described by the set of operations it can perform and for every block not more than one of these operations can be activated at a certain moment. There are two types of operations. For the asynchronous type, block input signals values influence output signal value instantly and in a continous manner. A synchronous operation can change the output signal value only after a special clock signal. The structure operates in steps, specified by microprogram instructions. Each step consists of two phases. During the asynchronous phase the structure ought to achieve a certain steady state and the synchronous one ends the step. All component blocks of the structure operate simultaneously. Thus, the final effect of a one-step operation /microinstruction/ cannot be calculated instantly, and checking, if a microinstruction works as it was designed to, is not a trite problem.

For a given structure, some operations may appear impossible to carry out. In this case, microprogram analysis ought to give some hints how to redesign this structure. A microprogram can be minimized by simplifying individual microinstructions. This means designing microinstructions which perform the same effective operation but activate fewer component blocks. The length of a microprogram can be reduced by minimizing its flow-chart. This can be done, for example, by introducing one microinstruction instead of two, consecutive ones. The above operations can be done on certain conditions concerning the structure component blocks, activated by the microinstructions being considered.

The presented model makes it possible to apply the microprogram verification method proposed in [1], and the ideas introduced in this paper are developed in [2].

2. ABSTRACT MODEL OF THE CONTROLLED STRUCTURE

Let $\mathbb{D}$ be an arbitrary vector of sets. For every $1 \leqslant i \leqslant l(\mathbb{D})$ i represents /one-to-one/ a certain block, a component of the structure and $\mathbb{D}_i$ is the domain of values which may appear in the block represented by i /for every vector x , $l(x)$ denotes the number of coordinates of x/. $\mathbb{D}$ is called the <u>structure states domain</u> and is fixed for this paper.

Further n will denote a natural number, f - a function and m - a vector of natural numbers. Objects of the form:

1° $(0,n,f,m)$

will be used to describe an asynchronous activity and objects of the form:

2° $(1,n,f,m)$

a synchronous activity of the block represented by n , performing the operation f on the values in blocks represented by $m_1, m_2, \dots, m_{l(m)}$.
Precisely, every object of the type 1° or 2° is an <u>elementary microoperation</u> over $\mathbb{D}$ iff it satisfies the following conditions:

- $1 \leqslant n \leqslant l(\mathbb{D})$
- $m \in \{1,2,\dots,l(\mathbb{D})\}^*$
- $l(m)$ equals the arity of f
- for $m \neq \mathcal{E}$, $\mathbb{D}_{m_1} \times \mathbb{D}_{m_2} \times \dots \times \mathbb{D}_{m_{l(m)}} \subseteq \text{Domain}(f)$ /$\mathcal{E}$ denotes the empty vector/
- $\text{Range}(f) \in \mathbb{D}_n$

and for the objects of the type 1° moreover:

- $(\forall 1 \leqslant i \leqslant l(m))[m_i \neq n]$.

Similarly, objects of the form:

3° (f,m)

are used for checking whether certain conditions, concerning the controlled structure are satisfied. Precisely, every object of the form 3° which satisfies:

- $m \in \{1,2,\dots,l(\mathbb{D})\}^+ \& (\forall 1 \leqslant i,j \leqslant l(m))[i < j \Rightarrow m_i < m_j]$
- $\mathbb{D}_{m_1} \times \mathbb{D}_{m_2} \times \dots \times \mathbb{D}_{m_{l(m)}} \subseteq \text{Domain}(f)$ (*)
- $\text{Range}(f) = \{0,1\}$

is an <u>elementary condition</u> over the structure states domain $\mathbb{D}$.

Every system of the form:

$$\mathbb{S} = (\mathbb{D},\mathbb{F},\mathbb{C})$$

where $\mathbb{D}$ is the structure states domain, $\mathbb{F}$ and $\mathbb{C}$ are arbitrary sets of elementary microoperations and conditions over $\mathbb{D}$, respectively, is called a structure over $\mathbb{D}$. $\mathbb{S}$ describes all possible values that can appear in the particular blocks and all possible operations, performed by these blocks, including blocks that represent the input signals to the structure. It also determines the possibilities of testing the states of the structure.

A subset F of the set $\mathbb{F}$ is called an action of the structure $\mathbb{S} = (\mathbb{D},\mathbb{F},\mathbb{C})$ if for every $1 \leqslant i \leqslant l(\mathbb{D})$ it contains not more than one elementary microoperation describing the activity of i.

An asynchronous action of F is a set $\underline{F} = \{(0,n,f,m) \in F\}$ and a synchronous action of F a set: $\overline{F} = F - \underline{F}$. They represent asynchronous and synchronous operations in F, respectively.

An elementary stage of the asynchronous phase of structure work under F is described by a function $[\underline{F}]: \mathbb{D} \xrightarrow[\text{total}]{} \mathbb{D}$ which is defined as follows:
for every $x,y \in \mathbb{D}$

$[\underline{F}](x) = y \iff \forall 1 \leqslant i \leqslant l(\mathbb{D})$
- if for every $(0,n,f,m) \in \underline{F}$, $n \neq i$ then $y_i = x_i$
- if $(0,i,f,m) \in F$ then $y_i = f(x_{m_1}, x_{m_2}, \ldots, x_{m_{l(m)}})$.

A function $[\overline{F}]$ analogically defined describes the synchronous phase of structure work under F.

Only so called "proper" actions are of practical importance as they contain no loops consisting of asynchronous elementary microoperations. This can be expressed using the following auxiliary notion:
sequence a is called an elementary microoperations sequence in action F iff
- $(\forall a_i)[a_i \in \underline{F}]$
- $(\forall i > 1)[a_{i-1} = (0,n,f,m) \,\&\, a_i = (0,n',f',m') \Rightarrow (\exists 1 \leqslant j \leqslant l(m))(n' = m_j)]$.

An action F of the structure $\mathbb{S} = (\mathbb{D},\mathbb{F},\mathbb{C})$ is proper iff every elementary microoperations sequence in F is finite. The maximum length of sequences in F is denoted by $d(F)$. For every proper action the structure achieves a steady state during the asynchronous phase of its work. This can be illustrated by the following feature of a proper action F:
for every natural number i, $[\underline{F}]^{d(F)} = [\underline{F}]^{d(F)+i}$.
Thus, for any initial state of the structure $d \in \mathbb{D}$, $[\underline{F}]^{d(F)}(d)$ describes the steady state of the structure after the asynchronous phase of work under F, and
$P_F = [\underline{F}]^{d(F)}[\overline{F}]$ - the effective operation performed by the structure under the proper action F.

3. MICROPROGRAMS IN A STRUCTURE

A certain physical structure determines all possible operational parts of microinstructions that can control the structure as well as the conditions that can be used in microprogram sequencing. "All possible conditions" refers to the closure of the set of elementary conditions according to Boolean operators. For an abstract structure $\mathbf{S} = (\mathbb{D},\mathbb{F},\mathbb{C})$ the the possible microinstruction operations are represented by all proper actions of $\mathbf{S}$ and the set of possible conditions by the set $\mathrm{Cond}(\mathbf{S})$, defined below. $\mathrm{Cond}(\mathbf{S})$ is the least set including the set $\mathbb{C}$ and closed according to operators: $\neg$, $\sqcup$ defined as follows:

for every $(f',m'), (f'',m'') \in \mathrm{Cond}(\mathbf{S})$:

- $\neg(f',m') = (g,m')$ where $(\forall d \in \mathbb{D})(g(d_{m'_1},d_{m'_2},\ldots,d_{m'_{l(m')}}) = 1 - f(d_{m'_1},d_{m'_2},\ldots,d_{m'_{l(m')}}))$
- $(f',m') \sqcup (f'',m'') = (f,m)$ where
  1. $\{m_1,m_2,\ldots,m_{l(m)}\} = \{m'_1,m'_2,\ldots,m'_{l(m')}\} \cup \{m''_1,m''_2,\ldots,m''_{l(m'')}\}$
  2. f and m satisfy conditions (*) /page 2/
  3. $(\forall d \in \mathbb{D})[f(d_{m_1},d_{m_2},\ldots,d_{m_{l(m)}}) = 1 \iff f'(d_{m'_1},d_{m'_2},\ldots,d_{m'_{l(m')}}) = 1 \vee \vee f''(d_{m''_1},d_{m''_2},\ldots,d_{m''_{l(m'')}}) = 1]$

Operators, corresponding to other Boolean functors / $\oplus$, $\wedge$, $\Rightarrow$,etc./, analogically defined, can be expressed by means of $\neg$ and $\sqcup$.

For every $c = (f,m)$ in $\mathrm{Cond}(\mathbf{S})$ and for every $d \in \mathbb{D}$, $c(d)$ denotes $f(d_{m_1},d_{m_2},\ldots,d_{m_{l(m)}})$.

Let L be an arbitrary set /fixed for this paper/ representing all possible labels in a microprogram. An abstract <u>microinstruction</u> over $\mathbf{S}$ is defined as a system of the form:

$$(l,F,c_1,l_1,c_2,l_2,\ldots,c_k,l_k)$$

where

- $l,l_1,l_2,\ldots,l_k \in L$ and for any $1 \leqslant i,j \leqslant k$, if $i \neq j$ then $l_i \neq l_j$
- F is an action of $\mathbf{S}$
- $c_1,c_2,\ldots,c_k \in \mathrm{Cond}(\mathbf{S})$.

l is an <u>entry label</u> of the microinstruction and l_i - an <u>exit label</u> indicating the microinstruction to be activated after the given one if condition c_i is satisfied /$1 \leqslant i \leqslant k$/. Such a system represents any microinstruction that can be applied to the structure $\mathbf{S}$ apart from its practical sense. However, microprograms will be built using <u>proper microinstructions</u> over $\mathbf{S} = (\mathbb{D},\mathbb{F},\mathbb{C})$ i.e. microinstructions of the form: $(l,F,c_1,l_1,c_2,l_2,\ldots,c_k,l_k)$ which satisfy the following conditions:

- F is a proper action of $\mathbf{S}$
- $(\forall d \in \mathbb{D})(\exists i!)[c_i(d) = 1]$.

Every object of the form:

$$M = (A,W)$$

is an abstract microprogram in the structure $\mathbb{S}$ iff

- $A \subseteq L$
- W is an arbitrary set of proper microinstructions over $\mathbb{S}$
- for every $w_1, w_2 \in W$ if $w_1 \neq w_2$ then the entry label of w_1 is different from the entry label of w_2 .

A is a set of entry labels of M .

4. MICROPROGRAM BEHAVIOUR

For every microprogram $M = (A,W)$ in the structure $\mathbb{S} = (\mathbb{D},\mathbb{F},\mathbb{C})$, a function: $\mathbb{B}_M : L \times \mathbb{D} \xrightarrow[\text{part.}]{} L \times \mathbb{D}$ describing one-step behaviour of M is defined as follows:

for every $a,b \in L$ and for every $e,f \in \mathbb{D}$

$\mathbb{B}_M(a,e) = (b,f)$ iff there exist $(a,F,c_1,l_1,c_2,l_2,\ldots,c_k,l_k) \in W$ and $1 \leqslant j \leqslant k$

$$\text{such that: } P_F(e) = f \text{ , } c_j([\underline{F}]^{d(F)}(e)) = 1 \text{ and } l_j = b \text{ .}$$

l is an exit label of M $/l \in L_{ex}(M)/$ iff l is an exit label of some microinstruction in W and is not an entry label of any microinstruction in W .

Resulting relation of M : $Res_M = \mathbb{B}_M^{*} \cap ((A \times \mathbb{D}) \times (L_{ex}(M) \times \mathbb{D}))$ describes the effective, input-output behaviour of M . It can be proved that Res_M is a function.

Let $M = (A,W)$ be an arbitrary microprogram and $W' \subseteq W$. l is an entry label of W' in M $/l \in L_{en}(W',M)/$ iff

- l is an entry label of some $w \in W'$
- $l \in A$ or l is an exit label of some $w' \in W - W'$.

Assume that microprograms M' and M'' differ on a certain subset of their microinstructions sets. The following theorem states the conditions for $Res_{M'} = Res_{M''}$.

Theorem 1

For every structure $\mathbb{S}$ and for every two microprograms $M' = (A,W')$ and $M'' = (A,W'')$ in $\mathbb{S}$

if

$Res_{(L_{en}(W'-W'',M'),W'-W'')} = Res_{(L_{en}(W''-W',M''),W''-W')}$

then

$Res_{M'} = Res_{M''}$.

5. MICROPROGRAM TRANSFORMATIONS

This section presents two examples of microprogram transformations which preserve its resulting relation. First, some auxiliary notions will be introduced.

Let $\mathbb{S}$ be an arbitrary structure. For every action F of $\mathbb{S}$:

- $a(F) = \{x \mid (\exists\, b,f,m)[(b,x,f,m) \in F]\}$
- $\xrightarrow[F]{}$ denotes relation in $a(F)$, defined as follows:
  for every $n,n' \in a(F)$

$n \xrightarrow[F]{} n'$ iff there exist such $(b,n,f,m),(b',n',f',m') \in F$ that

1. $n \in \{m'_1, m'_2, \ldots, m'_{1(m')}\} \cap a(\underline{F})$ or
2. $n' \in \{m_1, m_2, \ldots, m_{1(m)}\} \cap a(\overline{F})$

- $\xrightarrow[F]{}$ denotes relation in $2^{a(F)}$ defined as follows:

for every $A,B \subseteq a(F)$

$$A \xrightarrow[F]{} B \iff (\forall x \in A)(\forall y \in B)[\neg(y \xrightarrow[F]{} x)] \quad .$$

One of the possible microprogram transformations is putting one microinstruction instead of two, consecutive ones.

Theorem 2 Let S be an arbitrary structure.
For every microprogram: $M = (\{1\},\{(1,F_1,e),(e,F_2,c_1,l_1,c_2,l_2,\ldots,c_k,l_k)\})$ in S, if

1° $F_1 \cup F_2$ is an action

2° $a(F_1) \xrightarrow[F_1 \cup F_2]{} a(F_2)$

3° $a(\overline{F}_1) \cap \{n \mid (\exists i,j,f,m)[c_i = (f,m) \,\&\, m_j = n]\} = \Phi$

then

$M' = (\{1\},\{(1,F_1 \cup F_2,c_1,l_1,c_2,l_2,\ldots,c_k,l_k)\})$ is a microprogram in S and

$Res_M = Res_{M'}$.

The above theorem describes one of the possible microprogram transformations. Even though it concerns microprograms of a specific kind, according to the theorem 1 it can be applied to any microprogram containing two microinstructions which are to be joined. It can be also used when splitting microinstruction into smaller consecutive ones. This can be expressed with the help of the following:

Theorem 3
For every microprogram $M = (\{1\},\{(1,F,c_1,l_1,c_2,l_2,\ldots,c_k,l_k)\})$ in a structure S ,
every $A \subseteq a(F)$ such that $a(\overline{F}) \cap \{n \mid (\exists i,j,f,m)[c_i = (f,m) \,\&\, m_j = n]\} \subseteq A$
and $a(F) - A \xrightarrow[F]{} A$
and for every $e \notin \{1,l_1,l_2,\ldots,l_k\}$

$Res_M = Res_{M'}$

where

$M' = (\{1\},\{(1,F|(a(F) - A),e),(e,F|A,c_1,l_1,c_2,l_2,\ldots,c_k,l_k)\})$ is the microprogram in S and $F|A$ denotes the subset of F such that $a(F|A) = A$.

Similarly according to the theorem 1 the theorem 3 can be applied to some more complicated microprogram which contains the microinstruction to be split.

6. BIBLIOGRAPHY

[1]. A.Blikle, S.Budkowski A general program - verification method applied to microprograms, Proceedings of International Symposium on Fault-Tolerance Computing Pittsburg, Pa., June 21 - 23, 1976

[2]. I.Hansen, J.Leszczyłowski Structure-context approach to microprogram analysis I Computation Centre Polish Academy of Sciences Reports, 1976

RELATIONS BETWEEN PROGRAMS WITH DIFFERENT STORAGE REQUIREMENTS

M. D. HARRISON
OXFORD UNIVERSITY COMPUTING LABORATORY
PROGRAMMING RESEARCH GROUP
45 Banbury Road, Oxford, OX2 6PE, England.

1. Introduction

Milne and Strachey [1] have considered "similarity" between programs in terms of "standard" denotational semantics [2]. In this article we introduce their framework for expressing "similarity" relationships and then consider a class of situations where the ideas of [1] are not adequate. An alternative relation is required which involves the adoption of a new equivalent semantic description.

It may be said that two programs are similar if the effect of elaborating the two programs from the same initial state (input information, store and environment) is to give identical answers (i.e. the two programs demonstrate the same I/O behaviour). An example is expressible in terms of "standard" semantics. Similarity between two programs in a given language may exist when the standard semantic denotations of the two programs are functionally equivalent.

We are concerned with the replaceability of commands or expressions and wish to know when, given any admissible program context, the replacement of an expression or command by a "similar" expression or command gives the same answer on execution as would the original program. In particular we are interested in when we can prove that information stored in different but equivalent ways, can be used equivalently in a class of circumstances. For example, it may be necessary to prove that two programs which do the same thing with different representations of the same data structure are similar. The work described in [3,4,5] has motivated such an interest. It will be seen that the similarity described in [1] is not sufficient when relating programs which use the store differently.

For ease of explanation we do not admit data structures into our language. In considering whether different representations of data structures relate we first look at how the structure is embedded in the store and then check that canonical forms, which do not depend on store, simulate the same abstract structure. The first part of the consideration requires techniques which are similar to the problem we will deal with. A relation is defined which allows us to relate a value with an address holding that value. The relation is generalized in [6]. In §2 we summarise the underlying principles of the mathematical model upon which the semantic descriptions are based; §3 characterizes the languages which are used to exemplify this simpler problem. We then describe an idea of similarity in standard semantics; give examples of its use; and then, having demonstrated its shortcomings, go on to develop the alternative relation.

2. Basic Principles of the lattice theoretic approach.

The meaning of a programming language will be defined by denoting constructs in the language by continuous functions over complete lattices [2]. Many of the definitions underlying these principles will be assumed (e.g. "complete lattice", "continuous", "monotonic", fix). Definitions will be found in [1,2].

A "retraction" on a complete lattice D is a continuous function $r:D\to D$ with the property that $r=r\circ r$. A "retract" for r is the image of D under r; a retract is seen to be a complete lattice. A "universal domain" is a complete lattice Z associated with three retractions flat cross and arrow having associated retracts isomorphic with an infinite "flat" lattice, $Z\times Z$ and $Z\to Z$ respectively. $\times$ constructs a complete lattice of ordered pairs, $\to$ of continuous functions and $+$ the separated sum. Scott has proved that universal domains of this kind exist [7].

Notation: D is a domain (capital letter), $\underline{d}$ is a retraction corresponding with D (underlined small), $d\in D$ (small) and $\dot{d}$ is a binary relation on D.

Operations $+$, $\times$, $\to$ may be defined on the set of retractions of Z (a complete lattice) with the properties that:
$\text{Image}(\underline{d}_1+\underline{d}_2)\approx\text{Image}(\underline{d}_1)+\text{Image}(\underline{d}_2)$ etc. and $+$, $\times$, $\to$ are continuous on the domain of retractions of Z.

With these operations in mind it is possible to construct domains D which are recursively defined.

Example: $D\approx N+(D\times D)+(D\to D)$ in the context of Z where N is a flat lattice with some annotation to distinguish it from other flat lattices. Define F to be $\lambda\underline{d}.\underline{n}+(\underline{d}\times\underline{d})+(\underline{d}\to\underline{d})$ where the λ-notation is used in the usual way [1,2,7]. F is a continuous function mapping retracts into retracts and D = Image(fix F) is a domain because fix(F) is a retract.

Now it is possible to discuss the domains which will underly the languages used for purposes of exposition in this article.

3. Underpinnings of a class of languages.

We will choose elements from a language which is a member of a class of languages having the following semantic domains in common.

The store is defined to be a function $s \in S = L \to (T \times V)$ where L is a flat lattice with elements corresponding to the addresses of locations, and T is a flat lattice of truth values telling when a location is addressable. $v \in V = N+T+F$ where N is a flat lattice of integers, and $F = E \to K \to C$ a domain of abstractions. E is the domain of expressed values L+V, and includes locations which may hold values. C is the domain of continuations $C = S \to A$, a set of functions corresponding to the rest of the program; A is an unspecified domain of objects denoting output information; $K = E \to C$ comprises expression continuations which handle the evaluation of an expression in passing to the rest of the program. "Environments" are also defined as part of the semantic description $Env = (\underline{Ide} \to D) \times J$ where Ide is the syntactic domain of identifiers and J=K denotes the set of jumps ("goto"s for example) and D=E Finally when denoting declarations it is necessary to provide environment continuations $X = Env \to C$.

Data structures are not introduced. This extension adds only structural detail. We may define V to include $(V+(V \times V)+(V \times V \times V)+\ldots) = V^*$ and when "reveal" of §6 is defined suitably structures are adequately dealt with.

There will be three basic syntactic domains:

com∈Com: the domain of commands

examples: ide:=exp (assignments), while exp do com (while loops), com_1; com_2 (sequencing of commands), if exp do com (conditional command)

exp∈Exp: the domain of expressions.

examples: exp_1 dyad exp_2 (where dyad is a representative of the domain of dyadic operators), dec inside exp (a declaration of a variable inside an expression), copy exp (produces a new location in store and inserts a value corresponding with exp), basic values like numerals and truth values, com before exp (evaluates exp after doing the command).

dec∈Dec: the domain of declarations.

examples: ide=exp, dec_1 and dec_2 (two declarations in sequence)

The semantics of a language is described by three functions:

CC:Com→Env→C→C, EE:Exp→Env→K→C and DD:Dec→Env→X→C.

4. Similarity.

It is now possible to discuss relationships between terms (viz. commands, expressions and declarations). We will begin with a simple example, and by seeing its shortcomings, generalise the idea. Two terms are denotationally equivalent if their valuations are equal. That is, for any exp_1, $exp_2 \in$ Exp $exp_1 =_s exp_2$ iff $EE[\![exp_1]\!] = EE[\![exp_2]\!]$ etc. (for other valuations). Denotational equivalence is an equivalence relation and has substitution properties (in any context two terms denotationally equivalent may be substituted for one another without affecting the answer).

In many circumstances it will be useful to restrict the class of all possible contexts. It becomes necessary to define "context conditions" which are rather like Hoare's axioms [3]. Two commands are denotationally equivalent if for all $r \in Env, c \in C$ and $s \in S$ $CC[\![com_1]\!]rcs = CC[\![com_2]\!]rcs$. It is of interest to consider what happens when binary relations $\mathring{r}, \mathring{c}, \mathring{s}$ and $\mathring{a}$ are defined on Env, C, S and A, and it is said that com_1 and com_2 are related when $\mathring{r}\langle r_1,r_2\rangle$, $\mathring{c}\langle c_1,c_2\rangle$ and $\mathring{s}\langle s_1,s_2\rangle$ imply that $\mathring{a}\langle CC[\![com_1]\!]r_1c_1s_1, CC[\![com_2]\!]r_2c_2s_2\rangle$.

It will be useful to define some notational abbreviation which will make it more easy to reason about relations of this kind:

Definition. Let $\mathring{r}_1$ and $\mathring{r}_2$ be binary relations then $\mathring{r}'$ is related to $\mathring{r}''$ by $\mathring{r}_1 \Rightarrow \mathring{r}_2$ if for any x,y such that $x\mathring{r}_1y$ and for any x_1,y_1 for which $x\mathring{r}'x_1$ and $y\mathring{r}''y_1$ it is true that $x_1\mathring{r}_2y$.

Definition. A relation is restrictive if it is transitive and symmetric.

Properties. (i) $\mathring{r}_1, \mathring{r}_2$ symmetric then $\mathring{r}_1 \Rightarrow \mathring{r}_2$ is symmetric.

(ii) $\mathring{r}_1, \mathring{r}_2$ restrictive then $\mathring{r}_1 \Rightarrow \mathring{r}_2$ is restrictive.

It is necessary to specialise these relations. In the example of denotational equivalence we were relating continuous functions. We desire to construct relations from $\mathring{r}_1, \mathring{r}_2$.

$\mathring{r}_1 \to \mathring{r}_2$ with characteristic function $\lambda\langle f_1,f_2\rangle . \bigwedge\{\mathring{r}_2\langle f_1r_1,f_2r_2\rangle \mid \mathring{r}_1\langle r_1,r_2\rangle\}$ where $\bigwedge\{\ldots\}$ means a conjunction over all elements of the set specified by the brackets. It has already been shown that recursively defined domains may be constructed. Relations on recursively defined domains are not continuous or monotonic in general (because they involve equality). Following Milne [1] and Reynolds [8] a "predictor" is defined for a relation. A "predictor" maps successive levels of the relation (corresponding with each stage of the fixed point). If the relations at each stage of the development of the fixed point are directed complete (relation holds for each pair in an ascending chain implies the relation holds for the least upper bound of the chain) and "information is preserved" then it is proved that the limit relation exists, and is directed complete.

Property if $\mathring{r}_1, \mathring{r}_2$ are directed complete and exist over their domains then $\mathring{r}_1 \to \mathring{r}_2$ is directed complete and exists.

5. Examples of the generalisation.

(i) denotational equivalence

$com_1, com_2 \in$ Com $com_1 =_s com_2$ iff $\mathring{r} \to (\mathring{c} \to \mathring{c}) \langle CC[\![com_1]\!], CC[\![com_2]\!] \rangle$ where $\mathring{r}$ is the identity relation on Env and $\mathring{c}$ is the identity relation on C.

(ii) similarity of while loops.

Milne and Strachey [1] consider two examples of an expression which will yield factorial of n. They demonstrate that

k=1 and l=n inside((while l≥k do com_1; k:=0;l:=0)before m)

is denotationally equivalent with the same expression where com_1 is replaced by com_2. com_1 is m:=m×k;k:=k+1 and com_2 is m:=m×l;l:=l-1.

The proof is provided by using a recursion induction rule for while loops. For a definition of similarity, in which the relations on the environment and store ensure that k and l denote locations which are disjoint (k and l do not share) and the locations hold integers, it is proved that while l≥k do $com_1 \sim_s$ while l≥k do com_2. In the definition of $\sim_s$, components are involved which prevent the relations from being continuous. It can be shown that for most interesting cases $\sim_s$ forms of relation have "substitution" properties, are directed complete and restrictive.

6. "Revelatory" similarity.

It was suggested in the introduction that we are interested in situations where "equivalent" programs use store differently. We will give a very simple example of such a situation. It is intuitively clear that unless there is no available storage capacity x is similar to y = copy 0 inside (y:=x before y) in the sense that either could be used in a suitable context without differentiating the behaviour of the program. We wish to define a relation between expressions involving denotations of different storage use, i.e. if the store were "stripped away" equivalent values would be revealed.

It is necessary to relate states (P) (store/environment pairs)

$\mathring{p} = \lambda \langle p_1, p_2 \rangle . \bigwedge \{ \mathring{d} \langle \langle p_{1env}[\![ide]\!], p_1 \rangle, \langle p_{2env}[\![ide]\!], p_2 \rangle \rangle \mid ide \in \underline{Ide} \}$

p_{ienv} means a projection of p_i into Env. $\dot{d}$ is a relation on denotations and states (no longer binary relation)

$$\dot{d} = \lambda\langle\langle d_1, p_1\rangle, \langle d_2, p_2\rangle\rangle . \mathring{v}\langle \text{reveal}\langle d_1, p_{1store}\rangle, \text{reveal}\langle d_2, p_{2store}\rangle\rangle$$

$$\underline{\text{reveal}} = \underline{\text{fix}}(\lambda f . \lambda\langle d, s\rangle . d \in L \rightarrow (\underline{\text{area}}ds \rightarrow f\langle \underline{\text{hold}}ds, s\rangle, \underline{\text{error}}), d)$$

hold produces the contents of the location d in store s, area tests whether the location d is actually in the accessible part of the store s, and error is some element in V indicating a prohibited computation. These functions are primitive in the semantics. reveal is continuous and therefore does not "interfere" with the directed complete nature of $\dot{d}$. $\mathring{v}$ is a relation on V complicated by the component relating members of F. The method of dealing with F affects the semantic description to be discussed, but will not be considered here. Having defined the relation between states, it is necessary to relate terms. Two terms are to be related if when executed in the context of "similar" states, and of continuations which are related in similar states, provide answers which are related. The standard description of the class of languages abstracts the environment out. It is necessary to allow the continuation to be "sensitive" to the environment. This may be achieved by leaving the semantic structure as it is and pushing the current environment into the answer domain (not very nice) or by allowing the continuation to be a function of state. The latter possibility is chosen; a new semantics (proved congruent with the former in the sense of Milne[1]) is defined in which C = Env→S→A and K = E→C and semantic functions are defined

$$CC_A : \underline{\text{Com}} \rightarrow C \rightarrow C; \quad EE_A : \underline{\text{Exp}} \rightarrow K \rightarrow C; \quad DD_A : \underline{\text{Dec}} \rightarrow C \rightarrow C$$

and $\mathring{c} = \lambda\langle c_1, c_2\rangle . \bigwedge\{\mathring{a}\langle c_1 p_{1env} p_{1store}, c_2 p_{2env} p_{2store}\rangle \mid \dot{p}\langle p_1\ p_2\rangle\}$

thus $com_1, com_2 \in \underline{\text{Com}}$ $com_1 \sim_D com_2$ iff $\mathring{c} \rightarrow \mathring{c}\ \langle CC_A[\![com_1]\!], CC_A[\![com_2]\!]\rangle$ etc.

It can be shown, by the method already sketched, that these relations exist. In addition if the basic component $\dot{a}$ is restrictive then the relations are restrictive and, apart from terms involving assignment to global variables, there are some substitution properties.

7. Conclusion.

These relations are to be used as the basis for a syntactic calculus for proving relations between programs. It can be shown that for syntactic restrictions of terms, some similarities between terms imply "revelatory" similarity. Consequently these relations can be integrated into the more straightforward properties of the relations defined in terms of a more abstract semantics. The calculus and some applications to examples may be found in [6].

I am deeply indebted to Robert Milne. Thanks also to members of the Programming Research Group. The research was carried out using a U.K. Science Research Council Grant.

8. References

1. R. E. Milne and C. Strachey, A Theory of Programming Language Semantics. Chapman and Hall (Late 1976).

2. C. Strachey and C. Wadsworth, Continuations: A mathematical semantics for handling full jumps. Tech. Monog. PRG-11 Prog.Res.Group. Oxford 1974.

3. C. A. R. Hoare, Proof of a structured program: "The Sieve of Erosthenes". Computer Journal 15 4 November 1972.

4. J. Darlington, A Semantic approach to automatic program improvement. Exp.Prog.Reps. 27 School of A.I. Edinburgh 1972.

5. B. Liskov and S. Zilles, Programming with Abstract Data Types. SIGPLAN Notice 9:4 1974 .

6. M. D. Harrison, D.Phil. Thesis in preparation. Late 1976 Oxford.

7. D. Scott, Data Types as Lattices, Theoretical Computer Science, 1976.

8. J. Reynolds, On the Relation between direct and continuation semantics. Lecture Notes in Computer Science, vol.14, Springer-Verlag (1974) pp.141-156.

AN ALGEBRAIC APPROACH TO DATA TYPES, PROGRAM VERIFICATION, AND PROGRAM SYNTHESIS

Friedrich W. von Henke

Gesellschaft für Mathematik und Datenverarbeitung Bonn
5205 St.Augustin 1, W-Germany

Introduction. In investigating problems related to abstract programs one usually does not take into account the structure of the data a program is operating on; the theory of program schemata, for example, abstracts from data domains and the meaning of operations. In general, however, there is a certain correspondence between the structure of a program and the data structure. The correspondence is particularly obvious in the case of recursive data structures. Many LISP programs follow a scheme: separate cases for NIL and/or atoms and CONS-objects; recursive calls for the CAR/CDR of CONS-objects. For example, the function APPEND is simply an instance of the recursive definition scheme of functions that operate on linear lists,

```
        F = (LAMBDA (X Y)
   (1)       (COND ((NULL X) (G Y))
                   (T  (H (CAR X) (F (CDR X) Y))) ))
```

where G and H are some functions. Compare this with the following definition of the data type 'linear lists': "a linear list is either empty or composed of an atom and a linear list." Evidently, the recursive scheme (1) parallels the data structure directly. Surprisingly enough, this apparently trivial observation has had little impact on methods for generating programs and reasoning about programs. On the contrary, more recent work on program verification and automatic program synthesis does not make explicit use of the underlying structures, apart from applying structural induction. For example, current program generating systems have to "rediscover" the basic structure (sequence of cases, recursive calls etc.) each time a program is synthetized (cf. /MaW/). One reason for not utilizing the 'similarity' of program structures and data structures seems to be that this relationship has not been expressed hitherto in a mathematically precise way, so that it might be suitable as a basis for formal reasoning.

In this paper we relate program structures to recursive data types in a way that provides some insight into their mutual dependency. A suitable definition of data types leads to an interpretation in terms of universal algebra; programs whose structure is similar to the data structure are then representable as homomorphisms. The concept of homomorphic definability is investigated, and some of its consequences in connection with program generation and verification are discussed. Owing to lack of space the presentation has to be somewhat fragmentary and imprecise; a more detailed treatment of some problems can be found in /He1,He2/.

Data Types. The basis is a definition of data types by means of constructors, selectors and recognizers, following McCarthy's ideas of "abstract syntax" /McC/. For example, the data type linear lists of atoms is defined in a BNF-like notation by a listing of alternatives,

(2) llist := nil | comp(hd:atom, tl:llist)

Her nil is a constant, comp a constructor which takes an atom and a linear list as arguments, and hd and tl are the selectors associated with comp such that

(3) hd(comp(a,b)) = a, tl(comp(a,b)) = b for all a,b

(the primitives of the type may be regarded as abstract versions of LISP's NIL, CONS, CAR and CDR). Such a type can be interpreted as an absolutely free many-sorted or "heterogeneous" algebra /BiL/. In the example of llist, there are two sorts (atom and llist), a nullary (nil) and a binary (comp) operation. The algebra is generated by the 'base set' atom and the operations in the way commonly associated with word-algebras. Note that the selector functions hd and tl must not be taken as generators; because of the equalities (3) the resulting algebra would not be absolutely free.

In the following we do not distinguish between (abstract) programs and functions which are given in a constructive way. Structures and functions are expressed in terms of the Logic for Computable Functions (LCF) /Mi1, Mi2/. The logic LCF is particularly suited for expressing and proving problems arising in the mathematical theory of computation; furthermore, it has been implemented in form of an interactive theorem prover /Mi1,Ne/. Roughly speaking, the terms of LCF are the expressions of the λ-calculus, augmented by conditional expressions $p \Rightarrow q,r$ ("if p then q else r") and fixed points $\mu F.s(F)$ (minimal fixed point of $\lambda F.s(F)$). In addition, we have constants TT and FF denoting the truth values true and false respectively. (In this short paper we disregard undefined values and partial functions which can also be treated in the logic.)

<u>Homomorphisms</u>. A data type is characterized by the identity function in that it contains the basic information about the structure. E.g. for the type llist:

$$\text{(4)}\quad id_{llist} = \mu F.\ \lambda x.\ null(x) \Rightarrow \underline{nil},\ \underline{comp}(id_{atom}(hd(x)),\ F(tl(x))).$$

However, in order to be able to prove that id_{llist} is the identity on linear lists, we have to add further axioms like (3) which relate constructors, selectors and the 'recognizer' null to each other (cf. /McC, Mi2/). Now, all functions that are similar to the identity function in that their definitions have essentially the same structure can be characterized as <u>homomorphisms</u> from the algebra associated with the data type into an appropriate target domain (algebra). Moreover, there is a uniform way of representing homomorphisms: the generic nature of the source algebra entails that every homomorphism is uniquely determined by a function on the base set and the operations on the target algebra. Thus, by turning the primitives underlined in (4) into (global) parameters the identity function is converted into a definition scheme for homomorphisms on linear lists,

$$Lhom = \lambda f\ c\ op.\ \mu F.\ \lambda x.\ null(x) \Rightarrow c,\ op(f(hd(x)),\ F(tl(x))).$$

As an example, consider the function occur with occur(a,s)=TT iff the atom a occurs in the linear list s. occur is defined recursively by

$$occur = \mu F.\ \lambda a\ s.\ null(s) \Rightarrow FF,\ (hd(s)=a) \Rightarrow TT,\ F(a,\ tl(s)).$$

Note that the argument a is not changed throughout the recursion, so that it may be bound globally. Thus,

$$occur = \lambda a.\ Lhom((\lambda x.x=a),\ FF,\ \underline{or})$$

where <u>or</u> is the logical connective represented by <u>or</u> = λx y.x ⇒ TT,y. The example brings out important properties of the use of Lhom. First, Lhom is an extension functional, it extends a base function (here: equality on atoms) to the whole type. Second, the structure of the target algebra need not be stated explicitly; it may be deduced from the arguments of the extension functional. In the example, the constant FF and the operation <u>or</u> define a structure on the domain of truth values which corresponds to the one of llist.

<u>Homomorphic Definability</u>. In general, there are several different ways to represent a function as a homomorphism. Let us consider the function append. In analogy to occur, it can be represented as

$$\text{(5)}\quad append = \lambda x\ y.\ Lhom(id_{atom},\ y,\ comp)(x)$$

(Note the change in the order of arguments.) In (5) the argument y is a constant parameter. There is another way of interpreting the binary function append: it maps the recursion argument x onto a computation to be performed on y (this interpretation corresponds to the usual representation of n-ary functions in the λ-calculus by 'currying'.). Let $il = id_{llist}$ and $C = \lambda y\ f.\ comp(y) \circ f$. These functions induce an appropriate structure on the function domain (llist → llist), and we obtain an alternative representation of append,

(6) $append = Lhom(id_{atom}, il, C)$.

This technique of mapping elements homomorphically into function domains allows us to represent a wide class of functions, in particular functions with more than one non-constant argument. As an example, the 'iterative' reversal function is represented as

$$reverse = \lambda x.\ rev(x,nil)$$

where

$$rev = Lhom((\lambda z.comp(z,nil)), id_{llist}, g)$$
$$g = \lambda z\ f\ y.\ f \circ append(y,z)$$

In spite of the simplicity, the scheme of homomorphic definition is quite powerful. Call a function <u>homomorphically definable</u> if it can be represented as composition and application of homomorphisms; as in the examples, function domains may also be used as intermediate source and target domains. The following theorem shows that virtually all functions of interest in programming are definable by means of homomorphisms.

<u>Theorem</u>. All primitive recursive functions on a data type are homomorphically definable.

Remarks on the proof: We presuppose a natural extension of the notion 'primitive recursive' to functions on terms (see, e.g., /Ma/). The scheme of primitive recursive definition differs from homomorphic definition mainly in two respects: (a) it contains additional constant parameters; (b) the right-hand-side functions 'know' the argument, not only the value returned by the recursive calls. Global binding takes care of (a). The trick that solves (b) is to encode the argument into the returned value by means of conditional expressions, i.e. the recursion takes place in a function domain derived from the data type. For details, see /He2/.

<u>Applications</u>. What does it mean, in practice, for a function to be homomorphically definable? Generally speaking, on account of the

uniformity of definitions and the inherent properties of homomorphisms on generic structures, many problems can be solved in a uniform way or by simply referring to properties of the definition scheme. Let us demonstrate this by means of a few examples.

In proving properties of programs many properties have to be proved only once for the definition scheme. As an example, consider termination of programs. A homomorphism is defined on the domain described by the corresponding identity function; thus, it is already proved that the associated program always terminates for correct input. Even properties that apparently are not related at all to homomorphic definition can be proved from general properties of the definition scheme. Consider, for example, the functional Lhom. For every triple f,c,op of suitable arguments Lhom(f,c,op) is the unique extension of f satisfying the homomorphy conditions with respect to nil and comp. Let F_i = Lhom(f_i,c_i,comp) for i=1,2. It is proved easily that

$$(F_1 \circ F_2)(\text{nil}) = F_1(c_2)$$

and

$$(F_1 \circ F_2)(\text{comp}(a,b)) = \text{comp}((f_1 \circ f_2)(a), (F_1 \circ F_2)(b)) \quad \text{for any a,b}$$

Thus, by the uniqueness property we have

$$(7) \quad F_1 \circ F_2 = \text{Lhom}(f_1 \circ f_2, F_1(c_2)).$$

Now, instantiating (7) for append yields

$$\text{append}(\text{append}(a,b), c) = \text{append}(a, \text{append}(b,c))$$

that is, associativity of append is provable without induction directly from the homomorphic representation. Naturally, (7) implies similar properties of other functions; in fact, it is sort of a proof scheme.

Note that equality (7) also provides a scheme for merging two recursions, that is, it may be regarded as an 'optimizing transformation'. Such transformations are necessary as programs defined by composition of homomorphisms are well-structured, but tend to be inefficient. However, standard transformations are able to largely reduce inefficiency, for example by simplifying the recursion structure. Moreover, these transformations can already be applied to the definition schemes, thus yielding new and more efficient function definition schemes which, however, retain many of the advantages of the original ones.

Consider, for example, a general form of function iteration. By iteration we mean here that a function is to be applied repeatedly with a varying parameter. Such a form of iteration can be represented by homomorphic extension. Let f be a function from atoms into a function domain. Then

Iter(s)(f) := Lhom(f, id, ∘)(s)

maps a linear list s onto a composition of f's, for instance,

Iter((a,b,c))(f) = f(a)∘f(b)∘f(c).

Now, if for every atom a f(a) is a homomorphism from llist into llist which changes only the atoms in a list, say

f = Lhom(g,nil,comp),

then the computation of Iter(s)(f) requires as many recursions as there are elements in s. These recursions, however, can be combined to a single one, for

(8) Iter(s)(f) = Lhom(Iter(s)(g), nil, comp).

The proof of (8) is similar to the one of (7).

Homomorphic definition is able, to a certain extent, to replace a complex problem solving process in synthetizing programs. The homomorphic definition scheme - and other schemes derived from it - provides the 'frame'; the information to be filled in is the minimum required to specify the function explicitly and has to be supplied one way or other. A similar approach can also simplify generation of implicitly defined programs. This will be discussed in a subsequent paper.

The methods and techniques presented in this paper are mechanizable without great effort. The structure-oriented techniques complement - and may, to some extent, replace - the more heuristic approaches to verification and optimization as developed, for example, by Boyer and Moore /BoM/ and Burstall and Darlington /BuD/. They are intended to eventually serve as a basis of an interactive system that allows us to develop and verify well-structured and reliable programs.

References

/BiL/ G. Birkhoff and J.D. Lipson: Heterogeneous algebras. Journ. Comb. Theory 8 (1970), 115-133.

/BoM/ R.S. Boyer and J S. Moore: Proving theorems about LISP functions. Journ. of the ACM 22 (1975), 129-144.

/BuD/ R.M. Burstall and J. Darlington: Some transformations for developing recursive programs. Proc. Int. Conf. on Reliable Software, Los Angeles, 1975, 465-472.

/He1/ F.W. von Henke: On the representation of data structures in LCF. Memo AIM-267, Stanford University, 1975.

/He2/ F.W. von Henke: Recursive data types and program structures. 1976 (to appear).

/Ma/ F.K. Mahn: Primitiv-rekursive Funktionen auf Termmengen. Arch. math. Logik 12 (1969), 54-65.

/MaW/ Z. Manna and R. Waldinger: Knowledge and reasoning in program synthesis. Techn. Note 98, Stanford Research Institute, 1974.

/McC/ J. McCarthy: Towards a mathematical science of computation. Proc. IFIP Congr. 1962, 21-28.

/Mi1/ R. Milner: Logic for computable functions - description of an implementation. Memo AIM-169, Stanford University, 1972.

/Mi2/ R. Milner: Implementation and application of Scott's logic for computable functions. Proc. ACM Conf. on Proving Assertions about Programs, Las Cruces, New Mexico, 1972.

/Ne/ M. Newey: Formal semantics of LISP with applications to program correctness, (PhD thesis). Memo AIM-257, Stanford University, 1975.

ABOUT THREE EQUATIONAL CLASSES OF LANGUAGES BUILT UP BY SHUFFLE OPERATIONS

Matthias Höpner

Manfred Opp

Institut für Informatik, Universität Hamburg
D-2000 Hamburg 13, Schlüterstraße 70

Mazurkiewicz introduced in [6] a class of parallel, recursive program-schemes . He showed that the class of value-languages of such schemes is exactly the class of languages defined by equations within the algebra $(\mathcal{P}(X^*),\Omega')$, where $\Omega' = \{ \cup , \cdot , \between , (\{x\})_{x \in X \cup \{\Lambda\}} \}$ is the set of operations: union, concatenation, shuffle (of rank 2) and the nullary operations $\{x\}$.

In his paper Mazurkiewicz didn't answer questions concerning inter-relationships with known families of languages, as for instance: regular sets, value-languages of arbitrary parallel program schemes, or other classes of languages defined by shuffle operations.

To get some more results in this direction we investigate the following three families:

$\mathcal{L}_1 \subset \mathcal{P}(X^*)$ defined by equations using the set of operations:

$$\Omega^1 = \{ \cup , \cdot , \between , (\{x\})_{x \in X \cup \{\Lambda\}} \} .$$

We denote (as in Höpner[3][4]) by ' $\between$ ' the shuffle operation:

$$\between : \begin{cases} X^* \times X^* \longrightarrow \mathcal{P}(X^*) \\ (u,v) \longrightarrow \{u_1v_1u_2v_2\ldots u_nv_n \in X^* / \; n \in \mathbb{N},\; u_i,v_i \in X^*, \\ \qquad\qquad u_1\ldots u_n = u \text{ and } v_1\ldots v_n = v \} . \end{cases}$$

$\mathcal{L}_2 \subset \mathcal{P}(X^*)$ defined by equations using the set of operations:

$$\Omega^2 = \{ \cup , (f_x)_{x \in X}, \between , (\{x\})_{x \in X \cup \{\Lambda\}} \} .$$

The operation f_x means 'leftconcatenation with x', i.e.

$$f_x : \begin{cases} \mathcal{P}(X^*) \longrightarrow \mathcal{P}(X^*) \\ M \longmapsto \{x\} \cdot M \end{cases} .$$

$\mathcal{L}_3 \subset \mathcal{P}(X^*)$ defined by equations using the set of operations:

$$\Omega^3 = \{ \cup , \between , (\{x\})_{x \in X \cup \{\Lambda\}} \} .$$

(Whenever the term 'defined by equations is used, we mean the well-known representation of languages by components of minimal fixpoints of finite systems of such equations.)

After stating our main theorems concerning characterisations of the introduced language families (theorem (1) and (2)), hierarchy-relations (theorem (3)), normalform-theorem (theorem (4), without proof) we shall give proofs of theorem 2 and of a special closure result (cor. (13)).

We have chosen this sequence in our paper, because in the latter proofs we used the simplifying concept of congruent families (first introduced in Opp [8]) which for clearness reasons isn't worked out before summarizing our results.

(1) Theorem: $\mathcal{L}_3$ equals the family of commutative closures of the regular sets of X^* (denoted by $\mathcal{R}$). That means $\mathcal{L}_3 = \text{perm}(\mathcal{R}) := \psi^{-1}(\psi(\mathcal{R})) := \{L \subset X^* / L = \psi^{-1}(\psi(R)),\ R \in \mathcal{R}\}$, ψ is the Parikh-mapping.

Proof: From Höpner [4] we know that the family perm($\mathcal{R}$) equals the smallest family of languages that contains the letters and is closed with respect to union, shuffle and shuffle-iteration (defined by $M^{\ast} := \{\Lambda\} \cup M \cup (M \ast M) \cup (M \ast M \ast M) \cup \ldots$). Since M is the minimal fixpoint of the equation $X = X \ast M \cup \{\Lambda\}$ each member of the family perm($\mathcal{R}$) can be defined using equations with operations from Ω^3. The other direction follows from an inductive argument using the iterative construction of minimal fixpoints.

Obviously perm($\mathcal{R}$) contains noncontext-free languages, as for example the language $L = \text{perm}(\{abc\}^*)$, since $L \cap a^*b^*c^* = \{a^n b^n c^n / n \geq 0\}$.

Now we characterize the family $\mathcal{L}_2$ in terms of a class of languages already known.

(2) Theorem: $\mathcal{L}_2$ equals the family of images of Szilard-languages under alphabetical homomorphisms.

This family has been defined in Höpner [3] and is there called the family of '1-induced' languages. We abbreviate this above result by $\mathcal{L}_2 = \mathcal{H}_\alpha(\mathcal{S}_z) := \{L = h(S) / h$ an alphabetical homomorphism, $S \in \mathcal{S}_z$ (= the family of Szilard-languages of context-free grammars)$\}$.
(h is called alphabetical homomorphism, if $\forall x \in X$: $lg(h(x)) \leq 1$, coding, if $\forall x \in X$: $lg(h(x)) = 1$.)

To obtain theorem (2) we use the normalform theorem given in Höpner which shows that each member of $\mathcal{H}_\alpha(\mathcal{S}_z)$ can be obtained by a context-free grammar in Chomsky-normalform with certain labels. These normalform-theorems are used to show theorem(9) below, which together with theorem (11) implies theorem (2).

From the characterization of 1-induced languages as minimal solutions of equations we can get the finite representation using expressions that is given in Höpner [3][4]. As this is not done here, the reader is referred to the general ideas of Wand [9] and Bekic [1].

Using theorem (1) and theorem (2) we can show that the inclusion relations of the defined families are proper:

(3) Theorem: $\mathcal{L}_3 \subsetneqq \mathcal{L}_2 \subsetneqq \mathcal{L}_1$.

Proof: The proof is given by two counterexamples (the inclusions are obvious): The Λ-free Dyck-language D_1 over one pair of brackets $\{0,1\}$ is the minimal solution of the following Ω^2-equation:

$$X = X \between (f_0(\{1\})) \cup f_0(f_1(\{\Lambda\})) ,$$

but clearly isn't contained in $\mathcal{L}_3$.

The language $L = \{a^n b^n \;/\; n \geq 0\}$ as a context-free language is contained in $\mathcal{L}_1$ but not in $\mathcal{L}_2$, since each letter-bounded language of $\mathcal{L}_2$ is a regular set (see Höpner [4]).

D_1 is also the minimal solution of the equation

$$X = f_0(X \between \{1\}) \cup f_0(\{1\}).$$

It turns out that it is a general property of the family $\mathcal{L}_2$ that Λ-free languages within $\mathcal{L}_2$ can be defined as solutions of equations neither using the operator $\{\Lambda\}$ nor using shuffle without leftconcatenation. The following theorem stating this result has a quite complicated proof and may be found in Höpner, Opp [5].

(4) Theorem: Let $L \in \mathcal{L}_2$ be arbitrary. Then $L \setminus \{\Lambda\}$ can be defined as a solution of a system of equations using the set of operations:

$$\Omega^4 = \{ \cup , (g_x)_{x \in X}, (\{x\})_{x \in X}, (f_x)_{x \in X} \} , \; g_x \text{ is defined by}$$

$$g_x : \begin{cases} \mathcal{P}(X^*) \times \mathcal{P}(X^*) \longrightarrow \mathcal{P}(X^*) \\ (M_1, M_2) \longrightarrow x \cdot (M_1 \between M_2) . \end{cases}$$

(So g_x combines both shuffleoperation and leftconcatenation.)

Theorem (4) and theorem (2) show that for each language $L \in \mathcal{H}_\alpha(\mathcal{S}_z)$ the set $L \setminus \{\Lambda\}$ is a coding of some Szilard-language.

In order to compare the family $\mathcal{L}_1$ with value-languages of arbitrary parallel program schemes, we have to look at the family $\mathcal{Z}$ defined in

Höpner [3]. $\mathcal{Z}$ equals the family of homomorphic images of firing sequences of arbitrary Petri-nets and can be defined using (weak) counter automata. In Höpner [3][4] it is shown that $\mathcal{Z} = \mathcal{H}(\mathcal{S}_z \cap \mathcal{R})$ and is the least full, semi AFL generated by $\mathcal{S}_z$. Therefore $\mathcal{Z}$ also equals the least, full semi AFL generated by $\mathcal{L}_2$. We show:

(5) Theorem: The families $\mathcal{L}_1$ and $\mathcal{Z}$ are incomparable with respect to inclusion.

Proof: First note that the Parikh-image $\psi(L)$ is a semilinear set for each $L \in \mathcal{L}_1$. This follows from the characterization by equations. We know that $\mathcal{Z}$ contains a language M such that $\psi(M)$ is not a semilinear set. Therefore $\mathcal{Z} \not\subset \mathcal{L}_1$ holds.

On the other hand it is clear that the family $\mathcal{L}_1$ contains each context-free language which fails to be true for the family $\mathcal{Z}$. This follows from a result of Hack [2].

Similar observations show that $\mathcal{L}_1$ is not closed with respect to intersection with regular sets.

(6) Theorem: The families $\mathcal{L}_1, \mathcal{L}_2, \mathcal{L}_3$ are not closed with respect to intersection with regular sets.

Proof: For the language $L = \text{perm}(\{ab\}^*) \in \mathcal{L}_3$ the following holds: $L \cap a^*b^* \notin \mathcal{L}_2$. This shows the nonclosure of intersection with regular sets of both $\mathcal{L}_2$ and $\mathcal{L}_3$.

Now let us define the notions of congruences and congruent families in the general context of arbitrary multi-valued Ω-algebras (A,Ω). A multi-valued Ω-algebra is a usual Ω-algebra with multi-valued functions, i.e. for each $f \in \Omega$ with arity $a(f)=n$, f is a function of the following type:

$$f: \begin{cases} A^n \longrightarrow \mathcal{P}(A) \\ (a_1,..,a_n) \longmapsto f(a_1,..,a_n) \end{cases} .$$

(7) Definition: A partition $\mathcal{K} = \{K_1,..,K_r\}$ (or equivalence $\sim_{\mathcal{K}}$ by $x \sim_{\mathcal{K}} y \iff \exists i \in \{1,..,r\}: x,y \in K_i$) on A is called congruence of (A,Ω), if:

$$\forall n \in \mathbb{N}_0 \forall f \in \Omega_n \forall a_i,b_i \in A: \; (a_i \sim_{\mathcal{K}} b_i \text{ for } i=1,..,n \Longrightarrow$$
$$\exists j \in \{1,..,r\}: (f(a_1,..,a_n) \subset K_j \text{ and } f(b_1,..,b_n) \subset K_j)).$$

This definition yields the usual notion of congruences in the special case of single-valued Ω-algebras.

(8) Definition: Let (A,Ω) be a multi-valued Ω-algebra.

(a) $(f,t_1,..,t_n) \in \Omega_n \times A^n$ is called a decomposition of t in (A,Ω), if $t \in f(t_1,..,t_n)$.

(b) Dec(t) is the set of all decompositions of t.

(c) Let $\mathcal{F} = \{F_i \;/\; i \in I\}$, $F_i \subset A$, be a set of subsets of A. For each pair (t,F_i), $t \in F_i$, we define:

$$\mathrm{Dec}_{\mathcal{F}}(t,F_i) = \left\{(f,t_1,..,t_n) \in \mathrm{Dec}(t) \;/\; \exists\, i_1,..,i_n \in I : t_j \in F_{i_j} \text{ for } j=1,..,n \text{ and } f(F_{i_1},..,F_{i_n}) \subset F_i\right\}.$$

The following diagram illustrates this:

$$\begin{array}{ccccccc} t & \in & f(t_1 & , & \dots & , & t_n) \\ \cap & & \cap & & & & \cap \\ F_i & \supset & f(F_{i_1} & , & \dots & , & F_{i_n}) \end{array} .$$

(d) $\mathcal{F} = \{F_i \;/\; i \in I\}$, $F_i \subset A$, is called congruent family on (A,Ω), if: $\forall i \in I, \forall t \in F_i$: $(\mathrm{Dec}(t) \neq \emptyset \Longrightarrow \mathrm{Dec}(t,F_i) \neq \emptyset)$.

(e) In the special case $A = X^*$ (i.e. $(A,\Omega) = (X^*,\Omega)$) we introduce reducing congruent families (with the abbreviations $\mathrm{NTDec}(t) = \{(f,t_1,..,t_n) \in \mathrm{Dec}(t) \;/\; t_i \neq \Lambda,\; i=1,..,n\}$; $\mathrm{NTDec}_{\mathcal{F}}(t,F_i) = \mathrm{NTDec}(t) \cap \mathrm{Dec}_{\mathcal{F}}(t,F_i)$) as follows:
$\forall i \in I, \forall t \in F_i, \lg(t) \geqslant 2 : (\mathrm{NTDec}(t) \neq \emptyset \Longrightarrow \mathrm{NTDec}_{\mathcal{F}}(t,F_i) \neq \emptyset)$.

The powerset-algebra $(\mathcal{P}(A), (\hat{f}_\omega)_{\omega \in \Omega})$ of $(A, (f_\omega)_{\omega \in \Omega})$ is defined in the usual way by:

$$\hat{f}_\omega : \begin{cases} (\mathcal{P}(A))^{a(\omega)} \longrightarrow \mathcal{P}(A) \\ (A_1,..,A_{a(\omega)}) \longmapsto \bigcup\limits_{a_i \in A_i} f_\omega(a_1,..,a_{a(\omega)}) \end{cases} .$$

Clearly the $\hat{f}_\omega$ are countable continous on $(\mathcal{P}(A),\subset)$. For short we continue to write (A,Ω) resp. $(\mathcal{P}(A),\Omega)$ instead of $(A,(f_\omega)_{\omega \in \Omega})$ resp. $(\mathcal{P}(A),(f_\omega)_{\omega \in \Omega})$.

We start with characterizations of $\mathcal{L}_2$. Let $\mathcal{A}_2$ be the algebra (X^*,Ω^2), Ω^2 as mentioned above.

(9) Theorem: The reducing congruent families on $\mathcal{A}_2$ exactly saturate the class of alphabetical homomorphic images of the Szilard languages ($\mathcal{H}_\alpha(\mathcal{S}_z)$) of X^*.

Proof: As Höpner [3] has shown, the 1-induced languages can be constructed by reduced context-free grammars with labelings of the following form: $A \xrightarrow{\wedge} BC$, $A \xrightarrow{x} B$, $A \xrightarrow{x} \wedge$, where A,B,C are nonterminals of the context-free grammar and $x \in X \cup \{\wedge\}$.

(1) Let $L \in \mathcal{H}_\alpha(\mathcal{S}_z)$ be a 1-induced language derived from $G = (V,\emptyset,P,S,X)$, where P is the labelled rule-set as stated above. Now $\mathcal{F} = \{F_A \,/\, A \in V\}$, where F_A denotes the 1-induced language derived from $G_A = (V,\emptyset,P,A,X)$, forms a reducing congruent family.

(2) Let on the other hand $\mathcal{F} = \{F_i \,/\, i \in I\}$ be a reducing congruent family on $\mathcal{A}_2$. Then we define the following labelled context-free grammar $G_i = (V,\emptyset,P,A_i,X)$, $V = \{A_i \,/\, i \in I\}$,

$$P = \{A_k \xrightarrow{\wedge} A_i A_j \,/\, F_i \between F_j \subset F_k\} \cup \{A_j \xrightarrow{x} A_i \,/\, x \in X,\ f_x(F_i) \subset F_j\}$$

$$\cup \{A_i \xrightarrow{x} \wedge / \ x \in F_i,\ x \in X \cup \{\wedge\}\}.$$

It turns out that the set F_i, $i \in I$, is exactly the 1-induced language derived from G_i . Since $\mathcal{H}_\alpha(\mathcal{S}_z)$ is closed under union we obtain our statement.

Example: $X = \{0, 1\}$, $\mathcal{A}_2 = (X^*, \{\between, f_0, f_1, \{0\}, \{1\}, \{\wedge\}\})$. The Dyck-language $D_1 \in \mathcal{H}_\alpha(\mathcal{S}_z)$ has the following representation in terms of reducing congruent families: $\mathcal{F} = \{D_1, \{1\}\}$ is a reducing congruent family consisting of two elements, because

$\begin{matrix} t & \in & 01 & \between & t' \\ \cap & & \cap & & \cap \\ D_1 & \supset & D_1 & \between & D_1 \end{matrix}$	clearly holds true for arbitrary $t \in X^*$, $lg(t) \geqslant 2$, and	$\begin{matrix} 01 & = & f_0(1) \\ \cap & & \cap \\ D_1 & \supset & f_0(\{1\}) \end{matrix}$.

Now it is easy to see, that for the construction of languages $L \in \mathcal{H}_\alpha(\mathcal{S}_z)$, $L \ni \wedge$, it suffices to use grammars $G = (V,\emptyset,P,S,X)$ without rules of the form $A \xrightarrow{\wedge} \wedge$.(Let $\mathcal{F} = \{F_i \,/\, i \in I\}$ be a red. congruent family saturating L, then $\{F_i - \{\wedge\} / \ i \in I\}$ is a red. congruent family saturating $L - \{\wedge\}$.)

That is the reason too for omitting the nullary operator $\{\wedge\}$ in Ω_2-equations in constructing $\wedge$-free minimal fixpoints.

As further applications of the ideas in Opp [7][8] we derive conditions for the equivalence of the notions of 'equational' subsets and subsets saturated by reducing congruent families.

(10) Definition: lg (the usual length of words in X^*) is called 'length-mapping' for (X^*,Ω) , if:

(a) $\forall n \in \mathbb{N}, \forall f \in \Omega_n, \forall w_1,\ldots,w_n \in X^*: \min\{lg(w)/w \in f(w_1,\ldots,w_n)\} \geqslant lg(w_i)$ for all $i = 1,\ldots,n$; and '$>$' instead of '$\geqslant$', if $lg(w_i) > 0$ for $i = 1,\ldots,n$.

(b) $\Omega_0 = X \cup \{\Lambda\}$.

(c) Λ is not essential for POL($\mathcal{P}(X^*), \Omega$), i.e. none of the polynomials ($\neq \{\Lambda\}$) really needs $\{\Lambda\}$.

(d) $\forall\, w \in X^* \exists\, n \in \mathbb{N}\ \exists\, f \in \Omega_n\ \exists\, w_1,\ldots,w_n \in X^* : (\ lg(w) \geqslant 2 \Longrightarrow w \in f(w_1,\ldots,w_n)$ and $lg(w_i) < lg(w)$ for $i = 1,\ldots,n\ )$.

(11) Theorem: Let lg be a length-mapping for (X^*, Ω).
Then the equational subsets of (X^*, Ω) equal the subsets saturated by finite reducing congruent families.

For the idea of the proof the reader is referred to Opp [8].

From (9) and (11) we obtain the following proof of theorem (2): Since the four conditions of Definition (10) hold true for $\mathcal{A}_2$ we can applicate theorem (11).(Condition (c) of (10) follows from the equations $X \between \{\Lambda\} = \{\Lambda\} \between X = X$, and $f_x(\Lambda) = x$).

The following general property is valid for multi-valued Ω-algebras with length-mapping:

(12) Theorem: The intersection of a subset saturated by a (reducing) congruent family with a subset saturated by a congruence can be saturated by a (reducing) congruent family. Moreover: finiteness of the underlieing congruence and congruent family implies finiteness of the resulting congruent family.

Proof: Let (A,Ω) be a multi-valued Ω-algebra, $L \subset A$ be saturated by the (reducing) congruent family $\mathcal{F} = \{F_i \ / \ i \in I\}$, $K \subset A$ saturated by the congruence $\mathcal{K} = \{K_j \ / \ j \in J\}$. We show that $\mathcal{F} \wedge \mathcal{K} = \{F_i \cap K_j \ / \ i \in I,\ j \in J\}$ is a (reducing) congruent family:

Let $t \in F_i \cap K_j$ with $Dec(t) \neq \emptyset$. Now

$$\begin{array}{lll} t & \in & f(t_1,\ldots\ldots,t_n) \\ \pitchfork & & \quad\ \pitchfork \qquad\quad \pitchfork \\ F_i & \supset & f(F_{i_1},\ldots,F_{i_n}) \end{array} \qquad \text{and } K_j \supset f(K_{j_1},\ldots,K_{j_n})\ , \text{ where } t_i \in K_{j_i}\ ,$$

implies the following diagram:

$$\begin{array}{ccc} t & \in & f(\; t_1 \quad , \ldots , \quad t_n \quad) \\ \cap & & \quad\;\; \cap \qquad\qquad\quad \cap \\ F_i \cap K_j & \supset & f(F_{i_1} \cap K_{j_1}, \ldots , F_{i_n} \cap K_{j_n}) \; . \end{array}$$

Now we get special closure properties for the families $\mathcal{L}_1$, $\mathcal{L}_2$, and $\mathcal{L}_3$ by discovering the saturation capacity of congruences of finite index on $\mathcal{A}_1$, $\mathcal{A}_2$, and $\mathcal{A}_3$.

<u>(13) Corollary:</u> Let $L \in \mathcal{L}_i$, $i \in \{1,2,3\}$, $R \subset X^*$ be a commutative regular language, i.e. perm(R) = R. Then $L \cap R \in \mathcal{L}_i$.

<u>Proof:</u> The finite congruences of $\mathcal{A}_1$, $\mathcal{A}_2$, and $\mathcal{A}_3$ coincide and saturate exactly the commutative regular subsets of X^*. So we can apply the above theorem (12).

Literature

1 Bekić,H. Definable operations in general algebras and the theory of automata and flowcharts. IBM, Vienna, (1969).

2 Hack,M. Petri Net Languages, MIT Comp. Struct. Group Memo 124,(1975).

3 Höpner,M. Über den Zusammenhang von Szilardsprachen und Matrixgrammatiken, Inst.für Informatik,Univ.Hamburg,Tech. Rep. Nr 12,(1974).

4 Höpner,M. Families of Languages Defined by Shuffle Operations, submitted for publication,(1976).

5 Höpner,M.
Opp,M. Renaming and Erasing in Szilard Languages,Univ. Hamburg, Tech.Rep. to be published, (1976)

6 Mazurkiewicz,A.
Parallel Recursive Program Schemes, 4th Symp. MFCS Marianske Lazne, (1975).

7 Opp,M. Eine Beschreibung kontextfreier Sprachen durch endliche Mengensysteme, 2nd GI Conf. on Aut.Th. and Formal Lang.,Kaiserslautern,(1975).

8 Opp,M. Charakterisierungen erkennbarer Termmengen in absolut freien universellen Algebren, Diss.Hamburg, (1975).

9 Wand,M. Mathematical foundations of formal language theory, MIT, MAC TR - 108, (1973).

A MACHINE INDEPENDENT DESCRIPTION OF COMPLEXITY CLASSES, DEFINABLE BY NONDETERMINISTIC AS WELL AS DETERMINISTIC TURING MACHINES WITH PRIMITIV RECURSIVE TAPE OR TIME BOUNDS

H. Huwig
Abteilung Informatik
Universität Dortmund
D - 46 Dortmund 50

For the following let $\Sigma = \{\sigma_1,\dots,\sigma_k\}$ ($k\in\mathbb{N}$, $k \geq 2$) be a fixed alphabet. We call the free monoid over this alphabet Σ^* and it's unit e.
For $\sigma\in\Sigma$ the σ-th syntactic successor function λ_σ is defined by:
$\lambda_\sigma:\Sigma^* \to \Sigma^*$, $x\in\Sigma^* \Rightarrow \lambda_\sigma(x) = x\sigma$.
The function $\phi:\Sigma^* \to \mathbb{N}_0$

$$x \to \begin{cases} 0 & \text{if } x = e \\ i & \text{if } x = \sigma_i\in\Sigma \\ k\cdot\phi(x') + \phi(\sigma) & \text{if } x = x'\sigma\in\Sigma^*\Sigma \end{cases}$$

is a bijection. Thus there is one and only one function $\nu:\Sigma^* \to \Sigma^*$, for which the equality $\nu \circ \phi = \phi \circ N$ holds. (N denotes the successor function on the natural numbers) ν is called the primitive successor function.

Let Y be a fixed set. Then the class of relations, Rel(Y), defined by
$Rel(Y) = \{R \mid \exists r,t\in\mathbb{N}_0 : R \subset Y^r \times Y^t\}$ is an X-category with respect to the mappings $\circ, \times$: $Rel(Y) \times Rel(Y) \to Rel(Y)$, where $\circ$ means the composition of relations and $\times$ is defined by: $R \times S := \{((x_1,x_2),(y_1,y_2)) \mid (x_1,y_1)\in R \wedge (x_2,y_2)\in S\}$.
Fun (Y) := $\{R \mid R\in Rel(Y)$ and R is a function$\}$ is a sub-X-category of Rel(Y).

In order to get large classes of computable functions or relations, one has to introduce some kind of recursion. We choose very simple forms of recursion: The primitive and the syntactic iteration.

<u>Def 1</u>: Let $(R_\sigma)_{\sigma\in\Sigma}$ be a sequence of relations with $R_\sigma \subset X \times X$ for all $\sigma\in\Sigma$. A relation $S \subset (X \times \Sigma^*) \times X$ is called a <u>syntactic iteration of $(R_\sigma)_{\sigma\in\Sigma}$</u> iff the following axioms hold:

a) $S(x,e) = id(x)$

b) $\sigma\in\Sigma, x\in X \wedge y\in\Sigma^* \Rightarrow$
$S \circ (id \times \lambda_\sigma)(x,y) = R_\sigma \circ S(x,y)$

(As usual for a relation T, T(x) denotes $\{y \mid (x,y)\in T\}$ and id the identity relation.)

Def 2: Let R be a relation, $R \subset X \times X$, then a relation T is called a primitive iterated relation of R iff:

$T \subset (X \times \Sigma^*) \times X$, such that for all $x \in X$ and $y \in \Sigma^*$

a) $T(x,e) = id(x)$

and b) $T \circ (id \times \nu)\ (x,y) = R \circ T(x,y)$.

Lem 1: a) If $(R_\sigma)_{\sigma\in\Sigma}$ is a sequence of relations with $R_\sigma \subset X \times X$ for all $\sigma\in\Sigma$, then there exists one and only one relation S, which is the syntactic iterated relation of $(R_\sigma)_{\sigma\in\Sigma}$.

b) If all R_σ are functions, then so is S.

Proof: Remark, that $M(X) := \{L \mid L \subset X \times X\}$ is a monoid with respect to composition of relations. Since Σ^* is a free monoid, there is one and only one antihomomorphism $F:\Sigma^* \to M(x)$ which extends to Σ^* the mapping $f:\Sigma \to M(x)$, defined by $\sigma\in\Sigma \Rightarrow f(\sigma) = R_\sigma$.

Define a relation $S \subset (X \times \Sigma^*) \times X$ by

$((x,y),z) \in S \Leftrightarrow (x,z) \in F(y)$. By induction one can see, that S is a syntactic iterated relation of $(R_\sigma)_{\sigma\in\Sigma}$, and that any other relation, satisfying def 1 for $(R_\sigma)_{\sigma\in\Sigma}$, equals S.

b) results from the fact, that the functions form a submonoid of M(X).

Lem 2: a) If R is a relation with $R \subset X \times X$, then there exists one and only one relation T, which is the primitiv iterated relation of R.

b) If in addition R is a function, then so is T.

Proof: The proof roceeds in a similar way, as that of the previous lemma, if we consider Σ^* and M(X) to be 0,1-algebras.

Besides recursion one needs some basic functions.

Def 3: $G = \{c,\bar{c},d,v\}$ is the set of basic functions, where

$c:\{\emptyset\} \to \Sigma^*$, $c(\emptyset) = e$	is the constant function;
$\bar{c}:\Sigma^* \to \{\emptyset\}$, $c(x) = \emptyset$	is the projection;
$d:\Sigma^* \to \Sigma^* \times \Sigma^*$, $d(x) = (x,x)$	is the diagonalisation
$v:\Sigma^* \times \Sigma^* \to \Sigma^* \times \Sigma^*$, $v(x,y) = (y,x)$	is the inversion.

Next we make also use of the primitive predecessor function π, which is uniquely determined by $\pi:\Sigma^* \to \Sigma^*$ with $\pi \circ \nu = id$ and $\pi(e) = e$. The syntactic predecessor function κ is defined by: $\kappa:\Sigma^* \to \Sigma^*$ satisfying: $\sigma\in\Sigma \Rightarrow \kappa \circ \lambda_\sigma = id$ and $\kappa(e) = e$. Finally the relation U, defined below, is sufficient to introduce nondeterminism: $U = \{(x,y) \mid x\in\Sigma^* \wedge y\in\{e,\sigma_1\}\}$.

We are now ready to define the classes of primitive resp. syntactic iterated functions resp. relations. We abbreviate $\mathbb{R} := Rel(\Sigma^*)$ and $\mathbb{A} := FUN(\Sigma^*)$

Def 4: $\overline{\$}$, the class of syntactic iterated relations, is the smallest sub-X-category of $\mathbb{R}$, for which the following axioms hold:

($\bar{S}1$) $G \cup \{\kappa, U\} \cup \{\lambda_\sigma | \sigma\varepsilon\Sigma\} \subset \overline{\$}$

($\bar{S}2$) If the sequence $(R_\sigma)_{\sigma\varepsilon\Sigma}$ with $R_\sigma \varepsilon \overline{\$}$ has a syntactic iterated relation S, then $S\varepsilon\overline{\$}$.

$\$$, the class of syntactic iterated functions, is defined like $\overline{\$}$, but ($\bar{S}1$) replaced by:

(S1) $G \cup \{\kappa\} \cup \{\lambda_\sigma | \sigma\varepsilon\Sigma\} \subset \$$

$\overline{\mathbb{P}}$, the class of primitiv iterated relations, is the smallest sub-X-category of $\mathbb{R}$, for which the following axioms hold:

($\bar{P}1$) $G \cup \{\pi, \nu, U\} \subset \overline{\mathbb{P}}$.

($\bar{P}2$) $R\varepsilon\overline{\mathbb{P}}$ has a primitiv iterated relation T, then $T\varepsilon\overline{\mathbb{P}}$.

$\mathbb{P}$, the class of primitiv iterated functions, is defined like $\overline{\mathbb{P}}$, but ($\bar{P}1$) replaced by: (P1) $G \cup \{\pi, \nu\} \subset \mathbb{P}$.

Lem 3: $\overline{\mathbb{P}} \subset \overline{\$}$ and $\mathbb{P} \subset \$$

Proof: One can easily find syntactic iterated schemata for the functions π and ν. But then by definition of $\overline{\$}$ and $\overline{\mathbb{P}}$, it is sufficient to show, that $\overline{\$}$ is closed under primitive iteration: Take any relation $R\varepsilon\$$ with $R \subset \Sigma^{*r} \times \Sigma^{*r} (r\varepsilon\mathbb{N}_0)$ and define a sequence $(R_\sigma)_{\sigma\varepsilon\Sigma}$ by $\sigma\varepsilon\Sigma \Rightarrow R_\sigma = R$. By definition of $\overline{\$}$, S the syntactic iterated relation of $(R_\sigma)_{\sigma\varepsilon\Sigma}$ can be found in $\overline{\$}$. Let $f:\Sigma^* \to \Sigma^*$ be defined by $f(y) = \sigma_1^{\phi(y)}$. Clearly f is a syntactic iterated function. But then T, the primitive iterated relation of R is also in $\overline{\$}$, as the following equation shows:

$$T = S \circ (id_{\Sigma^{*r}} \times f).$$

Thus $\overline{\$}$ is closed under primitive iteration, i.e. $\overline{\mathbb{P}} \subset \overline{\$}$. Since f is a function, the prove also works for $\mathbb{P} \subset \$$.

In order to prove the other inclusions, we replace a sequence $(R_\sigma)_{\sigma\varepsilon\Sigma}$, with $R_\sigma \subset \Sigma^{*r} \times \Sigma^{*r}$ by a single relation R, which may be described in an informal way as follows:

$$R \subset (\Sigma^{*r} \times \Sigma^*) \times (\Sigma^{*r} \times \Sigma^*)$$

$R(x,z)$ = <u>if</u> $z\varepsilon\Sigma^*\{\sigma_1\}$ <u>then</u> $R_{\sigma_1} \times \kappa(x,z)$

<u>else</u> <u>if</u> $z\varepsilon\Sigma^*\{\sigma_2\}$ <u>then</u> $R_{\sigma_2} \times \kappa(x,z)$ ...

<u>if</u> $z\varepsilon\Sigma^*\{\sigma_2\}$ <u>then</u> $R_{\sigma_k} \times \kappa(x,z)$ <u>else</u> $id_{\Sigma^{*r}} \times id(x,z)$ <u>fi</u> ... <u>fi</u>.

Obviously for S the syntactic iterated relation of $(R_\sigma)_{\sigma\varepsilon\Sigma}$ and T the primitiv relation of R, the following equality holds:

$$S = T \circ (id_{\Sigma^*} \circ d).$$

Thus to prove, that $\overline{\mathbb{P}}$ is closed under syntactic iteration, it is essential to show, that we can construct the conditional statement in $\overline{\mathbb{P}}$.

Def 5: Let G,H be two relations, with $G,H \subset X \times X$ and F a relation with $F \subset X \times \Sigma^*$. We say, that S is built from F,G and H by conditional statement iff:

For all $(x,y)\varepsilon X \times X \Rightarrow$

$$(x,y)\varepsilon S \Leftrightarrow ((x,e)\varepsilon F \wedge (x,y)\varepsilon G) \vee$$
$$(\ z\varepsilon\Sigma^*\Sigma \text{ with } (x,z)\varepsilon F \wedge (x,y)\varepsilon H)$$

We write $(F \rightarrow G,H)$ instead of S.

Remark, that, if F is a function, then $(x,e)\varepsilon F \Rightarrow (x,z)\notin F$ for all $z\varepsilon\Sigma^*\Sigma$ and thus $(F \rightarrow G,H)$ is usual conditional statement in this case.

Lem 4: $F,G,H,\varepsilon\bar{\mathbb{P}}$ with the properties demanded in def 5, then: $(F \rightarrow G,H)\varepsilon\bar{\mathbb{P}}$

Proof: Define a relation $S_r \subset (\Sigma^{*r} \times \Sigma^{*r})^2$ by $(x',y')\varepsilon S_r(x,y) \Leftrightarrow x' = y' = y$. Obviously $S_r\varepsilon\mathbb{P}$, for all $r\varepsilon\mathbb{N}_o$. But then T_r, the primitive iterated relation of S_r is in $\mathbb{P}$. By introduction one shows:

$$(x',y')\varepsilon T_r(x,y,z) \Leftrightarrow$$
$$x' = x \wedge y' = y \text{ if } z = e$$
$$x' = y \wedge y' = y \text{ if } z \neq e.$$

Since $(F \rightarrow G,H) = T_r \circ (G \times H \times F) \circ \Delta_{r,3}$,

- with $\Delta_{r,3}:\Sigma^{*r} \rightarrow \Sigma^{*r} \times \Sigma^{*r} \times \Sigma^{*r}$

$$x \rightarrow (x,x,x)$$ -

$\Delta_{r,3}$ is in $\bar{\mathbb{P}}$ and $\bar{\mathbb{P}}$ is an X-category, it follows that $(F \rightarrow G,H)\varepsilon\bar{\mathbb{P}}$.

Theorem 1: $\bar{\mathbb{P}} = \bar{\$}$ and $\mathbb{P} = \$$

Proof: One shows that κ, the functions $\lambda_\sigma(\sigma\varepsilon\Sigma)$ as well as the functions $g_\sigma:\Sigma^* \rightarrow \Sigma^*$

$$x \rightarrow \begin{cases} e & \text{if} \quad x\varepsilon\Sigma^*\{\sigma\} \\ \sigma_1 & \text{if} \quad x\notin\Sigma^*\{\sigma\} \end{cases}$$

are in $\bar{\mathbb{P}}$. Then because of lemma 4 we can construct for each sequence $(R_\sigma)_{\sigma\varepsilon\Sigma}$ with $R_\sigma\varepsilon\bar{\mathbb{P}}$ the informally described R in $\bar{\mathbb{P}}$. The above mentioned equality between the syntactic iterated relation S of $(R_\sigma)_{\sigma\varepsilon\Sigma}$ and the primitive iterated relation T of R,

$S = T \circ (id_{\Sigma^{*r}} \times d)$, shows, that with T also S is in $\bar{\mathbb{P}}$, i.e. $\bar{\$} \subset \bar{\mathbb{P}}$.

Since the g_σ are functions, the proof also works for $\$ \subset \mathbb{P}$. The other inclusions were shown in lemma 3.

We want to divide $\mathbb{P}$, $\$$, $\bar{\mathbb{P}}$ and $\bar{\$}$ in complexity classes. For this purpose let $\bar{a}_i: \mathbb{N}_o \times \mathbb{N}_o \rightarrow \mathbb{N}_o$ be the i-th Ackermannfunction ($i\varepsilon\mathbb{N}_o$), and call $a_i:\Sigma^* \times \Sigma^* \rightarrow \Sigma^*$ that function, for which the equality $\phi \circ a_i = \bar{a}_i \circ (\phi \times \phi)$ holds. In addition we define $\bar{a}_{2a}: \mathbb{N}_o \times \mathbb{N}_o \rightarrow \mathbb{N}_o$ by $(x,y)\varepsilon\mathbb{N}_o \times \mathbb{N}_o \Rightarrow \bar{a}_{2a}(x,y) = x^{[lg_k y]}$ and a_{2a} by the equality $\phi \circ a_{2a} = \bar{a}_{2a} \circ (\phi \times \phi)$. We introduce a relation $\leq$ on Σ^* by $x \leq y \Leftrightarrow \phi(x) \leq \phi(y)$.

It is clear how $\leq$ is understood on cartesian products of Σ^* and we can define $\leq$ for two relations S and S' $(S,S' \subset \Sigma^{*r} \times \Sigma^{*t})$ by $S \leq S'$ iff $(x,y) \varepsilon S \Rightarrow \exists\, (x,y') \varepsilon S'$ with $y \leq y'$. We now are ready to introduce a Grzegorczyk hierarchy for all the classes $\$, \bar{\$}$, $\mathbb{P}$ and $\bar{\mathbb{P}}$.

Def 6: For $i \varepsilon \mathbb{N}_o \cup \{2a\}$ $\bar{\mathbb{F}}^i$ is the smallest sub-X-category of $\bar{S}$, for which the following axioms hold:

($\bar{F}$1) $G \cup \{\kappa, U, a_i\} \cup \{\lambda_\sigma | \sigma \varepsilon \Sigma\} \subset \bar{\mathbb{F}}^i$

($\bar{F}$2) If S, the syntactic iterated relation of a sequence $(R_\sigma)_{\sigma \varepsilon \Sigma}$ with $R_\sigma \varepsilon \bar{\mathbb{F}}^i$ is defined and there exists
$S' \varepsilon < G \cup \{\kappa, U, a_i\} \cup \{\lambda_\sigma | \sigma \varepsilon \Sigma\} >$ with $S \leq S'$, then: $S \varepsilon \bar{\mathbb{F}}^i$.

(For a set Y, <Y> means the smallest X-category containing Y).

It should be clear, how $\mathbb{F}^i, \mathbb{E}^i$, and $\bar{\mathbb{E}}^i$ the Grzegorczyk-classes of S, $\mathbb{P}$ and $\bar{\mathbb{P}}$ are defined.

Theorem 2:
a) $\bar{\mathbb{F}}^o = \bar{\mathbb{F}}^1, \mathbb{F}^o = \mathbb{F}^1, \bar{\mathbb{E}}^o \quad \bar{\mathbb{E}}^1, \mathbb{E}^o \quad \mathbb{E}^1$.
b) $\bar{\mathbb{F}}^i \subsetneq \bar{\mathbb{F}}^{i+1}, \mathbb{F}^i \subsetneq \mathbb{F}^{i+1}, \bar{\mathbb{E}}^i \subsetneq \bar{\mathbb{E}}^{i+1}, \mathbb{E}^i \subsetneq \mathbb{E}^{i+1}$. $(i \varepsilon \mathbb{N}_o)$
c) $\bar{\mathbb{F}}^2 \subsetneq \bar{\mathbb{F}}^{2a} \subsetneq \bar{\mathbb{F}}^3, \mathbb{F}^2 \subsetneq \mathbb{F}^{2a} \subsetneq \mathbb{F}^3$,
$\bar{\mathbb{E}}^2 \subsetneq \bar{\mathbb{E}}^{2a} \subsetneq \bar{\mathbb{E}}^3, \mathbb{E}^2 \subsetneq \mathbb{E}^{2a} \subsetneq \mathbb{E}^3$.

Proof: By a standard argument about the growth of the functions resp. relations.

Theorem 3:
a) $i \varepsilon \mathbb{N}_o$, $i \geq 3 \Rightarrow \mathbb{F}^i = \mathbb{E}^i, \mathbb{F}^i = \mathbb{E}^i$.
b) $j \varepsilon \{1,2,2a\} = \mathbb{F}^j \subset \mathbb{E}^j, \bar{\mathbb{F}}^j \subset \bar{\mathbb{E}}^j$.
c) equality holds in b iff $\mathbb{F}^j$ resp. $\mathbb{F}^j$ is closed under primitive iteration.

Proof: An inspection of the proof of theorem 1 shows, that the functions used, to simulate syntactic by primitive iteration can be found in $\mathbb{E}^o$. The function used in the other direction has exponential growth. This shows a) and b).
c) should be clear form the definition of $\bar{\mathbb{F}}^j$ and $\mathbb{E}^j$ resp. $\mathbb{F}^j$ and $\mathbb{E}^j$.

The different Grzegorczyk classes may be used to characterize the complexity of Turing machine computations. For this purpose let $|\ |: \Sigma^* \to \mathbb{N}_o$ be the homomorphism induced by $\sigma \varepsilon \Sigma \Rightarrow |\sigma| = 1$ and $|\ |_r: \Sigma^{*r} \to \mathbb{N}_o$ defined by $x = (x_1, \ldots, x_r) \to \max\{|x_\gamma| \,|\, \gamma \varepsilon [1,r]\}$. The time used for a Turing computation is measured in the usual way by a function $T': \Sigma^{*r} \to \mathbb{N}_o$ which factorized over $|\ |_r$, i.e. there is $T: \mathbb{N}_o \to \mathbb{N}_o$ such that $T' = T \circ |\ |_r$ holds. To each such function T we associate a function $\bar{T}: \Sigma^{*r} \to \Sigma^*$, for which the equality $|| \circ \bar{T} = T \circ ||_r$ holds. In the same way to each $S: \mathbb{N}_o \to \mathbb{N}_o$, measuring the tape used during a computation, we associate a function $\bar{S}$. It is well known, that in the deterministic case we can state the following theorem:

Theorem 4: a) $i \in \mathbb{N}$, $i \geq 3 \vee i \in \{2a\} \Rightarrow$

$f \in \mathbb{F}^i \Leftrightarrow$ There exists a Turing machine computing f within in the time bound $\bar{T}$ satisfying $\bar{T} \in \mathbb{F}^i$.

b) $i \in \mathbb{N}$, $i \geq 2 \quad i \in \{2a\} \Rightarrow$

$f \in \mathbb{E}^i \Leftrightarrow$ There exists a Turing machine computing f within the tape bound $\bar{S}$ and $\bar{S}$ satisfying $\bar{S} \in \mathbb{E}^i$.

c) $f \in \mathbb{F}^2 \Leftrightarrow$ There exists a Turing machine computing f within linear space and polynomial time.

Proof: A proof concerning time complexity is in [He]. c) can be found in [To].

Theorem 5: Theorem 4 holds in the nondeterministic case, if we replace $\mathbb{F}^i$ by $\bar{\mathbb{F}}^i$ and $\mathbb{E}^i$ by $\bar{\mathbb{E}}^i$

Proof: We only give an outline of the proof. The if-part works like the deterministic case. For the only-if-part remark, that we can replace the transition function δ of a Turing machine $\delta: K \to 2^K$ by a relation $\Delta \subset K \times K$. (K denotes the set of configuration of the Turingmachine, i.e. $K \subset Q \times \Sigma^{*r} \times \Sigma^{*s} \times \Sigma^{*t}$ with Q the finite set of states, Σ^{*r} representing the input tapes, Σ^{*s} the working tapes and Σ^{*t} the output tapes.) Since Q is a finite set Δ may be simulated by a relation $\bar{\Delta} \subset \bar{K} \times \bar{K}$ where $\bar{K} \subset \Sigma^{*} \times \Sigma^{*r} \times \Sigma^{*s} \times \Sigma^{*t}$. More over we can imagine $\bar{\Delta}$ to be a finite union of some functions $\bar{\delta}: \bar{K} \to \bar{K}$. i.e. $\bar{\Delta} = \bigcup_{\nu \in [1,n]} \bar{\delta}_\nu$. Encreasing time or tape bounds by a constant factor we can make the Turing machine using its tapes like pushdowns. But then the δ_ν can be built up from λ_σ and κ by $\circ, \times$ and conditional statements. Thus the δ_ν are in $\mathbb{E}^1 \cap \mathbb{F}^1$. Then to prove $\bar{\Delta} \in \bar{\mathbb{E}}^1 \cap \bar{\mathbb{F}}^1$, it is sufficient to show, that $\bar{\mathbb{E}}^1$ and $\bar{\mathbb{F}}^1$ are closed under union, since $\mathbb{E}^1 \subset \bar{\mathbb{E}}^1$ and $\mathbb{F}^1 \subset \mathbb{F}^1$ and $\delta_\nu \in \mathbb{E}^1 \cap \mathbb{F}^1$ $(\nu \in [1,n])$.

Now let R and S be two relations with $R, S \subset \Sigma^{*r} \times \Sigma^{*r}$ and consider $V = (U \to R, S)$, where U is the relation of definition 3. It is easy to show, that $V = R \cup S$, thus $\bar{\Delta} \in \bar{\mathbb{E}}^1$. Since conditional statements can also be constructed, with the help of syntactic iteration, $\bar{\Delta} \in \bar{\mathbb{F}}_1$ follows too.

Then the primitive iterated relation of $\bar{\Delta}$ can be found in $\bar{\mathbb{E}}^2$ and the syntactic iterated relation of the sequence $(R_\sigma)_{\sigma \in \Sigma}$ with $R_\sigma = \bar{\Delta}$ for all $\sigma \in \Sigma$ can be found in $\bar{\mathbb{F}}^2$.

From these relations the relation computed by the Turing machine is easily to be found by some coding using $\bar{T}$ resp. $\bar{S}$. Thus is clear, that the complexity of the computed relation F is already determined by the time resp. tape bound.

Theorem 6: a) The following statements are equivalent:

1) NP, the set of relations computable on a nondeterministic Turing machine within polynomial time bounds equals the set of functions computable on a nondeterministic Turingmachine within polynomial tape bounds.

2) NP is closed under primitive iteration

3) NP $\supset \mathbf{E}^{0}$

b) a) holds if we replace nondeterministic by deterministic Turing machines.

Proof: In either case the equivalence of 1) and 2) is a corollary of theorem 3 and theorem 4 resp. theorem 5. A proof for the equivalence of 3) in the deterministic case may be found in [Hu]. A slight modification of the proof works in the nondeterministic case.

Literature

[E] S. Eilenberg, C. Elgot, Recursiveness, Academic Press, New York and London, 1970

[G] A. Grzegorczyk, Some classes of recursive functions, Rozprawy Matematyczne, Warszawa 1953

[He] F.W. von Henke, K. Indermark, K. Weihrauch, Primitive recursice wordfunctions, Automata, Languages and Programming - Proceedings of a symposium organized by IRIA, North-Holland Publishing Company, Amsterdam, London, 1973

[Hu] H. Huwig, Beziehungen zwischen beschränkter syntaktischer und beschränkter primitiver Rekursion, Universität Dortmund, Dissertation 1976

[K] H. Kopp, Programmierung von Funktionen, Berichtsreihe der Abteilung Informatik der Universität des Saarlandes

[M] H. Müller, Klassifizierungen der primitiv-rekursiven Funktionen, Dissertation, 1974

[S] C.P. Schnorr, Rekursive Funktionen und ihre Komplexität, Teubner Studienbücher, Stuttgart 1974

[To] D.B. Thompson, Subrecursiveness: Machine-Independent Notions of Computability in Restricted Time and Storage, Mathematical Systems Theory, Vol.6, No.1, Springer-Verlag, New York, 1972

SCHEMES WITH RECURSION ON HIGHER TYPES

Klaus Indermark

Lehrstuhl für Informatik II, RWTH Aachen

Büchel 29 - 31, D - 51oo Aachen

1. Introduction

In program scheme theory it has been shown that recursion is a more powerful control structure than iteration: flowchart schemes are translatable into recursion schemes, but not vice versa. For a comprehensive treatment of this and related results see the books of ENGELFRIET |2| and GREIBACH |4|. These recursion schemes do not involve objects of higher functional types. In order to investigate the impact of higher types on the definition of lower type objects we introduce a class of program schemes which are based on typed combinators including fixed-point combinators.

These "combinator schemes" have two characteristic features:

1) Cartesian products are not eliminated by means of SCHÖNFINKEL's isomorphisms $((A \times B) \to C) \cong (A \to (B \to C))$ because this would lead to irrelevant higher types.

2) The schemes are completely uninterpreted in the sense of NIVAT |6|: <u>if</u> ... <u>then</u> ... <u>else</u> ... and predicate symbols do not occur; operation symbols will be interpreted as continuous operations on chain-complete partially ordered sets.

In this paper we define syntax and semantics of combinator schemes which originated from the author's lectures on recursive definitions |5|. Furthermore, we reduce this class of schemes to certain subclasses. Due to space limits proofs are omitted and will be published elsewhere.

2. Cartesian types

Types are names for sets. Starting from a set of base types we generate cartesian types by use of two binary operations. They will be interpreted as cartesian product and exponentiation.

For a given set I of <u>base types</u> we define the set <u>typ</u>(I) of <u>cartesian types over I</u> as the smallest class $K \subseteq (I \,\dot{\cup}\, \{[\,,\,],\ |\,,e\})^{+}$ such that

(i) $\{e\} \cup I \subseteq K$

(ii) $t_1, t_2 \in K \Rightarrow [t_1 \mid t_2] \in K$

(iii) $t_1, t_2 \in K \setminus \{e\} \Rightarrow t_1 t_2 \in K$.

<u>typ</u> (I) can be considered as the carrier of an algebra with operations $(t_1,t_2) \mapsto [t_1 \mid t_2]$, $(t_1,t_2) \mapsto t_1 t_2$ with unit e and $(\,) \mapsto e$. Moreover, this algebra is freely generated by I in the class of all algebras with two binary and one nullary operation where in addition one binary operation is associative with the nullary operation as its neutral element.

3. Typed combinators

Typed combinators are names for canonical elements of certain function spaces.

The set $\Gamma(I)$ of <u>combinators over I</u> is defined as the disjoint union of the following symbol sets:

(i) <u>composition combinators</u> $\{\underline{C \ \langle t_1,t_2,t_3\rangle} \mid t_\nu \in \underline{typ}(I)\}$

(ii) <u>tupling combinators</u> $\{\underline{T \ \langle t_1,t_2,t_3\rangle} \mid t_\nu \in \underline{typ}(I)\}$

(iii) <u>abstraction combinators</u> $\{\underline{K \ \langle t_1,t_2\rangle} \mid t_\nu \in \underline{typ}(I)\}$

(iv) <u>Schönfinkel combinators</u> $\{\underline{S \ \langle t_1,t_2,t_3\rangle} \mid t_\nu \in \underline{typ}(I)\}$

and $\{\underline{\$ \ \langle t_1,t_2,t_3\rangle} \mid t_\nu \in \underline{typ}(I)\}$

(v) <u>fixed-point combinators</u> $\{\underline{Y \ \langle t\rangle} \mid t \in \underline{typ}(I)\}$

Their meaning can be guessed from the notation and will be defined below. Since we deal with cartesian products we have included tupling and Schönfinkel combinators. Fixed-point combinators are required because infinite types, and therefore self-application, lay outside the scope of this paper.

According to its indices each combinator over I is given a type.
The mapping $\tau : \Gamma(I) \to \underline{typ}(I)$ is defined by

(i) $\underline{C\ <r,s,t>}\ \mapsto\ [[r\mid s][s\mid t]\mid[r\mid t]]$

(ii) $\underline{T\ <r,s,t>}\ \mapsto\ [[r\mid s][r\mid t]\mid[r\mid st]]$

(iii) $\underline{K\ <s,t>}\ \mapsto\ [t\mid[s\mid t]]$

(iv) $\underline{S\ <r,s,t>}\ \mapsto\ [[rs\mid t]\mid[r\mid[s\mid t]]]$

(v) $\underline{\$\ <r,s,t>}\ \mapsto\ [[r\mid[s\mid t]]\mid[rs\mid t]]$

(vi) $\underline{Y\ <t>}\ \mapsto\ [[t\mid t]\mid t]$

Syntactically, these types allow for typed combinations of combinators and operation symbols, whereas semantically they will indicate the corresponding function spaces.

4. Combinator schemes

Now, we can introduce the class of combinator schemes over an alphabet Ω of heterogeneous operation symbols as the typed combination closure of Ω and Γ. To be more precise let $\Omega(I)$ be a set of operation symbols over I typed by
$\tau : \Omega(I) \to [I^* \mid I]$.
The class rec($\Omega(I)$) of combinator schemes over $\Omega(I)$ is defined as the smallest subclass

$$K \subseteq (\Omega(I) \cup \Gamma(I) \cup \{(\ ,\ )\})^+ \quad \text{typed by} \quad \tau : K \to \underline{typ}(I) \quad \text{such that}$$

(i) $\Omega \cup \Gamma \subseteq K$

(ii) $S,S_1,\ldots,S_n \in K,\quad \tau(S) = [t_1 t_2 \ldots t_n \mid t],\quad \tau(S_\nu) = t_\nu,$

$1 \leq \nu \leq n \quad \Rightarrow (S\, S_1\, S_2 \ldots S_n) \in K$ with type t

The notation rec stands for "recursion". In fact, the fixed-point combinators will describe recursion on higher types.

5. Semantics

Types will be interpreted as chain-complete posets (cpo's), operation symbols as continuous operations, combinators as continuous operators, and combinations as applications.

The class cpo of all cpo's has the following property. For $A,B \in$ cpo we know that the set $(A \to B)$ of continuous functions from A to B w.r.t. point-wise ordering and the associative cartesian product $A \times B$ w.r.t. component-wise ordering belong again to cpo. By $\perp$ we denote the one-element cpo $\{\emptyset\}$ which is the neutral element of $\times$. Thereby, we can define for a given class $\mathfrak{K}$ of cpo's its <u>cartesian closure</u> <u>cart</u>($\mathfrak{K}$) as the smallest subclass of <u>cpo</u> that contains $\mathfrak{K} \cup \{\underline{\perp}\}$ and that is closed under exponentiation $(A,B) \mapsto (A \to B)$ and product $(A,B) \mapsto A \times B$.

Let $A := \{A^i \mid i \in I\} \subseteq \underline{cpo}$. A is called a <u>(continuous) interpretation of I</u> and it extends uniquely to all cartesian types over I:

The mapping $h_A : \underline{typ}(I) \to \underline{cart}(A)$ is determined by

$$\begin{aligned} i &\mapsto A^i \\ e &\mapsto \underline{\perp} \\ [s \mid t] &\mapsto (h_A(s) \to h_A(t)) \\ st &\mapsto h_A(s) \times h_A(t) \end{aligned}$$

For the uniqueness of h_A see the remarks in 2. on the algebraic character of <u>typ</u>(I). They prove h_A to be an algebra homomorphism.

Notation: We write A^t for $h_A(t)$ as in the case of base types and $\underline{obj}(A) := \{F \in A^t \mid t \in \underline{typ}(I)\}$.

An interpretation A of I implies the semantics of the typed combinators: The mapping $[\![\ ]\!]_A : \Gamma(I) \to \underline{obj}(A)$ is given by

$$[\![C<r,s,t>]\!]_A : A^{[r|s]} \times A^{[s|t]} \to A^{[r|t]},\quad (f,g) \mapsto \lambda x.\ g(f(x))$$

$$[\![T<r,s,t>]\!]_A : A^{[r|s]} \times A^{[r|t]} \to A^{[r|st]},\quad (f,g) \mapsto \lambda x.\ (f(x),\ g(x))$$

$$[\![K<s,t>]\!]_A : A^t \to A^{[s|t]},\quad f \mapsto \lambda x.\ f$$

$$[\![S<r,s,t>]\!]_A : A^{[rs|t]} \to A^{[r|[s|t]]},\quad f \mapsto \lambda x.\ \lambda y.\ f(x,y)$$

$$[\![\$<r,s,t>]\!]_A : A^{[r|[s|t]]} \to A^{[rs|t]},\quad f \mapsto \lambda(x,y).\ f(x)(y)$$

$$[\![Y<t>]\!]_A : A^{[t|t]} \to A^t,\quad f \mapsto \{f^n(\underline{\perp}) \mid n \in \mathbb{N}\}$$

It can be shown that all these objects are in fact continuous.

Now, let in addition $\phi : \Omega(I) \to \underline{obj}(A)$ be a type preserving mapping, i.e., $F \in \Omega,\ \tau(F) = [w \mid i] \Rightarrow \phi(F) \in (A^w \to A^i)$. Then, $\underset{\sim}{A} := (A;\phi)$ is called a <u>(continuous) interpretation of $\Omega(I)$</u>. It implies the semantics of combinator schemes as follows.

$$[\![\ ]\!]_{\underset{\sim}{A}} : \underline{rec}(\Omega(I)) \to \underline{obj}(A)$$

is determined by

(i) $[\![S]\!]_{\underset{\sim}{A}} := [\![S]\!]_A$ for $S \in \Gamma(I)$

(ii) $[\![S]\!]_{\underset{\sim}{A}} := \phi(S)$ for $S \in \Omega(I)$

(iii) $[\![(S\,S_1 \ldots S_n)]\!]_{\underset{\sim}{A}} := [\![S]\!]_{\underset{\sim}{A}} ([\![S_1]\!]_{\underset{\sim}{A}}, \ldots, [\![S_n]\!]_{\underset{\sim}{A}})$.

Finally, we define <u>equivalence</u> of schemes $S_1, S_2 \in \underline{rec}(\Omega(I))$ as usual:

$$S_1 \sim S_2 \iff [\![S_1]\!]_{\underset{\sim}{A}} = [\![S_2]\!]_{\underset{\sim}{A}} \text{ for every interpretation } \underset{\sim}{A} \text{ of } \Omega(I).$$

6. Reduction

The language of combinator schemes is rather redundant concerning equivalence. Therefore we shall reduce this language to equivalent sublanguages. For that purpose we first select a hierarchy of types:

$$I_o := I \quad \text{and} \quad I_{n+1} := [I_n^* \mid I_n] \qquad (n \in \mathbb{N})$$

and denote by $\underline{\text{rec}}(\Omega(I))^n$ the class of combinator schemes of degree n, i.e. their type is in I_n.

(1) It can be shown that every combinator scheme is "reducible" to some $S \in \underline{\text{rec}}(\Omega(I))^n$ by means of certain abstraction and application schemes.

In the next reduction step we construct for each $\underline{\text{rec}}(\Omega(I))^n$ a subclass $\underline{\mu\text{-rec}}(\Omega(I))^n$. This construction is based on the following combinator schemes.

Lemma For all $s, t_1, \ldots, t_r, u \in \underline{\text{typ}}(I)$ and $1 \leq \nu \leq r$ the class $\underline{\text{rec}}(\Omega(I))$ contains schemes $\underline{\pi < t_1, \ldots, t_r, \nu >}$, $\underline{\sigma < s, t_1, \ldots, t_r, u >}$, $\underline{\mu < s, t_1, \ldots, t_r, u >}$, $\underline{\kappa < s, u >}$, $\underline{\alpha < s >}$ and $\underline{1}$ which have for each interpretation $\underset{\sim}{A}$ of $\Omega(I)$ the following property:

$$[\![\underline{\pi < t_1, \ldots, t_r, \nu >}]\!]_{\underset{\sim}{A}} \; (a_1, \ldots, a_r) = a_\nu$$

$$[\![\underline{\sigma < s, t_1, \ldots, t_r, u >}]\!]_{\underset{\sim}{A}} \; (f, f_1, \ldots, f_r) = \lambda x. \;\; f(f_1(x), \ldots, f_r(x))$$

$$[\![\underline{\mu < s, t_1, \ldots, t_r, u >}]\!]_{\underset{\sim}{A}} \; (f, f_1, \ldots, f_r) = \lambda x. \;\; f(\mu y. \; (f_1(x,y), \ldots, f_r(x,y)))$$

$$[\![\underline{\kappa < s, u >}]\!]_{\underset{\sim}{A}} \; (f) = \lambda x. \; f(\;)$$

$$[\![\underline{\alpha < s >}]\!]_{\underset{\sim}{A}} \; (a) = \lambda(\;).\; a \quad \text{and} \quad |\underline{1}|_{\underset{\sim}{A}} = \bot \in A^e \quad .$$

The types should be clear from the context, e.g.: $\tau(\underline{\kappa < s, u >}) = [[e \mid u] \mid [s \mid u]]$.
If there is no danger of confusion type indices are dropped. In particular, we write $(\underline{\alpha}^n S)$ for n-fold abstraction.
According to their semantics these schemes are called projection schemes, substitution schemes, μ - substitution schemes, constant schemes, abstraction schemes and unit scheme.

Now, let $n \geq 1$. Denoting by $\Pi(I)^n$ and $\Sigma(I)^n$ the classes of projection and substitution schemes of degree n, respectively, we construct the class $B(\Omega(I))^n$ of base schemes of degree n by

$$B(\Omega(I))^1 \quad := \quad \Omega(I) \cup \Pi(I)^1$$

and

$$B(\Omega(I))^{n+1} \quad := \quad \{(\underline{\alpha}^n S) \mid S \in \Omega(I) \cup \Pi(I)^1\} \cup \Sigma(I)^{n+1} \cup \Pi(I)^{n+1} \quad .$$

Then, the class $\underline{\mu - rec}(\Omega(I))^n$ is defined as the smallest $L \subseteq \underline{rec}(\Omega(I))^n$ such that

(i) $B(\Omega(I))^n \subseteq L$

(ii) $S, S_1, \ldots, S_r \in L \Rightarrow (\underline{\sigma}\ SS_1 \ldots S_r) \in L$

(iii) $S, S_1, \ldots, S_r \in L \Rightarrow (\underline{\mu}\ SS_1 \ldots S_r) \in L$

(iv) $S \in L \Rightarrow (\underline{\kappa}\ S) \in L$

provided that the argument schemes have suitable types. (In the terminology of WAND |7| this is called the μ - clone of $B(\Omega(I))^n$.)
From normal form theorems for μ - clones it can be derived that

(2) $\underline{\mu - rec}(\Omega(I))^1$ is equivalent to the class of regular equation schemes with parameters in the sense of GOGUEN / THATCHER |3|,

and that

(3) $\underline{\mu - rec}(\Omega(I))^2$ is equivalent to the class of recursion equation schemes with operation parameters, a slight generalization of NIVAT's recursion schemes |6|.

Moreover, combinator schemes can be reduced to these schemes:

(4) For each $n \geq 1$ and $S \in \underline{rec}(\Omega(I))^n$ there is $m \geq 1$ and $S' \in \underline{\mu - rec}(\Omega(I))^{n+m}$ such that $S \sim \underbrace{(\ldots((S'\underline{1})\underline{1})\ldots\underline{1})}_{m}$.

Since we want to use higher types only as an auxiliary device for generating low level objects our interest concentrates on the class $\underline{rec}(\Omega(I))^1$ of "operational" combinator schemes. From (4) we know that every such scheme can be obtained from some higher-type μ - clone scheme by iterated applications. This leads to the following definition:

$$\underline{\mu - rec}(\Omega(I))^n_1 := \{\underbrace{(\ldots((S\,\underline{1})\underline{1})\ldots\underline{1})}_{n-1} \mid S \in \underline{\mu - rec}(\Omega(I))^n \, , \ \tau(S) \ \text{suitable}\}$$

Then we can prove the following hierarchy of schemes:

(5) $\underline{\mu - rec}(\Omega(I))^n_1$ is translatable into $\underline{\mu - rec}(\Omega(I))^{n+1}_1$.

Moreover, in DAMM |1| we find a proof of

(6) $\underline{\mu - rec}(\Omega(I))^2_1$ is not translatable into $\underline{\mu - rec}(\Omega(I))^1_1$.

It should be noted that (6) requires certain restrictions on Ω. E.g., if Ω contains only monadic function symbols the classes of (6) are intertranslatable.

7. Conclusion

This discussion leads to the problem whether the hierarchy of (5) is strict. A positive answer would demonstrate that procedures with recursion on higher types enlarge the computational power of a programming language.

This research is being continued in collaboration with Werner DAMM, and I take the opportunity to thank him for many helpful and stimulating discussions.

8. References

|1| DAMM, W.: Einfach-rekursive und rekursive Schemata mit stetigen Interpretationen - Diplomarbeit Bonn (1976)

|2| ENGELFRIET, J.: Simple Program Schemes and Formal Languages - Lecture Notes in Computer Science 2o (1974)

|3| GOGUEN, J.A., THATCHER, J.W.: Initial Algebra Semantics - IEEE Conf. Rec. SWAT 15 (1974), 63 - 77

|4| GREIBACH, S.A.: Theory of Program Structures: Schemes, Semantics, Verification - Lecture Notes in Computer Science 36 (1975)

|5| INDERMARK, K.: Theorie rekursiver Definitionen - Vorlesung, Universität Bonn (1975)

|6| NIVAT, M.: On the Interpretation of Recursive Program Schemes - IRIA - Rapport de Recherche 84 (1974)

|7| WAND, M.: A Concrete Approach to Abstract Recursive Definitions - in: Automata, Languages, and Programming (ed. NIVAT), Amsterdam (1973), 331 - 341

CONSTRUCTING ITERATIVE VERSION OF A SYSTEM OF RECURSIVE PROCEDURES

Jacek Irlik
Institute of Mathematical Machines "MERA", Katowice

In [1] and [2] some rules were presented which enabled one to find iterative versions of monadic recursive procedures of certain structure. The theory which has been developed by Mazurkiewicz an Blikle [3] was used to prove correctness of these rules and the rules were argued to be an initial form of more specific rules for recursion elimination from algol-like procedures.

In this paper a theorem is presented which enables one to construct an iterative version of a system of cooperating monadic recursive procedures, i.e. of such a system of procedures which can be described by a PD-algorithm. Thus, when compared to the previous papers, there is no restrictions on the structure of procedures being subject of the translation.

The theorem is preceded by definitions of some auxiliary notions and two lemmas.

Definition 1. Let V be an alphabet. We define the mapping

$$\mathrm{Top} : V^+ \Rightarrow V$$

by means of

(i) $a \in V \Rightarrow \mathrm{Top}(a) = a$,
(ii) $a \in V \wedge \alpha \in V^* \Rightarrow \mathrm{Top}(a\alpha) = a$.

Definition 2. Let V be an alphabet. We define the mapping

$$\mathrm{Tail} : V^+ \Rightarrow V^*$$

by means of

(i) $a \in V \Rightarrow \mathrm{Tail}(a) = \varepsilon$,
(ii) $a \in V \wedge \alpha \in V^* \Rightarrow \mathrm{Tail}(a\alpha) = \alpha$.

We have the following lemma.

Lemma 1. Let $A = (X, V, \sigma, P)$ be a PD-algorithm.

Let $\mathcal{B} = (X \times V^{*}, V \cup \{e, \hat{\sigma}, \hat{\varepsilon}\}, \hat{\sigma}, \hat{\varepsilon}, P_{\mathcal{B}})$ be an FC-algorithm where

$$
\begin{aligned}
P_B = & \{(a,\tilde{R},e) \mid (a,R,\varepsilon) \in P\} \cup \\
& \{(a,\tilde{R},b) \mid (a,R,b) \in P \wedge b \in V\} \cup \\
& \{(a,\tilde{R}\Gamma_{\gamma},b) \mid (a,R,b\gamma) \in P \wedge b \in V \wedge \gamma \in V^{+}\} \cup \\
& \{(e,\Lambda_a,a) \mid a \in V\} \cup \\
& \{(\hat{\sigma},S,\sigma),(e,F,\hat{\varepsilon})\}
\end{aligned}
$$

and

$$
\begin{aligned}
\Gamma_{\gamma} &= \{((x,\alpha),(x,\beta)) \mid x \in X \wedge \beta = \gamma\alpha\}, \\
\Lambda_a &= \{((x,\alpha),(x,\beta)) \mid x \in X \wedge \alpha \neq \varepsilon \wedge a = \mathrm{Top}(\alpha) \wedge \beta = \mathrm{Tail}(\alpha)\}, \\
\tilde{R} &= \{((x,\alpha),(x',\alpha)) \mid xRx' \wedge \alpha \in V^{*}\}, \\
S &= \{((x,\alpha),(x,\varepsilon)) \mid x \in X \wedge \alpha \in V^{*}\}, \\
F &= \{((x,\alpha),(x,\alpha)) \mid x \in X \wedge \alpha = \varepsilon\}.
\end{aligned}
$$

There is

$$((x,\alpha),(x',\varepsilon)) \in \mathrm{Res}_{\mathcal{B}} \iff (x,x') \in \mathrm{Res}_A .$$

Proof: The proof becomes obvious when computations of the two algorithms are compared.

Let us now introduce a mapping, denoted K, in the following way.

<u>Definition 3</u>. Let n be a positive integer. We define, for every integer k such that $1 \leq k \leq n$, the mapping

$$t_k : (J^{+})^{n+1} \to (J^{+})^{n+1}$$

by means of the formula

$$t_k(j_1,\ldots,j_n,d) = (j_1,\ldots,j_{k-1},j_k+d,j_{k+1},\ldots,j_n,2 \times d).$$

(We used J^{+} to denote the set of nonnegative integers.)

<u>Definition 4</u>. Let $V = \{a_1,\ldots,a_n\}$ be a finite alphabet. We define the mapping

$$K : V^{*} \to (J^{+})^{n+1}$$

by means of

(i) $K(\varepsilon) = (0,\ldots,0,1)$,

(ii) $K(a_k\alpha) = t_k(K(\alpha))$.

We have the following lemma concerning the introduced mapping.

<u>Lemma 2</u>. Let $V = \{a_1,\dots,a_n\}$, $\alpha \in V^*$ and let $K(\alpha) = (j_1\dots,j_n,d)$.
There are

(i) $\alpha = \varepsilon \iff d = 1$,

(ii) $\alpha \neq \varepsilon \wedge Top(\alpha) = a_k \iff d > 1 \wedge j_k \geq d \div 2 \wedge \forall_{m \neq k}\, j_m < d \div 2$,

(iii) $\alpha \neq \varepsilon \wedge Top(\alpha) = a_k \Rightarrow$

$$\Rightarrow K(Tail(\alpha)) = (j_1,\dots,j_{k-1},j_k - d\div 2, j_{k+1},\dots,j_n, d\div 2).$$

Proof: The proof is very simple and is omitted.

Lemma 1 and Lemma 2 imply the following theorem.

<u>Theorem</u>. Let $V = \{a_1,\dots,a_n\}$ be an alphabet and let $A = (X, V, \sigma, P)$ be a PD-algorithm.
Let $C = (X \times (J^+)^{n+1}, V \cup \{e, \hat{\sigma}, \hat{\varepsilon}\}, \hat{\sigma}, \hat{\varepsilon}, P_C)$ be an FC-algorithm where

$$\begin{aligned} P_C = \; & \{(a,\tilde{R},e) \mid (a,R,\varepsilon) \in P\} \cup \\ & \{(a,\tilde{R},b) \mid (a,R,b) \in P \wedge b \in V\} \cup \\ & \{(a,\tilde{R}\,\Gamma_{a_{k_1}\dots a_{k_m}},b) \mid (a,R,ba_{k_1}\dots a_{k_m}) \in P \wedge b \in V\} \cup \\ & \{(e,\Lambda_{a_k},a_k) \mid a_k \in V\} \cup \\ & \{(\hat{\sigma},S,\sigma),(e,F,\hat{\varepsilon})\} \end{aligned}$$

and where

$$\Gamma_{a_{k_1}\dots a_{k_m}} = \{((x,w),(x,w')) \mid x \in X \wedge w \in (J^+)^{n+1} \wedge w' = t_{k_1}(\dots(t_{k_m}(w))\dots)\},$$

$$\Lambda_{a_k} = \{((x,j_1,\dots,j_n,d),(x,j_1,\dots,j_{k-1},j_k - d\div 2, j_{k+1},\dots,j_n,d\div 2)) \mid d > 1 \wedge j_k \geq d\div 2 \wedge \forall_{m\neq k}\, j_m < d \div 2\},$$

$$\tilde{R} = \{((x,w),(x',w)) \mid xRx' \wedge w \in (J^+)^{n+1}\},$$

$$S = \{((x,j_1,\dots,j_n,d),(x,0,\dots,0,1)) \mid x \in X\},$$

$$F = \{((x,j_1,\dots,j_n,d),(x,j_1,\dots,j_n,d)) \mid d = 1\}.$$

There is

$$((x,j_1,\dots,j_n,d),(x',0,\dots,0,1)) \in Res_C \iff (x,x') \in Res_A.$$

Let $P_1,\dots,P_N$ be a system of cooperating monadic recursive procedures. The above theorem helps to construct an iterative procedure Q the call of which is, in the sense of the theorem, equivalent to the call of any of $P_1,\dots,P_N$. To construct the Q we must only declare some additional integer variables and introduce some operations of multiplication and division by two in the body of Q.

Example.

We have

```
procedure P1;
if p(x) then begin F1;P1;P2
             end
        else G1;
```

and

```
procedure P2;
if r(x) then begin F2;P2;P1
             end
        else G2;
```

We want now to have an iterative procedure Q which is equivalent to P_1. To do this we construct the following PD-algorithm to be a model of P_1.

$A = (X, V, \sigma_1, P)$ where $V = \{\sigma_1, \sigma_2\}$ and where

$$P = \{(\sigma_1, \pi F_1, \sigma_1\sigma_2), (\sigma_1, \bar{\pi} G_1, \varepsilon), (\sigma_2, \varrho F_2, \sigma_2\sigma_1), (\sigma_2, \bar{\varrho} G_2, \varepsilon)\}.$$

$(\pi = \{(x,x) \mid p(x)\},\ \varrho = \{(x,x) \mid r(x)\},\ \bar{\pi} = I - \pi,\ \bar{\varrho} = I - \varrho.)$

The theorem shows how to construct an FC-algorithm which is equivalent to the above one. It is

$C = (X \times (J^+)^3, V \cup \{\hat{\sigma}, \hat{\varepsilon}, e\}, \hat{\sigma}, \hat{\varepsilon}, P_C)$ where

$$P_C = \{(\sigma_1, \widetilde{\pi F_1} \Gamma_{\sigma_2}, \sigma_1), (\sigma_1, \widetilde{\bar{\pi} G_1}, e), (\sigma_2, \widetilde{\varrho F_2} \Gamma_{\sigma_1}, \sigma_2), (\sigma_2, \widetilde{\bar{\varrho} G_2}, e), (e, \Lambda_{\sigma_1}, \sigma_1), (e, \Lambda_{\sigma_2}, \sigma_2), (\hat{\sigma}, S, \sigma_1), (e, F, \hat{\varepsilon})\}.$$

The above algorithm is a model of the following procedure Q.

```
procedure Q;
begin integer j1,j2,d;
```

```
j1:=j2:=0; d:=1;
E1: while p(x) do begin j2:=j2+d; d:=2× d; F1
                  end;
    G1; go to E;
E2: while r(x) do begin j1:=j1+d; d:=2× d; F2
                  end;
    G2;
E : if d>1 then begin
                  if j1≥ d÷2 then begin d:=d÷2; j1:=j1 -d; go to E1
                                  end;
                  d:=d÷2; j2:=j2-d; go to E2
                  end
end;
```

The F's and the G's represent some arbitrary blocks which, however, must not contain calls of neither P_1 nor P_2 and must not contain go to' s leading outside these blocks. The resulting procedure Q can be easily brushed up. For example j_2 is a variable which can be removed together with the operations on it. The above text of Q was presented in order to exhibit its correspondence to the algorithm C.

References.

[1]. Irlik, J; Iterative Flowcharts For Some Recursive Procedures, CC PAS Reports 227, (1975),

[2]. Irlik, J; Translating Some Recursive Procedures Into Iterative Schemas, Proc. of 2nd Symp. on Programming, Paris (1976),

[3]. Blikle, A; Mazurkiewicz, A; An Algebraic Approach to Theory of Programs, Algorithms, Languages and Recursiveness, Proc. of MFCS'72 Symposium, Warsaw, Jadwisin (1972).

A METHOD USING A SET-THEORETICAL FORMALISM TO DESCRIBE THE SEMANTICS OF PROGRAMMING LANGUAGES

Walter Issel

Central Institute of Mathematics and Mechanics of the Academy of Sciences of GDR, 108 Berlin, GDR

In former papers ([1], [2], [3], [4]) a method to formalize different aspects of high-level programming languages was described. It is presented here in a more abstract, homogeneous form.

1. General principles of the method

Of the language L whose semantics is to be described the following is assumed to be given: Basic sets S_i, with i element of some index set IS, (numbers and strings of different kinds, names for variables etc.) L is operating upon by means of a set OPER of operations; a set SDS of denotations for the sets S_i (i.e. type-predicates); sets $SDELS_i$ of denotations for elements of the sets S_i (i.e. constants); a set SDOP of operations-symbols; a set LINK of functions linking the denotations with what they denote: CONST mapping constants to the corresponding (abstract) elements of the S_i and REP as inverse function to CONST, TY mapping SDS in $\{S_i\}_{i \in IS}$, OP mapping operation-symbols to operations, conversion functions governing the admissibility and the result of operations on operands of different types.

Now a formal set-theoretical language can be defined.
Basic symbols are: Symbols for variables (x,y,...), the elements of the sets SDS, $SDELS_i$, SDELOP, LINK, the symbols $\in$, = , the usual logical symbols $\neg, \wedge, \vee, \rightarrow, \exists, \forall$ and technical symbols. From this symbols terms and expressions are defined in the usual recursive manner.
The language is interpreted in the domain $\bigcup_{i \in IS} S_i \cup \bigcup_{i \in IS} SDELS_i \cup SDS \cup SDOP \cup AS$, AS is a set of auxiliary symbols most often marks to identify certain objects. All sets are assumed to be disjoint. The logical and set-theoretical symbols have the usual meaning, elements of the sets $SDELS_i$, SDS, SDOP, and AS (which are basic symbols and in the domain!) denote themselves, i.e. strings which get the desired

meaning by use of the functions of LINK which are interpreted as given by L.

By means of this interpretation, sets, functions, tuples, sequences of elements of the domain and other already described objects can be formed and operations can be defined. In the sequel appear:

$\{a_1,\dots,a_n\}$; $[a_1,\dots,a_n]$; $(a_1,\dots,a_n)$ - set; n-tuple; sequence of $a_1,\dots,a_n$.

$\{x|H(x)\}$; $\iota x(H(x))$-set of all x; the uniquely determined x; with H(x) true.

$x \epsilon M$; $x \underline{\epsilon} F$ - x is element of the set M; x is element of the sequence F.

$M \cup N$; $F \underline{\cup} x$ - union of the sets M, N; the sequence F concatenated with x.

COn(x); F(n); F⊖n - n-th component of x; n-th element of sequence F; n-th element of the sequence F from end of F.

Λ -the empty sequence.

RPCOMPn(M,N,K) replaces all n-th components of elements of $N \underline{\subseteq} M$ by K.

RMSEL(F,⊖n) removes the last n elements from sequence F.

Now define sets ot lists (i.e. finite sequences) for the storage of information and their changes during the elaboration, i.e. sequences of these sets or lists. To choose these sequences is quite arbitrary, partially this depends on L. Assume k lists $t_1,\dots,t_k$ and their sequences $t_1S,\dots,t_kS$ are to be defined. The k-tuple $[t_1,\dots,t_k]$ can be considered as the state of an abstract machine.

A finite set of "semantic bricks" is defined of the form

[mark 1, mark 2, numeration, DS_{ℓ_1} ..., DS_{ℓ_k}].

The marks (auxiliary symbols of AS) and the numeration (a tuple of integers) are used to recognise bricks in a brick-list, the $DS_{\ell_1},\dots,DS_{\ell_k}$ are definition-schemes for the $t_1,\dots,t_k$, exactly one for each of the $t_1,\dots,t_k$. A definition-scheme is a string which in the formalism is considered as element of AS (and, therefore, may appear in lists etc.), but which can be interpreted as denoting an object in the following way. A scheme for t_iS has the form

t_iS: $\langle$operation-symbol; arg_1;...;$arg_n\rangle$

where the terms $arg_1,\dots,arg_n$ (the operation denoted by the symbol is assumed to have n arguments) may contain variables $\bar{t}_1,\dots,\bar{t}_k$, FCOMP, THCOMP. The result of the "elaboration" of this scheme if it appears in brick B in the state $[t_1,\dots,t_k]$ is:

operation $(obj_1,\dots,obj_n)$,

with arg_i denoting obj_i, i.e., the term arg_i denotes obj_i after giving $\bar{t}_i$ the value t_i, FCOMP the first component of B, THCOMP the third component of B.

Example. Let $t_{\hat{i}}$ = (1,2) . The result of elaborating the scheme for $t_{\hat{i}}S$ in the brick [m1, m2, 10, $t_{\hat{i}}S$: $\langle \underline{\cup}$; $t_{\hat{i}}$; THCOMP$\rangle$, ...] is $t_{\hat{i}} \underline{\cup} 10$ = (1,2,10).

t_1 is assumed to be a list of bricks (command-list CL), t_2 to be a list of numerations (command-counting CC).

Now define a function AN which translates every program P of L into a corresponding list LB(P) of bricks, i.e., AN is some kind of syntactical analysis. Substrings of P (names, constants, operation-symbols etc.) can be stored as first marks in bricks of LB(P) and referred to by FCOMP.

The elaboration of P is recursively defined by the sequences t_iS (i = 1,...,k): $t_1S(0)$ = LB(P), $t_2S(0)$ = 1, $t_iS(0)$ for i = 2,...,k are assumed to be given.

If the $t_iS(n)$ are defined, then take the last element E of $t_2S(n)$ (a numeration) and elaborate in the state [$t_1S(n)$,...,$t_kS(n)$] the definition-schemes (in the order of their appearance) of that element B of $t_1S(n)$ (a brick) which has E as third component, thus n + 1-th elements $t_iS(n+1)$ are defined.

The elaboration is finished, i.e. all sequences are set constant, if there is no such B (an error or the end of P).

It is convenient to allow conditional, nested, or empty (which will be omitted) definition-schemes. An empty scheme for t_i lets t_i unchanged.

2. The method applied to ALGOL 60

For this application see [1], [2].

The basic sets S_i of ALGOL 60 are: the sets of integers, of real numbers, of Boolean values, of names. The forms and meanings of the constants and operation-symbols are well-defined, conversions are possible between real numbers and integers.

Six sequences are defined, the elements of which form states [CL, CC, IL, OL, VS, ST].

The input-list IL contains all values still to be read, the output-list OL contains all values written, the stack ST stores intermediate results. A value-set VS contains for all currently valid variables a 7-tuple

[mark, (new) name, type-predicate, block-level, value, l1, l2],

where l1, l2 are two lists to store subscripts of arrays or parameters of procedures, and a block-counting BLC: [BL, n] , where BL is a mark for "block-level" and n is the depth of block-nesting.
The function AN, as defined in [1] , translates a program P into a brick-list LB(P) in which the program appears as in reverse Polish notation.
The 0-th state is
[LB(P), (1), IL, $\wedge$, {[BL, 0]}, $\wedge$], IL is assumed to be given with P. Now the elaboration can start, the last element of CC is 1, therefore elaborate the first element of LB(P) = CL thus defining the next elements of the sequences, i.e., a new state, etc.

Example. To give an idea of the formalism, a small program P, LB(P) and its simplified elaboration shall be considered:
(in the bricks, for $\overline{CL}$,...,$\overline{ST}$ simply CL,...,ST is written)
begin real x; x:= 3.14 end , IL = $\wedge$.
AN translates this program as follows (the pairs [substring of P, corresponding brick] are shown)

1. [begin, block-begin]
2. [x, name in declaration]
3. [real, type-predicate]
4. [real x, declaration]
5. [x, used name]
6. [3.14, constant]
7. [x:= 3.14, assignment]
8. [begin ... end , block]
9. [begin ... end , program]

1. [BB, G, 1, VSS: ⟨ RPCOMP2; VS, {BLC}, CO2(BLC)+1 ⟩]
Marks: BB "block-begin", G "general mark", 1 is the numeration.
The second component of BLC (formally: $\iota x(x \in VS \wedge CO1(x) = BL)$), here [BL,0], is to be increased by 1: VS = {[BL,1]}.

2. [x, D,2, VSS: ⟨$\cup$; VS; {[UN, x, SU, CO2(BLC), SU, $\wedge$, $\wedge$]}⟩]
Marks: D "declaration", UN "unfinished name", SU "still unknown".
To VS an unfinished tuple for x is added:
VS = {[BL,1], [UN, x, SU, 1, SU, $\wedge$, $\wedge$]}.

By bricks 3 and 4 the type-predicate is inserted in all tuples with mark UN, this mark is changed to N ("name").

5. [x, U, 5, STS: ⟨ $\underline{\cup}$; ST; {x | $x \in VS \wedge CO2(x)$ = FCOMP}⟩]
Mark: U "used name". The set of n-tuples of VS whose second component (name) is the first component (FCOMP) of the current brick

forms the top element of the stack: ST = ({[N,x, real, 1, SU, Λ, Λ]}).

6. [3.14, G, 6, STS: ⟨ $\underline{\cup}$; ST; FCOMP⟩]
   ST = ({[N,x, real,1, SU, Λ,Λ]}, 3.14).

7. [EM, G, 7, VSS: ⟨RPCOMP5; VS; $\{x \mid x \in VS \wedge x \underline{\in} ST \ominus 2\}$; VALSTEL(ST⊖1)⟩,
   STS: ⟨ RMSEL; ST; ⊖2⟩]
   Mark: EM "empty mark". VALSTEL(x) is the value of a stack-element, = CO5(x), if x is a 7-tuple, = CONST(x) else. The top value of ST is inserted in VS in the fifth component of the tuple which is also in ST⊖2, i.e. the tuple for x, afterwards the stack is emptied:
   VS = {[BL,1], [N, x, 1, real, 3.14, Λ, Λ]}, ST = Λ.

Brick 8 removes from VS all elements which have been declared in the finished block, i.e. formally, which have CO2(BLC) as fourth component. BLC is decreased by one. Brick 9 sets all sequences constant.
If in a brick B a variable is declared or used, it appears as first component of B. A label is considered to be declared by its appearance. A jump to label M effects the command-counting to show the numeration of that brick which has M as first component. In the same way jumps to the marked parts of a conditional structure are performed.

After the handling of parameters at a procedure call, say by the brick with numeration n, the bricks of the body of the procedure, say with numerations k,...,l, are inserted in the command-list, with new numerations [n,k],...,[n,l], with the order $n < [n,k] < \ldots < [n,l] < n+1$.
At the end of the procedure the bricks with longest numerations are are removed. As numerations triples etc. may appear.
In order to identify names, i.e., to reflect the block-concept, at the begin of a block B for all names declared in B, in all first components of bricks in B these names are dynamically replaced by new ones. If a name is declared in a brick with numeration $[n_1,\ldots,n_l]$, its new name is the string consisting of the special symbol Z concatenated with itself $2^{n_1} \cdot 3^{n_2} \cdots p_l^{n_l}$-times ($p_l$ denotes the l-th prime number). These strings are elements of AS. Therefore, all names are at any time distinguished, even in procedures called recursively.
For the languages considered here (ALGOL 60, PL/I) it is sufficient to have the command-list changed during the elaboration only by the insertion of new names and insertion and removal of procedure bodies.

3. The method applied to PL/I

If only that part of PL/I is considered which is semantically a part of ALGOL 60 too, the model of section 2 can be used. Here PL/I list-processing is additionally to be taken into account, as in [4].

Because of the definition of operations in PL/I it is more suitable to think of PL/I as operating on pairs [bit-string s, type-predicate t] instead of abstract values, s representing a value of type t. The operations and conversions then happen between those pairs.

Therefore, as basic sets S_i names, bit-strings, and type-predicates appear, the constants are denotations for the pairs mentioned.

In PL/I it is possible to overlay by means of pointers and BASED-variables any part of the store, cutting out a bit-sequence there irrespective of what was there before. Therefore, it is convenient to have an addressable memory. Now seven sequences are defined, i.e. a state has the form [CL, CC, IL, OL, VS, ST, ME].
There is no essential diffence to the CL, CC, IL. OL, ST of section 2, of course every brick contains seven definition-schemes.

The memory ME is a sequence of a given fixed length of bits, beginning with a sequence of 0-bits. In it the current values of all variables are stored as bit-sequences according to the types of the variables. In VS the fifth (value-) components now give the addresses of the values in ME, not the values themselves. These addresses can be relative, determined by the values of pointers, which are adresses.

4. A generalization to describe PL/I-multitasking

If the list-processing is not taken into account, the basic model of section 2 can be used, as it is done in [3] and shall be done here.

Now the elaboration can branch, therefore, sets of sequences instead of single sequences are considered, one can think of a state for each task, with some lists shared by alls tasks.

To each task an element of the set SEQ of all finite sequences of integers is coordinated. The major task has sequence (1). If task t_1 has sequence $(z_1,\dots,z_n)$, task t_2 is a (direct) subtask of t_1 and $t_1',\dots,t_e'$ are exactly the subtasks of t_1 branching from t_1 before t_2, then t_2 has sequence $(z_1,\dots,z_n,l+1)$.

The states are of the form:

$$[\{CL_g\}_{g\in SEQ},\ \{CC_g\}_{g\in SEQ},\ IL,\ OL,\ VS,\ \{ST_g\}_{g\in SEQ}].$$

This means every task has its own control and elaboration, but input-list, output-list, and value-set are the same for all tasks. At the beginning, $CL_{(1)}$ is the brick-list corresponding to the program, $CC_{(1)} = 1$, IL is given by the program, $OL = ST_g = \Lambda$ $(g\in SEQ)$, $VS = \{[BL, 0, (1)]\}$. All other sequences, CL_g, CC_g $(g\in SEQ,\ g \neq (1))$ are empty until a new task, with sequence g, is created (by a special procedure-call). At the termination of a task it will be made inactive by inserting a special mark in its command-counting.
A brick contains definition-schemes for all elements of states, only for a finite subset of SEQ they are non-empty. In the value-set a tuple for a variable has as component the sequence of the task in which it was created, in order to prevent other than subtasks to use this variable. Each task has its own block-counting.

The recursive definition of the sequences is similar as before, but stages are determined at which the transition from state n to state n+1 takes place. This is done by assuming a function TIME(B,S) which is the time needed to elaborate brick B (which is considered to be indivisible) in the state S.
For each stage n, SWB(n) is the set of pairs of all bricks working (i.e. started, but not finished) after stage n together with their times of start, TCS(n) is the time to reach stage n.
Stage n+1 now is determined from stage n by the smallest time at which bricks of SWB(n) are finished, call this set SFB(n+1).

State n+1 is given by elaborating SFB(n+1) if this set is consistent, else nothing changes. A set of bricks $B_1,\ldots,B_k$ is "consistent" in state S, if the order of their elaboration in S is irrelevant, i.e. if $B_1(B_2(\ldots B_k(S)\ldots) = PERM(B_1,\ldots,B_k)\ (S)$, PERM denoting any permutation of the $B_1,\ldots,B_k$.
TASK-variables have priorities as values; if p tasks can work concurrently, p bricks of SFB(n+1) of tasks with top priorities are chosen.
WAIT-statements do not change anything until the corresponding EVENT-variables have suitable values.

The function TIME is left open. By choosing it properly, all sorts of merging processes in time can be achieved.

5. Conclusion

The method presented here is very convenient to describe operations and control of a program. On the other hand, to describe the block-structure in a set-theoretical formalism is not easy.

The method is related to the Vienna definition language (see e.g. [5]), Apart from the formalism and many algorithms used, the main difference is that here the elaboration is compiling rather than simulating.

References

1. Issel, W., Eine Methode zur Formalisierung der Semantik von Programmierungssprachen, Diss. B Humboldt-Universität zu Berlin, 1975.
2. Issel, W., A method to formalize the semantics of programming languages, Elektronische Informationsverarbeitung und Kybernetik 11 (1975), 228-239.
3. Issel, W., A model for PL/I-multitasking using a simulated time, Elektronische Informationsverarbeitung und Kybernetik 11 (1975), 239-252.
4. Issel, W., A model for PL/I list-processing using the method of semantic bricks, to appear in Elektronische Informationsverarbeitung und Kybernetik 12 (1976).
5. Lucas, P., Lauer, P., Stigleitner, H., Method and notation for the formal definition of programming languages, TR 25.087 IBM, 1968.

THE CUBIC SEARCH METHOD

Romuald Jagielski

University ofGdańsk
Institute of Mathematics
80-952, POLAND

Introduction

Scatter storage technique is a way of reducing the time required either for finding an item in table or for enterning an item into the table. The time will be minimal when an average number of probes per lookup and the time per probe is minimal. The access to memory is connected with a calculation of the item´s location. An address is obtained by transformation of the key of the desired item. All know hash functions are not ideal and collisions occur, i.e. cases in which two or more keys are mapped into the same initial address. Efficiency of scatter storage techniques depends very strongly on the used methods of resolving of collisions.

Methods for handling collisions are called search methods. Among them we are intersted in methods which do not require a separate area for collisions. The simlest search is the linear search in which the finding is performed according to linear scheme:

$$d_i = (d_o + ai) \pmod p$$

where d_o - an initial hash address, a - an integer constant usualy a=1 , p - table size, i=0,1,2,...,p-1 - steps of searching. Morris [1] has indicated that this is the worst strategy in use, since it is least effective because of clustering of items. In order to avoid clustering Maurer [2] suggested a quadratic search in which the search is according to quadratic dependence:

$$d_i = (d_o + bi + ci^2) \pmod p$$

where d_i, d_o, i the same as above, b, c - integer constans.Various algorithms were suggested, being in fact modifications of quadratic search (c.f. Radke [3] , Day [4], Batagelj [5]) for some types of primes p. Below is presented a new search method based on computation of cubic residues.

1. The cubic search

Effective searching in which every item will be probed exactly once is obtained when using a higher power residues for a prime modulus. If p is a prime, n a natural number > 1, then an integer a is called an n-th power residue for the modulus p whenever there exists an integer x such $x^n \equiv a \pmod p$. We profit from the following theorem, proved in [6, p.p. 257-258] :

Theorem : If p is a prime, n a natural number and $d=(n,p-1)$, then the number of different n-th power residues for the modulus p is $(p-1)/d + 1$.

Corollary : If $n=3$ and $d=1$, then the number of different cubic residues for a modulus p is exactly p. This assures that the whole table be searched.

The condition $d=1$ denotes that $p-1$ is relatively prime to 3; hence p should be a prime of the form $3k+2$, where k is a natural numbers. In [6] it is proved that there are infinitely many primes of the form $3k+2$.

2. Implementation of the method

When appling the cubic residues for searching in scatter storage we obtain a search sequence by increment of cubic residues for $i=0,1,2,\dots,p-1$:

$$d_i = (d_o + i^3)(\mathrm{mod}\ p) \qquad (1)$$

In the case when is too large number it is better to use:

$$d_i = \{ d_o + [i^2 (\mathrm{mod}\ p)\ i] \} (\mathrm{mod}\ p) \qquad (2)$$

Implementation of this method in ALGOL is show in Appendix A.

There exists a possibly of reducing the computation time of cubic residues by using the following difference schema for a sequence $y_i = i^3$. We have differences:

$$\Delta^{(1)} y_i = y_{i+1} - y_i = 3i^2 + 3i + 1 ,$$

$$\Delta^{(2)} y_i = \Delta^{(1)} y_{i+1} - \Delta^{(1)} y_i = 6i + 6 ,$$

$$\Delta^{(3)} y_i = \Delta^{(2)} y_{i+1} - \Delta^{(2)} y_i = 6 .$$

The cubic of next integer is computed by:

$$y_o = 0 ,$$

$$y_1 = 1 ,$$

. . .

$$y_{i+1} = y_i + \Delta^{(1)}_{i-1} + \Delta^{(2)}_{i-2} + \Delta^{(3)} , \qquad (3)$$

where : $\Delta^{(3)} = 6$ for all i ,

$$\Delta^{(2)}_o = 6 , \quad \Delta^{(2)}_i = \Delta^{(2)}_{i-1} + \Delta^{(3)} ,$$

$$\Delta^{(1)}_o = 1 , \quad \Delta^{(1)}_i = \Delta^{(1)}_{i-1} + \Delta^{(2)}_{i-1} .$$

Hence, the determining of successive addresses is reduced to a simple addition:

$$d_o = d_o ,$$

$$d_1 = d_o + 1 ,$$

. . .

$$d_{i+1} = (d_i + \Delta^{(1)}_{i-1} + \Delta^{(2)}_{i-2} + 6) \pmod p \qquad (4)$$

for $1 \leqslant i < p$.

In Appendix B there is a procedure which uses the method for searching of tables.

3. Some Experiments

For verifying and comparison with other methods the ALGOL procedures were used, as shown in the Appendixes. The experiments were done by a symulation sets of keys and hash coding for various values of table size for both cases: (a) the sequence of addresses is pseudorandom with random collisions, (b) pseudorandom address sequence has slots with some clusters of collision; all cases for a variable loading factor α $(0 < \alpha < 1)$. It seems from our experiments that the cubic search method is not worse than the linear method and the quadratic methods suggested by Radke [3]and Day [4], or often better. Especialy our method is much better then the previous ones in case when hash functions tend towards a clustering. The results of the experiments are shown in table 1.

Conclusion

We have proposed a new search method for scatter storage. The method based on cubic residues, for table size being a prime of the form p=3k+2, examines the whole table in the first p probes. The algorithm is simple and efficient, needs little probes per lookup.

Table 1

Average numbers of probes to retrieve an item

	(a)				(b)			
α	(1)	(2)	(3)	(4)	(1)	(2)	(3)	(4)
.50	1.43	1.57	1.39	1.38	13.55	4.14	2.43	1.95
.60	1.67	1.93	1.60	1.56	16.59	4.61	2.76	2.12
.70	2.12	2.25	1.86	1.78	21.00	5.50	3.14	2.19
.80	2.81	3.12	2.20	2.14	.	6.85	3.86	2.77
.85	3.60	3.40	2.47	2.34	.	7.64	4.29	3.02
.90	5.50	4.37	2.92	2.74	.	8.80	4.66	3.41
.95	10.72	5.81	3.59	3.34	.	10.40	5.38	4.05
.99	28.09	8.39	4.92	4.65	.	13.60	7.14	5.51

(1) linear search
(2) Radke's method
(3) Day's method
(4) cubic search

Reference

1. Morris, Robert Scatter storage techniques . Comm.ACM 11,1 (Jan. 1968), 34-44
2. Maurer, W.D. An improved hash code for scatter storage. Comm.ACM 11, 1 (Jan. 1968), 35-38
3. Radke, Charles E. The use of quadratic residue research, Comm.ACM 13, 2 (Feb. 1970), 103-105
4. Day, Colin A. Full table quadratic searching for scatter storage. Comm.ACM 13, 8 (Aug. 1970), 481-482
5. Batagelj V. The quadratic hash method when the table size is not a prime number. Comm. ACM 18,4 (Apr. 1975), 216-217
6. Sierpiński Wacław Elementary theory of numbers. Państwowe Wydawnictwo Naukowe, Warszawa, 1964

Appendix A

```
integer procedure ADDR (hash,i) ;
comment this procedure will calculate an address in scatter storage
        (0 ≤ ADDR < p) , p is a table size, starting from a initial
        hash address (hash) for a current probe of searching  i
        (i=1,2,...,p). The 1-st version of a procedure;
begin integer p,a ;
      a:=i×i  - ((i×i)÷p)×p ;
      ADDR:= hash + a×i  - ((hash + a×i)÷p)×p
end ADDR;
```

Appendix B

```
 integer procedure ADDR (hash,i) ;
comment  this procedure will calcule an address in scatter storage
         (0 ≤ ADDR < p) , p is a table size, starting from a initial
         hash address (hash) for a current probe of searching i
         (i=1,2,...,p). The 2-nd version of a procedure;
begin own integer a,b,c,p;
if i=1 then begin
a:=c:=1;
b:=0  end else begin
c:=c+a+b+6;
for c:=c while c≥ p  do c:=c-p;
b:= if b+6 < p then b+6 else b+6-p;
a:= if a+b < p then a+b else a+b-p
                end;
ADDR:= if hash +c < p then hash + c else hash+c-p
end ADDR;
```

VECTORS OF COROUTINES

Ryszard Janicki
Technical University of Warsaw

1. Introduction. By coroutines we mean program components able to interact in symmetric fashion. This concept is useful whenever an algorithm is best described and understood as a set of interlocked independent components. Such a case is of frequent occurrence in discrete event simulation. In this paper we introduce vectors of coroutines to be considered as mathematical models for really coroutines. This model allows to prove some properties of coroutines in the mechanical manner. Our approach is the following. Each component is represented by an algebraic system like Mazurkiewicz algorithm ([4], [5]) with a mechanism making possible an interaction.

A set of all functions computed by programs with recursive coroutines will be proved to contain a set of all functions computed by commonly used recursive programs.

2. Relations, languages and general algorithms. Let X,Y be sets. Each subset of $X \times Y$ is called a binary relation in $X \times Y$. For every relation R, xRy means $(x,y) \in R$. By Rel(X) we shall denote the set of all binary relation in $X \times X$, and by I we shall denote the identity relation in Rel(X). For every relations R,S we denote by RS the composition of R and S. A relation $R^* = \bigcup_{i=0}^{\infty} R^n$ is called the iteration of R.

Let Σ be a finite set, called alphabet. Finite sequences of symbols are called words. The empty word will be denoted by ε. If w,v are words, then wv is the concatenation of w and v. By Σ^* we denote the set of all words with elements in Σ. Each subset of Σ^* is called a language over Σ. Let Σ be an alphabet, L be a language over , F be a set of relation.

Every mapping $\varphi : \Sigma \longrightarrow F$ will be called an interpretation of L in F. Let φ^* be an extension of φ such that :

$$\varphi^* \varepsilon = I ,$$
$$\varphi^*(vr) = (\varphi^* v)(\varphi r) \qquad \text{for } v \in \Sigma^*,\ r \in \Sigma .$$

By $\varphi^* L$ we shall denote the relation: $\varphi^* L = \bigcup \{ \varphi^* w \mid w \in L \}$.

By a general algorithm we shall mean a system

$$A = (X , V , \delta , P) ,$$

where: X is a set (of object of A),

V is an alphabet (of control symbols of A),

$\sigma \in V$ (the initial symbol of A),

P is a finite set of pairs (Q,R), where $Q \subseteq V^* \times V^*$, $R \subseteq X \times X$.

Elements of P are called instructions.

The set $S_A = V^* \times X$ is called a set of states of A.
Let $Tr_A \subseteq S_A \times S_A$ be a relation such that :

$$(u,x)\ Tr_A\ (w,y) \iff [(\exists Q)(\exists R)\ \ (Q,R) \in P \text{ and } uQw \text{ and } xRy].$$

The relation Tr_A is called a transition relation of A.
A relation $Res_A \subseteq X \times X$, such that $x\ Res_A\ y \iff (\sigma,x)\ Tr_A^*\ (\varepsilon,y)$ is called a resulting relation of A.
General algorithms were originally defined by A.Mazurkiewicz [4].

Let $Q \subseteq V^* \times V^*$. We say that Q is :

(i) simple iff $(\exists a \in V)\ (\exists b \in V \cup \{\varepsilon\})\quad Q = \{(aw,bw) \mid w \in V^*\}$,

(ii) recursive iff $(\exists a \in V)\ (\exists u \in V^*)\quad Q = \{(aw,uw) \mid w \in V^*\}$,

(iii) complex iff $(\exists u_1 \in V^* - \{\varepsilon\}, u_2, u_3 \in V^*)\quad Q = \{(u_1 w, u_2 w u_3) \mid w \in V^*\}$.

We shall say that an algorithm $A=(X,V,\sigma,P)$ is finite-control (push-down, complex), iff $(Q,R) \in P$ implies Q is simple (recursive, complex resp.). Frequently we shall write FC-algorithm (PD-algorithm) instead of finite-control algorithm (push-down) algorithm .

It can be observed that FC-algorithms can be regarded as models for procedure-free programs, PD-algorithms as models for recursive programs. We shall show in this article that complex algorithms can be regarded as models for coroutines.

Let $F \subseteq Rel(X)$. A relation S is said to be finite-control (push-down, complex) computable from F, iff there is a finite-control (push-down, complex) algorithm $A=(X,V,\sigma,P)$ with properties :

(i) $S = Res_A$,

(ii) $(Q,R) \in P \implies R \in F \cup \{I\}$.

The class of all relations finite-control (push-down, complex) computable from $F \subseteq Rel(X)$ will be denoted by FC(F) (PD(F), C(F)).

Theorem 2.1.

$$(\exists X)\ (\exists F \subseteq Rel(X)) \qquad FC(F) \subsetneq PD(F) \subsetneq C(F) .$$

■

Theorem 2.2.
For each finite-control (push-down, complex) algorithm A there exists a regular (context-free, accepted by Turing machines)

language L and an interpretation φ such that :

$$Res_A = \varphi^* L \text{ .}$$

■

Theorem 2.3.

For each regular (context-free, accepted by Turing machines) language L there exists a finite-control (push-down, complex) algorithm A and an interpretation φ such that :

$$Res_A = \varphi^* L \text{ .}$$

■

3. Vectors of coroutines. Now we define a certain algebraic system which can be regarded as model for coroutines.

A vector of coroutines is a system $C = (i_0, A_1, \ldots, A_n)$ where: i_0 is integer ($1 \leq i_0 \leq n$) and i_0 will be called the number of initial coroutine,

A_i for $i=1,\ldots,n$ are coroutines, i.e. quadruples

$$A_i = (X, V_i, \sigma_i, P_i)$$

where: X is a set of objects (common for all coroutines),

V_i is an alphabet (of control symbols of A_i),

$\sigma_i \in V_i$ is an initial symbol of A_i,

P_i is a finite subset of the set

$$\{i\} \times \{1,2,\ldots,n\} \times Rel(V_i^*) \times Rel(X)$$

such that $((i,j),Q,R) \in P_i$ implies that if $i \neq j$ then $R=I$.

Instead of $((i,j),Q,R)$ we shall write $(i \mapsto j, Q, R)$. In other words elements of P_i have one of two forms: $(i \mapsto i, Q, R)$ or $(i \mapsto j, Q, I)$. The set P_i will be called a set of instructions of A_i.

If for $i=1,\ldots,n$ $(i \mapsto j, Q, R) \in P_i$ implies that Q is simple (recursive) then a vector C will be called a vector of finite-control coroutines (of push-down coroutines).

(abbr. vector of FC-coroutines and vector of PD-coroutines)

Vectors of FC-coroutines can be regarded as mathematical models for programs with not recursive coroutines ([1]), and vectors of PD-coroutines can be regarded as models for programs with recursive coroutines([2]).

The set $VS = \{1,\ldots,n\} \times V_1^* \times \ldots \times V_n^*$ is called a set of control states of C, and the set $S_C = VS \times X$ is called a set of states of C.

Let $num: VS \longmapsto \{1,\ldots,n\}$ be a function such that if $a=(i,v_1,\ldots,v_n) \in VS$ then $num(a)=i$.

Let $p: \{1,\ldots,n\} \times VS \longmapsto \bigcup_{i=1}^{n} V_i$ be a function such that

$$a=(i,v_1,\ldots,v_n) \in VS \text{ implies } (\forall k: 1 \leq k \leq n) \quad p(k,a)=v_k \text{ .}$$

By a transition relation of C we shall mean a relation $Tr_C \subseteq S_C \times S_C$ defined as follows:

$$(a,x)\ Tr_C\ (b,y) \iff [(\exists (num(a) \mapsto num(b),Q,R) \in P_{num(a)}) \text{ and } (\forall i: i \neq num(a), 1 \leq i \leq n)\quad p(i,a)=p(i,b) \text{ and } p(num(a),a)\ Q\ p(num(a),b) \text{ and } xRy] .$$

In other words Tr_C is such relation that :

$$(i,v_1,\ldots,v_i,\ldots,v_n,x)\ Tr_A\ (j,v_1,\ldots,w_i,\ldots,v_n,y) \iff [(\exists (i \mapsto j,Q,R) \in P_i)\quad v_i Q w_i \text{ and } xRy] .$$

A set $VT \subseteq VS$ such that $a \in VT$ implies $p(num(a),a)=\varepsilon$ will be called a set of terminal control states.

We put $a_0=(i_0,\delta_1,\ldots,\delta_n)$. The control state a_0 will be called an initial control state.

A relation $Res_C \subseteq X \times X$, such that

$$x\ Res_C\ y \iff (\exists a \in VT) \quad (a_0,x)\ Tr_C^*(a,y)$$

is called a resulting relation in C.

By a computation in C we shall mean a sequence of states $(s_0,s_1,\ldots,s_m,\ldots)$, finite or infinite, with the property $s_{i-1} Tr_C s_i$ for all $i \geq 1$.

From above definitions it follows that the following two conditions are equivalent :

(i) $x\ Res_C\ y$,

(ii) there exists a computation $(s_0,s_1,\ldots,s_m)$, $m \geq 0$, such that $s_0=(a_0,x)$, $s_m=(a,y)$ where $a \in VT$, and $s_{i-1} Tr_C s_i$ for $i=1,\ldots,m$.

Vectors of coroutines were originally defined by R.Janicki [1],[2].

<u>Example</u>. This example will be phrased in a certain not really existing Algol-like idiom which is an extension of Algol 60. Additional constructs are following: "<u>coroutine</u> name", "<u>resume</u> name" and "<u>call</u> name". The first construct is a declaration of a coroutine the second causes a revival of the coroutine "name" from a current reactivation point, and the third is a call of coroutine.

A mechanism of activity of a construct <u>resume</u> and a difference between <u>resume</u> and <u>call</u> were described precisely by A.Wang and O.J.Dahl [6].

Let Dl be a sequence of declarations and let $In_1,\ldots,In_5$ be sequences of substitution instructions. Consider the following program:

<u>begin</u> Dl;
<u>coroutine</u> C1;

```
  if p(x) then go to E;
  In₁; call C1; In₂; resume C2 ; In₃;
  E:end of coroutine C1;
  coroutine C2;
  if q(x) then go to E;
  In₄; resume C1; call C2; In₅;
  E:end of coroutine C2;
 call C1
end of program
```

We associate a suitable denotation of a relation to each of above instruction :

$$\underline{\text{if}}\ p(x)\ \underline{\text{then}}\ \underline{\text{go to}}\ E \longleftrightarrow R_1 , \qquad In_2 \longleftrightarrow R_3 ,$$
$$\underline{\text{if}}\ \neg p(x)\ \underline{\text{then}}\ \underline{\text{begin}}\ In_1\ \underline{\text{end}} \longleftrightarrow R_2 , \qquad In_3 \longleftrightarrow R_4 ,$$
$$\underline{\text{if}}\ q(x)\ \underline{\text{then}}\ \underline{\text{go to}}\ E \longleftrightarrow R_5 , \qquad In_5 \longleftrightarrow R_7 ,$$
$$\underline{\text{if}}\ \neg q(x)\ \underline{\text{then}}\ \underline{\text{begin}}\ In_4\ \underline{\text{end}} \longleftrightarrow R_6 .$$

To simplify the notation we shall write $(i\mapsto j, \alpha\mapsto u, R)$ instead of $(i\mapsto j, \{(\alpha w, uw) \mid w \in V_i^*\}, R)$. The following vector of PD-coroutines can be a model for the above program.

$$C = (1 , A_1 , A_2)$$

where: $A_1 = (X , \{\sigma_1, \alpha_1, \alpha_2, \alpha_3\} , \sigma_1 , P_1)$ and

$$P_1 = \{ (1\mapsto 1, \sigma_1\mapsto \varepsilon, R_1) , (1\mapsto 1, \sigma_1\mapsto \sigma_1\alpha_1, R_2) , (1\mapsto 1, \alpha_1\mapsto \alpha_2, R_3) , (1\mapsto 2, \alpha_1\mapsto \alpha_3, I) , (1\mapsto 1, \alpha_3\mapsto \varepsilon, R_4) \} ;$$

$A_2 = (X , \{\sigma_2, \beta_1, \beta_2\} , \sigma_2 , P_2)$ and

$$P_2 = \{ (2\mapsto 2, \sigma_2\mapsto \varepsilon, R_5) , (2\mapsto 2, \sigma_2\mapsto \beta_1, R_6) , (2\mapsto 1, \beta_1\mapsto \sigma_2\beta_2, I) , (2\mapsto 2, \beta_2\mapsto \varepsilon, R_7) \} .$$

Now, we formulate three theorems designating relationships between algorithms and vectors of coroutines.

Theorem 3.1.

For each FC-algorithm (PD-algorithm) C there exists a vector of FC-coroutines (PD-coroutines) C such that :

(i) $S_C = \{1\} \times S_A$,

(ii) $(\forall s_1, s_2 \in S_A)\quad s_1\ Tr_A\ s_2 \Longleftrightarrow (1,s_1)\ Tr_C\ (1,s_2)$. ∎

Theorem 3.2.

For each vector of FC-coroutines C there exists a FC-algorithm A such that: (i) $S_C \subseteq S_A$,

(ii) $Tr_C = Tr_A \mid S_C$,

(iii) $Res_C = Res_A$. ∎

Theorem 3.3.
For each vector of PD-coroutines C there exists a complex algorithm A such that : $Res_C = Res_A$. ■

The above theory proves that complex algorithms can be regarded as mathematical model for coroutines but the vector approach seems to be more natural.

4. Languages definable by coroutines. If in a vector of coroutines we replace a set of relations with an alphabet, the identity relation with the empty word, a composition of relations with a concatenation of words then we shall get a certain system generating a language.

By a quasigrammar we shall mean a system: $QG = (i_0, G_1, \ldots, G_n)$
where: i_0 is a number of initial grammar and $1 \leq i_0 \leq n$,
G_i for $i=1,\ldots,n$ are quadruples like grammars, i.e.

$$G_i = (\Sigma_i , V_i , \sigma_i , P_i)$$

where: Σ_i is an alphabet of G_i,
V_i is an alphabet of control symbols of G_i,
$V_i \cap \Sigma_i = \emptyset$,
$\sigma_i \in V_i$ is an initial symbol of G_i,
P_i is a finite subset of the set

$$\{i\} \times \{1,\ldots,n\} \times Rel(V_i^*) \times (\Sigma_i \cup \{\varepsilon\})$$

such that $((i,j),Q,r) \in P_i$ implies that if $i \neq j$ then $r=\varepsilon$.

The set P_i will be called a set of productions of G_i. As in preceding chapter instead of $((i,j),Q,r)$ we shall write $(i \mapsto j,Q,r)$. We put $\Sigma = \Sigma_1 \cup \ldots \cup \Sigma_n$. The set Σ will be called an alphabet of QG. Let p,num be functions defined in the chapter 2 and let VS, VT be sets defined in the chapter 2.

The set $SG = VS \times \Sigma^*$ we shall called a set of word states of QG.

By a transition relation of the quasigrammar QG we shall mean a relation $T \subseteq SG \times SG$ defined as follows :

$$(a,u)T(b,v) \iff [(\exists (num(a) \mapsto num(b),Q,r) \in P_{num(a)}) \text{ and } (\forall i: i \neq num(a), 1 \leq i \leq n) \quad p(i,a)=p(i,b) \text{ and } (p(num(a),a),p(num(a),b)) \in Q \text{ and } v=ur] .$$

The language $L_{QG} = \{ w \in \Sigma^* \mid (\exists b \in VT) \ (a_0,\varepsilon) \ T \ (b,w) \}$ where $a_0 = (i_0, \sigma_1, \ldots, \sigma_n)$ will be said to be generated by QG.

If $(i \mapsto j,Q,r) \in P_i$ for $i=1,\ldots,n$ implies that Q is simple (recursive) then a quasigrammar QG will be called a regular (context-free) quasigrammar. The set of all languages generable by regular, context-free quasigrammars will be denoted respectively by $\mathcal{L}_{RQ}$, $\mathcal{L}_{CFQ}$, and the class of regular, context-free, accepted by Turing machines will be denoted respectively by $\mathcal{L}_{R}$, $\mathcal{L}_{CF}$, $\mathcal{L}_{TM}$.

Theorem 4.1.
There is a context-free quasigrammar QG such that $L_{QG} = \{ a^n b^n c^n \mid n \geq 0 \}$. ■

Theorem 4.2.

$$\mathcal{L}_{RQ} = \mathcal{L}_{R} \subsetneq \mathcal{L}_{CF} \subsetneq \mathcal{L}_{CFQ} \subseteq \mathcal{L}_{TM} . \quad ■$$

Theorem 4.3.
For each regular (context-free) quasigrammar QG there exists a vector of FC-coroutines (of PD-coroutines) C and an interpretation φ such that : $Res_C = \varphi^* L_{QG}$. ■

Theorem 4.4.
For each vector of FC-coroutines (of PD-coroutines) C there exists a regular (context-free) quasigrammar QG and an interpretation φ such that : $Res_C = \varphi^* L_{QG}$. ■

The last two theorems show a conection between quasigrammars and vectors of coroutines. Using them we are able to interprete some facts from the formal language theory as facts concerning relations computable by vectors of coroutines.

5. Coroutines computability. In this chapter computability properties of vectors of coroutines will be presented.

Let $F \subseteq Rel(X)$. A relation S is said to be FC-coroutines (PD-coroutines) computable from F iff there is a vector of FC-coroutines (PD-coroutines) C with properties :

(i) $S = Res_C$,

(ii) $(i \mapsto j, Q, R) \in P_i \Longrightarrow R \in F \cup \{I\}$ for i=1,...,n.

The class of all relations FC-coroutines (PD-coroutines) computable from F will be denoted by VFC(F) (VPD(F)) .

Theorem 5.1.
$(\exists X)(\exists F \subseteq Rel(X)) \quad VFC(F) = FC(F) \subsetneq PD(F) \subsetneq VPD(F) \subseteq C(F)$.

Thus the programming by means of coroutines with recursivness gives greather defining posibilities than the ordinary recursive programming.

<u>6. Final comment.</u> Usually a computation is analysed from the point of view of the binary relation between an input and an output. In our model this relation is called the resulting relation. Many well-known problems in the theory of programming can be formulated in terms of resulting relation. For a vector C and an object x it is easy to find such an object y that $x \mathrm{Res}_C y$. It is not easy, howeever, to find some general properties of Res_C by virtue of its definition. For vectors of FC-coroutines we can adopt the method of label elimination ([1]), while for vectors of PD-coroutines a method like label elimination or tail relations ([4]) does not exist yet.

At the end we notice that some high level simulation languages as SOL, SIMULA 67 provide mechnisms for coroutine-like sequencing.

References.

[1] Janicki, R.: A Mathematical Model for Coroutines, CC PAS Reports 232, Warsaw, 1976.

[2] Janicki, R.: An Algebraic Approach to the Theory of Recursive Coroutines, Fundamenta Informatica, to appear.

[3] Mayoh, B.H.: Problems in the Modelling of Programming, Proc. Sym. on MFCS'72, Jablonna, 1972.

[4] Mazurkiewicz, A.: Recursive Algorithms and Formal Languages, Bull. Acad. Polon. Sci., Ser. Sci. Math. Astronom. Phys., XX, No 9, 799-803.

[5] Mazurkiewicz, A.: Algorithms and Grammars, manuscript, (not published).

[6] Wang, A., Dahl, O.J.: Coroutine Sequencing in a Block Structured Environment, BIT, 11, 1971, 425-449.

ONE - ONE DEGREES OF TURING MACHINES DECISION PROBLEMS

Joanna Jędrzejowicz
Institute of Mathematics
University of Gdańsk

In /1/ Shepherdson has proved that for any three recursively enumerable Turing degrees L_1, L_2, L_3 there exist a Turing machine such that halting, derivability and confluence problems are of degrees L_1, L_2, L_3 respectively. Overbeek /2/ has established this result for many--one degrees. Singletary /4/ has shown that this is best possible result in the sense that not all one - one degrees are represented by decision problems of Turing machines.
The object of this paper is to prove that the result for one - one degrees is true iff L_1, L_2, L_3 are degrees of cylinders.

1. Preliminaries and basic definitions.

Let D_x be a finite set with number x where

$D_x = \{x_1, \ldots x_k\}$, $x_1 < x_2 < \ldots < x_k$ and $x = 2^{x_1} + 2^{x_2} + \ldots + 2^{x_k}$.
Let τ be a pairing function and 1, r functions such that $\tau(1(x), r(x)) = x$. $A \times B$ will stand for the set $\{\tau(x,y) \quad x \in A,\ y \in B\}$. Let c_M be one - one enumeration of all configurations of Turing machine M, d_M - length of configuration and s_M a function defined as follows:

$$s_M x = \begin{cases} x & \text{if } c_M^{-1}(x) \text{ is a terminal configuration,} \\ c_M x^{(w)} & \text{otherwise where } w \text{ is a successor of configuration } c_M^{-1}(x). \end{cases}$$

For a Turing machine M we define following sets:

$H_M = \{c_M(w)$ for w leading to a terminal configuration$\}$

$D_M = \{\tau(c_M(w_1),\ c_M(w_2))$ for w_1 leading to $w_2\}$,

$CF_M = \{\tau(c_M(w_1),\ c_M(w_2))$ for w_1, w_2 leading to the same configuration$\}$.

We can easily establish following corollaries:

1 $D_M \neq \emptyset$ and $CF_M \neq \emptyset$:

$\tau(x,x) \in D_M \cap CF_M$ for any $x \in N$.

2 If $H_M \neq \emptyset$ then $CF_M \neq N$:

if w = uqv is a terminal configuration then for any symbol $A \neq B$ from the machine alphabet $\tau(c_M(w),\ c_M(wA)) \in \overline{CF_M}$.

3 $D_M \neq N$:

$D_M = N$ implies that for any configurations w_1, w_2 we have that w_1 leads to w_2, let w stand for the successor of configuration w_1 that is $w = c_M^{-1}(s_M(c_M(w_1)))$ then we must have that w leads to w_1 but it contradicts the assumption that there are infinitely many different successors of w_1.

4 If $H_M = N$ then D_M and CF_M are recursive subsets of N (different from $\emptyset$ and N following corollaries 1,2,3): if every configuration leads to a terminal configuration, then for any configurations w_1, w_2 we can effectively decide whether w_1 leads to w_2 before a terminal configuration and whether there exists a configuration w such that both w_1, w_2 lead to w.

We introduce the following definition:

configuration w of Turing machine M is called right shifting left shifting, if we have $s_M{}^n(c_M(w)) = c_M(w)$ for some $n \geq 1$, $s_M{}^n$ stands for n-th iteration of s_M, and besides, if b is a marker of the beginning (the end) of configuration w then starting from bw (wb) we obtain the word $bB^s w$ ($wB^s b$) for some $s > 0$.

Note that if $s_M{}^n(c_M(w)) = c_M(w)$ then the same command is applicable to both w and $c_M^{-1}(s_M{}^n(c_M(w)))$. This proves that if w is right shifting then for any $k > 0$: $c_M^{-1}(s_M{}^k(c_M(w)))$ is right shifting and can not be left shifting.

In the sequel we shall use following lemmas formulated in /3/:

i) A is a cylinder iff for any set B, $B \leq_m A$ implies $B \leq_{1-1} A$.

ii) A is a cylinder iff there exists a recursive function g such that

/$D_x \neq \emptyset$ and $D_x \subset A$ / implies $g(x) \in A - D_x$

/$D_x \neq \emptyset$ and $D_x \subset \bar{A}$ / implies $g(x) \in \bar{A} - D_x$

Overbeek proved following result /2/: for any three total recursive functions f_1, f_2, f_3 a machine M can be constructed such that tha halting problem is of the same many-one degree as the decision problem for the range of f_1, the confluence problem is of the same many-one degree as the decision problem for the range of f_2, the derivability problem is of the same many-one degree as the decision problem for the range of f_3.

Remark. In the proof the author assumes that the range of each of the functions f_1, f_2, f_3 is defferent from N.

Lemma 1. For any recursively enumerable many-one degrees L_1, L_2 different from $\{\emptyset\}$ and $\{N\}$ there existe a Turing machine M such that the halting, derivability and confluence problems are of many-one degrees $\{\emptyset\}$, L_1, L_2. The proof follows immediately from lemma 5 and lemma 6 of /2/.

Lemma 2. There exists a Turing machine M such that the halting, derivability and confluence problems are of many-one degrees $\{N\}$, L , L - where L is many-one degree of all recursive sets different from N and $\emptyset$.

This trivial lemma is established if we consider the Turing machine with only one instruction:

$$q_1 \; B \; A \; q_1$$

where A stands for any symbol different from the blank B.

2. Turing machine of given one-one degrees of decision problems.

Theorem 1. For any Turing machine M, the sets H_M, D_M and CF_M are cylinders.

Proof: According to lemma ii) for each set H_M, D_M and CF_M we need to construct a suitable function g. We define suitable functions conditionally and we assume that always in case * the smallest value of quantified variable, j, satisfying the condition, is taken.

Let $D_x = \{x_1, \ldots x_k\}$, $x = 2^{x_1} + \ldots + 2^{x_k}$,

A - any symbol from the machine alphabet different from the blank symbol B.

At first we shall prove that H_M is a cylinder.

Let $z = \sum_{j=1}^{k} d_M(x_j)$, $w_1 = c_M^{-1}(x_1)$

We define the function g_1 as follows:

$$g_1\,x = \begin{cases} t_1 \quad * & \text{if } (\exists j)\,(1 \leq j \leq k)(s_M(x_j) = t_1 \in \overline{D}_x) \\ c_M(wB^zA) = t_2 & \text{if } w_1 \text{ leads to a halt, where } w \text{ is the terminal form of } w_1 \\ c_M(w_1B^zA) = t_3 & \text{if } w_1 \text{ leads to left shifting configuration} \\ c_M(AB^zw_1) = t_4 & \text{otherwise} \end{cases}$$

From the above definitions it follows that $g_1(x) \in \overline{D}_x$.

Moreover if we are not in the case * then w_1 leads to a halt or to a looping configuration and the situation can be effectively tested. If w_1 is a halting configuration then $c_M^{-1}(t_2)$ is halting as well (in fact, it is terminal), otherwise the machine M will never stop for w_1 and so will do for $c_M^{-1}(t_3)$ and $c_M^{-1}(t_4)$.

The condition that w_1 leads left shifting configuration (which in case when * is not satisfied can be effectively tested) means that M will never examine the rightmost symbol A of $c_M^{-1}(t_3)$, similiary for w_1 leading to right shifting configuration or looping configuration which is not shifting.

It proves that H_M is a cylinder.

Now let $z = \max\left[\sum_{j=1}^{k} d_M(1(x_j)),\quad \sum_{j=1}^{k} d_M(r(x_j))\right]$.

$t_2 = \tau(n,n)$, where n is the number of any configuration longer than z (e.g. $n = c_M(AqB^z A)$, q is a state symbol)

$t_3 = \tau(1(x_1), n)$

$w_1 = c_M^{-1}(1(x_1))$

$w_2 = c_M^{-1}(r(x_1))$

We define recursive function g_2 as follows:

$$g_2\, x = \begin{cases} t_1 & * \text{ if } (\exists j)(1 \le j \le k)(\tau(s_M(1(x_j)),\ r(x_j)) = t_1 \in \overline{D}_x) \\ t_2 & \text{if } w_1 \text{ leads to } w_2 \\ t_3 & \text{otherwise} \end{cases}$$

From the above it follows that $g_2(x) \in \overline{D}_x$.

If $*$ is not satisfied then w_1 leads to a halt or looping configuration. Each can be effectively tested, as D_x is finite, and derivability problem for w_1 and w_2 can be solved.

Cleary, if $*$ is not satisfied then w_1 can lead only to configurations of length less then z, so we have $t_3 \notin \overline{D}_M$. It proves that D_M is a cylinder. It remains to prove that CF_M is a cylinder as well.

Let z, t_2, w_1, w_2 be defined as before and let

$t_3 = \tau(c_M(c_M^{-1}(s_M{}^k(1(x_1)))\ B^z A),\ r(x_1))$

$t_4 = \tau(c_M(w_1 B^{2z} A),\ r(x_1))$

$t_5 = \tau(c_M(AB^{2z} w_1),\ r(x_1))$

The function g_3 is defined below:

$$g_3\, x = \begin{cases} t_1 & * \text{ if } (\exists j)(1 \le j \le k)(\tau(s_M(1(x_j)),\ s_M(r(x_j))) = t_1 \in \overline{D}_x) \\ t_2 & \text{if } w_1, w_2 \text{ conflue} \\ t_3 & \text{if } w_1 \text{ leads to a halt} \\ t_4 & \text{if } w_1 \text{ leads to left shifting configuration} \\ t_5 & \text{otherwise} \end{cases}$$

It is obvious that $g_3(x) \in \overline{D}_x$.

If $*$ is not satisfied then both w_1 and w_2 lead to terminal configurations or looping configurations. Each can be checked and in this case it can be checked whether w_1 and w_2 conflue. If so, then obviously $g_3(x) = t_2 \notin CF_M$. Otherwise none of t_3, t_4, t_5 belongs to CF_M.

In fact if w_1 leads to a halt then $c_M^{-1}(s_M{}^k(1(x_1))\ B^z A)$ is terminal

and it does not conflue with w_2 as well.
If w_1 leads to looping configuration which is left shifting then the machine M started for $w_1B^{2z}A$ will never halt but it will lead to configurations of length greater than z so it will not conflue with w_2. Similarly in case when w_1 leads to looping configuration which is right shifting or is not shifting.
This completes the proof that H_M, D_M, CF_M are cylinders.
Theorem 2. For recursively enumerable one-one degrees L_1, L_2, L_3 of cylinders such that $L_1 \neq \{N\}$, $L_i \neq \{\emptyset\}$ and $L_i \neq \{N\}$ for i = 2,3 there exists a Turing machine M such that the halting problem is of one-one degree L_1, the derivability problem is of one-one degree L_2 and the confluence problem is of one-one degree L_3.
The proof follows immediately from Overbeek´s result, lemma i , lemma 1 and theorem 1.

References:

/1/ J.C.Shepherdson-Machine configuration and world problems of given degree of unsolvability, Z.math.Logik und Grund.Math.Bd.11,1965 /pp.149-175/.

/2/ R.Overbeek-The representation of many-one degrees by decision problems of Turing machines, Proc.London Math.Soc.,Jan.1973, pp. 167-192.

/3/ H.Rogers-Theory of recursive functions and effective computability, Mc Graw Hill Company 1967.

/4/ C.E.Hughes,R.Overbeek,W.E.Singletary-The many-one equivalence of some general combinatorial decision problems Bull.Amer.Math.Soc., 77,1971,pp.467-472.

HEURISTIC REPRESENTATION OF STATE-SPACE BY FINITE AUTOMATON

Jozef Kelemen
Department of Theoretical Cybernetics
Komensky University, 816 31 Bratislava
Czechoslovakia

INTRODUCTION

The heuristic methods for problem-solving are usually developed as the methods for determining the "realistic" (see Sec. 4) strategies of a search through the state-space. The goal of these methods is to reduce an extent of the search. The heuristic information is used as a basis for the construction of the strategies (see Sec. 2).

The starting point of our reasoning is the following idea: Each heuristic methods is developed on the basis of some a priori knowledges about the problem environment of a particular problem-solver; therefore each heuristics specifies some level of the knowledge of the problem environment. In this paper we shall use the heuristic information to make a representation of a state-space in this level of knowledge (in Sec. 3). In Sec. 4 we give a sufficient condition for a fact that a heuristicaly guided strategy is "realistic".

In the next section we shall introduce the basic notions and notations concerning the state-space problem-solving.

1. STATE-SPACE PROBLEM-SOLVING

The state-space problem-solving assumes the existence of a countable set S of states and a finite set F of operators which maps the state of S into themselves (see [3]).

Operators are partial functions from S into S. The set of all states in which $f \in F$ is applicable is denoted by $S_f \subseteq S$. The identity function id (for each $s \in S$, id(s) = s) is required to be an element of F. The state-space given in such a way is denoted by (S,F).

The problem in (S,F) is specified by a nonempty set $T \subseteq S$.

The elements of T represent the desired goal states.

The problem-solver is seen as a moving through the state-space in an attemp to reach one of a desired goal states. The problem-situation for a problem spacified in (S,F) by T is given whenever a start state $s_o \in S$, from which this moving begins, is fixed.

We use the following notation: $((S,F),T)$ for problem and for problem-situation $(s_o, ((S,F),T))$.

The solution of a given problem-situation is a finite sequence $\langle f_1, f_2, \ldots, f_n \rangle$ of operators such that $f_n(\ldots f_2(f_1(s_o))\ldots) \in T$. Of course, this expression is defined only when $s_o \in S_{f_1}$, $f_1(s_o) \in S_{f_2}$ etc. The number n is the length of the solution. The problem-situation is solvable iff there exists at least one its solution. We note that the problem-situation for $s_o \in T$ is solvable and its solution is a 1-element sequence $\langle id \rangle$.

2. HEURISTICS

Intuitively, the heuristics associates each state with the set of "advantageous" (for solving a given problem) operators. In this case the goal oriented strategy is based on a generation of immediately succesive states to a given state by these operators.

Formaly, we express a heuristics for a given problem in the following way:

Let $((S,F),T)$ be a problem and let $\bar{F} \subseteq 2^F$ be a set such that $\{\emptyset\} \in \bar{F}$ and $\{id\} \in \bar{F}$. The total function H from S onto $\bar{F}$ with the properties

i if $H(s) = F_i \in \bar{F}$ then $s \in S_f$ for each $f \in F_i$

ii $s \in T$ iff $H(s) = \{id\}$

is said to be a heuristic mapping (or shortly heuristics) for the problem $((S,F),T)$.

The equivalence between our definition of heuristics and the one given implicitly in [2] is established in [4] .

The heuristic mapping can be understood as a basis for the following reduction of state-space:

Let the set $S_f^H = \{s \in S_f : f \in H(s)\}$ be the restricted domain of $f \in F$. Let F^H be a set of operators with resristed domains obtained from F by H. The state-space (S, F^H) is said to be the reduced state-space of (S,F) by H.

A crucial property of heuristics is that the strategy determined by it is capable to solve the given problem-situation. This property is now formalized by a notion of useful heuristics:

Let H be a heuristic mapping for the problem $((S,F),T)$. H is <u>useful</u> for solving a given problem-situation $(s_o,((S,F),T))$ iff there exists at least one solution of a problem-situation $(s_o,((S,F^H),T))$.

3.HEURISTIC REPRESENTATION OF STATE-SPACE

The primary purpose in problem-solving should be better to understand the state-space, to find representation within which the problem-situations are easier to solve (cf. [5]) .

In this section the heuristic mapping is used to give a heuristic representation of state-space. This representation is presented on a form of a finite automaton.

Let $((S,F),T)$ be a problem. Let H be a heuristic mapping for this problem. Let $R_H \subseteq S \times S$ be an equivalence relation defined as follows:

$$(s,\ s') \in R_H \quad \text{iff} \quad H(s) = H(s') \quad .$$

Let $S/R_H = \{S_i \subseteq S : S_i = \{ s \in S : H(s) = F_i \in \bar{F} \} \text{for each } F_i \in \bar{F}\}$ be the factor set defined by the equivalence relation R_H. It is easy to see that there exists a total mapping p (the projection) from S onto S/R_H and that $s \in S_i$ iff $p(s) = S_i$.

For a given problem there exists $S_T \in S/R_H$ such that $S_T = T$ because $s \in T$ iff $H(s) = \{id\}$. For s_o, the start state of a problem-situation of a given problem, there exists $S_o \in S/R_H$ such that $s_o \in S_o$.

Let a ternary relation $E \subseteq S/R_H \times F \times S/R_H$ be defined as follows:

$$(S_i,\ f,\ S_j) \in E \quad \text{iff} \; \exists s_i \in S_i \; : \; f \in H(s_i) \text{ and } f(s_i) \in S_j \; .$$

The datas S/R_H, S_o, S_T and E determines a finite F-automaton $A = (S/R_H, S_o, S_T)$ where S/R_H is considered as a set of states of the automaton A, S_o as an initial state, S_T as a terminal state and the set E as a set of edges (see [1]) .

The automaton A is considered to be a <u>heuristic</u> <u>representation</u> of the state-space (S,F) for the problem-situation $(s_o,((S,F),T))$. This automaton , without the initial state S_o , represents heuristicaly the state-space for the given problem $((S,F),T)$.

The following theorem, proved in [4] , shows the mutual relations between the property of heuristics "to be useful" (for given problem-situation) and the crucial property of corresponding heuristic repre-sentation of state-space:

Theorem 1: A heuristics H is useful to solve a given problem-situation iff there exists a solution $\langle f_1, f_2, \ldots, f_n \rangle$ of the given problem-situation such that $f_1 f_2 \ldots f_n$ is an element of the behavior $|A| \subseteq F^*$ of related F-automaton.

Closing this section we note that a state-space (S,F) together with this related heuristic representation via an F-automaton create an S-machine of the type F (see [1]) .

4. THE "REALISTIC" STRATEGIES

The basic difficulty of the heuristicaly guided strategies of problem-solving defined in Sec. 2 is the fact that the number of generated states grows very rapidly depending on the length of a solution of a given problem-situation. When this growth is exponentially dependent on the length of the solution, it is "unrealistic" to employ a computer for solving a problem-situation using these strategies.

We shall call "realistic" those strategies for which the number of generated states grows at most polynomially with respect to the length of a solution.

Our following theorem answers a question when the heuristics determine a "realistic" strategy for solving given problem-situation.

Theorem 2: If each state of A is an element of at most one cycle$^+$ in A then the associated heuristic strategy is "realistic".

The outline of the proof:

1/ If there is no cycle in the automaton A then the number N_1 of generated states in (S,F) depends on the number of states of A and does not depend on the length of the solution.

2/ If there is only one cycle in A then the number of generated states is at most $N_1 + N_2$ where N_2 depends on the length of solution linearly.

3/ If there are k cycles in A then the number of generated states in (S,F) is at most $(N_1 + N_2)\, N_3$ where N_3 depends polynomially on the length of the solution of given problem-situation. The degree of the polynomial $(N_1 + N_2)\, N_3$ is equal to k + 1.

The complete proof is in [4] .

$^+$The path $S_1 f_1 S_2 f_2 \ldots f_{n-1} S_n$ is said to be a cycle in A iff $S_1 = S_n$. The states $S_1, S_2, \ldots, S_n$ are the elements of this cycle.

REFERENCES

[1] Eilenberg S.: Automata, Languages and Machines, Vol. A, Academic Press, New York, 1974

[2] Ernst G. W., Banerji R. B., Hookway R. J., Oyen R. A., Shaffer D. E.: Mechanical Discovery of Certain Heuristics, Case Western Reserve University, Jennings Computing Center, Report No.1136 - A, 1974

[3] Hunt E. B.: Artificial Intelligence, Academic Press, New York, 1975

[4] Kelemen J.: Heuristics as a Basis for Frame-Representation of State-Space (in Slovak) RNDr. Thesis, Komensky University, Bratislava, 1976

[5] Minsky M.: A Framework for Representing Knowledge, in Psychology of Computer Vision (ed.: P. H. Winston),McGraw Hill, New York, 1975

SEMIGROUP CHARACTERIZATIONS OF SOME LANGUAGE VARIETIES

Robert Knast

Mathematical Institute of the Polish Academy of Sciences,

61-725 Poznań, Poland

1. INTRODUCTION

This note aims at presenting some new results on semigroup characterizations of language varieties. The importance of these characterizations of languages lies in the fact that the algebraic decision procedures for deciding whether a regular language belongs to this variety or not, directly result from them. They also relate a language representation to the given variety of semigroups. In this way language hierarchies can be compared with semigroup hierarchies (see for example Brzozowski, Knast (1976).

We present two generalizations of the concept of local testability introduced in McNaughton and Papert's monograph (1971). Namely, the vector local testability taken from Simon (1972) and the periodic local testability (Knast (1976)). Next we give a list of correspondences between language and semigroup varieties including some correspondences connected with vector and periodic locally testable languages.

For an excellent and more general presenting of problems related to this note the reader is asked to look up Brzozowski (1976) or the book of Eilenberg (1976).

2. DEFINITION FRAMEWORK

Languages

Let Σ be a finite non-empty alphabet. $\Sigma^+(\Sigma^*)$ will denote the free semigroup (free monoid) generated by Σ. A language L is any subset of Σ^*.

The family of languages $\mathcal{L}$ over finite non-empty alphabets is called a $*$-variety iff $\mathcal{L}$ is closed (with respect to Σ^*) under boolean operations, left and right derivations (i.e. $L\in\mathcal{L}$ implies that $\{w|wa\in L, w\in\Sigma^*\}$, $\{w|aw\in L, w\in\Sigma^*\}\in\mathcal{L}$ for all $a\in\Sigma$) and inverse homomorphism (i.e. for two alphabets Σ_1^*,Σ_2^* if $h:\Sigma_1^*\to\Sigma_2^*$ is a homomorphism then $\Sigma_2^*\supset L\in\mathcal{L}$ implies $Lh^{-1}\in\mathcal{L}$).

In a similar way, if we consider languages as subsets of Σ^+ instead of Σ^*, we obtain a $+$-variety of languages.

For $x,v\in\Sigma^*$ we define $h(v,x)$ as follows: $h(x,v) = h$ ($h\geq 0$, an integer) if $x=u_ivw_i, u_iw_i\in\Sigma^*$ for $i=1,2,\ldots,h$, $|u_1|<|u_2|<\ldots<|u_h|$ and $x=uvw$, $u,w\in\Sigma^*$ implies $u\in\{u_1,u_2,\ldots,u_h\}$ ($h=0$ if $x\neq uvw$ for all $u,w\in\Sigma^*$), where $|u|$ denotes the length of $u, u\in\Sigma^*$.

Let $p\geq 0$ be an integer. We shall use the following functions:

$$\bar{h}(x,v) = \begin{cases} h(x,v), & \text{if } h(x,v)<2p \\ p+h(x,v)/\mathrm{mod}\ p, & \text{if } h(x,v)\geq 2p \end{cases}, \quad \underline{h}(x,v)=h(x,v)/_{\mathrm{mod}p}$$

where for $p=0$ we assume that for any integer h $h/\mathrm{mod}\ p=0$. Let $k\geq 1$, $m\geq 0$ be integers and let $w = (w_1,w_2,\ldots,w_n)\in(\Sigma^k)^m$, $w_i\in\Sigma^k$ for $i=1,2,\ldots,m$. We shall write $w\,\underline{\varepsilon}\,x$, $x\in\Sigma^*$ if there exist $u_1,u_2,\ldots,u_m,v_1,v_2,\ldots,v_m\in\Sigma^*$ such that $|u_1|<|u_2|<\ldots<|u_m|$ and $x = u_iw_iv_i$, $i=1,2,\ldots,m$. Let $\Sigma^{<k} = \{w|\,|w|\leq k, w\in\Sigma^*\}$, $\underline{p} = \{0,1,\ldots,p-1\}$.

Define the following functions:

$f_k:\Sigma^*\to\Sigma^{\leq k}$, $f_k(x)$ is k-length prefix of x (if $|x|\leq k$, then $f_k(x) = x$)

$t_k:\Sigma^*\to\Sigma^{\leq k}$, $t_k(x)$ is k-length suffix of x (if $|x|\leq k$, then $t_k(x) = x$)

$\mu_k^p:\Sigma^*\to 2^{\Sigma^k\times\underline{p}}$, $\mu_k^p(x) = \{(v,h)|(v,h)\in\Sigma^k\times\underline{p}$ and $\underline{h}(x,v) = h\}$

$m_k^p:\Sigma^*\to 2^{\Sigma^k\times\underline{2p}}$, $m_k^p(x) = \{(v,h)|(v,h)\in\Sigma^k\times\underline{2p}$ and $\bar{h}(x,v) = h\}$

$\mu_{m,k}:\Sigma^*\to 2^{(\Sigma^k)^m}$, $\mu_{m,k}(x) = \{w|w\in(\Sigma^k)^m$ and $w\,\underline{\varepsilon}\,x\}$.

Now we can define the following congruencess: for $x,y\in\Sigma^*$

$x \underset{k}{\rightarrow} y$ ($x \underset{k}{\leftarrow} y$) iff $f_{k-1}(x) = f_{k-1}(y)$ (respectively, $t_{k-1}(x) = t_{k-1}(y)$)

$x \underset{mk}{\sim} y$ iff (a) $x = y$ if $|x| < m+k-1$

(b) $f_{k-1}(x) = f_{k-1}(y)$, $t_{k-1}(x) = t_{k-1}(y)$

and $\mu_{m,k}(x) = \mu_{m,k}(y)$ otherwise.

$x \underset{p/k}{\sim} y$ iff $f_{k-1}(x) = f_{k-1}(y)$, $t_{k-1}(x) = t_{k-1}(y)$

and $m_k^p(x) = m_k^p(y)$

$x \underset{k/\text{mod } p}{\sim} y$ iff $f_{k-1}(x) = f_{k-1}(y)$, $t_{k-1}(x) = t_{k-1}(y)$

and $\mu_k^p(x) = \mu_k^p(y)$.

Basing on these congruences we have the following language + - varieties:

(1) A language L is <u>finite/cofinite</u> iff it is finite or its complement is finite,

(2) A language L is <u>definite (reverse definite)</u> iff it is a union of congruence classes of $\underset{k}{\rightarrow}$ (respectively, $\underset{k}{\leftarrow}$) for some k,

(3) A language L is <u>(strictly) p-periodicly k-testable</u> iff L is a union of congruence classes of $\underset{p/k}{\sim}$ (respectively, $\underset{k/\text{modp}}{\sim}$),

(4) A language L is <u>(strictly) p-periodicly locally testable</u> iff L is a union of congruence classes of $\underset{p/k}{\sim}$ (respectively, $\underset{k/\text{modp}}{\sim}$) for some k,

(5) A language L is <u>(strictly) periodicly locally testable</u> iff L is (strictly) p-periodicly locally testable for some p,

(6) A language L is <u>m,k - testable</u> iff it is a union of congruence classes of $\underset{m,k}{\sim}$,

(7) A language L is <u>m-locally testable</u> iff L is m,k-testable for some k,

(8) A language L is a <u>dot-depth one</u> language iff it is m-locally testable for some m,

(9) A language L is a <u>piecewise testable</u> language iff it is m,1-testable for some m.

By the remark in the definition of $\underline{h}$ $(\bar{h})$, if p=0 then $m_k^0(x)=m_k^0(y)$ for all $x,y\varepsilon\Sigma^*$. Hence, the family of 0-periodicly locally testable languages concides with the family of generalized definite languages (Ginzburg(1966)). Next the family of 1-periodicly locally testable or 1-locally testable languages is the same as the family of locally testable languages introduced in the McNaughton and Papert's monograph (1971).

Semigroups

For any language $L\subset\Sigma^*$ the syntactic congruence $\equiv_L$ is defined as follows: for $x,y\ \varepsilon\ \Sigma^*$

$x\equiv_L y$ iff for all $u,v\varepsilon\Sigma^*(uxv\ \varepsilon\ L$ iff $uyv\varepsilon L)$. The quotient semigroup $\Sigma^+/\equiv_L$ (monoid $\Sigma^*/\equiv_L$) is called the syntactic semigroup S_L (syntactic monoid M_L, respectively) of L. If S is a semigroup, then $S^1 = S\cup\{\Lambda\}$, where Λ is the identity and the multiplication in S is unchanged (if in S there is the identity, then $S^1 = S$). A family of finite semigroups (monoids) is an S-variety (an M-variety) iff it is closed under taking submonoids, homomorphism and finite direct products.

Next we shall deal with the following varieties of finite semigroups:

(1) a semigroup S is group-free iff it contains no groups other than the trivial one-element groups (or iff there is $m>0$ such that for all $a\ \varepsilon\ S$ $a^m = a^{m+1}$)

(2) a semigroup S is commutative iff for all $a,b\ \varepsilon\ S$ ab=ba

(3) a semigroup S is 0-$\mathcal{J}$-trivial iff for all $a,b\ \varepsilon\ S$

$$a=ab=ba$$

(4) a semigroup S is 1-$\mathcal{J}$-trivial iff for all $a,b\ \varepsilon\ S^1$

$$ab=aba \quad \text{and} \quad ab=ba$$

(5) a semigroup S is 2-$\mathcal{J}$-trivial iff for all $a,b,c\ \varepsilon\ S^1$

$$abca=abaca \quad \text{and} \quad (ab)^2=(ba)^2$$

(6) a semigroup S is $\mathcal{J}$-trivial iff there is $m>0$ such that for all $a,b \in S$ $a^m=a^{m+1}$ and $(ab)^m=(ba)^m$

(7) a semigroup S is an idemgroup iff for all idempotents e in S the subsemigroup eSe is a group.

(8) a semigroup S is $\mathcal{R}$-($\mathcal{L}$-) trivial iff there is $m>0$ such that for all $a,b \in S$ $(ab)^m=(ab)^m a$ (respectively, $(ab)^m=b(ab)^m$)

(9) a semigroup S is 0-$\mathcal{R}$-(0-$\mathcal{L}$-) trivial iff for all $a,b \in S$

$a=ab$ (respectively, $a=ba$)

We say that S is quasi commutative (i-$\mathcal{J}$-trivial, i=0,1,2, J-trivial) iff for all idempotents e in S the subsemigroup eSe is commutative (i-J-trivial, $\mathcal{J}$-trivial, respectively). We say that S is quasi 0-$\mathcal{R}$-(0-$\mathcal{L}$-) trivial iff for all idempotents e in S the subsemigroup eS (Se, respectively) is 0-$\mathcal{R}$-(0-$\mathcal{L}$-) trivial.

3. A LIST OF CORRESPONDENCES BETWEEN LANGUAGE AND SEMIGROUP VARIETIES.

The listed below correspondences are examples of a general result of Eilenberg (1976), that to each + -variety of languages corresponds an S-variety of semigroups and vice versa.
A correspondence from the list should be read as follows:
a language L belongs to a language + -variety iff its syntactic semigroup S_L is in a corresponding S-variety. Some of these correspondences can be considered as correspondences between * - and M-varieties (for details see original papers).

Language variety	Finite semigroup variety
(1) Aperiodic (star free) languages	group-free semigroups (Schützenberger (1965))
(2) Finite / confinite languages	quasi 0-($\mathcal{R}\wedge\mathcal{L}$)-trivial semigroups
(3) Definite(Reverse definite) languages	quasi 0-$\mathcal{L}$-(0-$\mathcal{R}$-) trivial semigroups

(4) Generalized definite languages O-locally testable languages	quasi O-$\mathcal{J}$-trivial(or O-($\mathcal{R}\cup\mathcal{L}$)-trivial) semigroups ((2)-(4) Perrin (1971), Zalcstein (1972), Brzozowski, Simon (1973))
(5) 1,1-testable languages	1-$\mathcal{J}$-trivial(or idempotent and commmutative)semigroups (Simon (1972))
(6) 2,1-testable languages	2-$\mathcal{J}$-trivial semigroups (Knast (1975))
(7) 1-locally testable languages	quasi 1-$\mathcal{J}$-trivial semigroups (Brzozowski,Simon(1973), McNaughton (I974))
(8) 2-locally testable languages	quasi 2-$\mathcal{J}$-trivial semigroups (Knast (1975))
(9) Piecewise testable languages	$\mathcal{J}$-trivial semigroups (Simon (1972), (1975)
(10) Dot-depth one languages	quasi $\mathcal{J}$-trivial semigroups (Simon (1972), Knast (1975))
(11) Periodicly 1-testable languages	commutative semigroups
(12) Periodicly locally testable languages	quasi commutative semigroups
(13) Strictly periodicly 1-testable languages	commutative groups
(14) Strictly periodicly locally testable languages	quasi commutative idemgroups ((11)-(14) Knast (1976))

Recently Brzozowski $(1975)_2$ investigating an analogy between the family of finite/cofinite languages and the family of piecewise testable languages, has found that $\mathcal{J}$-($\mathcal{R}$-,$\mathcal{L}$-) trivial monoids and aperiodic I-monoids (for the definition see this paper) are natural generalizations of syntactic semigroups of finite/cofinite (definite, reverse definite) and generalized definite languages. For the case of two letter alphabet ($\Sigma=\{0,1\}$) these monoids correspond to the $\oplus$-finite/cofinite (definite, reverse definite) and $\oplus$-generalized definite languages, where in the definition of these languages the extended alphabet $\Sigma_{\oplus}=\{0,1,0^+,1^+\}$ is used.

The ways of proving the correspondences listed above are various and generally, quite complex, but one of these ways can be applied to (4), (7), (8), (10), (12) and (14). This originates from Brzozowski, Simon (1973) with some modifications taken from Knast(1975). One of the steps of this way consists of a characterization of a variety of languages in terms of the decompositions of the reduced automata accepting these languages. So this step of proving these correspondences develops, in a way, the decomposition theory of automata. As an example: a language L is p-periodicly k-testable iff the reduced automaton accepting L can be covered by a cascade product of (k-1)-definite automaton and a parallel connection of p-comets (for details and definitions see Knast (1976)).

References

Brzozowski J.A.,(1975)$_1$,Run languages,Bericht Nr.87,Institut für Rechner-und Programstructuren,Gesellschaft für Matematik und Datenverarbeitung mbH,Bonn,Germany,17 pp.

Brzozowski J.A.,(1975)$_2$,On aperiodic I-monoids,Technical Report, University of Waterloo,Waterloo,Ont.,Canada.

Brzozowski J.A.,(1976),Hiererchies of aperiodic Languages,Revue Francaise d'Automatique,Informatique,Recherche Operetionnelle Série Rouge (Informatique Théorique)-to appear in no.3.

Brzozowski J.A.,Knast R.,(1976),The dot-depth hiererchy of star free languages is infinite,Technical Report,University of Waterloo, Waterloo,Canada.

Brzozowski J.A.,Simon I.,(1973),Characterizations of locally testable events,Discrete Mathematics,vol.4,pp.243-271.

Cohen R.S.,Brzozowski J.A.(1971),Dot-depth of star-free events, J.Computer and System Sc.,vol.5,pp.1-16.

Eilenberg S.(1974),Automata,languages,and machines,vol.A, New York, Academic Press, (1976) vol.B (in press)

Ginzburg A.,(1966),About some properties of definite,reverse definite and related automata,IEEE Trans.Electronic Computers EC-15,pp. 806-810.

Knast R.,(1975),Semigroups characterization of dot-depth one languages, unpublished manuscript.

Knast R.,(1976),Periodic and strictly periodic local testability, Technical Report,Institute of Mathematics,Polish Academy of Sciences,Poznań,Poland.

McNaughton R.,(1974),Algebraic decision procedures for local testability,Math.Systems Theory,vol.8,pp.60-76.

McNaughton R.,Papert S.,(1971),Counter-free automata,Cambridge,The MIT Press (MIT Research Monographs,65).

Perrin D.,(1971),Sur certains semigroupes syntaxiques,Séminaires de 'IRIA,Logiques et Automates,pp.169-177.

Schutzenberger M.P.,(1965),On finite monoids having only trivial subgroups,Inform. and Control,vol.8.pp.190-194.

Schützenberger M.P.,(1966),On a family of sets related to McNaughton's L-language,"Automata Theory",edited by E.R.Caianiello,New York, Academic Press.pp.320-324.

Simon I. ,(1972),Hierarchies of events with dot-depth one,Ph.D.Thesis, Dept.of Applied Analysis and Computer Science,University of Waterloo,Waterloo,Ont.,Canada.

Simon I.,(1975),Piecewise testable events,2nd GI-Proffesional Conference on Automata Theory and Formal Languages,Kaiserlautern, Germany.(To appear in Lecture Notes in Computer Science, Springer-Verlag,Berlin).

Zalcstein Y.,(1972),Locally testable languages,J.Computer and System Sc.,vol.6.pp.151-167.

Zalcstein Y.,$(1973)_1$,Locally testable semigroups, Semigroup Forum, vol.5.pp.216-227.

Zalcstein Y.,$(1973)_2$,Syntactic semigroups of some classes of star-free languages,"Automata,Languages and Programming", Proceedings of a Symposium,Rocquencourt,Amsterdam,North-Holland Publishing Company,pp.135-144.

ON MEMORY REQUIREMENTS OF STRASSEN's ALGORITHMS

Antoni Kreczmar
Warsaw University

Abstract. In the paper we analyse the memory problem of Strassen s algorithms for fast matrix multiplication and inversion.

1. Strassen-Winograd algorithm for multiplication 2x2 matrices.

Let us recall the famous algorithm for fast matrix multiplication. We consider two 2x2 matrices :

$$\begin{bmatrix} a & b \\ c & d \end{bmatrix} \qquad \begin{bmatrix} e & f \\ g & h \end{bmatrix}$$

with element from some noncommutative ring. In order to compute their product V.Strassen / 9 / proposed the algorithm, which afterwards improved by S.Winograd took the following form.

First we compute seven products:

$p_1 := a \cdot e \qquad p_2 := b \cdot g \qquad p_3 := (c+d-a) \cdot (h-f+e)$

$p_4 := (c+d) \cdot (f-e) \qquad p_5 := (a-c) \cdot (h-f)$

$p_6 := (b-c-d+a) \cdot h \qquad p_7 := d \cdot (g-h+f-e)$

Next in order to compute the whole product : $\begin{bmatrix} A & B \\ C & D \end{bmatrix}$

we must only perform the following additions:

$A := p_1+p_2 \qquad B := p_1+p_3+p_4+p_6$

$C := p_1+p_3+p_5+p_7 \qquad D := p_1+p_3+p_4+p_5$

Now if we have two nxn matrices by treating them as 2x2 matrices ,each of whose elements are n/2 x n/2 submatrices, then the product can be expressed in terms of sums and products of these submatrices. Hence using k-levels of recursion of Strassen's algorithm and multiplying the resulting 7^k pairs of submatrices classically, we obtain fast algorithm for multiplication matrices of any order n.

P.Fischer and R.Probert / 4 / showed that the optimal strategy for defining k gives the method whose arithmetic total cost is

$$K \cdot n^{\log_2 7}$$

where K varies between 3.732 and 4.537. A saving in comparison with the classical method is guaranteed for all even $n \geq 14$ and all $n \geq 35$.

2. Memory problem.

We leave the problem of arithmetical complexity of these algorithms, remembering that it has been the object of very intensive investigations for several last years. The problem which we analyse in the paper is the problem of memory size needed in such recursive algorithms. The reader can easily see that this method proposed in its original version is memory consuming. Every level of recursion requires a declaration of seven new auxiliary matrices of order n/2 and the eight matrix is needed for the result. Hence the straightforward application of Strassen's method needs at least:

$$n^2 + 8(n^2/4+n^2/16+.... \qquad) = 11/3\ n^2$$

of additional memory cells.

The memory problem will become less drastic if we try to construct an algorithm, which evaluates in 'in situ' way. Then arguments of a procedure may be treated as input as well as auxiliary and output variables.

We shall define the algorithm, which computes the same arithmetic expressions as in Strassen's method, but using only input variables: a,b,c,d,e,f,g,h and two auxiliary variables: x,y. The result of multiplication is put on the left or the right argument depending on the value of a Boolean control variable : left.

```
begin
   x:=c:=c+d;  y:=f:=f-e;  x:=x·y;  c:=c-a;  f:=h-f;
   y:=e;  a:=a·y;  d:=d-c;  e:=f-e;  y:=d;  e:=y·e;
   d:=d+c;  y:=g:=g-f;  d:=d·y;  g:=g+f;  y:=b;
   y:=y·g;  b:=b-c;  b:=b·h;  c:=c·f;  c:=c+a;  x:=x+c;
   if  left  then
   begin
      a:=a+y;  b:=b+x;  c:=c+d+e;  d:=e+x
   end  else
   begin
      h:=e+x;  g:=c+d+e;  f:=b+x;  e:=a+y
   end
end
```

If the above method is to be applied recursively, then every multiplication of the form:

$$p := q \cdot r$$

can be performed only under the inductive assumption, i.e. p must be either q or r and moreover that second argument which is not used as the output variable, has after the calculation undefined value, because it was used as an auxiliary variable in the process.

We can easily verify that our algorithm satisfies that inductive condition and it computes the product of two 2x2 matrices with elements from noncommutative ring.

Every step of recursion needs $2n^2/4^k$ additional memory cells, hence the whole method needs:

$$2\left(n^2/4 + n^2/16 + \dots\right) = 2/3\, n^2$$

of additional memory cells.

3. Matrix inversion algorithm.

Having the fast matrix multiplication algorithm we can applicate it to the matrix inverting problem.

Let

$$\begin{bmatrix} a & b \\ c & d \end{bmatrix}$$

be 2x2 matrix which we want to invert. V. Strassen / 9 / proposed the following algorithm. First calculate the values:

$p_1 := a^{-1}$ $p_2 := c \cdot p_1$ $p_3 := p_1 \cdot b$ $p_4 := c \cdot p_3$

$p_5 := p_4 - d$ $p_6 := p_5^{-1}$ $p_7 := p_3 \cdot p_6$ $p_8 := p_6 \cdot p_2$

$p_9 := p_3 \cdot p_8$ $p_{10} := p_1 - p_9$

Then the result

$$\begin{bmatrix} A & B \\ C & D \end{bmatrix}$$

can be obtained in the following way:

$A := p_{10}$ $B := p_7$ $C := p_8$ $D := -p_6$

Hence matrices may be also inverted in approximately $n^{\log_2 7}$ arithmetic operations by recursive partitioning and application of the above method.

Now we propose the following algorithm which is the simple transformation of Strassen's method.

```
begin
    a:=a^-1 ;   x:=a;   y:=c;   c:=c·x;   x:=a;
    b:=x·b;   x:=b;   y:=y·x;   d:=y-d;   d:=d^-1;
    x:=b;   y:=d;   c:=y·c;   y:=c;   y:=x·y;
    a:=a-y;   y:=d;   b:=b·y;   d:=-d
end
```

As in Strassen ,we assume that all recursively invoked inverses make sense,i.e. that none of the intermediate matrices are singular. Combining the method from §2 and the above one we obtain the algorithm which computes the inversion of matrices in nearly 'in situ' way. The reader can easily verify that all multiplications and inversions performed in our algorithm satisfy the inductive assumption.

Bibliography

/1/ Bunch J.,Hopcroft J.E. ,Triangular factorization and inversion by fast matrix multiplication,Math.Comp. 28,1974,231-236

/2/ Fiduccia C.M.,Fast matrix multiplication,Proc. 3rd Annual ACM Symposium on Theory of Computing,1971,45-49

/3/ Fiduccia C.M.,On obtaining upper bounds on the complexity of matrix multiplication,in Complexity of Computer Computations, N.Y.-London,1972,31-40

/4/ Fischer P.C.,Probert R.L.,Efficient procedures for using matrix algorithms,Proc. 2nd Coll.Aut.Lan.Prog.,1974,413-427

/5/ Fischer P.C.,Further schemes for combining matrix algorithms, Proc. 2nd Coll.Aut.Lan.Prog. ,1974,428-436

/6/ Hopcroft J.E.,Kerr L.R.,On minimizing the number of multiplications necessary for matrix multiplication,SIAM J.Ap.Math., 20 ,1971,30-36

/7/ Hopcroft J.E.,Musinski J.,Duality in determining the complexity of noncommutative matrix multiplication,Proc. 5th Annual ACM Symposium on Theory of Computing,1973 ,73-87

/8/ Kerr L.R.,The effect of algebraic structure on the computational complexity of matrix multiplications,Ph.D.Thesis,Cornell Un.

/9/ Strassen V.,Gaussian elimination is not optimal,Num.Math.13,1969 354-356

/10/ Winograd S.,On the multiplication of 2x2 matrices,Linear Algebra and its applications, 4,1971,381-388

DETERMINISM IN CONCURRENT SYSTEMS

Włodzimierz Kwasowiec
Computation Centre of the PAS
PKiN, Skr.poczt.22, 00-901 Warszawa, Poland

1. Introduction.

The aim of the paper is to examine the problem of determinism in concurrent systems. In order to do this we have to say what the concurrent system is. The second purpose of the paper is a definition of the concurrent system in such a general way that it will be able to make the starting point for investigations of various properties of the systems.

There is a number of papers concerning parallelism but they deal mainly with parallel programs (e.g. Dijkstra [2], Hoare [3], Mazurkiewicz [5]) and only a few with parallel systems (Mazurkiewicz [6], Petri [8]). We might say about the equivalence between parallel programs and systems but programs remain only simulators of real systems. Sometimes it is impossible to simulate a system by a program because of infinite number of system components.

The following model of the concurrent system is proposed. We assume that there is a number of arbitrary objects (e.g. points of our space) each of which is in a certain state. The operation of an object consists in a transformation of the object from its actual state to another state. Objects may operate sometimes by themselves (independently) and sometimes may cooperate (they are interdependent during changing their actual states). Petri nets (Petri [8]) turned out to be very useful tool for the description of the control (its framework) of the system. We can not use tools applied for sequential operation of objects. I tried to define the control otherwise (by means of so called concurrent relation) but it gave me less class of systems than the present one.

The definition of the concurrent system takes the origin in Mazurkiewicz's idea of concurrent programs ([5]). Next due to Mazurkiewicz [5] and Winkowski [9] we can define a process as a graph which describes the system behaviour in a possible pass of its operation (the definition is a little different).

Let us take an arbitrary system. After some actions other actions are performed and the system always "knows" is to be executed in a given moment (although we, who observe the system, may not know how it is going on). So it is very important to examine determinism of systems. We shall deal with determinism in the mentioned sense of the only one choice of actions to be executed in a given state of the system. Not in the sense of non-deterministic precedence of the execution of parallel actions (Mazurkiewicz [4]).

Proofs of theorems will not be given in that paper. They will be published elsewhere.

2. Denotation.

Let R be an arbitrary binary relation. For an arbitrary set Z we denote

$$R(Z) = \{ t : \quad zRt \quad \text{for a certain} \quad z \in Z \},$$

$$R^{-1}(Z) = \{ t : \quad tRz \quad \text{for a certain} \quad z \in Z \}.$$

If Z is a one-element set $Z = \{z\}$, we shall write $R(z)$, $R^{-1}(z)$.

By R^* we shall mean the transitive closure of the relation R.

If Z_1, Z_2 are sets, then $Z_1 R Z_2$ denotes that $z_1 R z_2$ holds for all $z_1 \in Z_1$ and $z_2 \in Z_2$.

By Dom(R) we shall denote the domain of the relation R (in particular, R may be a function), i.e. the set of all x such that xRy for a certain y.

3. Concurrent systems.

By a concurrent system we mean a triple $U = \langle I, T, \varphi \rangle$, where I is a set of indices - names of objects, T is the control framework and φ is the control semantics. Now we are going to explain the components of concurrent systems.

3.1. Objects.

I is an arbitrary set. We adopt that elements of the set I are names of objects (assigned uniquely to objects).

An arbitrary object i (from here objets will be identified with their names) will be characterized, following an idea of Pawlak [7], by a set of its states S_i and a set of its possible actions Π_i which consists of functions $\pi_i : S_i \longrightarrow S_i$. Therefore in this sense we can write

$$i = \langle S_i , \Pi_i \rangle .$$

Let us denote $S = \bigcup_{i \in I} S_i$ and $\Pi = \bigcup_{i \in I} \Pi_i$.

3.2. Control framework.

The control framework T is a Petri net $T = \langle Q, C, R \rangle$, where Q, C are arbitrary sets, R is a relation $R \subseteq Q \times C \cup C \times Q$ and we assume that the following conditions are satisfied:

(3.2.1) $Q \cap C = \emptyset$,

(3.2.2) for each $q \in Q$ $R^{-1}(q) \neq \emptyset$,

(3.2.3) for all $q_1, q_2 \in Q$ either $R^*(q_1) \cap R^*(q_2) \neq \emptyset$

or $(R^{-1})^*(q_1) \cap (R^{-1})^*(q_2) \neq \emptyset$.

Condition (3.2.2) states that, in the future meaning, each action has to have arguments. Condition (3.2.3) assures us of the connectivity of the net T.

3.3. Control semantics.

Let us denote by A the set of all partial functions $a: I \longrightarrow \Pi$ such that $a(i) \in \Pi_i$ for $i \in Dom(a)$. So $a(i)$ is an action from Π_i.

The control semantics φ consists of two functions $\varphi = \langle \varphi_1, \varphi_2 \rangle$

$$\varphi_1 : Q \longrightarrow A$$
$$\varphi_2 : C \longrightarrow 2^I$$

satisfying for each q Q the following conditions:

(3.3.1) $\quad Dom(\varphi_1(q)) \subseteq \bigcup_{c \in R^{-1}(q)} \varphi_2(c) \;=\; \bigcup_{c \in R(q)} \varphi_2(c)$,

(3.3.2) $\quad$ if $c_1 \neq c_2$ and either $c_1, c_2 \in R^{-1}(q)$ or $c_1, c_2 \in R(q)$, then $\varphi_2(c_1) \cap \varphi_2(c_2) = \emptyset$.

Therefore the control semantics to each $c \in C$ assigns a set of objects and to each $q \in Q$ assigns a set of actions. The first condition says that actions should be executed on correspondent objects. The second condition states that none "parallel" c_1, c_2 must contain the same object, because otherwise an object could be in two different states simultaneousely.

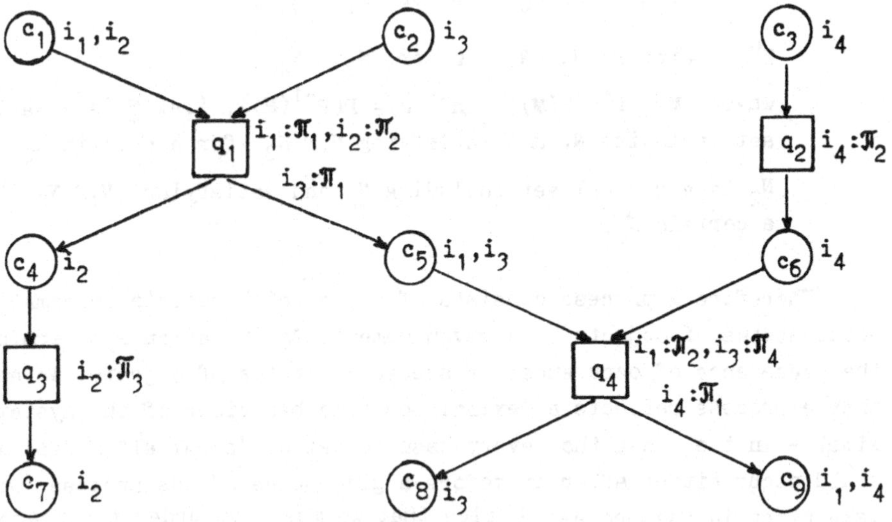

Fig.1. An example: a fragment of a concurrent system.
(Colons separate arguments and values of functions.)

4. Processes.

Let us denote by F the set of all partial functions $f\colon I \longrightarrow S$ satisfying $f(i) \in S_i$ for $i \in Dom(f)$.

Def. By a process of the system U we shall mean a graph together with a function $G = \langle N, P, g \rangle$, where N is a set of nodes, P is a relation $P \subseteq N \times N$ and g is a function $g\colon N \longrightarrow C \times F$, which may be presented as two functions $g = \langle g_1, g_2 \rangle$ where $g_1\colon N \rightarrow C$ and $g_2\colon N \longrightarrow F$. We require that the process G consist of a maximal connected (in the sense of linking by the relation P) set of nodes which satisfies the following conditions:

(4.1) $\quad Dom(g_2(n)) = \varphi_2(g_1(n)) \qquad$ for each $n \in N$,

(4.2) $\quad N_1 P\, N_2 \quad$ if there exists $q \in Q$ such that $g_1(N_1) = R^{-1}(q)$, $g_1(N_2) = R(q)$ and for each object $i \in \varphi_2(g_2(N_1))$ there exist $n_1 \in N_1$, $n_2 \in N_2$ such that

$$g_2(n_2)(i) = \begin{cases} [\varphi_1(q)(i)]\,([g_2(n_1)](i)) & \text{if } i \in Dom(\varphi_1(q)), \\ [g_2(n_1)](i) & \text{if } i \in Dom(\varphi_1(q)) , \end{cases}$$

(4.3) $\quad$ if $N_1 P\, N_2$ and $N_3 P\, N_4$ then the following conditions hold

1° $\quad$ either $\check{N}_1 \cap \check{N}_3 = \emptyset$ or $\check{N}_1 = \check{N}_3$,

2° $\quad$ either $\hat{N}_2 \cap \hat{N}_4 = \emptyset$ or $\hat{N}_2 = \hat{N}_4$,

where $\check{M} = P^{-1}(P(M))$ and $\hat{M} = P(P^{-1}(M))$, i.e. $\check{N}_1$ is a maximal set including N_1 and satisfying $N_1 P\, N_2$ for a certain N_2, and $\hat{N}_2$ is a maximal set including N_2 and satisfying $N_1 P\, N_2$ for a certain N_1.

Therefore a process consists of nodes which contain information about states of objects at a given moment. The relation P determines the precedence of occurences of succesive states of objects. We adopt that a process reflects a maximal possible behaviour of the system. Maximal - in the sense that every case (a set of "parallel" nodes) which could occur either after or before a given case of the process will take place in the process. Notice that we must not order the process sequentially (instead the above graph) if we want to preserve the nature of concurrency.

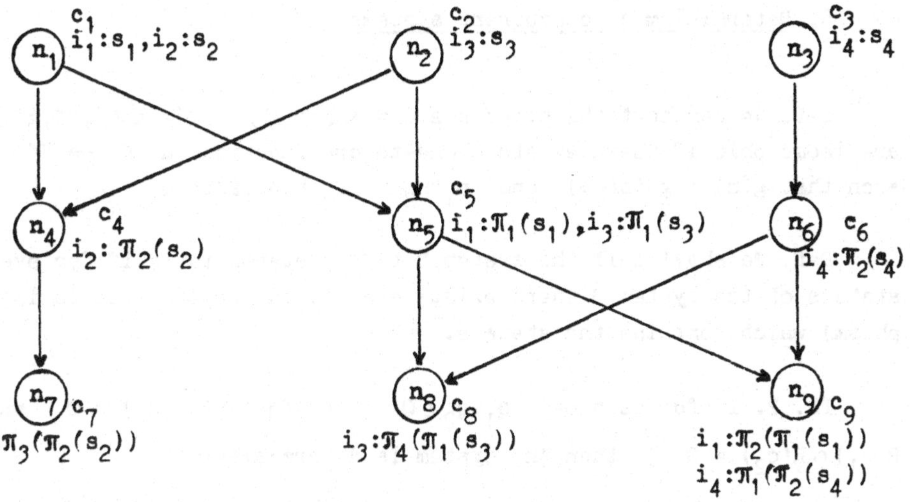

Fig.2. An example: a fragment of a process corresponding to the part of the concurrent system of fig. 1.

Def. We shall call nodes n_1, n_2 of the process G to be concurrent if neither $n_1 P n_2$ nor $n_2 P n_1$.

Def. By a case of the process G we mean a maximal set of nodes of G which are concurrent in pairs.

Def. By a state of the system U we mean a set $s \subseteq C \times F$ composed of all pairs which are values assigned by g to all nodes of a case of a certain process. In such instance we shall say that the process contains the state s.

Th. 1. For all n_1, n_2 which are concurrent

$$\varphi_2(g_1(n_1)) \cap \varphi_2(g_1(n_2)) = \emptyset \quad .$$

Corollary 1. For an arbitrary state s of the system U
$\bigcup \{f: \ (c,f) \in s\}$ is a function.

This property says that in each state of the system U each object may appear at most once.

5. Determinism of concurrent systems.

Def. We say that the processes $G = \langle N,P,g \rangle$, $G' = \langle N',P',g' \rangle$ are isomorphic if there exists a one-to-one function $h: N \longrightarrow N'$ such that $g(n) = g'(h(n))$ and $n_1 P n_2$ iff $h(n_1)P'h(n_2)$.

Def. We shall call the system U to be deterministic if for every state s of the system U there exists exactly one process (up to isomorphism) which contains the state s.

Th. 2. If for each pair $q_1, q_2 \in Q$ $\quad R^{-1}(q_1) \cap R^{-1}(q_2) = \emptyset$ and $R(q_1) \cap R(q_2) = \emptyset$, then the system is deterministic.

Now we shall define the consequence relation P_{con} between cases cases of the process. The relation will determine which case may occur after a given case of the process.

Def. $N_1 P_{con} N_2$ if we can present $N_1 = \bigcup_{j \in J} N_{1,j}$, $N_2 = \bigcup_{j \in J} N_{2,j}$ such that for each $j \in J$ $\quad N_{1,j} P N_{2,j}$.

Note that we allow the identity into the consequence relation of a process. We do this because looking at the time behaviour of the system there exists an interval of time within which no changes are made on the actual state.

Th. 3. For an arbitrary process $\quad P^* \subseteq P_{con}$.

Th. 4. If $P_{con} = P$ for each process of the system, then the system is deterministic.

Thus theorems 2,4 give us two different sufficient conditions for a system to be deterministic. The conditions intersect but none of them contains the other one. The main problem is to give such a sufficient condition which is necessary simultaneousely.

References

[1] Brinch Hansen, P., A Comparison of Two Synchronizing Concepts , Acta Informatica, Vol.1, 1972, 190 - 199.

[2] Dijkstra, E.W., Cooperating Sequential Processes, in Programming Languages, ed. by F. Genuys, Academic Press, London and New York, 1968.

[3] Hoare, C.A.R., Parallel Programming: an Axiomatic Approach,Stanford Artificial Intelligence Laboratory, Memo AIM-219, October 1973.

[4] Mazurkiewicz, A., Parallel Recursive Program Schemes, Lecture Notes 32, Springer Verlag, 1975.

[5] Mazurkiewicz, A., Invariants of Concurrent Programs, Proc.Conf. INFOPOL-1976, Warsaw, 1976.

[6] Mazurkiewicz, A., On Concurrent Processes, to appear.

[7] Pawlak, Z., Fundamentals for Computer Science, Proc.Symp. MFCS-72, Warsaw-Jabłonna, 1972.

[8] Petri, C.A., Concepts of Net Theory, Proc.Symp. MFCS-73, High Tatras, 1973.

[9] Winkowski, J., On Sequential Modelling of Non-Sequential Processes, this issue.

GENERATING CONTROL MECHANISMS BY RESTRICTIONS

K. Lautenbach and H. Wedde
Gesellschaft fuer Mathematik und Datenverarbeitung
D-5205 St. Augustin 1, Schloss Birlinghoven

0. The Concept of Mutual Exclusion

Programming techniques for handling mutual exclusion problems, e.g. the reader-writer-problem, are normally very laborious. This is especially so when compared with the elementary nature of mutual exclusion of states on which problems of this type are based upon. One reason is that programming languages were developped in accordance with the event-oriented character of computer instructions. Thus it is difficult to describe state-oriented phenomena. In this paper we shall give a new approach to such problems. It is based on the concept of mutual exclusion which we look at as a binary relation of inhibition between elementary states (called phases). Hereby also the role of events will change: While in event-oriented system descriptions the holding of a well-defined set of elementary conditions is equivalent to the possibility of occurrence of an elementary event, in our way of description every elementary event may occur which does not lead to a collision with the inhibition structure: a "complementary" view of events.

Despite the formal character of our model we want to point out that we see it as a programming concept in the context described above. It is conceivable to use the inhibition structure to provide additional semantical information for a compiler. There are good reasons to believe that this is only the first step towards writing "complementary" programs by using the inhibition structure alone. The compilation of such programs into an event-oriented form can be regarded as solved in its main parts.

1. Loosely Coupled Systems

The concept of Loosely Coupled Systems (LCS) is a method to formalize the interdependence between the components of a real system. It is due to C.A. PETRI. The components, called parts, are represented by sets which have nearly no internal structure. The reason for this is that we are more interested in the interdependence between parts than in their inner structure. The elements of the parts are called phases.

Let B be the (finite) set of parts; P the set of all phases; we require of our model the following properties:

1.1 $\bigcup_{b \in B} b = P$; 1.2 $\forall_{b_1,b_2 \in B} (b_1 \neq b_2 \Longrightarrow b_1 \cap b_2 = \emptyset)$.

So the parts are pairwise disjoint sets of phases, and B is a partition of P. The form of interdependence we speak about here is given in the following way: Given any two distinct parts b_1, b_2: For some phases $p_1 \in b_1$; $p_2 \in b_2$, we say that p_1 and p_2 cannot hold together. This mutual exclusion relation is called coupling relation between b_1 and b_2 and denoted by $K\langle b_1 b_2\rangle$. So we have:

1.3 $K\langle b_1 b_2\rangle \subseteq b_1 \times b_2$; $K\langle b_1 b_2\rangle = (K\langle b_2 b_1\rangle)^{-1}$.

$K\langle b_1 b_2\rangle$ is a binary and "symmetrical" relation. It is convenient to extend the notion of a coupling relation to the case where $b_1=b_2=:b$:

1.4 $\quad K\langle bb\rangle := (b \times b)\setminus id\langle b\rangle.$

(Two different phases of a part b cannot hold together.) Now we define a _global coupling relation K_ which is symmetrical as follows:

1.5 $\quad K := \bigcup_{b_1,b_2 \in B} K\langle b_1 b_2\rangle.$

In any system situation - called _case_ - every part will be in exactly one phase. So, if C is the set of all cases, we characterize C by:

1.6 $\quad \forall_{c\in C} \; c \subseteq P$; (Cases are sets of phases.)

1.7 $\quad \forall_{b\in B} \forall_{c\in C} \; |b \cap c| = 1$; (In any part there is exactly one phase belonging to a given case.)

1.8 $\quad \forall_{c\in C} \forall_{p_1,p_2\in c} \; (p_1,p_2) \notin K.$ (Two phases of a case cannot be coupled.)

So the cases are the maximal sets of phases which are pairwise "compatible". A loosely coupled system (LCS) is a quadruple (P,B,C,K) with the properties 1.1 to 1.8.

To describe the system behaviour of LCS we use a concept of event which is compatible with the coupling structure in the sense just pointed out. So events must be transitions between allowed situations (cases), and they are changes between phases in this context. To be more precise we shall use the concept of _elementary events_ for describing the changing of phases within a single part. We do not wish to admit as elementary events such case changes where the cases are reachable from one another only by coincident changes of phases in two parts b_1 and b_2. For this would imply an additional inhibition structure, beyond the coupling structure given above. So the existence of an elementary event in a given case means that the part b where the event may occur has a certain _slack_ with respect to all other parts. It should be noted that this independency of parts that our model permits is fundamental for the concept of modularization.

Formally speaking, we say that a pair (c_1,c_2) of cases $c_1,c_2 \in C$ determines an _elementary event_ iff

1.9 $\quad |c_1\setminus c_2| = |c_2\setminus c_1| = 1.$

Let $\{p\} := c_1\setminus c_2$; $\{q\} := c_2\setminus c_1$. It is obvious that p and q belong to the same part. For the elementary event e which is determined by (c_1,c_2) we have $e = (p,q)$, i.e., e transforms the system state c_1 into c_2. Obviously $\overline{e} := (q,p)$ transforms c_2 into c_1. - The _case graph_ of a LCS has the cases as nodes. Two cases c_1,c_2 are joined by an undirected edge iff there is an elementary event which transforms c_1 into c_2. For example in fig. 1, we have an LCS representing the mutual exclusion of the critical sections s_1,s_2,s_3 of the processes P_1,P_2,P_3. As the critical sections of the P_i are the only phases which underlie the mutual exclusion, the parts P_i each have only two phases: s_i as the critical section phase and r_i as the phase representing the states outside the critical section. Iff two phases in different parts are coupled this is indicated by an edge. As the case graph shows there is no case which contains more than one critical section phase.

The elementary events (r_2,s_2) and (r_3,s_3) which may occur in the case $\{r_1,r_2,r_3\}$ exclude one another. A dependency like this is called _conflict_. If we remove the edge (s_2,s_3) (fig.2), we see, however, that both events may occur in arbitrary order, and we may also think that they take place coincidentally. We shall call this independency of events concurrency.

In formal terms: Let $c_0,c_1,c_2 \in C$; $c_0\backslash c_1 = \{p_1\}$; $c_1\backslash c_0 =: \{q_1\}$; $c_0\backslash c_2 =: \{p_2\}$; $c_2\backslash c_0 =: \{q_2\}$. The elementary events (p_1,q_2) and (p_2,q_2) are concurrent (with respect to c_0) iff $(q_1,q_2) \notin K$. It can be shown [4] that this property is equivalent to the independency of events described above. On the other hand the concurrency of events as just defined means a certain independency of the parts in which they occur - in the sense that these parts are loosely coupled. The organization of the mutual exclusion in fig.1 is decentralized. But we can give an elementary representation of the "modern" centralized form of the mutual exclusion (fig.3). We use one control part cp where the number of phases corresponds to the number of critical sections. The function of this part can mainly be interpreted as a monitor in the sense of DIJKSTRA [1] and HOARE [2]: If one of the processes P_i is in its critical section s_i there is exactly one phase of cp in any such case. On the other hand: If none of the P_i is in its phase s_i the "monitor" part can be in any of its phases as shown in the corresponding case graph (fig. 3).

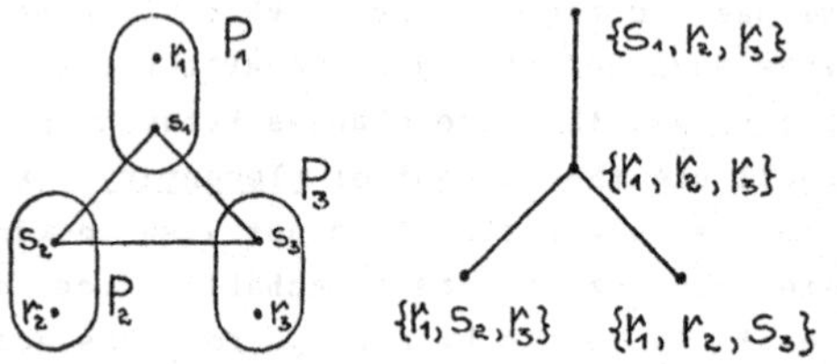

L C S case graph

Figure 1

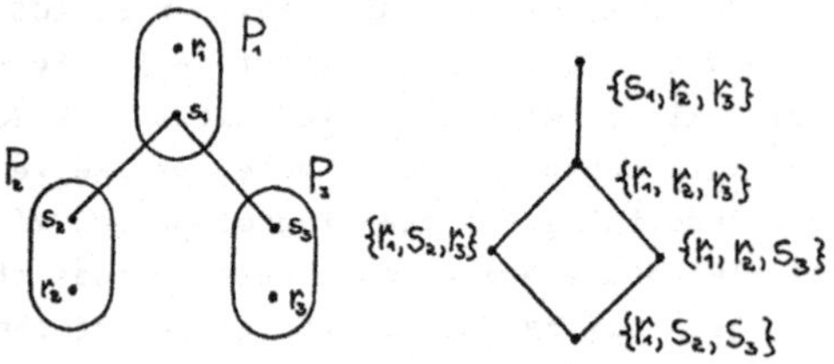

L C S case graph

Figure 2

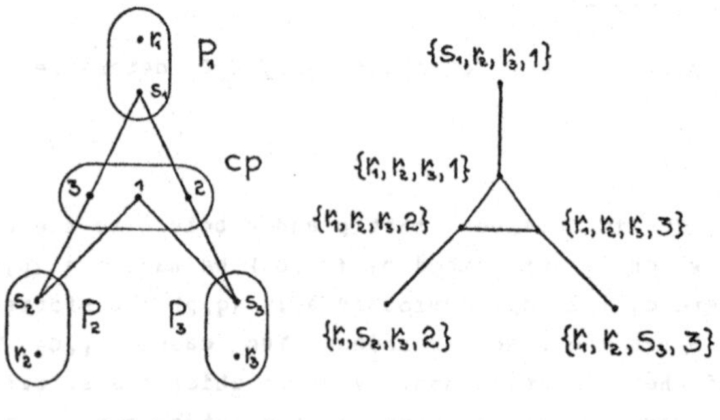

L C S case graph

Figure 3

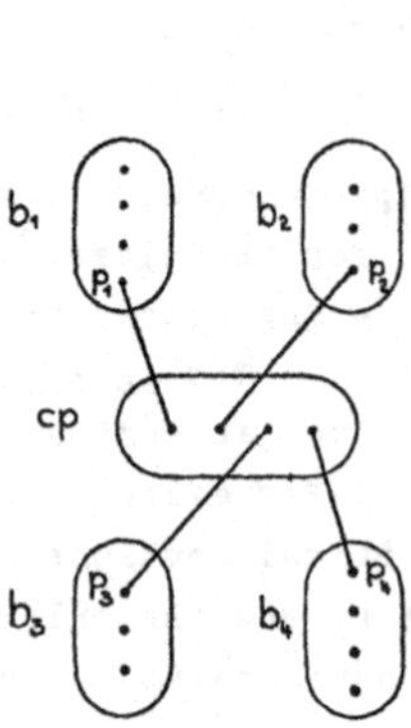

Figure 4

2. Elementary Restrictions

We now wish to introduce a modeling technique to describe the flow of influence from one class of parts to other ones. Though the coupling relation is symmetrical these influences normally will be asymmetrical.

Fig. 4 gives an idea of how to influence the behaviour of a system component "in the direction of" coupling edges (and not at the level of events): The cases of this LCS are characterized by the fact that at most three of the n = 4 phases p_i; $1 \le i \le n$ may belong to a common case; or equivalently:

2.1 $\forall_{c \in C} \; \exists_{1 \le i \le n} \; p_i \notin c.$

(It can be shown that this restriction on $b_1, \ldots, b_n$ cannot be represented without the aid of a "control" part for $n \ge 3$.) This symmetrical formula can be replaced by an asymmetrical one: We divide $b_1, \ldots b_n$ into two classes $S := \{b_i \mid 1 \le i \le n\}$ and $T := \{b_i \mid k+1 \le i \le n\}$. (Take k = 2 in fig.4.) Equivalently to 2.1 we can write:

2.2 $\forall_{c \in C} \; (\forall_{1 \le i \le k} \; p_i \in c \Rightarrow \exists_{k+1 \le j \le n} \; p_j \notin c).$

I.e. if all elements of S are in their "critical" phase then there is some element of T which cannot be in its "critical" phase. Another example:

2.3 $\forall_{c \in C} \; (\exists_{1 \le i \le k} \; p_i \notin c \Rightarrow \forall_{k+1 \le j \le n} \; p_j \in c).$

I.e., if not all elements of S are in their "critical" phase then in all elements of T the "critical" phase must hold. For k = 2, n = 4 there is an example in fig.5. The general form of these __elementary restrictions__ is the following: Let for $1 \le i \le n$ and $c \in C$ $A(i,c)$, $A'(i,c)$ be one of the formulas $p_i \in c$ or $p_i \notin c$; let #, #' be one of the quantifiers $\forall$ or $\exists$. Then we write:

2.4 $\forall_{c \in C} \; (\#_{1 \le i \le k} \; A(i,c) \Rightarrow \#'_{k+1 \le j \le n} \; A'(j,c)).$

It can be shown that for every such elementary restriction, there exists an LCS which realizes this restriction. Moreover such an LCS contains only one control part - in addition to the parts $b_1, b_2, \ldots, b_n$ -, and the coupling relations associated with this part can be constructed in a simple way. We regard these LCS as elementary "inhibition macros". - We can prove the following properties (see [3]): Let $c, c_1, c_2 \in C$.

a) If the premise of 2.4 does not hold for c all the elementary events which do not lead to a holding of the premise may occur (i.e. the regulation induced by 2.4 is "loose enough");

b) Let neither the premise nor the conclusion of 2.4 hold for c_1; let the premise hold for c_2. Then c_2 cannot be reached from c_1 __before__ fulfilling the conclusion of 2.4.

Furthermore: the restriction 2.4 holds for every LCS which contains the constructed LCS as a subsystem. This __modularity__ property admits that some parts b_i may be a component of different restrictions, and such restrictions cannot be cancelled by coupling other parts to the b_i.

As we have seen in 2.1 and 2.2 we have various equivalent formulas for a given formula of type 2.4, especially the logical contraposition. But there is only one LCS for all equivalent formulas of type 2.4. So the formulas can be regarded as interpretations of that LCS, and for the purpose of modeling one can take the most convenient one. As a consequence we get a pendant for b): Before falsifying the conclusion of a formula by elementary events it is necessary to falsify the premise.

Restrictions of the form 2.4 may be rather pathological, e.g. contradictions. But if nothing is prescribed about the validity of the conclusion in case that the premise does not hold, the LCS representation of the formula will admit all situations and operations described in a) and b).

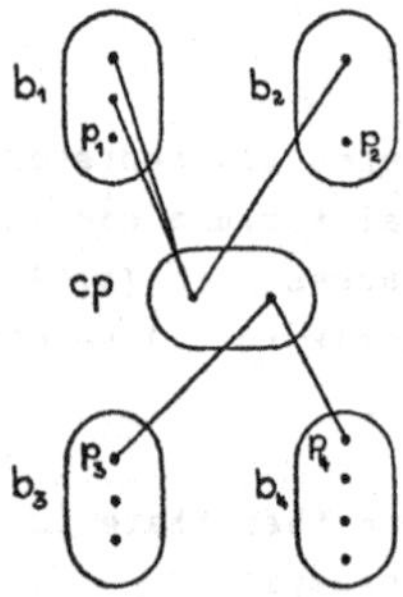

Figure 5

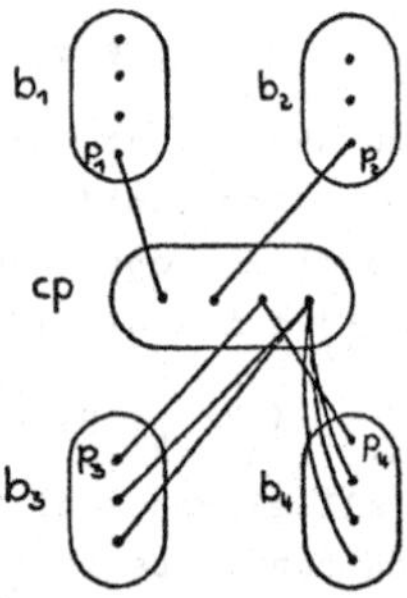

Figure 6

3. Conditional Elementary Restrictions

To represent more complex inhibition structures we need an extension of our construction technique. As a first step we build up a type of restrictions of the following general form:

Let $n \geq 3$ and $I_1, I_2, \ldots, I_n$ be pairwise disjoint index sets; for $i \in I_1 \cup \ldots \cup I_n$ we have a part b_i and a phase $p_i \in b_i$. Let $c \in C$ for the LCS to be constructed and $A_1(i,c), A_2(i,c), \ldots, A_n(i,c)$ be one of the formulas $p_i \in c$ or $p_i \notin c$; let $\#^1, \#^2, \ldots, \#^n$ be one of the quantifiers $\forall$ or $\exists$. We formulate:

3.1 $$\forall_{c \in C} \left(\#^1_{i \in I_1} A_1(i,c) \Longrightarrow \left(\#^2_{i \in I_2} A_2(i,c) \Longrightarrow \left(\ldots \Longrightarrow \#^{n-2}_{i \in I_{n-2}} A_{n-2}(i,c) \Longrightarrow \right.\right.\right.$$
$$\left.\left.\left. \Longrightarrow \left(\#^{n-1}_{i \in I_{n-1}} A_{n-1}(i,c) \Longrightarrow \#^n_{i \in I_n} A_n(i,c) \right) \ldots \right)\right)\right).$$

We see that the elementary restriction

$$\#^{n-1}_{i \in I_{n-1}} A_{n-1}(i,c) \Longrightarrow \#^n_{i \in I_n} A_n(i,c)$$

depends on the condition

$$\#^{n-2}_{i \in I_{n-2}} A_{n-2}(i,c),$$

and the validity of this conditional elementary restriction is similarly conditional. Example: Let $I_1 := \{1,2\}$; $I_2 := \{3,4\}$; $I_3 := \{5,6\}$; furthermore $b_3 = b_5$; $b_4 = b_6$; $p_3 = p_5$; $p_4 = p_6$. Let the restriction be

$$\forall_{c \in C} \left(\forall_{i \in I_1} p_i \in c \Longrightarrow \left(\exists_{i \in I_2} p_i \in c \Longrightarrow \forall_{i \in I_2} p_i \in c \right)\right) \qquad \text{or}$$

$$\forall_{c \in C} \left(\left(\forall_{i \in I_1} p_i \in c \wedge \exists_{i \in I_2} p_i \in c \right) \Longrightarrow \forall_{i \in I_2} p_i \in c \right).$$

The corresponding LCS is shown in fig.6. Here we have influences from b_1, b_2, b_3, b_3 on b_5, b_6, but this is a form of reaction because of $b_5 = b_3$; $b_6 = b_4$.

In general, we need only one control part to build an LCS which contains the b_i and which realizes 3.1. Furthermore these LCS have all properties just pointed out for elementary restrictions (see [3]).

4. Phase substitutions

In addition to the conditioning of elementary restrictions there is another simple rule to generate new control structures. First we give the general form of the new restrictions:

Let $I_1, I_2, \dots, I_k, I_{k+1}, \dots I_n$ be pairwise disjoint index sets. For every $i \in I_j$; $1 \le j \le n$ we have a part b_i and a phase $p_i \in b_i$. Let for $1 \le j \le n$ $z_j := \{p_i | i \in I_j\}$. For $c \in C$ let $A(i,c)$, $A'(i,c)$ be one of the formulas $z_i \subseteq c$, $z_i \not\subseteq c$, $z_i \cap c = \emptyset$, $z_i \cap c \neq \emptyset$; let $\#, \#'$ be one of the quantifiers $\forall$, $\exists$. Then our restriction form is

4.1 $$\forall_{c \in C} \left(\#_{1 \le i \le k} A(i,c) \Longrightarrow \#'_{k+1 \le j \le n} A'(j,c) \right).$$

So we have an elementary restriction form but the phases p_i of the formulas in 2.4 are substituted by the phase sets z_i. As an example we take $n = 4$; $k = 2$; $I_1 := \{1,2,3\}$; $I_2 := \{4,5\}$; $I_3 := \{6,7,8\}$; $I_4 := \{9,10\}$. Our formula is:

4.2 $$\forall_{c \in C} \left(\exists_{1 \le i \le 2} z_i \subseteq c \Longrightarrow \exists_{3 \le j \le 4} z_j \not\subseteq c \right).$$

The corresponding LCS (for special parts b_i) is found in fig.7. The framed subsystem is the LCS representation for the elementary restriction which corresponds to the form in 4.2:

4.3 $$\forall_{c \in C} \left(\exists_{1 \le i \le 2} q_i \in c \Longrightarrow \exists_{3 \le j \le 4} q_j \notin c \right).$$

So our construction can be built up in two elementary steps: (1) construction of the LCS corresponding to the elementary restriction; (2) substitution by coupling every part B_i with certain b_j. This procedure can be continued. It is interesting that in doing such constructions we are always at the same representational level. So we have a flexible construction method. Again the constructed LCS have all properties pointed out for elementary restrictions (see [3]).

5. Example

Let us regard the following problem: All processors of two classes $P =: \{P_1, P_2\}$ and $Q =: \{Q_1, Q_2, Q_3\}$ have phases r,s,t,u. Nothing is asserted about their behaviour; e.g. all processors may work cyclically. If there are processors of P and Q running in the cyclic mode r,s,t,u and if there is a case which contains the r-phases of these processes, then the Q-processors must not enter their s-phase before the P-processors have not entered their s-phase. If processors of P and Q are running in the reversed cyclic mode u,t,s,r and processors of both classes are in their s-phase, then the P-processors must not enter their r-phase before the Q-processors have not done so. Apart from this, P- and Q-processors must not disturbe one another when they are running cyclically.

A solution is shown in fig.8. The control part m enforces the required precedence. A Q-processor can only be disturbed if a P-processor remains in its r-phase. So we have to guarantee that in some situations no P-processor is in its r-phase. This is done by the control part synP and its coupling to the P-parts: If one of the P-processors is running in any cyclic mode and wants to enter the t-phase the other one must have left the r-phase. That means that in each turn of a processor in cyclic mode there is at least one case in which no P-processor is in its r-phase.

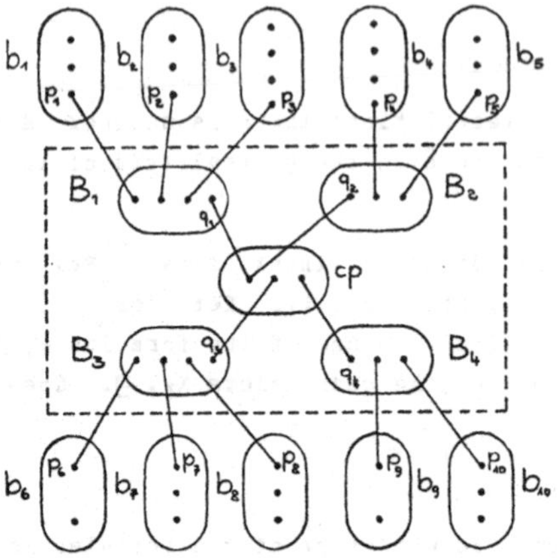

Figure 7

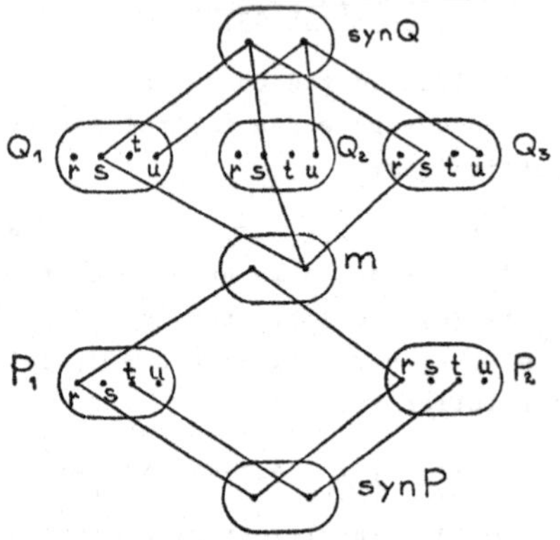

Figure 8

So a certain kind of synchronization is induced if both P-processors are working cyclically. On the other hand any of the P-processors may remain arbitrarily long in s or u while the other one is running. The mechanism given by synQ and the related coupling relation works similarly. The formal restrictions are the following:

Precedence (control part m): Let $b_1 := P_1$, $b_2 := P_2$, $b_3 := Q_1$, $b_4 := Q_2$, $b_5 := Q_3$; let p_1, p_2 the r-phases of b_1, b_2, resp.; let p_3, p_4, p_5 the s-phase of b_3, b_4, b_5, resp.. We have the restriction form:

$\forall_{c\in C} \; (\exists_{1\le i\le 2} \; p_i \in c \Longrightarrow \forall_{3\le j\le 5} \; p_j \notin c)$ (elementary restriction).

Synchronization of P-processors (control part synP): Let $b_1 = b_3 := P_1$, $b_2 = b_4 := P_2$; let p_1, p_2 the r-phases of b_1, b_2, resp.; let p_3, p_4 the t-phases of b_3, b_4, resp.. We have the restriction form:

$\forall_{c\in C} \; (\exists_{1\le i\le 2} \; p_i \in c \Longrightarrow \forall_{3\le j\le 4} \; p_j \notin c)$ (elementary restriction).

The synchronisation of the Q-processors is also elementary.- It was our aim to point out by this example that elementary restrictions are a powerful tool for handling coordination problems. It should be mentioned that by using conditional elementary restrictions and phase substitution methods, the range of coordination problems representable by our approach, can be further extended.

References

[1] Dijkstra,E.W.: Hierarchical Ordering of Sequential Processes; Acta Informatica 1(1971); p. 115-138

[2] Hoare,C.A.R.: Monitors: An Operating System Structuring Concept; CACM Vol. 17 No. 10(1974); p. 549-557

[3] Lautenbach,K. and Wedde,H.: Loosely Coupled Systems - a New Formal Concept to Generate Control Mechanisms for Concurrent Processes; GMD-ISF, Technical Report (1976)

[4] Wedde,H.: Lose Kopplung von Systemkomponenten (German); Berichte der GMD No. 96: Bonn 1975

ON DIAGNOSIS OF ALGORITHMICAL PROCESSES

J.W. Łąski

Instytut Informatyki, Politechnika Gdańska

Gdańsk, Majakowskiego 11/12, Poland

1. Introduction

The diagnosis of computer hardware emerged in the late fifties and since then has been established as a well-defined discipline within the framework of computer sciences. This purely engineering area has been developing almost independently from the other important discipline, namely, software testing and debugging. It is felt, however, that both - the hardware diagnosis and software testing have much more in common than it is generally perceived. It is the purpose of this note to put forward some fundamental mathematical ideas related to diagnosis of algorithmical processes as the abstract models of real computational ones.

2. The model of a computer system.

A computing module m_i, will be denoted by the triple $m_i = \langle X_i, Y_i, h_i \rangle$ where X_i, Y_i - the input and output data respectively, $val(X_i) \in D_i^x$, $val(Y_i) \in D_i^y$, $\left(val(U)\right.$ - the valuation of a variable $\left.U\right)$, and $h_i \subseteq D_i^x \times D_i^y$ - the transformation relation assigned to m_i, symbolically $[m_i] = H_i$. A computing system $\sum$ is the sixtuple $\sum = \langle M, S, D, C, R_d, R_c \rangle$ where $M = \{m_i\}$ is the set of modules, $S = \underset{i}{X}(X_i \times D_i^x) \times (Y_i \times D_i^y)$ - is the set of states, $D = \{d_{ij}\}$ - the set of data flow predicates, $C = \{c_{ij}\}$ - tne control flow predicates (both over S), $R_c \subseteq (M \times S) \times M$, $R_d \subseteq (M \times S) \times M$ - the control and data flow relations respectively. These relations provide for independent data exchange and control flow among modules, and are defined as follows: for any m_i, $m_j \in M$, $s \in S$

$$(m_i, s)\ R_c\ m_j \iff (\exists x,y)\ x\ Hiy \wedge s_y^i = y \wedge c_{ij}(s)$$

$$(m_i, s)\ R_d\ m_j \;=\; (\exists x,y)\ x\ Hiy \wedge s_y^i = y \wedge d_{ij}(s)\ ,$$

where s_y^i - the projection of s onto the output variable of m_i. In other word, $(m_i, s)\ R_c\ m_j$ iff s can be obtained as a result of m_i, satisfying simultaneously the control predicate $c_{ij}(s)$.

A similar interpretation holds for R_d.

These relations describe the potential data and control flows and therefore they refer to the static aspects of our model. To come nearer to its dynamic properties we define actions that fake place when to any triple (m_i, s, m_j) tests for R_d and R_c are applied: if they pass then 1/ $s_x^j := sel(s_y^i)$ where $sel(u)$ is a selection operator that chooses some subcomponents of u, 2/ modul m_j is activated.

This leads to the concept of a computation process defined as the set $G = \{g_i\}$ of all sequences of the type $g_i = m(o)\,s(o)\,m(1)\ \ldots,$ $m(i)\,s(i)\,m(i+1)\ldots$, where $m(i) \in M$, $s(i) \in S$ - are the modul activated and state obtained at a given abstract moment of time i, and $[m(i), (s)(i)]\ R_c\ m_j$, $[m(i), s(i)]\,R_d\ m_j$.

If for a pair $\langle m(k), s(k)\rangle$ there is no such m_l that $[m(k), s(k)]\ R_c m_l$ holds then the process stops giving the value $s(k)$ as its result.

The set $P \subseteq S \times S$ containing all the pairs u,v for which there exists a finite computation transforming u into v is referred to as the global resulting relation [1], [2].

The resulting relation P can be expressed in terms of the basic operators H_i; the actual form of the expression for P depends upon the data and control relations R_d and R_c, therefore $P = f[H_1, H_2, \ldots, H_n; R_d, R_c]$. In the particular case of the structured control flow R_c is restricted to some well-defined control structures like sequencing, selection and iteration and then the expression for P is a regular one.

3. Erroneous processes.

Consider a permanent fault e belonging to the class $E = \{e_i\}$ of admissible errors. It can either affect the system $\sum$ /the static case/ or the process G /the dynamic case/. In the first case it is a function $e : \sum \mapsto \sum_e$, where $\sum_e$ - the erroneous version of $\sum$, in the second case $e : G \mapsto G_e$. The static errors fall into the following three categories: 1/ functional errors, affecting the transformation relations H_i-s, i.e. being of the form $e : H_i \mapsto H_i^e$, 2/ data errors, affecting the system data base, $e : S \rightarrow S$, and 3/ control errors influencing the relation R_c, $e : R_c \mapsto R_c^e$ /note that an error in the data flow relation R_d can be formally interpreted as a data error/. The dynamic errors do not change the system initially since they occur in a random fashion during a computation; however, having ocurred they can mutilate the system data base and manifest themselves later as static ones.

If we restrict ourselves to the class of single errors /as opposed to the multiple ones/ then the above three types of errors can be defined more precisely.

4. The diagnosis of processes.

Let A be the set of diagnostic decisions; then

the diagnostic function $F : \{G_i\} \times A \rightarrow A$ is actually a testing operator that assigns a decision /the test outcome/ to a specified subset of computational sequences; such a subset $T \subseteq G_i$ is referred to as the diagnostic test. There are two principal aims to be achieved by the test, namly : 1/ detection, i.e. deciding whether we deal with G_o /the pattern process/ or with one of the G_i - s, and 2/ localization i.e. knowing that the process we deal with is erroneons one to determine its actual version G_i. Realization of these tasks depends strongly upon the types of errors involved. Therefore, to be more specific we restrict ourselves to the functional single-error case. Consider then an operator $H \in \{H_i\}$ and its erroneous version H_e . As far as the observeability criterion is concerned we deal with two kinds of tests, namely:

1 input-output ones /IO-tests/ when $T \subseteq H \cup H_e$ and

2 output tests /O-tests/, when $T \subseteq R_g \left(H \cup \bar{H}_e\right)$.

Introducing two predicates $p(x)$ and $q(x)$ referred to as the input and output diagnostic predicates respectively we define the IO-test for H with respect to H_e as follows

$$T_{io}\left[H,H_e\right] y = p(x) \wedge x \left[H \cup H_e\right] y \wedge q(y) \Rightarrow$$

$$\Rightarrow x\, Hy \wedge \neg x\, H_e\, y$$

or relationally $T_{io}\left[H,H_e\right] = Ip \left(H \cap \bar{H}_e\right) \quad Iq$, where $I_r \overset{df}{=} \{(x,x) \mid r(x)\}$.

For the O-test we have

$$x \in T_o[H,H_e] \Leftrightarrow q(x) \Rightarrow (\exists z) zH\, x \wedge z\bar{H}_e y \wedge p(x)$$

or relationally $T_o[H,H_e] = q \wedge p\,[H \wedge \bar{H}_e]$.

Definition. A test T_1 is said to be stronger than T_2, $T_1 \geqslant T_2$, iff implications satisfied for T_1 are simultaneously satisfied for T_2.

Proposition 1. For any predicates p and q, $T_{io}[H,H_e] \geqslant T_o[H,H_e]$.

Proof is straightforward if we note that $x\, T_{io}\, y$ implies $p(x) \wedge q(y)$, and therefore $y \in T_o$.

The correctnes tests introduced above allow for verifying the hypothesis that the process failed in a priori specified way. Any single element belonging to the tests is thus a basis for drawing diagnostic conclusions. However, they do not guarantee the total verification of the process against the all possible errors. In the case of the elementary /basic/ operators the total verification can be achieved by applying the exhaustive testing procedure, i.e. by checking all the elements of H.

Proposition 2. If H is a basic /nondecomposable/ operator then the correction tests T_c contains one element being the H itself, i.e. $T_c[H] = H$.

If R is a decomposable operator, then its correctnes can be verified by checking independently those elementary operators that constitute R and the corresponding data and control flow relations. However, because of restricted observeability of the process it is sometimes impossible to apply this approach directly. In such cases the global testing can offer a solution. Its main idea is as follows: given a proces G with its resulting relation $P = f[H_1, H_2, .., H_n]$ check the correction of H_i on the base of G. Assume then that due to a fault there are two versions of $H_i - H_{io}$ and H_{i1}.

Definition. By the global test for H_{io} with respect to H_{i1} we mean the relation

$$T_g[H_{io}, H_{i1}] = I_\varphi f[H_1, .., H_{io}, .., H_n] \cap \bar{f}[H_1, .., H_{i1}, .., H_n] \; I_\psi$$

where φ and ψ - the global input and output predicates respectively. By restricting H_{io} and H_{i1} through the predicates $p(x)$, $q(x)$, where $p(x) = Dom(H_{io}) \cap Dom(H_{i1})$, $q(x) = R_g(H_{io}) \cap \bar{R}_g(H_{i1})$ we obtain the proper global or physically realizable test

$$T_p[H_{io}, H_{i1}] = f[H_1, .., I_p H_{io} I_q, .., H_n] \cap \bar{f}[H_1, .., I_p H_{i1} I_q, .., H_n] .$$

Of some interest is also the idea of the induced global test T_i, defined as the global image of the local test $T_l[H_{io}, H_{i1}]$, i.e.

$$T_i[H_{io}, H_{i1}] = I_\lambda f[H_1, .., H_{i-1}, T_l[H_{io}, H_{i1}], H_{i+1}, .., H_n] \; I_\varepsilon ,$$

where λ and ε - some predicates. To find out the relationships between those tests it is necessary to introduce the concept of the decomposition of the resulting relation P with respect to an operator H_i. It is understood as a subset $P_i \subseteq P$ generated by all computations G_i going though H_i, represented as the composition of three relations $P_i = \alpha_h(H_i) \, \alpha_f(H_i) \, \alpha_t(H_i)$, where: 1/ $\alpha_h(H_i)$ is the relation generated by the process until H_i is activated the first time, 2/ $\alpha_f(H_i)$ corresponds to that part of the set of sequences G_i when H_i is active and, perhaps - is iterated several times, 3/ $\alpha_t \, H_i$ represents that portion of G_i which starts after the last activation of H_i. These three relations are referred to as the head, functional and tail relations respectively, all with respect to H_i.

Theorem 1. If $\alpha_t(H_i) = H_i$ i.e. is activated once then $T_p \subseteq T_g$ /$T_p \geq T_g$/.

Proof. Assume that $x\ T_p\ y$ holds. Then

$$x\, T_p y = (\exists\, u,v)\, x\, \alpha_h(H_i)\, u \wedge u\, I_p u \wedge u\, H_{io} v \wedge v\, I_q\, v$$
$$\wedge v\, \alpha_t(H_i)\, y \wedge (\forall u_1, u_2)\, [x\, \bar{\alpha}_h(H_i) u_1 \vee u_1\, Ip\, u_1$$
$$\vee u_1 \bar{H}_{i1} u_2 \vee u_2\, \bar{I}_q\, u_2 \vee u_2\ \ \bar{I}_q\, u_2 \vee u_2\, \bar{\alpha}_t(H_i)\, y]$$

If $I_p \neq \emptyset$ then $(\forall u_1, u_2)[x\, \bar{\alpha}_h(H_i) u_1 \vee u_1\, \bar{I}_p\, u_1 \vee u_2\, \bar{I}_q\, u_2]$ cannot hold and therefore, must be $(\forall u_1, u_2)\, u_1 \bar{H}_{i1} u_2$, which means that $x\ T_g y$.

Lemma. If $\lambda = \varepsilon = S$ and p,q are the maximal predicates then $T_g \subseteq T_i$.

Proof: straightforward.

Lemma and Theorem 1 lead to the

Theorem 2: For the maximal predicates p,q

$$T_p \subseteq T_g \subseteq T_i\ .$$

References

1. Mazurkiewicz A., Proving Properties of Processes, PAS Reports, 134/1973
2. Łąski J., Tests for Algorithmic Processes, in "System Diagnosis and Reliability", Scientific Papers of the Institute of Technical Cybernetics of Wrocław Technical University, 34, 9, 1976, pp.75-85.

ON SOME PROPERTIES OF CYCLIC AUTOMATA AND THEIR EXTENSIONS

Bolesław Mikołajczak
Institute of Control Engineering
Technical University of Poznań
60-965 Poznań, Poland

This paper deals with algebraic properties of cyclic automata under different transformations. Especially we investigate the relationship between endomorphisms semigroup of cyclic transitive automata and endomorphisms semigroup of fixed analogs of their extensions. We characterize also algebraic properties of g-transformation of cyclic automata.

First we quote or introduce some definitions and notations to be used later. We assume that terms finite automaton and strictly periodic automaton are known [3,4].

A finite automaton $A=(S,\Sigma,M)$ is said to be cyclic [7] iff

$$\exists_{s_0 \in S} \forall_{s \in S} \exists_{x \in I} \quad s=M(s_0,x),$$

where s_0 is called the generator of A, and I is an input free semigroup with the operation of concatenation as a composition. Let R^* be a relation between elements of I such that xR^*y iff for every $s \in S$ $M(s,x)=M(s,y)$. The set of all equivalence classes with respect to R^* will be denoted $\overline{I(A)}$ and called a characteristic semigroup of A.

Let $A=(S,\Sigma,M)$ and $B=(U,\Sigma,N)$ be automata. A pair (g,h) of mappings is called state-input homomorphism if g maps S into U and Σ into Σ and

$$\forall_{s \in S} \forall_{\sigma \in \Sigma} \quad g(M(s,\sigma))=N(g(s),h(\sigma))$$

If g and h are one-to-one and onto, then a pair (g,h) is called a state-input isomorphism. If A=B, then (g,h) is called state-input endomorphism and state-input automorphism, respectively. If h=id., then g is called homomorphism, isomorphism, endomorphism and automorphism, respectively.

Let $A^0=(S^0,\Sigma,M^0), A^1=(S^1,\Sigma,M^1),\dots,A^{q-1}=(S^{q-1},\Sigma,M^{q-1})$ be finite automata such that $|S^0|=|S^1|=\dots=|S^{q-1}|$ and let pairs of functions $(g_i,h_i), i=0,1,\dots,q-1$ be one-to-one and onto such that

$$g_0: S^0 \longrightarrow S^1,\ g_1: S^1 \longrightarrow S^2,\ \dots,\ g_{q-1}: S^{q-1} \longrightarrow S^0,\quad h_i: \Sigma \longrightarrow \Sigma$$

for $i=0,1,\dots,q-1$. A strictly periodic automaton $V=(S^+,\Sigma,M^+)$ is called a generalized periodic sum of $A^0,A^1,\dots,A^{q-1}$ associated with pairs of functions $(g_i,h_i), i=0,1,\dots,q-1$ if $S^+=(S^0,S^1,\dots,S^{q-1})$, $M^+=(M_0^+,M_1^+,\dots,M_{q-1}^+)$, where $M_i^+ : S^i \longrightarrow S^{i+1(\mathrm{mod}\ q)}$, $i=0,1,\dots,q-1$ and

$$\forall_{s\in S^i}\ \forall_{\sigma\in\Sigma}\quad M_i^+(s,\sigma)=g_i(M^i(s,h_i(\sigma))).$$

We denote $V=\mathrm{comp}_q(A^0,A^1,\dots,A^{q-1})$. If $h_0\equiv h_1\equiv\dots\equiv h_{q-1}\equiv h$, then V is called a restricted periodic sum of $A^0,A^1,\dots,A^{q-1}$. If $h\equiv$id., then V is called a periodic sum of $A^0,A^1,\dots,A^{q-1}$(see [3,4]). If (g_i,h_i), $i=0,1,\dots,q-1$ are state-input isomorphisms of A^0 onto $A^i=(S^i,\Sigma,M^i)$, $i=0,1,\dots,q-1$, then

$$\forall_{s\in S^i}\ \forall_{\sigma\in\Sigma}\quad M_i^+(s,\sigma)=g_{i+1(\mathrm{mod}\ q)}(g_i)^{-1}(M^i(s,h_i(\sigma)))$$

and V is called a generalized extension of A^0 associated with (g_i,h_i), $i=0,1,\dots,q-1$. If $h_0\equiv h_1\equiv\dots\equiv h_{q-1}\equiv h$, then V is called a restricted extension of A^0. If $h\equiv$id., then V is called an extension of A^0(see [8]). Of course, a generalized extension is a special case of a generalized periodic sum, namely $(g_i,h_i)=(g_{(i+1)\mathrm{mod}\ q}(g_i)^{-1},h_i)$.

A fixed analog V^* of a strictly periodic automaton $V=(S',\Sigma,M')$, where $S'=(S_0',S_1',\dots,S_{T-1}')$ and $M'=(M_0',M_1',\dots M_{T-1}')$, is a finite automaton (S^*,Σ,M^*), where

$$S^* = \bigcup_{t=0}^{T-1} S'_t \text{ , and } M^* : S^* \times \Sigma \longrightarrow S^*$$

is a transition function defined for all $s \in S'_t$, and $\sigma \in \Sigma$ and $t \in \{0,1,\ldots,T-1\}$ as $M^*(s,\sigma)=M'_t(s,\sigma)$.

An automaton $A=(S,\Sigma,M)$ is said to be transitive with respect to semigroup of endomorphisms $E(A)$ and state s of S iff for every s' of S there exists $\varphi \in E(A)$ such that $s'=\varphi(s)$.

Let us introduce a relation R on S of $A=(S,\Sigma,M)$, namely

$$s_1Rs_2 \quad \text{iff} \quad \exists_{x,y \in I} \quad M(s_1,x)=s_2 \text{ and } M(s_2,y)=s_1 \text{ .}$$

R is an equivalence relation, but not a congruence. Therefore an automaton $A_R=(S_R,\Sigma,M_R)$, defined as

$S_R=\{B_i : B_i \in \pi\}$, where $\pi=\{B_0,B_1,\ldots,B_{k-1}\}$ is a partition generated by R, and for every B_i of π and every $\sigma \in \Sigma$

$$M_R(B_i,\sigma)=\{B_j : M(s,\sigma) \in B_j \text{ and } s \in B_i\}$$

and $i,j \in \{0,1,\ldots,k-1\}$, is undeterministic.

Now we construct a family of partially defined automata associated with A and R, namely $A_i=(B_i,\Sigma,M_i)$, where $B_i \in \pi$, and

$$\forall_{s \in B_i} \ \forall_{\sigma \in \Sigma} \quad M_i(s,\sigma) = \begin{cases} M(s,\sigma) & \text{if } M(s,\sigma) \in B_i \\ \text{undefined} & \text{otherwise} \end{cases} \text{ .}$$

A_i are said to be components of A.

An automaton $A_g=(S,\Sigma,M_g)$ is said to be g-transformation of automaton $A=(S,\Sigma,M)$ iff for every s of S and every $\sigma \in \Sigma$ $M_g(s,\sigma)=M(g(s),\sigma)$, where $g \in G(A)$ ($G(A)$ is a group of automorphisms of A).

Now we can state the main results of our paper.

Theorem 1 . Let $A=(S,\Sigma,M)$ be a cyclic automaton. A fixed analog of extension (restricted extension) $V_A=(S',\Sigma,M')$ is cyclic iff all fixed analogs $V^*_{A_i}$ of extensions V_{A_i} of the components A_i of A are connected

Proof. LET $V^*_A=(S^*,\Sigma,M^*)$ be a fixed analog of $V_A=(S',\Sigma,M')$.

If V_A^* is cyclic, then V_A^* is connected and $V_{A_i}^*$ are strongly connected. On the other side if A is cyclic, then A_i are strongly connected from the definition of R. Therefore $V_{A_i}^*$ are also strongly connected and cyclic. From the definition of R follows that A_R is connected, and $(V_A^*)_R$ is also connected (there exists an isomorphism between A_R and and $(V_A^*)_R$, namely $\delta : S_R \longrightarrow S_R^*$ such that

$$\forall_{B_i \in S_R} \quad \delta(B_i)=\{B_i^j \; : \; j=0,1,\dots,q-1 \text{ and } B_i^j=\{g_j(s) \; : \; s\in B_i\}\} \;).$$

From connectedness of $(V_A^*)_R$ and strong connectedness of $V_{A_i}^*$ follows that V_A^* is cyclic. <u>Q.E.D.</u>

<u>Lemma 1</u>. Let $A=(S,\Sigma,M)$ be a finite automaton, let $V_A=(S',\Sigma,M')$ be a connected extension of A (connected restricted extension of A), let $V_A^*=(S^*,\Sigma,M^*)$ be a fixed analog of an extension, then characteristic semigroup $\overline{I(A)}$ of A is isomorphic with a homomorphic image of the characteristic semigroup $\overline{I(V_A^*)}$ of V_A^*.

<u>Proof.</u> If $\bar{x}\in\overline{I(V_A^*)}$, then $f_{\bar{x}}^{V_A^*}(s')=M^*(s',x)$; similarly if $\bar{y}\in\overline{I(A)}$, then $f_{\bar{y}}^{A}(s)=M(s,y)$ for every $s'\in S^*$ and every $s\in S$. Function $f_{\bar{y}}^{A}$ maps S into S and function $f_{\bar{x}}^{V_A^*}$ maps S_i' into $S'_{i+|x|(\mathrm{mod}\ q)}$ for every $s'\in S_i'$, $i=0,1,\dots,q-1$, where $S'=(S_0',S_1',\dots,S_{q-1}')$. Now we introduce a mapping $h : S^* \longrightarrow S^*$ defined as follows:

$$\forall_{s\in S_i'} \quad \forall_{\bar{y}\in\overline{I(A)}} \qquad h(s)=g_{i+|y|(\mathrm{mod}\ q)}f_{\bar{y}}^{A}((g_i)^{-1}(s))$$

We note that $h(s)=f_{\bar{y}}^{V_A^*}(s)$ because V_A^* is connected. We have proved that if $\bar{x}\in\overline{I(V_A^*)}$, then $\bar{x}\subseteq\bar{y}\in\overline{I(A)}$. On the other hand, we introduce a sequence of mappings $h_i : S\longrightarrow S$ for $i=0,1,\dots,q-1$ defined as follows:

$$\forall_{s\in S} \quad \forall_{\bar{x}\in\overline{I(V_A^*)}} \qquad h^i(s)=(g_{i+|x|(\mathrm{mod}\ q)})^{-1}f_{\bar{x}}^{V_A^*}g_i(s) \quad .$$

We note that $h_i(s)=f_{\bar{x}}^{A}(s)$ because V_A^* is connected. We define homomorphism φ of the semigroup $\overline{I(V_A^*)}$ onto the semigroup $\overline{I(A)}$ as follows:

$$\varphi(\bar{x})=\bar{y} \quad \text{iff} \quad \bar{x}\subseteq\bar{y}\ , \text{ where } \bar{x}\in\overline{I(V_A^*)} \text{ and } \bar{y}\in\overline{I(A)}\ .$$

The equivalent definition of the homomorphism φ is following:

$$\underset{\bar{x}\in \overline{I(V_A^*)}}{\forall} \varphi(\bar{x})=\bar{y} \quad \text{iff} \quad \underset{s\in S}{\forall} h_{\bar{y}}(s)=(g_{i+|x|(\text{mod } q)})^{-1} f_{\bar{x}}^{V_A^*} g_i(s)$$

where $h_{\bar{y}}(s)$ is equal $h(s)$ for $\bar{y}$, and $i=0,1,\ldots,q-1$. With the homomorphism φ a partition π on the semigroup $\overline{I(V_A^*)}$ is associated such that

$$\bar{x}_1 \equiv \bar{x}_2(\pi) \quad \text{iff} \quad \varphi(\bar{x}_1)=\varphi(\bar{x}_2) .$$

Obviously, π has a substitution property. Therefore, according to the basic theorem on homomorphisms [2], there exists an isomorphism ψ such that $\varphi = \rho\psi$, where ρ is a canonical homomorphism. A proof for connected restricted extension of A is similar, and therefore omitted.

Q.E.D.

Theorem 2. Let $A=(S,\Sigma,M)$ be cyclic transitive automaton with respect to semigroup of endomorphisms $E(A)$ and generator s_0, and let fixed analog $V_A^*=(S^*,\Sigma,M^*)$ of an extension $V_A=(S',\Sigma,M')$ (of a restricted extension) be cyclic, then there exists a homomorphism of the semigroup of endomorphisms $E(V_A^*)$ onto the semigroup of endomorphisms $E(A)$.

Proof. We have immediately that $E(A)$ is isomorphic to $\overline{I(A)}$ (see [6]); because of lemma 1, $\overline{I(A)}$ is a homomorphic image of $\overline{I(V_A^*)}$. Therefore $E(A)$ is a homomorphic image of $\overline{I(V_A^*)}$. Q.E.D.

Theorem 3. Let $A=(S,\Sigma,M)$ be a cyclic automaton with respect to generator s_0. g-transformation $A_g=(S,\Sigma,M_g)$ of A is cyclic iff $g\equiv g^2$.

Proof. Let A and A_g be cyclic automata; then from the definition we have

$$\underset{s_0\in S}{\exists}\ \underset{s\in S}{\forall}\ \underset{x\in I}{\exists} \quad s=M(s_0,x)$$

and

$$\underset{s_0'\in S}{\exists}\ \underset{s'\in S}{\forall}\ \underset{x\in I}{\exists} \quad s'=M_g(s_0',x)$$

where $s_0'=g(s_0)$ and $s'=g(s)$; then we can write as follows

$$\underline{g(s)}=s'=M_g(s_0',x)=M(g(s_0'),x)=M(g(g(s_0)),x)=g(M(g(s_0),x))=g^2(M(s_0,x))=$$
$$=\underline{g^2(s)} \text{ ,and therefore } g\equiv g^2.$$

On the other hand, let $g\equiv g^2$ and let A be a cyclic automaton, then

$s' = g(s) = g^2(s) = g^2(M(s_0,x)) = g(M(g(s_0),x)) = g(M(s_0',x)) = M_g(s_0',x)$ Q.E.D.

References

1 . Beyga,L., g-transformation of automata (unpublished work)

2 . Clifford,A.H., and Preston,G.B., The Algebraic Theory of Semigroups, Vol.I and II, Amer.Math.Soc., Providence, Rhode Island, 1961

3 . Grzymała-Busse,J.W., On the periodic representation and the reducibility of periodic automata, JACM 16,3(1969),432-441.

4 . Grzymała-Busse,J.W., On the endomorphisms of finite automata, MST, 4,4(1970),373-384.

5 . Inose,T., Masunaga,Y., Noguchi,S., Oizumi,J., A semigroup theoretic consideration about the structure of automata,II, Proc. 3rd Hawaii Int. Conf. on System Sciences,1970

6 . Inose,T., Masunaga,Y., Noguchi,S., Oizumi,J., Extension of the semigroup-theoretic consideration on its structure of automata specified by endomorphism grouping, Systems,Computers,Controls, 2,5 (1971),673-681.

7. Masunaga,Y., Noguchi,S., Oizumi,J., A characterization theorem for the class of automata with transitive endomorphisms semigroups, The Transacitons of the Institute of Electronics and Communication Engineers of Japan, Abstracts, 57,1(1974),22-23.

8 . Mikołajczak,B., On linear realization of finite automata extensions (to appear)

COMPILER GENERATION USING DENOTATIONAL SEMANTICS

P. D. Mosses

Oxford University Computing Laboratory
Programming Research Group

45 Banbury Road, Oxford, England OX2 6PE.

INTRODUCTION

This paper is a sequel to "The Semantics of Semantic Equations", which was presented at MFCS '74 [1]. There we argued that any notation for giving precise and unambiguous definitions of programming languages should have a formal definition itself; and we introduced MSL, a formally-defined version of the Scott-Strachey notation of semantic equations [2]. It was noted that, by virtue of its formal definition, MSL is amenable to computer-processing - a property not shared by the original Scott-Strachey notation.

Here we shall describe the use of MSL as the semantic language of a compiler-generating system (currently being developed at Oxford and Aarhus). The reader need not be familiar with the details of MSL, only with its essential properties:

(i) it is an applicative, expression-based, non-imperative language;

(ii) it is suitable for describing the denotational semantics of programming languages;

(iii) it can be used to describe (but not necessarily define) its own (meta-) semantics; and

(iv) it is possible (and practicable) to translate it into a primitive functional language such as Scott's LAMBDA [3].

The system is flexible and could use any semantic notation with the above properties.

First of all, we shall describe our basic approach to compiler generation, separating the concept of a *correct* compiler from that of a *useful* one. Then we shall show how the system is able to *meta-compile* semantic descriptions in MSL, and to *evaluate* (i.e. execute) programs on data to produce output. Finally the *practicality* of the system will be discussed.

BASIC APPROACH

A (standard) denotational semantics for a programming language specifies a function from programs to abstract values, giving to each phrase in the language a value depending on the values of its sub-phrases. These values, which are usually elements of higher-type function spaces, are denoted directly using λ-notation. The semantics is as abstract as possible, and avoids simulating particular implementation mechanisms (such as stacks or closures).

From our point of view here, the important thing is what a denotational semantics does *not* do: it does not postulate some abstract (or real) machine and specify a mapping from programs to sequences of instructions. How, then, can it be used in "compiler-generation", if it doesn't mention the code the compiler is to generate?

There are two possible approaches:

(i) Choose a "universal" object code with a well-defined semantics. Then to generate a compiler from a given denotational semantics for some programming language, find code sequences which simulate the abstract meanings of the phrases of the language, and construct a compiler which produces these code sequences.

(ii) Take a more abstract view of compiling:
instead of *Compiler* : *Progs* → *Code* (i.e. sequences of instructions)
consider *Compiler* : *Progs* → *Input-Output-fns*.
Thus, an abstract compiler does not transform an (abstract) program text into an (abstract) sequence of instructions; rather it transforms it into the abstract input-output-fn represented by those instructions. The concrete version of such an abstract compiler produces denotations (i.e. representations) of input-output-fns from denotations of programs - it is just an implementation of a denotational semantics.

We take the second approach, which leads to a particularly unified system producing compilers which are automatically correct.

GENERATION OF CORRECT COMPILERS

We start by considering the simplest system imaginable. Let *PL-Semantics-MSL* be the text of a semantic description in MSL of a programming language PL, denoting an abstract semantic function, mapping programs to input-output-fns; and let *Program-PL* be the text of a PL program.
Then the MSL-expression:

$$\textit{PL-Semantics-MSL}[\![\textit{Program-PL}]\!] \tag{1}$$

denotes the input-output-fn which is the meaning of *Program-PL*. Hence the operation of inserting the text *Program-PL* in (1) produces the denotation of input-output-fn from a program, and so it is an implementation of an abstract compiler for PL. Expression (1) could be called the "code" of *Program-PL*.

Clearly there is a negligible amount of work in producing such a "compiler", and in using it to "compile" a program - but the important thing is the validity and automatic correctness of this operation. Note that the correctness does not come from the simplicity of the operation, but from the direct use of our ultimate arbiter of correctness, the denotational semantic definition.

USEFUL COMPILERS

The "code" produced by our correct compiler is in general rather long - it is always at least as long as the "listing" (in MSL) of the compiler. One could consider a useful compiler to be one which produces code whose length is (directly) proportional to the length of the source program. For our compiler above to become useful, it must produce as code a reduced version of the MSL-expression (1); but to remain correct, it should not change the abstract value (input-output-fn) denoted by the code. It would be possible to implement such a value-preserving reduction for MSL expressions directly; however it is more convenient to make use of the simpler reduction rules of LAMBDA [3], by transforming *PL-Semantics-MSL* and *Program-PL* into LAMBDA-expressions *PL-Semantics-LAMBDA* and *Program-PL-LAMBDA* (the former denoting a semantic function, the latter denoting a sequence of characters). Provided that these transformations into LAMBDA are themselves correct (value-preserving) and that we have an effective reduction algorithm for LAMBDA, then the operation of LAMBDA-reducing

Program-LAMBDA =
PL-Semantics-LAMBDA (Program-PL-LAMBDA) (2)

can be considered as a correct and "useful" compiler.

META-COMPILATION

It is trivial to transform a program text *Program-PL*, which is a sequence of characters, into a LAMBDA-expression *Program-PL-LAMBDA* denoting it (e.g. a LAMBDA-tuple of integers). The transformation from *PL-Semantics-MSL* (a text) to *PL-Semantics-LAMBDA* (denoting the corresponding semantic function) is more difficult, as it effectively consists of the meta-compilation of MSL.

The ability to do this meta-compilation correctly comes from the fact that the canonical definition of the semantics of MSL is itself basically a LAMBDA-expression, *MSL-Semantics-LAMBDA* - it denotes a mapping from texts of semantic descriptions (in MSL) to the described semantic functions. Thus we can take

PL-Semantics-LAMBDA =
MSL-Semantics-LAMBDA (PL-Semantics-MSL-LAMBDA) (3)

where we have again used the trivial transformation from texts to LAMBDA. The LAMBDA-expression in (3) could be taken, as it stands, as the "code" of our compiler for PL; however, it is possible to use LAMBDA-reduction, as in (2), to make our meta-compiler "useful".

In [1] we gave a circular description of the semantics of MSL, i.e. a text *MSL-Semantics-MSL*. We can use meta-compilation to establish the consistency of this circular description with the definition *MSL-Semantics-LAMBDA*:

MSL-Semantics-LAMBDA (MSL-Semantics-MSL-LAMBDA) (4)

must denote the same (meta-semantic) function as *MSL-Semantics-LAMBDA*. This does hold, and indeed the reduction algorithm reduces (4) to an expression identical to *MSL-Semantics-LAMBDA*.

EVALUATION

Having obtained the code *Program-LAMBDA* by compiling *Program-PL*, we can then evaluate, or run, the code on a particular input. All that we need is *Input-LAMBDA*, which might be written directly in LAMBDA, or else compiled into LAMBDA from some data-description language. Then

$$\textit{Program-LAMBDA (Input-LAMBDA)} \qquad (5)$$

can be reduced to yield *Output-LAMBDA*.
Comparison with (2) and (3) shows that we are just using the same mechanism as before - application followed by reduction.

PRACTICALITIES

Pure LAMBDA, although powerful, is not sufficiently compact for use in the present system. An extension, LAMB (described briefly in [1]), is used instead. LAMB includes integers, tuples and associated operators as primitive, and it also has the least fixpoint operator as primitive (so that the code of programs with loops, etc. can be reduced to normal form).

For expository purposes the structure of the system has been simplified above by ignoring syntax analysis. Semantic functions in denotational semantics are essentially defined on parse-trees, rather than on program texts. A compiler is then the composition of a parser and a semantic function. Parsers are specified in a BNF-like notation, but although the eventual aim is to treat BNF just like any other language and use the system to compile it into LAMB-expressions (denoting parsing functions, from texts to trees), the present version of the system uses BCPL programs to generate and interpret parsing tables.

SUMMARY

We have described how it is possible to generate "correct compilers" from denotational semantic definitions. They are "correct" in that they conform exactly to the canonical formal definition of a language, its denotational semantics - whether they are meaningful, or are what the author of the semantics intended, is a different question (similarly every legal ALGOL program could be said to be "correct"). They are "compilers" in that they can be viewed either as implementations of "abstract compilers", or else (less abstractly) as generators of code for the LAMBDA-machine.

It is hoped that the compiler-generator system will find applications in the following areas:

(i) "Debugging" complex semantic descriptions;

(ii) Teaching fundamental concepts of programming languages, by means of denotational semantics; and

(iii) Designing programming languages, using denotational semantics for canonical definitions.

Note that efficiency is not essential in these areas!

The system is being actively developed, to make the syntax analysis part more portable. Also the notation MSL will need to improve before it is an acceptable "publication language" for denotational semantics. Because of this, the reader cannot be referred to an up-to-date User's Guide to the system at the time of writing. However, a detailed description of an early version may be found in [4], along with the original definitions of MSL and LAMB.

ACKNOWLEDGEMENTS

The work reported here was supported by a grant from the British Science Research Council.

REFERENCES

[1] MOSSES, P.D. *The Semantics of Semantic Equations.* Proc.Symp. on Math.Found.Comp.Sci., Jadwisin, 1974, Lect.Notes Comput.Sci. 28, pp.409-422, Springer-Verlag, 1975.

[2] SCOTT, D.S.; STRACHEY, C. *Toward a Mathematical Semantics for Computer Languages.* Proc.Symp. on Comput. and Automata, Poly.Inst.Brooklyn, 1971; Tech.Mono. PRG-6, Oxford Univ.Comput.Lab., 1971.

[3] SCOTT, D.S. *Data Types as Lattices.* Proc. Logic Conf., Kiel, 1974, Lect.Notes 499, pp.579-651, Springer-Verlag, 1976.

[4] MOSSES, P.D. *Mathematical Semantics and Compiler Generation.* D. Phil. Thesis, Univ. of Oxford, 1975.

ON DIVERGENCE PROBLEM FOR PROGRAM SCHEMAS

V.A.Nepomniaschy
Computing Center, Siberian Division, USSR Academy of Sciences,
Novosibirsk 630090, USSR

1. INTRODUCTION

Study of decision problems plays an important role in the theory of program schemas and similar to them discrete processors. A central one of these problems is the strong equivalence problem [1] - [4]. Let S_0 be a schema which loops for all interpretations. For any schema the divergence problem is the problem of its equivalence to S_0. For a new class of program schemas it is natural to study the equivalence problem starting with the divergence problem since the undecidability of the first one follows from the undecidability of the second.

We consider classes of program schemas [3] with variables x_1,x_2 (location symbols), 0-ary function symbol θ and unary function symbols $\omega, \omega_1, \omega_2$, unary and binary predicate symbol p. The classes of program schemas are determined by bases, i.e. by sets of allowed assignment statements of the form $x_i:=\theta$, $x_i:=x_j$, $x_i:=\omega(x_i)$, $x_i:=\omega_i(x_i)$ and test statements of the form $p(x_i)$, $p(x_1,x_2)$ $(i=1,2)$. The purpose of the present paper is to study effect of basis structure on decidability of the divergence problem in corresponding classes of schemas.

2. BASES WITH UNDECIDABLE DIVERGENCE PROBLEM

It was shown in [2]-[4] that the divergence problem is undecidable in the class of schemas over the basis $B_0 = \{x_1:=\omega(x_1),\ x_2:=\omega(x_2),\ x_1:=x_2,\ p(x_1),\ p(x_2)\}$. This result is strengthened in the following theorem.

THEOREM 1. The divergence problem is undecidable in the class of schemas over the basis $B_1 = \{x_1:=\omega(x_1),\ x_2:=\omega(x_2),\ x_1:=x_2,\ p(x_1)\}$.

Now, bases whose test depends on both x_1 and x_2 are considered. It is known that there exists such a basis with undecidable divergence problem. Actually, it was shown in [5], [6] that the divergence problem is undecidable in the class of schemas over the basis $B_2 = \{x_1:=\omega(x_1),\ x_2:=\omega(x_2),\ x_1:=\theta,\ x_2:=\theta,\ p(x_1,x_2)\}$. The following question naturally arises: how does replacement of $x_i:=\theta$ by $x_i:=x_j$ affect the above result. The following theorem and theorem 5 give the answer to this question.

THEOREM 2. The divergence problem is undecidable in the class of schemas over the basis $B_3 = \{x_1 := \omega(x_1),\ x_2 := \omega(x_2),\ x_1 := x_2,\ x_2 := \theta,\ p(x_1, x_2)\}$.

The following lemma is used to prove Theorems 1, 2.

LEMMA 1. Suppose, given a two-tape Minsky machine T, one can effectively construct a schema S_T from a class of schemas Σ which diverges if and only if machine T loops (starting with empty tapes). Then the divergence problem is undecidable in the class of schemas Σ.

3. DECIDABLE CASES FOR MONADIC SCHEMAS

Let R(S) be a set of all paths of schema S each of which leads from the input node to the output one and corresponds to some interpretation.

The decidability of the emptiness problem in the class of one-way nondeterministic stack automata (Theorem 8.2 [7]) implies the following lemma.

LEMMA 2. Suppose, given a schema S from a class of schemas Σ, one can effectively construct one-way nondeterministic stack automaton accepting the set R(S). Then the divergence problem is decidable in the class Σ.

The following Theorem is established by means of this lemma.

THEOREM 3. The divergence problem is decidable in the classes of schemas over the bases $B_4 = \{x_1 := \omega_1(x_1),\ x_2 := \omega_2(x_2),\ x_1 := x_2,\ p(x_1),\ p(x_2)\}$, $B_5 = \{x_1 := \omega_1(x_1),\ x_2 := \omega_2(x_2),\ x_1 := x_2,\ x_2 := x_1,\ p(x_1)\}$.

Comparison of bases B_4 and B_5 with B_1 shows that for decidability of the divergence problem in the class of schemas over B_4 and B_5 it is essential that different variables are changed by means of different function symbols.

4. STACK AUTOMATA WITH A SPECIAL COUNTER

To prove the decidability of the divergence problem in classes of schemas whose tests depend on both x_1 and x_2 we need strengthening of lemma 2. For this purpose a more general class of automata is introduced which is a class of one-way nondeterministic stack automata with a special counter. This counter is used only to execute a special operation over stack. Until this operation is complete, an automaton is in a state q from a special set Q_0, stack head scans the top symbol and there are no moves on the input tape. At first stack is made empty and the number n of those stack symbols which belong to the special set N_q is stored in the counter. Then n symbols from N_q are written in the stack ($N_q \cap N_{q'} = \emptyset$ for $q \neq q'$ and $q, q' \in Q_0$). The process of writing is nondeterministic and at each step the counter is decreased by 1. The operation is complete when number 0 appears on the counter.

Note that a stack automaton with a special counter accepts the language $L_0 = \{ w_1 * w_1 * w_2 * w_2 \ldots * w_m * w_m * \mid m = 1,2,3\ldots$; arbitrary words $w_1, w_2, \ldots, w_m$ in alphabet $\{0,1\}$ are of the same length$\}$. We suppose that the language L_0 is not accepted by any stack automaton (without a counter).

THEOREM 4. The emptiness problem is decidable in the class of one-way nondeterministic stack automata with a special counter.

COROLLARY. Suppose, given a schema S from a class of schemas Σ, one can effectively construct a stack automaton with a special counter accepting the set R(S). Then the divergence problem is decidable in the class Σ.

Theorem 4 follows from lemmas 3,4.

LEMMA 3. Given a stack automaton with a special counter accepting a language L, one can effectively construct a pushdown automaton with a special counter accepting a language L' such that L' is empty if and only if L is empty.

LEMMA 4. Given a pushdown automaton with a special counter, one can effectively construct a pushdown automaton (without a counter) such that both automata accept the same language.

So lemma 4 shows that the class of languages accepted by pushdown automata with a special counter coincides with the class of context-free languages.

5. DECIDABLE CASES FOR SCHEMAS WITH BINARY TESTS

The following theorem is established by means of the corollary from Theorem 4.

THEOREM 5. The divergence problem is decidable in the classes of schemas over the bases $B_6 = \{x_1 := \omega(x_1),\ x_2 := \omega(x_2),\ x_1 := x_2,\ x_2 := x_1,\ p(x_1, x_2)\}$, $B_7 = \{x_1 := \omega(x_1),\ x_2 := \omega(x_2),\ x_1 := x_2,\ x_1 := \theta,\ p(x_1, x_2)\}$.

Note that Theorem 5 implies Theorem 1 [8] about the decidability of the divergence problem in the class of schemas over the basis $B_8 = \{x_1 := \omega(x_1),\ x_2 := \omega(x_2),\ x_1 := \theta,\ p(x_1, x_2)\}$.

Comparison of basis B_6 with B_1 shows that for decidability of the divergence problem in the class of schemas over B_6 it is essential that the test should be dependent on all variables used in this basis.

REFERENCES

1. A.P.Ershov "Theory of Program Schemata", Proc. of IFIP Congress 71, North Holland, 1972.
2. A.A.Letichevsky "Functional Equivalence of Discrete Processors III" Cybernetics, No.1, 1972 (in Russian).
3. D.C.Luckham, D.M.R.Park, M.S.Paterson "On Formalised Computer Programs", Journal of Computer and System Sci., v.4, No.3, 1970.
4. M.S.Paterson "Decision Problems in Computational Models", Proc. of ACM Symposium on Proving Assertions about Programs, New Mexico, 1972.
5. G.N.Petrosyan "On a Basis of Operators and Predicates with Unsolvable Problem of Emptiness", Cybernetics, No.5, 1974 (in Russian).
6. A.B.Godlevsky "On One Case of Special Problem of Functional Equivalence over Memory", Cybernetics, No.3, 1974 (in Russian).
7. A.V.Aho, J.D.Ullman "The Theory of Languages", Mathematical Systems Theory, v.2, No.2, 1968.
8. A.B.Godlevsky "Some Special Cases of Automata Halting and Functional Equivalence Problems", Cybernetics, No.4, 1973 (in Russian).

ON THE PARSING OF LL-REGULAR GRAMMARS

Anton Nijholt
Department of Mathematics
Free University, Amsterdam, The Netherlands*

1. INTRODUCTION

Culik II and Cohen [1] introduced the class of LR-regular grammars, an extension of the LR(k) grammars. In [2] and [3] the same idea is applied to the class of LL(k) grammars and the LL-regular grammars were introduced. The idea is that the parsing is done with a two-scan parsing algorithm. The first scan of a sentence w to be parsed, called the pre-scan, is done by a Moore machine (reading w from right to left) and yields a string of symbols which is the input for a deterministic push-down transducer (dpdt). In the case of an LR-regular grammar G the result of the pre-scan is a sentence of an LR(0) grammar G' which can be constructed from G, and the parsing can be done with regard to this LR(0) grammar. In the case of an LL-regular grammar it is possible to construct a strict deterministic grammar [8] and after the pre-scan has been performed the parsing can be done with regard to this grammar. However a more efficient method can be given since it can be shown that the parsing can be done with a 1-predictive parsing algorithm or even with a simple LL(1) parsing method (see section 3 and [2]).
The classes of LR-regular and LL-regular grammars have some similar properties as the classes of LR(k) and LL(k) grammars. Moreover, sometimes the proofs of these properties need only slight adaptions. In this paper the proofs are omitted. In [2] proofs, and some properties and examples not given here, can be found. In the remainder of this section we give some notations and definitions. In section 2 we list some properties and the main part of this paper is in section 3 where we consider the parsing of LL-regular grammars.

A (reduced) context-free grammar (cfg) is denoted by $G = (N,T,P,S)$, $V = N \cup T$; we will denote elements of N by A,B,C,...; elements of T by a,b,c,...; elements of T^* by ...w,x,y,z; elements of V^* by $\alpha,\beta,\gamma,\delta,\ldots$; ε denotes the empty string. A regular partition of T^* is a partition of T^* of finite index and such that each block is a regular set. The states of a Moore machine (with input alphabet T) define a regular partition of T^* [4].

* The research reported in this paper has been carried out at the Department of Applied Mathematics of the Twente University of Technology, Enschede.

The following definition can be found in [6] and in a generalized form in [5].

DEFINITION 1. (Left-cover)

Let G and G' be cfgs, G = (N,T,P,S), G' = (N',T,P',S') and L(G) = L(G'). G' left-covers G if there is a homomorphism h from P' to P^* (extended to P'^*) such that

(1) if $S' \overset{\rho'}{\underset{\ell}{\Longrightarrow}} w$, then $S \overset{h(\rho')}{\underset{\ell}{\Longrightarrow}} w$, and

(2) for all ρ such that $S \overset{\rho}{\underset{\ell}{\Longrightarrow}} w$, there exists ρ' such that $S' \overset{\rho'}{\underset{\ell}{\Longrightarrow}} w$ and $h(\rho') = \rho$.

In this definition ρ and ρ' denote the concatenations of the productions used in the left-most derivations.

2. LL-REGULAR GRAMMARS, AN EXTENSION OF LL(k) GRAMMARS

DEFINITION 2. (LL-regular grammar)

Let G = (N,T,P,S) be a cfg, π a regular partition of T . G is said to be an LL(π) grammar if, for any two left-most derivations of the forms

(i) $S \overset{*}{\underset{\ell}{\Longrightarrow}} wA\alpha \underset{\ell}{\Longrightarrow} w\gamma\alpha \overset{*}{\Longrightarrow} wx$,

(ii) $S \overset{*}{\underset{\ell}{\Longrightarrow}} wA\alpha \underset{\ell}{\Longrightarrow} w\delta\alpha \overset{*}{\Longrightarrow} wy$,

where $x \equiv y \pmod{\pi}$, then we may conclude $\gamma = \delta$. A cfg G is said to be LL-regular or LLR if there exists such a partition π of T^*.

The class of grammars introduced in [3] is in fact a subclass of our class of LLR grammars. We prefer to call those grammars strong LLR grammars to obtain a framework analogous to the LL(k) and strong LL(k) grammars. If we replace in definition 2 each occurrence of w and α in (i) by w_1 and α_1 and in (ii) by w_2 and α_2 respectively, then we obtain the definition of a strong LL(π) grammar. It will be clear that every strong LLR grammar is LLR and easily can be verified that every LL(k) grammar is LLR.

Example 1. Cfg G with only productions S → aAaa|bAbaa|bAbab and A → bA|b is neither LL nor strong LLR. However G is LLR. A regular partition for G is given in section 3.

THEOREM 1.

a. Every LLR grammar is unambiguous

b. No LLR grammar is left-recursive

c. It is decidable whether a cfg is LL(π) for a given regular partition π.

Since every left-recursive grammar can be covered by a non-left-recursive grammar [7] in some cases it may be useful to see if elimination of left recursion yields an LL(π) grammar for some regular partition π. Theorem 1c. can be proved in a way such that it amounts to the construction of the parsing algorithm. This algorithm will be discussed in the following section.

The following two theorems have proofs which differ only in details of proofs for LL(k) and LR(k) grammars as given in [6].

THEOREM 2.

Every LL(π) grammar, where π is a left congruence, is an LR(π) grammar.

Since a left congruence can always be found by refining of the partition we may say that every LLR grammar is also an LRR grammar. This inclusion is proper.

Example 2. Cfg G with only production $S \rightarrow Cc$, $C \rightarrow Cb|b$ is LR(0) and hence LRR, but G is not LLR.

THEOREM 3.

Every LLR grammar G, such that $\varepsilon \notin L(G)$, has an equivalent LLR grammar G' in Greibach normal form (GNF). Moreover G' left-covers G.

Like the equivalent theorem for LL(k) grammars this theorem is useful in showing that a language may be non-deterministic. The LLR languages are properly contained in the LRR languages. For example, the language $L = \{c^n d^n,\ c^{n+l} d^n \mid n > 1,\ l \geq 1\}$ is a deterministic language, and therefore LRR, but it has no LLR grammar in GNF.

3. PARSING OF LL-REGUALR GRAMMARS

An LL-regular grammar can be parsed, after a regular pre-scan from right to left has been performed, by using a strict deterministic parsing method [2]. This section however is devoted to a generalization of the LL(k)-parsing method. This generalization is such that any LL(π) grammar can be parsed, after a regular pre-scan from right to left has been performed, with a 1-predictive parsing algorithm.

First we need the following definition, in which π is a regular partition of T^*, $\pi = \{B_0, B_1, \ldots, B_n\}$ and $\alpha \in V^*$.

DEFINITION 3.

$BLOCK(\alpha) = \{B_k \in \pi \mid L(\alpha) \cap B_k \neq \emptyset\}$. If $B_i, B_j \in \pi$, then $B_i \,\Box\, B_j = \{B_k \in \pi \mid B_k \cap (B_i.B_j) \neq \emptyset\}$, where $B_i.B_j$ denotes the usual concatenation of sets of strings.

Let $L_1, L_2 \subseteq \pi$, then $L_1 \,\Box\, L_2 = \{B_k \in \pi \mid B_k \in B_i \,\Box\, B_j,\ B_i \in L_1 \text{ and } B_j \in L_2\}$.

Notice that $L(\alpha)$ is a context-free language (cfl), B_k is a regular set and therefore $L(\alpha) \cap B_k$ is a cfl. Hence it is decidable whether $L(\alpha) \cap B_k$ is non-empty [4].

This definition, together with lemma 1 we will give below, enables us to introduce the generalized parsing method.

LEMMA 1.

a. $BLOCK(\alpha\beta) = BLOCK(\alpha) \,\Box\, BLOCK(\beta)$.

b. Let $G = (N,T,P,S)$ be a cfg and suppose $A \rightarrow \beta$ and $A \rightarrow \gamma$ are in P, $\beta \neq \gamma$. G is not

$LL(\pi)$ iff there is a derivation $S \overset{*}{\underset{\ell}{\Longrightarrow}} wA\alpha$ and
$(BLOCK(\beta) \boxdot BLOCK(\alpha)) \cap (BLOCK(\gamma) \boxdot BLOCK(\alpha)) \neq \emptyset$.

Analogous to the theory of LL(k) parsing we define functions $T_{A,L}$ on partition π (these functions are called the $LL(\pi)$-tables), where A is a nonterminal and L is a set of blocks. These functions satisfy the following conditions.

(1) $T_{A,L}(B_k)$ = error, if there is no production $A \to \alpha$ in P such that $BLOCK(\alpha) \boxdot L$ contains B_k.

(2) $T_{A,L}(B_k) = (A \to \alpha, [L_1,L_2,\ldots,L_m])$, if $A \to \alpha$ is the unique production in P such that $BLOCK(\alpha) \boxdot L$ contains B_k. If $\alpha = x_0C_1x_1C_2\ldots C_mx_m$, $m \geq 0$, $C_i \in N$ and $x_i \in T^*$, then $L_i = BLOCK(x_iC_{i+1}\ldots C_mx_m) \boxdot L$, $(0 \leq i \leq m)$.

(3) $T_{A,L}(B_k)$ = undefined if there are two or more productions $A \to \alpha_1$ and $A \to \alpha_2$, $\alpha_1 \neq \alpha_2$, such that $(BLOCK(\alpha_1) \boxdot L) \cap (BLOCK(\alpha_2) \boxdot L)$ contains B_k.

Now it will be clear that if cfg G is $LL(\pi)$ and there is a derivation $S \overset{*}{\underset{\ell}{\Longrightarrow}} wA\alpha \overset{*}{\Longrightarrow} wx$, then $T_{A,L}(B_k)$, where $x \in B_k$ and $L = BLOCK(\alpha)$, will uniquely determine which production is to be used to expand A.

Starting with $LL(\pi)$-table $T_0 = T_{S,\{B_0\}}$, where $B_0 = \{\varepsilon\}$, it is possible to determine the set T(G) of all relevant $LL(\pi)$-tables of G. In the example at the end of this section T(G) is given for the cfg of example 1.

With the $LL(\pi)$-tables as input the following algorithm constructs a 1-predictive parsing table.

In this algorithm we use the partition $\pi_0 = \{aT^* \mid a \in T\} \cup \{\varepsilon\}$ and we require that partition π for which the parsing table is constructed is a refinement of π_0. We let $\pi = \{B_0,B_1,\ldots,B_n\}$, where $B_0 = \{\varepsilon\}$. It is always possible to obtain such a partition π if G is LLR. The condition $\pi \subseteq \pi_0$ is introduced to prevent the parsing algorithm (see algoritm 2) from giving left parses for sentences which do not belong to L(G). To each block in π we assign a unique number $(0,1,2,\ldots,n)$, and we let π also denote the set of these numbers. These numbers will be the output alphabet of the Moore machine in the parsing algorithm.

To each production in P we also assign a unique number and we let P also denote the set of these numbers.

ALGORITHM 1. (construction of a 1-predictive parsing table)

Input: $LL(\pi)$ grammar $G = (N,T,P,S)$, $\pi \subseteq \pi_0$ and the set T(G).

Output: a parsing table Q for G,

$$Q: (T(G) \cup T \cup \{\$\}) \times \pi \to ((T(G) \cup T)^* \times P) \cup \{pop, accept, error\}$$

Method:

(1) if $A \to x_0C_1x_1C_2x_2\ldots C_mx_m$ is the i-th production in P and $T_{A,L}$ is in T(G), then for every B_j such that $T_{A,L}(B_j) = (A \to x_0C_1x_1C_2x_2\ldots C_mx_m, [L_1,L_2,\ldots,L_m])$ we have $Q(T_{A,L},j) = (x_0T_{C_1,L_1}x_1T_{C_2,L_2}x_2\ldots T_{C_m,L_m}x_m,i)$.

(2) $Q(a,j)$ = pop, if $w \in B_j$ implies that the first symbol of w is a.

(3) $Q(\$,0)$ = accept

(4) otherwise $Q(X,j)$ = error, for X in $T(G) \cup T \cup \{\$\}$ and block B_j.

Now we are prepared to give the parsing algorithm. We let w^R denote the string w in a reversed order, $B_j^R = \{w^R \mid w \in B_j\}$ and $\pi^R = \{B_j^R \mid B_j \in \pi\}$. For convenience we assume that G is $LL(\pi)$, where π is a left congruence. We assume the reader is familiar with the construction of a Moore machine M_π which defines by its states the right congruence π^R. M_π will perform the pre-scan from right to left.

ALGORITHM 2. (1-predictive parsing algorithm)

Input: $LL(\pi)$ grammar $G = (N,T,P,S)$, parsing table Q and Moore machine M_π. The string $w = a_0a_1\ldots a_ia_{i+1}\ldots a_m \in T^*$ has to be parsed.

Output: The left parse for w if $w \in L(G)$, otherwise 'error'.

Method:

(1) Apply M_π to w^R such that if $a_ia_{i+1}\ldots a_m$ is in block B_j, then the to B_j^R corresponding state of M_π gives output j. The result is a string $w_\pi = j_0j_1\ldots j_m \in \pi^*$.

(2) A configuration is a triple $(x, X\alpha, \psi)$, where

  i. x represents the unused portion of the original input string w_π.

  ii. $X\alpha$ represents the string on the pushdown list (with X on top), $X\alpha \in (T(G) \cup T)^*\$$.

  iii. ψ is the string on the output tape.

  The initial configuration is $(w_\pi, T_0\$, \varepsilon)$, where $T_0 = T_{S,\{B_0\}}$, the accept configuration is $(\varepsilon, \$, \rho)$ where ρ is the left parse of w with respect to G.

(3) A move $\vdash$ is defined on the configurations as follows:

  i. $(jx, T_k\alpha, \psi) \vdash (jx, \beta\alpha, \psi i)$, $T_k \in T(G)$ and $Q(T_k,j) = (\beta,i)$.

  ii. $(jx, a\alpha, \psi) \vdash (x, \alpha, \psi)$, $a \in T$ and $Q(a,j)$ = pop.

  If none of these moves can be done, hence $Q(X,j)$ = error, then the parsing ceases.

Example 3. Cfg G with only productions 1. $S \to aAaa$, 2. $S \to bAbaa$, 3. $S \to bAbab$, 4. $A \to bA$ and 5. $A \to b$. The table below gives a regular partition for G which satisfies the conditions of the two algorithms.

π							
B_0	$\{\varepsilon\}$	B_6	$bbbT^*b$	B_{12}	$babT^*b$	B_{18}	$\{bab\}$
B_1	$aaaT^*$	B_7	$bbaT^*a$	B_{13}	$\{b\}$	B_{19}	$\{ba\}$
B_2	$aabT^*$	B_8	$bbaT^*b$	B_{14}	$\{bb\}$	B_{20}	$\{a\}$
B_3	$abaT^*$	B_9	$baaT^*a$	B_{15}	$\{bbb\}$	B_{21}	$\{aa\}$
B_4	$abbT^*$	B_{10}	$baaT^*b$	B_{16}	$\{bba\}$	B_{22}	$\{ab\}$
B_5	$bbbT^*a$	B_{11}	$babT^*a$	B_{17}	$\{baa\}$		

In the LL(π)-tables we only display the non-error entries.

T_0	$= T_{S,\{B_0\}}$
B_3	$S \to aAaa$, $[\{B_{21}\}]$
B_4	$S \to aAaa$, $[\{B_{21}\}]$
B_5	$S \to bAbaa$, $[\{B_{17}\}]$
B_6	$S \to bAbab$, $[\{B_{18}\}]$

T_1	$= T_{A,\{B_{21}\}}$
B_5	$A \to bA$, $[\{B_{21}\}]$
B_7	$A \to bA$, $[\{B_{21}\}]$
B_{17}	$A \to b$, $[\emptyset]$

T_2	$= T_{A,\{B_{17}\}}$
B_5	$A \to bA$, $[\{B_{17}\}]$
B_7	$A \to b$, $[\emptyset]$

T_3	$= T_{A,\{B_{18}\}}$
B_6	$A \to bA$, $[\{B_{18}\}]$
B_8	$A \to b$, $[\emptyset]$

Parsing table Q. (only the entries of T_0, T_1, T_2 and T_3 are given)

Q	3	4	5	6	7	8	17
T_0	aT_1aa, 1	aT_1aa, 1	bT_2aa, 2	bT_3bab, 3	-	-	-
T_1	-	-	bT_1, 4	-	bT_1, 4	-	b, 5
T_2	-	-	bT_2, 4	-	b, 5	-	-
T_3	-	-	-	bT_3, 4	-	b, 5	-

Let us apply algorithm 2 on w = abbaa.

(1) applying M_π yields 4.7.17.21.20

(2) $(4.7.17.21.20,\ T_0\$,\ \varepsilon) \vdash (4.7.17.21.20,\ aT_1aa\$,\ 1) \vdash (7.17.21.20,\ T_1aa\$,\ 1)$
$\vdash (7.17.21.20,\ bT_1aa\$,\ 14) \vdash (17.21.20,\ T_1aa\$,\ 14) \vdash (17.21.20,\ baa\$,\ 145)$
$\overset{*}{\vdash} (\varepsilon,\ \$,\ 145)$, and hence 145 is the left parse for abbaa.

Note. It is possible to show that if G is in GNF then we can construct from parsing table Q a simple LL(1) grammar G_π with properties:

(i) $\{[M_\pi(w^R)]^R \mid w \in L(G)\} \subseteq L(G_\pi)$,

(ii) if $w \notin L(G)$ then $[M_\pi(w^R)]^R \notin L(G_\pi)$, and

(iii) there exist homomorphisms h and g such that if ρ is a left parse for $w_\pi \in L(G_\pi)$ then h(ρ) is a left parse for $w = g(w_\pi) \in L(G)$.

From these properties and from theorem 3 it follows that every LLR grammar can be parsed, after a regular pre-scan has been performed, with respect to a simple LL(1) grammar.

Acknowledgements:

I am grateful to prof. L. Verbeek who gave me the opportunity to do this work.

References.

1. Čulik II K. and Cohen R., LR-regular grammars - an extension of LR(k) grammars, J. Comput. System Sci.7, (1973), No. 1, 66-96.

2. Nijholt A., Regular extensions of some classes of grammars, T.W. mem. No. 100, september 1975, Twente University of Technology.

3. Jarzabek S. and Krawczyk T., LL-regular grammars, Information Processing Letters, Vol. 4, No. 2, november 1975, 31-37.

4. Hopcroft J.E. and Ullman J.D., "Formal languages and their relation to automata", Add. Wesley, Reading, M.A., 1969.

5. Nijholt A., On the covering of parsable grammars, T.W. mem. No. 96, september 1975, Twente University of Technology.

6. Aho A.V. and Ullman J.D., "The theory of parsing, translation and compiling", Vols. I and II, Prentice Hall, Englewood Cliffs, 1972 and 1973.

7. Nijholt A., On the covering of left-recursive grammars, T.W. mem. No. 127, april 1976, Twente University of Technology.

8. Harrison M.A. and Havel I.M., Strict deterministic grammars, J. Comput. System Sci. 7, (1973), No. 3, 237-277.

THE CHARACTERISTIC POLYNOMIAL OF A FINITE AUTOMATON

D. Perrin
Université Paris VII
Departement de Mathématiques
T. 45-55, 2, place Jussieu, 75221 PARIS CEDEX 05

ABSTRACT

We study certain decompositions of a finite automaton in relationship with the factorisations of a polynomial associated to it.

INTRODUCTION

Let $\mathcal{A} = \langle S, X\rangle$ be a strongly connected finite automaton with S a set of states and X as (input) alphabet. We recall that $\mathcal{A}$ is said to be *synchronizing* if there exists at least one word f which, starting from any state $s \in S$, leads to the same fixed state* ; in the other case, the automaton will be said to be *asynchronous*. Any asynchronous automaton may be covered by a cascade product of a group-automaton by a synchronizing one, as in the Krohn-Rhodes theory (see [6], for example) ; indeed, it is sufficient to remark that the transition semigroup of the automaton may be faithfully represented by its Schützenberger representation over its minimal ideal (see [2]). However, such a covering does not lead to a reasonable construction of asynchronous automata and one is led to consider wider classes of asynchronous automata than the group's one. Let us say that a strongly connected (s.c.) automaton is *nilgroup* if there exists an integer n such that all words of length n define an application of the same rank r ; the case $n = 0$ is that of the groups and that of $r = 1$ corresponds to the definite automata of [7]. These automata play an important role in the study of certain variable-length encodings ([12]) and we gave an explicit construction of them in [10], chapter III. The purpose of this paper is to study the reduction of asynchronous automata to nilgroup and synchronizing ones by means of techniques introduced in [13] and that we recall now.

Denote by μx the $S \times S$ matrix asociated with the mapping : $x \in X$: $(\mu x)_{s,t} = 1$ if $sx = t$ and 0 otherwise. Calling M the matrix $M = \sum_{x \in M} x \ \mu x$ (considered as a matrix with elements in the ring $Z[X]$ of polynomials in the (conmuting) variables $x \in X$), we call *characteristic polynomial* of the automaton $\mathcal{A}$ the polynomial $\Delta = \det(I - M)$.

We shall see, as a consequence of the Perron-Frobenius theorem [5], that $1-\alpha X = 1 - \sum_{x \in X} x$ divides Δ with a multiplicity equal to the number of s.c. subautomata of $\mathcal{A}$; now we shall derive of the proof of the main result of [13] the follo-

(*) the minimum length of such a word may be bounded by a polynomial of degree 3 in Card(S) - see [1].

wing theorem : *if the quotient* $\frac{\Delta}{1-\alpha X}$ *is irreducible in* $Z[X]$, *then the s.c. automaton* A *is either synchronizing or nilgroup.* This result is motivated by the fact that if an automaton A has an homomorphic image B , then the characteristic polynomial of B divides that of A , and thus if $\frac{\Delta}{1-\alpha X}$ is irreducible, the automaton A is certainly irreducible (except, as we shall see, for the case of definite automata). Unfortunatly, as we will show by an example, there exists irreducible automata that are neither synchronizing nor nilgroup.

We shall, in conclusion, make a few remarks about the point that motivated the use of the characteristic polynomial in [13], that is to say the relationship between it and the languages which are the stabilizers of the states of the automaton.

THE FACTOR $1 - \alpha X$

Recall that an automaton $A = < S, X >$ is said to be strongly connected (s.c.) if, for any states $s,t \in S$, there exists at least a word $f \in X^*$ such that $s.f = t$ (we note with a simple point the action of X^* on S). We will denote by α the natural homomorphism of the free monoid X^* into $Z[X]$, extended by linearity to finite subsets of X^* ; one then has :

Proposition 1. *The characteristic polynomial of* A *is divisible by* $1 - \alpha X$ *with multiplicity equal to the number of s.c. subautomata of* A .

Proof. Let π be a mapping of X into the interval $]0,1[$ of real numbers such that $\sum_{x \in X} \pi(x) = 1$, and P be the matrix :

$$P = \sum_{x \in X} \pi(x)\ \mu x.$$

We show that $1 - \alpha X$ divides Δ with the same multiplicity that $\lambda - 1$ divides $\det(\lambda I - P)$, the characteristic polynomial of P . Let in fact $d(\lambda) = \det(\lambda I - P)$ and l be the multiplicity of $1 - \alpha X$ in $\Delta = (1 - \alpha X)^l\ \Gamma$; then the value of Δ when subsituing $\pi(x)\lambda$ to $x \in X$ is a polynomial $\delta(\lambda)$ such that :

(1) $d(\lambda) = \delta(\frac{1}{\lambda})\lambda^{\mathrm{card}(S)}$ (2) $\delta(\lambda) = (1 - \lambda)^l\ \gamma(\lambda),\ \gamma(1) \neq 1$ which shows that l is the multiplicity of $\lambda - 1$ in $d(\lambda)$.

Now it is well known that the subspace formed by the eigenvectors corresponding to the eigenvalue 1 of a finite Markov chain is of dimension equal to the number of closed subsets of the set of states of the chain (see [4], p. 356) ; and the multiplicity of the eigenvalue 1, that is to say l , is equal to this dimension because this subspace has got a stable complement, namely the subspace of $Z[S]$ spanned by the non recurrent states (i.e. the ones that do not belongto a s.c. subautomaton of A) and diferences $s - t$, where s and t belong to the same s.c. subautomaton.

Let us recall that an automaton $A = < S, X >$ is called *definite* if there exists an integer n such that each word f of length n defines an application of rank 1 : $\forall f \in X^n$, $\forall s,t \in S$, $sf = tf$ (see [7], [9]). The following property will be used below:

Proposition 2. *The characteristic polynomial of* A *is equal to* $1-\alpha X$ *iff* A *is definite.*

Proof. If A is a definite automaton, there exists an integer n such that $\sum_{f\in X^n} f\,\mu f$ is a matrix with all its lines equal between then. This implies that M^n which is equal to $\sum_{f\in X^n} \alpha f\,\mu f$, is a matrix of rank one ; thus all but one of its eigenvalues are 0 and one has $\det(I - M) = 1 - \alpha X$.

Conversely, if $\Delta = 1 - \alpha X$, then M has a power M^n which is of rank one and therefore A is definite.

Remark. One calls *generalized definite* an automaton A such that there exists an integer n satisfying : for any $u,v \in X^n$ and $f \in X^*$, uv and ufv define the same application of S in itself (see [9] for example). Then one may generalize the above result to : A *is generalized definite iff* $\Delta = (1 - \alpha X)^r$.

MAIN RESULT

Let now A be a strongly connected automaton, Δ its characteristic polynomial, and put $\Delta = \Gamma(1 - \alpha X)$.

Theorem : If Γ *is irreducible in* $Z[X]$ *either* A *is synchronizing or it is nil-group.*

Proof. Let J be the set of subsets of S which are the minimal images of A, that is to say the sets Sf, for $f \in X^*$, which are of minimal cardinality. Then the action of X on J defines a new automaton noted A_1; if one calls V_1 the subspace of $V = Z[S]$ spanned by the $v_I = \sum_{s\in I} s$, for $I \in J$, then V_1 is stable by μ and the restriction of μ to V_1 is equal to the representation μ_1 associated with A_1 ; let μ_2 be the representation induced by μ on the quotient $V_2 = V/V_1$ and $\Delta_2 = \det(I - \sum_{x\in X} x\,\mu_2\,x)$; one has $\Delta = \Delta_1 \Delta_2$, where Δ_1 is the characteristic polynomial of A_1. Now if Γ is irreducible, then either $\Delta_1 = 1-\alpha X$, or $\Delta_2 = 1$; we saw that $\Delta_2 = 1-\alpha X$ iff A_1 is a definite automaton ; but this means that, for an integer $n \in N$, one has for all $f \in X^n$, and $I,J \in J$, $If = Jf$; as A is s.c., S is the union of the minimal images and thus Sf itself is a minimal image ; whence A is nilgroup if $\Delta_1 = 1-\alpha X$.

Now if $\Delta_2 = 1$, then $M_2 = \sum_{x\in X} x\,\mu_2\,x$ is nilpotent and thus there exists an $n \in N$ such that, for all $f \in X^n$, $Vf \subset V_1$. This implies, since A is s.c., that $V = V_1$; but the dimension of V_1 is at most $\mathrm{Card}(S) - r + 1$, where r is the cardinality of the minimal images : let in fact I_o be a minimal image and V_o the subspace spanned by the elements of I_o ; the subspace $V_o \cap V_1$ is of dimension 1 because if $v \in V_o \cap V_1$ and e is a word of image I_o, then $v\mu e = \alpha v_{I_o}$, and this implies $v = \alpha \sum_{s\in I} s$, as e defines a permutation on I_o. We thus derive of $V = V_1$ that $r = 1$ or, equivalently that A is synchronizing.

Example 1. Let A be the following automaton, given by the transitions of the letters x and y ; its characteristic polynomial may be computed as :

S	1	2	3	4	5
x	2	3	1	1	3
y	4	5	1	5	1

$\Delta = (1-\alpha X)\ (1+x+x^2+xy+x^2y+y+y^2+y^2x)$; the second factor is irreducible over $Z[X]$ and A is in fact nilgroup

Example 2. The following example shows that there exists automata that are neither nilgroup nor synchronizing, without possessing any non trivial homomorphic image* ;

S	1	2	3	4	5	6	7	8	9
x	2	3	1	1	3	8	9	3	1
z	4	6	7	5	1	4	1	5	1

in fact A is not synchronizing because the minimal images are of rang 3 : they are {1,2,3}, {1,4,5}, {4,6,7}, {1,8,9}; on the other hand, A is not nilgroup as $(xy)^k$ is of rank 5 for any k .
The characteristic polynomial of A is correspondingly found to be divisible by 1 + xy (on this example, see [10], chapter V).

CONCLUDING REMARKS

We point out here some problems about the relationship between Δ and the languages that are the stabilizers of the states of A .

1. Let us denote by A_s the prefix code generating the stabilizer of the state $s \in S : A_s^* = \{ a \in A^* | \, sa = s\}$. It is shown in [13] that, if A_s is finite, then $1 - \alpha A_s = \Delta^{(*)}$; more generally, let us put $1 - \alpha A_s = \frac{P}{Q}$ where $P,Q \in Z[X]$ are two polynomials without common factor, and α is extended to regular languages (see [3]). Now one has $1 - \alpha A_s = N_{s,s}$, where N is the inverse of I - M, and thus P must divide Δ ; one does not have $P = \Delta$, even if A is reduced with respect to s, as shown in the following example :

S	1	2	3	4	5
x	2	1	1	1	2
y	4	3	1	5	4

one has : $1 - A_1 = \frac{1 + x}{1 - y}(1 - \alpha X)$, while :

$$\Delta = (1 + y)(1 + x)(1 - \alpha X)$$

We conjecture that, if A is a group automaton, one has $P = \Delta$.

2. Let A be a group automaton ; if the asociated permutation group is not 2-transi-

(*) it is to be noted that no such example can be found if the cardinality of the minimal images is 2 ; indeed, it is shown in [11] that if the permutation group defined by the automata on a minimal image is regular, then the automaton possesses a non-trivial homomorphic image which is either a group automaton or synchronizing.

tive, then the representation μ can be reduced (cf. [14] p. 86) and Γ will split into two factors. It is not true that, conversely, if the group is 2-transitive, then Γ is irreducible as one sees in the following example : Let $\mathcal{A}$ be the automaton defined by the two permutations : $x = (1245)$, $y = (123465)$; the stabilizer of 1 is generated by a prefix code A which is of the form $A = B\tilde{B}$, where B is the prefix code consisting of the left factors b of A which satisfy $1b = 4$ and $\tilde{B}$ is the mirror image of B. Thus $1 - \alpha A = (1 - \alpha B)^2$ and consequently Γ factors although the group generated by x and y is the symetric group S_6. We conjecture that if the number of states, that is to say the degree of the group, is prime then this cannot occur.

REFERENCES

[1] ČERNÝ J. - On directable automata, *Kybernetica, 7* (1971) 289-298

[2] CLIFFORD A.H. and G.B. PRESTON - *The Algebraic Theory of Semigroups*, Vol. 1, Amer. Math. Soc. (1961)

[3] EILENBERG S. - *Automata, Languages and Machines*, Vol. A, Academic Press (1974)

[4] FELLER W. - *An Introduction to Probability Theory and its Applications*, Vol. 1, Wiley Publ. in Statistics (1957)

[5] GANTMACHER F-R. - *Théorie des Matrices* (translated from Russian) Paris, Dunod (1966)

[6] KROHN K.K., J.L. RHODES and R. TILSON - The prime decomposition theorem of the algebraic theory of machines, in *Algebraic Theory of Machines, Languages and Semigroups* (M.A. Arbib ed.) Academic Press (1968) 81-125

[7] PERLES M., RABIN M.O. and E. SHAMIR - The theory of definite automata, *IEEE Trans. on E.C., 12* (1963) 233-243

[8] PERRIN D. - Codes Conjugués, *Information and Control, 20*, 3 (1972) 222-231

[9] PERRIN D. - Sur certains semigroupes syntaxiques, in *Logique et Automates*, Seminaires IRIA (1971) 169-177

[10] PERRIN D. - *Codes Bipréfixes et Groupes de Permutations*, Thèse, Paris (1975)

[11] PERROT J-F. - Une Théorie Algébrique des Automates finis monogènes, *Symposia Mathematica, XV* (1975) 201-244

[12] SCHUTZENBERGER M.P. - On a special class of recurrent events, *Annals of Math. Stat., 32* (1961) 1201-1213

[13] SCHUTZENBERGER M.P. - Sur certains sous-monoïdes libres, *Bull. Soc. Math. de France, 93* (1965) 209-223

[14] WIELANDT H. - *Finite Permutation Groups*, Academic Press (1964)

(*) Thus, if A_s and A_t are both finite, one has $A_s = A_t$; in fact, we showed in [8] that one has in this case $A_s = UV$, $A_t = VU$, for two prefix codes U and V.

ERROR DETECTION USING REGULAR LANGUAGES

P. Prusinkiewicz
Institute of Computer Science, Warsaw Technical University
Nowowiejska 15/19, 00-665 Warsaw, Poland

ABSTRACT.

The paper introduces formal definitions of sets of errors detectable and undetectable by a language. A method is given for determining these sets, when the language and a set of all possible errors are known. The method uses finite automata to define languages and sets of errors.

KEY WORDS: error detection, finite automata, transductions.

1. A FORMULATION OF THE PROBLEM.

Let V be an alphabet, V^* - set of all words over V. We call a pair $(L,\hat{L})\in(V^*)^2$ a transmission over V; L can be interpreted as a word sent to, and $\hat{L}$ - received from an information channel. The identity relation $[V^*]$ in V^* is called the set of correct transmissions. A relation $P\subset(V^*)^2-[V^*]$ is called a set of all possible errors [7]. Thus, $C \underset{\Delta}{=} P\cup[V^*]$ is the set of all the transmissions in consideration.

Let $\mathcal{L}\subset V^*$ be a language over V. We denote $\bar{\mathcal{L}} \underset{\Delta}{=} V^*-\mathcal{L}$. Then

$$D \underset{\Delta}{=} P\cap\mathcal{L}\times\bar{\mathcal{L}} = [\mathcal{L}]\circ P\circ[\bar{\mathcal{L}}] \quad /1/$$

/where the symbol $\circ$ is the operator of composition of relations/ is called the set of errors detectable by the language $\mathcal{L}$;

$$U \underset{\Delta}{=} P\cap\mathcal{L}\times\mathcal{L} = [\mathcal{L}]\circ P\circ[\mathcal{L}] \quad /2/$$

is called the set of undetectable errors.

Determining D and U for a given $\mathcal{L}$ and P is a fundamental problem in coding theory [3], although so far it has not been formulated in the form of equations /1,2/. This problem /closely related to that of transformations of formal languages/ has been solved for many different, but usually small classes of languages or sets of errors /cf. [3 - 6]/. This paper presents a more general approach to the problem.

2. A SOLUTION OF THE PROBLEM.

To define $\mathcal{L}$ and P we will use 1- and 2-input automata respectively. An n-input finite automaton is understood as a system

$$A \underset{\Delta}{=} \langle V^n,S,F,s_0,I\rangle \quad /3/$$

where: V - the /input/ alphabet, S - the set of states, $F\subset S$ - the set of final states, $s_0\in S$ - the initial state, $I\subset V^n\times S^2$ - the set of instructions. We assume that the sets V, S, F and I are finite.

We use the symbol $\tilde{I}$ to denote the <u>generalized set of instructions</u> defined as follows:

1. $(v_1,\dots,v_n,s_i,s_k)\in I \Longleftrightarrow (v_1,\dots,v_n,s_i,s_k)\in\tilde{I}$ /4/

2. $(\exists s_j\in S)[(L_1,\dots,L_n,s_i,s_j)\in\tilde{I} \wedge (v_1,\dots,v_n,s_j,s_k)\in I] \Longleftrightarrow$ /5/
$\Longleftrightarrow (L_1v_1,\dots,L_nv_n,s_i,s_k)\in\tilde{I}$

where the juxtaposition /Lv/ signifies concatenation.

We use the symbol def(A) to denote the <u>set</u> /or <u>relation</u>/ <u>defined by the automaton A</u>:

$$\mathrm{def}(A) \underset{\Delta}{=} \{(L_1,\dots,L_n)\in(V^*)^n \mid (\exists s_k\in F)(L_1,\dots,L_n,s_o,s_k)\in\tilde{I}\} \qquad /6/$$

Let $A = \langle V,S,F,s_o,I\rangle$ be a 1-input finite automaton. The <u>extension of A</u> is defined as the 2-input finite automaton

$$\lceil A\rceil \underset{\Delta}{=} \langle V^2,S,F,s_o,I_r\rangle \qquad /7/$$

where $(v_1,v_2,s_i,s_k)\in I_r \Longleftrightarrow [v_1=v_2 \wedge (v_1,s_i,s_k)\in I]$ /8/

Let $A = \langle V^n,S_a,F_a,s_{oa},I_a\rangle$ and $B = \langle V^m,S_b,F_b,s_{ob},I_b\rangle$ be finite automata. The <u>composition of A and B</u> is defined as the finite automaton

$$A\bullet B \underset{\Delta}{=} \langle V^{n+m-2},S_a\times S_b,F_a\times F_b,(s_{oa},s_{ob}),I_{ab}\rangle \qquad /9/$$

where $(v_1,\dots,v_{n-1},v_{n+1},\dots,v_{n+m-1},(s_{ai},s_{bi}),(s_{ak},s_{bk}))\in I_{ab} \Longleftrightarrow$ /10/
$\Longleftrightarrow (\exists v_n\in V)[(v_1,\dots,v_n,s_{ai},s_{ak})\in I_a \wedge (v_n,\dots,v_{n+m-1},s_{bi},s_{bk})\in I_b]$

The following theorems can be proved /see subdivision 5/:

<u>Theorem 1</u>. $\mathcal{L} = \mathrm{def}(A) \Longleftrightarrow [\mathcal{L}] = \mathrm{def}(\lceil A\rceil)$

<u>Theorem 2</u>. $\mathrm{def}(A)\circ\mathrm{def}(B) = \mathrm{def}(A\bullet B)$

Let $\mathcal{L} = \mathrm{def}(A)$, $\overline{\mathcal{L}} = \mathrm{def}(\overline{A})$, $P = \mathrm{def}(B)$. From eqs. /1,2/, considering theorems 1 and 2, it follows:

$$D = \mathrm{def}(\lceil A\rceil\bullet B\bullet\lceil\overline{A}\rceil) \qquad U = \mathrm{def}(\lceil A\rceil\bullet B\bullet\lceil A\rceil) \qquad /11/$$

Eqs. /11/ make it possible to determine the automata defining D and U when A and B are known. The automaton $\overline{A}$ defining $\overline{\mathcal{L}}$ can be found from A using the procedure described in [1]. In particular, for a deterministic automaton $A = \langle V,S,F,s_o,I\rangle$, $\overline{A} = \langle V,S,S-F,s_o,I\rangle$.

From the definitions introduced above it follows that the class of relations /and therefore - the class of sets of errors/ in consideration is restricted to length-preserving transductions [2]. We will remove this restriction without changing the definitions of operations on automata /composition and extension/.

Let e be a symbol from outside V, called the <u>empty letter</u>. In the "augmented" alphabet $\mathbf{V} \underset{\Delta}{=} V\cup\{e\}$ we define a <u>relation</u> of e-equivalence.

denoted by $\underset{e}{=}$, as follows:

$$\mathbf{l}_1 \underset{e}{=} \mathbf{l}_2 \Longleftrightarrow (\exists z, p_0, \ldots, p_z, q_0, \ldots, q_z \geq 0)(\exists v_1 \ldots v_z \in V^*)$$

$$\left(\mathbf{l}_1 = e^{p_0} v_1 e^{p_1} \ldots e^{p_{z-1}} v_z e^{p_z} \wedge \mathbf{l}_2 = e^{q_0} v_1 e^{q_1} \ldots e^{q_{z-1}} v_z e^{q_z}\right) \qquad /12/$$

where e^p is a /sub/word composed of p consecutive letters e.

We extend the notion of e-equivalence to n-tuples of words:

$$(\mathbf{l}_1, \ldots, \mathbf{l}_n) \underset{e}{=} (\mathbf{l}'_1, \ldots, \mathbf{l}'_n) \Longleftrightarrow (\forall\, 0 \leq i \leq n)\ \mathbf{l}_i \underset{e}{=} \mathbf{l}'_i \qquad /13/$$

Let us consider an automaton $\mathbf{A} = \langle \mathbf{V}^n, S, F, s_0, I \rangle$. We call $\mathbf{A}$ an <u>e-automaton</u>, iff

$$(\forall s \in S)(e, \ldots, e, s, s) \in I \qquad /14/$$

We use the symbol DEF($\mathbf{A}$) to denote the <u>generalized set</u> /or <u>relation/ defined by the e-automaton A</u>:

$$\mathrm{DEF}(\mathbf{A}) \underset{\bar{A}}{=} \{(L_1, \ldots, L_n) \in (V^*)^n \mid$$
$$[\exists(\mathbf{l}_1, \ldots, \mathbf{l}_n) \underset{e}{=} (L_1, \ldots, L_n)]\ (\mathbf{l}_1, \ldots, \mathbf{l}_n) \in \mathrm{def}(\mathbf{A})\} \qquad /15/$$

Obviously, the generalized relations may be not-length-preserving transductions. For instance, for $V = \{0,1\}$, if $(001, 1e0) \in \mathrm{def}(\mathbf{A})$ then $(001, 10) \in \mathrm{DEF}(\mathbf{A})$.

For e-automata $\mathbf{A}$ and $\mathbf{B}$ the theorems 3 and 4, similar to 1 and 2, can be proved.

<u>Theorem 3</u>. $\mathcal{L} = \mathrm{DEF}(\mathbf{A}) \Longleftrightarrow [\mathcal{L}] = \mathrm{DEF}([\mathbf{A}])$

<u>Theorem 4</u>. $\mathrm{DEF}(\mathbf{A}) \circ \mathrm{DEF}(\mathbf{B}) = \mathrm{DEF}(\mathbf{A} \bullet \mathbf{B})$

Thus, for given e-automata $\mathbf{A}$ and $\mathbf{B}$, which define /in the generalized way/ the language $\mathcal{L}$ and the set of errors P in consideration, the set of detectable errors D and the set of undetectable errors U can be expressed as follows:

$$D = \mathrm{DEF}([\mathbf{A}] \bullet \mathbf{B} \bullet [\bar{\mathbf{A}}]) \qquad U = \mathrm{DEF}([\mathbf{A}] \bullet \mathbf{B} \bullet [\mathbf{A}]) \qquad /16/$$

3. AN EXAMPLE.

Let us consider a language $\mathcal{L}$, which in coding theory is called the <u>parity check code</u> [3], and a set P of <u>single deletion errors</u> [6]. The e-automata $\mathbf{A}$ and B defining $\mathcal{L}$ and P are shown in fig. 1 and 2. As usual, we denote the initial state by a short unlabelled arrow, and the final states - by a double circle. In labels of 2-input automata we use the symbol / to separate the first and the second input letter.

We ought to find the e-automata $[\mathbf{A}] \bullet \mathbf{B} \bullet [\bar{\mathbf{A}}]$ and $[\mathbf{A}] \bullet \mathbf{B} \bullet [\mathbf{A}]$, which define the sets D and U. This can be done in steps; the results are shown in fig. 3 - 8. For clarity, the states aAb and bAa, not accessible from the

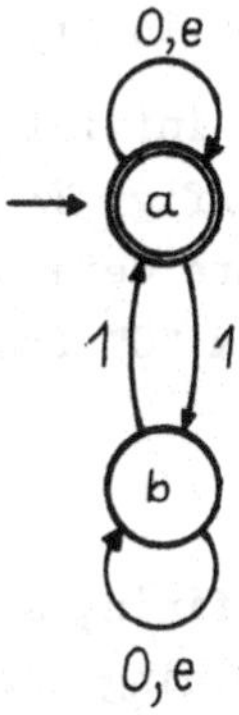

Fig. 1
Automaton **A**

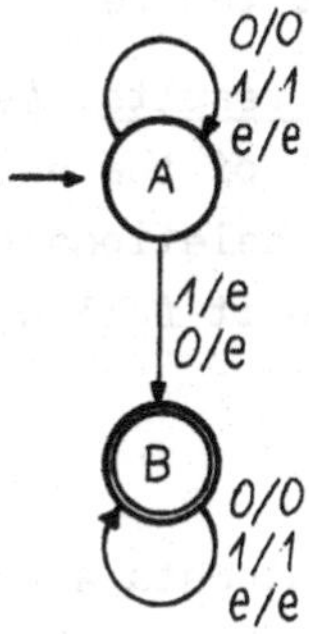

Fig. 2
Automaton **B**

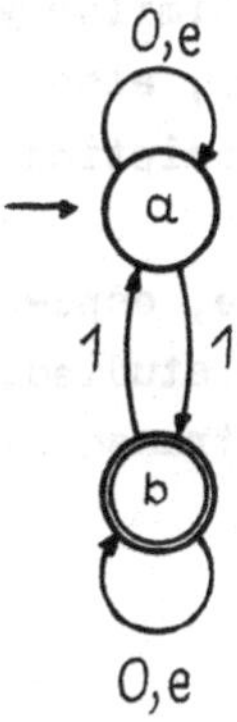

Fig. 3
Automaton
$\bar{\mathbf{A}}$

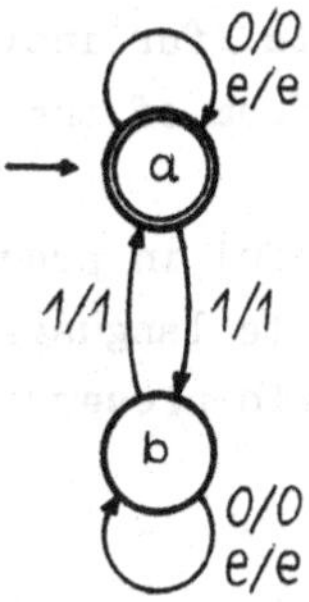

Fig. 4
Automaton
⌈**A**⌉

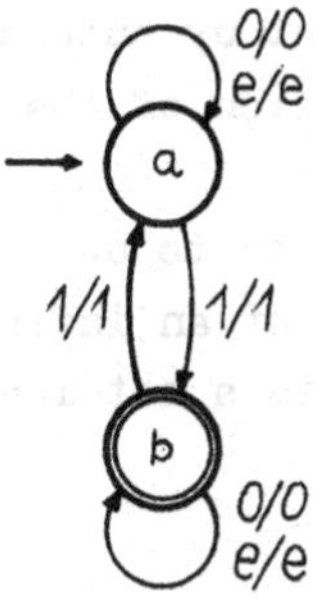

Fig. 5
Automaton
⌈$\bar{\mathbf{A}}$⌉

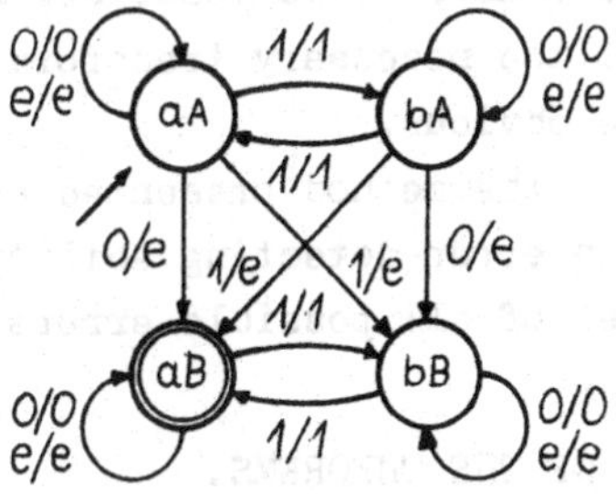

Fig. 6
Automaton
⌈**A**⌉• **B**

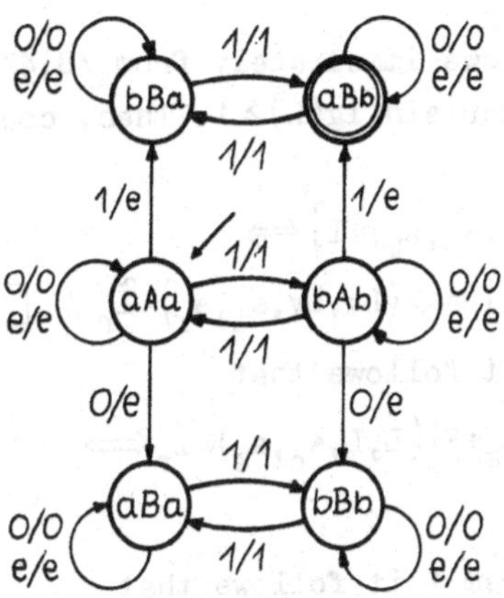

Fig. 7
Automaton ⌈**A**⌉•**B**•⌈$\bar{\mathbf{A}}$⌉

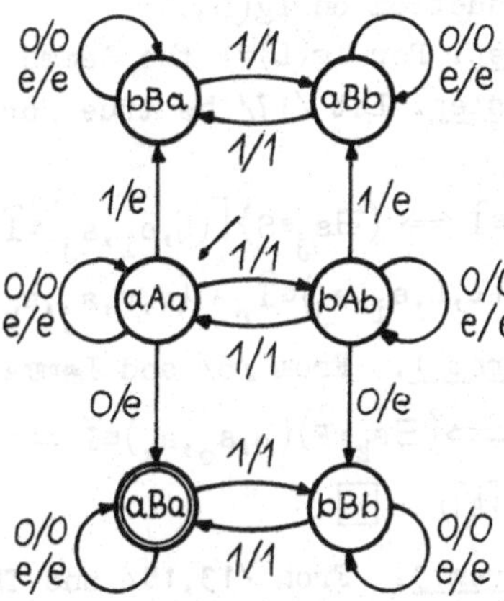

Fig. 8
Automaton ⌈**A**⌉•**B**•⌈**A**⌉

initial state aAa, and the related arcs are not shown in fig. 7, 8.

Interpretation of the results. As each path from the initial state aAa to the final state aBb of the e-automaton $\lceil \mathbf{A} \rceil \bullet \mathbf{B} \bullet \lceil \tilde{\mathbf{A}} \rceil$ /fig. 7/ contains one arc labelled 1/e, deletions of a "1" from $L \in \mathcal{L}$ are detectable errors. Similarly, from fig. 8 it follows that deletions of a "0" from $L \in \mathcal{L}$ are undetectable errors.

4. CONCLUSIONS.

For given finite automata A and B /or **A** and **B**/ defining a language $\mathcal{L}$ and a set of all possible errors P, the automata defining the set of detectable errors D and the set of undetectable errors U can easily be found.

When $\mathcal{L}$ and P are defined not by automata /for instance, verbally/, the problem of synthesising A and B /**A** and **B**/ may not be trivial. Similarly, when D and U have to be described not by automata /for instance, also verbally/, the necessary transformation of the form of the description may not be obvious.

However, the method presented seems to be useful in practice, especially when error-detecting ability of an infinite language is studied, and the set of all possible errors is a not-length-preserving transduction.

5. PROOFS OF THE THEOREMS.

Let us denote the length of a word L by lg(L).

Lemma 1. If A is 1-input automaton, then

$$(L,s_i,s_k)\in\tilde{I} \Longleftrightarrow (L,L,s_i,s_k)\in\tilde{I}_r \qquad /17/$$

Proof - by induction on lg(L).

Initial step. For lg(L)=1 the lemma follows immediately from /8,4/.

Induction step. Let /17/ be true for a certain $lg(L)\geqslant 1$. Then, considering /5/,

$$(Lv,s_i,s_k)\in\tilde{I} \Longleftrightarrow (\exists s_j\in S)[(L,s_i,s_j)\in\tilde{I} \wedge (v,s_j,s_k)\in I] \Longleftrightarrow$$

$$\Longleftrightarrow (\exists s_j\in S)[(L,L,s_i,s_j)\in\tilde{I}_r \wedge (v,v,s_j,s_k)\in I_r] \Longleftrightarrow (Lv,Lv,s_i,s_k)\in\tilde{I}_r \qquad \square$$

Proof of Theorem 1. From /6/ and Lemma 1 it follows that

$$L\in def(A) \Longleftrightarrow (\exists s_k\in F)(L,s_o,s_k)\in\tilde{I} \Longleftrightarrow (\exists s_k\in F)(L,L,s_o,s_k)\in\tilde{I}_r \Longleftrightarrow$$

$$\Longleftrightarrow (L,L)\in def(\lceil A \rceil) \qquad \square$$

Proof of Theorem 3. From /13,15/ and Theorem 1 it follows that

$$L\in DEF(\mathbf{A}) \Longleftrightarrow (\exists \mathbf{L} \underset{e}{=} L)[\mathbf{L}\in def(\mathbf{A}) \Longleftrightarrow [\exists(\mathbf{L},\mathbf{L}) \underset{e}{=} (L,L)]\,(\mathbf{L},\mathbf{L})\in def(\lceil \mathbf{A} \rceil) \Longleftrightarrow$$

$$\Longleftrightarrow (L,L)\in DEF(\lceil \mathbf{A} \rceil) \qquad \square$$

Lemma 2. If $A = \langle V^2, S_a, F_a, s_{oa}, I_a\rangle$ and $B = \langle V^2, S_b, F_b, s_{ob}, I_b\rangle$ then

$$(L_1, L_2, (s_{ai}, s_{bi}), (s_{ak}, s_{bk})) \in \tilde{I}_{ab} \Longleftrightarrow$$
$$\Longleftrightarrow (\exists L \in V^*)[(L_1, L, s_{ai}, s_{ak}) \in \tilde{I}_a \wedge (L, L_2, s_{bi}, s_{bk}) \in \tilde{I}_b]$$

Proof - by induction on $lg(L)$ - is analogous to the proof of Lemma 1 and therefore will be omitted.

Proof of Theorem 2 /for A and B being 2-input automata/. From /6,9/ and Lemma 2 it follows that

$$(L_1, L_2) \in def(A \bullet B) \Longleftrightarrow$$
$$\Longleftrightarrow [\exists (s_{ak}, s_{bk}) \in F_a \times F_b](L_1, L_2, (s_{oa}, s_{ob}), (s_{ak}, s_{bk})) \in \tilde{I}_{ab} \Longleftrightarrow$$
$$\Longleftrightarrow (\exists s_{ak} \in F_a)(\exists s_{bk} \in F_b)(\exists L \in V^*)[(L_1, L, s_{oa}, s_{ak}) \in \tilde{I}_a \wedge (L, L_2, s_{ob}, s_{bk}) \in \tilde{I}_b] \Longleftrightarrow$$
$$\Longleftrightarrow (\exists L \in V^*)[(L_1, L) \in def(A) \wedge (L, L_2) \in def(B)] \Longleftrightarrow (L_1, L_2) \in def(A) \circ def(B) \quad \square$$

The proof of Theorem 4 is much more complicated than the three preceding ones. This proof basis on some concepts from [2].

We will need some auxiliary notions.

For a given n, in the set $(V^*)^n$ we define the immediate predecessor relation $<$:

$$(\mathbf{L}_1, \dots, \mathbf{L}_n) < (\mathbf{L}_1', \dots, \mathbf{L}_n') \Longleftrightarrow (\exists d, d' \geqslant 0)(\forall 1 \leqslant i \leqslant n)(\exists \mathbf{l}_i, \mathbf{l}_i' \in V^*)$$
$$[lg(\mathbf{l}_i) = d \wedge lg(\mathbf{l}_i') = d' \wedge \mathbf{L}_i = \mathbf{l}_i \mathbf{l}_i' \wedge \mathbf{L}_i' = \mathbf{l}_i e \mathbf{l}_i'] \qquad /18/$$

Considering this definition and in the case of Lemma 4′ also eqs. /5,6,14/, the following lemmas can be proved:

Lemma 3′. $[lg(\mathbf{L}_1) = lg(\mathbf{L}_2) \wedge \mathbf{L}_1 < \mathbf{L}_1'] \Longrightarrow (\exists \mathbf{L}_2' \in V^*)(\mathbf{L}_1, \mathbf{L}_2) < (\mathbf{L}_1', \mathbf{L}_2')$

Lemma 4′. If **A** is an e-automaton, then

$$[(\mathbf{L}_1, \dots, \mathbf{L}_n) \in def(\mathbf{A}) \wedge (\mathbf{L}_1, \dots, \mathbf{L}_n) < (\mathbf{L}_1', \dots, \mathbf{L}_n')] \Longrightarrow (\mathbf{L}_1', \dots, \mathbf{L}_n') \in def(\mathbf{A})$$

Using the relation $<$ we define the partial ordering relation $\leqslant$:

1. $(\mathbf{L}_1, \dots, \mathbf{L}_n) \leqslant (\mathbf{L}_1, \dots, \mathbf{L}_n)$ /19/

2. $[(\mathbf{L}_1, \dots, \mathbf{L}_n) \leqslant (\mathbf{L}_1', \dots, \mathbf{L}_n') \wedge (\mathbf{L}_1', \dots, \mathbf{L}_n') < (\mathbf{L}_1'', \dots, \mathbf{L}_n'')] \Longrightarrow$
$\Longrightarrow (\mathbf{L}_1, \dots, \mathbf{L}_n) \leqslant (\mathbf{L}_1'', \dots, \mathbf{L}_n'')$ /20/

By induction on $d = lg(\mathbf{L}_i') - lg(\mathbf{L}_i)$, lemmas 3′ and 4′ can easily be generalized as follows:

Lemma 3. $[lg(\mathbf{L}_1) = lg(\mathbf{L}_2) \wedge \mathbf{L}_1 \leqslant \mathbf{L}_1'] \Longrightarrow (\exists \mathbf{L}_2' \in V^*)(\mathbf{L}_1, \mathbf{L}_2) \leqslant (\mathbf{L}_1', \mathbf{L}_2')$

Lemma 4. If **A** is an e-automaton, then

$$[(\mathbf{L}_1, \dots, \mathbf{L}_n) \in def(\mathbf{A}) \wedge (\mathbf{L}_1, \dots, \mathbf{L}_n) \leqslant (\mathbf{L}_1', \dots, \mathbf{L}_n')] \Longrightarrow (\mathbf{L}_1', \dots, \mathbf{L}_n') \in def(\mathbf{A})$$

Lemmas 5 and 6 join the notion of partial ordering with e-equivalence.

Lemma 5. $\mathbf{L}_1 \underset{e}{=} \mathbf{L}_2 \Longrightarrow (\exists \mathbf{L} \in \mathbf{V}^*)(\mathbf{L}_1 \leqslant \mathbf{L} \wedge \mathbf{L}_2 \leqslant \mathbf{L})$

Proof. Considering /12/, the words $\mathbf{L}_1$ and $\mathbf{L}_2$ can be represented as:

$$\mathbf{L}_1 = e^{p_0} v_1 e^{p_1} \ldots e^{p_{z-1}} v_z e^{p_z} \qquad \mathbf{L}_2 = e^{q_0} v_1 e^{q_1} \ldots e^{q_{z-1}} v_z e^{q_z}$$

Let $\mathbf{L} = e^{p_0} e^{q_0} v_1 e^{p_1} e^{q_1} \ldots e^{p_{z-1}} e^{q_{z-1}} v_z e^{p_z} e^{q_z}$. Then $\mathbf{L}_1 \leqslant \mathbf{L}$ and $\mathbf{L}_2 \leqslant \mathbf{L}$ □

Lemma 6. $[\lg(\mathbf{L}_1) = \lg(\mathbf{L}_2) \wedge \lg(\mathbf{L}_3) = \lg(\mathbf{L}_4) \wedge \mathbf{L}_2 \underset{e}{=} \mathbf{L}_3] \Longrightarrow$

$$\Longrightarrow (\exists \mathbf{L}_1', \mathbf{L}', \mathbf{L}_4' \in \mathbf{V}^*)[(\mathbf{L}_1, \mathbf{L}_2) \leqslant (\mathbf{L}_1', \mathbf{L}') \wedge (\mathbf{L}_3, \mathbf{L}_4) \leqslant (\mathbf{L}', \mathbf{L}_4')]$$

Proof follows immediately from lemmas 3 and 5.

Lemma 7. $[(L_1, L) \in \mathrm{DEF}(\mathbf{A}) \wedge (L, L_2) \in \mathrm{DEF}(\mathbf{B})] \Longleftrightarrow$

$$\Longleftrightarrow [\exists (\mathbf{L}_1, \mathbf{L}, \mathbf{L}_2) \underset{e}{=} (L_1, L, L_2)][(\mathbf{L}_1, \mathbf{L}) \in \mathrm{def}(\mathbf{A}) \wedge (\mathbf{L}, \mathbf{L}_2) \in \mathrm{def}(\mathbf{B})]$$

Proof $\Longleftarrow$ follows from /15/; $\Longrightarrow$ follows from /15/ and lemmas 6, 4.

Proof of Theorem 4 /for $\mathbf{A}$ and $\mathbf{B}$ being 2-input automata/. Considering /15/, Theorem 2 and Lemma 7,

$$(L_1, L_2) \in \mathrm{DEF}(\mathbf{A} \cdot \mathbf{B}) \Longleftrightarrow [\exists (\mathbf{L}_1, \mathbf{L}_2) \underset{e}{=} (L_1, L_2)](\mathbf{L}_1, \mathbf{L}_2) \in \mathrm{def}(\mathbf{A} \cdot \mathbf{B}) \Longleftrightarrow$$

$$\Longleftrightarrow [\exists (\mathbf{L}_1, \mathbf{L}_2) \underset{e}{=} (L_1, L_2)](\exists \mathbf{L} \in \mathbf{V}^*)[(\mathbf{L}_1, \mathbf{L}) \in \mathrm{def}(\mathbf{A}) \wedge (\mathbf{L}, \mathbf{L}_2) \in \mathrm{def}(\mathbf{B})] \Longleftrightarrow$$

$$\Longleftrightarrow (\exists L \in V^*)[(L_1, L) \in \mathrm{DEF}(\mathbf{A}) \wedge (L, L_2) \in \mathrm{DEF}(\mathbf{B})] \Longleftrightarrow (L_1, L_2) \in \mathrm{DEF}(\mathbf{A}) \circ \mathrm{DEF}(\mathbf{B}) \quad \square$$

6. REFERENCES.

[1] A. Blikle: Automaty i gramatyki. Wstęp do lingwistyki matematycznej. 1971 Warszawa.

[2] C. C. Elgot, J. E. Mezei: On relations defined by generalized finite automata. IBM J. Res. Develop. pp. 47 - 68, January 1965.

[3] W. W. Peterson: Error-correcting codes. 1961 New York.

[4] W. B. Smith: Error detection in formal languages. J. Comp. Syst. Sci. vol. 4 pp. 385 - 405, 1970.

[5] R. E. Stearns, J. Hartmanis: Regularity preserving modifications of regular expressions. Inf. Control vol. 6 pp. 55 - 69, 1963.

[6] M. C. Thomason: Errors in regular languages. IEEE Trans. Comput. vol. C-23 pp. 597 - 602, June 1974.

[7] S. Winograd: Input error limiting automata. J. ACM vol. 11 pp. 338 - - 351, 1964.

ON A RELATIONSHIP BETWEEN PROGRAMS OF ADDRESS MACHINES AND MAZURKIEWICZ ALGORITHMS

Zbigniew Raś
University of Warsaw
Institute of Mathematics
00-901 Warsaw, Poland

Introduction

One of the principal problems of mathematical foundations of computer science is the investigation of the essential properties of programs for computing mavhines. We can separate here three main currents:

(1) a study of properties of programs from the point of view of the computer in which they are realized (see [1,4,8,13,16,18])
(2) a study of properties of programs from the point of view of the language in which they are written (see [2,3,6,15,17])
(3) a study of properties of programs independently from a computer in which they are realized and from the language in which they are written (see [5,7,10,11]).

A study of programs from the point of view of the computer is strictly related to a finding a mathematical model of a computer. On the basis of this model we define a program. A study of programs from the point of view of a language is related to finding a formal language such that some of its elements are interpreted as programs. A study of programs independently from a computer in which they are realized and a language in which they are written is related to a finding of an abstract model of a program in which we can describe all interesting attributes of programs. These three above currents we can describe by using the following pictures:

(1)

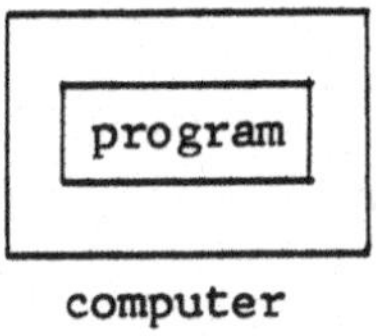

(2)

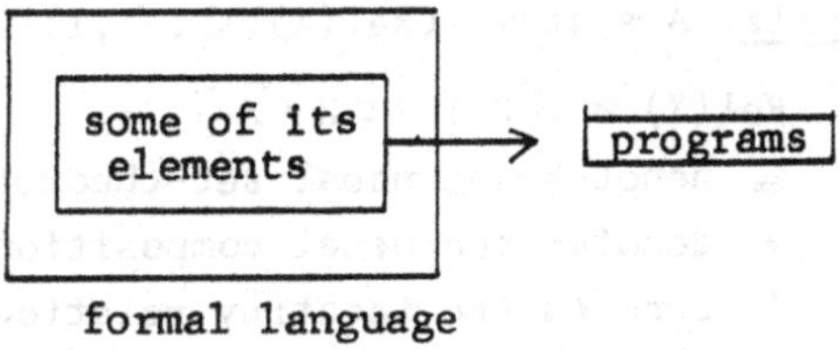

(3)

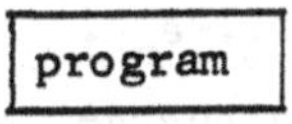

Therefore, in the first case we define a program on the basis of a computer whereas in the second and in the third case the program is defined without a notion of a computer. It seems that without a computer we can not describe all the properties and possibilities of programs because new machines are constantly constructed whereas we investigate the same models of programs. Thus the possibilities of machines are from year to year greater as possibilities of programs. On the other hand introducing a model of a computer restricts liberty of acceptance of a model program because in this case we introduce a notion of a program inside a computer. So it is natural to investigate the relationships between these three currents. In this paper we are going to give some relationships between the first and the third approach.

As a model of a program we are going to take a Mazurkiewicz algorithm (see [10]). As a model of a computer we are going to accept a stored program computer (SPC) due to Pawlak (see [14]). On the basis of this model we are going to investigate the notion of a program due to Ras (see [16]).

A category of FC-algorithms.

In this part a notion of a FC-algorithm over a net (see [5]) will be recalled and a definition of a homomorphism will be proposed. Some simple properties related to homomorphisms will be given. It appears that if we take homomorphisms as morphisms and FC-algorithms over nets of relations as objects we obtain a category which we shall denote by FCR.

By a net we shall mean any system $N = (U, \leq, \circ, e)$ where:

(1) $(U, \leq)$ is a complete lattice

(2) $(U, \circ, e)$ is a monoid with unit e

(3) a binary relation $\circ$ is additive and continous

(4) for any $a \in U$, $a \cdot \underline{0} = \underline{0} \cdot a = \underline{0}$, where $\underline{0} = \bigcap U$.

Example. A system $(Rel(X), \subseteq, \circ, I)$ where:

(1) $Rel(X) = \{R : R \subset X \times X\}$

(2) $\subseteq$ denotes the usual set-theoretic inclusion

(3) $\circ$ denotes the usual composition

(4) I denotes the identity relation

is a net.

Let us assume that $N = (U, \leq, \circ, e)$ is a net and $a_i \in U$ for $i \leq n$. We adopt the following notation: $C[a_1, \ldots, a_n] = a_1 \cdot \ldots \cdot a_n$.

By a FC-algorithm over $N = (U, \leq, \circ, e)$ we mean any system $A = (V,$

$\alpha_1, \varepsilon, P)$ where:

(1) $V = \{\alpha_1, \dots, \alpha_n\}$ is the set of labels

(2) ε is the empty sequence

(3) P is a set of instructions of the form (α_i, a, z) where $z \in V \cup \{\varepsilon\}$ and $a \in U$

(4) α_1 is a distinguished element called an initial label.

Each finite sequence of instructions $(\alpha_{i1}, a_1, \alpha_{i2})(\alpha_{i2}, a_2, \alpha_{i3}) \dots (\alpha_{i\,n-1}, a_{n-1}, \alpha_{in})(\alpha_{in}, a_n, \varepsilon)$ will be called α_{i1}-run of A.

The sequence $a_1, \dots, a_n$ is called α_{i1}-trace of A.

Let $Tr(\alpha_i)$ denotes the set of all α_i-traces of A. So the outcome of $Tr(\alpha_i)$ will be the join $\bigcup\{C(t) : t \in Tr(\alpha_i)\}$ since any two traces can be considered as independent executions of the algorithm. Therefore $Res_A = \bigcup\{C(t) : t \in Tr(\alpha_1)\}$ describes the behaviour of A and is called the result element of A.

Let us consider two FC-algorithms $A_i = (V_i, \alpha_i, \varepsilon, P_i)$ over $N_i = (Rel(X_i), \subseteq, \circ, I)$, $i = 1,2$.

A function $f : X_1 \longrightarrow X_2$ will be called a homomorphism from A_1 to A_2 if the following condition holds:

if $(x,y) \in Res_{A1}$ then $(f(x), f(y)) \in Res_{A2}$

for any $x, y \in X_1$.

<u>Proposition</u>. Let A_1, A_2, A_3 be FC-algorithms over $(Rel(X_i), \subseteq, \circ, I)$ for $i=1,2,3$ respectively.

(1) if $f_1 : X_1 \longrightarrow X_2$ and $f_2 : X_2 \longrightarrow X_3$ are homomorphisms from A_1 to A_2 and from A_2 to A_3 respectively then $f_1 \cdot f_2 : X_1 \longrightarrow X_3$ is a homomorphism from A_1 to A_3.

(2) $id_{A1} : X_1 \longrightarrow X_1$ (i.e. $id_{A1}(x) = x$ for each $x \in X_1$) is a homomorphism.

(3) whenever the composition makes sense, we have $(f_1 \cdot f_2) \cdot f_3 = f_1 \cdot (f_2 \cdot f_3)$, $id_{A1} \cdot f_1 = f_1$, $f_1 \cdot id_{A2} = f_1$.

<u>Proposition</u>. If we take FC-algorithms over nets of relations as objects and homomorphisms as morphisms we obtain a category MAR.

Denote now by $Fun(X)$ the subset of $Rel(X)$ defined as follows: $R \in Fun(X)$ iff $R \in Rel(X)$ and R is a function.

The net $(Fun(X), \subseteq, \circ, I)$ will be called the net of functions over X.

Let us consider a class of FC-algorithms over nets of functions satisfying the condition:

(*) if $A = (V, \alpha_1, \varepsilon, P)$ is a FC-algorithm over $(Fun(X), \subseteq, \circ, I)$

and (a,R_1,z) , $(a,R_2,z) \in P$ then $R_1 = R_2$.

Proposition. If we take FC-algorithms over nets of functions satisfying the condition (*) as objects and homomorphisms as morphisms we obtain the full subcategory of MAR. We will denote it by MAF.

Definition. Let $A_1 = (V_1, \alpha_1, \mathcal{E}, P_1)$, $A_2 = (V_2, \alpha_2, \mathcal{E}, P_2)$ be arbitrary FC-algorithms over $(Rel(X_1), \subseteq, \circ, I)$, $(Rel(X_2), \subseteq, \circ, I)$ respectively. Then: $A_1 \cdot A_2$ is defined iff $V_1 \cap V_2 = 0$.
In this case $A_1 \cdot A_2 = (V, \alpha, \mathcal{E}, P)$ is the FC-algorithm over $(Rel(X_1 \cup X_2), \subseteq, \circ, I)$ where:

(1) $V = V_1 \cup V_2$
(2) $\alpha = \alpha_1$
(3) $P = P_2 \cup \{(a,R,b) : (a,R,b) \in P_1$ and $b \neq \mathcal{E}\} \cup \{(a,R,\alpha_2) : (a,R,\mathcal{E}) \in P_1\}$.

Proposition. Let us assume that $A_i = (V_i, \alpha_i, \mathcal{E}, P_i)$ for $i=1,2$ are FC-algorithms over $(Rel(X), \subseteq, \circ, I)$ and $A_1 \cdot A_2$ is defined. Then : $Res_{A1 \circ A2} = Res_{A1} \circ Res_{A2}$.

Proposition. Let $A_i = (V_i, \alpha_i, \mathcal{E}, P_i)$, $A_i' = (V_i', \alpha_i', \mathcal{E}, P_i')$ be FC-algorithms over $(Rel(X), \subseteq, \circ, I)$, $(Rel(X'), \subseteq, \cdot, I)$ respectively , $i=1,2$. Let $f : X \longrightarrow X'$ be a homomorphism from A_1 to A_1' and from A_2 to A_2' . Then : if $A_1 \cdot A_2$, $A_1' \circ A_2'$ are determined then $f : X \longrightarrow X'$ is a homomorphism from $A_1 \circ A_2$ to $A_1' \cdot A_2'$.

A category of programs of address machines

In this part a notion of a SPC being some modification of an address machine due to Pawlak (see [14]) will be proposed. A notion of a program and of a computation will be given. Also a definition of a homomorphism of programs will be proposed. It appears that if we take programs of address machines as objects and homomorphisms as morphisms we obtain a category, which will be denoted by AM .

By an address machine we shall mean an ordered sequence $M = (A,B,C,R,\varphi,1)$ where :

(1) A , B are arbitrary sets called the set of addresses and the alphabet
(2) $C = B^{[A]}$ where $B^{[A]}$ is the set of all partial functions from set A to set B . Set C will be called the set of states.
(3) $R \subset C^C$ is an arbitrary set called the set of instructions .
(4) $\varphi : B \longrightarrow R$ is a partial function called the coding function.
(5) $1 \in A$.

The transition function of M is defined as follows : $\pi(c) =$

$(\varphi(c(c(1))))(c)$ where $c \in C$. This function will be called the action of M .

By a computation of M we mean any finite or infinite sequence $c_1, c_2, \ldots$ of states such that :

(1) $(\forall i)(\ c_{i+1} = \pi(c_i)\ )$

(2) if c_n is the end state of this sequence then $c_n \notin D_\pi$.

By a program of M we understand any triple $P = (U,a,b)$ such that :

(1) $U \subset A \times R$ is a function , $card(D_U) < \aleph_0$.

(2) $a \in D_U$, $b \in A - D_U$.

Let $U \subset A \times R$ be a function. By C^U we denote the following set :

$C^U = \{c \in C : (\forall a \in D_U)(\ (a,c(a)) \in U\ )$ and $(\forall a \notin D_U)(\ c(a) \notin R\ )\}$

Clearly the set C^U is the set of states which contain exactly the function U understanding as a program.

We shall say that c_2 is a W-widening of c_1 if the following conditions hold :

(1) $c_2/D_{c_1} = c_1$ and $c_2 \in C^W$

(2) $D_{c_2} - D_{c_1} \subset D_W$.

By a SPC we shall mean an address machine $M = (A,B,C,R,\varphi,1)$ such that :

(1) $(\forall c \in C)(\ c \in C^U \longrightarrow \pi(c) \in C^U\ )$

(2) if c_2 is a W-widening of c_1 then $\pi(c_2)$ is a W-widening of $\pi(c_1)$ if only W-widening of $\pi(c_1)$ exists..

Let $P = (U,a,b)$ be an arbitrary program and $p = c_1,\ldots,c_n$ a computation such that $c_1 \in C^U$. We say that p is over a function $W \subset A \times R$ if there exists a W-widening of c_i for every $i \leq n$.

With every program $P = (U,a,b)$ we associate now some set of computations over W denoted by $C^P_{M,W}$ and defined as follows :

$p \in C^P_{M,W}$ iff $p = c_1,\ldots,c_n$ is a computation over W and $c_1(1) = a$ and $c_n(1) = b \in Dom(W - U)$ and $c_1 \in C^U$.

The resulting function $Res^W_P \subset C \times C$ of P is defined as follows :

$(c,c')\ Res^W_P$ iff $(\exists\ p = c_1,\ldots,c_n \in C^P_{M,W})(\ c_1 = c$ and $c_n = c')$

We shall write also Res_P instead of Res^W_P .

Let us assume that $P_i = (U_i,a_i,b_i)$ is a program of M_i for $i = 1,2$. A function $f : C_1 \longrightarrow C_2$ will be called a homomorphism from P_1 to P_2 if the following condition holds :

if $(c,c') \in Res_{P_1}$ then $(f(c),f(c')) \in Res_{P_2}$.

Proposition. If we take programs of SPC as objects and homomorphisms as morphisms we obtain a category which we shall denote by AM .

Let $M = (A,B,C,R,\varphi,1)$ be any SPC. For any (a_1,r_1) , $(a_2,r_2) \in W$ we adopt :

$(a_1,r_1)\ N_W\ (a_2,r_2)$ iff $(\exists c_1,c_2 \in C^W)(\forall i)[\ (a_i,r_i) = (c_i(1), \varphi(c_i(c_i(1)))\ )$ and $\pi(c_1) = c_2\ ]$.

By DU we denote the transitive closure of N_U in U .

Let us assume that $P_1 = (U_1,a_1,b_1)$, $P_2 = (U_2,a_2,b_2)$ are arbitrary programs of M and $W : A \longrightarrow R$. We adopt :

$P_1 \cdot_W P_2$ is determined iff

(1) $U_1 \cap U_2 = 0$, $U_1 \cup U_2 \subset W$, $b_1 = a_2$

(2) $\mathrm{Dom}(N_W(U_1) \cap U_2) = \{a_2\}$, $N_W(U_2) \cap U_1 = 0$.

If $P_1 \cdot_W P_2$ is determined then we put $P_1 \cdot_W P_2 = (U_1 \cup U_2, a_1, b_2)$.

We shall say that a program P is W-decomposable if there exists programs P_1 , P_2 such that $P = P_1 \cdot_W P_2$. In opposite case P is said to be W- atom .

Proposition. Let $P = (U,a,b)$ be an arbitrary program and $U \subset W$.
(1) if DW is an equivalence relation on U or card(U) = 1 then P is a W-atom .
(2) if DW is a connective relation on U then: P is an W-atom iff DW is an equivalence relation on U or card(U) = 1 .

Proposition. Let $P_i = (U_i,a_i,b_i)$, $i = 1,2$ be arbitrary programs and $P_1 \cdot_W P_2$ is determined. Then

$\mathrm{Res}^W_{P_1 \cdot W P_2} = \mathrm{Res}^W_{P_1'} \cdot \mathrm{Res}^W_{P_2'}$

where $P_1' = (U_1 \cup U_2, a_1, b_1)$, $P_2' = (U_1 \cup U_2, a_2, b_2)$.

Proposition. Let $f : C \longrightarrow C'$ be a homomorphism from P_1 to P_1' and from P_2 to P_2' . Let us assume that $P_1 \cdot_{W_1} P_2$ and $P_1' \cdot_{W_2} P_2'$ is determined. Then f is a homomorphism from $P_1 \cdot_{W_1} P_2$ to $P_1' \cdot_{W_2} P_2'$.

Proposition. there exists a full subcategory of AM which is equivalent to MAF .

References.

1. Amoroso S., Bloom St., A model of a digital computer, Symposium on Computers and Automata, Brooklyn, 1971

2. de Backer J.W., Recursive procedures, Mathematical Center Tracts 24

Mathematisch Centrum Amsterdam, 1971

3. de Backer J.W., Scott D., A theory of programs in outline of join work by J.W. de Bakker and Dana Scott, Vienna 1979

4. Bartol W., Raś Z., Skowron A., Theory of computing systems, to appear

5. Blikle A., An extended approach to mathematical analysis of programs, CC PAS REPORTS, 1974

6. Cadiou J.M., Recursive definitions of partial functions and their computations, Stanford University, Report STAN-266-72

7. Eilenberg S., Automata, languages and machines, Volume A, Academic Press. 1974

8. Elgot C.C., Robinson A., Random-access stored-program machines, an approach, to programming languages, Journ. ASM, 11, 1964

9. Kalmar L., Les calculatrices automatiques comme structures algebriques, Previsions, calculs et realites , Paris 1965

10. Mazurkiewicz A., Proving algorithms by tail functions, Inf. Cont. 18, 220-226, 1971

11. Mazurkiewicz A., Iteratively computable relations, Bull. Acad. Polon Sci., Ser. Sci. Math. Astronom. Phys. 20, 793-798, 1972

12. Mitchell B., Theory of categories, Academic Press, 1965

13. Pawlak Z., On the notion of a computer, Logic. Meth. and Phil. of Science, 255-267, 1968

14. Pawlak Z., A mathematical model of a digital computer, Proc. Conf. Theory of Autom. and Formal Lang., Boon 1973

15. Rasiowa H., On ω^+-valued algorithmic logic and related problems, Supplement to Proc. of Symp. and Summer School on Mathematical Foundations of Computer Science, High Tatras, September 3-8, 1973

16. Raś Z., Classification of programs of SPC, Lectures Notes in Computer Science, 3rd Symposium at Jadwisin, June 17-22, 1974

17. Salwicki A., Formalized algorithmic languages, Bull. Acad. Polon. Sci., Ser. Math. Astronom. Phys. 18, 1972

18. Wagner E.G., Bounded action machines: toward an abstract theory of computer structure, Journ. of CSS, 2, 13-75, 1968 .

DIJKSTRA'S PREDICATE TRANSFORMER, NON-DETERMINISM, RECURSION, AND TERMINATION

W.P. de ROEVER

Université de Rennes (France)
Mathematisch Centrum, Amsterdam (Netherlands)

Abstract : An in both arguments continuous characterization of DIJKSTRA's weakest--precondition operator wp (R)(p) is investigated. A relationship between wp and full recursion is given. By way of example, a method for expressing total correctness of non-deterministic recursive procedures by means of inductive assertion patterns is presented and shown to be adequate (complete), thus refining work of de BAKKER's and MEERTENS'.

0. SURVEY AND SOME RELATED IDEAS

0.1. *Survey*

0.1.1. First a definition of Dijkstra's weakest-precondition operator wp, with functional dependence determined by $\lambda R.\lambda p.\lambda x.\ ((wp(R)(p))(x))$, is given, which reflects his original verbal (as opposed to axiomatic) characterization. Continuity of wp(R) in R is proved, using the Egli-Milner order. Following DIJKSTRA [7], continuity of wp(R)(p) in p holds, provided in case R's non-determinism is infinite in input x also $xR\perp$ holds, with $\perp$ expressing the presence of a non-terminating computation.
0.1.2. Then both the usual relationships between the composition, non-deterministic choice, and conditional operators and wp are stated, and the relationship between wp and arbitrary (non-iterative ones included) recursive procedures using least fixed points of predicate-transformer transformations is proved.
0.1.3. Finally I demonstrate, using the schema for the control structure of the Towers of Hanoi, (1) how total correctness of (non-deterministic) recursive procedures can be expressed using inductive assertion patterns only, and (2) that the presented method is *adequate* (,or, as some authors prefer,*complete*). Formulation and proving validity and adequacy of the general method will be published elsewhere.

0.2. *Some related ideas*

0.2.1. Dijkstra's observation of continuity of wp(R)(p) in p, provided R's non-determinism is finitely bounded,is an essential step forward. HOARE recently characterized wp using operational means [11, 12].
0.2.2. In a letter to Dijkstra, SCOTT shows how the wp-oriented approach to defining the semantics of program constructs can be reconciled with the Scott-Strachey approach [17];PLOTKIN [14] is the most profound 1975 study in that field.
0.2.3. BURSTALL, MEERTENS and (Jerry) SCHWARTZ each told me about related ideas for proving total correctness using inductive assertions (;none of them considered adequacy, however). Indeed, the inductive assertion patterns of section 3 give a foundation for Burstall's method for proving termination [5], and generalize that method to (non-determinism and) full recursion. Good formal studies on recursion, non-determinism, and termination are HITCHCOCK & PARK [10] and de BAKKER [2].

Acknowledgements. After STRACHEY's untimely death, Joe STOY provided me the opportunity for giving the Michaelmas term 'Introduction to programme correctness' at the Programming Research Group, Oxford, during which the above ideas were expounded. Dana SCOTT gave me access to his correspondence on predicate transformers. Chris WADSWORTH suggested an improvement.

The research reported in this paper has been carried out at the Programming Research Group, Oxford, on a grant from the Netherlands Organization for the Advancement of Pure Research (Z.W.O.), and at I.R.I.S.A., Université de Rennes.

1. DIJKSTRA'S WEAKEST-PRECONDITION OPERATOR

1.1. *Introduction*

There exists some confusion about the proper characterization of Dijkstra's weakest-precondition operator. This can be understood as follows :

DEFINITION 1.1. *Let* R *vary over binary relations over some domain* D, *and* p *over total predicates over* D. *Then* op *is defined by* $\underline{op} \underset{DEF}{=} \lambda R.\lambda p.\lambda x.\ \forall y[(x,y) \in R \rightarrow p(y)] \wedge \exists y[(x,y) \in R \wedge p(y)]$ □ . Then in case non-determinism occurs *) op, although satisfying Dijkstra's axioms in [6], does not reflect his intended meaning as expressed by :

"... *we shall use the notation wp(R,p) ... to denote the weakest precondition on the initial state of the system such that activation of* R *is guaranteed to lead to a properly terminating activity leaving the system in a final state satisfying the post-condition* p (op.cit.)."

Why do his axioms not reflect his intended meaning ? Let op (R)(p)(x) be true, and R describe the Input/Output behaviour of some program construct S. Then :

(1) There exists a terminating computation since $\exists y[(x,y) \in R \wedge p(y)]$ is true.

(2) However , this does *not* eliminate for S the possibility of a non-deterministically branching off non-terminating compution in x, since that possibility is not reflected in the above-used classical notion of binary relations to describe the I/O behaviour of programs :As observed in MILNER [13], although a terminating computation does contribute an input-output pair to R, a non-terminating computation does not contribute anything to R, and hence its presence cannot be deduced from R.

Dijkstra's continuous, as we shall see, intuition is captured in

DEFINITION 1.2. *Let* R *vary over subsets of* $D{\times}D \cup (D\cup\{\perp\}) \times \{\perp\}$ *containing* $\langle\perp,\perp\rangle$, *and* p *over total predicates over* D. *Then* wp *is defined by*

$$wp \underset{DEF}{=} \lambda R.\lambda p.\lambda x.\ \forall y[(x,y) \in R \rightarrow (p(y) \wedge \neg(y=\perp))].\ {**})\ \square$$

Remarks :(1) Since $(x,\perp) \in R$ intends to express the presence of a non-terminating computation, 'Scott's bottom' $\perp$ is needed [18]. Hence the $(D\cup\{\perp\} \times \{\perp\}$ factor above guarantees that a non-terminating computation does not terminate.

(2) The intended use of a total predicate p above should not be confused with that of possibly partial predicates r occurring in conditionals ; these are represented as follows :

DEFINITION 1.3. *Let* r *be a partial predicate over* D. *Then* r *is represented by the pair* (r^+,r^-) *of total predicates over* D, *defined as follows :* $r^+(x)$ = true *iff*

*) The deterministic case is simple : then R denotes the graph of a function, and op reduces to $\lambda R.\lambda p.\lambda x.\forall y[(x,y)\in R \wedge p(y)]$, an operator which is studied in an axiomatic setting in de BAKKER & de ROEVER [4], and related to call-by-value in de ROEVER [15, 16].

**)As remarked by EVTIMOV, restriction to predicates p satisfying $p(\perp)$ = false, reduces wp to $\lambda R.\lambda p.\lambda x.\ \forall y\ [(x,y) \in R \rightarrow p(y)]$.

$r(x)$ = true, *and* $r^+(x)$ = false *otherwise, and* $r^-(x)$ = true *iff* $r(x)$ = false, *and* $r^-(x)$ = false *otherwise.* □

In [6], Dijkstra defines the semantics of some programming constructs using wp. SCOTT agrees with this principle [17], and even applies it by defining the semantics of jumps in analogy with STRACHEY & WADSWORTH [19] using predicates in stead of continuations and introducing environments. However, before one is justified in doing so, *continuity* of wp in its arguments must be obtained - a natural requirement in view of Scott's own work on programming semantics ; by SCOTT [18] it is sufficient to demonstrate this separately for each argument.

1.2. *Continuity of wp in R*

The introduction of $\perp$ forces one to define an appropriate approximation-relation $\leq$ between relations as considered in definition 1.2. above. Such a definition is provided by EGLI [8], and PLOTKIN [14] (who attributes it to MILNER). In both publications, a relation is described by a function of inputs to nonempty *sets* of outputs. First an approximation relation $\leq_{E-M}$, the Egli-Milner order, is defined between these sets of outputs :

DEFINITION 1.4. *Let* V_1 *and* V_2 *be subsets of* $D\cup\{\perp\}$. *Then* $V_1 \leq_{E-M} V_2$ *just in case* (i) *if* $\perp \in V_1$ *then* $V_1 - \{\perp\} \subseteq$ *(set-theoretical inclusion!)* V_2, *and* (ii) *if* $\perp \notin V_1$ *then* $V_1 = V_2$. □

Remark : An intuitive justification of $\leq_{E-M}$ is given in section 1.3. □

It can be checked that $\leq_{E-M}$ is a complete partial order ; e.g., let $\{V_i\}_{i\in N}$ be a collection of sets satisfying $V_i \leq_{E-M} V_{i+1}$, then its least upper bound $\bigvee_{i=0}^{\infty} V_i$ exists : if $\perp \in V_i$ for all $i \in N$ then $\bigvee_{i=0}^{\infty} V_i = \bigcup_{i=0}^{\infty} V_i$ (set-theoretical union!), otherwise, if $\perp \notin V_{i_0}$, where i_0 is the smallest such index i, by definition $V_{i_0} = V_{i_0+1} = \ldots = V_{i_0+n} = \ldots$, $n \in N$, and hence $\bigvee_{i=0}^{\infty} V_i = V_{i_0}$.

Secondly, the complete partial order $\leq$ between functions R with these output sets as values is defined by : $R_1 \leq R_2$ iff, for all inputs x, $R_1(x) \leq_{E-M} R_2(x)$.

Next we prove that wp is continuous in R. For all R considered in definition 1.2. wp(R) denotes a transformation of total predicates ; hence we first need a complete partial order for total predicates.

DEFINITION 1.5. *Let* p *and* q *be total predicates over* $D\cup\{\perp\}$. *Then* $p \leq q$ *just in case* $(p(x) \rightarrow q(x))$ *is* true *for all* x. □

Remark : Alternatively, {false, true} is considered as the (trivially) complete lattice $\emptyset$ ordered by false $\sqsubseteq$ true. Then it is clear that the least upper bound $\bigvee_{i=0}^{\infty} p_i$ of a chain $p_i \leq p_{i+1}$, $i\in N$, can be computed elementwise. □

Let $\{R_i\}_{i\in N}$ satisfy $R_i \leq R_{i+1}$, $i\in N$. Since $wp(\bigvee_{i\in N} R_i) = \bigvee_{i\in N} wp(R_i) \Longleftrightarrow$ for all p, $wp(\bigvee R_i)(p) = \bigvee wp(R_i)(p) \Longleftrightarrow$ for all p and x, $wp(\bigvee R_i)(p)(x) = \bigvee wp(R_i)(p)(x)$, two cases occur :

(a) $\perp \in R_i(x)$ for all $i\in N$. Then $\perp \in (\bigvee R_i)(x)$ and $wp(\bigvee R_i)(p)(x)$ = false = $wp(R_i)(p)(x)$, for $i\in N$. Thus $\bigvee wp(R_i)(p)(x)$ = false.

(b) $\perp \notin R_{i_0}(x)$, with i_0 the smallest such index i. Then $(\vee R_i)(x) = R_{i_0}(x)$ and $wp(\vee R_i)(p)(x) = wp(R_{i_0})(p)(x)$; as $R_{i_0}(x) = R_{i_0+n}(x)$, $n\in N$, and $wp(R_i)(p)(x) =$ $\underline{false}$ for $i<i_0$, $\vee wp(R_i^0)(p)(x) = wp(R_{i_0}^0)(p)(x)$ follows.

1.3. *Continuity of wp in p*

As can be checked, wp is *monotone* in p. However, wp is not necessarily continuous in p : Let $R(x) = N$ and $p_i(y) = y \leq i$, $i \in N$; then $p_i \leq p_{i+1}$, $i \in N$, and $\overset{\infty}{\underset{i=0}{\vee}} p_i = \lambda y.\underline{true}$; hence $wp(R)(\vee p_i)(x) = \underline{true} \neq \underline{false} = wp(R)(p_i)(x) = (\vee wp(R)(p_i))(x)$. With this example in mind, we ask ourselves, as Dijkstra did in [7] : "*Are such relations R whose non-determinism is unbounded in some points* x *and who satisfy* $\perp \notin R(x)$ *indeed computed by programs ?*"

Our assumptions are that (1) elementary statements are bounded in their non-determinism, and (2) the non-deterministic choice operator $\cup$ is binary (,e.g., $\overset{\infty}{\underset{i=0}{\cup}} T_i$ is no programming construct). Then the answer to the above question is NO (cf. [7]) : *Since under our assumptions all computation sequences for a given input* x *can be ordered as a finitary tree, by König's lemma an infinite number of outputs (nodes) is only possible if an infinite computation sequence occurs in that tree, i.e., if* $\perp \in R(x)$ (*see* PLOTKIN [14]) ! Therefore, in our example above $N \subseteq R(x)$ dictates $R(x) = N\cup\{\perp\}$ if R is to be programmable.

And if we restrict ourselves in definition 1.2. to programmable relations R, i.e., $|R(x)| = N$ *implies* $\perp \in R(x)$, continuity of wp in p can be proved indeed, cf. DIJKSTRA [7].

Intuitive justification of $\leq_{E-M}$: Let P be a recursive procedure with body $\mathbf{T}(P)$ built up from elementary statements with finitely bounded non-determinism, and P(x) be infinite. Then $\perp \in P(x)$ follows, and $wp(P)(q)(x) = \underline{false}$, irrespective of q. Let $\Omega = \lambda x.\perp$, then $P = \overset{\infty}{\underset{i=0}{\vee}} T^{(i)}$, where $T^{(0)} = \Omega$ and $T^{(i+1)} = T(T^{(i)})$(;$T^{(i)}$ describes the I/O behaviour of P restricted ro recursion depth $\leq i$). By continuity of wp, $wp(P) = wp(\overset{\infty}{\underset{i=0}{\vee}} T^{(i)}) = \overset{\infty}{\underset{i=0}{\vee}} wp(T^{(i)})$, since $T^{(i)} \leq T^{(i+1)}$, $i \in N$. Thus $wp(P)(q)(x) = \underline{false}$ is already evident for all finite approximations T^i to P since $wp(T^i)(q)(x) = \underline{false}$ irrespective of q. Hence $\perp \in T^i(x)$, $i \in N$.

In this light, the intuitive meaning of $\perp$ becomes : "*Given more time, new values may still be computed, for the machine hasn't stopped calculating yet.*" Using this conception, the Egli-Milner order captures exactly that a to-some-recursion-depth *truncated* set of outputs V_1 with $\perp \in V_1$ may be still improved to a set V_2 with $V_1 - \{\perp\} \subseteq V_2$, by increasing the recursion depth, but that if $\perp \notin V_1$ the information is perfect already, and therefore machine calculation stopped (cf. EGLI [8]).

1.4. *Continuity of wp in x*

Since $D\cup\{\perp\}$ is just considered as a flat lattice, for $y \in D$ the only element x s.t. $x \sqsubseteq y$ is $x = \perp$; as $wp(R)(p)(\perp) = \underline{false}$, and $\underline{false} \sqsubseteq \underline{true}$ in $\emptyset$, the result follows.

Summary : If in definition 1.2. the relations R are considered as functions of inputs to sets of outputs satisfying *if* R(x) *is infinite then* $\perp \in R(x)$, then wp defined by $\lambda R.\lambda p.\lambda x.\forall y(y \in R(x) \rightarrow (p(y) \wedge \neg (y=\perp)))$ is continuous in its arguments.

2. SOME PROGRAMMING CONSTRUCTS AND THEIR RELATION WITH WP

2.1. *Some programming constructs*

2.1.1. *Syntax.* Elementary statement constants are denoted by A, A_1, A_2,..., relation variables by X, X_1, X_2,..., and predicate constants for conditionals by r, r_1, r_2, ... From these, composite constructs T, called *schemes*, are formed using composition ";", non-deterministic choice "$\cup$", conditionals "<u>if</u> ... <u>then</u> ... <u>else</u> ... <u>fi</u>", and least fixed point variable binding operators μ ... [...] in order to express recursion ; a typical example of a scheme is

μX[<u>if</u> r <u>then</u> A_1 ; X ; A_2 ; X ; A_3 <u>else</u> A_4 <u>fi</u> $\cup$ A_5].

2.1.2. *Semantics*. Let D be some domain then

(i) *elementary constants* are interpreted by sets V s.t. $\{(\perp,\perp)\} \subseteq V \subseteq D\times D \cup \{(\perp,\perp)\}$ and $\{y|(x,y) \in V\}$ is finite for all $x \in D$, and

(ii) *variables* by sets V s.t. $\{(\perp,\perp)\} \subseteq V \subseteq D\times D \cup (D\cup\{\perp\}) \times \{\perp\}$ and if $\{y|(x,y) \in V\}$ is infinite then $(x,\perp) \in V$, for all $x \in D$;

(iii) *composition* is interpreted as relational composition : $(x,z) \in T_1 ; T_2$ iff $\exists y[(x,y) \in T_1$ and $(y,z) \in T_2]$, *non-deterministic choice* as union of relations, and *conditionals by*: $(x,y) \in$ <u>if</u> r <u>then</u> T_1 <u>else</u> T_2 <u>fi</u> iff (a) r(x) is undefined and $y = \perp$, or (b) r(x) = <u>true</u> and $(x,y) \in T_1$, or (c) r(x) = <u>false</u> and $(x,y) \in T_2$, with r denoting (an arbitrary *predicate constant* denoting) a partial predicate over D.

(iv) $\mu X[T(x)]$ with X denoting an arbitrary relation variable, is interpreted as the least fixed point of the transformation $X \mapsto T(X)$.

2.1.3. As is wellknown, $\mu X[T(X)] = \bigcup_{i=0}^{\infty} T^{(i)}$ with $T^{(i)} \leq T^{(i+1)}$, and $T^{(i)}$ defined in def. 1.3, see, e.g., de BAKKER [2]. I feel free to switch from a relation R as subset of values of some cartesian product $D_1\times D_2$, to a function R from $D_1\cup\{\perp\}$ to nonempty subsets of $D_2\cup\{\perp\}$, made total by using $\{\perp\}$ as value for R(x) in case in the relational picture $\{y|(x,y) \in R\}$ is empty (; i.e., first the relation is made total, and then its functional description is considered). Also I shall blur the distinction between operational body-replacement reasoning about a recursive procedure P with body T(P), and mathematical least fixed point reasoning using $\mu X[T(X)]$, since the two are in accord (,e.g., see de ROEVER [16]). Indeed, one can justify operational reasoning about $\mu X[T(X)]$, a point well brought forward in GORDON [9].

2.2. ... *and their relation with wp*

The following properties can be checked :

(i) $wp(T_1;T_2) = wp(T_1) \circ wp(T_2)$, with "o" denoting functional composition, ... (2.1.)

(ii) $wp(T_1 \cup T_2) = \lambda q.wp(T_1)(q) \wedge wp(T_2)(q)$, abbreviated to $wp(T_1) \wedge wp(T_2)$,... (2.2.)

(iii) $wp(\underline{if}\ r\ \underline{then}\ T_1\ \underline{else}\ T_2\ \underline{fi}) = \lambda q.((r^+ \wedge wp(T_1)(q) \vee (r^- \wedge wp(T_2)(q)))$,
abbreviated to $(r^+ \wedge wp(T_1) \vee (r^- \wedge wp(T_2))$, with (r^+,r^-) as defined in def. 1.3. ...(2.3)

Using a suggestion of WADSWORTH's, $wp(\mu X[T(X)])$ can be expressed as the least fixed point of a transformation predicate transformers ; the general case should be clear from the following example :

Let $T(X) \equiv \underline{if}\ r\ \underline{then}\ A_1 ; X ; A_2 ; X ; A_3\ \underline{else}\ A_4\ \underline{fi} \cup A_5$.

Then $wp(T(X)) = ((r^+ \wedge wp(A_1) o wp(X) o wp(A_2) o wp(X) o wp(A_3)) \vee (r^- \wedge wp(A_4))) \wedge wp(A_5)$

Since $\wedge$, $\vee$ and o denote continuous operations, we may consider the least fixed point $\mu\tilde{X}[\tilde{T}(\tilde{X})]$ of the continuous transformation

$$\tilde{X} \mapsto \underbrace{((r^+ \wedge wp(A_1) o \tilde{X} o wp(A_2) o \tilde{X} o wp(A_3)) \vee (r^- \wedge wp(A_4))) \wedge wp(A_5)}_{\tilde{T}(\tilde{X})}$$

between predicate transformers.

Let $\tilde{\Omega} \underset{DEF}{=} \lambda p.\lambda x.\underline{false}$, $\tilde{T}^{(0)} \underset{DEF}{=} \tilde{\Omega}$ and $\tilde{T}^{(j+1)} = \tilde{T}(\tilde{T}^{(j)})$. Then $\tilde{T}^{(i)} = wp(T^{(i)})$ can be proved by induction on i. Hence $wp(\mu X[T(X)]) = wp(\bigvee_{i=0}^{\infty} T^{(i)}) = \bigvee_{i=0}^{\infty} \tilde{T}^{(i)} = \mu\tilde{X}[\tilde{T}(\tilde{X})]$ follows..(2.4)

3. EXPRESSING TOTAL CORRECTNESS OF RECURSIVE PROCEDURES BY INDUCTIVE ASSERTION PATTERNS

3.1. *Introduction*

Suppose $p \leq wp(\underbrace{\mu X[\underline{if}\ r\ \underline{then}\ A_1 ; X ; A_2 ; X ; A_3\ \underline{else}\ A_4\ \underline{fi}]}_{\mu T})(q)$ ... (3.1)

holds for some interpretation with domain D. Then the problem posed, and answered, in this section is : "*How can* (3.1) *be expressed by inductive assertions without using least fixed point operators ?*"

If we could find predicates p_0, q_0, p_0', q_0', p_1, q_1, p_2, q_2, s.t.

$$\left.\begin{array}{l} \text{(i) } p \leq r^+ \vee r^-, \\ \text{(ii) } p \wedge r^+ \leq p_0,\ p_0 \leq wp(A_1)(p_1),\ p_1 \leq wp(\mu T)(q_1),\ q_1 \leq wp(A_2)(p_2), \\ \qquad p_2 \leq wp(\mu T)(q_2),\ q_2 \leq wp(A_3)(q_0),\ q_0 \leq q \text{ and} \\ \text{(iii) } p \wedge r^- \leq p_0',\ p_0' \leq wp(A_4)(q_0'),\ q_0' \leq q, \end{array}\right\} (3.2)$$

are satisfied, (3.1) follows, since

$p_0 \leq wp(A_1)(p_1) \leq$ (monotonicity of wp in 2nd argument) $wp(A_1)(wp(\mu T)(q_1))$
$\leq$ (id.)$wp(A_1)(wp(\mu T)(wp(A_2)(p_2))) \leq$ (id.)$wp(A_1)(wp(\mu T)(wp(A_2)(wp(\mu T)(q_2))))$
$\leq$ (id.)$wp(A_1)(wp(\mu T)(wp(A_2)(wp(\mu T)(wp(A_3)(q_0))))) = wp(A_1;\mu T;A_2;\mu T;A_3)(q_0)$
$\leq$ (id.)$wp(A_1;\mu T;A_2;\mu T;A_3)(q)$, by (ii), and

$p_0' \leq wp(A_4)(q_0') \leq$ (id.)$wp(A_4)(q)$, by (iii), and hence, by (i),

$p \leq (r^+ \wedge wp(A_1;\mu T;A_2;\mu T;A_3)(q) \vee (r^- \wedge wp(A_4)(q)) =$ (by(2.3) and fixed point property) $wp(\mu T)(q)$.

However, the problem with $p_1 \leq wp(\mu T)(q_1)$ and $p_2 \leq wp(\mu T)(q_2)$ is that they still contain μT. If similarly as we related $\{p,q\}$ to $\{p_0,q_0,p_0',q_0',p_1,q_1,p_2,q_2\}$ we could also find predicates $\{p_{i0},q_{i0},p_{i0}',q_{i0}',p_{i1},q_{i1},p_{i2},q_{i2}\}$ related to $\{p_i,q_i\}$, i = 1,2, again (3.1) follows, with those two inclusions removed ; but then the same objection holds for $p_{ij} \leq wp(\mu T)(q_{ij})$, $i,j = 1.2$!

By systematically removing μT in this vein, we end up with the following infinite expansion, as observed in de BAKKER & MEERTENS [3] :

For all *indices* $\sigma \varepsilon \{0,1,2\}^*$,

$$\left.\begin{array}{l}\text{(i)}\ \ p=p_\varepsilon,\ q_\varepsilon=q,\ p_\sigma \leq r^+ \vee r^-,\\ \text{(ii)}\ p_\sigma \wedge r^+ \leq p_{\sigma 0},\ p_{\sigma 0} \leq wp(A_1)p_{\sigma 1},\ q_{\sigma 1} \leq wp(A_2)p_{\sigma 2},\ q_{\sigma 2} \leq wp(A_3)q_{\sigma 0},\ q_{\sigma 0} \leq q_\sigma,\\ \text{(iii)}\ p_\sigma \wedge r^- \leq p'_{\sigma 0},\ p'_{\sigma 0} \leq wp(A_4)q'_{\sigma 0},\ q'_{\sigma 0} \leq q_\sigma.\end{array}\right\} \quad (3.3)$$

QUESTION : If we can find predicates p_σ, p'_σ and q_σ, q'_σ for $\sigma\varepsilon\{0,1,2\}^*$, satisfying (3.3), then what does that imply ?

ANSWER : It eliminates the possibility for inputs x s.t. p(x)=true that computation of $\mu T(x)$ is undefined because at some *finite* recursion depth r, A_1, A_2, A_3, or A_4 are undefined in some intermediate state ; just following the elementary computations by the corresponding assertions of (3.3) guarantees that all elementary transitions are well-defined, and that, in case of termination, the output satisfies q.

QUESTION : What about the global problem of infinite regression due to an infinite number of inner recursive calls ?

ANSWER : First define well-foundedness of a relation R in x as follows :

DEFINITION 3.1 *Let* $\{\langle\perp,\perp\rangle\} \subseteq R \subseteq D\times D \cup (D\cup\{\perp\}) \times \{\perp\}$, *and* $x \varepsilon D$. *Then* R *is well-founded in* x *iff there exists no infinite sequence* $\{x_i\}_{i=0}^{\infty}$ s.t. $x=x_0$, $(x_i, x_{i+1}) \varepsilon R$ *and* $x_i \neq \perp$, $i \varepsilon N$.□

Then infinite regression can be eliminated by requiring that $A_1 \cup A_1;\mu T;A_2$ is well-founded in those x s.t. p(x) holds, since $A_1 \cup A_1;\mu T;A_2$ describes *all* possible state-transformations in between a call of μT and the constituent inner recursive calls of μT. □

In (3.2) the infinite expansion applies to $p_i \leq wp(\mu T)q_i$, i=1,2. When do we need p_1 ? After the transformation A_1 in-between-a-recursive-call-and-some-constituent-inner-recursive-call has been performed. When do we need p_2 ? After the transformation $A_1;\mu T;A_2$ in-between-a-recursive-call-and-some-constituent-inner-recursive-call has been performed. Thus, the transitions of p to p_1, p_1 to p_{11}, and p_2 to p_{21}, are related to A_1, and the transitions of p to p_2, p_1 to p_{12}, and p_2 to p_{22} are related to $A_1;\mu T;A_2$. This can be mathematically expressed by introducing *index-transformations* f, g, h and i, and rewriting (3.3) as follows, cf. de BAKKER & MEERTENS [3] :

$$\begin{array}{l}\text{(i)}\ \ p=p_\varepsilon,\ q_\varepsilon=q,\ p_\sigma \leq r^+ \vee r^-,\\ \text{(ii)}\ p_\sigma \wedge r^+ \leq p_{f(\sigma)},\ p_{f(\sigma)} \leq wp(A_1)p_{g(\sigma)},\ q_{g(\sigma)} \leq wp(A_2)p_{h(\sigma)},\ q_{h(\sigma)} \leq wp(A_3)q_{f(\sigma)},\\ \qquad q_{f(\sigma)} \leq q_\sigma,\\ \text{(iii)}\ p_\sigma \wedge r^- \leq p_{i(\sigma)},\ p_{i(\sigma)} \leq wp(A_4)q_{i(\sigma)},\ q_{i(\sigma)} \leq q_\sigma.\end{array}$$

Now, if we could transfer the well-foundedness of the state-transformation $A_1 \cup A_2;\mu T;A_2$ to well-foundedness of the index-information $\lambda\sigma.f(\sigma)\vee g(\sigma)\vee h(\sigma)\vee i(\sigma)$, we would have eliminated infinite regression. However, the problem with the in (3.3) suggested choices for f, g, h and i is that the latter expression is not well-founded in any $\sigma\varepsilon\{0,1,2\}^*$. We must therefore look for another index set for which well-foundedness of these index-transformations can be made to hold :

If we find an index set I, partial index-transformations f, g, h, i : $I\to I$, parametrized (or indexed) predicates $\pi,\kappa : I\to(D\to\{\underline{true},\underline{false}\})$, and a partial mapping $\sum : D\to I$ (in order to find an index to start with) satisfying :

$$\left.\begin{array}{ll}
(A_1) & \text{if } p(x)=\underline{true} \text{ then } \sum(x) \text{ is defined and } \pi(\sum(x))(x) \text{ holds, and similarly} \\
 & \kappa(\sum(x))(y) \text{ implies } q(y), \\
(A_2) & \text{(i)}\ \ \pi(\sigma) \leq r^+ \vee r^-, \\
 & \text{(ii)}\ \pi(\sigma)\wedge r^+ \leq \pi(f(\sigma)),\ \pi(f(\sigma)) \leq wp(A_1)\pi(g(\sigma)),\ \kappa(g(\sigma)) \leq wp(A_2)\pi(h(\sigma)), \\
 & \qquad \kappa(h(\sigma)) \leq wp(A_3)\kappa(f(\sigma)),\ \kappa(f(\sigma)) \leq \kappa(\sigma), \\
 & \text{(iii)}\ \pi(\sigma)\wedge r^- \leq \pi(i(\sigma)),\ \pi(i(\sigma)) \leq wp(A_4)\kappa(i(\sigma)),\ \kappa(i(\sigma)) \leq \kappa(\sigma), \\
 & \qquad \text{for all } \sigma\varepsilon I, \\
(A_3) & \text{such that } \lambda\sigma.f(\sigma)\vee g(\sigma)\vee h(\sigma)\vee i(\sigma) \text{ is well-founded on } \{\sum(x)\mid p(x)\},
\end{array}\right\} \quad (3.4)$$

we have succeeded in expressing (3.1) without using least fixed point operators. This can be understood as follows :

-(A_1) guarantees that execution of μT in x with p(x)=<u>true</u> can be parallelled by finding a starting predicate $\pi(\sum(x))$ satisfied in x, and similarly the fact that $(\kappa(\sum(x))(y)\to q(y))$ holds implies for the on the index level step-by-step reflected calculation of the state-transformation level that ending with $\kappa(\sum(x))$ satisfied implies q.

-(A_2) guarantees that, once the starting predicate $\pi(\sum(x))$ is satisfied, the encountered intermediate predicates $\pi(\sigma)$ and $\kappa(\sigma)$ are satisfied, and the encountered elementary state-transformations or tests do not lead to undefined results (,p(x)=<u>true</u>).

-(A_3) prohibits infinite regression by global means when starting with index $\sum(x)$ s.t. p(x) holds.

Since *partial* index-transformations are involved in expressing (A_2), caution must be exercised in interpreting (A_2) ; e.g., satisfaction of $\pi(f(\sigma)) \leq wp(A_1)\pi(g(\sigma))$ implies that for all $x\varepsilon D$ and $\sigma\varepsilon I$, if $f(\sigma)$ is well-defined and $\pi(f(\sigma))x$ holds then $g(\sigma)$ is well-defined and $(wp(A_1)\pi(g(\sigma)))x$ holds. Connoisseurs should justify the following version of (A_2) :

$\pi \leq r^+\vee r^-$, $\pi\wedge r^+ \leq \pi\circ f$, $\pi\circ f \leq wp(A_1)\circ\pi\circ g$, $\kappa\circ g \leq wp(A_2)\circ\pi\circ h$,
$\kappa\circ h \leq wp(A_3)\circ\kappa\circ f$, $\kappa\circ f \leq \kappa$, $\pi\wedge r^- \leq \pi\circ i$, $\pi\circ i \leq wp(A_4)\circ\kappa\circ i$, $\kappa\circ i \leq \kappa$.

Thus the infinite assertion pattern (A_2) can be expressed using a finite number of inclusions by increasing the function level.

The proof of *validity* of the method, in particular that satisfaction of (3.4) implies satisfaction of (3.1), is omitted.

3.2. *Example*

The following provides an example of a total-correctness proof based on a simplified version of (3.4) :

EXAMPLE (modified - de BAKKER [1]) :Let $P(n,t)$ be defined by

$P \Leftarrow$ <u>if</u> $n>0$ <u>then</u> $n := n-1$; P ; $t := t+1$; P ; $n := n+1$ <u>else</u> <u>fi</u>

(P computes the number of necessary disc movements for the recursive solution of the Towers of Hanoi puzzle). We want to establish $P(n,t) = (n, t+2^n-1)$.

Let I consist of pairs (ν,τ) of natural numbers, define indexed predicates π and κ by $\pi(\sigma)(x)=\pi(\nu,\tau)(n,t)=\{n=\nu,t=\tau\}$, $\kappa(\sigma)(x)=\kappa(\nu,\tau)(n,t)=\{n=\nu,t=\tau+2^\nu-1\}$, define index-transformations Q_1 and Q_2 - one for each constituent inner recursive call of P's body - by $Q_1(\sigma)=Q_1(\nu,\tau)=(\nu-1,\tau)$, $Q_2(\sigma)=Q_2(\nu,\tau)=(\nu-1,\tau+2^{\nu-1})$, and define $\sum$ by $\sum(n,t)=(n,t)$.

Then the reader should verify the following :

(A_1) $\pi(\sum(n,t))(n,t)=$<u>true</u>, ($\kappa(\sum(\nu,\tau))(n,t)$ itself expresses the output predicate already),

(A_2) (i) $\pi(\nu,\tau)(n,t) \leq n>0 \vee n=0$,

(ii) $\pi(\nu,\tau)(n,t) \wedge n>0 \leq (wp(n:=n-1)\pi(\nu-1,\tau))(n,t)$,

$\kappa(\nu-1,\tau)(n,t) \leq (wp(t:=t+1)\pi(\nu-1,\tau+2^{\nu-1}))(n,t)$,

$\kappa(\nu-1,\tau+2^{\nu-1})(n,t) \leq (wp(n:=n+1)\kappa(\nu,\tau))(n,t)$,

(iii) $\pi(\nu,\tau) \wedge n=0 \leq (wp(Identity)\kappa(\nu,\tau))(n,t)$,

(A_3) $Q_1 \cup Q_2$ is well-founded on I.

Therefore we conclude that $P(n,t)=(n,t+2^n-1)$ holds.

3.3. *Adequacy (or completeness) of the proposed method*

Satisfaction of $p \leq wp(\mu X[T(X)])q$ -(3.1)- implies that each computation sequence of $\mu X[T(X)]$ starting in x with $p(x)=$<u>true</u> must terminate, in particular that they are *not infinite*. Since (the initial parts of) these sequences are made longer by going deeper into the recursion, this very fact prohibits infinite regression by an infinite number of inner recursive calls. The initial parts of these sequences therefore provide the basis for the looked-for domain of indices I ; define $\sum(x)$ by $\langle x\rangle$.

On the computational level, going one step deeper into recursion results in applying a state-transformation S_i describing a transition in between a recursive call and a constituent inner recursive call of the procedure body T : there is one such transition S_i for each textually contained inner recursive call of T, say N in all. With I as chosen above, on the index-transformation level these S_i, $i=1,..,N$, describe therefore all possible ways for lengthening a computation sequence $\langle x_0,\dots,x_k\rangle$ to $\langle x_0,\dots,x_k,S_i(x_k)\rangle$; hence we define the index-transformations Q_i essentially by, *provided* $S_i(x_k)$ *is defined*, $Q_i(\langle x_0,\dots,x_k\rangle)=\langle x_0,\dots,x_k,S_i(x_k)\rangle$, $i=1,\dots,N$. Then (3.1) guarantees well-foundedness of $\bigcup_{i=1}^{N} Q_i$ in one-element sequences $\langle x\rangle$ s.t. $p(x)$ holds.

The reader should check that satisfaction of (3.1) therefore implies that I, $\sum$, f, g, h and i, and π and κ defined below, satisfy (3.4) :

(i) $I \underset{\mathrm{DEF}}{=} (D \cup \{+,-\})^*$, $\sum : x \mapsto \langle x \rangle$.

(ii) *f, g, h and i are defined by :*

If $r(x_k)$ is <u>true</u> then $f(\langle x_0,\ldots,x_k \rangle)=\langle x_0,\ldots,x_k,+ \rangle$; if $A_1(x_k)$ is defined then $g(\langle x_0,\ldots,x_k \rangle)=\langle x_0,\ldots,x_k,A_1(x_k) \rangle$; if $A_2(\mu T(A_1(x_k)))$ is defined then $h(\langle x_0,\ldots,x_k \rangle)=\langle x_0,\ldots,x_k,A_2(\mu T(A_1(x_k))) \rangle$; and if $r(x_k)$ is <u>false</u> then $i(\langle x_0,\ldots,x_k \rangle)=\langle x_0,\ldots,x_k,- \rangle$; in all other cases the index-transformations are undefined.

(iii) *π and κ are defined by :*

$$\pi(\langle x_0,\ldots,x_k,(+/-)^*) \rangle)(x)=p(x_0) \wedge \left(\bigwedge_{i=1}^{k-1}(x_i,x_{i+1}) \in (A_1 \cup A_1;\mu T;A_2)\right) \wedge x=x_k \wedge (r^+(x_k)/r^-(x_k))^*)$$

and

$$\kappa(\langle x_0,\ldots,x_k,(+/-)^*) \rangle)(x)=p(x_0) \wedge \left(\bigwedge_{i=0}^{k-1}(x_i,x_{i+1}) \in (A_1 \cup A_1;\mu T;A_2)\right) \wedge (x_k,x) \in \mu T \wedge (r^+(x_k)/r^-(x_k))^*),$$

and if $x_k \notin \{+,-\}$ then

$$\pi(\langle x_0,\ldots,x_k \rangle)(x)=p(x_0) \wedge \left(\bigwedge_{i=0}^{k-1}(x_i,x_{i+1}) \in (A_1 \cup A_1;\mu T;A_2)\right) \wedge x=x_k, \text{ and}$$

$$\kappa(\langle x_0,\ldots,x_k \rangle)(x)=p(x_0) \wedge \left(\bigwedge_{i=0}^{k-1}(x_i,x_{i+1}) \in (A_1 \cup A_1;\mu T;A_2)\right) \wedge (x_k,x) \in \mu T.$$

4. REFERENCES

[1] de BAKKER, *Fixed pt.appr. in sem.*, Found.Cptr.Sc., MCT63, Math.Centre, A'dam (75).

[2] de BAKKER, *Termination of nondet.progr.*, Proc.3rd coll.Aut., Lang.& Progr., Edinb.(76).

[3] de BAKKER & MEERTENS, *Completeness ind.assertion method*, JCSS <u>11</u>,3 (75).

[4] de BAKKER & de ROEVER, *Calculus for rec.progr.schemes*, Proc.1st coll.Aut., Lang. & Progr., North-H. (72).

[5] BURSTALL, *Prog.proving as hand sim. with little induction*, Inf. Processing 74, North-H.

[6] DIJKSTRA, *Guarded commands*, CACM <u>18</u>,8 (75).

[7] DIJKSTRA, *A discipline in programming*, Pr.Hall (76).

[8] EGLI, *A math. model for non-det. comp.*, Forsch. Inst. ETH Zurich (75).

[9] GORDON, *Op. reasoning & den. sem.*, <u>in</u> Proving & improving programs, IRIA (75).

[10] HITCHCOCK & PARK, *Induction rules and proofs of termination*, <u>in</u> (see[4]).

[11] HOARE, *A model for progr. lang. sem.*, corrected draft, jan.76, Belfast.

[12] HOARE, *Some prop. of non-det. comp.*, manuscript, march 76, Belfast.

[13] MILNER, *Processes : a math. model for comp. agents*, Proc. Bristol 73 Logic Coll, North-H.

[14] PLOTKIN, *A powerdomain construction*, Dept. Art. Int., Univ. of Edinb. (75).

[15] de ROEVER, *Rec. progr. schemes : sem. & proof th.*, MCT, Math.Centre, A'dam (76).

[16] de ROEVER, *Rec. & par. mech. : ax. approach*, Proc. 2nd coll. Aut.,Lang & Progr., Springer C.Sc. 14 (74).

[17] SCOTT, *Continuous lattices*, Proc.7th Dalhousie Conf., Springer Lect. Notes.

[18] SCOTT, Private communication (75).

[19] STRACHEY & WADSWORTH, *Continuations*, Techn. Monogr. PRG-11, Progr. Res. Group, Oxford (74).

---

*) Whichever case applies.

CONTEXT-FREE PROGRAMMED GRAMMARS AND ETOL SYSTEMS

G. Rozenberg
Department of Mathematics
University of Antwerp,UIA
Wilrijk 2610 Belgium

D. Vermeir
Department of Applied Economics
University of Leuven,KUL
Leuven Belgium

ABSTRACT

The relationship between ETOL systems and context-free programmed grammars is investigated. The characterization of the class of ETOL languages, and its main subclasses (EOL, EDTOL, EDOL) in terms of various subclasses of the class of context-free programmed grammars is provided. Then an extension of the notion of an ETOL system is investigated. In this way a characterization of the class of context-free programmed languages is provided.

0. INTRODUCTION

The main feature that distinguishes L systems (see, e.g. [2] and [5] from Chomsky grammars (see, e.g., [7]) is that whereas in the former case the rewriting is done in the parallel fashion (meaning that all occurences of all symbols in a string are rewritten in a single derivation step), in the later case it is done sequentially (only one occurence of one symbol is rewritten in a single derivation step).

Trying to understand the essential differences between the nature of parallel and sequential rewriting one compares various "representative" classes of both kinds (see, e.g., [1], [2], [4], [8] and [9]). The class of ETOL systems forms perhaps the central class among various families of L systems without interactions (see, e.g., [6]). It is well known (see [4]) that ETOL systems are strictly more powerful in their language-generative power than context-free grammars. Hence the natural trend to locate (as precisely as possible) ETOL systems among various extensions of context free grammars.

Context-free programmed grammars (see [3]) are undoubtlessly among the most natural and interesting extensions of context free grammars (see also [7]). They are still sequential in nature, meaning that in a single derivation step only one symbol is rewritten.

It was proved in [4] that the class of ETOL languages is strictly included in the class of (Λ-free) context-free programmed grammars. Then it was noticed in [10] that the class of ETOL systems is included even in the class of unconditional transfer context-free programmed grammars.

This paper examines closely the relationship between context-free programmed grammars and ETOL systems. We concentrate on two questions :

1) What restriction should be put on the generating mechanism of context free

programmed grammars so as to equalize their language generating power with the language generating power of ETOL systems?

2) What extension should be added to the generating mechanism of ETOL systems so as to equalize their language generating power with the language generating power of context-free programmed grammars?

The answer to the first question is provided by Theorem 1 and the answer to the second by Theorem 3. Thus we get the feeling that there is a quite natural relationship between ETOL systems and context-free programmed grammars.

Because of the restrictions on the size of this paper, we state here only our main results and the proofs are omitted. The full version of this paper will be published elsewhere.

I. PRELIMINARIES

We assume the reader to be familiar with the rudiments of formal language theory (e.g. in the scope of [7]) and with the basics of L systems theory (e.g. in the scope of [2]). In particular the reader should be acquainted with the notions of a context free programmed grammar (see also [3]) and of an ETOL system (see also [4]).

A context-free programmed grammar (abbreviated as c.f.p. grammar) is written in the form $G = \langle V_N, V_T, P, S \rangle$ where V_N is its nonterminal alphabet, V_T its terminal alphabet, P its set of rules and S its axiom. If $\pi = (i),\ A \rightarrow \alpha,\ S(i),\ F(i)$ is a rule in G then we reffer to $A \rightarrow \alpha$ as the production of π (and we write $Prod(\pi) = A \rightarrow \alpha$ or $Prod(i) = A \rightarrow \alpha$). We use $LH(\pi)$ or $LH(i)$ to denote A and $RH(\alpha)$ or $RH(i)$ to denote α. We also say that π rewrites A.

An ETOL system is written in the form $G = \langle V, \mathcal{R}, S, \Sigma \rangle$ where V is its alphabet, $\mathcal{R}$ its set of tables, S its axiom and Σ its terminal (target) alphabet.

We use $\mathcal{L}(ETOL)$, $\mathcal{L}(EDTOL)$ and $\mathcal{L}(EOL)$ to denote the classes of ETOL, EDTOL and EOL languages respectively. We use $\mathcal{L}(CFP)$ and $\mathcal{L}(UCFP)$ to denote the classes of context-free programmed and unconditional transfer context-free programmed (abbreviated u.t.c.f.p.) languages. When $\mathcal{L}(X)$ denotes the class of languages generated by type X c.f.p. grammars then we write $\mathcal{L}_\Lambda(X)$ to denote the usual Λ-free restriction. Also all equalities between languages considered in this paper are "Λ-adjusted" meaning that we write $K_1 = K_2$ if $K_1 \cup \{\Lambda\} = K_2 \cup \{\Lambda\}$.

II. ITERATIVE CONTEXT-FREE PROGRAMMED GRAMMARS

Now we aim at characterizing ETOL languages by c.f.p. grammars. We shall put certain restrictions on c.f.p. grammars which will "adjust" their language generative power so that it will be equal to the language generative power of ETOL systems.

Definition 1. Let G be a c.f.p. grammar and let $\pi = (i),\ A \rightarrow \alpha,\ S(i),\ F(i)$ be a rule in G. We say that π is label-iterative if $S(i) = \{i\}$.

We shall use Ind(A) to denote the set of labels of all rules which are rewriting A and which are not label-iterative.

Definition 2. Let G be a c.f.p. grammar. We say that G is iterative if

1) Whenever (i), $A \to \alpha$, S(i), F(i) and (j), $A \to \beta$, S(j),F(j) are rules in G which are not label-iterative then S(i) = S(j) = Ind(A) and F(i) = F(j).
2) Whenever (i), $A \to \alpha$, S(i), F(i) is a rule in G and F(i) contains the label of a rule (k),$B \to \beta$, S(k), F(k) which is not label-iterative, then Ind(B) $\subseteq$ F(i).

If G is an iterative c.f.p. grammar then we refer to all its rules that are not label-iterative as symbol iterative. If π = (i), $A \to \alpha$, S(i), F(i) is a symbol-iterative rule then we also say that π is an A-iterative rule. Since, for a given A, all A-iterative rules have the same success and the same failure field we can reffer to them using S(A) and F(A) respectively.

We use $\mathcal{L}$(CFP-ITER) to denote the class of languages generated by iterative c.f.p. grammars.

Definition 3. A c.f.p. grammar is called label-iterative if it consists of label-iterative rules only.

We use $\mathcal{L}$(CFP-LITER) to denote the class of languages generated by label-iterative c.f.p. grammars.

Definition 4. An iterative c.f.p. grammar G is called almost circular if its nonterminals can be ordered as a chain $A_1, \ldots, A_n$ and then

1) The control of G is of the form

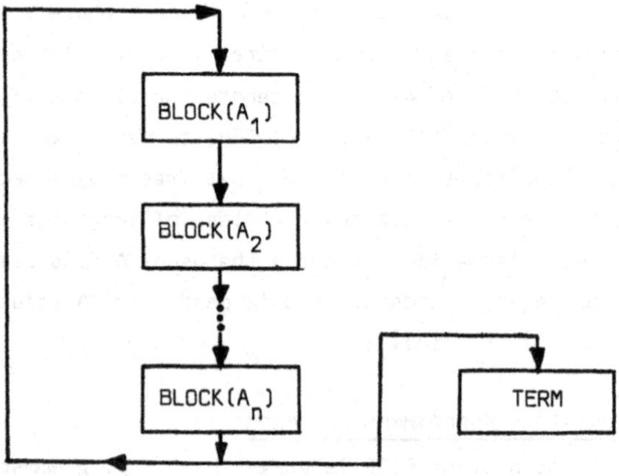

where each BLOCK(A_j) consists of either a single label-iterative rule or a set of A_j-iterative rules and TERM is a (may be empty) sequence of label-iterative rules with the productions of the form $A \to a$ where A is a nonterminal and a is a terminal.

2) If $A \to \alpha$ is the production of any rule in G then α does not contain an occurrence of A.

We use $\mathcal{L}$(CFP-ACITER) to denote the class of languages generated by almost circular c.f.p. grammars.

Definition 5. Let G be an almost circular iterative c.f.p. grammar with the control structure as follows

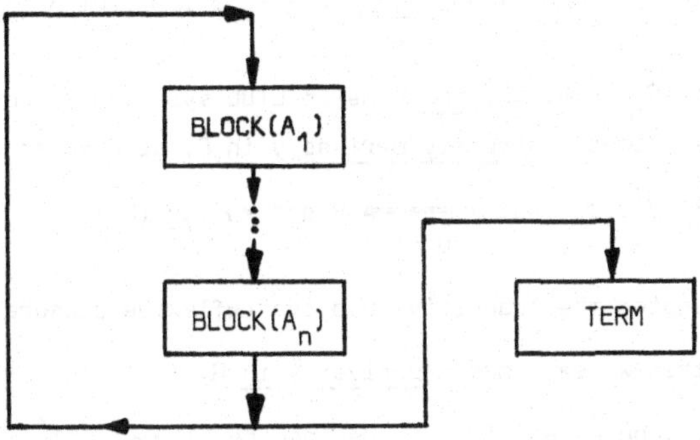

We say that G is deterministic if

1) for each $1 \leq j \leq n$, BLOCK(A_j) consists of a single label-iterative rule,
2) for each $1 \leq j \leq n$, if $A_j \to \alpha_j$ is the production of the rule from BLOCK(A_j) then α_j does not contain an occurrence of a terminal symbol,
3) if $A \to a$ and $B \to b$ are productions of different rules from TERM then $a \neq b$.

We use $\mathcal{L}$(CFP-DACITER) to denote the class of languages generated by deterministic almost circular c.f.p. grammars.

Theorem 1.

$\mathcal{L}$(CFP-ITER) = $\mathcal{L}_\Lambda$(CFP-ITER) = $\mathcal{L}$(ETOL) = $\mathcal{L}$(EPTOL)

$\mathcal{L}$(CFP-LITER) = $\mathcal{L}_\Lambda$(CFP-LITER) = $\mathcal{L}$(EDTOL) = $\mathcal{L}$(EPDTOL)

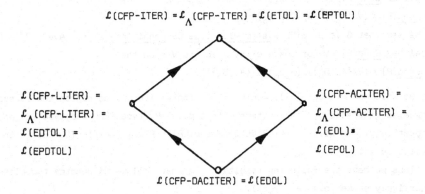

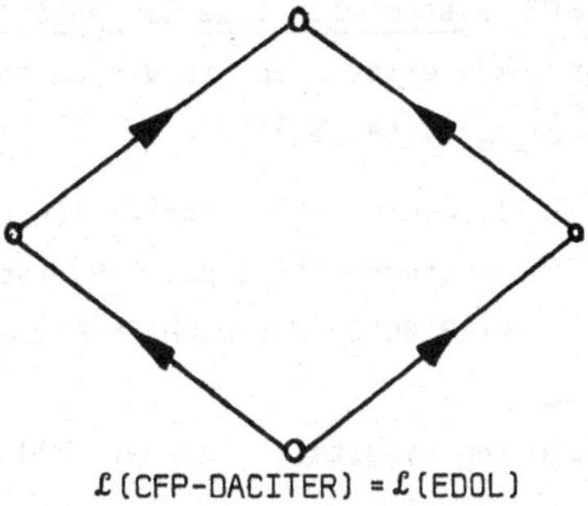

$\mathcal{L}$(CFP-ACITER) = $\mathcal{L}_\Lambda$(CFP-ACITER) = $\mathcal{L}$(EOL) = $\mathcal{L}$(EPOL)

$\mathcal{L}$(CFP-DACITER) = $\mathcal{L}$(EDOL)

III. ETOL SYSTEMS WITH CONDITIONS

Now we turn to our second question : what extension should be added to the generative mechanism of ETOL systems so as to equalize their language generative power with the language generative power of context-free programmed grammars?

To this aim we introduce the notion of an ETOL system with conditions.

Definition 6. An ETOL system with conditions is a construct $G = \langle V, \mathcal{R}, S, \Sigma, \underline{Cond} \rangle$ where $H = \langle V, \mathcal{R}, S, \Sigma \rangle$ is an ETOL system (called the underlying system of G and denoted by Und(G)) and Cond is a function from $\mathcal{R}$ into the set 2^{V^*} of languages over V.

Definition 7. Let $G = \langle V, \mathcal{R}, S, \Sigma, \underline{Cond} \rangle$ be an ETOL system with conditions.

1) Let $x, y \in V^*$. We say that x directly derives y in G, denoted as $x \underset{G}{\Rightarrow} y$, if there exists a table P in $\mathcal{R}$ such that $x \underset{Und(G)}{\overset{P}{\Longrightarrow}} y$ and $x \in \underline{Cond}(P)$

2) As usual $\underset{G}{\overset{*}{\Longrightarrow}}$ denotes the transitive and the reflexive closure of the relation $\underset{G}{\Longrightarrow}$. If $x \overset{*}{\Longrightarrow} y$ then we say that x derives y in G.

3) The language of G, denoted as L(G), is defined by $L(G) = \{x \in \Sigma^* : S \underset{G}{\overset{*}{\Longrightarrow}} x\}$.

Actually for purpose of this paper we will need very simple kind of conditions only. These are introduced in the next definition. Please note that all the types of conditions we consider are special cases of a very simple subclass of regular languages namely this of chain events of Yoeli (see [11]). We will see that already that simple conditions increase enormly the generative power of ETOL systems.

Definition 8. Let $G = \langle V, \mathcal{R}, S, \Sigma, \underline{Cond} \rangle$ be an ETOL system with conditions.

1) We say that G is an ETOL system with type STAR conditions if for every P in $\mathcal{R}$ there exists a subset V_P of V such that $\underline{Cond}(P) = V_P^*$.

2) We say that G is an ETOL system with type PROG conditions if for every P in $\mathcal{R}$ either $\underline{Cond}(P) = V^*$ or there exists a symbol A_P in V such that $\underline{Cond}(P) = (V/\{A_P\})^* \{A_P\} (V/\{A_P\})^*$.

3) We say that G is an ETOL system with type CS conditions if for every P in $\mathcal{R}$ either $\underline{Cond}(P) = V^*$ or there exist A_P, B_P in V such that $\underline{Cond}(P) = (V/\{A_P, B_P\})^* \{A_P B_P\} (V/\{A_P, B_P\})^*$.

We will use $\mathcal{L}$(ETOL-STAR), $\mathcal{L}$(ETOL-PROG) and $\mathcal{L}$(ETOL-CS) do denote the classes of languages generated by ETOL systems with type STAR, type PROG and type CS conditions respectively. We will use $\mathcal{L}$(EPTOL-STAR), $\mathcal{L}$(EPTOL-PROG) and $\mathcal{L}$(EPTOL-CS) in the obvious sense.

Thus we have the following results. (In what follows $\mathcal{RE}$ denotes the class of recursively enumerable languages).

Theorem 2. $\mathcal{L}$(ETOL-STAR) = $\mathcal{L}$(ETOL) = $\mathcal{L}$(EPTOL-STAR) = $\mathcal{L}$(EPTOL).

Theorem 3. 1) $\mathcal{L}$(CFP) = $\mathcal{L}$(EPTOL-PROG).

2) $\mathcal{RE}$ = $\mathcal{L}$(ETOL-PROG).

Theorem 4. 1) $\mathcal{L}$(CS) = $\mathcal{L}$(EPTOL-CS).

2) $\mathcal{RE}$ = $\mathcal{L}$(ETOL-CS).

REFERENCES

[1] A.Ehrenfeucht, G.Rozenberg and S.Skuym, A relationship between ETOL and EDTOL languages, to appear in Theoretical Computer Science.

[2] G.T.Herman and G.Rozenberg, Developmental systems and Languages, North Holland Publ. Comp. 1975.

[3] D.Rosenkrantz, Programmed grammars and classes of formal languages, J.Assoc. Comput. Mach., 16,107-131,1969.

[4] G.Rozenberg, Extension of tabled OL systems and languages, Int.J.Comp.Inf. Sciences, 2,311-334,1973.

[5] G.Rozenberg, A.Salomaa (eds.), L systems, Springer Verlag, 1974.

[6] G.Rozenberg, A.Salomaa, Mathematical theory of L systems, to appear in Progress in Information Processing, J.Ton (ed.).

[7] A.Salomaa, Formal Languages, Academic Press, 1975.

[8] A.Salomaa, Parallelism in rewriting systems, Lecture Notes in Computer Science No. 14, 523-533, Springer Verlag, 1974.

[9] S.Skyum, On decomposing languages defined by parallel devices, to appear in SIAM Journal on Computing.

[10] J.van Leeuwen, The membership question for ETOL languages is polynomially complete, Inf. Proceeding Letters, 3,138-143.

[11] M.Yoeli, Canonical representations of chain events, Information and Control, 8,180-189,1965.

CONTEXT-FREE ALGEBRA: A MATHEMATICAL DEVICE FOR COMPILER SPECIFICATION

Teodor Rus
I.T.C. Filiala Cluj,
Str.Soporului Nr.53,
3400 Cluj-Napoca, Rumania

§1. The lack of naturally in today man-machine communication is determined by imposing to the user the implemented languages by the constructor. To meet all the user's needs, the languages become very complex and hence the efficiency of the compilers and produced programs by compilers become very low and the lack of naturally in man-machine communication is growing up.

To remove the lack of naturally in man-machine communication, the computers wouldn't be equiped with imposed implemented languages, but they would be equiped with a natural tool for language specification and with an universal algorithm which acts on specified language by the natural tool and produces its compiler into machine language. On this way each user would have a chance to implement his natural language, according to his problems.

The natural tool for language specification can be get by a deeply mathematical study of the concept of language. A language has to be understood as a triple $\langle S,C,h \rangle$ where C is the language structure of contents or the language's semantics, S is the language structure of forms or expressions or the language's syntax and $h:S \longrightarrow C$ is an evaluation morphism.

Because the support of an algebraic structure with the purpose of semantics for a language has to be a very heterogeneous class of objects, we have to look for a heterogeneous algebraic structure, in short HAS, as natural tool for language specification.Then C would be such a HAS and S would be the free word HAS in the class of similarity determined by C.

To get such HAS we shall give first the concept of basis.

A basis for a HAS is a mechanism to specify HAS support and HAS operations. A basis can be itself a HAS.

The above concept of basis for a HAS guide us to the following HAS hierarchy:

i. An universal algebra $\mathcal{A} = \langle A, \Omega, \varphi : \Omega \longrightarrow N\rangle$ is a HAS of hierarchy order zero.

ii. Any HAS of hierarchy order i can be a basis for a HAS of hierarchy order i+i.

Examples of HAS.

a). Higgins's Σ - algebras [1] can be given by the following HAS hierarchy:

i. The chosen basis is an universal algebra $B = \langle I, \Omega, \varphi : \Omega \rightarrow N\rangle$

ii. A Σ - algebra is a triple $\mathcal{A} = \langle A, B, f\rangle$ where B is the chosen basis above.

The support A is specified by B as a family of sets indexed by I, $A = (A_i)_{i \in I}$. The operations on A are specified by the operations $\omega \in \Omega$ on I by means of the following rule:

To each $\omega \in \Omega$, $\varphi(\omega) = n$, i.e. $\omega : I^n \rightarrow I$ correspond a family of operations on A. If we denote this family by Σ_ω then

$$\Sigma_\omega = \left\{ f_{\omega_{i_1 i_2 \ldots i_n i}} : A_{i_1} \times A_{i_2} \times \ldots \times A_{i_n} \rightarrow A_i \,\middle|\, (i_1, i_2, \ldots, i_n) \in \in \mathrm{Domain}(\omega) \text{ and } i = \omega(i_1, i_2, \ldots, i_n) \right\}$$

Hence, an operation on A is determined by a triple $\langle n = \varphi(\omega), i_1 i_2 \ldots i_n i, \omega \rangle$ called operation scheme, where $(i_1, i_2, \ldots, i_n) \in \mathrm{Domain}(\omega)$ and $i = \omega(i_1, i_2, \ldots, i_n)$.

If Σ is the set of all operation scheme defined by the basis B then a Higgins Σ - algebra become a triple $\mathcal{A} = \langle A, \Sigma, f\rangle$ where A and Σ are specified by a given universal algebra as above.

b). The heterogeneous algebra considered by Birkhoff and Lipson [2] can be given by the following HAS hierarchy:

i. The chosen basis is an universal algebra together with a family of functions

$$B = \langle I, \Omega, \varphi : \Omega \rightarrow N, \gamma : \Omega \rightarrow I, \{ \tau_\omega : [1, 2, \ldots, \varphi(\omega) \rightarrow I\} \omega \in \Omega \rangle$$

ii. The next level of HAS hierarchy is a triple $\mathcal{A} = \langle A, B, f\rangle$ where the support A is specified by support of B as a family $A = (A_i)_{i \in I}$ and for each $\omega \in \Omega$, B specifies f_ω as an operation on A, namely

$$f_\omega : A_{\tau_\omega(1)} \times A_{\tau_\omega(2)} \times \ldots \times A_{\tau_\omega(\varphi(\omega))} \longrightarrow A_{\gamma(\omega)}$$

In this case the operator scheme Σ is the set of all triples

$$\langle n = \varphi(\omega), \tau_\omega(1) \ \tau_\omega(2) \ldots \tau_\omega(\varphi(\omega)) \gamma(\omega), \omega \rangle, \omega \in \Omega$$

and hence the Birkhoff&Lipson's heterogeneous algebras are the triples

$$\mathcal{A} = \langle A = (A_i)_{i \in I}, \Sigma, f \rangle$$

§2. A context-free algebra, used by us as natural tool for language specification is given by the following HAS hierarchy:

i. The chosen basis is a triple $B = \langle I, S, \mathcal{Z} \rangle$ where I and S are nonempty sets, $I \cap S = \emptyset$ and $\mathcal{Z}$ is a binary relation on $I^+ \times S^+ \cup \{\varepsilon\}$, i.e. $\mathcal{Z} \subseteq I^+ \times S^+ \cup \{\varepsilon\}$, such that if $(i,s) \in \mathcal{Z}$ then $\lambda(i) = \lambda(s)$ where is the function which associates to a word its length.

ii. A context-free algebra is a triple $\mathcal{A} = \langle A, B, f \rangle$ or if $\Sigma = \{ \langle n, i_1 i_2 \ldots i_n i_{n+1}, s_1 s_2 \ldots s_n s_{n+1} \rangle \mid (i_1 i_2 \ldots i_n i_{n+1}, s_1 s_2 \ldots s_n s_{n+1}) \in \mathcal{Z}, n \in N \cup \{o\} \}$ then a context-free algebra is a triple $\mathcal{A} = \langle A = (A_i)_{i \in I}, \Sigma, f \rangle$ where f associates to every $\sigma \in \Sigma$, $\sigma = \langle n, i_1 i_2 \ldots i_{n+1}, s_1 s_2 \ldots s_{n+1} \rangle$ a function

$$f_\sigma : A_{i_1} \times A_{i_2} \times \ldots \times A_{i_n} \longrightarrow A_{i_{n+1}}$$

called heterogeneous operation on A.

For $\sigma \in \Sigma$, $\sigma = \langle n, i_1 i_2 \ldots i_n i_{n+1}, s_1 s_2 \ldots s_n s_{n+1} \rangle$, $d(\sigma) = \{ i_1, i_2, \ldots, i_n \}$ is called domain, $t(\sigma) = \{ i_{n+1} \}$ is called codomain and $c(\sigma) = (s_1, s_2, \ldots, s_n, s_{n+1})$ is called state word or operation symbol distributed on its operands [3].

A basis $B = \langle I, S, \mathcal{Z} \rangle$ is finite if $I, S, \mathcal{Z}$ are finite sets.

Lemma 1. If $B = \langle I, S, \mathcal{Z} \rangle$ is a finite basis then it defines a CF-grammar.

Proof: The CF-grammar defined by B is $G_B = \langle V, V_t, P, V_n \rangle$ where:

$V_n = I$;

$V_t = S$; $V = V_n \cup V_t$

$P = \{ i \longrightarrow s_1 i_1 s_2 i_2 \ldots s_n i_n s_{n+1} \mid (i_1 i_2 \ldots i_n i, s_1 s_2 \ldots s_n s_{n+1}) \in \mathcal{Z} \}$

G_B constructed above is a CF-grammar accepting any nonterminal symbol as start symbol or axiom. In the next, by CF-grammar we shall understand such a grammar.

Lemma 2. Any CF-grammar $G = \langle V, V_t, P, V_n \rangle$ defines a finite basis B_G for a context-free algebra.

Proof: Let $B_G = \langle I, S, \mathcal{Z} \rangle$ be the defined basis by G. Then $I = V_n$, $S = \{ s_1, s_2, \ldots, s_{n+1} \mid A_{n+1} \rightarrow s_1 A_1 s_2 A_2 \ldots s_n A_n s_{n+1} \in P, s_i \in V_t^*, A_i \in V_n, i = 1, \ldots, n \}$

$\mathcal{E} = \{(A_1A_2\ldots A_{n+1}, s_1s_2\ldots s_{n+1}) \mid A_{n+1} \rightarrow s_1A_1s_2A_2\ldots s_nA_ns_{n+1} \in P$
$s_i \in V_t^*,\ A_i \in V_n,\ n = 1,2,\ldots,\ n+1\}$

__Theorem 1.__ If $G = \langle V, V_t, P, V_n \rangle$ is a CF-grammar and
$L(G) = \{ w \in V_t^* \mid \exists A \in V_n \ \&\ A \overset{*}{\Longrightarrow} w\}$
is the language specified by G, then L(G) is a context-free algebra specified by B_G.

__Proof:__ Let $[A] = \{x \in V_t^* \mid A \overset{*}{\Longrightarrow} x\}$ be the set of language sentences which are derived from A as start symbol. Then L(G) is a family of (not necessarly disjoint) sets indexed by V_n, $L(G) = ([A])_{A \in V_n}$
Hence L(G) can be viewed as a context-free algebra, namely
$L(G) = \langle ([A])_{A \in V_n}, \Sigma_G, f)\rangle$ where Σ_G is supplied by B_G and for each $\sigma \in \Sigma_G$, $\sigma = \langle n, A_1A_2\ldots A_nA_{n+1}, s_1s_2\ldots s_ns_{n+1}\rangle$, f_σ is the function
$$f_\sigma : [A_1] \times [A_2] \times \ldots \times [A_n] \longrightarrow [A_{n+1}]$$
defined by the rule: for every $a_k \in [A_k]$, $k=1,2,\ldots,n$ $f_\sigma(a_1,a_2,\ldots,a_n) = \sigma(a_1,a_2,\ldots,a_n) = s_1a_1s_2a_2\ldots s_na_ns_{n+1} \in [A_{n+1}]$.

The language's context-free algebra is called naturale structure of the language.

Let $X = (X_i)_{i \in I}$ a family of finite sets and $B = \langle I, S, \mathcal{E}\rangle$ a finite basis be given. Denote by $W(X) = (W_i(X))_{i \in I}$ the family of words generated by a finite operator scheme Σ over B in symbols of X, where $W_i(X)$ is defined by the rules:

i. If $x \in X_i$ then $x \in W_i(X)$;

ii. If $\sigma \in \Sigma$, $\sigma = \langle o, i, s$ then $s \in W_i(X)$;

iii. If $\sigma \in \Sigma$, $\sigma = \langle n, i_1i_2\ldots i_ni, s_1s_2\ldots s_ns_{n+1}\rangle$ and $w_k \in W_{i_k}(X)$, $k=1,2,\ldots,n$ then $w = s_1w_1s_2w_2\ldots s_nw_ns_{n+1} \in W_i(X)$;

vi. Nothing else belong to $W_i(X)$.

__Theorem 2.__ If $X = (X_i)_{i \in I}$ is a family of finite sets and Σ is an operator scheme over a finite basis $B = \langle I, S, \mathcal{E}\rangle$ then there exists a CF-grammar G such $L(G) = W(X)$.

__Proof:__ $G = \langle I \cup S \cup X,\ S \cup X,\ P,\ I\rangle$ where P is defined as follows:

1. If $x \in X_i$ then $i \rightarrow x \in P$
2. If $(i_1i_2\ldots i_ni_{n+1}, s_1s_2\ldots s_ns_{n+1}) \in \mathcal{E}$ then
   $i_{n+1} \longrightarrow s_1i_1s_2i_2\ldots s_ni_ns_{n+1} \in P$

To prove that L(G)=W(X) we can use the induction on word length to show the inclusions $W(X) \subseteq L(G)$ and $L(G) \subseteq W(X)$. W(X) is called a word context-free algebra in symbols of X generated by Σ.

As it is shown in [4], L(G) is the initial object in the category of all context-free algebras over a given finite basis. Actually, L(G) can be specified as a word context-free algebra in symbols of the family of empty sets, i.e. $L(G)=\langle \emptyset=(\emptyset_i)_{i\in I}, \Sigma_G, f\rangle$, or forgeting f because of its definition, $L(G)=\langle \emptyset=(\emptyset_i)_{i\in I}, \Sigma_G\rangle$.

§3. Let $G=\langle V,V_t,P,V_n\rangle$ be a given CF-grammar and Σ_G the operator scheme supplied by the basis defined by G. If $L(G)\neq\emptyset$ then $\{\sigma\in\Sigma_G \mid d(\sigma)=\emptyset\}\neq\emptyset$. If $J\subseteq V_n$ then we call type construction, in short TC(J), the operation to build the following set:

$TC(J)=\{j\in V_n \mid \sigma=\langle n,i_1i_2\ldots i_nj,s_1s_2\ldots s_ns_{n+1}\rangle\in\Sigma_G \,\&\, (i_1,i_2,\ldots,i_n)\in J^n\}$

Then we can define the following cascade of subsets in V_n:

$I_o\subseteq V_n$, $I_o=\{i \mid \sigma\in\Sigma_G,\ d(\sigma)=\emptyset\}$;

$I_k\subseteq V_n$, $I_k=I_{k-1}\cup TC(I_{k-1})$, $k=1,2,\ldots$

For a finite basis, as is our case, there exists an m called basis hierarchy order, such that $TC(I_m)=\emptyset$, and hence $I_o\subseteq I_1\subseteq\ldots\subseteq I_m=$ $=V_n$.

Now we can split the set Σ_G into the subsets $\Sigma_o, \Sigma_1, \ldots,$ Σ_m, and Σ' by the following rules:

$$\Sigma_o=\{\sigma\in\Sigma \mid d(\sigma)=\emptyset\}$$

$$\Sigma_1=\{\sigma\in\Sigma \mid d(\sigma)\neq\emptyset \text{ and } d(\sigma)\subseteq\bigcup_{\sigma'\in\Sigma_o} t(\sigma')\}.$$ For $i=1,2,\ldots,m$

$$\Sigma_i=\{\sigma\in\Sigma \mid d(\sigma)\not\subseteq\bigcup_{\sigma'\in\bigcup_{j=0}^{i-2}\Sigma_j} t(\sigma') \,\&\, d(\sigma)\subseteq\bigcup_{\sigma''\in\bigcup_{j=0}^{i-1}\Sigma_j} t(\sigma'')\}$$

It is easy to see that for $o\leq i, j\leq m$, $i\neq j$, $\Sigma_i\cap\Sigma_j=\emptyset$. Then $\Sigma_G=\Sigma_o\cup\Sigma_1\cup\ldots\cup\Sigma_m\cup\Sigma'$. If $\Sigma'=\emptyset$ then Σ_G is a simplified operator scheme. According to the language generated by G we can always assume that Σ_G is simplified because the elements in Σ' doesn't generate any element in L(G). $\Sigma_o, \Sigma_1, \ldots, \Sigma_m$ are called the hierarchy classes of Σ_G.

Let us now use the following notations:

$W^o=\langle\emptyset, \Sigma_o\rangle$;

$W^1=\langle W^o, \Sigma_1\rangle$;

....

$W^m=\langle W^{m-1}, \Sigma_m\rangle$.

Then the following take place:

Lemma 3. If $L(G) \neq \emptyset$ then $W^o \neq \emptyset$ and is a finite set.

Lemma 4. For each i, $o \subseteq i \subseteq m$, W^i is generated by W^{i-1} and freely generated by W^o.

Lemma 5. $W^m = W(\emptyset) = L(G)$.

It follows that L(G) can be splited on the levels $L_o, L_1, \ldots, L_m$ such that L_o is a finite set of words, $L_o \subseteq L_1 \subseteq \ldots \subseteq L_m = L(G)$ and for each i, $o < i \leqslant m$, L_i is generated by L_{i-1} and freely generated by L_o.

§4. To use the above results for compiler specification we have to interpret an operation scheme $\sigma \in \Sigma_G$,

$$\sigma = \langle n, i_1 i_2 \ldots i_n i, s_1 s_2 \ldots s_n s_{n+1} \rangle$$

as a pattern $F(\sigma) = [\, s_1 i_1 s_2 i_2 \ldots s_n i_n s_{n+1};\ i \,]$ where $s_1, s_2, \ldots, s_n, s_{n+1}$ are fixed parts and $i_1, i_2, \ldots, i_n$ are parameters parts of the pattern. A pattern match processing determined by $F(\sigma)$ on a string x is an operation to isolate all the substrings $s_1 i_1 s_2 i_2 \ldots s_n i_n s_{n+1}$ in x and to substitute them by i. If there exists no such substrings in x then pattern matching process fails [5].
Let FILT(X,F,R) be such a pattern matching process, where R=o if the pattern matching process fails and R≠o otherwose.

Assume now that the corresponding patterns to $\Sigma_o, \Sigma_1, \ldots, \Sigma_m$ have been organized as a table called TUSO, such that TUSO(i,j) is the jth pattern supplied by Σ_i Denoting by CREP(i,j) the repetition coefficient associated to TUSO(i,j) and GREP(i) the repetition coefficient associated to Σ_i. the parsing algorithm for L(G) can be given as the following algol-bastard procedure:

```
procedure FASTANAL(string X,F,VN, integer M,I, integer array
                   N[o:M], GREP[o:M],CREP[o:M ,1:N[I]] ,
                   string array TUSO[o:M, 1:N[I]]),
     begin integer RS,RT,J; I:=o;
           Lo: RT:=o; J:= 1;
           L1: RS:=o; F:= TUSO(I,J); FILT(X,F,RS);
               while RS≠o do
                     begin
                        RT:=RT+1; if CREP(I,J)≥J then go to
                        L2 else begin
                                   J:=CREP(I,J); go to L1;
                     end        end
```

```
L2: if J < N[I] then begin J:=J+1; go to L1; end
          while RT≠o do begin if GREP(I) ≥ I then go to L3
             else begin I:=GREP(I); go to Lo; end end
L3: if I < M then begin I:=I+1; go to Lo; end else
          if X ∈ VN then CORRECT else ERROR;
end
```

Assuming now that L(G) is an absolutely free HAS the correctness of FASTANAL follows from the results above. For the case when L(G) is not absolutely free HAS the solution is given in [4,6] .

Considering that the operation schemes are macrooperations, we can associate to them appropriate macrobodies in a given macro-language [7] and if FILT has also the function to extend macro which correspond to the used pattern, then we get a compiler. TICS-system, a technology for compiler construction has been implemented following the above ideas.

References:

1. P.J. Higgins, Algebras with a Scheme of Operators, Math. Narichten,27(1963/64), pp.115-132.
2. G.Birkhoff, J.D.Lipson, Heterogeneous algebras, J. Comb. Theory, 8(1970):1, pp. 115-133,
3. T. Rus, $\sum S$ - algebra of a formal language, Bull. Math. de la Soc. Sci. de la R.S.Roumanie, 15(63)(1972):2, pp. 227-235.
4. W.S.Hatcher, T. Rus, Context-Free Algebra, submited to Journal of Cybernetics, 1976.
5. D.E.Knuth, J.H.Morris,Jr. V.R.Pratt, Fast Pattern Matching in Strings, STAN-CS-74-440, August 1974.
6. T. Rus, Language specification by generators and relations (rumanian), submited to Ed. Academiei R.S.R., Bucureşti, 1976.
7. P.J.Brown, Macro Processors and Techniques for Portable Software, John Wiley & Sons, London 1974.

ON THE LOWER BOUND FOR MINIMUM COMPARISON SELECTION

Peter Ružička , Juraj Wiedermann

Computing Research Centre
Dúbravská 3 , 885 31 Bratislava
Czechoslovakia

Introduction

Given a set X of n distinct objects and an integer k, $0 < k \leq n$, the selection problem is to determine the minimum number $V_k(n)$ of pairwise comparisons needed to select the k-th largest element of X (shortly k θ X).

This problem has received a considerable interest in the past few years [1,2,4] . The number $V_k(n)$ has been determined exactly for k = 1 and 2. Furthermore, $V_k(n) \leq n-k+(k-1).\lceil \log_2(n-k+2) \rceil$ is known by Hadian and Sobel to be an upper bound for the general case, i. e. for all n and k. The search for progressively faster general methods for this problem has culminated in the linear worst-case algorithm by Blum, Floyd, Pratt, Rivest and Tarjan. They proved an upper bound for $V_k(n)$ to be 5.4305 n.

Although this is the most efficient known general algorithm, there is an intuitive feeling that the constant of proportionality can be considerably improved. In order to make it possible to determine how the given algorithm is close to the optimality, lower bounds on the complexity have been examined. Indeed, at the present time there are hardly any mathematical techniques available for proving the optimality or even establishing any non-trivial lower bounds on the complexity of some of the commonest combinatorial problems and thus ad hoc techniques have been devised for special problems.

Among the few general methods for specifying non-trivial lower bounds for the selection problem, a significant position is occupied by an adversary approach ascribed to Blum at el and improved by Yao.

The best previously known upper bound up to the quaternian was published by Hyafil [2] who generalized Knuth´s intriguing idea of proving the optimality $V_2(n)$ by means of oracle strategy. In this paper a definition and some basic characteristics are given to handle the general oracle model based on the so called basic strategy and ruled by a certain sequence of constants. This approach yields a general framework for proving correctness of the whole class of oracles and it allows us to specify the lower bound for this general class considering the sequence of constants $c_1, c_2, \dots, c_{k-1}$ as $V_k(n) \geq n-1+\sum_{s=1}^{k-1} \lfloor \log_2 c_s \rfloor$. Further an optimal oracle for the underlying class is discussed and also the lower bound for the optimal constants is indicated. This new lower bound supersedes the best known lower bounds up to the quaternian for infinitely many values of k and n.

General lower bound

An oracle may be viewed as an "adversary" of the selection algorithm, which, following its own deterministic strategy, is trying to force the selection algorithm to make as many comparisons as possible. This is done by giving clever responses to the requests concerning the relation between any two elements.

Various oracle strategies are known from the literature. For our purposes the particular oracle strategy is described, the so called basic strategy, in which the relation between two elements is determined by means of weight function.

Definition 1.
Weight function $f_t(a)$, $a \in X$, in the t-th comparison is recursively defined as follows:

1. $f_0(a) = 1$
2. if $f_t(a) \geq f_t(b)$, $t > 0$, then $f_{t+1}(a) = f_t(a) + f_t(b)$, $f_{t+1}(b) = 0$ and $f_{t+1}(x) = f_t(x)$ for all $x \neq a$, $x \neq b$, $x \in X$

Definition 2.
Basic strategy (BS) is a prescription determining the relation a:b in the t-th comparison with respect to the weight function f as follows:

$a > b$	if $f_t(a) > f_t(b)$
$a < b$	if $f_t(a) < f_t(b)$
arbitrary	otherwise

The oracle strategy can be viewed as a deterministic process ruled by the basic strategy which for an arbitrary pair of elements from X decides the relation between these elements satisfying antisymmetry and transitivity.

Definition 3.
BS oracle $\sigma(k,n) = \langle X,f,C \rangle$ is a deterministic device where

- X is a linearly ordered set,
- f is a weight function,
- C denotes a nondecreasing sequence of constants $c_1, c_2, \dots, c_{k-1}$ preserving $\sum_{s=1}^{k-1} c_s < n$.

$\sigma(k,n)$ operates on two sets L and N, $L \cup N = X$, and L is initially empty. For any $a,b \in X$ in the t-th comparison $\sigma(k,n)$ acts in the following way:

1. if $a,b \in N$, $f_t(a) > f_t(b)$, then
   a. if $f_t(a) + f_t(b) > c_{|L|}$, then $f_{t+1}(d) := f_t(d)$ for all $d \in X$, $N := N - \{a\}$, $L := L \cup \{a\}$, where a becomes the minimal element in the set L
   b. if $f_t(a) + f_t(b) \leqslant c_{|L|}$, then the basic strategy is applied
2. if $a \in L$, $b \in N$, then $a > b$ and $f_{t+1}(d) := f_t(d)$ for all $d \in X$
3. if $a,b \in L$, then a:b is known (oracle maintains a total ordering in L after 1a) and $f_{t+1}(d) := f_t(d)$ for all $d \in X$

To recap briefly the previous definition, as long as the oracle deals with the elements from N, it follows BS until the sum of weights of compared elements is greater than $c_{|L|}$. Then the oracle removes the greater element from the set N and places it in the set L. Afterwards it continues following BS.

Further we prove BS oracle to be correct - i. e. it never terminates before determining k-1 elements greater than k θ X and k θ X is not found before the oracle ceases.

Property 1.
If $\sum_{s=1}^{k-1} c_s < n$ and $|L| < k-1$, then $\sum_{a \in N} f_t(a) > \sum_{s=|L|+1}^{k-1} c_s$

Proof:
For every $t \geqslant 0$ it obviously holds $\sum_{b \in L} f_t(b) \leqslant \sum_{s=1}^{|L|} c_s$, and thus

$$n = \sum_{a \in N} f_t(a) + \sum_{b \in L} f_t(b) \leqslant \sum_{a \in N} f_t(a) + \sum_{s=1}^{|L|} c_s .$$

Exploiting the assumption $\sum_{s=1}^{k-1} c_s < n$ we get

$$\sum_{a \in N} f_t(a) \geqslant n - \sum_{s=1}^{|L|} c_s > \sum_{s=1}^{k-1-|L|} c_{|L|+s} .$$

Property 2.
If $\sum_{s=1}^{k-1} c_s < n$, $|L| < k-1$, $c_s \leqslant c_{s+1}$ for $s=1,2,\dots,k-2$, then $|L| + |P| >$ $> k-1$ where $P = \{ a \in N \mid f_t(a) > 0 \}$.

Proof:

By the property 1 and the assumption it follows

$$\sum_{a\in N} f_t(a) = \sum_{a\in P} f_t(a) > \sum_{s=1}^{k-1-|L|} c_{|L|+s} > (k-1-|L|)\, c_{|L|+1}$$

Since for all $a\in P$ it holds $f_t(a) \leqslant c_{|L|+1}$, for the other side we have $\sum_{a\in P} f_t(a) \leqslant |P|\, c_{|L|+1}$. Combining both sides of relations we get $(k-1-|L|)\, c_{|L|+1} < |P|\, c_{|L|+1}$ from where the required claim follows.

Proof of the correctness of BS oracle.

FACT 1. We have to prove that as long as $|L| < k-1$ there is enough weightings for the elements in N to make comparisons which promote elements into the set L. But this is exactly what the property 1 claims.

FACT 2. We have to prove that while $|L| < k-1$, $k \theta X$ cannot be determined by the selection algorithm.

Proof: Let the selection algorithm find $k \theta X = a$ and let $|L| < k-1$. Then

- if $a\in L$, then from the construction of the oracle it follows that a is greater than at least $|N| = n-|L|$ other elements. Following the assumption, $n-|L| > n-k+1$ implying that $a \neq k \theta X$, a contradiction
- if $a\in N$ and $f_t(a) = 0$, then by the property 2 there exist more than k-1 elements greater than a, a contradiction
- if $a\in P$, then since $|P| + |L| > k-1$ and $|L| \leqslant k-2$ we have $|P| > 1$ meaning there exists also an element $b\in P$, $b \neq a$, uncompared with the element a, thus the selection algorithm cannot know $a = k \theta X$

Furthermore, our goal is to determine the general lower bound for BS ruled oracles. Here the important role is played by the notion of the crucial comparison.

Definition 4.

The crucial comparison for an element $a\in X$, $a \neq k \theta X$, is the first comparison a:b such that $b = k \theta X$ or $a<b<k \theta X$ or $k \theta X<a<b$.

In general, the decision whether a comparison is a crucial comparison or not can be resolved only after all comparisons have been made and $k \theta X$ has been selected. However, for an arbitrary $a\in X$, $a \neq k \theta X$, each algorithm selecting $k \theta X$ must determine whether $a > k \theta X$ or $a < k \theta X$. This proves

Property 3.

A selection algorithm has to make precisely n-1 crucial comparisons to select $k \theta X$, where $|X| = n$.

In establishing the lower bound, we start from the basic estimate $V_k(n) \geqslant n-1+ \sum_{a\in L} \lceil \log_2 f_t(a) \rceil$ following from the fact that n-1 crucial comparisons as well as at least $\lceil \log_2 f_t(a) \rceil$ noncrucial comparisons for each element $a > k \ \theta \ X$ are necessary ($\lceil \log_2 f_t(a) \rceil$ is the minimal number of comparisons performed by a with $f_t(a)$ being its weight).

First of all we show how the number of comparisons for the given element can be estimated:

<u>Property 4.</u>
If $f_t(a) \geqslant f_t(b)$, $f_t(a) + f_t(b) > 2^j + \mathcal{E}$, $0 \leqslant \mathcal{E} < 2^j$, $j>0$, then $\lceil \log f_t(a) \rceil \geqslant j$.

<u>Proof:</u>
Note first that following the assumptions we get $\lceil \log_2 f_t(a) \rceil > \log_2(2^{j-1} + \mathcal{E}/2)$. Consider either $\mathcal{E} = 0$, and then obviously $\lceil \log_2 f_t(a) \rceil \geqslant j$, or $0 < \mathcal{E} < 2^{j-1}$, and in that case we obtain $\lceil \log_2 f_t(a) \rceil > \log_2 2^{j-1}(1+ \mathcal{E}/2^j) = j-1+\mathcal{E}_1$ where $0 < \mathcal{E}_1 < 1$; so $\lceil \log_2 f_t(a) \rceil \geqslant j$.

Assuming $a\in L$ we know there exists say the t-th comparison a:b such that both $f_t(a) \geqslant f_t(b)$ and $f_t(a) + f_t(b) > c_{|L|} = c_i$ hold. The constant c_i can be written in the form $c_i = 2^{\lfloor \log_2 c_i \rfloor} + \mathcal{E}$, where $0 \leqslant \mathcal{E} < 2^{\lfloor \log_2 c_i \rfloor}$. Using the previous property it is apparent that the following assertion can be made.

<u>Consequence 1.</u>
If $a\in L$, then $\lceil \log_2 f_t(a) \rceil \geqslant \lfloor \log_2 c_i \rfloor$ for an appropriate constant c_i, $1 \leqslant i \leqslant |L|$.

The previous consequence enables us to formulate the following important assertion

<u>Theorem 1</u> (general lower bound)
For any BS oracle $\mathcal{O}(k,n) = \langle X, f, \{c_1, c_2, \ldots, c_{k-1}\} \rangle$ it holds

$$V_k(n) \geqslant n - 1 + \sum_{s=1}^{k-1} \lfloor \log_2 c_s \rfloor .$$

<u>Optimal lower bound</u>

Oracles constructed by Blum and Hyafil form special cases of our approach. Considering sequences of constants $c_s = 2$ or $c_s = 2^{\lceil \log_2 n/(2(k-1)) \rceil}$ for s = 1,2,...,k-1, the estimations

$$V_k(n) \geqslant n+k-2 \quad \text{or} \quad V_k(n) \geqslant n-k+(k-1) \lceil \log_2 n/(k-1) \rceil$$

can be reached respectively.

Now we raise the following question: What sequence of constants maximizes the lower bound estimation ?

Definition 5.
BS oracle $\sigma(k,n)=\langle X,f,\{c_1,\dots,c_{k-1}\}\rangle$ is optimal (with respect to the basic strategy) if and only if

$$\sum_{s=1}^{k-1} \lfloor \log_2 c_s \rfloor = \max\{\sum_{s=1}^{k-1} \lfloor \log_2 a_s \rfloor \mid \sum_{s=1}^{k-1} a_s < n,\ a_s > 0\} \qquad (A)$$

In the following property the general characterization for the sequence of constants for an optimal BS oracle is given. Generally the maximality condition of the sum $\sum \lfloor \log c_s \rfloor$ is equivalent to that of $\sum c_s$ (providing $\sum c_s < n$). However, our aim is to construct the optimal constants in as simple a manner as possible ; so a more special case where all constants are balanced (meaning that the difference of their logarithms does not exceed one) is shown.

Property 5.
For an arbitrary n and k there exists a nondecreasing sequence of constants $c_1, c_2, \dots, c_{k-1}$, each of them being the power of two, such that the condition (A) holds if and only if

$$\sum_{s=1}^{k-1} c_s = \max\{\sum_{s=1}^{k-1} a_s \mid \sum_{s=1}^{k-1} a_s < n,\ \left|\lfloor \log_2 a_i \rfloor - \lfloor \log_2 a_j \rfloor\right| \leqslant 1,\ 1 \leqslant i,j \leqslant k-1\} \qquad (B$$

Proof:
The proof is straightforward but long and tedious and therefore it is omitted here; it can be found in [5].

In order to determine constants of an optimal BS oracle it is sufficient to consider only those which are balanced and are powers of two; hence $\log_2 c_i/c_j \leqslant 1$, and thus $1 \leqslant c_i/c_j \leqslant 2$ for $j \leqslant i$. Proceeding from Hyafil constants we get

Consequence 2.
For any n and k, $k \leqslant n$, the sequence of constants $c_1,\dots,c_{k-1}$ for an optimal BS oracle is given by

$c_i = 2^{d-1}$ $\quad i=1,2,\dots,2\,(k-1)+1-\lceil n\,2^{-d+1}\rceil = r$

$c_j = 2^d$ $\quad j=r+1,\dots,k-1$

where $d = \lceil \log_2 n/(k-1) \rceil$.

Theorem 2.
The minimal number of comparisons necessary to compute the k-th largest element from a linearly ordered set of n elements is lower-**bounded by the** function

$$B_k(n) = n-2k+d(k-1)+\lceil n2^{-d+1}\rceil$$

$k \geqslant 2$, where $d = \lceil \log_2 n/(k-1) \rceil$.

Analysis of the lower bound

Denote the upper bound for $V_k(n)$ due to Hadian and Sobel by $HS_k(n)$, and let $\Omega_k(n) = HS_k(n) - B_k(n)$.

Property 6.
$\Omega_2(n) = 0$ for $n \geqslant 2$.

In the case of the third element our general lower bound is equal to the best known result in [4] where the case k = 3 was specially analyzed:

Property 7.

$$\Omega_3(n) = \begin{cases} 0 & n = 2^s+1 \\ 2 & 2^s+1 < n \leqslant 3.2^{s-1} \\ 1 & 3.2^{s-1} < n \leqslant 2^{s+1} \end{cases}$$

The case k = 4 was not specially considered. By theorem 2 we get

Property 8.

$$\Omega_4(n) = \begin{cases} 3 & 3.2^{s-1} \leqslant n < 2^{s+1} \\ 2 & 2^{s+1} \leqslant n \leqslant 2^{s+1}+2 \\ 5 & 2^{s+1}+2 < n < 5.2^{s-1} \\ 4 & 5.2^{s-1} \leqslant n < 3.2^s \end{cases} \qquad s \geqslant 1$$

Property 9.

$$\Omega_k(n) \leqslant (k-1)\lceil \log_2(k-1) \rceil \qquad k \geqslant 2$$

The best previously known general lower bound for $3 < k < n/4$ is due to Hyafil [2] : $H_k(n) = n-k+(k-1)\lceil \log_2 n/(k-1) \rceil$.

Property 10.
Within the interval $n/2^{s+1}+1 < k \leqslant n/2^s$, s=2,3,... it holds

$$1 \leqslant B_k(n) - H_k(n) < k-1$$

where the right side of the inequality cannot be improved.

Thus, the new lower bound $B_k(n)$ is strictly greater than the best previously known general lower bounds for an infinite many values of n and k.

References.

1. Blum M., Floyd R. W., Pratt V., Rivest R., and Tarjan R., Time bounds for selection. JCSS 7 (Aug. 1973), 448 - 461
2. Hyafil L., Bounds for selection. IRIA. Rapport de Recherche n° 77. 1974
3. Knuth D. E., The art of computer programming. Volume 3. Sorting and Searching. Addison - Wesley publishing company. 1973
4. Pratt V. and Yao F. F., On lower bounds for computing the i-th largest elements. Proceedings of the Fourteenth Symposium on Switching and Automata Theory, 1973
5. Ružička P., Wiedermann J., **Algorithms of partial ordering. Technical Report CRC Bratislava, June 1976.**

COMPUTATIONAL PROCESSES GENERATED BY PROGRAMS WITH /RECURSIVE/ PROCEDURES AND BLOCK STRUCTURES.

A. Salwicki /Warsaw University/

T. Müldner /Institute of Computing Machines/

0. The language ALGOL is one of the most known programming languages, however, as far as we know, yet not a full description of its semantics is given. The purpose of this paper is to give the definition of the language ALGOL1, which is a restriction of the language ALGOL, and to give a full description of the semantics of this language. In this way, we believe, we illustrate our idea of semantics of a program with block structure and procedures. In §1 we give the description of ALGOL1 syntax, in §2 we describe semantics of this language and in §3 we define a computation of a program and give an example. Some connections between ALGOL and ALGOL1 and also full, formalized syntax will be given in [3] .

1. ALGOL1 syntax.

By the language ALGOL1 we shall understand the ordered pair consisting of the alphabet and the set of well-formed expressions /called programs/ Alphabet is the union of the set of identifiers, the set of primitive functors and predicates and the set of auxiliary signs.

By the identifier we shall understand the finite sequence

$$a_1a_2\ldots a_ra_{r+1}\ldots a_s$$

where $1 \leq r < s$, a_1 and a_r are letters, a_i are letters or digits for $i = 2,3,..,r-1$, and a_i are digits for $i = r+1,r+2,..,s$.

Let n be such identifier and let us denote by N an identifier of the form $a_1a_2..a_r0$, and by k the value of the integer $a_{r+1}..a_s$. In the sequel identifier n will be also called the k-th copy of the identifier N.

Let V denote the set of all identifiers.

Primitive functors /predicates/ are the names of functions /relations/ occurring in the language ALGOL e.g. + =

The set of auxiliary signs consists of the following elements:

<u>begin</u> <u>end</u> <u>beginblock</u> <u>endblock</u> <u>if</u> <u>then</u> <u>else</u> <u>while</u> <u>do</u> <u>goto</u> <u>real</u> <u>integer</u> <u>Boolean</u> <u>label</u> <u>array</u> <u>of</u> <u>procedure</u> <u>value</u> := : ; ,( ) [ ]

Let S be the set of substitutions i.e. the set of all expressions of the form

x := AE /AE - arithmetic expression/

x := BE /BE - Boolean expression/

where x is an identifier /we use notions: arithmetic expression and

Boolean expression in its intuitive sense, for exact definition see [1] or [3] , these notions correspond to the notions of term and quantifier-free formula respectively/.

Let J be the set of statements i.e. the least set satisfying following conditions:

1. $J \supset S$,
2. if $n \in V$ then goto $n \in J$,
   /such expression will be called a jump statement/,
3. if $p, a_1, a_2, \ldots, a_k \in V$ /or a_i are arithmetic/Boolean/ expressions/ then $p(a_1, a_2, \ldots, a_k) \in J$
   /such expression will be called a procedure statement, $a_1, \ldots, a_k$ will be called actual parameters of this procedure/,
4. if $n \in V$, $I \in J$ then $n{:}I \in J$,
   /such expression will be called a statement labeled by the label n/
5. if $I_1, I_2, \ldots, I_k \in J$ then begin $I_1; I_2; \ldots I_k$ end $\in J$
   /such expression will be called a compound statement/,
6. if $I_1, I_2 \in J$ then if BE then I_1 else $I_2 \in J$
   /such expression will be called a conditional statement/,
7. if $I \in J$ then while BE do $I \in J$
   /such expression will be called an iterative statement/,
8. if $P_1, P_2, \ldots, P_k \in J$ then beginblock $D; P_1; P_2; \ldots P_k$ endblock $\in J$
   /such expression will be called a block, $P_1, \ldots, P_k$ will be called statements contained in the given block/
   where D is a declaration of identifiers, it means a finite sequence of expressions from the set $D_1 \cup D_2 \cup D_3 \cup D_4$ /every such expression will be called a declaration of the identifier n as an identifier of a type given in declaration, and denoted by d(n)/, where:

   D_1 - the set of declarations of variable identifiers of primitive type i.e. expressions of the form
   integer n ; or real n ; or Boolean n ;

   D_2 - the set of declarations of label identifiers i.e. expressions of the form
   label n ;

   D_3 - the set of declarations of procedure identifiers i.e. expressions of the form
   procedure $n(f_1, f_2, \ldots, f_k)$; value $f_{i_1}, \ldots f_{i_n}$; $s(f_1); \ldots s(f_k)$; B ;
   where n is an identifier /called procedure identifier/, $f_1, f_2, \ldots, f_k$ are identifiers /called formal parameters of the given procedure/, $\{i_1, \ldots, i_n\} \subset \{1, \ldots, k\}$, $s(f_1), \ldots, s(f_k)$ are specifications of identifiers $f_1, \ldots, f_k$, B is a statement - see [3] .

/we shall say that $f_{i_1},..,f_{i_n}$ are called by value, the other parameters are called by name, and the expression

$(f_1,..,f_k)$;<u>value</u> $f_{i_1},..,f_{i_n}$; $s(f_1)$;.. $s(f_k)$; B ;

is the text of given procedure/,

D_4 - the set of declarations of array identifiers i.e. expressions of the form

⟨declaration of type of k-dim. array⟩ ⟨identifier⟩

where the declaration of type of k-dim. array is defined inductively:

⟨declar. of type of 1-dim. array⟩ ::= <u>array</u> $[l_1:u_1]$ <u>of</u> ⟨primitive type⟩ ,

⟨declar. of type of k-dim. array⟩ ::= <u>array</u> $[l_k:u_k]$ <u>of</u> ⟨declar. of type of (k-1)-dim. array⟩ .

We accept that :

1.1. If an identifier in block B occurs, but the declaration of this identifier in B does not occur, then such occurrence is called nonlocal for block B. By a scope of identifier n /which is declared in a block B/ we shall understand all statements contained in the block B except of those blocks contained in B in which declaration of identifier n is repeated. An occurrence of identifier n is called local for block B if identifier n is declared in this block and this occurrence takes place in statement which is in the scope of identifier n.

/for further assumptions see [3] /.

2. ALGOL1 semantics.

By a realization of the language ALGOL1 we shall mean an arbitrary mapping R such that

a/ to every primitive type R assigns a set:

<u>real</u> a set $|\text{real}| \subset \mathbb{R}$ /$\mathbb{R}$ - the set of real numbers/,

<u>integer</u> a set $|\text{integer}| \subset \mathbb{Z}$ /$\mathbb{Z}$ - the set of integer numbers/,

<u>Boolean</u> a set $|\text{Boolean}| = \{\mathbf{0}, \mathbf{1}\}$ /$\mathbf{0}$ - false, $\mathbf{1}$ - true/.

b/ to every primitive functor /predicate/ R assigns a function /relation/ on an appropriate set,

e.g. realization of the functor + may be a function $|\text{real}| \times |\text{real}| \to |\text{real}|$ which realize an adding of real numbers.

In the sequel we shall consider the fixed realization R.

By a valuation we shall understand an arbitrary mapping

$v : V \to |\text{real}| \cup |\text{integer}| \cup |\text{Boolean}| \cup |\text{expression texts}|$

where the set $|\text{expression texts}|$ is a subset of the set of all expressions /i.e. all finite sequences of elements of alphabet/, such that v assigns identifiers of type:

<u>real</u> to elements of the set |real| ,

<u>integer</u> to elements of the set |integer| ,

<u>Boolean</u> to elements of the set |Boolean| ,

<u>label</u> and <u>procedure</u> to elements of the set |expression texts|

In every fixed expression of the language only a finite set of identifiers occurs, so during computation of its value it is enough to have a restriction of a mapping v to this set. Hence a mapping v /or rather its graph/ can be written in the form as in the following example:

v :

a0	b1b32	cdc2	g5	A0[1]	A0[2]	A0[3]
0	1.2	0	(a);<u>integer</u> a; a:=a+1;	2	3	4

Let us denote

if $a_1, a_2, .., a_k, a_{k+1}, .., a_s \in V$, $v_1: \frac{a_1 | \dots | a_k}{- | \dots | -}$, $v_2: \frac{a_{k+1} | \dots | a_s}{- | \dots | -}$

$v_3: \frac{a_1 | \dots | a_s}{- | \dots | -}$

then

$v_1 \oplus v_2 = v_3$.

Let w be an arbitrary expression. Then by $[a_1/b_1, \dots, a_n/b_n]w$ we shall denote an expression obtained from w by simultaneous replacement of all occurrences of the identifiers $a_1, .., a_n$ in w with corresponding identifiers $b_1, .., b_n$, /see [4] p.152/. If B is an arbitrary block, then by $[a_1/b_1, \dots, a_n/b_n]_B w$ we shall denote an expression obtained from w by simultaneous replacement of all occurrences of identifiers $a_1, .. a_n$ in w which are local for block B with corresponding identifiers $b_1, . b_n$.

3. Computation of ALGOL1 program.

Let K be an ALGOL1 program and let v be a valuation of identifiers which occurrences in this program are nonlocal.

We shall define a computation of the program K at the valuation v /and realization R/. We assume the existence of the block counter l, the initial value of which is equal to the greatest number of the copy of an identifier occuring in the program K.

By a configuration we shall understand an ordered pair (v,X) where v is a valuation, X is an expression /the configuration corresponds to the temporary state of a computational process: a valuation defines the memory state and an expression X defines the list of statements which are to be executed/.

By a computation of program K we shall understand a finite sequence of configurations

$$(v_1,K_1),\ (v_2,K_2),\ \ldots,\ (v_n,K_n)$$

such that

$v_1 = v$, $K_1 = K$, $K_n = \emptyset$, for $i = 1,2,\ldots n-1$; $(i+1)$-th configuration depends on the valuation v_i and the initial elements of expression K_i, namely:

the configuration (v, TX) depending on T passes to configuration:

/a/ (v_1, X') if T: __beginblock__ $d(a_1);\ldots d(a_k);P_1;\ldots P_n$ __endblock__

where

Let l be the present value of the block counter and let

$P_i' = [a_1/a_1(l+1),\ldots,a_k/a_k(l+1)]_T P_i$.

Then

$$X' = P_1';\ldots P_n';\ X$$

$$v_1 = v \oplus \frac{a_1(l+1)}{-}\Big|\ \ldots\ldots\ \Big|\frac{a_k(l+1)}{-}$$

Initial values of identifiers $a_i(l+1)$ except of label and procedure identifiers are accedintal. Initial value of a procedure identifier is equal to the text of this procedure modified in the same way as every P_i, value of a label identifier n is equal to the expression consisting of all statements which occur in expression X', starting from the statement labeled by the identifier $n(l+1)$, to the end of expression X'.

Next, value of the block counter is increased by one, $l:=l+1$.

/b/ $(v, K_1;\ldots K_n;X)$ if T: __begin__ $K_1;\ldots K_n$ __end__

/c/ (v_1, X) if T: $a:=w$;

where valuation v_1 is obtained from the valuation v by a substitution a value of the expression w on the value of the identifier a.

/d/ (v, Y) if T: __goto__ b;

where $Y = v(b)$.

/e/ $(v, p'X)$ if T: $p(a_1,\ldots,a_k)$,

where

if the declaration of procedure p is the following:

__procedure__ $p(f_1,\ldots,f_k)$;__value__ $f_{i_1},\ldots,f_{i_n}$; $s(f_1);\ldots s(f_k)$; A ;

then p' is a modified procedure body i.e. is of the form:

__beginblock__ $d(f_{i_1});\ldots d(f_{i_n});f_{i_1}:=a_{i_1};\ldots f_{i_n}:=a_{i_n}$; A' __endblock__

where $\{j_1,\ldots,j_s\} = \{1,\ldots,k\} - \{i_1,\ldots,i_n\}$,

$$A' = [f_{j_1}/a_{j_1},\ldots\ldots,f_{j_s}/a_{j_s}]_{p'} A .$$

/f/ $\begin{cases}(v, I_1; X) \\ (v, I_2; X)\end{cases}$ if T: **if** BE **then** I_1 **else** I_2 and $\begin{cases} v(BE) = 1 \\ v(BE) = 0 \end{cases}$

/g/ $\begin{cases}(v, I; \textbf{while } BE \textbf{ do } I; X) \\ (v, X)\end{cases}$ if T: **while** BE **do** I and $\begin{cases} v(BE) = 1 \\ v(BE) = 0. \end{cases}$

Example.

We give an example of a program in which a recursive procedure is called, /0-th copy of ident. i.e. $a_1..a_s0$ will be written as $a_1..a_s$/.

```
K: beginblock procedure S(n,w); integer n,w;
           beginblock integer j; if n≤c then w:=c else begin
                               S(n-c,j);  w := n*j ;      end
           endblock
     S(a,b);
   endblock
```

We shall show a computation of the program K with the initial values of identifiers a,b,c /which occurrences in K are nonlocal/:

v: | a | b | c |
|---|---|---|
| 3 | 0 | 1 |.

1=1 (v1:v⊕ $\frac{S1}{(n,w); \textbf{integer } n,w; \textbf{beginblock integer } j; \textbf{if } n \leq c \textbf{ then}}$ 'S1(a,b)
w:=c **else begin** S1(n-c,j);w:=n*j **end endblock**)

1=1 (v1, **beginblock integer** j;**if** a≤c **then** b:=c **else begin** S1(a-c,j);
b:=a*j **end endblock**)

1=2 (v2:v1⊕$\frac{j2}{-}$, **if** a≤c **then** b:=c **else begin** S1(a-c,j2);b:=a*j2 **end**)

1=2 (v2, **begin** S1(a-c,j2); b:=a*j2 **end**)

1=2 (v2, S1(a-c,j2); b:=a*j2)

1=2 (v2, **beginblock integer** j; **if** a-c≤c **then** j2:=c **else begin**
S1(a-c-c,j); j2:=(a-c)*j **end endblock** b:=a*j2)

1=3 (v3:v2⊕ $\frac{j3}{-}$, **if** a-c≤c **then** j2:=c **else begin** S1(a-c-c,j3);
j2:=(a-c)*j3 **end** b:=a*j2)

1=3 (v3, **begin** S1(a-c-c,j3); j2:=(a-c)*j3 **end** b:= a*j2)

1=3 (v3, S1(a-c-c,j3); j2:=(a-c)*j3; b:=a*j2)

```
l=3 (v3, beginblock integer j; if a-c-c≤c then j3:=c else begin
         S1(a-c-c-c,j); j3:=(a-c-c)*j;end endblock j2:=(a-c)*j3;
         b:= a*j2                                                )

l=4 (v4:v3⊕ j4/-, if a-c-c≤c then j3:=c else begin S1(a-c-c-c,j4);
                 j3:=(a-c-c)*j4 end j2:=(a-c)*j3; b:=a*j2;       )

l=4 (v4, j3:=c; j2:=(a-c)*j3; b:=a*j2)

l=4 (v5: a | b | c | S1   | j2 | j3 | j4 , j2:=(a-c)*j3; b:=a*j2)
         3 | 0 | 1 | text | -  | 1  | -

l=4 (v6: a | b | c | S1   | j2 | j3 | j4 ,  b:=a*j2)
         3 | 0 | 1 | text | 2  | 1  | -

l=4 (v7: a | b | c | S1   | j2 | j3 | j4 ,  ∅)
         3 | 6 | 1 | text | 2  | 1  | -
```

Final remarks.
The semantics of ALGOL given here is aimed as a standard /primary/ version of semantics. This standard is satisfactory for an analysis of programs from user's point of view, furthermore it makes a basis for next versions of semantics more helpful in compiler construction. This paper is a starting-point to the ALGOL 60 axiomatization /see [2] / The experience gained during this work will be applied in the LOGLAN project. LOGLAN is a name for the new universal programming language with concurrent computations and precisely defined semantics.

References.

[1] Naur,P /ed./ Revised Report on the Algorithmic Language ALGOL 60 Comm. ACM 6,1 /Jan. 1963/, pp.1-17.

[2] Mirkowska,G ; Salwicki,A. A complete axiomatic characterization of algorithmic properties of block-structure programs with /recursive/ procedures - the same volume.

[3] Müldner,T ; Salwicki,A. Computational processes generated by programs with /recursive/ procedures and block structures - to appear in Fund. Informaticae.

[4] Rasiowa,H ; Sikorski,R. Mathematics of metamathematics - Warsaw /1963/.

[5] Salwicki,A. Programmability and Recursiveness /an application of algorithmic logic to procedures/ - to appear in Dissertationes Mathematicae.

AN ALGEBRAIC FRAMEWORK FOR THE STUDY OF THE SYNTACTIC MONOIDS
APPLICATION TO THE GROUP LANGUAGES

J. SAKAROVITCH

C.N.R.S.

Institut de Programmation

France

Abstract We study here a category whose objects are the pairs (M,P) where M is a monoid and P a subset of M. This gives a suitable algebraic framework for studying the relationships between the properties of a language and those of its syntactic monoid, specially in the case of the infinite syntactic monoids as we did in [12, 13, 14] . Some results of Anisimov [1] can be improved within this framework.

Introduction

In this communication, we present briefly the algebraic framework we have set up in [13] order to study the syntactic monoids of the context free languages and we give an application to the Anisimov's group languages (cf. [1]).
A complete version of the paper, with full proofs and some more related results (particularly a new presentation of the Eilenberg's theorem on the varieties of regular languages [5]) will appear in Semigroup Forum.

Recall that if L is a language (i.e. a subset) of the free monoid X^* the syntactic monoid of L is the quotient of X^* by its coarsest congruence for which L is saturated.

The theory of syntactic monoids originated in the work of M.P. Schützenberger (1955) and has been developped for the rational (i.e. regular) languages which can be defined - and this is the fundamental theorem of Kleene - as the languages whose syntactic monoid is finite. The main part of the theory consists in the characterization of various classes of rational languages by their syntactic monoids : these are results of Mc Naughton, Zalcstein, Brzozowski and Simon, following the main theorem on "star-free" languages of Schützenberger [15].

The study of (infinite) syntactic monoids of non-regular languages and more precisely of the context-free languages is much more recent ([11], [12]) and is faced from the outset with one major difficulty : according to the following fact, it is not possible to characterize the family of the context-free languages, or even a subfamily of it, by a family of syntactic monoids.

Fact 1 Some monoids are syntactic monoid of both context-free and non context-free languages.

Example 1 A language and its complement have the same syntactic monoid. It is well known that the family of context-free languages is not closed under complementation.

Example 2 Let Z be the group of the integers and S a non-recursively enumerable set of integers.
Let $X = \{x, y\}$ be an alphabet and D_1^*, the 'Dyck language over one letter', defined by :

$$D_1^* = \{w \in X^* \mid |w|_x = |w|_y\}$$

($|w|_x$ denotes the number of letter x in the word w).
The syntactic monoid of D_1^* is isomorphic to Z. So Z is a quotient of X^* and let φ be the canonical homomorphism from X^* onto Z. The language $L = \varphi^{-1}(S)$ is non-recursively enumerable and its syntactic monoid is Z as well.

However, deep relationships do exist between the properties of a context-free language and the structure of its syntactic monoid and we have shown some of them, mainly related with the property of determinism, in [12] and [14]. These relationships have been established after the following fundamental lemma :

Lemma 1 : *If two languages have the same syntactic monoid and the same image in this syntactic monoid, then each one is the image of the other in an inverse homomorphism.*

The relation between two languages : 'each one is an inverse homomorphic image of the other' is a quite natural equivalence relation over the class of all languages : every family of the Chomsky's hierarchy and of its usual refinements (deterministic, linear, one counter,...context-free languages for example) is closed under this equivalence relation.
This fact led us to study the pairs made of a monoid and of a subset of it, pairs which we call pointed-monoids and these pairs will give us the suitable framework for studying infinite syntactic monoids.

I - Pointed-monoids

Definition 1 A pointed-monoid is a pair (M,P), denoted M_P in the sequel, where M is a finitely generated monoid and where P is any subset of M.

An homomorphism of pointed-monoids $\varphi : M_P \to N_Q$ is an homomorphism of monoids $\varphi : M \to N$ such that $\varphi^{-1}(Q) = P$.
The pointed-monoids and their homomorphisms form a category. The notions of congruence, quotient, substructure, and division are defined for the pointed-monoids as for any other algebraic structure.

<u>Définition 2</u> The syntactic pointed-monoid of M_P, denoted $\mathcal{M}(M_P)$, is the quotient of M_P by its coarsest congruence (called also the syntactic congruence of M_P and which is different from the universal equivalence on M, unless P is equal to M or to $\emptyset$).

If the syntactic congruence of M_P is the identity on M, M_P is said to be syntactic or P is said to be disjunctive in M.
Recall [16] that the syntactic congruence of M_P, denoted σ_P, is characterized by :

$$\forall p,q \in M \qquad p \equiv q \quad [\sigma_P] \Leftrightarrow \{ \forall u,v \in M \qquad upv \in P \Leftrightarrow uqv \in P \}$$

<u>Remark</u> The pointed-monoids are a particular case of the *abstract machines* defined and studied by Krohn and Rhodes [8] and by Give'on [7]. The normal form of an abstract machine is exactly in this case the syntactic pointed-monoid of a pointed-monoid.

<u>Proposition 1</u> If $\Theta : M_P \to N_Q$ then $\mathcal{M}(M_P)$ divides $\mathcal{M}(N_Q)$.

We shall say that two pointed-monoids M_P and N_Q *exchange by homomorphism* if there exist $\varphi : M_P \to N_Q$ and $\psi : N_Q \to M_P$.

We then slightly alter the classical definition of a language :

<u>Definition 3</u> A language is a pointed-monoid whose support is free.

The fundamental lemma 1 of the introduction becomes :

<u>Lemma 1'</u> *If two languages have the same syntactic pointed-monoid, they exchange by homomorphism.*

This lemma is of constant use in the demonstrations on syntactic monoids (see [12, 13,14]) : for studying a language X_L^* whose syntactic pointed-monoid is M_P, one can choose a set T of generators of M, adapted to the structure of M, and then study the inverse image of P in the canonical homomorphism of T^* onto M.

The converse of Lemma 1 is not true. One can state the following :

<u>Proposition 2</u> [8] *Two languages exchange by homomorphism if, and only if, their syntactic pointed-monoids divide each other.*

If, in the proposition 2, we restrict the languages to be regular we get the following corollary :

<u>Corollary</u> [7] *Two regular languages exchange by homomorphisme if, and only if, their syntactic pointed-monoids are isomorphic.*

The question then arises, to know if it is possible to strengthen the proposition 2 when the languages are restricted to be context-free. The answer is negative as we will show now.

Let X_L^* be a language, $M_P = \mathcal{M}(X_L^*)$ its syntactic pointed-monoid, and $\varphi : X_L^* \to M_P$ the syntactic homomorphism. Let $\Theta : X_L^* \to X_L^*$ be an endomorphism of the language X_L^*. From Proposition 1 follows that M_P divides M_P, i.e. there exists N_Q such that

i) there exists $\alpha : N_Q \to M_P$ surjective and $\beta : N_Q \to M_P$ injective

ii) there exists $\gamma : X_L^* \to N_Q$ surjective such that $\varphi = \alpha \circ \gamma$ and $\varphi \circ \Theta = \beta \circ \gamma$

It is useful to express this property under the following equivalent form :

<u>Lemma 2</u> Let Θ be an endomorphism of a language X_L^*. Let M_P be the syntactic pointed-monoid of X_L^* and φ the syntactic homomorphism

i) The following allways holds :

$$\forall\, p,q \in X^* \quad \varphi(\Theta(p)) = \varphi(\Theta(q)) \Rightarrow \varphi(p) = \varphi(q). \tag{1}$$

ii) The converse implication

$$\forall\, p,q \;\; X^* \quad \varphi(p) = \varphi(q) \Rightarrow \varphi(\Theta(p)) = \varphi(\Theta(q)) \tag{2}$$

holds if, and only if, there exists $\delta : M_P \to M_P$ such that $\delta \circ \varphi = \varphi \circ \Theta$.

If (2) holds, we shall say that Θ *commutes* with φ.

<u>Fact 2</u> There exist endomorphisms of context-free languages which do not commute with the syntactic homomorphisms.

<u>Example 3</u> Let $X = \{x,y,z\}$ be an alphabet and $\Theta : X^* \to X^*$ defined by $\Theta(x) = xz$, $\Theta(y) = y$, and $\Theta(z) = z$.

Let $L = L_1 \cup L_2$ be the language defined by

$L_1 = \{(xz^*)^n yz^n \; ; \; n \in N\}$, and $L_2 = \{yxz^n xz^m yz^* \; ; \; n,m \in N, \; n < m\}$.

One easily checks that $\Theta(L_1) = L_1 \cap \Theta(X^*)$. Then $\Theta^{-1}\Theta(L_1) = L_1$ as Θ is injective and thus $L_1 = \Theta^{-1}(L_1)$. For the same reasons $L_2 = \Theta^{-1}(L_2)$ and $\Theta : X_L^* \to X_L^*$ is endomorphism of the language X_L^*.

We have $xyz \equiv x^2 y z^2 \ [\sigma_L]$ and

$$\Theta(xyz) = xzyz \not\equiv xzxzyz^2 = \Theta(x^2 y z^2) \ [\sigma_L]$$

since $yx.xzyz \in L$ and $yx.xzxzyz^2 \notin L$.

Thus Θ does not commutes with the syntactic homomorphism of X_L^*.

X_L^* is a linear , one-counter deterministic context-free language.

The fact 2 is equivalent to the fact that the Proposition 2 cannot be strengthen for the context-free language (and even for usual subfamilies of context-free languages as example 3 shows).

II - The group languages

Definition 4 A group language is a language whose syntactic pointed-monoid is G_1, where G is any group and 1 the neutral element of G.

This definition is the same than the one given by Anisimov ([1] , [2], and [3]). The theorem 3, or 3', of [1] is an immediate corollary of the lemma 1' above and we shall improve it.

Recall first two classical notions : rational transduction and residually finite group.

As defined by Nivat [10] , a rational transduction from X^* into Y^* is a mapping from $\mathcal{P}(X^*)$ into $\mathcal{P}(Y^*)$ with the main property that the image of a rational (resp. context-free) language by a rational transduction is a rational (resp. context-free) language . Two languages are said to be rationally equivalent if each one is the image of the other in a rational transduction. This notion is widely used for the study of the families of languages ([6]) and especially of the subfamilies of the context-free languages (see [4] for example).

A group G is residually finite if for any element g of G different from the neutral element, there exists a normal subgroup of G of finite index which doesnt contain g. The free groups are residually finite, the direct product of residually finite groups in residually finite [9].

We then can state :

Theorem 1 *Let* G *be a residually finite group. The languages whose syntactic pointed-monoids are* G_F, *where* F *is any finite subset of* G, *are all rationnally equivalent.*

Theorem 1 is a corollary of the two following lemmas each one of its own interest.

<u>Lemma 3</u> Let G be a group and F any rational subset of G.
Any language whose syntactic pointed-monoid is G_F, is the image in a rational transduction of a language whose syntactic pointed-monoid is G_1.

<u>Lemma 4</u> Let G be a residually finite group, F any finite subset of G, and X_L^* a language whose syntactic pointed-monoid is G_F. For each element f of F, there exists a rational language X_K^* such that the syntactic pointed-monoid of $X_{L \cap K}^*$ is G_f.

References

[1] ANISIMOV A.V. Sur les langages à groupes (en russe) , Kibernetika, Kiev, 1971, n°4, 18-24 ; trad. anglaise in Cybernetics.

[2] ANISIMOV A.V. Languages over free groups, in MFCS'75, Lecture Notes in Computer Science n°32, Springer Verlag, 1975, 167-171.

[3] ANISIMOV A.V. and SEIFERT F.D., Zur algebraischen Charakteristik der durch kontext-freie Sprachen definierten Gruppen, E.I.K. 11, 1975, 695-702.

[4] BOASSON L. On the largest full sub-AFL of the full AFL of Context-Free Languages, in MFCS'75, Lecture Notes in Computer Science n° 32, Springer Verlag, 1975, 194-198.

[5] EILENBERG S. <u>Automata languages and machines</u>, Vol. B, to appear.

[6] GINSBURG S. <u>Algebraic and automata-theoretic properties of formal languages</u>, North Holland, 1975.

[7] GIVE'ON Y. On some properties of free monoids with applications to automata theory, J. of Comput. and System Sci. 1, 1967, 137-154.

[8] KROHN K.B. et RHODES J.L. Algebraic theory of Machines I, Trans. Amer. Math. Soc. 116, 1965, 450-464.

[9] MAGNUS W. Residually finite groups, Bull. Amer. Math. Soc., 75, 1969, p. 305-316.

[10] NIVAT M. Transductions des langages de Chomsky, Ann. Inst. Fourier, Grenoble, 18, 1968, 339-456.

[11] PERROT J-F. Monoïdes syntactiques des langages algébriques, to appear in Acta Informatica.

[12] PERROT J-F. et J. SAKAROVITCH Langages algébriques déterministes et groupes abéliens, in Automata Theory and Formal Languages 2nd GI Conference, Lecture notes in Computer Science 33, Springer Verlag, 1975, 20-30.

[13] SAKAROVITCH J. Monoïdes syntactiques et langages algébriques, Thèse 3e cycle Math. Univ. Paris VII, 1976.

[14] SAKAROVITCH J. Sur les monoïdes syntactiques des langages algébriques déterministes, communication to the III rd International Colloquium on Automata, Languages and Programming, Edinburgh 1976, to appear in Lecture Notes in Computer Science, Springer Verlag.

[15] SCHUTZENBERGER M.P. On finite monoids having only trivial subgroup, Information and control 8, 1965, 190-194.

[16] TEISSIER M. Sur les équivalences régulières dans les demi-groupes, C.R. Acad. Sci. Paris, 232, (1951), 1987-1989.

Mailing address : J. Sakarovitch
Université Pierre et Marie Curie
Institut de Programmation
Tour 55-65 - 4, place Jussieu
75230 Paris Cedex 05
France

DEGREES OF PARALLELISM IN COMPUTATIONS

V.Yu. Sazonov
Institute of Mathematics,
Novosibirsk 90, USSR

Abstract

This paper is concerned with the class of sequentially computable finite type functionals and its enrichments by adding some parallel functionals of various power.

Introduction

The notion of sequentially and parallelly computable functionals was introduced earlier by the author[4,5,6]. Also the class of effectively-sequential finite type functionals was found to coincide with the class of functionals expressible in D.Scott's algorithmic language LCF (Logic for Computable Functions, see 2 and §I below). This is an answer to the Scott's question on expressibility in LCF [2].

The results of the paper are connected with another question of D.Scott [2]: What parallel functionals can be reasonably added to LCF? He pointed out the parallel disjunction OR as one of candidates. M.B. Trachtenbrot proved [8,9] that all effective functions of the types $(o,o,\ldots,o\rightarrow o)$, where o - numerical type, are expressible in LCF + OR. But it follows from our paper that all effective finite type functionals (Ju.L. Ershov [I]) can be obtained only if we also add the so-called parallel existential quantifier $\exists$ which is functional of the type $((o\rightarrow o)\rightarrow o)$.

As OR and $\exists$ are mutually not expressible in LCF we have at least two incomparable degrees of parallelism. Some other degrees and connections between them are represented in Figure I of theorem 3. To be more exact, degrees of parallelism form an upper semilattice, and Figure I represents its finite subsemilattice. Thus more orless natural landmarks are arrenged in the set of degrees.

For multiplace numerical functions some analogous results on expressibility and nonexpressibility by means of superpusition operator or superposition and recursion operators were stated earlier by M.B. Trachtenbrot [7,8,9]. But in this paper expressibility is understood in some different sense. Here the only method of expressing functionals by other ones is the operation of application of a function to an argument of suitable types, both operators - superposition and recursion (the least fixed point operator) - being trivially expressible in LCF. Besides the mentioned above result on expressibility in LCF + + OR of multiplace numerical functions we note M.B.Trachtenbrot's example of three place function being effective and sequential but not effectively-sequential([8], theorem 4, and also [9]). At the end of §2 we give two analogous examples in which effectiveness also play an essential part. These examples deliver some new degrees of parallelism different from the degrees given in Figure I.

Following D.Scott we may state the task of characterisation of the class of functionals expressible in LCF + f, where f is functional belonging to this or that degree of parallelism. For some degrees given in Figure I such characteristics are obtained in terms of the strategies of sequential and parallel computation introduced by the author in [4,5]. It is characterisation in terms of the strategies on which Figure I is mainly based. As the technique of the computational strategies is rather cumbersome we confine oneselves to it and give no proofs.

The author is thankful to professor B.A.Trachtenbrot who has read the manuscript of the paper and made a number of valuble remarks.

§I. Functionals of finite types and language LCF

We follow D.Scott[3] in definition of finite type functionals and language LCF.

Let $D_0 = \{0, I, 2, \ldots, \bot\}$ be the set partially ordered by binary relation $\sqsubseteq$: $\bot$ - the least, so-colled <u>undefined</u>, element; the other numbers in D_0 are parwise incomparable. We read $x \sqsubseteq y$ as "x is less defined or equal to y". The undefined element $\bot$ iformally denotes an infinite computational process.

<u>Types</u> are built up from the basic type o by the rule: if α and β are types, then $(\alpha \to \beta)$ is type. We take the abbreviation $(\alpha_1, \alpha_2, \ldots$ $\ldots, \alpha_n \to \beta)$ for the type $(\alpha_1 \to (\alpha_2 \to \ldots (\alpha_n \to \beta) \ldots))$. Every type α can be uniquelly represented in the form $(\alpha_1, \alpha_2, \ldots, \alpha_n \to o)$.

For every type α we define a partially ordered set $(D_\alpha, \sqsubseteq)$ of functionals of the type α . $(D_0, \sqsubseteq)$ has been defined. Let $D_{(\gamma \to \delta)} \underset{df}{\equiv} [D_\gamma \to$ $\to D_\delta]$, where $[D_\gamma \to D_\delta]$ denotes the set of monotonic and continuous functions [I,2,3] from D_γ to D_δ. The result of application of a function $f \in D_{(\gamma \to \delta)}$ to an argument $x \in D_\gamma$ lies in D_δ and is denoted by fx. The partial order $\sqsubseteq$ on $D_{(\gamma \to \delta)}$ is pointwise: $f \sqsubseteq g \underset{df}{\Longleftrightarrow} (\forall x \in D_\gamma)(fx \sqsubseteq gx)$ Every D_α has the least, undefined, element $\bot_\alpha$ ($\bot_o = \bot$, $\bot_{(\gamma \to \delta)} x = \bot_\delta$). It is useful to note, that partial order $\sqsubseteq$ on functionals of the type

$\alpha = (\alpha_1, \alpha_2, \ldots, \alpha_n \to o)$ can be defined equivalently by the condition:
$f \sqsubseteq g \underset{df}{\Longleftrightarrow} (\forall x_1 \in D_{\alpha_1}, \ldots, \forall x_n \in D_{\alpha_n})(fx_1 \ldots x_n \sqsubseteq gx_1 \ldots x_n)$.

<u>Constants of the language LCF</u> are the following ones: $0, \perp \in D_o$, $Z, \sigma_+, \sigma_- \in D_{(o \to o)}$ (zero, undefined, the predicate "to be zero", the functions of the unit addition and subtraction), if $\in D_{(o,o,o \to o)}$ (conditional function), $K_{\alpha\beta} \in D_{(\alpha,\beta \to \alpha)}$, $S_{\alpha\beta\gamma} \in D_{((\alpha,\beta \to \gamma),(\alpha \to \beta),\alpha \to \gamma)}$ (combinators), $Y_\alpha \in D_{((\alpha \to \alpha) \to \alpha)}$ (the least fixed point operator).

What one can say about the functionals expressible in LCF, that is the functionals obtainable from LCF constants by the finite number of applications? First we stop at the notion of effectiveness.

Effective finite type functionals [I] are defined with the help of finite functionals (Ju.L.Ershov's f-elements [I]). A functional $a \in D_\alpha$ is <u>finite</u>, if for any increasing sequence $a_1 \sqsubseteq a_2 \sqsubseteq \ldots$ of elements from D_α $a \sqsubseteq \bigsqcup_{i=1}^{\infty} a_i$ imply $a \sqsubseteq a_i$ for some i. At more detailed investigation [I] it may be found that the finite functionals are really constructive objects. In particular we can discuss effective sequences of finite functionals of a given type α. Every functional $x \in D_\alpha$ can be represented in the form $x = \bigsqcup_{i=1}^{\infty} a_i$, where $a_1, a_2, \ldots \in D_\alpha$ is an increasing sequence of finite elements. A functional $x \in D_\alpha$ is called <u>effective</u>, if there exists an effective sequence $\{a_i\}$ which approximates it. All the constants of LCF are effective. It is not difficult to show that if $f \in D_{(\alpha \to \beta)}$ and $x \in D_\alpha$ are effective functionals, then functional $fx \in D_\beta$ is also effective. Therefore only effective functionals are expressible in LCF. As examples of effective functionals non-expressible in LCF we point out <u>parallel disjunction</u> $OR \in D_{(o,o \to o)}$ and <u>parallel existential quantifier</u> $\exists \in D_{((o \to o) \to o)}$:

$$ORxy = \begin{cases} I, \text{ if } x = I \text{ or } y = I, \\ 0, \text{ if } x = 0 \text{ and } y = 0, \\ \perp \text{ in other cases;} \end{cases}$$

$$\exists f = \begin{cases} 0, \text{ if } f\perp = 0, \\ I, \text{ if } fx = I \text{ for some } x \in D_o, \\ \perp \text{ in other cases.} \end{cases}$$

Let us explain by the example of parallel disjunction OR what its parallelism is. One can not begin computation of ORxy with any one of the arguments. It can be $\perp$ and the other - I, the value of ORxy being I. As $\perp$ denotes an infinite process we should newer know the value of the other argument. Therefore we would obtain $ORxy = \perp$ in contradiction to the above. The next conclusion follows: both arguments x and y should be computed parallel or that is essentially the same, the computation should begin with one of the arguments chosen undeterministically.

In contrast to OR the conditional function ifxyz can be computed sequentially: first compute x; if $x = I$ then compute y and set $ifxyz = y$; if $x = 0$ then compute z and set $ifxyz = z$. Note that the choice of the next arguments and resulting value is effective here. That is why we call the function if as effectively-sequential.

In [4,5,6] the class of <u>sequential</u> functionals and its subclass of <u>effectively-sequential</u> functionals of finite types (and also for some type-free model of D.Scott [4,5]) were defined. There was stated also the following

<u>Theorem I</u>. a) All effectively-sequential functionals, and only they, are expressible in LCF.

b) All sequential functionals, and only they, are expressible in $LCF + D_{(o\to o)}$.

<u>§2. Degrees of parallelism</u>

The presence of the combinators S and K in LCF causes the following equivalence: f_I is expressible in $LCF + f_2 \Longleftrightarrow$ there exists an expressible in LCF (that is effectively-sequential) functional G such that $f_I = Gf_2$. Here $G \in D_{(\alpha\to\beta)}$ if $f_I \in D_\beta$ and $f_2 \in D_\alpha$. If both sides of the equivalence are true we write $f_I \leqslant_{sq} f_2$ and say that f_I <u>sequentially reduces</u> to f_2. $\leqslant_{sq}$ is evidently preorder on the set $\bigcup D_\alpha$. Equivalence relation induced by the preorder is denoted by $\equiv_{sq}$. Related classes of the equivalence are called <u>degrees of parallelism</u>. As usual it is easy to show that degrees of parallelism form an upper semilattice. The join of any degrees f_I and f_2 is denoted by $f_I \oplus f_2$. The set of the functionals expressible in LCF form evidently the least degree of parallelism. The next theorem gives three nontrivial degrees.

<u>Theorem 2</u>. a) All effective functionals are expressible in $LCF + OR + \exists$.

b) All functionals are expressible in $LCF + OR + \exists + D_{(o\to o)}$.

c) OR and $\exists$ are not mutually expressible in $LCF + D_{(o\to o)}$.

Thus OR and $\exists$ give two incomparable degrees, and $OR \oplus \exists$ gives the greatest degree among all effective degrees (i.e. degrees containing effective functionals).

We indicate some more degrees of parallelism. Let us define functionals $\sigma \in D_{(o,o\to o)}$, $V, V' \in D_{(o,o,o\to o)}$, $\exists_n \in D_{((o\to o)\to o)}$ $(n \geqslant 0)$, $T_{OR} \in D_{(((o,o\to o)\to o)\to o)}$, $T_{\exists_n} \in D_{((((o\to o)\to o)\to o)\to o)}$ $(n \geqslant 0)$ by the following equalities:

$$\sigma x_I x_2 = \begin{cases} 0, \text{ if } x_I = 0 \text{ or } x_2 = 0, \\ \bot, \text{ if } x_I \neq 0 \text{ and } x_2 \neq 0; \end{cases}$$

$$Vx_1x_2x_3 = \begin{cases} x_i, \text{ if } x_i = x_j \text{ for some } j \neq i, \\ \bot, \text{ if } x_i \neq x_j \text{ for all } j \neq i; \end{cases}$$

$$V'x_1x_2x_3 = \begin{cases} 3n, \text{ if } x_1 = x_2 = 3n, \\ 3n+1, \text{ if } x_1 = x_3 = 3n+1, \\ 3n+2, \text{ if } x_2 = x_3 = 3n+2, \\ \bot \text{ in other cases;} \end{cases}$$

$$\exists_n f = \begin{cases} 0, \text{ if } f\bot = 0, \\ 1, \text{ if } fx = 1 \text{ for some } x \in \{0,1,\dots,n\}, \\ \bot \text{ in other cases;} \end{cases}$$

$$T_h G = \begin{cases} 0, \text{ if } Gh = 0, \\ \bot, \text{ if } Gh \neq 0 \end{cases} \qquad (h = OR, \exists_n).$$

Note that so-called <u>voting function</u> V was introduced by M.B.Trachtenbrot [7,8,9].

<u>Theorem 3</u>. The finite lattice in Fig. I is an upper subsemilattice of the upper semilattice of all degrees of parallelism.

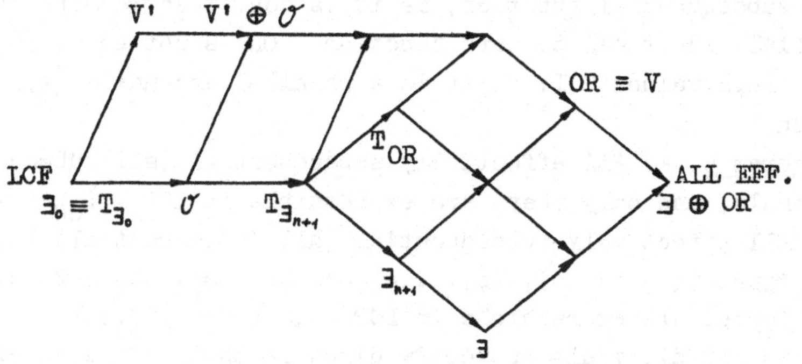

Figure I.

In particular it is asserted that $\exists \oplus OR \equiv \exists \oplus V'$, $\exists_0 \lneq \exists_1 \equiv \exists_2 \equiv \equiv \exists_3 \equiv \dots$, $V' \oplus \sigma \lneq V' + T_{\exists_{n+1}} \lneq V' \oplus T_{OR}$, etc.

If in the definition of sequential reducibility $\leqslant_{sq}$ the functional G is allowed to be any expressible in LCF + $D_{(o \to o)}$ (i.e. any sequential) then everything from the above, including theorem 3, remains true with a minor exception. Namely: I) the least degree will now consist of all functionals expressible in LCF + $D_{(o \to o)}$, and 2) $\exists \oplus OR$ will be the greatest degree among all degrees.

The next two examples deliver some new effective degrees of parallelism different from the given ones in Figure I. Let A and B be any recursively inseparable and recursively enumerable sets, and "$x \in B$ in y steps" is predicate taking the value I if in some fixed enumerating process of B x occurs in ctep y, and - the value 0 in the opposite case. Let further k be a total numerical function nonmajorable by any recursive function and such that the set $\{(x,y): x \leqslant k(y)\}$ is recursively enumerable. Let us define a function $r \in D_{(o,o \to o)}$ and a functional $H \in D_{((o\to o)\to o)}$ by the following equalities:

$$rxy = \begin{cases} 0, \text{ if } \perp \neq x \in A, \\ \text{"}x \in B \text{ in } y \text{ steps"}, \text{ if } x \neq \perp \text{ and } y \neq \perp, \\ \perp, \text{ if } x = \perp \text{ or } (\perp \neq x \notin A \;\&\; y = \perp); \end{cases}$$

$$Hf = \begin{cases} 0, \text{ if } f\perp \neq \perp, \\ I, \text{ if for some } x \neq \perp \;\; \perp \neq f0 \neq fx \neq \perp \text{ and } x \leqslant k(f0), \\ \perp \text{ in other cases.} \end{cases}$$

Theorem 4. a) Function r is effective and expressible in LCF + + $D_{(o\to o)}$ but nonexpressible in LCF + T_{OR}.

b) Functional H is effective and expressible in LCF + OR + $D_{(o\to o)}$, but nonexpressible in LCF + OR.

A functional f is called subsequential, if $f \sqsubseteq g$ for some sequential functional g. If f is also effective and g - effectively-sequential then f is called effectively-subsequential. For example, $\mathcal{O}$ is effectively-subsequential function, as it is contained in effectively-sequential, identical to zero function. OR is not subsequential as on the truth values 0,I,$\perp$ it is a parallel and maximally defined function.

Theorem 5. a) All effectively-subsequential (all subsequential) functionals, and only they, are expressible in LCF + T_{OR} (+ $D_{(o\to o)}$).

b) All effectively-subsequential (all subsequential) functionals of the types $((o\to o)\to o)$, $(o,\ldots,o\to o)$, and only those functionals of the types, are expressible in LCF + $\mathcal{O}$ (+ $D_{(o\to o)}$).

It is not difficult to verify directly that r is an effective and sequential but not effectively-subsequential function. This and theorem 5 a) easily imply theorem 4 a). In the introduction the example from [8] of an effective and sequential, but not effectively-sequential function was mentioned. This function in opposite to r is effectively-subsequential.

References

I. Ershov, Ju.L., Computable functionals of finite types, Algebra i Logika, II, No4 (I972), 367–437.
2. Scott, D., A type-theoretical alternative to CUCH, ISWIM, OWHY, Oxford University, I969.
3. Scott, D., Continuous lattices, in Toposes, Algebraic Geomrtry and Logic, Lecture Notes in Mathematics N274, I972, 97-I36.
4. Sazonov, V.Yu., Sequentially and parallelly computable functionals (extended abstract), in λ-Calculus and computer Science Theory, Proc. of the Symp. held in Rome, I975, Lect. Notes in Comp. Sci., 37, I975, 3I2-3I8.
5. Sazonov, V.Yu., Sequentially and parallelly computable functionals, Sibirskiĭ Matematičeskiĭ Žurnal, XVII, No3 (I976), 648-672 (in Russian).
6. Sazonov, V.Yu., On expressibility and computability of objects in D.Scott's language LCF, Third All-Union Conference on Mathematical Logic, Novosibirsk, I974, I9I-I94 (in Russian).
7. Trachtenbrot, M.B., On interpreted functions in program schemes, in Sistemnoe i teoretičeskoe programmirovanie, Novosibirsk, I973, I88-2II (in Russion).
8. Trachtenbrot, M.B., On representation of sequential and parallel functions, in Vyčislitel'naja matematika i programmirovanie, Novosibirsk, I974, 74-80 (in Russian).
9. Trachtenbrot, M.B., On representation of sequential and parallel functions, in Proc. of 4th Symp. on Mathematical Foundations of Computer Science, Lect. Notes in Comp. Sci., 32, I975, 4II-4I7.

ON ADAPTABILITY OF A SYSTEM OF PROGRAMS

A. Schurmann
Institute of Mathematics
University of Gdansk
80-952, Poland

1. Introduction

Many problems concerning construction of optimalprogramming systems have practically no effective solutions. On the other hand, using software engineering methods, we are able to design large programming systems which seems to be "optimal" from the practical point of view. May we treat these software engineering techniques as methods for obtaining solutions near to the optimal ons? In other words, can we develop in programming theory efficient methods for approximate solutions ? This note is an attempt to give a positive answer to this question.

2. Basic notions

By a memory we mean a non-empty set C of vectors. An operation defined on the memory C is a partial computable function $r:C\rightarrow C$. Let L denote a set of symbols called labels. An instruction is a word of the form $l:r(X)$, where $l\in L$, r denotes amoperation defined on memory C and X denotes a subset of C. A machine defined on memory C is a system $M=\langle I,D,O,V,\mu\rangle$, where $I,O\subset D\subset C$, I and O are disjoint sets (called the sets of input states and output states, respectively), V is a set of instructions and $\mu:(D-O)\rightarrow V$ is a partial function (called the transition function) with the property: if $\mu(c)=r$ then c belongs to the domain of r (abbr.: $c\in \mathrm{dom}(r)$). By op(M) we shall denote the set of operations of machine M, i.e. $r\in \mathrm{op}(M)$ iff there exists an instruction $l:g(X)\in V$ such that $g=r$.

We define functions fun and arg as follows: if q denotes the instruction $l:r(X)$ then $\mathrm{fun}(q)=r$ and $\mathrm{arg}(q)=X$. By a computation of machine M beginning with x_1 we mean the sequence $\mathrm{com}(M)(x_1)=x_1,x_2,\ldots,x_k,\ldots$ such that $x_1\in I$, $x_i\in D-O$, $x_i\in \mathrm{arg}(\mu(x_i))$ and $x_{i+1}=[\mathrm{fun}(\mu(x_i))](x_i)$. If $x_k\in O$ then x_k is the result of this computation. By the state function of machine M we mean the partial function $\mathrm{st}(M):I\rightarrow O$ defined as follows: $\mathrm{st}(M)(x)=z$, if z is the result of $\mathrm{com}(M)(x)$

=undefined, otherwise.

We say that machine M computes partial function $f:C\rightarrow C$ if $\mathrm{dom}(f)\subseteq \mathrm{dom}(\mathrm{st}(M))$ and f is a restriction of function $\mathrm{st}(M)$.

A program of machine M is any subset P of the set of instructions V with the following property: for all $s,w \in P$, if $s \neq w$ then $lab(s) \neq lab(w)$, where $lab(s)$ denotes the label of instruction s. Sequence $c_1,\ldots,c_k,\ldots$ is a computation of program P beginning with c_1 (abbr.: $com(P)(c_1)$) if: $\mu(c_i) \in P$, $c_i \in arg(\mu(c_i))$ and $c_{i+1}=[fun(\mu(c_i))](c_i)$, for $i=1,2,\ldots$ If the above conditions hold for $i<k$ and, $c_k \in O$ or $\mu(c_k) \notin P$ then c_k will be called the result of $com(P)(c)$. We define the state function $st(P)$ of program P analogously as the state function of a machine.

Definition 1([11]). By a system of programs (abbr.: spr) of machine $M=\langle I,D,O,V,\mu\rangle$ we mean the sequence of ordered sets

(1) $\langle P(i,1),\ldots,P(i,n_i),P(i),V_{i+1}\rangle$, for $i=1,\ldots,n$,

with the following properties:

i. $V_1=V$,
   V_{i+1} is a set of instructions of the form $l:st(P(i,j))(X)$, where $P(i,j)\subset V_i$ are programs, for $j\leqslant n_i$;

ii. for some non-empty sets I_i, $O_i \subset D$, $M_i=\langle I_i,D,O_i,V_{i+1},st(P(i))\rangle$ are machines, where $P(i)\subset V_i$ is a program, for $i=1,\ldots,n$.

In the sequel we omit the sets V_i and we shall write the spr (1) as follows: $\mathcal{P}=\{P(i,j),P(i) \mid i\leqslant n, j\leqslant n_i\}$. By a computation of spr $\mathcal{P}$ we will mean the computation of machine M_n. The above definition implies that spr $\mathcal{P}$ consists of a set of hierarchically structured programs $P(i,j)$ such that programs from the i-th level call only programs from the lower levels.

Now we shall introduce the notions of adaptation of programs and spr. Let $sp(M,f)$ denote the set of all programs of machine M which compute function f.

Definition 2. By the adaptation of a program $P\in sp(M,f)$ to a program $Q\in sp(H,g)$ we shall mean a transformation $\alpha: sp(M,f)\rightarrow sp(H,g)$ such that $Q=\alpha(P)$.

Next we shall give a measure of effort required to perform the adaptation.

Definition 3. By the measure of adaptation of program P by transformation α we shall mean the value $am(P,\alpha)$, where function am satisfies the following conditions:

i. $am(P,\alpha)\geqslant 0$; if $\alpha(\emptyset)$ is not empty program then $am(\emptyset,\alpha)>0$, where $\emptyset$ denotes the empty program;

ii. if $P=P_1\cup P_2$ and $P_2=\alpha(P)$ then $am(P,\alpha)=0$;

iii. if $P=P_1\cup P_2\cup P_3$, $\alpha(P)=P_1\cup P_2\cup T$, $\beta(P)=P_1\cup G\cup T$ and $G\neq P_2$ then $am(P,\beta)>am(P,\alpha)$;

iv. if $\alpha(P)=\beta(\gamma(P))$ then $am(P,\alpha)=am(P,\gamma)+am(\gamma(P),\beta)$.

We should interpret the function $am(P,\alpha)$ as the effort needed to obtain program $\alpha(P)$ from program P. Condition (ii) says that if program $\alpha(P)$ is a part of program P then no effort is needed to obtain the program $\alpha(P)$ from program P. Condition (iii) express the property that the effort needed to obtain the program $P_1 \cup P_2 \cup T$ from the program $P_1 \cup P_2 \cup P_3$ is less than or equal to the effort needed to obtain the program $P_1 \cup G \cup T$ from the program $P_1 \cup P_2 \cup P_3$. Condition (iv) says that if a program $\alpha(P)$ is obtained from program P in two steps, then the effort needed to obtain $\alpha(P)$ is the sum of the efforts needed in the first and in the second step.

Let sps(M,f) denote the set of all spr of machine M which compute function f.

Definition 4. By the adaptation of spr (abbr.: asp transformation) $\mathcal{P}=\{P(i,j),P(i) \mid i\leq n, j\leq n_i\} \in sps(M,f)$ to a spr $\mathcal{Q}=\{Q(i,j),Q(i) \mid i\leq m, j\leq m_i\} \in sps(H,g)$ we shall mean a system of program transformations $\mathcal{T}=\{\mathcal{T}(i,j),\mathcal{T}(i) \mid i\leq m, j\leq m_i\}$ with the following properties:

$$Q(i)=\mathcal{T}(i)(P(i)), \quad Q(i,j)=\mathcal{T}(i,j)(P(i,j)), \text{ for } i=1,\dots,m, \ j=1,\dots,m_i.$$

In this case we shall write $\mathcal{Q}=\mathcal{T}(\mathcal{P})$

Definition 5. Let the notation of Definition 4 be valid. By the measure of adaptation of spr $\mathcal{P}$ by asp transformation $\mathcal{T}$ we shall mean the value $ams(\mathcal{P},\mathcal{T})$ defined as follows

$$(2) \qquad ams(\mathcal{P},\mathcal{T})=\textstyle\sum_{i=1}^{m}[am(P(i),\mathcal{T}(i))+\sum_{j=1}^{m_i} am(P(i,j),\mathcal{T}(i,j))].$$

We should consider formula (2) as one of the possible measures of the effort required to perform asp transformations.

3. Problem and the approximate solution

Problem. Suppose there are given machines M, H_e and functions f, g_e, for e=1,...,w, such that if $i\neq j$ then $H_i\neq H_j$ or $g_i\neq g_j$. Design spr $\mathcal{A}\in sps(M,f)$ and determine asp transformations $\omega_e: sps(M,f)\rightarrow sps(H_e,g_e)$, $e\leq w$, such that

$$\textstyle\sum_{e=1}^{w} ams(\mathcal{A},\omega_e)\leq\sum_{e=1}^{w} ams(\mathcal{P},\mathcal{T}_e),$$

for all spr systems $\mathcal{P}\in sps(M,f)$ and all asp transformations $\mathcal{T}_e: sps(M,f)\rightarrow sps(H_e,g_e)$, $e\leq w$.

In general we have not an efficient method to solve this problem. But we may seek approximate solutions. Below a general outline of an algorithm for such solution is given. More precisely, the algorithm presents a general description of spr $\mathcal{Q}\in sps(M,f)$ and of asp transformations φ_e, $e\leq w$, which approximate the spr $\mathcal{A}$ and asp transformations ω_e, respectively, in the sense that $\sum_{e=1}^{w} ams(\mathcal{Q},\varphi_e)$ approximates $\sum_{e=1}^{w} ams(\mathcal{A},\omega_e)$. It must be noted that the approximation error is not known.

We shall assume that, for f, we know the high-level macrooperations $f_1,\ldots f_k$ such that the algorithm with this operations computes function f. In other words, we assume that there are given high-level macro-operations $f_1,\ldots,f_k$ such that f is computable by a machine F with the set of operations $op(F)=\{f_i \mid i=1,\ldots,k\}$. Analogously, we assume that, for every g_e ($e\leq w$), there are given high-level macrooperations g_{ej}, $j=1,\ldots,j_e$, such that function g_e is computable by a machine G_e with the set of operations $op(G_e)=\{g_{ej} \mid j=1,\ldots,j_e\}$. Futher we assume that $op(F)\cap op(G_e)\neq\emptyset$, for $e\leq w$.

Below we shall use partial spr. Let $\mathcal{P}=\{P(i,j),P(i) \mid i\leq n, j\leq n_i\}$ be an spr. By a partial spr we mean a set $\mathcal{T}=\{T(i,j),T(i) \mid i\leq m, j\leq n_i\}$ such that $T(i,j)=P(i,j)$ or $T(i,j)=\emptyset$, $T(i)=P(i)$ or $T(i)=\emptyset$. Let $\mathcal{R}=\{R(i,j),R(i) \mid i\leq m, j\leq m_i\}$ be a partial spr. We define operations $\leftarrow$ and $\dot{-}$ as follows. $\mathcal{T}\leftarrow\mathcal{R}$ will denote the partial spr $\mathcal{S}=\{S(i,j),S(i) \mid i\leq v, j\leq v_i\}$, where $v=\max(n,m)$ and

$S(i)=T(i)$ if $R(i)=\emptyset$, otherwise $S(i)=R(i)$,

$S(i,j)=T(i,j)$ if $R(i,j)=\emptyset$, otherwise $S(i,j)=R(i,j)$.

$\mathcal{T}\dot{-}\mathcal{R}$ will denote the partial spr $\mathcal{U}=\{U(i,j),U(i) \mid i\leq n, j\leq n_i\}$, where

$U(i)=T(i)$ if $T(i)\neq R(i)$, otherwise $U(i)=\emptyset$,

$U(i,j)=T(i,j)$ if $T(i,j)\neq R(i,j)$, otherwise $U(i,j)=\emptyset$.

Let $\mathcal{P}=\{P(i,j),P(i) \mid i\leq n, j\leq n_i\}$ be an spr. We shall say that programs from a set $B\subseteq\{P(v),P(v,1),\ldots,P(v,n_v)\}$ depend only from operations of the set $B_0\subseteq\{st(P(e,1)),\ldots,st(P(e,n_e))\}$ if the following conditions hold:

i. for $u=1,\ldots,v-e$, there exists subset $B_u\subseteq\{P(e+u,1),\ldots,P(e+u,n_{e+u})\}$ such that programs from B_u contain only instructions of the form $l:st(E)(X)$, where $E\in B_{u-1}$,

ii. $B\subseteq B_{v-e}$.

Let N_e denote the set $op(F)\cap op(G_e)$, for $e\leq w$, and let N denote the sum $N_1\cup\ldots\cup N_w$. If P is a program and q a function then we shall write $st(P)=q$ to denote the property that $st(P)(x)=q(x)$ for $x\in dom(q)$.

<u>Algorithm</u>. Construction of spr $\mathcal{Q}\in sps(M,f)$ and of asp transformations φ_e such that $\varphi_e(\mathcal{Q})\in sps(H_e,g_e)$.

a. Design spr $\mathcal{Q}'=\{Q'(i,j),Q'(i)\mid i\leq n, j\leq n_i\}$ of machine M and asp transformations β_e, $e\leq w$, with the following properties:

a.1. for every function $q\in N$ there exists $j\leq n_n$ such that $st(Q'(n,j))=q$, where n_n is the number of elements of the set N;

a.2. $\beta_e(\mathcal{Q}')$ is an spr of machine H_e such that, for some $v(e)<n$, $V_e\subseteq B_e$, where $B_e=\{st(Q'(v(e),j))\mid j\leq n_{v(e)}\}$, $V_e=\{st(T_e(m_e,j))\mid j\leq e_{m_e}\}$ and $\{T_e(i,j),\ T_e(i)\mid i\leq m_e, j\leq e_i\}=\beta_e(\mathcal{Q}')$, for $e\leq w$;

a.3. programs from the set $\{Q'(n,j)\mid j\leq n_n$ and there exists function $q\in N_e$ such that $st(Q'(n,j))=q\}$ depend only from operations of the set V_e;

a.4. the number $\sum_{e=1}^{w} ams(\mathcal{Q}',\beta_e)$ is as small as possible.

b. Design partial spr $\mathcal{S}=\{S(i,j),S(i)\mid i\leq n, n_i<j\leq k_i\}$ with the following properties:

b.1. $\mathcal{Q}'\leftarrow\mathcal{S}\in sps(M,f)$;

b.2. for every function $q\in F-N$ there exists j $(n_n<j\leq k_n)$ such that $st(S(n,j))=q$, where k_n-n_n equals the number of elements of the set F-N.

c. $\mathcal{Q}:=\mathcal{Q}'\leftarrow\mathcal{S}$.

d. Delete from spr $\mathcal{Q}'$ all programs $Q'(i,j)$ which do not necessery to compute functions from $op(G_e)$; more precisely, design asp transformation $\gamma_e=[\gamma(i,j),\gamma_e(i)\mid i\leq n, j\leq n_i\}$ in the following way:

d.1. $[\gamma_e(n,j)](Q'(n,j))=Q'(n,j)$, if $st(Q'(n,j))\in N_e$,

$=\emptyset$, otherwise,

for $j\leq n_n$;

d.2. if, for program $Q'(i,j)$, there exists $u\leq n_{i+1}$ such that program $[\gamma_e(i+1,u)](Q'(i+1,u))$ contains an instruction of the form $1:st(Q'(i,j))(X)$ then $[\gamma_e(i,j)](Q'(i,j))=Q'(i,j)$; otherwise $[\gamma_e(i,j)](Q'(i,j))=\emptyset$; for $i=n-1,n-2,\ldots,v(e)$ and $j=1,\ldots,n_i$;

d.3. $\gamma_e(i)(Q'(i))=Q'(i)$, for $i=1,\ldots,n$,

$[\gamma_e(i,j)](Q'(i,j))=Q'(i,j)$, for $i=1,\dots,v(e)-1$, $j=1,\dots,n_i$.

e. Let $\mathcal{K}_e=\{K_e(i,j),K(i) \mid i\leq n, j\leq n_i\}=\gamma_e(Q')$. Design asp transformation γ'_e such that if $\mathcal{K}'_e=\{K'_e(i,j),K'_e(i) \mid m_e<i\leq s, j\leq s_i\}=\gamma'_e(\mathcal{K}_e)$ then: $s=n-v(e)+m_e$, $s_i=n_i-v(e)+m_e$, $K'_e(i,j)=K_e(i-v(e)+m_e,j)$, for $j=1,\dots$ $\dots,s_i$ and $K'_e(i)=K_e(i-v(e)+m_e)$, for $m_e<i\leq s$.

f. $\mathcal{W}_e:=\mathcal{K}'_e\leftarrow\beta_e(Q')$.

Comment: $\mathcal{W}_e$ is an spr of machine H_e which computes functions from N_e.

g. Design partial spr $\mathcal{U}_e=\{U_e(i,j),U_e(i) \mid i\leq s, t_i<j\leq p_i\}$ of machine H_e (i.e. design asp transformation σ_e such that $\sigma_e(\emptyset)=\mathcal{U}_e$) with the following properties:

g.1. $\mathcal{W}_e\leftarrow\mathcal{U}_e\in sps(H_e,g_e)$,

g.2. $\{st(U_e(s,j)) \mid j=t_s+1,\dots,p_s\}=op(G_e)-N_e$, where $t_i=e_i$ if $i\leq m_e$, otherwise $t_i=s_i$.

h. Define asp transformation φ_e as follows: $\varphi_e(Q):=\mathcal{W}_e\leftarrow\mathcal{U}_e$.

Corollary. asp transformation φ_e has the following form

$$\varphi_e(Q) = [\gamma'_e(\gamma_e(Q \div S))\leftarrow\beta_e(Q\div S)]\leftarrow\sigma_e(\emptyset)$$

and satisfies the condition $\varphi_e(Q)\in sps(H_e,g_e)$.

Theorem. $ams(Q,\varphi_e)=ams(Q',\beta_e)+ams(\emptyset,\sigma_e)$.

Using q times the above Algorithm we may obtain a sequence $(Q'_i,\beta_{ei},\sigma_{ei})$, $i\leq q$, where Q'_i and β_{ei} are the spr and the asp transformation, respectively, specified in (a), and σ_{ei} is the asp transformation specified in (g). According to the Algorithm, the i-th element of this sequence defines the spr Q_i and the asp transformation φ_{ei}. Using the given Theorem, we may choose , from the sequence (Q_i,β_{ei}), the approximation subsequence (Q_{i_u},φ_{ei_u}) such that

$$\Sigma^{w}_{e=1}\, ams(Q_{i_{u+1}},\varphi_{ei_{u+1}}) < \Sigma^{w}_{e=1}\, ams(Q_{i_u},\varphi_{ei_u}).$$

References

1. Schurmann A.: On portability of abstract programming systems, CC PAS Reports 211, (1975).

A MATHEMATICAL MODEL OF PARALLEL INFORMATION PROCESSING

A. Skowron

Institute of Mathematics
Warsaw University
Poland

Introduction

In the paper we present a mathematical model of information processing (which includes parallel processing as well). The basic motivation for our considerations (as compared to [4], [5]) lies in the fact that the realization of elementary programs (which corresponds to programs with one assignment statement) as well as that of programs obtained through sequential, parallel and conditional composition and through iteration is a process rather than a function.

We introduce basic notions concerning parallel programs and define their semantics, using the notion of a process. We also state some properties of the parallel program semantics. The theory of parallel programs will be presented in [6].

An example is given to illustrate the application of the notions introduced in the paper. Using the language of parallel programs we formulate tasks for cellular matrix [3].

1. Notation and auxiliary notions

We denote sequences by $d, d', \ldots$; while elements of sequences are denoted by $c, c', \ldots$. $|d|$ stands for the length of a sequence d; first (d) represents the first element of d, last (d) is the last element of d, when it is finite. If $d = c_1 \ldots c_n \ldots$, then let $\tilde{d} = d$ when for no n, $c_n = c_{n+1}$, and $\tilde{d} = c_1 \ldots c_p$ otherwise, where $p = \min_k (c_k = c_{k+1})$. The empty sequence is denoted by ε. When $\tilde{d}$ is finite, we denote by end (d) the last element of $\tilde{d}$.

We define now the operation of sequential composition of sequences (denoted by $\circ$) and the operation of parallel composition of sequences (denoted by $\|$). Let $d = c_1 \ldots c_n \ldots$, $d' = c_1' \ldots c_n' \ldots$.

Then $d \circ d' = d$, when $|\tilde{d}| = \infty$; and $d \circ d' = c_1 \ldots c_k c_2' \ldots c_n' \ldots$, when $\tilde{d} = c_1 \ldots c_k$ and $c_k = c_1'$ (where $k \geq 1$). In all other cases, $d \circ d' = \varepsilon$.

If c and c' are functions from A into B, then let $R_{cc'} = \{a \in A : c(a) \neq c'(a)\}$. If c, c', c'' are functions from A into B and $R_{cc'} \cap R_{cc''} = \emptyset$, then let

$$\|(c, c', c'') = c' | R_{cc'} \cup c'' | R_{cc''} \cup c | (A - (R_{cc'} \cup R_{cc''})).^{1)}$$

The parallel composition of c' and c'' with c is undefined when $R_{cc'} \cap R_{cc''} \neq \emptyset$.

If $d = c_1 c_2' \ldots c_n' \ldots$, $d' = c_1 c_2'' \ldots c_n'' \ldots$ and d,d' are sequences of functions from A into B, then - assuming that for all $i \geq 2$ the parallel composition of c_i' and c_i'' with c_i is defined - let $d \| d' = c_1 c_2 \ldots c_n \ldots$, where $c_i = \|(c_{i-1}, c_i', c_i'')$. In all other cases $d \circ d' = \varepsilon$.

2. The memory.

A memory is an ordered triple $P = (A,B,C)$, where A is a set of addresses (variables), B is an alphabet and $C \subset B^A$. The elemensts of C are called states (valuations). If $a \in A$ and $c \in C$, then $c(a)$ is called the contents of the address a in the state c (the value of the variable a under the valuation c).

C^∞ stands for the set of all infinite sequences over C. C^* is the set $C^\infty \cup \{\varepsilon\}$.

3. Operations on subsets of C^*

We introduce here operations on subsets of C^* which will be fundamental for our subsequent considerations on parallel program semantics. These operations are: sequential composition (;), parallel composition (‖), conditional composition with respect to a condition α ($Cond_\alpha$) and iteration

1) $f | A$ is the function f reduced to the set A.

with respect to a condition α (It_α). If $T,T' \subset C^*$, then $T\,;\,T' = \{d \circ d' : d \in T \wedge d' \in T' \wedge d \circ d' \neq \varepsilon\} \cup A_\varepsilon$, where $A_\varepsilon = \{\varepsilon\}$ when $\varepsilon \in T \cup T'$ or if for some $d \in T$ such that $0 < |\tilde{d}| < \infty$, $d \circ d' = \varepsilon$ for every $d' \in T'$; in all other cases $A_\varepsilon = \emptyset$.
If $T,T' \subset C^*$, then $T \parallel T' = \{d \parallel d' : d \in T \wedge d' \in T' \wedge (\text{first}(d) = \text{first}(d') \vee d = \varepsilon \vee d' = \varepsilon)\}$.

<u>Proposition 1</u> If $T,T',T'' \subset C^*$, then $(T;T');T'' = T;(T';T'')$ and $(T \parallel T') \parallel T'' = T \parallel (T' \parallel T'')$.

Let $T,T' \subset C^*$ and let α be an open formula, α_R its realization in the memory (A,B,C) (i.e. [5] α_R is a function from C into $\{0,1\}$). Then $\text{Cond}_\alpha(T,T') = \{d \in T : \alpha_R(\text{first}(d)) = 1\} \cup \{d' \in T' : \alpha_R(\text{first}(d')) = 0\} \cup B_\varepsilon$, where $B_\varepsilon = \{\varepsilon\}$ if $\varepsilon \in T \cup T'$ and $B = \emptyset_\varepsilon$ otherwise. The set $It_\alpha(T)$ is defined as the join of sets $I_\alpha(T)$ and $I_\varepsilon(T)$. $I_\alpha(T)$ is the set of all sequences $d \in C^\infty$ for which one of the following conditions holds:

1° there exist a $p > 1$ and $d_1, \ldots, d_p \in T - \{\varepsilon\}$ such that $d = d_1 \circ \ldots \circ d_p$, where for $i \leqslant p-1$ $|\tilde{d}_i| < \infty$, $\alpha_R(\text{end}(d_i)) = 1$ and $|\tilde{d}_p| = \infty$ or $\alpha_R(\text{end}(d_p)) = 0$;

2° there exists an infinite sequence $d_1 d_2 \ldots$ over $T - \{\varepsilon\}$ such that for $i = 1,2,\ldots$, $|\tilde{d}_i| < \infty$ and $\alpha_R(\text{end}(d_i)) = 1$ and for every $p \geqslant 1$ there exists a $d' \in C^\infty$, with $d_1 \circ \ldots \circ d_p \circ d' = d$.

$I_\varepsilon(T) = \{\varepsilon\}$ when $\varepsilon \in T$ or when there exists a sequence $d \in T$ for which none of the conditions 1°, 2° holds. Otherwise $I_\varepsilon(T) = \emptyset$.

4. <u>Processes</u>

A set $T \subset C^\infty$ is called a process if for every $c \in C$ there exists at most one sequence $d \in T$ such that $\text{first}(d) = c$ and for every $d \in T$ if $d = c_1 c_2 \ldots$ and $c_i = c_{i+1}$ for some i, then $c_k = c_{k+1}$ for $k > i$.

<u>Proposition 2</u>. Let $T,T' \subset C^\infty$ be processes and let α be an open formula with a realization in the memory $P = (A,B,C)$. Then

a) if $\varepsilon \notin T;T'$, then $T;T'$ is a process,

b) if $\varepsilon \notin T \parallel T'$, then $T \parallel T'$ is a process,

c) if $\varepsilon \notin \text{Cond}_\alpha(T,T')$, then $\text{Cond}_\alpha(T,T')$ is a process,

d) if $\varepsilon \notin It_\alpha(T)$, then $It_\alpha(T)$ is a process.

5. Parallel programs and their realizations

Let E be a set of assignment instructions of the form

$$x_1 \leftarrow \tau_1, \ldots, x_k \leftarrow \tau_k \quad (k > 0),$$

where $x_1, \ldots, x_k$ are pairwise distinct variables and $\tau_1, \ldots, \tau_k$ are terms constructed in the usual way from the functional symbols, variables and auxiliary symbols.

A program is defined as follows:

1° $[\Phi]$ is an (elementary) program for any $\Phi \in E$;

2° if Φ , Ψ are programs and α is an open formula, then $[\Phi;\Psi]$, $[\Phi \| \Psi]$, [<u>if</u> α <u>then</u> Φ <u>else</u> Ψ] , <u>while</u> α <u>do</u> Φ] are programs, too ;

3° only the expressions obtained by finite applications of rules 1° and 2° to expressions from the set E are programs.

Let $P = (A,B,C)$ be a memory and let I be an interpretation of basic functional symbols and basic predicates in the memory P. This interpretation may be extended in the usual way onto all terms. To each assignment instruction $\Phi \in E$ we assign in the usual way ([5]) the function Φ_I from C into C, called its realization.

A realization R_I (with respect to an interpretation I) of parallel programs is defined as follows:

1° $R_I[\Phi] = \{(c, \Phi_I(c), \Phi_I(c), \ldots) : c \in C\}$ for $\Phi \in E$,

2° if Φ and Ψ are programs and α is an open formula, then $R_I[\Phi ; \Psi] = R_I\Phi \; ; R_I\Psi$, $R_I[\Phi \| \Psi] = R_I\Phi \| R_I\Psi$,
$R_I[$ <u>if</u> α <u>then</u> Φ <u>else</u> $\Psi] = \mathrm{Cond}_\alpha(R_I\Phi, R_I\Psi)$,
$R_I[$ <u>while</u> α <u>do</u> $\Phi] = \mathrm{It}_\alpha(R_I\Phi)$.

A program Φ is called semantically correct (with respect to an interpretation I) iff $\varepsilon \notin R_I\Phi$.

<u>Theorem 1</u> If Φ is a semantically correct program (with respect to an interpretation I), then $R_I\Phi$ is a process.

Programs are equivalent with respect to an interpretation I (which we denote by $\Phi \sim_I \Psi$) iff $R_I\Phi = R_I\Psi$. Using the realization R we may define the function computable by a program Φ (denoted $O(\Phi)$) :

$$O(\Phi) = \{(c,c') \in C^2 : (\exists d)_{R_I} \; (\mathrm{first}(d) = c \wedge \mathrm{end}(d) = c')\}.$$

<u>Proposition 3</u> Let Φ, Φ', Φ'' be programs and I their interpretation. Then $[[\Phi;\Phi'];\Phi''] \sim_I [\Phi;[\Phi';\Phi'']]$ and $[[\Phi \| \Phi'] \| \Phi''] \sim_I [\Phi \| [\Phi' \| \Phi'']]$.

6. Example

6.1 Cells

A cell is an ordered quintuple $K = (A,B,C,Q,P)$ such that (A,B,C) is a memory, Q is a finite set of control states and $P : Q \times C \to C$. Furthemore we assume that $A = \{a_1,a_2,a_3,a_4,a_5,a_6\}$, $B = \{0,1\}$, $Q = \{S,W,ZZ,ZW,PZ,ZP,PW,WP\}$ and $P_q(c) = \varphi(q)_I$ for $c \in C$ and $q \in Q$, where φ is defined in table 1 and I is an interpretation defined in table 2. In the sequel we shall consider a set of cells $\{Kr\}_{r \in U \times J}$, where $U \times J$ is a set of indices. Then instead of $S, W, \ldots$ and $a_1, a_2, \ldots, a_6$ we shall write $S_r, W_r, \ldots$ and $a_{1r}, \ldots, a_{6r}$, correspondingly.

φ :

S	$a_4 \leftarrow a_4$
W	$a_4 \leftarrow a_2, a_2 \leftarrow a_4$
ZZ	$a_6 \leftarrow f_z(a_1,a_4,a_5)$
ZW	$a_6 \leftarrow f_z(a_2,a_4,a_5)$
PZ	$a_6 \leftarrow f_p(a_1,a_4,a_5)$
ZP	$a_6 \leftarrow f_p(a_4,a_1,a_5)$
PW	$a_6 \leftarrow f_p(a_2,a_4,a_5)$
WP	$a_6 \leftarrow f_p(a_4,a_2,a_5)$

Table 1

0,1 – 0-ary functional symbols interpreted as constants 0 and 1

$$f_z(b_1,b_2,b_3) = \begin{cases} 0 & \text{if } b_1 \neq b_2 \vee b_3 = 0 \\ 1 & \text{if } b_1 = b_2 \wedge b_3 = 1, \end{cases}$$

$$f_p(b_1,b_2,b_3) = \begin{cases} 0 & \text{if } b_1 = b_2 \wedge b_3 = 0 \vee b_1 > b_{} \\ 1 & \text{if } b_1 = b_2 \wedge b_3 = 1 \vee b_1 < b_{} \end{cases}$$

Table 2

6.2 Cellular matrix

A cellular matrix M is an ordered pair $(\{Kr\}_{r \in U \times J}, w)$, where $U = \{1,\ldots,n\}$, $J = \{1,\ldots,m\}$, Kr is a cell for $r \in U \times J$ and w is a function from the set A of all addresses of cells Kr for $r \in U \times J$ into A /called constrains function/. Let for $r \in U \times J$ $l(r) = r + (0,-1)$, $p(r) = r + (0,1)$, $g(r) = r + (-1,0)$. In our example we consider constrains function w defined as follows: for $r \in U \times J$ we assume $w(a_{1r}) = a_{1g(r)}$, $w(a_{2r}) = a_{3g(r)}$ when $g(r) \in U \times J$; $w(a_{1r}) = a_{1r}$, $w(a_{2r}) = a_{2r}$ otherwise; $w(a_{5r}) = a_{6l(r)}$

---

1 $0 < 1$, if $s, s' \in \{0,1\}^m$ then $s < s'$ iff there exist strings $s_1, s_2, s_3 \in \{0,1\}^*$ and $b, d \in \{0,1\}$ such that $s = s_1 b s_3$, $s' = s_2 d s_3$ and $b < d$.

when $l(r) \in U\times J$, $w(a_{5r}) = a_{5r}$ otherwise; $w(a_{6r}) = a_{5p(r)}$ when $p(r) \in U\times J$, $w(a_{6r}) = a_{6r}$ otherwise ; $w(a_{3r}) = a_{4r}$; $w(a_{4r}) = a_{3r}$.

A function $c : A \rightarrow B$, where A is the set of addresses of a cellular matrix M is called a memory state of M iff for every $a \in A$, $c(a) = c(w(a))$ and $c \mid A_r$ is a memory state of the r-th cell of M. We denote by C_M the set of all memory states of M.

A control state of M is a matrix $q = (q_r)_{p \in U\times J}$ such that q_p is a control state of the cell K_p for $p \in U\times J$. A control state q of M is said to be admissible, if $q(c) \in C_M$ for $c \in C_M$, where $q(c) = \bigcup_{p \in U\times J} I(r_p)(c_p)$, $c_p = c \mid A_p$ and $I(r_p)$ is the realization of the instruction of K_p, assigned to the control state q_p (table 1).

A function $f : C_M \rightarrow C_M$ is computable by a cellular matrix M if for every $c \in C_M$ there exists a sequence $q_1 \ldots q_k$ of ad - missible control states of M such that $f(c) = (q_k \ldots q_2(q_1(c))\ldots)$.

If $c \in C_M$ and $q_1 \ldots q_k \ldots$ is a sequence of admissible control states of a cellular matrix M, then the sequence $c, q_1(c), q_2(q_1(c)), \ldots$ will be called a computation of M. Now we featured examples of programs such that functions computable by these programs are computable by M (assuming that we consider an interpretation of functional symbols defined in table 2 and predicates defined below).

$S_{i,1} \parallel \ldots \parallel S_{i,m}$	P_i
$W_{i,1} \parallel \ldots \parallel W_{i,m}$	WY_i
$ZZ_{i,1} ; \ldots ; ZZ_{i,m}$	ZZ_i
$ZW_{i,1} ; \ldots ; ZW_{i,m}$	ZW_i
$PZ_{i,1} ; \ldots ; PZ_{i,m}$	PZ_i
$ZP_{i,1} ; \ldots ; ZP_{i,m}$	ZP_i
$PW_{i,1} ; \ldots ; PW_{i,m}$	PW_i
$WP_{i,1} ; \ldots ; WP_{i,m}$	

$(i = 1, \ldots, n)$

Table 3

$P_1 \parallel \ldots \parallel P_n$	PAM
$ZZ_1 \parallel \ldots \parallel ZZ_n$	ZRZ
$ZW_1 \parallel \ldots \parallel ZW_n$	ZRW
$PZ_1 \parallel \ldots \parallel PZ_n$	PPZ
$ZP_1 \parallel \ldots \parallel ZP_n$	PZP
$PW_1 \parallel \ldots \parallel PW_n$	PPW
$WP_1 \parallel \ldots \parallel WP_n$	PWP

Table 4

Let n be a pair number. By WYP we shall denote the program $P_1 \parallel G_2 \parallel P_2 \parallel \ldots \parallel P_{n-1} \parallel G_n$ while WYN is the program $P_1 \parallel P_2 \parallel G_3 \parallel P_3 \parallel \ldots \parallel G_{n-1} \parallel P_n$, where G_i is of the form [<u>if</u> α_i <u>then</u> WY_i <u>else</u> P_i] for $i=1,2,\ldots,n$ and $\alpha_{\mathbb{R}}(c) = 1$ iff $c(a_{6,(i,m)}) = 0$. A sorting program for strings included in the rows of the matrix M (with respect to $<$) is defined as follows:

$$\underbrace{PPZ \; ; \; WYP}_{1} \; ; \; \underbrace{PPZ \; ; \; WYN}_{2} \; ; \; \ldots \; ; \; \underbrace{PPZ \; ; \; WYP}_{n-1} \; ; \; \underbrace{PPZ \; ; \; WYN}_{n} \; .$$

Proposition 4 If Φ is a program and I is an interpretation of Φ such that for every $d \in R_I\Phi$ d is a computation of the cellular matrix M, then Φ is a semantically correct program (with respect to an interpretation I).

References

[1] Codd E. , Cellular automata, New York, 1968.
[2] Kahn G. , The semantics of a simple language for parallel programming, IFIP 1974, pp. 471-475.
[3] Muraszkiewicz M. , Nonnumerical algorithms information processing and methods of their realizations in matrix functional units, [in Polish], Ph. D. thesis , Warsaw 1976.
[4] Peterson J.L. , Bredt T.H. , A comparison of models of parallel computation, IFIP 1974, pp. 466-470.
[5] Salwicki A. , Formalized algorithmic logic, Bull. Acad. Polon. Sci., Sér. Sci. Math. Astronom. Phys. , 18 (1970), 227 - 231.
[6] Skowron A. , The theory of parallel programs /to appear/.

P O W E R D O M A I N S

M.B.Smyth
Department of Computer Science
University of Warwick
Coventry, England

1. INTRODUCTION

A non-deterministic process yields, for a given input, a set of possible outputs belonging to some domain D. Thus, in order to apply the methods of fixpoint semantics, we want to be able to regard the subsets (though not necessarily <u>all</u> the subsets - see Sec.3 below) of D as themselves forming a domain, the <u>powerdomain</u> of D. Exactly as in the case of deterministic computation, the domain of meanings of programs in a language will be obtained as the solution of a recursive domain equation. In addition to the usual domain-forming operations, however, we will now have the powerdomain operation $\mathcal{P}[\ ]$. A typical equation involving $\mathcal{P}$ is:

$$R = S \rightarrow \mathcal{P}[S + (S \times R)] \qquad (1)$$

where S is an appropriate domain of "states". (This example is discussed in [1]). Our main aim is to develop a method of solution for equations such as (1).

Of course, the details of the solution depend on the definition chosen for . Our approach to defining is to ask: what is a "finite piece of information" about the result of a non-deterministic computation? Then we will define the ordering between subsets of the output domain by:

$S \sqsubseteq S' =_{df}$ every (finite) piece of information that is true of the result of a computation, given that S is the set of possible outcomes, is also true when S' is the set of possible outcomes. (2)

It turns out that this approach yields two plausible definitions of the powerdomain.

This paper originated as attempt to derive the results of Plotkin [1] in a simple and concise manner. The simplification we have achieved can be attributed mainly to the completely new approach to defining the orderings in the powerdomain. As to content, the main innovations in the present work are: the definition of a weak powerdomain operator $\mathcal{F}_0[\ ]$, which appears to be adequate for most purposes, and which has a particularly simple theory (Sec.4); and the material on categories in Sec.7.

The treatment here is rather sketchy, and most proofs are omitted. For the full version, the reader should consult [2].

2. DOMAINS, PREDOMAINS

In this paper, a domain is required to be an algebraic cpo with countable basis (that is, with countably many finite, or isolated, elements). We shall also need to consider predomains - defined the same way as domains, except that the orderings are required only to be preorders (rather than partial orders). All the notions usually defined for domains generalize in a trivial way to predomains; they can indeed be usefully generalized to categories, as we shall see in the final section.

Notation. If $(P,\leq)$ is any pre-ordered set (predomain), then $[P]$ will denote the quotient poset (domain) $(P/\equiv, \leq/\equiv)$; if $x \in P$, then $[x]$ is the equivalence class containing x; and if $f:P \to P'$ is a monotone function from P to a pre-ordered set P', then $[f]:[P] \to [P']$ is the (monotone) function satisfying $[f][x] = [f(x)]$ (for all $x \in P$).

3. FINITELY GENERABLE SETS

Not every subset of an output domain D can occur as the set of possible outcomes of a non-deterministic computation. Following Plotkin, we restrict attention to processes having only finite non-deterministic branching. Thus the set of possible execution sequences (for a given input) can be arranged in a finitary tree. If the nodes of the tree are labelled with the intermediate results attained in the appropriate execution sequence, then the labels along any branch form an increasing sequence of finite elements of D.

There follows an example of a flowchart program with a simple non-deterministic choice node ($\vee$), together with the appropriate tree of intermediate results. The possible "outputs" of the program are strings in {0,1}. (The output domain is the domain Ω of finite and infinite strings in {0,1}, with the subsequence ordering.) Λ is the null string.

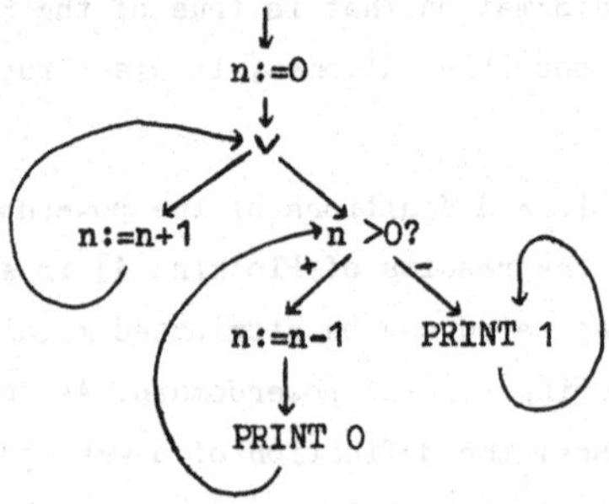

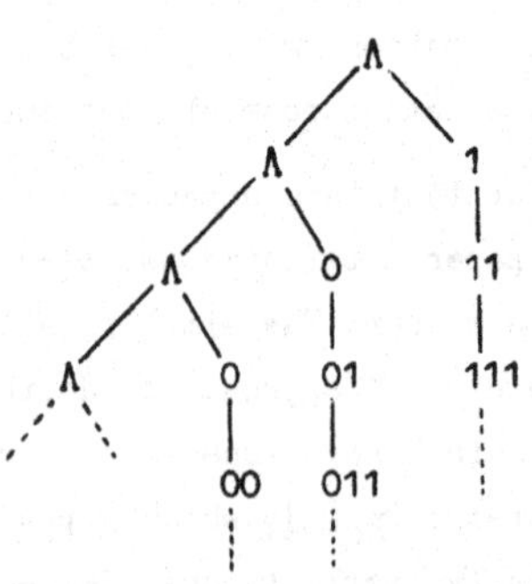

The set of possible outcomes is the set of "limits" along paths of the tree, namely $\{\Lambda\} \cup \{0^n1^\omega \mid n \geq 0\}$. This suggests:

Definition 1. Let D be a domain, and T a (node-)labelled finitary tree satisfying (i) for each node t the label $l(t) \in D$; (ii) T has no terminating branches ; and (iii) if t' is a descendant of t in T, then $l(t) \sqsubseteq l(t')$. Let L be the function which assigns to each (infinite) path through T the lub of the labels occurring along the path. We say that T is a generating tree over D, which generates the set $S = \{L(\pi) \mid \pi \text{ is a path through } T\}$. A set $S \subseteq D$ is finitely generable (f.g.) if it is generated by some tree T. The class of f.g. subsets of D is denoted $\mathfrak{F}(D)$.

If the labels of a generating tree are thought of as (possible) partial results of a non-deterministic computation, these labels should be finite elements of the output domain D. Let us call a generating tree strict if all its labels are finite. Then it is easily shown that every f.g. set can be generated by a strict tree.

Another easy result is that if X is a f.g. subset of domain D, and $f: D \to D'$ is continuous, then $f(X)$ is f.g. For, by transforming all the labels of any generating tree for X by f, we obtain a generating tree for $f(X)$.

Notation. If T is a generating tree, we denote by T_n the cross-section of T at depth n (that is, the set of labels of nodes at depth n).

4. ORDERINGS

As a "finite piece of information" it seems appropriate to take a non-empty finite set of finite elements of the output domain D (that is, a possible cross-section of a generating tree); let M(D) be the collection of such sets. What, exactly, is the information that is conveyed by an element A of M(D)? It appears that this may be construed in more than one way, and that (2) is ambiguous. Specifically, A may be considered

(i) as information about the outcome (that is, information which must be true of the actual outcome); or

(ii) as information about the f.g. set of all possible outcomes.

According to (i), the information given by A is:

$$\forall x \in S \; \exists a \in A \quad a \sqsubseteq x \tag{3}$$

where S is the set of (possible) outcomes. Abbreviating (3) as $A \sqsubseteq_O S$, version (ii) can be formalizes as:

$$A \sqsubseteq_O S \;\; \& \;\; \forall a \in A \; \exists x \in S \quad a \sqsubseteq x \tag{4}$$

which is abbreviated as $A \sqsubseteq_M S$ (the "Milner ordering").

By way of further explanation of (4) we note: if A is regarded as a cross-section of a generating tree at, say, depth n, then (4) gives all the information which can be gleaned about the set S of outcomes by analysing the computation to depth n.

In accordance with this analysis, we have two preorders $_O$, $_M$ for (D), given by:

$$S \sqsubseteq_O S' \equiv_{df} \forall A \in M(D).\; A \sqsubseteq_O S \to A \sqsubseteq_O S'$$

$$S \sqsubseteq_M S' \equiv_{df} \forall A \in M(D).\; A \sqsubseteq_M S \to A \sqsubseteq_M S' .$$

Theorem 1. Under each of the preorders $\sqsubseteq_0, \sqsubseteq_M$, $\mathcal{F}(D)$ is a predomain, with $M(D)$ as the set of finite elements.

We omit the detailed proof, noting only that it proceeds by way of two lemmas:

Lemma 1. Suppose that X is a f.g. set, generated by tree T, that $A \in M(D)$, and $A \sqsubseteq_0 X$. Then $A \sqsubseteq_0 T_m$ for some cross-section T_m. The same holds with $\sqsubseteq_0$ replaced by $\sqsubseteq_M$. (The proof is by an application of Konig's lemma).

Lemma 2. If X is generated by tree T, then X is a lub of the set of cross-sections of T (with respect to either of the preorders $\sqsubseteq_0, \sqsubseteq_M$).

Theorem 2. $\sqsubseteq_M$ coincides (on $\mathcal{F}(D)$) with the preorder $\sqsubseteq$ defined in [1], p.11.

These results are proved in [2]. The next theorem, of which the proof is a straight forward verification, lists some elementary properties of the orderings.

Theorem 3. For $X \subseteq D$ (D a domain), let $RC(X) = \{y \mid \exists x \in X\ x \sqsubseteq y\}$ and $Con(X) = \{y \mid \exists x,z \in X\ x \sqsubseteq y \sqsubseteq z\}$. Then we have:

(i) $X \sqsubseteq_0 Y \rightarrow X \sqsubseteq_0 Y$; $X \sqsubseteq_M Y \rightarrow X \sqsubseteq_M Y$

(ii) a) $X \simeq_0 RC(X)$; $X \simeq_0 Y$ iff $RC(X) = RC(Y)$

b) $X \simeq_M Con(X)$; $X \simeq_M Y$ iff $Con(X) = Con(Y)$.

From this theorem we see that any f.g. set over D which contains the least element $\perp$ is equivalent, in the weak ($\sqsubseteq_0$) ordering, to $\{\perp\}$. If this seems unsatisfactory, it should be recalled that an analysis in terms of $\sqsubseteq_0$ is intended to give us information about the outcome of which we can be certain; from this point of view a computation which may fail to yield any result is as good as worthless.

The preorder $\sqsubseteq_M$ also requires us to make some identifications which may seem unwelcome. For example, the f.g. set $X_0 = \{\Lambda\} \cup \{0^n1^\omega \mid n \geq 0\}$, discussed in Sec.3, must be identified with $X_0 \cup \{0^\omega\}$ - as noted in [1]. On the other hand, it seems that no more refined ordering than $\sqsubseteq_M$ could be computationally meaningful. The way out of this impasse is to observe that we have more than a mere ordering of data: we have a category of data - in which the morphisms correspond (roughly speaking) to the different ways in which the arcs may be drawn between successive cross-sections of a generating tree. The details of this approach are currently being worked out by D.Lehmann.

5. SPECIAL FUNCTIONS

We can now show that several special functions, needed for the interpretation of non-deterministic programs, are continuous. First we remark that a function $f: D \rightarrow D'$, where D, D' are predomains, is continuous iff, for every $x \in D$, $f(x)$ is a lub of $f(x_{fin})$, where $x_{fin} = \{a \mid a \text{ is finite } \& \ a \sqsubseteq x\}$. Now suppose $g: D \rightarrow D'$ is continuous, where D, D' are domains, and consider the extension $\hat{g}$ of g to $\mathcal{F}(D)$, defined by:

$\hat{g}(X) = g(X)$. Then $\hat{g}$ is continuous (w.r.t. either preorder), by the following argument. Any f.g. set X has a strict generating tree T, and (by Lemma 2) X is a lub of $\{T_n\}$. Thus $\{T_n\}$ is cofinal with X_{fin}. Since $\hat{g}$ is monotonic on $M(D)$, $\{\hat{g}(T_n)\}$ is cofinal with $\hat{g}(X_{fin})$. Since $\hat{g}(X)$ is a lub of $\{\hat{g}(T_n)\}$ (recalling that the transform of T by g is a generating tree for $\hat{g}(X)$), $\hat{g}(X)$ is a lub of $\hat{g}(X_{fin})$.

A similar argument establishes the continuity of Union: $\mathfrak{F}(D)^2 \to \mathfrak{F}(D): \langle X,Y\rangle \mapsto X \cup Y$ and of Singleton: $D \to \mathfrak{F}(D): x \mapsto \{x\}$. Plotkin considers also a "big union" function which, in effect, forms the union of a f.g. set of f.g. sets. The treatment of this function is a little more complex; see [2].

6. CLOSURE PROPERTIES

In order to handle recursive domain equations, we must ensure that the class of domains considered is closed under suitable sum, product, function-space and powerdomain constructions. Let us say that a domain D has bounded joins if every pair of finite elements of D that is bounded in D has a lub in D. If D has bounded joins, then so has $\mathfrak{F}_0[D]$: if $A,B \in M(D)$ and $\{A,B\}$ is bounded, then

$$[A] \sqcup [B] = [\{a \sqcup b \mid a \in A \ \&\ b \in B \ \&\ \{a,b\} \text{ is bounded in } D\}].$$

It is well-known (e.g.[3]) that if D,D' have bounded joins then so has the domain $[D \to D']$ of continuous functions. Closure under sum and product is trivial. Hence the class of domains having bounded joins is suitable, if we work with $\mathfrak{F}_0$.

For $\mathfrak{F}_M$ (which is in effect Plotkin's powerdomain constructor) the situation is more difficult. $\mathfrak{F}_M[D]$ need not have bounded joins, even when D has ([1],p.15). To handle this case we will introduce, following Plotkin, the SFP objects ("SFP" is an abbreviation for "sequence of finite partial orders").

Definition 2. An injection $f:D \to D'$, where D,D' are cpo's, is called an embedding if f has a continuous adjoint $f':D' \to D$.

- Equivalently, f is an embedding if there is a continuous $f':D' \to D$ such that $\langle f,f'\rangle$ is a projection pair, i.e.: $f' \circ f = I_D$ and $f \circ f' \sqsubseteq I_{D'}$.

An embedding sequence is a sequence $\langle D_n, p_n\rangle$, where each $p_n:D_n \to D_{n+1}$ is an embedding. CPO is the category of cpo's and continuous maps; CPO^E is the subcategory of CPO with maps restricted to be embeddings. An ω-system in a category C is a functor from the (partially) ordered set $\omega = 0 \leq 1 \leq \ldots$ into C.

Notation. If p is an embedding, we denote the adjoint of p by p'. If $\langle A_m, p_m\rangle$ is an embedding sequence, define the maps $p_{mn}:A_m \to A_n$ by:

$$p_{mn} = \begin{cases} p_{n-1} \cdots p_m & \text{if } n > m \\ I_{A_m} & \text{if } n = m \\ p'_n \cdots p'_{m-1} & \text{if } n < m \end{cases}$$

Thus the embedding sequence $\langle A_m, p_m\rangle$ determines the ω-system (in CPO^E) $\langle A_m, p_{mn}\rangle_{m \leq n}$.

The following theorem summarizes some well-known facts about embedding sequences:

Theorem 4. (i) Let $\Sigma = \langle D_m, p_m \rangle$ be an embedding sequence of cpo's. Let D_∞ be the inverse limit of Σ; that is , D_∞ is the set $\{\langle x_m \rangle \mid \forall m.\ x_m \in D_m\ \&\ p'_m(x_{m+1}) = x_m\}$, with the ordering defined componentwise by the orderings of the D_m. Then D_∞, together with the embeddings $i_m : D_m \to D_\infty$ defined by $i_m(x) = \langle p_{mn}(x) \rangle_{n \in \omega}$, is a colimit of Σ (strictly, of the ω-system associated with Σ) in CPO^E. If each D_m is a domain with basis (set of finite elements) D^O_m, then D_∞ is a domain with basis $D^O_\infty = \bigcup_m i_m(D^O_m)$.

(ii) Let $\langle D_m, p_m \rangle, \langle E_m, q_m \rangle$ be embedding sequences of cpo's. For each m, define $F_m : [D_m \to E_m] \to [D_{m+1} \to E_{m+1}]$ by $F_m(f) = q_m \circ f \circ p'_m$. Then $\langle [D_m \to E_m], F_m \rangle$ is an embedding sequence, and its colimit (as constructed in (i)) is isomorphic with $[D_\infty \to E_\infty]$.

By Theorem 4(ii), the operator $\to$ commutes with the taking of colimits of ω-systems in CPO^E. The same is true for suitably-defined sum and product operators. That it holds also for the powerdomain operator $\mathcal{F}_M$ is the content of:

Theorem 5. If D is a colimit of $\langle D_m, p_m \rangle$, then $\mathcal{F}_M[D]$ is a colimit of $\langle \mathcal{F}_M[D_m], [p_m] \rangle$.

Proof. The basis of $\mathcal{F}_M[D]$ is $B = [M(D)]$, which is (Theorem 4) $[\bigcup_m i_m(M(D_m))]$, while the basis of $\operatorname{colim}\langle \mathcal{F}_M[D_m], [p_m] \rangle$ is $B' = \bigcup_m [i_m][M(D_m)]$. But there is an obvious order-preserving bijection between B and B'; hence $\mathcal{F}_M[D] \cong \operatorname{colim}\langle \mathcal{F}_M[D_m], [p_m] \rangle$.

Definition 3. Colimits of ω-systems of finite cpo's in CPO^E are called SFP objects.

A finite cpo is trivially a domain, and so by Theorem 4(ii) every SFP object is a domain. The sum, product, function space and powerdomain of finite domains are obviously finite, and so (cf. the remarks preceding Theorem 5) the class of SFP objects is also closed under these operations.

7. CATEGORIES, DOMAIN EQUATIONS

In this section we show that several notions and results about cpo's/domains generalize to categories. The main application is an improved account of the category-theoretic solution of recursive domain equations (see [1] for references).

In fact, the notions: poset, least element, monotone function, increasing sequence, continuous function, finite element, (countably) algebraic cpo generalize respectively to: category, initial object, functor, ω-system, ω-continuous functor, finite object, (countably) algebraic category. The first four pairs in this comparison are familiar, the other three are explained by:

Definition 3. Let C,C' be categories admitting ω-colimits. A functor $F : C \to C'$ is weakly ω-continuous if, whenever X is a colimit object for an ω-system Q in C, then FX is a colimit object for FQ. An object $A \in C$ is finite if, for any ω-system $\langle A_n \rangle$ in C with colimit $\langle X, i_n : A_n \to X \rangle$, the following holds: for any arrow $u : A \to X$ and for any sufficiently large n, there is a unique arrow $v : A \to A_n$ such that $u = i_n \circ v$.

Let K be a category having an initial object and at most countably finite objects. We say that K is <u>(countably) algebraic</u> provided (1)every object of K is a colimit of an ω-system of finite objects, and (2)every ω-system of finite objects has a colimit in K.

<u>Remarks</u>. (Strong) ω-continuity of F would require preservation of colimit <u>diagrams</u> (not just objects). Strictly, finiteness should be formulated in terms of directed systems (not just ω-systems); what we have defined is <u>ω-</u> finiteness. The name "algebraic category" is provisional (it conflicts with established usage). Purely for convenience, the definition does not stipulate that K admits ω-colimits; this will follow as Theorem 6.

<u>Example</u>. The category SFP^E of SFP objects and embeddings is countably algebraic, with the finite domains as finite objects. The functor $Fun:(SFP^E)^2 \to SFP^E$, defined on objects by $Fun(D,E) = [D \to E]$ and on arrows $p:D \to D'$, $q:E \to E'$ by $Fun(p,q) = \lambda f:D \to E.\ q \circ f \circ p'$, is weakly ω-continuous, by Theorem 4. The functor $\mathcal{P}:SFP^E \to SFP^E$, defined on objects by $\mathcal{P}(D) = \mathcal{F}_M[D]$ and on arrows by $\mathcal{P}(f) = [\ \hat{f}\ ]$, is weakly ω-continuous, by Theorem 5. (With a little more effort we could show that these functors are (strongly) ω-continuous). Continuous Sum and Product functors are readily defined.

<u>Theorem 6</u>. Every algebraic category admits ω-colimits.

<u>Theorem 7</u>. Let C be a category admitting ω-colimits, with initial object Ω. Let $F:C \to C$ be weakly ω-continuous. Then there is an object X such that $FX \cong X$ and such that for any Y with arrow $p:FY \to Y$ there is an arrow from X to Y.

<u>Proof-outline</u>. Take X as colimit of the ω-system $\Sigma = \Omega \xrightarrow{f} F\Omega \xrightarrow{Ff} F^2\Omega \to \ldots$. It is clear that Σ has the same colimit(s) as $F\Sigma$; hence (by weak ω-continuity of F) $X \cong FX$. Any arrow $p:FY \to Y$ can be used to construct a cone from Σ to Y; thus, by the colimit property, we have an arrow from X to Y.

It follows from this theorem that any equation of the form $D \cong F(D)$, where F is (weakly) continuous (for example, Equation (1),Sec.1) has a solution in SFP^E which is minimal, in the sense that it may be embedded into any other solution.

It is perhaps worth pointing out that under the assumption of full ω-continuity of F the conclusion of Theorem 7 can be strengthened, so as to characterize the <u>least</u> fixpoint of F by a universal property; this of course yields unique (up to isomorphism) minimal solutions for equations.

<u>References</u>

[1] Plotkin, G., A Powerdomain Construction, D.A.I. Research Report NO.3, University of Edinburgh (1975).

[2] Smyth, M.B., Powerdomains, Theory of Computation Report, University of Warwick (1976).

[3] Constable, R., and Egli, H., Computability Concepts for Programming Language Semantics, 7th Annual ACM Symposium on Theory of Computing (1975), 98-106.

ON THE DOMAIN OF ITERATION IN ITERATIVE ALGEBRAIC THEORIES

J. Tiuryn
Institute of Mathematics
Warsaw University
00-901 Warszawa PKiN IXp
Poland

We assume the reader is familiar with the paper by Elgot (1975) and especially with such notions as algebraic theory (in the sence of Lawvere (1963)) , iterative theory , ideal morphism in an iterative theory , power ideal morphism , normal description etc.

By e_i^n: [1] $\longrightarrow$ [n] we shall denote the i-th basic morphism with target [n] $(1 \leq i \leq n)$. If I is an iterative theory then :

1) The set of all morphisms in I with source [k] and target [n] will be denoted by $I_{k,n}$.

2) DomI will be the set of all morphisms in $\bigcup_{s,p} I_{s,s+p}$ which have a conditional iteration , i.e. a morphism g: [s] $\longrightarrow$ [s+p] belongs to the set DomI iff the equation $x = g(x,e_1^p,\ldots,e_p^p)$ has a unique solution in $x \in I_{s,p}$ (this unique solution will be denoted by g^+).

It is known (c.f. Elgot(1975) , prop. 4.2.1) that if g: [s] $\longrightarrow$ [s+p] is a power ideal morphism in an iterative algebraic theory I then it has a conditional iteration (i.e. $g \in$ DomI) . At first we shall characterize power ideal morphisms in iterative theories by their structural properties (theorem A) ; as a corollary , we shall prove that formal composition and iteration of power ideal normal descriptions (with the tack being power ideal) give again power ideal normal descriptions. This answers in affirmative the question posed by Elgot(1975) (p.230). The second theorem (theorem B) describes (by structural properties) the domain of iteration in any iterative algebraic theory.

A morphism $f = (f_1,\ldots,f_s)$: [s] $\longrightarrow$ [s+p] in an iterative theory I is said to contain a loop iff there exists a sequence of distinct elements $i_1,\ldots,i_n \in$ [s] $(1 \leq n \leq s)$ such that $f_{i_j} = e_{i_{j+1}}^{s+p}$ for $j=1,\ldots,n-1$ and $f_{i_n} = e_{i_1}^{s+p}$.

Now we are ready to formulate our first theorem.

<u>THEOREM A</u> Let I be an ideal theory and f: [s] $\longrightarrow$ [s+p] a morphism in I The following conditions are equivalent :

(i) f is power ideal ;

(ii) f does not contain a loop and if f_i is a base morphism component of f then $f_i = e_k^{s+p}$ and $1 \leq k \leq s$.

Proof

"$\Rightarrow$" First , suppose that f_{i_0} is a base morphism component of f such that $f_{i_0} = e_{s+j_0}^{s+p}$.

We prove by induction on k that

(1) $f_{i_0}(f, e_{s+1}^{s+p}, \ldots, e_{s+p}^{s+p})^k = f_{i_0}$, for all $k \in \{0, 1, \ldots\}$.

For k=0 this is obvious. Suppose that $f_{i_0}(f, e_{s+1}^{s+p}, \ldots, e_{s+p}^{s+p})^k = f_{i_0}$. Then

$f_{i_0}(f, e_{s+1}^{s+p}, \ldots, e_{s+p}^{s+p})^{k+1} = f_{i_0}(f, e_{s+1}^{s+p}, \ldots, e_{s+p}^{s+p})(f, e_{s+1}^{s+p}, \ldots, e_{s+p}^{s+p})^k =$

$e_{s+j_0}^{s+p}(f, e_{s+1}^{s+p}, \ldots, e_{s+p}^{s+p})^k = f_{i_0}(f, e_{s+1}^{s+p}, \ldots, e_{s+p}^{s+p})^k = f_{i_0}$.

Hence (1) is proved. It follows from (1) that f is not power ideal since for all $k \in N$ the i_0-th component of $f(f, e_{s+1}^{s+p}, \ldots, e_{s+p}^{s+p})^k$ is a base morphism.

Suppose now that f contains a loop. There exists a sequence of distinct elements $i_1, \ldots, i_n \in [s]$ $(1 \leq n \leq s)$ such that $f_{i_j} = e_{i_{j+1}}^{s+p}$ for $j=1, \ldots, n-1$ and $f_{i_n} = e_{i_1}^{s+p}$. We prove by induction on k that

(2) $f_{i_j}(f, e_{s+1}^{s+p}, \ldots, e_{s+p}^{s+p})^k$ is a base morphism for $1 \leq j \leq n$ and for all $k \in N$.

Again this is obvious for k=0. Suppose that $f_{i_j}(f, e_{s+1}^{s+p}, \ldots, e_{s+p}^{s+p})^k$ is a base morphism for some $j \in \{1, \ldots, n-1\}$. Then

$f_{i_j}(f, e_{s+1}^{s+p}, \ldots, e_{s+p}^{s+p})^{k+1} = f_{i_j}(f, e_{s+1}^{s+p}, \ldots, e_{s+p}^{s+p})(f, e_{s+1}^{s+p}, \ldots, e_{s+p}^{s+p})^k =$

$e_{i_{j+1}}^{s+p}(f, e_{s+1}^{s+p}, \ldots, e_{s+p}^{s+p})(f, e_{s+1}^{s+p}, \ldots, e_{s+p}^{s+p})^k = f_{i_{j+1}}(f, e_{s+1}^{s+p}, \ldots, e_{s+p}^{s+p})^k$

is a base morphism. For j=n the proof is almost the same.

It follows from (2) that f is not power ideal which completes the "$\Rightarrow$" proof.

"$\Leftarrow$" Suppose the condition (ii) is satisfied. We shall show that $f(f, e_{s+1}^{s+p}, \ldots, e_{s+p}^{s+p})^s$ is an ideal morphism.

Let $i \in [s]$; if f_i is an ideal morphism then obviously the morphism $f_i(f, e_{s+1}^{s+p}, \ldots, e_{s+p}^{s+p})^s$ is ideal as well. Suppose f_i is a base morphism. Then , from (ii) we have that $f_i = e_{k_1}^{s+p}$ and $1 \leq k_1 \leq s$. Since f does not contain a loop we may construct a sequence $k_1, \ldots, k_n$ $(1 \leq n \leq s)$ such that $k_j \in [s]$ $(j=1, \ldots, n)$, $f_{k_j} = e_{k_{j+1}}^{s+p}$ for $j=1, \ldots, n-1$ and f_{k_n} is an ideal morphism. Then

$f_i(f,e^{s+p}_{s+1},\dots,e^{s+p}_{s+p})^s = e^{s+p}_{k_1}(f,e^{s+p}_{s+1},\dots,e^{s+p}_{s+p})(f,e^{s+p}_{s+1},\dots,e^{s+p}_{s+p})^{s-1} =$
$f_{k_1}(f,e^{s+p}_{s+1},\dots,e^{s+p}_{s+p})^{s-1} = \dots = f_{k_n}(f,e^{s+p}_{s+1},\dots,e^{s+p}_{s+p})^{s-n}$
is ideal , f_{k_n} being ideal.

Q.E.D.

If $f_D: [s]\longrightarrow[s+p]$ and $f_E: [t]\longrightarrow[t+q]$ are tacks of normal descriptions $D:[n]\xrightarrow[s]{}[p]$ and $E:[p]\xrightarrow[t]{}[q]$ then the tack of the formal composition (c.f. Elgot(1975)) is defined by :

$f_{DE}=(f_D(e^{s+t+q}_1,\dots,e^{s+t+q}_s,g_E(e^{s+t+q}_{s+1},\dots,e^{s+t+q}_{s+t+q})),f_E(e^{s+t+q}_{s+1},\dots,e^{s+t+q}_{s+t+q}))$

where $g_E: [p]\longrightarrow[t+q]$ is the bind of E.

If $f_D: [s]\longrightarrow[s+n+p]$ is the tack and $g_D: [n]\longrightarrow[s+n+p]$ is the bind of a normal description $D:[n]\xrightarrow[s]{}[n+p]$ with f_D being power ideal and $g_D = h(e^{s+n+p}_1,\dots,e^{s+n+p}_s)$ for some morphism $h: [n]\longrightarrow[s]$ then the tack of the formal iteration of D is defined as follows

$$f_{D^+} = f_D(e^{s+p}_1,\dots,e^{s+p}_s,h(e^{s+p}_1,\dots,e^{s+p}_s),e^{s+p}_{s+1},\dots,e^{s+p}_{s+p}).$$

COROLLARY If f_D and f_E are power ideal (where D and E are normal descriptions) then :

(i) f_{DE} is power ideal ;

(ii) f_{D^+} is power ideal.

Proof

(i)Observe that $f_{DE}: [s+t]\longrightarrow[s+t+q]$. Suppose that for some $i\in[s+t]$ $e^{s+t}_i f_{DE}$ is a base morphism. Let us consider two cases.

I. Assume $1\leq i\leq s$.

This means that $e^{s+t}_i f_{DE} = e^s_i f_D(e^{s+t+q}_1,\dots,e^{s+t+q}_s,g_E(e^{s+t+q}_{s+1},\dots,$
$e^{s+t+q}_{s+t+q})) = e^{s+t+q}_{i_1}$.

The last equality holds since $e^s_i f_D$ must be a base morphism (say, $e^{s+p}_{i_1}$) and $1\leq i_1\leq s$, f_D being power ideal.

It is easy to see that the sequence $i,i_1,\dots,i_k$ obtained by iterating the above construction is a loop for f_{DE} iff the same sequence is a loop for f_D.

II. Let now $s<i\leq s+t$ $(i=j+s\ ,\ 1\leq j\leq t)$.

In this case we have

$e^{s+t}_{s+j}f_{DE} = e^t_j f_E(e^{s+t+q}_{s+1},\dots,e^{s+t+q}_{s+t+q}) = e^{s+t+q}_{s+j_1}$.

The last equality holds since $e^t_j f_E$ must be a base morphism (say, $e^{t+q}_{j_1}$) and $1\leq j_1\leq t$, f_E being power ideal.

Also , it is easy to see that the sequence $s+j,s+j_1,\dots,s+j_n$ is a loop for f_{DE} iff the sequence $j,j_1,\dots,j_n$ is a loop for f_E.

So we have proved that if $e^{s+t}_i f_{DE}$ is a base morphism (say, e^{s+t+q}_k)

then $1 \leq k \leq s+t$. Moreover , if $i_1,\ldots,i_k$ is a loop for f_{DE} then $1 \leq i_j \leq s$ for $j=1,\ldots,k$ or $s < i_j \leq s+t$ for $j=1,\ldots,k$. In the first case the sequence $i_1,\ldots,i_k$ is a loop for f_D and in the second case the sequence $i_1-s,\ldots,i_k-s$ is a loop for f_E. Thus f_{DE} satysfies the condition (ii) of the theorem A and it must be a power ideal.

(ii) The proof of (ii) is implicitly contained in the previous one (the idea is the same as in the case I of (i)).

Q.E.D.

An iterative algebraic theory I is said to be nontrivial provided $card(I_{1,0}) \geq 1$. For iterative theories it is equivalent to the condition $card(I_{1,n}) \geq n+1$ for some $n \in N$.

Now we are ready to present our second result.

THEOREM B Let I be an iterative algebraic theory.

a). If I = N then

(a1) DomI $I_{s,s} = \emptyset$ for $s \geq 1$; $I_{0,0} \subset$ DomI ;

(a2) $I_{s,s+1} \subset$ DomI for $s \geq 0$;

(a3) $I_{s,s+p} \cap \mathrm{DomI} = \{f \in I_{s,s+p} : f \text{ contains no loop}\}$ for $p \geq 2$, $s \geq 0$;

b). If I is nontrivial and $card(I_{1,0}) > 1$ then

(b1) $I_{s,s+p} \cap \mathrm{DomI} = \{f \in I_{s,s+p} : f \text{ contains no loop}\}$ for $p \geq 0$, $s \geq 0$;

c). If I is nontrivial and $card(I_{1,0}) = 1$ then

(c1) $I_{s,s} \subset$ DomI for $s \geq 0$;

(c2) $I_{s,s+p} \cap \mathrm{DomI} = \{f \in I_{s,s+p} : f \text{ contains no loop}\}$ for $p \geq 1$, $s \geq 0$.

Proof

The statements (a1) , (a2) and (c1) are obvious. The condition (a1) holds since $I_{1,0} = \emptyset$ and $I_{0,0} = \{1_0\}$ whenever I = N. Moreover in this case $I_{1,1} = \{1_1\}$ what proves (a2). The condition (c1) immediately follows from the assumption $card(I_{1,0}) = 1$.

The proof which follows is valid for (a3) , (b1) and (c2). First we show that

(3) $I_{s,s+p} \cap \mathrm{DomI} \subset \{f \in I_{s,s+p} : f \text{ contains no loop}\}$

Suppose $f: [s] \longrightarrow [s+p]$ has an iteration and contains a loop $i_1,\ldots,i_n$. Let $g = (g_1,\ldots,g_s): [s] \longrightarrow [p]$ be the unique solution of the equation

(4) $x = f(x, e^p_1,\ldots,e^p_p)$

In the cases (a3) , (b1) and (c2) the set $I_{1,p}$ has at least two elements. Let $h \in I_{1,p}$ be a morphism such that $h \neq g_{i_1}$. Let $f_{j_1},\ldots,f_{j_r}$ be all the ideal components of f (obviously $0 \leq r \leq s$). Consider two cases.

I. $r > 0$.

We shall define a new morphism $\hat{f}: [r] \longrightarrow [r+p]$ as follows. Let $1 \leq k \leq r$, then $e^r_k \hat{f} = f_{j_k} b$, where $b: [s+p] \longrightarrow [r+p]$ is defined as below.

$$(5) \qquad b_i = \begin{cases} h(e^{r+p}_{r+1},\dots,e^{r+p}_{r+p}) & \text{if } 1\le i\le s \text{ and } i\notin\{j_1,\dots,j_r\} \\ e^{r+p}_k & \text{if } i=j_k,\ 1\le k\le r \\ e^{r+p}_{r+i-s} & \text{if } s<i\le s+p \end{cases}$$

Obviously $\hat{f}$ is an ideal morphism so it has an iteration. Denote by $(a_1,\dots,a_r)$ the iteration of $\hat{f}$. It means that

$$e^r_k\hat{f}(a_1,\dots,a_r,e^p_1,\dots,e^p_p) = a_k \quad \text{for } k=1,\dots,r.$$

On the other hand $e^r_k\hat{f}(a_1,\dots,a_r,e^p_1,\dots,e^p_p) = f_{j_k}c$, where $c\colon [s+p]\longrightarrow[p]$ and from (5) c is described by :

$$c_i = \begin{cases} h & \text{if } 1\le i\le s \text{ and } i\notin\{j_1,\dots,j_r\} \\ a_k & \text{if } i=j_k,\ 1\le k\le r \\ e^p_{i-s} & \text{if } s<i\le s+p \end{cases}$$

Hence , from the above construction it follows that a morphism $\tilde{g}\colon[s]\longrightarrow[p]$ defined by $e^s_i\tilde{g} = c_i$ for $i=1,\dots,s$ is another solution of the equation (4).

II. <u>r=0.</u>

It means that the morphism f does not contain ideal components at all. So , in this case it is easy to see that the morphism $\tilde{g} = (h,\dots,h)\colon[s]\longrightarrow[p]$ is a solution of (4). In both cases we obtain a contradiction which proves the inclusion (3).

To show the inclusion in the opposite direction let us take any loop-free morphism $f\colon[s]\longrightarrow[s+p]$. Let $f_{i_1},\dots,f_{i_r}$ be all the ideal components of f.

For $k\in[r]$ we define a set $R_k\subset[s]$ in the following way : $m\in R_k$ iff there exists a sequence $n_1,\dots,n_v$ $(v\in[s]$, $n_i\in[s]$ for all $i\in[v])$ such that

(6) $n_1=m$, $n_v=i_k$ and $f_{n_i} = e^{s+p}_{n_{i+1}}$ for $i\in[v-1]$

Observe that $i_k\in R_k$ for all $k\in[r]$ and $R_k\cap R_{k'}=\emptyset$ for $k\ne k'$.

Subsequently , for $k\in[p]$ we define a set $D_k\subset[s]$ in the following way : $m\in D_k$ iff there exists a sequence $n_1,\dots,n_v$ $(2\le v\le s$, $n_i\in[s]$ for all $i\in[v-1]$ and $n_v\in[p])$ such that

(7) $n_1=m$, $n_v=k$, $f_{n_i} = e^{s+p}_{n_{i+1}}$ for all $i\in[v-2]$ and $f_{n_{v-1}} = e^{s+p}_{s+n_v}$.

Notice that the sets in the family $\{R_1,\dots,R_r,D_1,\dots,D_p\}$ are pairwise disjoint (some of the sets in this family are possibly empty) and $\bigcup_{i=1}^{p} D_i \cup \bigcup_{i=1}^{r} R_i = [s]$.

Define a morphism $g\colon[r]\longrightarrow[r+p]$ in the following manner :

$g_k = f_{i_k}(c,d)$ for $k\in[r]$, where $d = (e^{r+p}_{r+1},\dots,e^{r+p}_{r+p})\colon[p]\longrightarrow[r+p]$ and $c\colon[s]\longrightarrow[r+p]$ is defined as follows :

$$(8) \qquad c_m = \begin{cases} e_k^{r+p} & \text{if } m \in R_k \\ e_{r+k}^{r+p} & \text{if } m \in D_k \end{cases}$$

Obviously the morphism g is an ideal one. We shall show that the morphism $c(g^+,e_1^p,\dots,e_p^p) : [s] \longrightarrow [p]$ is the unique solution of the equation (4). First we show that

1. It is a solution of (4).

Let $m \in R_k$. So there exists a sequence $n_1,\dots,n_v$ with the properties described by (6). If v=1 then $m=i_k$ and

$f_{i_k}(c(g^+,1_p),1_p) = f_{i_k}((c,d)(g^+,1_p)) = g_k(g^+,1_p) = e_k^r g^+ =$

$e_k^{r+p}(g^+,1_p) = e_{i_k}^s c(g^+,1_p)$.

Here (and later) 1_p denotes the morphism $(e_1^p,\dots,e_p^p)$.

If $v>1$ then $f_m = e_{n_2}^{s+p}$. Hence (observe that $n_2 \in R_k$ as well)

$f_m(c(g^+,1_p),1_p) = e_{n_2}^{s+p}(c(g^+,1_p),1_p) = e_{n_2}^s c(g^+,1_p) = e_m^s c(g^+,1_p)$.

Now , let $m \in D_k$. There exists a sequence $n_1,\dots,n_v$ with the properties as in (7). If v=2 then $f_m = e_{s+k}^{s+p}$ and we have

$f_m(c(g^+,1_p),1_p) = e_{s+k}^{s+p}(c(g^+,1_p),1_p) = e_k^p = e_m^s c(g^+,1_p)$.

If however , $v>2$ then $f_m = e_{n_2}^{s+p}$ and $n_2 \in D_k$. So , in this case :

$f_m(c(g^+,1_p),1_p) = e_{n_2}^{s+p}(c(g^+,1_p),1_p) = e_{n_2}^s c(g^+,1_p) = e_m^s c(g^+,1_p)$.

Thus we have proved that $c(g^+,1_p)$ is a solution of the equation (3).

2. $c(g^+,1_p)$ is the unique solution of (3).

Suppose $a: [s] \longrightarrow [p]$ is any morphism such that $a_m = f_m(a,1_p)$ for all $m \in [s]$. We shall show that $a = c(g^+,1_p)$.

Let $m \in D_k$. Then there exists a sequence $n_1,\dots,n_v$ with the properties described by (7) . If v=2 then $f_m = e_{s+k}^{s+p}$ and we have : $e_m^s a =$ $f_m(a,1_p) = e_{s+k}^{s+p}(a,1_p) = e_k^p = e_m^s c(g^+,1_p)$.

If $v>2$ then $f_m = e_{n_2}^{s+p}$ and $n_2 \in D_k$. Moreover we have : $e_m^s a = f_m(a,1_p) =$ $e_{n_2}^{s+p}(a,1_p) = e_{n_2}^s a$. By induction we obtain that in this case :

$e_m^s a = e_{n_2}^s a = \dots = e_{n_{v-1}}^s a$. Besides , from the previous case we have :

$e_{n_{v-1}}^s a = e_{n_{v-1}}^s c(g^+,1_p) = e_m^s c(g^+,1_p) = e_k^p$. The second equality holds (by (8)) since n_{v-1} and m are in a common set D_k. Thus we have shown :

(9) $e_m^s a = e_m^s c(g^+,1_p) = e_k^p$ for all $m \in D_k$.

Suppose now that $m \in R_k$. Then there exists a sequence $n_1,\dots,n_v$ satisfying (6). As in the previous case it may be proved that

$e^s_{n_1} a = e^s_{n_2} a = \dots = e^s_{n_v} a$; and thus we obtain that

(10) $\quad e^s_m a = e^s_{i_k} a \quad$ for all $m \in R_k$

Let $b = (e^s_{i_1} a, \dots, e^s_{i_r}) : [r] \longrightarrow [p]$. We shall prove that

(11) $\quad g(b, 1_p) = b$

First we show that

(12) $\quad (c,d)(b,1_p) = (a,1_p)$

Let $m \in R_k$, then $e^{s+p}_m (c,d)(b,1_p) = e^s_m c(b,1_p) = e^{r+p}_k (b,1_p) = e^s_{i_k} a = e^s_m a = e^{s+p}_m (a,1_p)$ (the fourth equality holds by (10)).

If $m \in D_k$ then $e^{s+p}_m (c,d)(b,1_p) = e^s_m c(b,1_p) = e^{r+p}_{r+p}(b,1_p) = e^p_k = e^s_m a = e^{s+p}_m (a,1_p)$ (the fourth equality holds by (9)).

If $s < m \leqslant s+p$ (say, $m = s+j$) then $e^{s+p}_m (c,d)(b,1_p) = e^p_j d(b,1_p) = e^{r+p}_{r+j}(b,1_p) = e^p_j = e^{s+p}_m (a,1_p)$.

Thus (12) is proved. Applying (12) we obtain : $g(b,1_p) = (f_{i_1}, \dots, f_{i_r})(c,d)(b,1_p) = (f_{i_1}, \dots, f_{i_r})(a,1_p) = (e^s_{i_1} a, \dots, e^s_{i_r} a) = b$ which proves (11). Hence $b = g^+$ and

$e^s_{i_k} a = e^r_k b = e^r_k g^+ = e^{r+p}_k (g^+, 1_p) = e^s_{i_k} c(g^+, 1_p)$.

Now, by (8), (10) and the above equality we may see that $a = c(g^+, 1_p)$ is the unique solution of (4) and thus it is an iteration of f, which completes the proof of the theorem.

Q.E.D.

As a corollary we obtain

COROLLARY If I is a nontrivial iterative theory and $card(I_{1,0}) > 1$, then a morphism $f: [s] \longrightarrow [s]$ $(s \geqslant 0)$ has a conditional iteration iff it is power ideal.

Proof By the theorem A a morphism $f: [s] \longrightarrow [s]$ is power ideal iff it does not contain a loop. Now the proof follows from the theorem B (b1).

Q.E.D.

REFERENCES

1. S.L. Bloom, C.C. Elgot : The existence and construction of free iterative theories. Report RC 4937, IBM Watson Research Center, New York (1974).

2. F.W. Lawvere : Functorial semantics of theories. Proc. Nat. Acad. Sci., Vol. 50, No. 5, 869 - 872, (1963).

3. C.C. Elgot : Monadic computation and iterative algebraic theories. Logic Colloquium '73, H.E. Rose, J.C. Shepherdson ed., North Holland 175 - 230, (1975).

THE INFLUENCE OF THE DATA PRESENTATION ON THE COMPUTATIONAL POWER OF MACHINES

Rutger Verbeek and Klaus Weihrauch

Institut für Informatik, Universität Bonn

Address: Informatik I, Wegelerstr. 6, 53oo Bonn, W-Germany

Abstract: The influence of the data presentation on the computational complexity of functions is studied from a general point of view. The main emphasis lies on transformations T_ν induced by bijective changes ν of the presentation. Several sufficient conditions are given for very complex functions f such that $T_\nu^{-1}(f)$ is simple for an appropriate ν. On the other hand there are intrinsicially difficult functions that cannot be transformed into simple functions by any T_ν. Usually several functions shall be transformed simultaneously into simple functions. The following result gives a strong limitation of the power of data change: If T_ν is such that any primitive recursive (p.r.) f remains p.r., then no not p.r. function can be transformed into a p.r. function.

1. BASIC DEFINITIONS

F := class of arithmetical functions.

$F^{(k)}$:= class of k-ary arithmetical functions $(k \in \mathbb{N})$.

fh := $\lambda x_1 \dots x_k \left[f(h(x_1),\dots,h(x_n)) \right]$ for $f \in F^{(k)}$, $h \in F^{(1)}$.

Π := $\{f \in F^{(1)} \mid f \text{ bijective}\}$.

$T_\nu(f)$:= $\nu f \nu^{-1}$ for $f \in F$, $\nu \in \Pi$.

$\beta : \mathbb{N} \to \{0,1\}^*$, $\beta(i)$ = binary notation of i.

Let m be a machine (k input tapes, one output tape, tape alphabet $\Sigma = \{0,1\}$) which computes $g : (\Sigma^*)^{\times k} \to \Sigma^*$. Suppose $g\beta(\mathbb{N}) \subseteq \beta(\mathbb{N})$. Then M computes the arithmetical function $h := \beta^{-1} g$. [HU 69]

R_1 := $\{f \in F^{(1)} \mid f \text{ total recursive}\}$.

E_n := n-th Grzegorczyk class [BL 74] [S 74] [G 53].

E := class of elementary functions = E_3.

$\langle x,y \rangle := \frac{1}{2}(x+y)(x+y+1)$.

$f_3(x) := 2^x$, $f_{n+1}(x) := f_n^x(1)$ $(n \geq 3)$ "n-th Ackermann function".

2. INTRODUCTION

The aim of this paper is to study the dependence of the computational complexity of classes K and $T_\nu(K)$, where $K \subseteq F$ and $\nu \in \Pi$. Let K be the class of functions computed by some class M of (restricted) machines. Then $T_\nu(K)$ is the class of functions computed by M if $\nu^{-1}(x)$ is used as the presentation for x. The transformation T_ν simply describes a change of data presentation (input-output (I/O) encoding). Thus the influence of I/O encodings on the computational power of resource bounded machines is studied. The choice of the I/O encoding should depend on the class of functions to be computed [AHU 74] . For multiplication and division of integers, for example, the prime decomposition presentation might be reasonable, while for addition and substraction the binary presentation is reasonable. Is there a presentation such that both, addition and multiplication of integers, can be performed fast? We cannot answer this particular question, but similar problems will be treated from a general point of view. Looking at the usual definitions of the functions (arithmetical or word-) computed by automata [HU 69] it is difficult to find purely mathematical reasons for the choice of the used "data presentation". This is obvious for finite automata (e.g. unary, binary, or prime decomposition presentation of numbers) but is still true for Turingmachines. (There are, of course, good physical reasons for the choice of the binary presentation.) Therefore, one should also look for presentation-invariant properties of different types of automata.

The first two theorems are on less restricted types of data presentation. For the rest of the paper we shall assume that ν is a bijection. For any 0-1 valued function f there is $\nu \in \Pi$ such that $T_\nu^{-1}(f)$ is gsm-computable (generalized sequential machine [HU 69]). We give other sufficient conditions for an arbitrarily complex function f such that $T_\nu^{-1}(f)$ is elementary [G 53] for some $\nu \in \Pi$. There is a log n-tape-computable function h such that $T_\nu^{-1}(h)$ is not dpa-computable (deterministic pushdown automaton) for any $\nu \in \Pi$. Furthermore, a "strong compression theorem" [B 67] is proved. For any (tape constructable) function u (a tape constructable function u_1 and) a function f can be constructed with (f is u_1-tape-computable but) $T_\nu^{-1}(f)$ is not u-tape computable for any $\nu \in \Pi$. Thus, there are intrinsically very complicated functions. In the last theorems the simultaneous transformation of a set of functions is studied. There is a function f such that $T_{\nu'}(f)$ is elementary for some ν', but $T_\nu(s)$ is not elementary whenever $T_\nu(f)$ is elementary

($s(x) := x+1$). The most interesting theorem probably is the following one. There is a class $K \subsetneq F$ such that $T_\nu^{-1}(K) \subsetneq K$ for some $\nu \in \Pi(\mathbb{N})$. But for the class $Pr \subset F$ (primitive recursive functions) we have $T_\nu^{-1}(Pr) = Pr$, whenever $T_\nu^{-1}(Pr) \subseteq Pr$.

3. NUMBERINGS AND GÖDELIZATIONS

Up to now, we have only mentioned the change of presentation by a bijection. We introduce the more general concepts of numberings and gödelizations.

Def. 3.1: Any surjection $\nu : \mathbb{N} \to \mathbb{N}$ is called a numbering (of $\mathbb{N}$) [E 73]. For functions $f,g \in F$ we say "f is computed by g with respect to ν", iff $f\nu = \nu g$. Any injection $gn : \mathbb{N} \to \mathbb{N}$ is called a gödelization (of $\mathbb{N}$). For functions $f,g \in F$ we say "f is computed by g with respect to gn", iff $gn\ f = g\ gn$.

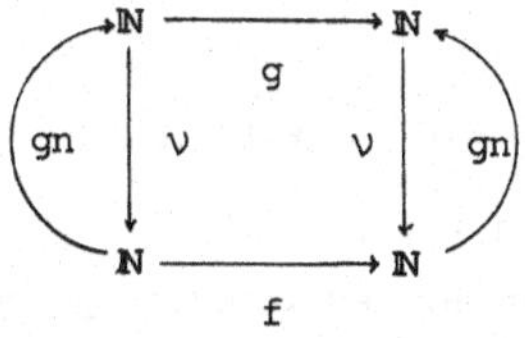

The following theorem shows, that the unrestricted use of numberings cannot yield interesting results. (But see the remark after Theorem 5.3)

Theorem 3.1: Suppose $K \subset F$, K at most denumerable. Then there is a numbering ν with: $(\forall f \in K)(\exists g \in F$, gsm-computable$)\ f\nu = \nu g$. (We allow generalized sequential machines with several one-way input tapes.)

Proof: Suppose $K = \{f_i \mid i \in \mathbb{N}\} \subset F^{(1)}$. Let $\tau : \Sigma^* \to \mathbb{N}$ be defined by

$$\tau(0^m) = 0$$

$$\tau(0^{n_0}\,1\,0^{n_1}1 \ldots 1\,0^{n_k}) = f_{n_1} f_{n_2} \ldots f_{n_{k-1}}(n_k) \quad (k \geq 1),$$

and set

$\nu := \tau\beta$. Suppose $i \in \mathbb{N}$. Define $g_i : \Sigma^* \to \Sigma^*$ by

$g_i(0^m) := 1\,0^i\,1,$

$g_i(0^m\,1\,w) := 1\,0^i\,1\,w.$

Thus g_i is gsm-computable. Set $h_i := \beta^{-1} g_i \beta$. These definitions imply $f_i \nu = \nu h_i$. We did not require $f_i \neq f_j$ for $i \neq j$. Thus K may be finite. If K contains functions with several arguments, the proof is similar.

Q. E. D.

The proof shows that all the difficulties can be shifted into the numbering. The following simple lemma is fundamental for several proofs.

Lemma 3.1: For $f \in F^{(1)}$ let $gr(f) := (\mathbb{N}, B)$ with $B := \{(x, f(x)) \mid x \in \mathbb{N}\}$ be the graph of f. Suppose $f, g \in F^{(1)}$, let $gn : \mathbb{N} \to \mathbb{N}$ be injective. Then:
$gn\ f = g\ gn \iff (gn : gr(f) \to gr(g)$ is a graph-monomorphism$)$.

Thus, $gr(f)$ is isomorphic to $gr(T_\nu(f))$ for any $\nu \in \Pi$ and any $f \in F^{(1)}$. Theorem 3.2 shows that unrestricted use of gödelizations cannot yield interesting results, whenever single functions are to be transformed.

Theorem 3.2: There is a gsm-computable $h \in F^{(1)}$ with:
$(\forall f \in F^{(1)})(\exists gn : \mathbb{N} \to \mathbb{N}$, injective$)\ gn\ f = h\ gn$
(Here again the whole difficulty of f is shifted into an appropriate gn)

Proof: (idea) Suppose $f \in F^{(1)}$. Then $gr(f)$ consists of at most denumerably many connected components. Each component has at most one directed cycle. Each node has at most denumerable many immediate predecessors. There is a universal graph $G = (\mathbb{N}, G')$ such that $gr(f)$ can be isomorphically embedded into G for any $f \in F^{(1)}$. It is not difficult to construct a gsm computing $h \in F^{(1)}$ such that G is isomorphic to $gr(h)$. This proves the theorem.

Q. E. D.

4. TRANSFORMATIONS OF SINGLE FUNCTIONS

In this chapter we shall assume throughout $\nu \in \Pi$. Theorem 4.1 says that any $f \in F^{(1)}$ with finite range can be transformed into a gsm-mapping.

Theorem 4.1: Suppose $f \in F^{(1)}$ with card (range f) $< \infty$. Then there is $\nu \in \Pi$ with $T_\nu^{-1}(f)$ gsm-computable.

Proof: Let us consider f is o-1 valued with $f^{-1}(0)$ and $f^{-1}(1)$ infinite (otherwise the theorem is trivial). There is $\nu \in \Pi$ with $\nu(i) \in f^{-1}(0)$ if i even, $\nu(i) \in f^{-1}(1)$ if i odd. Define $g : \Sigma^* \to \Sigma^*$ by $g(\varepsilon) := \varepsilon$, $g(w\,0) := \beta\nu^{-1}(0)$, $g(w\,1) = \beta\nu^{-1}(1)$ for any $w \in \Sigma^*$ and set $h := \beta^{-1} g \beta$. The functions g and h are gsm-computable, and $T_\nu(h) = f$ can be shown easily. The general case is proved similarly.

Q. E. D.

Also the next three theorems show that computationally very complicated functions can be transformed into simple functions.

Theorem 4.2: Suppose $f \in F^{(1)}$ with (1) $\lambda\, u\, v\, w\, x \left[f^u(v) = f^w(x) \right]$ is an elementary predicate and (2) $(\exists k)$ card $\{f^i(k) \mid i \in N\} = \infty$. Then there is $\nu \in \Pi$ with $f \in T_\nu(E)$. (The Ackermann functions satisfy (1) and (2)).

For the proof first a numbering ν' is constructed with $f\nu' = \nu' g$ for some $g \in E$. From ν' a bijection ν is derived with $\nu \equiv_e \nu'$ (: $\Longleftrightarrow$ $(\exists e_1, e_2 \in E)\nu = \nu' e_1$ and $\nu' = \nu e_2$). From this $T_\nu^{-1}(f) \in E$ follows immediately.

Theorem 4.3: Suppose $f \in F^{(1)}$ with (1) $(\forall k) f < k,0> = <k,0>$, (2) $f(\mathbb{N}) = <\mathbb{N},0>$, and (3) $(\forall k)$ card $f^{-1}<k,0> = \infty$. (There are arbitrarily complex functions with these properties). Then there is $\nu \in \Pi$ with $f \in T_\nu(E)$.

The proof is quite easy.

Theorem 4.4: Suppose $f \in \Pi \cap R_1$. Suppose one of the following conditions holds:

(1) $gr(f)$ has an infinite cycle.

(2) There is $e \in E$, injective, with $(\forall n \in \mathbb{N})$ ($gr(f)$ has a cycle with $e(n)$ nodes).

Then there are $\nu \in \Pi$ and $g \in E$ with $f = T_\nu g$ and $g^{-1} \in E$.

By Lemma 3.1 it is sufficient to construct $g \in E$ (with $g^{-1} \in E$) with $gr(g)$ isomorphic to $gr(f)$, i.e. for any n, $1 < n < \infty$, g and f must have the same number of cycles of length n. The function g is constructed by gradually computing the lengths of all the finite cycles of f. The conditions (1) or (2) are used for padding if the information comes too slowly. The number of infinite cycles is supplied as an initial information. The condition $g^{-1} \in E$ can be satisfied easily.

The next theorems show that there are functions which cannot be transformed into easily computable functions whatever transformation T_ν is used. These functions are "intrinsically" very complicated.

Theorem 4.5: Define f by $f(n) := \lfloor \log \lfloor \log \lfloor \log n \rfloor \rfloor \rfloor$. Then f is log n-tape-computable but $T_\nu^{-1}(f)$ is not gsm-computable for any $\nu \in \Pi$.

Theorem 4.6: Define f by $f(i) = m$ iff $f_4(3m) \leq i < f_4(3(m+1))$, $f_4 = 4^{th}$ Ackermann function. Then f is log n-tape-computable but $T_\nu^{-1}(f)$ is not dpa-computable (deterministic pushdown transducer) for any $\nu \in \Pi$.

The idea of the proofs is as follows. Let $FS = \{f \in F^{(1)} \mid (\forall n) \text{ card } f^{-1}(n) < \infty\}$ the class of unary functions with "finite surjectivity". Using the pumping lemma it can be shown that ($f_o \in PS$ and f_o dpa-computable) implies $(\forall n)$ card $f_o^{-1}(n) < g(n)$ for some function g. The "type of surjectivity" is invariant under transformations T_ν (Lemma 3.1). But the above defined function f does not have sufficiently many small classes $f^{-1}(n)$, thus $T_\nu(f_o) \neq f$ for all dpa-computable f_o and all $\nu \in \Pi$. The same method is used to prove Theorem 4.5. The next theorem is a generalization of these results. It is a very strong kind of compression theorem.

Theorem 4.7: For any $u \in R_1$ there is $u_1 \in R_1$ with

$$(\exists h \in L_{u_1})(\forall f \in L_u)(\forall \nu \in \Pi) h \neq T_\nu(f).$$

u_1 and h can be constructed from u. ($L_u := \{f \in F^{(1)} \mid f$ is computable on a u-tape-bounded Turingmachine). For increasing tape-constructable u, u_1 is roughly of magnitude $u^{(x^2)}(1)$.

For the proof the class $FC := \{f \in \Pi \mid gr(f)$ has only finite cycles and for any $n \geq 1$, $gr(f)$ has at most one cycle with n nodes$\}$ is considered. For any $f \in FC \cap L_u$ a subset of the cycle lengths can be enumerated by a not too complicated function $g \in L_{u_2}$ "sufficiently" fast. By diagonalization over all such functions g (and some more) a function g', which also enumerates cycle lengths, is constructed. The diagonalization is defined such that for any of the above function g there is $n \in \mathbb{N}$ such that g enumerates n but g' does not. Thus the permutation defined by g' is different from any $f \in FC \cap L_u$. Let $h \in FC$ be such that g' exactly enumerates the cycle lengths of h. Such a function h can be constructed from g'. Of course, $h \in L_{u_1}$ for an appropriate u_1. The details of the proof are complicated.

Theorem 4.7 has a simple consequence:

Corollary: There is $h \in E_{n+1}$ such that $h \notin T_\nu(E)$ for any $\nu \in \Pi$, if $n \geq 3$.

5. SIMULTANEOUS TRANSFORMATION OF FUNCTIONS

So far we only have considered the transformation of a single function (exception Theorem 3.1). If we want to transform several functions simultaneously into simple functions there might appear contradicting conditions for ν although every function can be transformed into a simple function separately.

Theorem 5.1: For any $h \in R_1$ there is $f \in R_1$ with $f(x) > h(x)$ infinitely often such that $\{f,s,pred\}$ $T_\nu(E)$ for some $\nu \in \Pi$ (s = successor, pred = predecessor).

As in Theorem 4.1 it can be shown that any finite set of finite valued functions can be transformed simultaneously into a set of simple functions. In these cases the different conditions for ν are compatible. The next single lemma is used for the following theorems.

Lemma 5.1: Suppose $\nu \in \Pi$ with $T_\nu^{-1}(s) \in E_n$. Then $\nu^{-1} \in E_{n+1}$.
As a first consequence the following can be proved.

Theorem 5.2: $\exists\, f \in E_{n+1}$, f 0-1 valued, with

$$T_\nu^{-1}(\{f,s\}) \nsubseteq E_n \quad \text{for any } \nu \in \Pi.$$

By Theorem 4.1 f can be transformed into E_3, s also, but not f and s together. A similar result can be obtained from the corollary of Theorem 4.7 for the pair $\{f_{n+1}, e\}$, where e is an elementary "universal single step function". Again f_{n+1} and e can be transformed into simple functions separately (Theorem 4.4), $n \geq 3$.

It would be desirable to have transformations that leave as many functions simple as possible and in addition make some other difficult functions simple.

By the following Lemma there may be situations of this kind.

Lemma 5.2: There is a class $K \subseteq F^{(1)}$, closed under substitution with $T_\nu^{-1}(K) \subsetneq K$ (or $T_\nu(K) \subsetneq K$) for some $\nu \in \Pi$.

But Theorem 5.2 already shows that there are strong limitations.

In contrast to Lemma 5.2 is the following fundamental theorem.

Theorem 5.3: Suppose $T_\nu^{-1}(Pr) \subseteq Pr$ for some $\nu \in \Pi$. Then $T_\nu^{-1}(Pr) = Pr$. (Pr = class of primitive recursive functions). In addition $\nu \in Pr$ and $\nu^{-1} \in Pr$.

It is proved that $f \in T_\nu(Pr) \setminus Pr$ implies the existence of an 0-1 valued $g \in T_\nu(Pr) \setminus Pr$. This is a contradiction to Lemma 5.1 .

Thus, if we change our data presentation by a bijection and require that every $f \in Pr$ is transformed into $f' \in Pr$, then no other function is transformed into Pr. Theorem 5.3 is even true under weaker conditions.

Corollary: Let $gn \in F^{(1)}$ be a gödelization, suppose $(\forall f \in Pr)(\exists f' \in Pr)\ gn\, f = f' gn$. Then there is no $g \in F \setminus Pr$ with $(\exists g' \in Pr)\ gn\, g = g' gn$.

A similar corollary can be obtained for numberings ν if we require that $\nu^{-1}(0)$ is an primitive recursive set.

REFERENCES

[AHU 74] Aho, Hopcroft, Ullman, The design and analysis of computer algorithms, Addison Wesley, 1974.

[B 67] M. Blum, A machine-independent theory of the complexity of recursive functions, J. Assoc. of Comput. Mach. 14 (1967), 322 - 336.

[BL 74] Brainerd, Landweber, Theory of computation, Wiley, New York, 1974.

[E 73] J.U. Ersov, Theorie der Numerierungen I, Zeitschrift f. Math. Logik und Grundlagen der Math., 19 (1973), 289 - 388.

[G 53] A. Grzegorczyk, Some classes of recursive functions, Rozprawy Mathematyczne 4 (1953), 1 - 45.

[HU 69] Hopcroft, Ullman, Formal languages and their relation to automata, Addision Wesley, 1969.

[S 74] C.P. Schnorr, Rekursive Funktionen und ihre Komplexität, Teubner, Stuttgart, 1974.

ON SEQUENTIAL MODELLING OF NON-SEQUENTIAL PROCESSES

Józef Winkowski
Computation Centre of PAS
00-901 Warsaw, PKiN, P.O.Box 22, Poland

Abstract

The aim of this paper is to answer the question whether all properties of discrete non-sequential processes can be expressed and proved in the framework of sequential descriptions of such processes. The paper deals only with the processes which can be defined in terms of Petri nets.

The rules according to which a process is running are represented by a Petri net. The process itself is identified with a Petri net of occurrences of conditions and events of this net. A characterization of these two nets, and of relationships between them, constitutes a theory of the process. Such a theory is objective in the sense of Petri.

A sequential description of a non-sequential process is a description of this process from the point of view of an external observer. The observer identifies the process with a sequence of occurrences of global states of the Petri net representing the rules of the process. A characterization of the last net, of the sequence of global net state occurrences, and of relationships between these two objects, is just a sequential description of the process, or a sequential theory of it. Such a theory is subjective in the sense of Petri.

The main result of the paper is that the objective theory of a process from a broad class of processes can be modelled in a subjective theory. It implies that the foundamental question of the paper may be answered positively for a class of processes.

Introduction

There is a number of ideas how to describe discrete non-sequential processes and to prove their properties. Some of these ideas (like those of Karp and Miller [5], Milner [8], Mazurkiewicz [6]) consist in replacing parallelism by nondeterminism and considering non-sequential processes in a sequential way. Others (like those of Petri [9], Genrich [3,4], Mazurkiewicz [7]) do not allow such simplification and insist on considering non-sequential processes as they are. The question arises whether the first approach is less powerful than the second or not.

To answer the question we take into consideration any non-sequential process P (in an intuitive sense). Next, we formulate two theories of P : one, say T, called an objective theory, which characterizes the process P as non-sequential one, and another, say T′, called a subjective theory, which characterizes P from the point of view of an external observer, i.e., as a sequential non-deterministic process. Then we show that the objective theory T can be modelled in that subjective T′ in such a way that every theorem remains true. This means that all the properties of the process which can be formulated and proved in the objective theory T can be formulated and proved in the subjective theory T′ as well.

We assume that the rules according to which the process P is running are represented by a Petri net N which we call a schema of P. Since for discrete non-sequential processes from a very broad class we are able to imagine such a net, this assumption does not seem to be very restrictive.

The schema N does not need to be specified completely. We specify it by some axioms which give a theory T_0 of it.

The objective theory T of P is constructed by extending T_0 by some new notions and axioms. This is made by describing P in terms of the Petri net N, a Petri net M of occurrences of conditions and events of N, and the function F which assigns conditions and events of N to their occurrences in M. The net M should not contain any conflict, any cycle, any infinite path with no beginning, any bounded infinite path with no end, and it should be maximal in a certain sense.

The subjective theory T' of P is also an extension of T_0. It is constructed by adding new notions and axioms to T_0 so that all possible sequences of occurrences of global states of N be characterized. The global states of N are defined as sets of simultaneously observed holding conditions.

All these theories are constructed as some extensions of the Zermelo - Fraenkel set theory that includes the usual definitions of the set Nat of the natural numbers, the natural ordering $\leqslant$ of Nat, and necessary arithmetical operations. Every extension is obtained by adding new relations, assuming for each n-ary relation R the axiom

$$(\exists x)((x_1,\ldots,x_n)\in x \Longleftrightarrow R(x_1,\ldots,x_n))$$

identifying such a relation with a (unique) set $\bar{R}$ such that

$$(x_1,\ldots,x_n)\in \bar{R} \Longleftrightarrow R(x_1,\ldots,x_n)$$

and characterizing the introduced relations by appropriate axioms. Modellings are supposed to preserve unchanged all the formulas of the set theory.

A schema description

According to our definition, the schema of the process P is a Petri net N. Thus, it is a quadruple

$$N = (C,E,Pre,Post)$$

where C,E are two disjoint sets with non-empty union, and $Pre \subseteq C \times E$, $Post \subseteq E \times C$. The elements of C are called conditions, those of E are called events. Each c with $(c,e) \in Pre$ is called a precondition of e. Each c with $(e,c) \in Post$ is called a postcondition of e.

The schema N can be specified (may be not completely) by a theory T_0. To construct such a theory we add to the set theory the relations C,E,Pre,Post with the following meaning :

C(x) : x is a condition
E(x) : x is an event

Pre(x,y) : x is a precondition of y
Post(x,y) : y is a postcondition of x

and characterize these relations (after identifying them with the sets they determine) by the axioms :

(1) $C \cap E = \emptyset$
(2) $C \cup E \neq \emptyset$
(3) $Pre \subseteq C \times E$
(4) $Post \subseteq E \times C$

Next, we add other relations and axioms if it is necessary for specifying the schema N. The resulting theory is just the theory T_0 we have in mind. Models of the theory T_0 are those of the set theory with some distinguished C,E,Pre,Post which constitute some appropriate Petri nets. There may exist models which are different from that with C,E,Pre,Post as in N.

<u>The objective theory T</u>

The objective theory of the process P is a description of : the schema N of P, a Petri net M of <u>occurrences</u> of conditions and events of N, and the function F which assigns conditions and events of N to their occurrences in M.

The schema N is described by the theory T_0. Thus, it remains to extend T_0 to a theory T in such a way that to specify in T the net M and the function F. To this end we add to the theory T_0 unary relations Q,U and binary relations pre,post,F, and identify these relations with some sets. Next, we join to T_0 axioms which state the following :

(5) M = (Q,U,pre,post) is a Petri net
(6) M is conflict-free, i.e.,

$$(\forall p \in Q)(\forall u \in U)(\forall v \in U)((pre(p,u) \,\&\, pre(p,v) \Longrightarrow u=v) \,\&\, (post(u,p) \,\&\, post(v,p) \Longrightarrow u=v))$$

(7) M contains no cycle, i.e., the reflexive and transitive closure $\preccurlyeq$ of the following relation

$$pRq \Longleftrightarrow (\exists u \in U)(pre(p,u) \,\&\, post(u,q))$$

in Q is a partial ordering of Q

(8) M does not contain any infinite path with no beginning, i.e., every non-empty subset of Q has a minimal element

(9) M does not contain any bounded infinite path with no end, i.e., every non-empty subset of Q with an upper bound has a maximal element

(10) F is a function that assigns a condition c of N to every condition p of M (the condition c to its occurrence p) and an event e of N to every event u of M (the event e to its occurrence u) in such a way that the pre- and postconditions of an occurrence of an event are in one-to-one correspondence with the pre- and postconditions of the event; more precisely :
(a) $F(Q) \subseteq C$
(b) $F(U) \subseteq E$
(c) $pre(p,u) \Longrightarrow Pre(F(p),F(u))$
(d) $post(u,p) \Longrightarrow Post(F(u),F(p))$
(e) $F(u)=e \,\&\, Pre(c,e) \Longrightarrow (\exists p)(pre(p,u) \,\&\, F(p)=c)$
(f) $F(u)=e \,\&\, Post(e,c) \Longrightarrow (\exists p)(post(u,p) \,\&\, F(p)=c)$
(g) $pre(p,u) \,\&\, post(u,q) \Longrightarrow F(p) \neq F(q)$
(h) $p \not\preccurlyeq q \,\&\, q \not\preccurlyeq p \,\&\, p \neq q \Longrightarrow F(p) \neq F(q)$

(11) M and F are maximal in the following sense :
let s be a case in M (by a <u>case</u> in M we mean a maximal subset of concurrent conditions of M; by <u>concurrent</u> conditions of M we mean such conditions which are not in the relation $\preccurlyeq$ one with another); if there is an event e of N such that
$(\forall c{:}Pre(c,e))(\exists p \in s)(F(p)=c) \,\&\, (\forall c{:}Post(e,c))(\forall p \in s)(F(p) \neq c)$
then there is an event u of M such that
$(\forall p{:}pre(p,u))(p \in s) \,\&\, (\forall p{:}post(u,p))(\forall q{:}p \preccurlyeq q)(q \notin s)$

The theory we have obtained in this way is just the required objective theory T. It is easy to prove that some very natural properties of the process P are involved in T. For instance, we have

<u>Proposition</u> 1 The set of the occurrences of a condition of N is a chain with respect to $\preccurlyeq$.

<u>Proposition</u> 2 If s is a case which contains all the preconditions of an occurrence u of an event e, and does not contain any of the postconditions of u or conditions which are later than postconditions of u, then all the preconditions of e have occurrences in s and all the postconditions of e do not have occurrences in s.

Proposition 3 If s is a case which contains all the preconditions of an occurrence u of an event e, and does not contain any of the postconditions of u or conditions which are later than postconditions of of u, and if there are postconditions of u, then the set

$$s'=\{p \in Q:\ (p \in s \ \&\sim pre(p,u)) \vee post(u,p)\}$$

is a case.

The subjective theory T′

The subjective theory T′ of the process P is a description of this process from the point of view of an observer. The observer considers the process P as a sequence of consecutive occurrences of global states of the net N. Each of the global states is a subset $s \subseteq C$ of the conditions which are observed as holding simultaneously. The state changes in P are considered as consisting of so called firings of events. An event is said to be fireable in a state s when all of its preconditions hold (i.e., are in s) and all of its postconditions do not hold (i.e., do not belong to s). Only fireable events may fire. In the case of a conflict, i.e., of several fireable events with common pre- or postconditions, only one of the events may fire. Any firing of an event e consists in changing the current state s into another state s′. The preconditions of e (which hold, i.e., belong to s) become not holding conditions (they are not included in s′). The postconditions of e (which do not hold, i.e., do not belong to s) become holding conditions (they are included in s′). The remaining conditions of s and s′ are the same (i.e., conditions which are not pre- or postconditions of e do not change). Any state change of the process P consists of one or more event firings. The process P continues while there are events which are fireable. Otherwise it terminates.

The subjective theory T′ of P is just a characterization of P like the above. The net N is characterized by the theory T_0. Thus, T′ is an extension of T_0. To construct T′ we number the consecutive state occurrences and identify these occurrences with their numbers. In this way we get a set Time of the state occurrences. Then we introduce the following primitive notions :

Holds(c,t) (c holds at t)
Fires(e,t) (e fires at t)

Fireable(e,t) (e is fireable at t)
Untouched(c,t) (c is not a pre- or postcondition of an event which fires at t)

and characterize them by appropriate axioms.

Formally, we add to the theory T_0 the relations Time, $\leq$,Holds, Fires,Fireable,Untouched, identify them with some sets, and characterize by axioms which state the following :

(5´) Time is the set Nat of the natural numbers or a non-empty initial segment of Nat

(6´) $\leq$ is the natural ordering of Time

(7´) Holds $\subseteq C \times$ Time

(8´) Fires $\subseteq E \times$ Time

(9´) $\mathrm{Fireable}(e,t) \Longleftrightarrow (\forall c{:}\mathrm{Pre}(c,e))\,\mathrm{Holds}(c,t)\ \&\ (\forall c{:}\mathrm{Post}(e,c))\sim\mathrm{Holds}(c,t)$

(10´) $\mathrm{Untouched}(c,t) \Longleftrightarrow (\forall e{:}\mathrm{Pre}(c,e))\sim\mathrm{Fires}(e,t)\ \&\ (\forall e{:}\mathrm{Post}(e,c))\sim\mathrm{Fires}(e,t)$

(11´) $(\exists e)\,\mathrm{Fireable}(e,t) \Longrightarrow (\exists e)\,\mathrm{Fires}(e,t)$
(if there are fireable events the some of them fire)

(12´) Fires $\subseteq$ Fireable
(only fireable events may fire)

(13´) $\mathrm{Fires}(e,t) \Longrightarrow t+1 \in \mathrm{Time}\ \&\ (\forall c{:}\mathrm{Pre}(c,e))\sim\mathrm{Holds}(c,t+1)\ \&\ (\forall c{:}\mathrm{Post}(e,c)\ \mathrm{Holds}(c,t+1)$
(if an event e fires then the process has a continuation and the preconditions of e do not hold and the postconditions of e hold at the next state occurrence)

(14´) $t \in \mathrm{Time}\ \&\ t+1 \in \mathrm{Time} \Longrightarrow (\exists e)\,\mathrm{Fires}(e,t)\ \&\ (\forall c{:}\mathrm{Untouched}(c,t))\,(\mathrm{Holds}(c,t+1) \Longleftrightarrow \mathrm{Holds}(c,t))$
(the only way to continue the process is firing of an event; holding of the conditions which are not pre- or postconditions of an event which fires do not change)

(15´) $((\mathrm{Pre}(c,e)\ \&\ \mathrm{Pre}(c,f)) \vee (\mathrm{Post}(e,c)\ \&\ \mathrm{Post}(f,c))\ \&\ \mathrm{Fires}(e,t)\ \&\ \mathrm{Fires}(f,t) \Longrightarrow e=f$
(if two different events have a common pre- or postcondition then at most one of them fires)

As result, we get a subjective theory of the process P and this theory is consistent if T_0 is (it has a model as that described in Winkowski [11]). However, such a theory appears too weak to modell T in it. This is so because there may be events which could fire but they wait to infinity. Thus we must join to the constructed theory an axiom excluding such situations. It suffices to join the following one :

(16′) there is no event e such that every precondition c of e holds for $t \geqslant t_c$ with some $t_c \in$ Time, and every postcondition c of e does not hold for $t \geqslant t_c$ with some $t_c \in$ Time

This gives just the subjective theory T′ we need. Unfortunately, because of the axiom (16′), the theory T′ can be inconsistent for some T_0. Then any modelling of T in T′ is trivial and worthless. Whether T′ is consistent depends on T_0. In this paper we do not engage in investigations of consistency of T′. We may only say that T′ is consistent if the net N does not contain any event with infinitely many pre- or postconditions.

<u>Modelling of T in T′</u>

By <u>modelling</u> of a theory T in another theory T′ we mean an assignment μ of formulas (terms) of T′ to the formulas (terms) of T that preserves free variables (term variables), logical operations (substitutions), and theorems. A more detailed definition can be found in Winkowski [12]. If such a modelling exists then all the theorems of T can be interpreted and proved in T . Thus, every model of T′ has all the properties of models of T which can be formulated in T. In particular, having such a model we can construct a model of T. Hence, T is consistent if only T′ is consistent.

To construct a modelling of the objective theory T in the subjective theory T′ we take the identity modelling of T_0 in T_0 and extend it to a correspondence μ between the formulas and constants of T and those of T′. Namely, we define :

$\mu(Q(p))$ as

$$(\exists c)(\exists m)(p=(c,m) \,\&\, \sim \mathrm{Holds}(c,m-1) \,\&\, (\forall n{:}m \leqslant n)\mathrm{Holds}(c,n)) \vee$$
$$(\exists c)(\exists m)(\exists n)(p=(c,m,n) \,\&\, m \leqslant n \,\&\, \sim \mathrm{Holds}(c,m-1) \,\&\, \sim \mathrm{Holds}(c,n+1) \,\&\, (\forall k{:}m \leqslant k \leqslant n)\mathrm{Holds}(c,k))$$

$\mu(U(u))$ as $(\exists e)(\exists m)(u=(e,m) \,\&\, \mathrm{Fires}(e,m))$

$\mu(pre(p,u))$ as

$$\mu(Q(p)) \,\&\, \mu(U(u)) \,\&\, (\exists c)(\exists e)(Pre(c,e) \,\&\, (\exists m)(\exists n)(p=(c,m,n) \,\&\, u=(e,n)))$$

$\mu(post(u,p))$ as

$$\mu(Q(p)) \,\&\, \mu(U(u)) \,\&\, (\exists c)(\exists e)(Post(e,c) \,\&\, ((\exists m)(p=(c,m+1) \,\&\, u=(e,m)) \vee (\exists m)(\exists n)(p=(c,m+1,n) \,\&\, u=(e,m))))$$

$\mu(F(x)=y)$ as

$$\mu(Q(x)) \,\&\, ((\exists m)(x=(y,m)) \vee (\exists m)(\exists n)(x=(y,m,n))) \vee \mu(U(x)) \,\&\, (\exists m)(x=(y,m)))$$

and extend this definition on other formulas so that :

$$\mu(\sim\alpha) = \sim\mu(\alpha), \quad \mu(\alpha \,\&\, \beta) = \mu(\alpha) \,\&\, \mu(\beta),$$
$$\mu(\alpha \vee \beta) = \mu(\alpha) \vee \mu(\beta), \quad \mu((\exists x)\alpha) = (\exists x)\mu(\alpha),$$
$$\mu((\forall x)\alpha) = (\forall x)\mu(\alpha)$$

In other words, we define an occurrence of a condition of N as an object that represents this condition and an interval of its holding, and an occurrence of an event of N as an object that represents a firing of this event. Our main result is the following.

Modelling Theorem The correspondence μ is a modelling of the objective theory T in the subjective theory T´.

A detailed proof is given in Winkowski [13].

Conclusions

Due to Modelling Theorem we may say that, for a broad class of discrete non-sequential processes, parallelism can be replaced by nondeterminism with no loss of possibilities to formulate and prove properties of processes. This enables one to study non-sequential processes using well developed methods which are elaborated to deal with sequential processes. In particular, various approaches which base on describing non-sequential processes in a sequential way appear to be justified. Of course, the result is not any argument for rejecting the approaches in which non-sequential processes are considered in an objective way. They are always valuable because they help us to understand the real nature of non-sequential processes.

References

1. Baer, J.L., A Survey of Some Theoretical Aspects of Multiprogramming, Computing Surveys, Vol 5, No 1, March 1973
2. Brinch Hansen, P., Concurrent Programming Concepts, Computing Surveys, Vol 5, 1973
3. Genrich, H.J., Einfache nicht-sequentielle Prozesse, BMBW-GMD-37, Bonn, 1971
4. Genrich, H.J., Extended Simple Regular Expressions, in Proc. of MFCS'75 Symp., Marianske Lazne, Lecture Notes in Comp. Sc. 32, Springer-Verlag, 1975
5. Karp, R.M. and Miller, R.E., Parallel Program Schemata, JCSS 3(2)
6. Mazurkiewicz, A., Parallel Recursive Program Schemes, in Proc. of MFCS'75 Symp., Marianske Lazne, Lecture Notes in Comp. Sc. 32, Springer-Verlag, 1975
7. Mazurkiewicz, A., Invariants of Concurrent Programs, to appear
8. Milner, R., An Approach to the Semantics of Parallel Programs, Unpublished Memo, Computer Science Department, University of Edinburgh, 1973
9. Petri, C.A., Interpretations of Net Theory, GMD, Bonn, 1975, presented at MFCS'75 Symp., Marianske Lazne, 1975
10. Shapiro, R.M. and Saint, H., A New Approach to Optimization of Sequencing Decisions, Ann. Rev. in Aut.Prog., Vol 6, P 5, 1970
11. Winkowski, J., Formal Theories of Petri Nets and Net Simulations, CC PAS Reports 242, 1976
12. Winkowski, J., Towards an Understanding of Computer Simulation, CC PAS Reports 243, 1976
13. Winkowski, J., On Sequential Modelling of Parallel Processes, to appear in CC PAS Reports

EQUIVALENCE AND OPTIMIZATION OF RECURSIVE PROGRAM SCHEMATA

Zbigniew Zwinogrodzki
Institute of Informatics and Automatics of AGH, Cracow.

Introduction

Most of the papers concerning program schemata have been devoted to studying methods as effective as possible for the recognition of equivalence of program schemata, their optimization, semantic correctness and desequention. Unfortunately except for the paper by A.A.Letichevsky /[1]/ each of these problems was discussed independently of the others. Two concepts of recursive program schemata equivalence are proposed in this paper: the so-called O-equivalence and QF-equivalence. The definition of O-equivalence contains all the based procedures of optimization of recursive program schemata. The relation of O-equivalence is decidable. For some sets of program schemes the concept of O-equivalence is more general than concepts of program schemata equivalence defined in [2] and [3]. It points to the glaring fact that each attempt at generalization of O-equivalence which gives a decidable relation has to include stronger procedures of optimization than these which are in this paper. The concept of QF-equivalence is more general than every concept of program schemata equivalence which was used until now. In spite of this fact, it seems to be a quite "natural" concept for users of computers.

This paper is a synopsis of the first chapter of [4]. The task of [4] is to show that definitions "maximally asynchronous" recursive program schema, "optimum" recursive program schema and the most general decidable concepts of program schemata equivalence are slight modyfications of one another.

Recursive program schemata, F- and QF- equivalences.

The following sets of letters are given:

the set of variables: $X = \{x_1, x_2, \dots\}$,

the set of functional letters: $T_L = \{\emptyset, \emptyset^+, \emptyset^-, t_1, t_2, \dots\}$,

the set of cycles: $F_L = \{f_\infty, f_1, f_2, \dots\}$,

the set of predicative letters: $P_L = \{p_1, p_2, \dots\}$

and a function $\arg: T_L \cup F_L \cup P_L \to N$, where N is a set of non-negative integers such that for every $i = 1, 2, \dots \arg(f_i) > 0, \arg(f_\infty) = \arg(\emptyset) = 0, \arg(\emptyset^+) = \arg(\emptyset^-) = 1$. The value $\arg(L)$ is called the number of arguments of L.

The set of <u>terms</u> Ter and the set of <u>formulas</u> For are least sets such that

(i) $X \subset Ter$, (ii) if $a_1,\dots,a_m \in Ter$, $arg(L) = m$ then if $L \in T_L \cup F_L$ then $L(a_1,\dots,a_m) \in Ter$ and if $L \in P_L$ then $L(a_1,\dots,a_m) \in For$.

Letters $a, a_1, a_2, \dots$ are used as variables for terms, letters $F, F_1, F_2, \dots$ are used as variables for formulas and letters $L, L_1, L_2, \dots$ are used as variables for letters.

Let $Exp = Ter \cup For$. Elements of Exp are called <u>expressions</u> and denoted by means of letters $E_1, E_2, \dots$. E is a <u>reduced expression</u> iff E does not contain any cycle. We assume Ter_0 to be the set of all reduced terms and For_0 to be the set of all reduced formulas. $Exp_0 = For_0 \cup Ter_0$.

We define a relation $\lhd$ in the set Exp as follows: (i) $E \lhd E$, (ii) if $E = L(a_1,\dots,a_m)$ then for every $i = 1,\dots,m$ $a_i \lhd E$, (iii) if $E_1 \lhd E_2$ and $E_2 \lhd E_3$ then $E_1 \lhd E_3$. If $E_1 \lhd E_2$ we say E_1 <u>occurs in</u> E_2 and if E_1 does not occur in E_2 we write $E_1 \not\lhd E_2$.

The sign $>E$ denotes the first letter from the left occurring in E.

A <u>recursive program schema</u> is defined as a sequence of inscriptions

$$RS = \left(f_i(x_1,\dots,x_n) = \text{if } E_i^0 \text{ then } E_i^1 \text{ else } E_i^2 \right), i = 1,\dots,m$$

where $E_i^e \in Ter$, $e = 1,2$, $E_i^0 \in For$ and expressions E_i^e, $e = 1,2,3$ are constructed by means of letters belong to the set $\{x_1,\dots,x_n\} \cup \cup \{f_\infty, f_1,\dots,f_m\} \cup T_L \cup P_L$ only. Moreover every two elements of RS are different , $>E_i^1 = \emptyset^+$, $>E_i^2 \neq \emptyset^-$ and letters $\emptyset^+, \emptyset^-$ occur in RS only in these positions.

<u>Example 1</u>: Sequences

$$\begin{aligned} RS_1 = \Big(f_1^0(x_1,x_2) &= \text{if } p_1^1 \text{ then } \emptyset^+(f_3^1(x_1,x_2)) \text{ else } \emptyset^-(f_2^1(x_1,x_2)), \\ f_2(x_1,x_2) &= \text{if } p_2^1 \text{ then } f_5^1(x_1,t_1^2) \text{ else } t_2^1(t_3^1(t_1^1)) \ . \\ f_3(x_1,x_2) &= \text{if } p_2^1(x_1) \text{ then } f_4^1(x_1,x_2) \text{ else } f_3^3(x_1,x_2), \\ f_4(x_1,x_2) &= \text{if } p_1^2 \text{ then } f_3^2(t_2^5(x_1),x_2) \text{ else } f_2^2(t_2^2(x_1),x_2) \ , \\ f_5(x_1,x_2) &= \text{if } p_3^1(x_2) \text{ then } t_2^3(t_3^3(x_1)) \text{ else } t_2^4(t_3^2(x_1)) \Big), \end{aligned}$$

$$RS_2 = \Big(f_1^0(x_1,x_2) = \text{if } p_2^1(x_1) \text{ then } \emptyset^+(f_2^1(t_3^1(x_1),x_2)) \text{ else } \emptyset^-(f_2^2(t_3^2(t_1^1), t_3^3(t_3^4(t_1^2)))) , f_2(x_1,x_2) = \text{if } p_1^1 \text{ then } f_2^3(x_1,x_2) \text{ else } t_2^1(x_1) \Big)$$

are recursive program schemata in the case when all upper-right indices are ignored at **this point.**

We assume that $E_1[E_2/E_3] = E$ iff (i) if $E_2 \not\sqsubset E_1$ then $E = E_1$, (ii) if $E_2 = E_1$ then $E = E_3$ (iii) if $E_2 \sqsubset E_1$ and $E_1 = L(a_1,\dots,a_m)$ then $E = L(a_1[E_2/E_3],\dots,a_m[E_2/E_3])$.

We say that $L(a_1,\dots,a_n)$ is <u>the reduceable term in E</u> iff $L(a_1,\dots,a_n)$ is the last term from the left in E such that $a_1,\dots,a_n \in Exp_o$ and $L \in F_L$.

W mean by <u>a substitution</u> every function $\sigma: Exp \to Exp$ such that $\sigma: X \to Ter$ and if $E = L(a_1,\dots,a_m)$ then $\sigma(E) = L(\sigma(a_1),\dots,\sigma(a_m))$.

Let $\bar{f}_j(x_1,\dots,x_n) = S_1, S_2, \dots$ be a sequence such that every element S_i is a finite sequence of expressions or expressions denoted by brackets constructed recursively in the followin way: (i) $S_1 = (f_j^o(x_1,\dots,x_n))$,

(ii) if $S_m = E_1,\dots,E_k,(E_{k+1}),(E_{k+2}),\dots,(E_l)$ then (ii$_1$) if $E_{k+1} \in Exp_o$ then $S_{m+1} = E_1,\dots,E_k,E_{k+1},(E_{k+2}),\dots,(E_l)$, (ii$_2$) if $f_i^r(a_1,\dots,a_n)$ is a reduceable term in E_{k+1} then $S_{m+1} = E_1,\dots,E_{k+1},(e_s\sigma(E_i^o))$,

$(E_{k+1}[f_i^r(a_1,\dots,a_n)/\sigma(E_i^s)]),(E_{k+2}),\dots,(E_l)$, where for every $m = 1,\dots,n$ $\sigma(x_m) = a_m$, $s > 0$ and $e_1 = +, e_2 = -$, (iii) if every element of S_m is **a reduced expression and $f_{oo} \notin E_k$ then** S_m is the last element of $\bar{f}_j(x_1,\dots,x_n)$.

$\bar{f}_j$ is the least sequence such that if $S_m = E_1,E_2,\dots,E_k,(E_{k+1}),\dots,(E_l)$ is an element of $\bar{f}_j(x_1,\dots,x_n)$ then $E_1,E_2,\dots,E_k$ is a subsequence of $\bar{f}_j$.

Every sequence $\bar{f}_1$ is called <u>a path of RS</u>.

Let H be a function defined on $F_L \cup P_L$ such that for every predicative symbol L of m arguments H(L) is a total function mapping Ter_o^m into $\{1,0\}$ and for every functional letter L $H(L) = L$. The function H is called <u>a Herbrand interpretation of RS.</u>

We mean by a <u>recursive program</u> every pair (RS,H).

Let σ_o be a substitution such that $\sigma_o: X \to Ter_o$. The value $E(H,\sigma_o) = E$ is defined recursively as: (i) if $E \in X$ then $E(H,\sigma_o) = E$, (ii) if $E = L(a_1,\dots,a_m)$ then $E(H,\sigma_o) = H(L)(a_1(H,\sigma_o),\dots,a_m(H,\sigma_o))$. It is easy to see that if $E \in For_o$ then $E(H,\sigma_o) \in \{1,0\}$ and if $E \in Ter_o$ then $E = E(H,\sigma_o)$.

A path[RS] of RS is <u>confirmed by an interpretation H and a sub-</u>

stitution σ_0 /in abbreviation/ $[RS](H,\sigma_0)$ / iff for every formula $eF \in [RS]$ such that $F \in Exp_0$ if $e = +$ then $F(H,\sigma_0) = 1$ and if $e = -$ then $F(H,\sigma_0) = 0$.

If a path $[RS]$ is finite, E is the last element of $[RS]$ such that $E = \emptyset^e$, $e = +,-$, then we write $[RS] = E$ and if not we write $[RS] = \infty$.

So every recursive program (RS,H) defines a partial function $FRS(H) : Ter_0^n \rightarrow Ter_0$ such that for every σ_0 if $[RS](H,\sigma_0) = a$ then $FRS(H)(\sigma_0(x_1),\ldots,\sigma_0(x_n)) = a$ and if $[RS](H,\sigma_0) = \infty$ then the value $FRS(H,\sigma_0)$ is not defined.

RS is <u>F-equivalent</u> to RS` /in abbreviation RS =/F/RS` / iff for every H $FRS(H) = FRS`(H)$.

Schemes RS_1 and RS_2 given in Example 1 are F-equivalent.

Undecidability of the relation =/F/ was first proved in [5] and [6]. Moreover every relation of equivalence defined for program schemata is undecidable if the definition of this relation contains the general quantifier: for every interpretation H .../[7] .It was attempted to avoid the undecidability of =/F/ by means of three sorts of additional constraints: /1/ on the class of program schemata /e.g. [8], [9]/, /2/ on the concept of program schemata equivalence /e.g. [2], [3]/, /3/ on the class of interpretations /e.g. [10] /. Though the relation =/F/ was accepted as the most general concept of program schemata equivalence in all the above-mentioned investigations it seems useful to introduce a samewhat more general concept of program schemata equivalence than F-euqivalence.

Let L_{RS} be a set of all letters which occur in RS. Then RS $\prec$ RS` iff for every interpretation H there exists such interpretation H` that for every $L \in L_{RS}$ $H(L) = H`(L)$ and $FRS(H`) = FRS`(H`)$.

We say RS is <u>quasi-functional equivalent to RS`</u> /in abbreviation RS =/QF/ RS`/ iff RS $\prec$ RS` and RS` $\prec$ RS.

Of course if $L_{RS} = L_{RS`}$ then RS =/F/RS` iff RS =/QF/RS`. "Naturalness" of QF-equivalence can be illustrated by means of the following simple schemes.

<u>Example 2:</u> Schemes

$RS_3 = (f_1(x_1) = \text{if } p_1 \text{ then } a_1 \text{ else } \emptyset^-(f_2(x_1)), f_2(x_1) = \text{if} p_4 \text{ then } a_1 \text{ else } a_2)$,

$RS_4 = (f_1(x_1) = \text{if } p_1 \text{ then } a_1 \text{ else } a_2)$,

where $a_1 \neq a_2$ are QF-equivalent but not F-equivalent.

The relation =/QF/ is not transitive. For schemes

$RS_5 = (f_1(x_1) = \text{if } p_1 \text{ then } a_1 \text{ else } a_2)$, $RS_6 = (f_1(x_1) = \text{if } p_4 \text{ then } a_1 \text{ else } a_2)$, $RS_7 = (\text{if } p_1 \text{ then } a_2 \text{ else } a_1)$

where $a_1, a_2 \in Ter_0$ and $a_1 \neq a_2$, RS_5 =/QF/ RS_6, RS_6 =/QF/ RS_7 but RS_5 is not QF-equivalent to RS_7. Of course RS_5 and RS_6 are not F-equivalent in spite of the fact that these schemes seem to be identical.

We say RS is <u>free</u> iff for every path $[RS]$ there exists such interpretation H and a substitution σ_0 that $[RS](H, \sigma_0) = [RS]$.
<u>Hypothesis</u>: Set $\{(RS, RS') \mid RS$ =/QF/ RS', RS and RS' are free$\}$ is decidable.

<u>O-eqivalence</u>

Let us suppose that all occurences of letters in RS are numerated as in Example 1 and S is a finite subsequence of $[RS]$. We distinguish now two symbols L^i and L^j. We say that f^i_j is <u>eliminated in S m times</u> iff S contains only m elements $E_{i_1}, \ldots, E_{i_m}$ such that for every $i_k, k=1,\ldots,m$ there exists such element $E_r \in S$, $r < i_k$, that $E_{i_k} = E_r[f^i_j(a_1,\ldots,a_n)/\sigma(E^e_i)]$ where $\sigma(x_m) = a_m$, $m = 1,\ldots,n$ and $1 \leqslant e \leqslant 2$.
The symbol $[\![RS]\!]$ denotes the longest initial segment of $[RS]$ such that every cycle in RS is eliminated in $[\![RS]\!]$ at most n+1 times. A sequence $[\![RS]\!]$ is <u>unclosed</u> iff the last element of $[\![RS]\!]$ is not reduced or there are two reduced formulas F_k, F_l such that $+F_k, -F_l \in [\![RS]\!]$ and $F_k \doteq F_l$, where $\doteq$ denotes the identity of expressions with precision to upper-right indexes and symbols $\emptyset^+, \emptyset^-$.

A letter L is said to be <u>passive in RS</u> iff one of the following two conditions is fulfilled: (i) L occurs only in unclosed sequences , (ii) L does not occur in any reduced expression occuring in a sequence $[\![RS]\!]$.

Let us do the following eliminations in RS: (i) if for every j f^j_i is passive in RS we exclude the i'th equation and we substitute f_∞ for every expression E^e_j, $0 \leqslant e \leqslant 2, 1 \leqslant j \leqslant m$, such that for some k $f^k_i(a_1,\ldots,a_n) \lhd E^e_j$, (ii) if t^j_i is passive in RS and $> a = t^j_i$ we substitute $\emptyset$ for a, (iii) we exclude all equations of the forms: $f_i(x_1,\ldots,x_n)$ = if f_∞ then E^1_i else E^2_i, $f_i(x_1,\ldots,x_n)$ = if E^0_i then f_∞ else f_∞.

Let us suppose that set RS is closed with respect to the rules (i) - (iii). Then we mean by $/f_i/$ the longest initial segment of $\bar{f}_i$ such that every cycle is eliminated in $/f_i/$ at most once.

If $e_1F_1, \ldots, e_kF_k, E$ is the subsequence of $/f_i/$ containing the last element and all reduced elements of $/f_i/$ and $f_\infty \not\lhd E$ then the triplet $(\{e_1F_1,\ldots,e_kF_k\}, E, i)$ is <u>a component of RS.</u>

Let C_{RS} be the set of all components of RS. We mean by <u>the canonic</u>

and for every k $f_i^k(a_1,\dots,a_n) \not\subset E'$. (ii) we substitute every two components $(Z\cup\{+F\},E_1,i),(Z\cup\{-F\},E_2,i)$ by the component (Z,E,i) ,if $E_1 \doteq E_2$

We say RS is <u>O-equivalent to</u> RS /in abbreviation RS =/O/ RS'/ iff CRS $\doteq$ CRS'.[1]

It is easy to prove that

Thi If RS =/O/ RS' then RS =/F/ RS'.

<u>Example 3</u>: For schemes given in Example 1:

$$[\![RS_1]\!]_1 = f_1^0(x_1,x_2),-p_1^1,\emptyset^-\left(f_2^1(x_1,x_2)\right),-p_2^1(x_1),\emptyset^-\left(t_2^1\left(t_3^1\left(t_1^1\right)\right)\right),$$

$$[\![RS_1]\!]_2 = f_1^0(x_1,x_2),-p_1^1,\emptyset^-\left(f_2^1(x_1,x_2)\right),+p_2^1(x_1),\emptyset^-\left(f_5^1(x_1,t_1^2)\right),+p_3^1(t_1^2),$$
$$\emptyset^-\left(t_2^3\left(t_3^3(x_1)\right)\right),$$

$$[\![RS_1]\!]_3 = f_1^0(x_1,x_2),-p_1^1,\emptyset^-\left(f_2^1(x_1,x_2)\right),+p_2^1(x_1),\emptyset^-\left(f_5^1(x_1,t_1^2)\right),-p_3^1(t_1^2),$$
$$\emptyset^-\left(t_2^4\left(t_3^2(x_1)\right)\right),$$

$$[\![RS_1]\!]_4 = f_1^0(x_1,x_2),+p_1^1,\emptyset^+\left(f_3^1(x_1,x_2)\right),-p_2^2(x_1),\emptyset^+\left(f_3^3(x_1,x_2)\right)\dots$$

$$[\![RS_1]\!]_5 = f_1^0(x_1,x_2),+p_1^1,\emptyset^+\left(f_3^1(x_1,x_2)\right),+p_2^2(x_1),\emptyset^+\left(f_4^1(x_1,x_2)\right),-p_1^2,\dots$$

$$[\![RS_1]\!]_6 = f_1^0(x_1,x_2),+p_1^1,\emptyset^+\left(f_3^1(x_1,x_2)\right),+p_2^2(x_1),\emptyset^+\left(f_4^1(x_1,x_2)\right),+p_1^2,\dots$$

$$[\![RS_2]\!]_1 = f_1^0(x_1,x_2),+p_2^1(x_1),\emptyset^+\left(f_2^1\left(t_3^1(x_1),x_2\right)\right),-p_1^1,\emptyset^+\left(t_2^1\left(t_3^1(x_1)\right)\right)$$

$$[\![RS_2]\!]_2 = f_1^0(x_1,x_2),+p_2^1(x_1),\emptyset^+\left(f_2^1\left(t_3^1(x_1),{}_2\right)\right),+p_1^1,\emptyset^+\left(f_2^3\left(t_3^1(x_1),x_2\right)\right),$$
$$-p_1^1,\dots$$

$$[\![RS_2]\!]_3 = f_1^0(x_1,x_2),+p_2^1(x_1),\emptyset^+\left(f_2^1\left(t_3^1(x_1),x_2\right)\right),+p_1^1,\emptyset^+\left(f_2^3\left(t_3^1(x_1),x_2\right)\right),$$
$$+p_1^1,\emptyset^+\left(f_2^3\left(t_3^1\left(t_3^1(x_1)\right),x_2\right)\right),\dots$$

$$[\![RS_2]\!]_4 = f_1^0(x_1,x_2),-p_2^1(x_1),\emptyset^-\left(f_2^2\left(t_3^2(t_1^1),t_3^3\left(t_3^4(t_1^2)\right)\right)\right),-p_1^1,\emptyset^-\left(t_2^1\left(t_3^2(t_1^1)\right)\right)$$

$$[\![RS_2]\!]_5 = f_1^0(x_1,x_2),-p_2^1(x_1),\emptyset^-\left(f_{22}^2\left(t_3^2(t_1^1),t_3^3\left(t_3^4(t_1^2)\right)\right)\right),+p_1^1,\dots$$

Sequences ended with points are unclosed. Letters $f_3^1, f_3^2, f_3^3, f_4^1$ are passive in Rs_1 and letters $f_2^3, t_3^3, t_3^4, t_1^2$ are passive in RS_2. Therefore the reduced schemes RS_1 and RS_2 are respectively:

1/Y≐Z iff for every E∈Y there exists E'∈Z such that E≐E' and inversely.

$$RS_1 = \Big(f_1^0(x_1,x_2) = \text{if } p_1^1 \text{ then } f_\infty \text{ else } \emptyset^-\big(f_2(x_1,x_2)\big),$$

$$f_2(x_1,x_2) = \text{if } p_2^1(x_1) \text{ then } f_5^1(x_1,t_1) \text{ else } t_2^1(t_3^1(t_1^1)),$$

$$f_5(x_1,x_2) = \text{if } p_3^1(x_2) \text{ then } t_2^3(t_3^3(x_1)) \text{ else } t_2^4(t_3^1(x_1))\Big),$$

$$RS_2 = \Big(f_1^0(x_1,x_2) = \text{if } p_2^1(x_1) \text{ then } \emptyset^+\big(f_2^1(t_3^1(x_1),x_2)\big) \text{ else } \emptyset^-\big(f_2^2(t_3^2(t_1^1)$$

$$f_2(x_1,x_2) = \text{if } p_1^1 \text{ then } f_\infty \text{ else } t_2^1(x_1)\Big) .$$

Canonic forms of RS_1 and RS_2 are sets:

$$CRS_1 = \{(\{-p_1^1, +p_2^1(x_1)\}, \emptyset^-(t_2^3(t_3^3(x_1))), 1), (\{-p_1^1, -p_2^1(x_1)\}, \emptyset^-(t_2^1(t_3^1(t_1^1))), 1\}$$

$$CRS_2 = \{(\{-p_1^1, +p_2^1(x_1)\}, \emptyset^+(t_2^1(t_3^1(x_1))), 1), (\{-p_1^1, -p_2^1(x_1)\}, \emptyset^-(t_2^1(t_3^2(t_1^1))), 1\}$$

Then $RS_1 =/0/ RS_2$. It is a well-known fact that every flowchart can be reduced to a recursive program schema but not inversely. So it is possible to compare 0-equivalence with these concepts of program schemata equivalence which are proposed in [2] and [3]. Schemes RS_1 an RS_2 can be reduced to flowcharts. These flowcharts are not equivalent any sens fixed in [2] and [3]. A more precise comparison of these concepts is given in [4].

References

[1] A.A.Letichevsky: Equivalence and optimization of programs, Internationa Symposium on Theoretical Programming, 5 Lecture Notes in Computer Scinence Springer-Verlag, Berlin-Heidelberg-New York, 1974.

[2] V.E.Itkin: Logiko-termalnaja ekwiwalentnost schem program, "Kibernetika Kiev, No1 /1972/, /in Russian/.

[3] Donald M.Kaplan: Regular Expressions and the Equivalence of Programs, Journal of Computer and System Sciences, vol3 /1969/.

[4] Zbigniew Zwinogrodzki: Equivalence, optimization and asynchronization o program schemata /to be published/.

[5] M.S.Paterson: Program Schemata, Machine Intelligence 3, Edinburgh Univ. Press /1968/.

[6] A.A.Letichevsky: Funkcjonalnaja ekvivalentnost diskretnych preobrazovan "Kibernetika", Kiev, No1/1969/ and No2/1970/.

[7] V.E.Itkin and Z.Zwinogrodzki: On Program Schemata Equivalence, Journal o Computer and System Sciences, vol6, No1/1972/.

[8] K. Indermak: On Ianov schemes with one memory location, Proceedings of MFCS Symposium High Tatras, 1973.

[9] E.Ashcroft, Z.Manna, A.Pnueli: Decidable Properties of Monadic Functiona Schemes, Journal of Associ. for Com.Machinery, vol.20, No3 /1973/

[10] A.Kreczmar: Problemy efektywności logiki algorytmicznej, University of Warsaw, 1974/doctor's thesis, in Polish/ .

OBSERVABILITY CONCEPTS IN ABSTRACT DATA TYPE SPECIFICATION

V. Giarratana, F. Gimona and U. Montanari

Istituto di Scienze dell'Informazione, University of Pisa, Italy.

1) Introduction

Structured programming [1] is a widely accepted methodology for producing reliable software which is based on a hierarchy of virtual machines going from a virtual machine oriented towards the problem to be solved to the actual available programming language.

Every virtual machine is implemented in terms of the lower machines and in general extends them with respect to both control and data. An interesting and very promising extension mechanism is the CLUSTER construct [2] which allows to define a new abstract data type and the operations on it, but completely hides this information to the user of the new type, thus guaranteeing full protection and ease of change. Similar constructs are also provided by a rapidly growing number of new programming languages based on the same ideas (see for instance [3]).

Beside hiding irrelevant information, a good extension mechanism should make sure that relevant information is actually passed, namely that the use of an abstract type is consistent with its definition. To achieve this goal, for every abstract type a specification should be provided serving as an interface between the user and the implementor [4]. Among the various formal and informal techniques which can be used to this purpose, the so-called axiomatic or algebraic approach is very popular [5-7].

In this approach, a set of axioms is used to define a congruence (and thus a partition) on the word algebra of all terms which can be constructed with the operations to be specified. The congruence classes are assumed to be (isomorphic to) the possible distinct values of the types. Therefore, to prove the correctness of an implementation, one should prove that the above congruence classes and the encodings of the values used in the actual representation are isomorphic [7].

In this paper we criticize the above "congruence semantics" since we feel that axioms are just a formalism among many others, and thus their semantics should be defined only reflecting their external behaviour. Congruence classes, instead, are strictly related to proofs, i.e. to the computations of the axiomatic formalism. Here we give a "functional" definition of semantics instead, and characterize the class of all equivalent representations and its structure. We treat also the case of incomplete specifications, which was skipped by most previous research [6]. In particular, we find that there are pairs of equivalent representations which are not isomorphic and not even homomorphic, thus giving evidence of the restrictiveness of the above criterion for the correctness of implementations.

2) Background

In this section we introduce few basic concepts centered on the notions of heterogeneous algebra [8] and of initial algebra [9]. An heterogeneous algebra $A=[S,F]$ is a pair, in which:

a) $S=\{S_i | i\in I_S\}$ is a family of phyla. Phylum S_i is called by a name i taken from a set I_S of phyla names.

b) $F=\{f_j | j\in I_F\}$ is a set of operations of finite n-arity. For specifying the domain and the range of every f_j, we give two functions $d:I_F\to I_S^*$ and $r:I_F\to I_S$. Thus if $d(j)=(i_1,i_2,\dots,i_{n(j)})$ and $r(j)=k$, we have $f_j:S_{i_1} X\ S_{i_2} X \dots X\ S_{i_{n(j)}}\to S_k$

In particular, if $d(j)=\lambda$, the empty string, then f_j is a nullary operation, or a costant.

To be concrete, in this paper phyla will be interpreted as data types, while the elements of set S_i will be seen as the possible values of a variable of type name i. Thus functions d and r give the types of the operations in A.

For example, arithmetic (with equality) is an heterogeneous algebra $I_S=\{I,B\}$, $S_I=\{0,1,2,\dots\}$, $S_B=\{T,F\}$; $I_F=\{zero,succ,sum,mult,eq\}$, d(zero) = (), r(zero) = I, d(succ) = (I), r(succ) = I, d(sum) = (I,I), r(sum) = I, d(mult) = (I,I), r(mult)=I,

d(eq) = (I,I), r(eq) = B and where the functions f_{zero}, f_{succ}, f_{sum}, f_{mult}, f_{eq} have the usual definition.
A suggestive way of giving names and operation types (i.e. the syntactical part of the algebra definition, but not the actual semantics of the operations) is to use an AND-OR graph [10]. For instance we see in Fig. 1 the syntactic graph of arithmetic.

FIG. 1

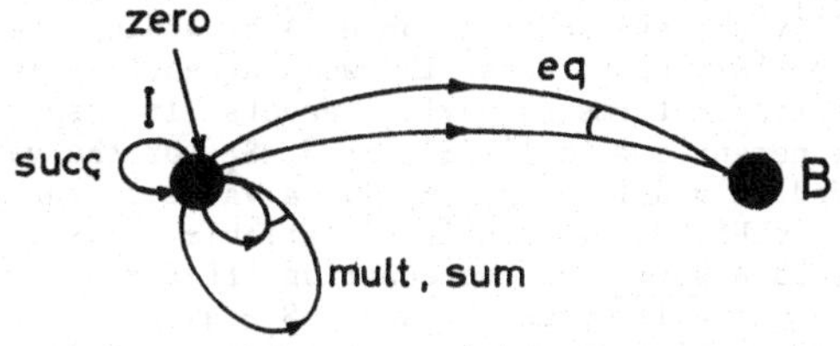

Two algebras A' and A" are called similar iff they have the same syntactic graph, i.e. iff they have the same phyla and operation names and the same operation types, $I_S'=I_S''=I_S$, $I_F'=I_F''=I_F$, d'=d"=d, r'=r"=r.
Given two similar algebras A' and A", a morphism from A' to A" is a family of function $H=\{h_i | i\in I_S\}$, $h_i: S_i' \to S_i''$, $i\in I_S$, such that for all function names $j\in I_F$, $d(j)=(i_1,i_2,\dots,i_{n(j)})$, $r(j)=k$, we have

$$f_j'' \circ (h_{i_1},h_{i_2},\dots,h_{i_{n(j)}}) = h_k \circ f_j'$$

As usual, morphisms which are injective, surjective or bijective are called monomorphisms, epimorphisms and isomorphisms respectively.

A congruence on an algebra A is a family $E=\{E_i | i\in I_S\}$ of equivalence relations, one for each phylum of A, with the following substitution property. For every $f_j\in F$ we must have

$$x_i\ E_i\ y_i;\ x_i,y_i\in S_i;\ i=i_1,i_2,\dots,i_{n(j)} \text{ implies}$$

$$f_j(x_{i_1},x_{i_2},\dots,x_{i_{n(j)}})\ E_k\ f_j(y_{i_1},y_{i_2},\dots,y_{i_{n(j)}})$$

It easy to see [8] that, given an algebra A, there exists a one-to-one correspondence between epimorphisms from A and congruences on A. In fact, given an epimorphism from A to A', the images in S_i of the elements of S_i' form the equivalence classes of a congruence, and viceversa A is epimorphic to the quotient algebra A' obtained from A by merging all elements equivalent according to some given congruence. For instance, if we define on the integer phylum of arithmetic the equivalence relation

$$x\ E_I\ y \quad \text{iff remainder}(x,3) = \text{remainder}(y,3)$$

and we further assume

$$T\ E_B\ F$$

then we get a congruence. The corresponding epimorphism is, of course, given by:

$$h_I(x) = \text{remainder}(x,3)$$

and

$$h_B(T) = h_B(F) = \lambda$$

Given a class C of similar algebras, we say that an algebra $\bar{A}$ is initial (final) in C iff there exists exactly one morphism from $\bar{A}$ to any A∈C (from any A∈C to $\bar{A}$). Initiality is a very interesting property. In fact it is possible to see [9] that i) if two algebras $\bar{A}'$ and $\bar{A}''$ are both initial in C, then they are isomorphic; and ii) if $\bar{A}'$ is initial in C and $\bar{A}''$ is isomorphic to $\bar{A}'$, also $\bar{A}''$ is initial in C.

The class of all similar algebras has an initial algebra T, called word algebra or Herbrand Universe consisting of all symbolic terms (or trees) which can be constructed, starting from the constants, using the operation names and respecting the operation types. In T every phylum is a recognizable (or regular, or equational) language of terms (or trees) [11]. Making reference to the syntactic graph, the phylum of T of name i is the set of solution trees generated by the graph, starting from node i [10]. The unique morphism H from T to A may be called an interpretation morphism, and it assigns some element of S_i to every term of the phylum of T of name i.

To express concisely some general properties of algebras, it is often convenient to introduce variables and equations. Given an algebra A and a family of sets of variables $X=\{X_i | i\in I_S\}$, one want to define the variable terms. To do this, it is enough to modify the syntactic graph of A by adding the variables to the proper phyla as new nullary operations. The word algebra T(X), obtained in this way, has the desired variable terms as phyla elements. It easy to see, using initiality, that any assignement $\alpha = \{\alpha_i | i\in I_S\}$, $\alpha_i : X_i \to S_i$, of the variables x_i to elements of S_i can be extended in a unique way to give a value to each variable term.

An equation <LHS,RHS> is a pair of variable terms taken from some phylum i of T(X). An algebra A satisfies the equation iff for every assignment α of the variables in X, the variable terms LHS and RHS evaluate to the same element of S_i. Given a set of equations ε, we may construct, as follows, an algebra A_ε which is initial in the class C of all the algebras which satisfy all the equations in ε.

i) Algebrically. The equations define relations R_i on the phyla of T. Let R'be the least (i.e. finer) congruence on T such that R_i' are coarser than, or equal to, R_i.

ii) Logically. Consider the equation as axioms LHS=RHS, and use as inference rules the standard rules of variable assignment and of substitution of equals. Then $x \; R_i' \; y$ iff you can prove x = y.

In both cases, A_ε is the quotient algebra of T with respect to R'.

3) The semantics of abstract data types

Usually to give the semantics of a program written in some formalism is to define some mathematical object computed by the program. For instance, the semantics of a grammar or of an acceptor may be the language defined, while the semantics of an ALGOL program is the (partial) function returning the final state in terms of the initial state. When giving the semantics of abstract data types, the situation is more complicated, since we must define both some functions (i.e. the operations) and their domains.

If abstract data types were to be defined "ab initio", little more could be added to the previous section. For instance, imagine to have to define the type "group element". The syntatic part of the definition would consist of a single phylum name, of a diadic operation named composition, of a monadic operation called inverse, and of some (possibly infinite) constants (among which the unity). The semantic part of the definition is the equation set ε, the axioms of groups. The group elements would then be the elements of the only phylum of the initial algebra A_ε, i.e. the elements of the free group generated by the above constants.

However, abstract data types, as pointed out in the introduction, are usually defined in terms of known types. Thus the definition of types as initial algebras, as carried on by Goguen et al. [7] does not seem to capture the right concept. Infact programs using abstract data types in their inside will still accept as data, and give back as results, only values of the known types. Thus the algebra of the abstract types and of their operations may have any convenient strutture which does insure the desired behaviour of the whole program, not necessary the finest structure satisfying the axioms, as assured by the initial algebra construction.

Therefore we feel that the mathematical objet which must be defined in order to give the semantics of an abstract data type definition (or specification) is a function which assigns a value to the terms of known type of the word algebra.

More precisely, let us assume to have to define some new types and the opetations on them in terms of some old types. Since we know the type of every operation, we may construct a syntactic graph where the nodes are partitioned in two classes I_S^N and I_S^O.

Furthermore, since we are going to define only operations related to the new types, we may assume that for all function names $j\in I_F$, either $d(j)\cap I_S^N \neq \emptyset$ or $r(j)\in I_S^N$ or both. Moreover according to the type (old or new) of the result, we partition also the operations in two sets: $j\in I_F^O$ if $r(j)\in I_S^O$ and $j\in I_F^N$ if $r(j)\in I_S^N$.

Finally, we explicitely add constant names to I_F^O corresponding to all the known values of the old types. Let us call QUOTE (x) the constant corresponding to the value x and UNQUOTE (y) the value corresponding to the constant y. For instance in fig. 2 we see the syntactic graph corresponding to the definition of the type "stack of integers". There I_S^N ={STACK}, I_S^O ={I,B}, I_F^N ={NEWSTACK, POP, PUSH, SERROR}, I_F^O ={ZERO, ONE, TWO,...,TOP, IERROR, TRUE, FALSE, BERROR, EMPTY}.

FIG. 2

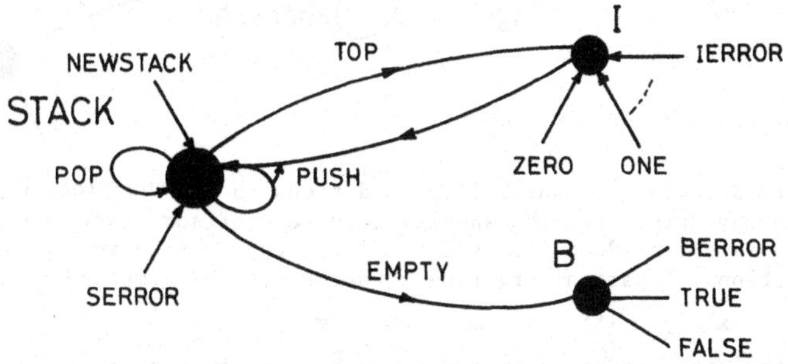

We can now consider the word algebra T generated by the syntactic graph. The terms obtained in this way are exactly all the expressions which can ever appear in a program using the abstract type. We are now ready to give our key definition.
Definition I. A specification of a set of abstract data types having a given syntactic graph is any family of functions

$$\overline{H} = \{\overline{h}_i \mid i \in I_S^O\}$$

$$\overline{h}_i : S_i^T \to S_i^! \cup \alpha$$

where S_i^T is the phylum of the word algebra of name i, $S_i^!$ is the set of values of the known type of name i and α represents don't care conditions. Functions $\overline{h}_i$ must satisfy the following consistency conditions:

a) let y be any constant of old type:

(3.1) $\overline{h}_i(y) = \text{UNQUOTE}(y)$

b) let y be any term of old type, let $\overline{h}_i(y) \neq \alpha$ and let t(x) be any variable term of old type

(3.2) $\overline{h}_k(t(\text{QUOTE}(\overline{h}_i(y)))) = \overline{h}_k(t(y))$

c) let y be any term of old type and let $\overline{h}_i(y) = \alpha$; then a constant z_y must exist, such that for all variable terms t(x) of old type with $\overline{h}_k(t(y)) \neq \alpha$, we have

(3.3) $\overline{h}_k(t(y)) = \overline{h}_k(t(z_y))$

A specification is called complete iff α does not appear in the range of functions $\overline{h}_i$.

Let us add some comments. Functions $\overline{h}_i$ are actually a "black-box" specification. When the value of some expression y is not specified (i.e. when $\overline{h}$ (y) evaluates to α), it means that the user of the new type believes never to need the value of expression y in his programs, and thus gives an extra degree of freedom to the implementor. Condition a) assures that to every constant will be assigned the corresponding value. Condition b) assures that the value assigned to a term must be consistent with the values assigned to all its subterms. Condition c) assures that for every term with a don't care condition, there exists at least a possible value UNQUOTE (z_y).

As an example, we give the case of a (string) language with don't care conditions. We have two old types, B and V (V is the alphabet) and one new type, STRING of characters. Function $\overline{h}_I$ associates a value T, F or don't care to every expression as

MEMBER (ADDCHAR (ADDCHAR (... (ADDCHAR (s_o,b) ...), a), a)

namely to every string on {a,b}

FIG. 3

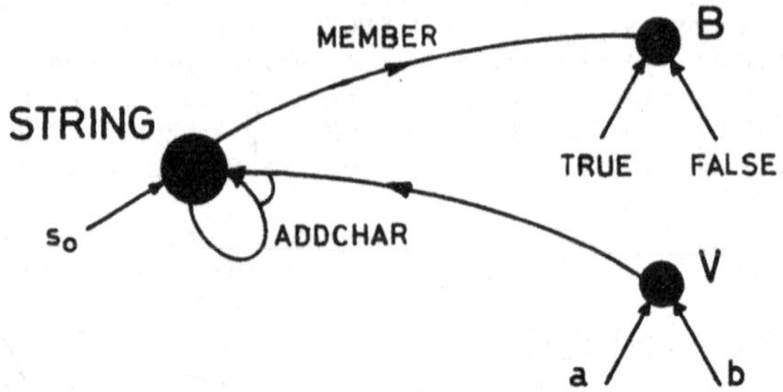

Besides obvious computability conditions on the functions $\overline{h}_i$, further constraints on them may arise from the special structure of some type. For instance, an extra value ω is often added to, say, the integers, to take into account nonterminating computations. A partial ordering structure is then imposed as follows:

$$x \subseteq y \quad \text{iff} \quad x = \omega \quad \text{or} \quad x = y$$

A monotonicity condition on functions $\overline{h}_i$ must then hold. Let x_1 and x_2 be integer constants. We must have

$$\overline{h}_i\ (x_1) \subseteq \overline{h}_i\ (x_2) \rightarrow \forall t(x),\ \ \overline{h}_i(t(x_1)) \subseteq \overline{h}_i(t(x_2))$$

where $t(x)$ is any variable term.

Let us consider the class R_t of all algebras A with a given syntactic graph and satisfying the following conditions.

i) Every element of every phylum is reachable, namely it can be obtained by evaluating some expression with no variables. This means that the single morphism from T to A (remember that T is initial) must be an epimorphism.

ii) Every phylum S_i of old type (namely with $i \in I_S^O$) must contain as elements exactly all the values of that type.

iii) The nullary functions must return the values obtained by unquoting their name.

Algebras $A \in R_t$ are called total representations of the defined abstract data types. This definition is quite natural. For instance, any (irredundant) implementation of the abstract data types in terms of lower level data types (supported by the standard programming language) is a total representation in the above sense.

We are now ready to define the semantics of an algebra $A \in R_t$. Let us consider the unique epimorphism from T to A namely the family of functions

$$H = \{h_i \mid i \in I_S\} \qquad h_i : S_i^T \rightarrow S_i$$

where S_i^T is the phylum of name i of the word algebra T. The semantics of A is the family

$$H' = \{h_i \in H \mid i \in I_S^O\}$$

Given a representation algebra $A \in R_t$ with its semantics H' and a specification $\overline{H}$, we say that A satisfies $\overline{H}$ iff for all $i \in I_S^O$, and for all $x \in S_i^T$ we have

$$\overline{h}_i\ (x) = h_i\ (x) \quad \text{whenever} \quad \overline{h}_i\ (x) \neq \alpha.$$

We now state the following straightforward theorem.

Theorem 3.1 - All total representation algebras satisfying a complete specification have the same semantics.

Given a specification $\overline{H}$, it is possible to obtain easily an algebra B which contains the same information. Infact let us define in T the following family of equivalence relations. For every phylum of name $i \in I_S^O$ and for every pair $x, y \in S_i^T$ we have

$$x \equiv y \quad \text{iff} \quad = \overline{h}_i(x) = \overline{h}_i(y) \neq \alpha$$

while for every phylum of name in I_S^N all the terms are by now in different classes. Let us then take the congruent closure $\equiv^B$ of $\equiv$ and let B be the quotient algebra of T with respect to $\equiv^B$.

From $\overline{H}$ it is also possible to define inductively another algebra L as follows.

a) For all phyla of old type. The value returned by any nullary function f_j^L, $d(j)=\lambda$, $r(j)=i\in I_S^O$ is the value corresponding to its name, i.e.

$$f_j^L\,(\,)=\overline{h}_i(j)=\text{UNQUOTE}\ (j)$$

Thus all the values of the old type of name i belong to the phylum S_i^L.
For all phyla of new type. The value returned by any nullary function f_j^L, $d(j)=\lambda$, $r(j)=i\in I_S^N$ is, like in the word algebra T, its name, which thus belongs to the phylum S_i^L.

b) For all phyla of old type. Let $j\in I_F^O$ be any function name, let $(i_1,i_2,\ldots,i_{n(j)})=d(j)$ be its domain and $k=r(j)\in I_S^O$ be its range. Let $(s_1,s_2,\ldots,s_{n(j)})$, $s_e\in S_{i_e}^L$, $1\leq e\leq n(j)$ be any list of arguments. Then if s_e is a value of an old type, let s_e'=QUOTE(s_e), else let $s_e'=s_e$.
If $\overline{h}_k(f_j^T(s_1',s_2',\ldots,s_{n(j)}'))=s_k\neq\alpha$, then we define

$$f_j^L(s_1,s_2,\ldots,s_{n(j)})=s_k$$

else we define

$$f_j^L(s_1,s_2,\ldots,s_{n(j)})=f_j^T(s_1',s_2',\ldots,s_{n(j)}')$$

thus the symbolic term $f_j^T(s_1',s_2',\ldots,s_{n(j)}')$ belongs to the phylum S_k^L.
For all phyla of new type. Let $j\in I_F^N$ be any function name, let $(i_1,i_2,\ldots,i_{n(j)})=d(j)$ be its domain and $k=r(j)\in I_S^N$ be its range. Let $(s_1,s_2,\ldots,s_{n(j)})$, $s_e\in S_{i_e}^L$, $1\leq e\leq n(j)$ be any list of arguments. Then if s_e is a value of an old type, let s_e'= QUOTE(s_e), else let $s_e'=s_e$. We define

$$f_j^L(s_1,s_2,\ldots,s_{n(j)})=f_j^T(s_1',s_2',\ldots,s_{n(j)}')$$

thus the symbolic term $f_j^T(s_1',s_2',\ldots,s_{n(j)}')$ belongs to the phylum S_k^L.

c) The phyla of L contain only the elements obtained with the construction above, which thus completely defines all the functions f_j^L, $j\in I_F$.

In short, L is obtained from the word algebra T by evaluating subexpressions bottom up as much as possible using the specification $\overline{H}$. We can prove the following theorem.

Theorem 3.2. Algebras B and L are isomorphic.

Outline of the proof.

It is possible to see that due to condition (3.2), in every congruence class of $\equiv^B$, there exist a smallest term which is either the element of L corresponding to the class or its quotation. Q.E.D.

Algebra L shows that there exist algebras with the given syntactic graph and closely related to some given specification $\overline{H}$, which are not, in general, total representations. Infact L is a total representation only if $\overline{H}$ is complete. Thus we introduce the concept of the class R_s of symbolic representations. An algebra $A\in R_s$ must satisfy the same conditions i) and iii) above, but condition ii) is substituted as follows.

ii') Every phylum S_i of old type (namely with $i\in I_S^O$) must contain as elements at least all the values of that type.

As we saw in the L case, the extra values of the old phyla have the meaning of don't care, unevaluated expressions.

Again, let $H=\{h_i \mid i\in I_S\}$ be the unique epimorphism from T to $A\in R_s$. The semantics of A is the family

$$H'=\{h_j\in H \mid i\in I_S^O\}.$$

Given a specification $\overline{H}$, we say that A satisfies $\overline{H}$ iff for all $i\in I_S^O$ and for all $x\in S_i^T$ we have

$$\overline{h}_i(x)=h_i(x)\quad\text{whenever } \overline{h}_i(x)\neq\alpha.$$

Note that an algebra A which is a total representation satisfying $\overline{H}$ is also a symbolic representation satisfying $\overline{H}$.

Given a specification $\overline{H}$, the construction of L shows that there exists at least one symbolic representation which satisfies $\overline{H}$. The following theorem proves that there always exists also at least one total representation satisfying $\overline{H}$.

Theorem 3.3. Given a specification $\overline{H}$ satisfying its consistency conditions, there always exists a total representation A satisfying $\overline{H}$.

Proof

Let us consider any specification $\overline{H}'$ obtained from $\overline{H}$ by letting $\overline{h}_i'(y)$=UNQUOTE (z_y) when $\overline{h}_i(y)=\alpha$, and where z_y is any constant satisfying the condition (3.3). It is immediate to see that $\overline{H}'$ is a specification since it satisfies consistency condition b), i.e. (3.2). Furthermore it is easy to see that every (symbolic) representation satisfying $\overline{H}'$ satisfies also $\overline{H}$. But $\overline{H}'$ is a complete specification, and thus the algebra L constructed from it, is a total representation. Q.E.D.

4. The structure of the family of representation algebras.

Given a syntactic graph and a specification $\overline{H}$, we are now interested in studying the structures of the families $R_s^{\overline{H}}$ and $R_t^{\overline{H}}$ of all symbolic and total representations satisfying $\overline{H}$. We can prove the following important theorem.

Theorem 4.1. Let us consider a specification $\overline{H}$ and let us construct the corresponding algebra L. For every algebra A in the class $R_s^{\overline{H}}$ of all symbolic representations satisfying $\overline{H}$, there exists an unique epimorphism from L to A. Thus L is initial in $R_s^{\overline{H}}$.

Proof: Let us consider the congruences C^B and C^A on the word algebra $\underset{\sim}{T}$ corresponding to B (and thus to L since B and L are isomorphic) and to A. Let $\equiv^B$ and $\equiv^A$ be the families of congruence relations corresponding to C^B and C^A, and let $\equiv$ be the family of equivalence relations defined as

$$x \equiv y \quad \text{iff} \quad \overline{h}_i(x)=\overline{h}_i(y) \neq \alpha .$$

Since A satisfies the specification $\overline{H}$, we have that $\equiv \rightarrow \equiv^A$. But $\equiv^B$ is the congruent closure of $\equiv$ by construction and thus $\equiv^B \rightarrow \equiv^A$. Therefore it exists an epimorphism from B and thus from L, to A. Q.E.D.

As a consequence of the above theorem instead of any algebra A in $R_s^{\overline{H}}$ we may consider the corresponding congruence $\equiv^A$ on L.

It may be useful to notice that such congruences are exactly all those congruences on L which put in different classes all the values of old types. Thus it will never happen that $3 \equiv^A 5$, but it may happen that $3 \equiv^A t$, where t was a don't care condition according to $\overline{H}$.

Since all congruences on L are a poset (infact are a complete lattice [1]), we have the following corollary.

Corollary. The families $R_s^{\overline{H}}$ and $R_t^{\overline{H}}$ of representation algebras are partially ordered sets with respect to the existence of an epimorphism.

While on $R_t^{\overline{H}}$, in general, nothing more can be said, the structure of $R_s^{\overline{H}}$ can be further specified as follows.

Theorem 4.2. The family $R_s^{\overline{H}}$ of all symbolic representation algebras with a given syntactic graph and satisfying a given specification $\overline{H}$ is a (lower) complete semilattice having as universal lower bound the algebra L constructed from $\overline{H}$.

Proof: The class of the congruences on L putting in different classes the values of old types is evidently closed with respect to congruence intersection. Furthermore, L is the universal lower bound by the initiality proved in theorem 4.1. Q.E.D.

To give an example, let us consider as syntactic graph the graph in Fig. 3. A particular algebra A_1 may be determined by specifying the phyla

$S_V^1=\{a,b\}$

$S_B^1=\{T,F,U\}$

$S_{STRING}^1=\{1,2,3,4,5\}$

and the results of the operations

$f^1_a(\ )=a$

$f^1_b(\ )=b$

$f^1_{TRUE}(\ )=T$

$f^1_{FALSE}(\ )=F$

$f^1_{S_o}(\ )=1$

x \ y	a	b
1	2	3
2	2	3
3	5	1
4	5	1
5	4	1

$f^1_{ADDCHAR}(x,y)=$

x	
1	F
2	U
3	F
4	T
5	F

$f^1_{MEMBER}(x)=$

It should be clear that the above symbolic algebra A_1 is essentially a finite-state automaton with a don't care condition. To make the example more concrete, let us assume that the specification $\overline{H}$ coincides with the semantics H'_A of A, for example:

$$\overline{h}_B(MEMBER(ADDCHAR(S_o,a)))=\alpha$$

while

$$\overline{h}_B(MEMBER(ADDCHAR(S_o,b)))=F$$

The initial algebra L is infinite instead. Since there is no function name in the syntactic graph mapping B into STRING, the phylum S^L_{STRING} coincides with S^T_{STRING}, i.e. the (terms representing) strings are all in different classes. Phylum S^L_B contains, besides T and F, also an infinite number of unevaluated terms representing don't care conditions, e.g.

$MEMBER(ADDCHAR(S_o,a))$

$MEMBER(ADDCHAR(ADDCHAR(S_o,a),a))$

$MEMBER(ADDCHAR(ADDCHAR(ADDCHAR(S_o,b),b),a))$

By merging states 1 and 2 one gets from A_1 the following algebra A_2.

$S^2_B=\{T,F\}$; $S^2_{STRING}=\{[1,2],3,4,5\}$

$f^2_{S_o}(\ )=[1,2]$

x \ y	a	b
[1,2]	[1,2]	3
3	5	[1,2]
4	5	[1,2]
5	4	[1,2]

$f^2_{ADDCHAR}(x,y)=$

x	
[1,2]	F
3	F
4	T
5	F

$f^2_{MEMBER}(x)=$

Algebra A_2 is thus a <u>total</u> representation satisfying $\overline{H}$, i.e. $A_2 \in R_t^{\overline{H}}$, and may be obtained from A_1 with the following epimorphism:

$h_V(a)=a$, $h_V(b)=b$, $h_B(T)=T$, $h_B(F)=F$, $h_B(U)=F$

$h_{STRING}(k)$:= <u>if</u> k=1,2 <u>then</u> [1,2] <u>else</u> k.

By applying standard minimization techniques [12] to algebra A_1 one obtains the following algebra A_3:

$S_B^3=\{T,F\}$; $S_{STRING}^3=\{[1,3], [2',4], [2'',5]\}$

$f_{S_o}^3(\ )=[1,3]$

$f_{ADDCHAR}^3(x,y)=$

x \ y	a	b
[1,3]	[2",5]	[1,3]
[2',4]	[2",5]	[1,3]
[2",5]	[2',4]	[1,3]

$f_{MEMBER}^3(x)=$

x	
[1,3]	F
[2',4]	T
[2",5]	F

Algebra A_3 is still a total representation satisfying $\overline{H}$, but in S_B^3 some of the expressions left unspecified in S_B^L evaluate to T and others to F.
For instance we have:

$f_{MEMBER}^3(f_{ADDCHAR}^3(f_{S_o}^3, f_a^3))=F$

$f_{MEMBER}^3(f_{ADDCHAR}^3(f_{ADDCHAR}^3(f_{S_o}^3, f_a^3), f_a^3))=T.$

Algebras A_2 and A_3 are a good example for showing that, in general, the poset $R_t^{\overline{H}}$ is not a lower semilattice. Infact the intersection $A_4=A_2 \cap A_3$, and all the lower bounds of both A_2 and A_3, are in $R_s^{\overline{H}}$ but not in $R_t^{\overline{H}}$. We have

$S_B^4=\{T,F,U',U''\}$; $S_{STRING}^4=\{1,2',2'',3,4,5\}$

$f_{S_o}^4(\ )=1$

$f_{ADDCHAR}^4(x,y)=$

x \ y	a	b
1	2"	3
2'	2"	3
2"	2'	3
3	5	1
4	5	1
5	4	1

$f_{MEMBER}^4(x)=$

x	
1	F
2'	U'
2"	U"
3	F
4	T
5	F

Algebra A_2 can be obtained from A_4 with the following epimorphism.

$h'_B(U')=h'_B(U'')=F$; $h'_{STRING}(k)$:= <u>if</u> k=1,2',2" <u>then</u> [1,2] <u>else</u> k.

Conversely, A_3 can be obtained from A_4 as follows.

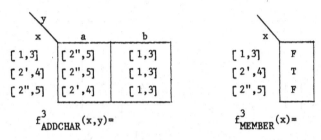

$h''_B(U')=T$; $h''_B(U'')=F$; $h''_{STRING}(k):=$ if $k=1,3$ then $[1,3]$ else if $k=2',4$ then $[2',4]$ else $[2'',5]$.

Furthermore, it is not true the conjecture that any algebra having a semantics equal to a given specification $\overline{H}$ is initial in $R_s^{\overline{H}}$. Infact there is no morphism from A_1 to A_3. Finally, in general both $R_s^{\overline{H}}$ and $R_t^{\overline{H}}$ are not upper semilattices (and thus $R_s^{\overline{H}}$ is not a lattice). Here the union is, as usual, the operation between algebras corresponding to congruence union on their images in L. Infact, for instance the union $A_1 \cup A_3$ is the following algebra A_5.

$S_B^5=\{[T,F]\}$; $S_{STRING}^5=\{[1,3], [2,4,5]\}$; $f_{TRUE}^5=f_{FALSE}^5=[T,F]$; $f_{S_0}^5(\ )=[1,3]$

$f_{ADDCHAR}^5(x,y)=$

x \ y	a	b
[1,3]	[2,4,5]	[1,3]
[2,4,5]	[2,4,5]	[1,3]

$f_{MEMBER}^5(x)=$

x	
[1,3]	[T,F]
[2,4,5]	[T,F]

However, algebra A_5 is not a representation algebra since it merges the values T and F in the phylum B. The above examples show that the results proved in the corollary to theorem 4.1 and in theorem 4.2 cannot be made stronger in general. However in the special case where $\overline{H}$ is a complete specification (i.e. without don't care conditions) and thus when $R_t^{\overline{H}}=R_s^{\overline{H}}$ we can prove the following result.

Theorem 4.3. The family $R_t^{\overline{H}}$ of all total representation algebras with a given syntactic graph and satisfying a given complete specification $\overline{H}$ is a lattice.

Proof: Since $R_t^{\overline{H}}=R_s^{\overline{H}}$, then $R_t^{\overline{H}}$ is a lower semilattice according to theorem 4.2. We prove that if A' and A" belong to $R_t^{\overline{H}}$, then also $A=A' \cup A''$ belongs to $R_t^{\overline{H}}$. Infact, let $\equiv', \equiv''$ and $\equiv$ be the congruences on L corresponding to A',A" and A respectively. It is easy to see that we have $x\equiv y$ iff there exists a chain

$$x=x_1\equiv x_2\equiv\ldots\equiv x_k=y$$

such that for every r, $r=1,2,\ldots,k-1$, there exists a variable term

$t_r(z_1,z_2,\ldots,z_h)$ with

$$t_r(z'_1,z'_2,\ldots z'_h)=x_r \quad \text{and} \quad t_r(z''_1,z''_2,\ldots,z''_h)=x_{r+1}$$

and where for every s, $s=1,2,\ldots,h$, z'_s and z''_s are suitable values depending on r with

$$z'_s\equiv' z''_s \quad \underline{\text{or}} \quad z'_s\equiv'' z''_s .$$

Let us now assume that the element $x=x_1$ is a value of old type and let us consider the term $t_1(z''_1,z'_2,z'_3,\ldots,z'_h)$. Since either $z'_1\equiv' z''_1$ or $z'_1\equiv'' z''_1$, in both cases we will have

$$x_1=t_1(z'_1,z'_2,\ldots,z'_h)=t_1\ (z''_1,z'_2,z'_3,\ldots,z'_h)$$

because both $\equiv'$ and $\equiv''$ are congruences which have one element per class for the values of old type. Similarly we can show

$$t_1(z''_1,z'_2,z'_3,\ldots,z'_h)=t_1\ (z''_1,z''_2,z'_3,\ldots,z'_h).$$

Thus eventually we have $x_1=x_2$ and therefore, iterating the construction, x=y. But since in this way we have proved that $x\equiv y$ (with x value of old type) implies x=y, we can conclude that also $\equiv$ puts the values of old types in distinct classes, and thus $A\in R_t^{\overline{H}}$. Q.E.D.

One may ask now if the lattice $R_t^{\overline{H}}$ has a universal upper bound when $\overline{H}$ is complete. To this purpose, let us define on L the relation $\equiv^U$ defined as follows:

(4.1) $x \equiv^U y$ iff $\forall t$, $t(x)=t(y)$

where $t(z)$ is any expression specifying operations in L and giving result in a phylum of old type. We can now prove the following theorem.

Theorem 4.4. Relation $\equiv^U$ defined above is a congruence relation.
Proof: Relation $\equiv^U$ is clearly reflexive and symmetric. It is also transitive, since if $x \equiv^U w \equiv^U y$ then for all t we have $t(x)=t(w)=t(y)$.
Thus $\equiv^U$ is an equivalence relation. For showing that it is also a congruence, let $f^L(z_1,z_2,\dots,z_k)$ be any function of L. We must show that if $z'_r \equiv^U z''_r$, $r=1,\dots,k$, then also

(4.2) $f^L(z'_1,z'_2,\dots,z'_k) \equiv^U f^L(z''_1,z''_2,\dots,z''_k)$..

Infact, let us assume

$$f^L(z'_1,z'_2,\dots,z'_k) \not\equiv^U f^L(z''_1,z'_2,\dots,z'_k).$$

Then there exists an expression such that

$$t(f^L(z'_1,z'_2,\dots,z'_k)) \neq t(f^L(z''_1,z'_2,\dots,z'_k)).$$

But then we have found an expression t'

$$t'(w)=t(f^L(w,z'_2,\dots,z'_k))$$

such that $t'(z'_1) \neq t'(z''_1)$

against the hypothesis $z'_1 \equiv^U z''_1$. Thus we have

$$f^L(z'_1,z'_2,\dots,z'_k) \equiv^U f^L(z''_1,z'_2,\dots,z'_k).$$

Iterating the above construction, and for the transitivity of $\equiv^U$, we thus obtain (4.2).
Q.E.D.

To the congruence $\equiv^U$ on L we can now associate the algebra U. We can prove the following theorem.

Theorem 4.5. Given any algebra $A \in R_t^{\overline{H}}$ there exists a unique epimorphism from A to U. Furthermore, $U \in R_t^{\overline{H}}$. Thus U is final in the class $R_t^{\overline{H}}$.
Proof: First we prove that $U \in R_t^{\overline{H}}$. Infact from (4.1) assuming x and y to be values of old type and letting $t(z)=z$, we get

$$x \equiv^U y \quad \text{implies} \quad x=y.$$

To prove the rest of the theorem, we show that

$$x \equiv^A y \quad \text{implies} \quad x \equiv^U y$$

where $\equiv^A$ is the congruence on L corresponding to A. Infact assume $x \not\equiv^U y$ and $x \equiv^A y$. Then there exists an expression $t(z)$ such that $t(x) \neq t(y)$ but $t(x) \equiv^A t(y)$, i.e. $A \notin R_t$. Q.E.D.

From theorems 4.2, 4.3 and 4.5 we can thus derive the following theorem.

Theorem 4.6. The family $R_t^{\overline{H}}$ of all total representation algebras with a given syntactic graph and satisfying a given complete specification $\overline{H}$, is a complete lattice having as universal lower and upper bounds the algebras L and U respectively.

References

[1] Dahl, O.J., Dijkstra, E.W. and Hoare, C.A.R., Structured Programming, Academic Press, 1972.

[2] Liskov, B., A Note on CLU, MIT project MAC Computation Structures Group Memo 112, Cambridge, Mass., November 1974.

[3] Wulf, W.A., ALPHARD: Towards a Language to Support Structured Programs, Dept. of Computer Science, Carnegie-Mellon University, Pittsburgh, April 1974.

[4] Liskov, B. and Zilles, S., Specification Techniques for Data Abstraction, IEEE Transactions on Software Engineering, Vol. SE-1, No 1, March 1975, pp.7-19.

[5] Zilles, S., Algebraic Specification of Data Types, MIT Project MAC Progress Report XI, Cambridge, 1973-74, pp.52-58.

[6] Guttag, J.V., The Specification and Application to Programming of Abstract Data Types, PhD Thesis, University of Toronto, Dept. of Computer Science, 1975, also Computer System Research Group Technical Report CSRG-59, September 1975.

[7] Goguen, J.A., Thatcher, J.W., Wagner, E.C. and Wright, J.B., Abstract Data Types as Initial Algebras and the Correctness of Data Representation.

[8] Birkhoff, G. and Lipson, J.D., Heterogeneous Algebras, Journal of Combinatorial Theory, 8, 1970, pp.115-133.

[9] Goguen, J.A. and Thatcher, J.W., Initial Algebra Semantics, 1974 IEEE Switching and Automata Theory Conference, New Orleans, pp.63-77.

[10] Montanari, U., Data Structures, Program Structure and Graph Grammars, Lecture Notes of the Course on "Data and Program Structures: Syntax and Semantics" May 3-15, 1976, Erice, Italy.

[11] Thatcher, J.W., Tree Automata: An Informal Survey, in: Currents in Computing, Prentice-Hall, 1973, pp.143-172.

[12] McCluskey, E.J., Introduction to the Theory of Switching Circuits, McGraw-Hill, New York, 1965.

THE CALCULUS OF FACTS

Hartmann J. Genrich and Gerda Thieler-Mevissen
Gesellschaft fuer Mathematik und Datenverarbeitung
- Institut fuer Informationssystemforschung -
Postfach 1240, D-5205 St.Augustin 1, B.R.D.

Summary

Nets of conditions and events ('special' Petri nets) are widely used models of dynamic systems. They represent the causal structure of the concurrent operation and co-operation of the components of a system. In this paper we introduce a net theoretic version of the first-order predicate calculus. Its purpose is to offer a formal language for expressing the relationship between a net model and the modelled system, and to provide rules for deriving the logical consequences of such an interpretation in a way that the results are expressed in the same language as the model, namely the net language. By this we permit the use of symbolic logic as part of a general formalism for the analysis and specification of dynamic systems. We show how 'static' logic can be correctly applied even in those practically important dynamic contexts where certain sentences change their truthvalues in a not fully specified order. As a useful by-product the graphical representation of nets induces a very natural graphical representation of the predicate calculus.

1. The Petri net calculus of facts

A quadruple $N = \langle S,T;Z,Q\rangle$ of two sets S and T and two binary relations $Z \subseteq S\times T$, $Q \subseteq S\times T$ is called a net iff $S\cap T=\emptyset$, $Z\cup Q\neq\emptyset$, $dom(Z\cup Q)=S$, and $ran(Z\cup Q)=T$. Under the basic interpretation of nets [1], the members of S are called conditions and are used to represent the effects of processes. Conditions sometimes hold and sometimes don't such that a case of the system can be represented by a 'marking' $M:S\rightarrow\{0,1\}$ telling for each condition $c\in S$ whether, in this case, c holds $(M(c)=1)$ or not. The elements of T are called transitions and denote classes of coincident changes of condition holdings. A transition $t\in T$ may occur according to the transition rule which is illustrated in the following diagram. Conditions are represented by circles ('places') ○ carrying a 'marker' iff the condition holds in the present case, transitions are represented by boxes □ and the elements of the flow relation $F = Z \cup Q^{-1}$ by arcs →:

Effect of an occurrence of a transition t with preconditions a,b and postconditions c,d.

Fig.1

Given a transition net N with the class [M] of all markings (cases) into which the initial marking M can be transformed by means of transition occurrences, the following two statements about a transition t with preconditions $p_1,\ldots,p_m$ and postconditions $q_1,\ldots q_n$ are equivalent (by virtue of the transition-rule):

- In no case is the transition rule applicable to t (t is 'dead');
- In every case, the sentence $[\neg p_1 \vee \ldots \vee \neg p_m \vee q_1 \vee \ldots \vee q_n]$ is true (where the atomic sentences p_i, or q_j, mean: p_i [q_j] holds).

Sentences about a system which are true in all cases we shall call factually valid propositions, or facts for short; thus transitions without any occurrence represent facts. In our graphical representation we denote facts by ▯, while events (transitions which have an occurrence) are denoted by ▭.

For the rest of this section we concentrate on that part of a system description which constitutes a net of conditions and facts (fact net). Each finite fact net is the representation of a valid proposition, namely the conjunction of 'or-clauses' represented by the single facts. And the converse is true, too: Each proposition P can be represented by a fact net. If P is a tautology, it contains at least one atomic sentence c such that P is equivalent to $[\neg c \vee c]$ which is represented by  . Otherwise P has an equivalent conjunctive normal form each clause of which can be represented by a single fact; the union of all facts then represents P.

By means of two net transformations - called expansion and resolution - logical consequences of the given fact net can be derived. These rules are illustrated in the following diagram in which ⤳ means: To a fact net containing the configuration on the left side, the fact on the right side may be added as a logical consequence (each system for which the given facts hold, also satisfies the fact to be added).

Expansion:

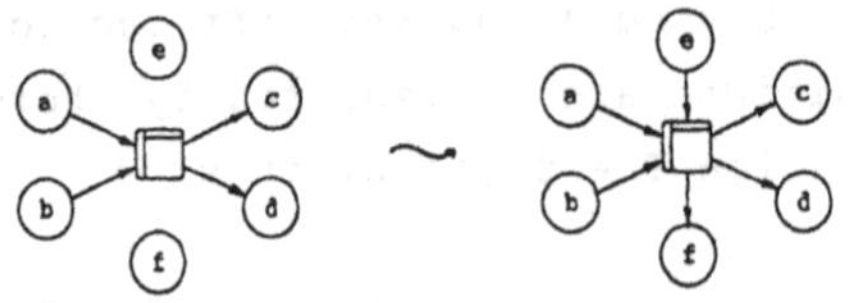

A given fact may be extended to include more conditions.

Resolution:

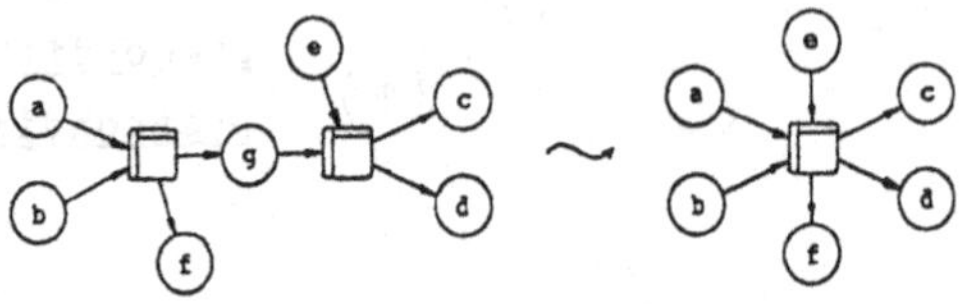

Two facts connected by a 'bridge' can be put together.

Fig. 2

The fact nets together with these two derivation rules constitute a Petri net version of the propositional calculus. It can be shown [2] that the rules are consistent and complete: All nets which can be derived from a given fact net by means of these rules consist of facts only, and all nets which represent the logical consequences of the given facts are derivable. In particular, a given proposition can be proved to be a consequence of a system of facts by adding the representation of its negation and deriving from the whole net the 'isolated fact' which represents a contradiction (it is a fact by derivation, but the transition rule is applicable to it - even in all cases). An important property of the transformations is that they act only locally, so all derivations can be made without knowing the whole net.

The net representation of the propositional calculus can be extended to a calculus for first-order predicate logic. As it is well known, every formula of predicate logic can be transformed into an equivalent prenex normal form, where the matrix (the part without quantifiers) is in conjunctive normal form; by means of Skolem functions (schemes for globally bound individual names) replacing the existential quantifiers we get an equivalent quantifier-free form in which all individual variables are understood to be generalized. (For all these transformations see [3].)

Each such quantifier free form of a first-order formula constitutes a net $<P,C;Z,Q>$ called a first-order fact net: P is the set of all instances of predicates and C is the set of all clauses; for $p \in P$ and $c \in C$, the pair (p,c) belongs to Z iff the negation of p occurs in c, and (p,c) belongs to Q iff p itself occurs in c. For practical purposes the graphical representation of these nets can be simplified in the following way: all instances of the same predicate are mapped onto one place while the arcs are labelled with the respective list of arguments. The following picture shows a simple example (which becomes meaningful in the next section):

Formula:

$$\bigwedge i\ [C(i) \rightarrow \bigvee x\ [R(x) \wedge U(i,x) \wedge \bigwedge j\ [U(j,x) \rightarrow i=j]]]$$

Prenex normal form:

$$\bigwedge i \bigvee x \bigwedge j\ [[\neg C(i) \vee R(x)] \wedge [\neg C(i) \vee U(i,x)] \wedge [\neg C(i) \vee \neg U(j,x) \vee i=j]]$$

Quantifier-free clauses	Fact net	Simplification
(1) $\{\neg C(i), R(r\langle i\rangle)\}$; (2) $\{\neg C(i), U(i,r\langle i\rangle)\}$; (3) $\{\neg C(i), \neg U(j,r\langle i\rangle), i=j\}$	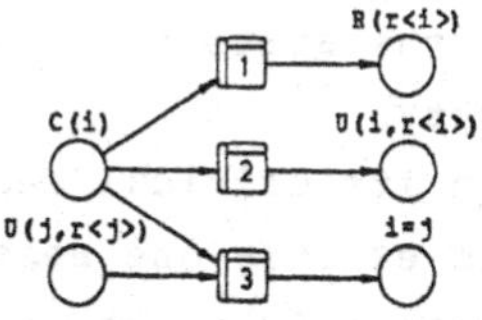	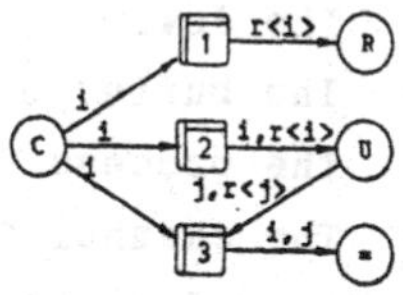

Fig.3

The special role of variables as locally bound individual names, in contrast to the globally bound names is expressed by the following <u>substitution rule</u> for the derivation of first-order facts:

<u>Substitution</u>: Let $v_1,\ldots,v_n$ be the variables of a given fact, and let $t_1,\ldots,t_n$ be arbitrary individual names (terms). If, simultaneously for all i, all occurrences of v_i are replaced by a copy of t_i, then the result is a fact too; it can be added to the given fact net as a logical consequence.

Together with the expansion and the resolution rule of the (propositional) fact calculus we have a Petri net version of the first-order predicate calculus. This could be extended to first-order logic with equality by formulating another derivation rule analogous to paramodulation [3]. For many practical applications it might be sufficient to state the equivalence relation property of the predicate constant = by adding to any fact net containing an instance of = the following net:

(1) $\bigwedge x\ x=x$	$\{x=x\}$	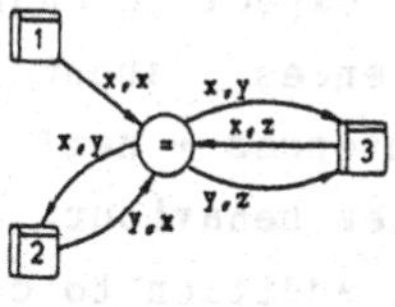
(2) $\bigwedge x \bigwedge y\ [x=y \rightarrow y=x]$	$\{\neg x=y, y=x\}$	
(3) $\bigwedge x \bigwedge y \bigwedge z\ [x=y \wedge y=z \rightarrow x=z]$	$\{\neg x=y, \neg y=z, x=z\}$	

Fig.4

2. The use of facts in modelling dynamic systems

In the previous section we interpreted conditions as atomic sentences such that the holdings of a condition represented the truth and the non-holdings represented the falsehood of the associated sentence. This interpretation led us to a net theoretic version of the first-order predicate calculus. Normally the user of a net model expresses the relationship between the net and some real or planned system in an informal way; he assigns a meaning to conditions by associating with them sentences like:

- The device D is in the state s.
- The buffer B is empty.
- The process P is in its critical section.
- The channel C holds exactly one message for the agent A.

Some of these sentences might be too complex to be treated as atomic; we therefore shall use the language of first-order predicate logic for formalizing sentences like above. This will enable us to derive the consequences of a given interpretation of a net model in a systematic way. Using the net representation of the predicate calculus will ensure, that all results of a derivation are expressed in the same language as the system model, namely the language of nets.

Assume we have formulated some first-order sentences which shall be used to assign a meaning to a given net of events and conditions. In order to express the connection between such a sentence, denoted by Σ, and the net, we use the following notation in the graphical representation:

Ⓒ$\rightarrow\Sigma$ In all cases in which c holds Σ is understood to be true; a holding of c is an <u>affirmation</u> of Σ, or, if Σ is of the form $\neg\Sigma'$, a <u>negation</u> of Σ'.

Ⓒ$\leftarrow\Sigma$ c holds in all cases in which Σ is true; c holds under the <u>premise</u> Σ.

Ⓒ$\leftrightarrow\Sigma$ c holds in exactly those cases in which Σ is true (Ⓒ$\rightarrow\Sigma$ and Ⓒ$\leftarrow\Sigma$)

The direction 'net $\rightarrow$ sentences' may be, for example, related to the notion of <u>observing</u> a system; the holdings of conditions make our sentences about the system true or false. In contrast to this, we do not expect to change the condition holdings by uttering true or false sentences about the system. Therefore the implication 'sentences $\rightarrow$ net' may be seen in connection with the <u>prognosis</u> of system behaviour.

In addition to connecting sentences with changing truthvalues to conditions we also wish to add certain 'invariants', i.e. sentences

which hold for the whole system or even a class of systems of the same
type. These are indicated by prefixing a ! sign. By means of the
technique introduced in the previous section the first-order
inscriptions of a given net can be transformed into a net of
(established or intended) first-order facts. The inscriptions and the
formal derivation of their logical consequences thus become part of
the description of dynamic systems in terms of the language of nets.

A well known simple example, the _mutual_exclusion_ of two processes,
shall illustrate the use of the net representation of the predicate
calculus for the purposes of system modelling. In Fig.5(a) we show the
net of two simple cyclic processes to which a fact is added specifying
a mutual exclusion of the two processes: They must not be concurrently
in their respective 'critical' phases c_1 and c_2. This specification is
satisfied, for example, by the system shown in Fig.5(b).

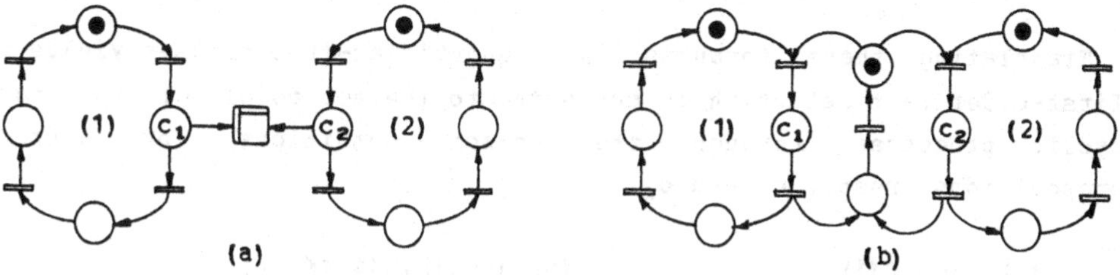

Fig.5

In practice this mutual exclusion may arise from the circumstance
that in their critical phases both processes need a resource which
cannot be used by more than one process at the same time but of which
at most one item is available. This interpretation is now formalized
by means of the language of symbolic logic:

$\bigvee x [R(x) \wedge U(1,x) \wedge \bigwedge i [U(i,x) \rightarrow i=1]]$

$![1 \neq 2]$
$!\bigwedge x \bigwedge y [R(x) \wedge R(y) \rightarrow x=y]$

$\bigvee y [R(y) \wedge U(2,y) \wedge \bigwedge j [U(j,y) \rightarrow j=2]]$

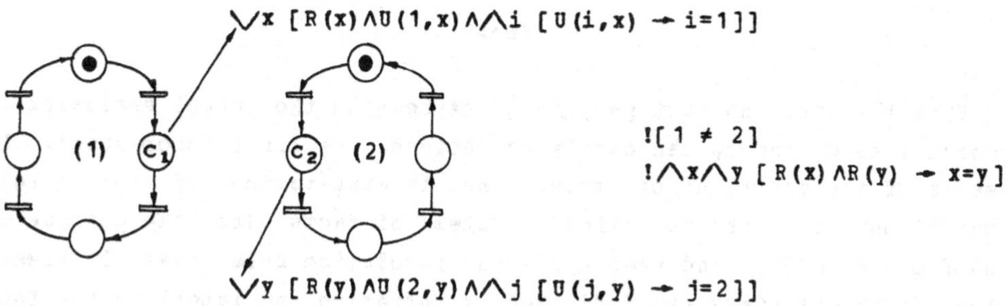

Note: R(x) means, that the thing x is a resource of type R;
          U(i,x) means, that the process i is using the resource x.

Fig.6

The sentences associated with c_1 and c_2 have exactly the same structure: they tell why the phases c_1 and c_2 are 'critical'. This can be used for simplifying the interpretation by introducing the concept of a critical phase in a formal way:

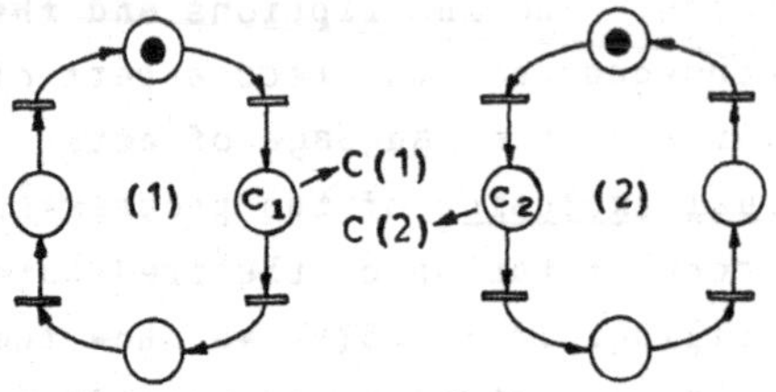

$!\,[1 \neq 2]$

$!\bigwedge i\ [C(i) \rightarrow \bigvee x\ [R(x) \wedge U(i,x)]]$

$!\,(\bigwedge i,j,x,y)[U(i,x) \wedge U(j,y) \wedge i\neq j \rightarrow x\neq y]$

$!\bigwedge x \bigwedge y\ [R(x) \wedge R(y) \rightarrow x=y]$

Note: C(i) means, that the process i is in a critical phase; R(x), U(i,x) as in Fig.6.

Fig.7

Translating these formulas into quantifier-free clauses yields a first-order fact net which is connected to the net model of the two cyclic processes through the common conditions, or atomic propositions, resp., c_1 and c_2.

(1) $\{\neg c_1, C(1)\}$

(2) $\{\neg c_2, C(2)\}$

(3) $\{\neg 1=2\}$

(4) $\{\neg C(i), R(r\langle i\rangle)\}$

(5) $\{\neg C(i), U(i,r\langle i\rangle)\}$

(6) $\{\neg U(i,x), \neg U(j,y), \neg x=y, i=j\}$

(7) $\{\neg R(x), \neg R(y), x=y\}$

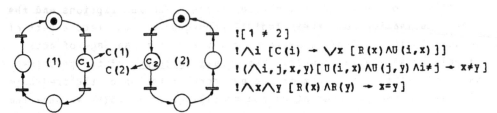

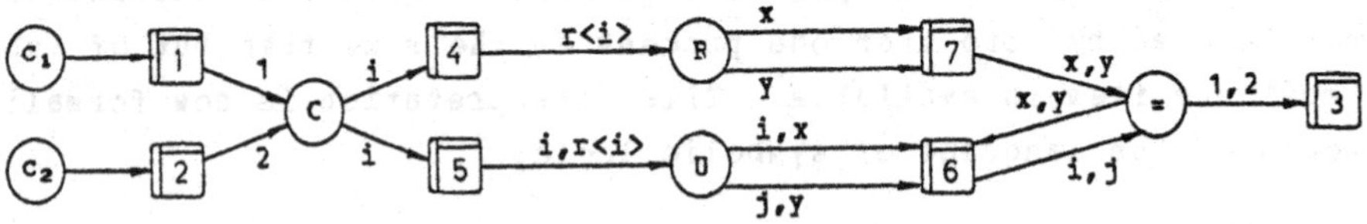

Fig.8

From this net the fact $[\neg c_1 \vee \neg c_2]$ expressing the mutual exclusion of conditions c_1 and c_2 can easily be derived. We first 'propagate', by means of the substitution rule, the interpretation of the single conditions through the whole system of facts (for the purpose of unification [3]), and then apply the resolution rule several times. The different steps are indicated by numbering and labelling the fact boxes in an appropriate way:

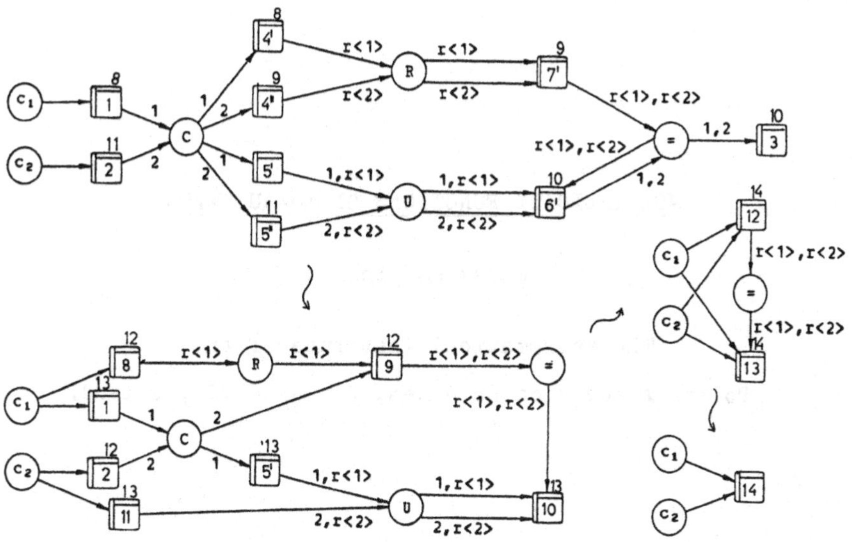

Fig.9

Conclusion

The method presented above permits the full use of (propositional and) first-order predicate logic in contexts where temporally and causally independent changes may occur, as e.g. in a computer system with components widely distributed in space. Static and sequentially changing systems are included as special cases. The method is, of course, independent of its graphical representation and not intended for such simple cases like the one used to illustrate this paper. Since all transformations of fact nets only act upon local configurations, an algorithm for the computer aided derivation of first-order facts could be directly based upon the graphical representation and used via a display in an interactive way.

References

1. Petri,C.A.: Interpretations of Net Theory.
   Internal Report ISF-75-07, GMD Bonn (1975)
2. Thieler-Mevissen,G.: The Petri Net Calculus of Predicate Logic.
   Internal Report (in preparation), GMD Bonn (1976)
3. Chang,C; Lee,R.: Symbolic Logic and Automated Theorem Proving.
   Academic Press, New York and London (1973)

MULTIPLICITY FUNCTIONS ON ω-AUTOMATA

Marek Karpiński

The Mathematical Institute of the

Polish Academy of Sciences, Poznań 61725, Poland.

ABSTRACT. We formulate some results on Function-and Recognition Multiplicities of ω-automata.

INTRODUCTION

The multiplicity notion of (nondeterministic) automata on finite words has been studied extensively in [3], [14].

Here we investigate the multiplicities of finite-state devices with the ω-rule of definability. We prove the Equality Problem of ω-Automata Multiplicities to be decidable. We also outline some results on their Recognition Multiplicities.

1. NOTATION

We shall adhere to the terminology and notation of [12], [13]. ω denotes the set of natural numbers. An ordinal is identified with the set of all its predecessors. $|A|$ and $P(A)$ denote the cardinality and the power set of A. For a mapping $f : A \rightarrow B$, we denote

$$In(f) = \{b \mid b \in B, |f^{-1}(b)| \geq \omega\}.$$

Given a (nondeterministic) automaton $\mathfrak{A} = \langle S, M, s_0, F \rangle$, $M : S \times \sum \rightarrow P(S)$, and an ω-sequence $v \in \sum^{\omega}$, an $\mathfrak{A}$-run on v is any function $r : \omega \to S$ such that $r(0) = s_0$ and $r(i+1) \in M(r(i),v(i))$ for every $i \in \omega$. $\mathfrak{A}$ accepts v (in Büchi's sense [1]) if there is an accepting (acc.) $\mathfrak{A}$-run on v such that $In(r) \cap F \neq \emptyset$. $L_\omega(\mathfrak{A})$ stands for all $v \in \Sigma^\omega$ accepted by $\mathfrak{A}$. ($Rn(\mathfrak{A},v)$, $Rn^{acc}(\mathfrak{A},v)$ are the sets of all $\mathfrak{A}$-runs, and all acc. $\mathfrak{A}$-runs on v.) $A \subseteq \Sigma^\omega$ is ω-regular if for some automaton $\mathfrak{A}$, $A = L_\omega(\mathfrak{A})$.

In [14] Schützenberger introduced the notion of ($\alpha < \omega$) - multiplicity functions (Z-, N-, $\mathcal{B}$-subsets) (see also Eilenberg [3]). It lies near at hand how the appropriate definition for $\alpha = \omega$-automata should go: The (ω-)multiplicity of $\mathfrak{A}$ is a function $[\mathfrak{A}] : \Sigma^\omega \to \omega+1$ ($= \omega \cup \{\omega\}$) such that $[\mathfrak{A}](v) = |Rn^{acc}(\mathfrak{A},v)|$. (The weak (w.) multiplicity $w[\mathfrak{A}]$ of $\mathfrak{A}$ is a function $w[\mathfrak{A}] : \Sigma^\omega \to \omega+1$, $w[\mathfrak{A}](v) = |Rn(\mathfrak{A},v)|$.)

Now, given a class B of ω-regular subsets $A \subseteq \Sigma^\omega$, the (recognition) multiplicity of a set B is the least ordinal range of multiplicity functions defining B, i.e. the ordinal $\sup_{A \in B} \inf_{\mathfrak{A}} \{[\mathfrak{A}](\Sigma^\omega) \mid [\mathfrak{A}](\Sigma^\omega) \in \omega,\ A = L_\omega(\mathfrak{A})\}$. The w.multiplicity of B is defined in the same way, as the ordinal $\sup_{A \in B} \inf_{\mathfrak{A}} \{w[\mathfrak{A}](\Sigma^\omega) \mid w[\mathfrak{A}](\Sigma^\omega) \in \omega,\ A = L_\omega(\mathfrak{A})\}$.

Intuitively speaking, the multiplicity γ ($< \omega$) of a class $B \subseteq P(\Sigma^\omega)$ is the measure of a minimal runs space required for all finite-state computations on B :: For a class B it is necessary to carry out at least $\gamma - 1$ parallel ω-computations.

2. MULTIPLICITY OF ω-REGULAR SETS

If the multiplicity of an ω-regular class $B \subseteq P(\Sigma^\omega)$ is equal to 2 (i.e. for every set $A \in B$ there exists an automaton $\mathfrak{A}$ such that $A = L_\omega(\mathfrak{A})$ and $|Rn^{acc}(\mathfrak{A},v)| \in \{0,1\}, v \in \Sigma^\omega$), then we call it fine.

It is well known that the multiplicity and the w.multiplicity of regular sets $A \subseteq \Sigma^*$ are both fine, however a simple arguments behind this utterly fail in the ω-case.

Basing on the fact observed in [7] on the limitary determinism of ED sets, we prove that still, the multiplicity of ω-regular sets is <u>fine</u>. Moreover, their w.multiplicity is settled to equal 3.

Theorem 1. The class of ω-regular sets is of fine multiplicity (=2).

Theorem 2. The class of ω-regular sets is of w.multiplicity 3.

Theorems 1,2 reduce the minimal space of parallel computations on ω-regular sets, to 1 and 2, accordingly.

2. SOLVABILITY RESULT

We prove the recursive solvability of the <u>ω-Equality Problem</u>.

Theorem 3. ([9]). There exists an (elementary recursive) procedure for deciding for any two automata $\mathfrak{A}, \mathfrak{B}$ whether $[\mathfrak{A}] = [\mathfrak{B}]$.

Proof. We shall introduce the notion of <u>infinite</u> tree automata (M.O. Rabin [12],[13]) in their n-ary formulation.

Let us have a (nondeterministic) automaton $\mathfrak{A} = \langle S, M, s_0, F\rangle$ over Σ, and a number n equal to or greater than $|S|$. Construct an n-ary <u>tree automaton</u> ([12]) $\mathcal{T}\mathfrak{A} = \langle \bar{S}, \bar{M}, s_0, \bar{F}\rangle$, $\bar{F} \subseteq P(\bar{S})$, over $\Sigma \times \{0,1\}$. Put $\bar{S} = S \times \{\alpha\}, \alpha \notin S$. Now for a given set $A \subseteq S$ denote by $\Gamma(A) \subseteq \bigtimes_{i<n} \bar{S}$ the set of all n-tuples $\langle s_1, \dots, s_n\rangle$ such that the <u>sequence</u> $s_1 \dots s_k$, $0 \leq k \leq n$, obtained from $s_1, \dots, s_n$ by deleting all its α's occurrences, is a <u>permutation</u> of some subset of A. The transition function $\bar{M} : \bar{S} \times \Sigma \to P(\bigtimes_{i<n} \bar{S})$ is defined by

$$\bar{M}(s, \langle \sigma, 1\rangle) = \Gamma(M(s,\sigma)) \quad \text{if } s \in S,$$
$$= \emptyset \qquad \text{otherwise ;}$$

and

$$M(s,\langle\sigma,0\rangle) = \{\langle\alpha,\dots,\alpha\rangle\} \text{ if } s = \alpha,$$
$$= \emptyset \qquad \text{otherwise.}$$

Furthermore, let $\bar{F} = \{A \mid A \ni \alpha \text{ or } A \cap F \neq \emptyset\}$. $T(\mathcal{L}\mathfrak{A})$ denotes the set of all infinite (n-ary) $\sum \times 2$-trees defined by $\mathcal{L}\mathfrak{A}$ (in a sense of [12], [13]). For every $\sum \times 2$-tree from $T(\mathcal{L}\mathfrak{A})$, the number of paths corresponding to the $\{1\}$-cylindrification of every $x \in L_\omega(\mathfrak{A})$ is less than or equal to $[\mathfrak{A}](x)$.

Now, given any pair of automata $\mathfrak{A}_i = \langle S_i, M_i, s_{oi}, F_i\rangle$, $i = 1,2$, we denote $n = \max(|S_1|, |S_2|)$. The above construction associates with $\mathfrak{A}_1, \mathfrak{A}_2$, and a number n, the tree automata $\mathcal{L}\mathfrak{A}_1$, and $\mathcal{L}\mathfrak{A}_2$. It can be verified, by the previous observation, that the identity $[\mathfrak{A}_1] = [\mathfrak{A}_2]$ is always equivalent to the condition $T(\mathcal{L}\mathfrak{A}_1) = T(\mathcal{L}\mathfrak{A}_2)$, and hence, (elem. recursively) solvable by [12].

3. MULTIPLICITY SETS (MSs).

A set $A \subseteq \sum^\omega$ is a MS if there is an automaton $\mathfrak{A}$ and an ordinal α such that

$$A = L(\mathfrak{A},\alpha) = \{x \mid [\mathfrak{A}](x) > \alpha\}.$$

Theorem 4. Given a set $A \subseteq \sum^\omega$, A is a MS if and only if it is ω-regular.

Theorem 4, via the results of [1], yields the following

Theorem 5. There exists an effective procedure for deciding for every automaton $\mathfrak{A}$ and an ordinal α whether $L(\mathfrak{A},\alpha) = \emptyset$.

Theorem 6. Given any two automata $\mathfrak{A}, \mathfrak{B}$ and ordinals α, β, there exists an effective procedure for deciding whether
$L(\mathfrak{A},\alpha) = L(\mathfrak{B},\beta)$ $(L(\mathfrak{A},\alpha) \subseteq L(\mathfrak{B},\beta))$.

4. FUNCTIONAL MSs

A set $A \subseteq \Sigma^{\omega}$ is a Functional (F) MS if there exist two automata $\mathfrak{A}, \mathfrak{B}$ such that

$$A = L(\mathfrak{A},\mathfrak{B}) = \{x \mid [\mathfrak{A}](x) > [\mathfrak{B}](x)\} .$$

It will turn out that the above notion of FMSs enlarges quite drastically the largest up to now known, class of 'definable' subsets of Σ^{ω}.

Theorem 7. There is a FMS $A \subseteq \Sigma^{\omega}$ such that the only expansion $A = \bigcup_{i<n} B_i C_i^{\omega}$, $n<\omega$, $C_i \subseteq \Sigma^*$ regular sets, holds for $B_i \subseteq \Sigma^*$ - context-sensitive (not regular).

Every ω-regular set $A \subseteq \Sigma^{\omega}$ possesses a regular expansion ([1]), and therefore we get

Theorem 8. The class of ω-regular sets is a proper subfamily of FMSs.

Now we shall give closer characterization of FMSs.

Theorem 9. The family of FMSs is closed under complementation, and this is the only boolean operation the FMSs are closed under. FMSs are not closed under projections.

Theorem 10. Given any pair of automata $\mathfrak{A}, \mathfrak{B}$, it is undecidable whether $L(\mathfrak{A},\mathfrak{B}) = \emptyset$.

The proofs of these two theorems employ the mechanism of formal power series (and some connected results of Schützenberger [15], Fliess [4], and Karpiński [8]).

A problem on the place of MFSs in the Borel hierarchy on 2^{ω} (cf. [10]) remains open.

REFERENCES

1. J.R. Büchi, On a decision method in restricted second order arithmetic, Proc. Internat. Congr. Logic, Method. and Philos. Sci. 1960, Stanford Univ. Press, Stanford, California, 1962, pp. 1-11.

2. J.R. Büchi, Decision methods in the theory of ordinals, Bull. Amer. Math. Soc. 71 (1965), 767-770.

3. S. Eilenberg, Automata, languages, and machines, Vol.A, Academic Press, New York, 1974.

4. M. Fliess, Propriétés booléennes des langages stochastiques, Math. Systems Theory 7 (1974), 353-359.

5. J. Hartmanis and R.E. Stearns, Sets of numbers defined by finite automata, Amer. Math. Monthly 74 (1967), 539-542.

6. F.A. Hosch and L.H. Landweber, Finite delay solutions for sequential conditions, Proc. Symp. Automata, Languages, Programming, Paris 1972, North-Holland, Amsterdam, 1973, 45-60.

7. M. Karpiński, Almost deterministic ω-automata with existential output condition, Proc. Amer. Math. Soc. 53 (1975), 449-452.

8. M. Karpiński, Note on Multiplicity Languages, Manuscript (1975).

9. M. Karpiński, The Equality Problem of ω-Automata Multiplicities is Decidable, to appear.

10. L.H. Landweber, Decision problems for ω-automata, Math. Systems Theory 3 (1969), 376-384.

11. R. McNaughton, Testing and generating infinite sequences by a finite automaton, Information and Control 9 (1966), 521-530.

12. M.O. Rabin, Decidability of second-order theories and automata on infinite trees, Trans. Amer. Math. Soc. 141 (1969), 1-35.

13. M.O. Rabin, Automata on infinite objects and Church's problem, Amer. Math. Soc., Reg. Conf. Ser. Math. 13 (1972), 1-22.

14. M.P. Schützenberger, Certain elementary families of automata, Proc. Symp. Math. Theory of Automata, Polytechnic Institute of Brooklyn, 1962, 139-153.

15. M.P. Schützenberger, Parties rationnelles d'un monoïde libre, Actes Congrès Internat. Math. Nice 3 (1970), pp. 281-282, Gauthier-Villars, Paris, 1971.

A COMPLETE AXIOMATIC CHARACTERIZATION OF ALGORITHMIC PROPERTIES OF BLOCK-STRUCTURED PROGRAMS WITH PROCEDURES

G.Mirkowska,A.Salwicki
Warsaw University, Mathmematical Dept. PKiN p.850
00-901 Warszawa / POLAND

In order to investigate properties of programs on an axiomatic basis one needs 1° a language L which is adequate for expressing algorithmic properties of programs, 2° a deductive system S /usually defined by the sets of axioms and inference rules/ such that a/ S is consistent , b/ S is complete. The consistency and completeness of S are usually proved with respect to a given semantics of the language L.

The problem of axiomatization was completely solved for programs without procedures in Mirkowska [3] , Banachowski [1] . Many other authors gave axiomatic systems, too, however, each of these systems either is inadequate since there is a property of programs inexpressible in the language of the system, or it is incomplete.

Here we present a formalized system of algorithmic logic for block-structured programs with procedures. Definitions and proofs are sketched only, for full text see [4].

1.LANGUAGE

A language L which enables to express most known algorithmic properties of programs is defined as an extension of languages considered in Mirkowska[3] and Müldner,Salwicki [5].

A well formed expression of the language L is either

- a term /you may it also conceive as an simple arithmetic expression of ALGOL, however, without procedures defined by a programmer/
- a quantifier-free formula/ simple Boolean expression of ALGOL/
- a program in a sense of [3,1,5]

  We are treating text of procedure as a text constant and declaration of procedure as an assignment of this text constant to the name of the procedure.
- a formula that contain a program.

Since the common definitions of terms, quantifier-free formulas and programs can be found in [6,3,5], we limit ourselves to the definition of the set FSF of formulas.

The set FSF is the least set of expressions such that

fsf1/ every quantifier-free formula is in FSF,

fsf2/ if K is a program and α is a formula then the expression $K\alpha$ is in FSF,

fsf3/ the set FSF is closed with respect to propositional connectives $\neg$ /negation/, $\wedge$ /conjunction/, $\vee$ /disjunction/, $\Rightarrow$ /implication/.

Examples

$+(x, \cdot(z,y))$ $\cdot(-(x,y), +(x,y))$ are terms written in a prefix form

```
begin x:= + x + z·y ; a:= a∨ x < y end
if a then z:= (x-y)(x+y) else z:=x fi
beginblock real x; integer n,m;
   procedure p(z,y); real z,y; while z < n do z:=z+y; m:=0;
   p(m,x);
endblock
```

are programs.

```
begin x:=x+2y ; a:=a∨ x < y end y > x ⇒ a
beginblock real x; integer n,m;
   procedure p(z,y); real z,y; while z < n do z:=z+y;
   m:=0; p(m,x)
endblock m=n
```

are formulas.

2. SEMANTICS

We are basing on the notions of realization of a language and valuation of variables [6,3] . Programs are interpreted as partial functions. Let R denotes a realization. Given a program K and a valuation v determine a /unique/ computation [5] . We conceive the realization K_R of the program K as the partial function defined on the set of valuations. For a valuation v the function K_R is defined iff the computation starting from the (v,K) configuration is finite. The value K_R v is the valuation v′ of the last configuration $(v', \emptyset)$ in the computation.

The value of a formula of the form $K\alpha$ is computed as follows:

$$(K\alpha)_R(v) = \begin{cases} \alpha_R(K_R(v)) & \text{if } v' = K_R(v) \text{ is defined} \\ \mathbb{O} \quad (\text{false}) & \text{otherwise} \end{cases}$$

The full definition of the realization of terms, formulas and programs is left to the reader [cf 3,5,1].

The notions of satisfiability, validity, of model etc are defined in a common way.

Let us remark that formulas $K \mathbb{1}$, $\alpha \Rightarrow K\beta$

$(m > 0 \wedge n > 0) \Rightarrow [\underline{\text{while}}\ n \cdot n > m\ \underline{\text{do}}\ n := n-1]\ n \cdot n \leq m \wedge (n+1)\cdot(n+1) \geq m$

do express the properties of programs: stop, correctness w.r.t. α, β i.e. they are valid iff programs possess corresponding properties.

3. AXIOMS AND INFERENCE RULES

The set of logical axioms contains the following schemes:

I all schemes of axioms of propositional calculus, [6]

II all schemes of axioms of algorithmic logic, schemes with iteration-quantifiers or generalized terms are excluded here [3]

III scheme of axiom of while instruction

$$s[\underline{\text{while}}\ \alpha\ \underline{\text{do}}\ K]\beta \Leftrightarrow s(\neg\alpha \wedge \beta \vee \alpha \wedge K[\text{while}\ \alpha\ \underline{\text{do}}\ K]\beta)$$

here s denotes a finite sequence / may be empty/ of substitutions, also called assignment instructions.

IV scheme of axiom of block

$$s[\underline{\text{beginblock}}\ D_1 \ldots D_m;\ I_1 \ldots I_n\ \underline{\text{endblock}}]\alpha \Leftrightarrow s\,s'\,I_1' \ldots I_n'\,\alpha$$

where s'denotes a substitution which for every procedure name p declared in $D_1 \ldots D_m$ declarations associates with it the text constant of declared procedure,

s is a finite sequence of substitutions,

$I_1' \ldots I_n'$ are instructions that arise from $I_1 \ldots I_n$ instrutions by replacing all the identifiers local [5] for the block in question by identifiers not occurring in the lefthand side.

Before we formulate the last scheme of axioms let us introduce the notion of $Mod_a T$ - a procedure text T modified by an actual parameter list a. Let p be a name of procedure, T_p its text, a - a list of actual parameters in a p(a)procedure instruction.

By $Mod_a T_p$ we denote the instruction arising from T_p in the following way:

1° the instruction T_p is bracketed by beginblock, endblock to form a block,

2° all identifiers occurring in the value part are declared in the block,

3° for everyformal parameter occurring in the value part an instruction of the form <formal parameter>:= <actual parameter>is inserted in front of T_p instruction,

4° all remaining formal parametrs are replaced textually by corresponding actual parametrs /call by name/.

V the scheme of axiom of procedure instruction

$$s\ p(a)\alpha \Leftrightarrow s\left[Mod_a T_p\right]\alpha$$

where s is a finite sequence of substitutions and contains a substitution of T_p for the procedure name p.

We admit the following inference rules

$$\text{r1}\quad \frac{\alpha,\ \alpha \Rightarrow \beta}{\beta} \qquad\qquad \text{r2}\quad \frac{\alpha \Rightarrow \beta}{K\alpha \Rightarrow K\beta}$$

$$\text{r3}\quad \frac{\{s[\text{if } \alpha \text{ then } K]^i(\neg\alpha \wedge \beta) \Rightarrow \mu\}_{i\in\omega}}{s[\text{while } \alpha \text{ do } K]\ \beta \Rightarrow \mu}$$

ω - the set of natural numbers

The next rule of inference needs some denotations. Let p be a procedure instruction. By Der p(a) we shall denote a set of instructions equivalent to p(a) . In the sequel we shall write Der shortly.

Der is the last set of instructions such that

1. $Mod_a T_p \in$ Der,
2. if $J \in$ Der and q(b) is a procedure instruction occurring in instruction J then the instruction J′ which arise from J by replacement of the instruction q(b) by $Mod_b T_q$ is an element of Der.

For every instruction J by $\hat{J}$ we shall denote a new instruction which arises from J by replacement of all procedure instructions occurring in J by the always looping instruction while true do begin end

$$\text{r4}\quad \frac{s\{\hat{J}\alpha \Rightarrow \mu\}\quad J\in \text{Der}}{s[p(a)]\alpha \Rightarrow \mu}$$

The logical axioms and inference rules define a consequence operation C, for any set of specific /nonlogical axioms/ X by C(X) we shall denote the set of all formulas that can be proved from X. Proofs are finite path trees, it may be a proof with infinitely many vertices. The rules r3 and r4 can not be replaced by any finitistic rule [3] From this follows, frequently observed, a necessity of proving of the existence of proofs instead of constructing them.

4. COMPLETENESS THEOREM

Let $\mathcal{T}$ denotes a formalized algorithmic theory

$$\mathcal{T} = \langle L, C, A \rangle$$

where L is the language of the theory $\mathcal{T}$,
C is the consequence operation,
A is a set of specific /nonlogical/ axioms.

Theorem For any consistent theory $\mathcal{T}$ and a formula $\alpha \in L$ the following conditions are equivalent:

/ i/ α is a theorem of $\mathcal{T}$,

/ii/ α is valid in every model of $\mathcal{T}$.

In order to investigate properties of ALGOL programs one should as specific axioms assume algorithmic axioms of natural numbers and axioms of formally real field [2]

REFERENCES

[1] Banachowski, L., Extended algorithmic logic and properties of programs, Bull.Acad.Pol.Sci., Ser.Math.Astr.Phys. 23 1975 ,325-330
[2] Kreczmar, A., Programmability in fields, to appear in Fundamenta Informaticae
[3] Mirkowska, G., On formalized systems of algorithmic logic, Bull. Acad.Pol.Sci., Ser.Math.Astr.Phys. 21 1971 ,421-428
[4 Mirkowska, G., Salwicki, A., Algorithmic properties of block structured programs with procedures, to appear in Fundamenta Informaticae
[5] Müldner, T., Salwicki, A., Semantics of block-structured programs this volume
[6] Rasiowa, H., Sikorski, R., Mathematics of metamathematics, PWN, Warszawa, 1963